KNOWLEDGE ENCYCLOPEDIA

SPACE!

NASA

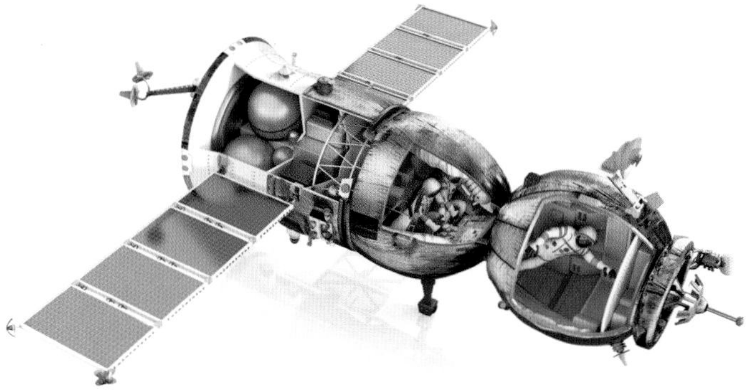

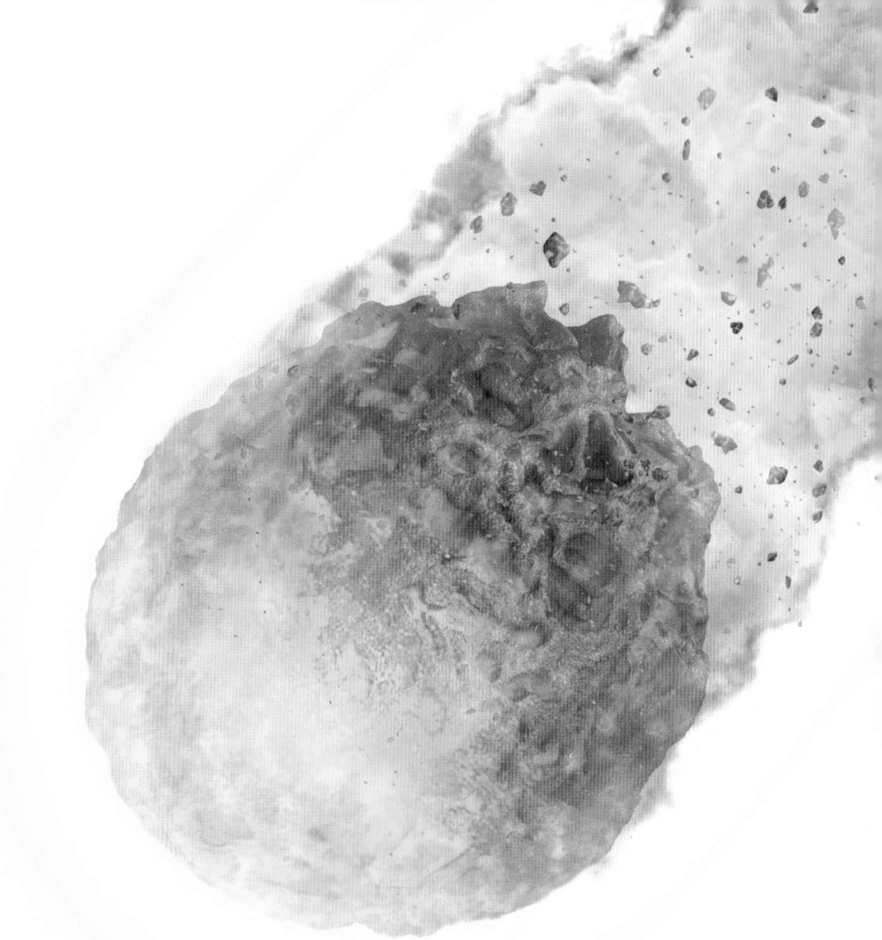

KNOWLEDGE ENCYCLOPEDIA

SPACE!

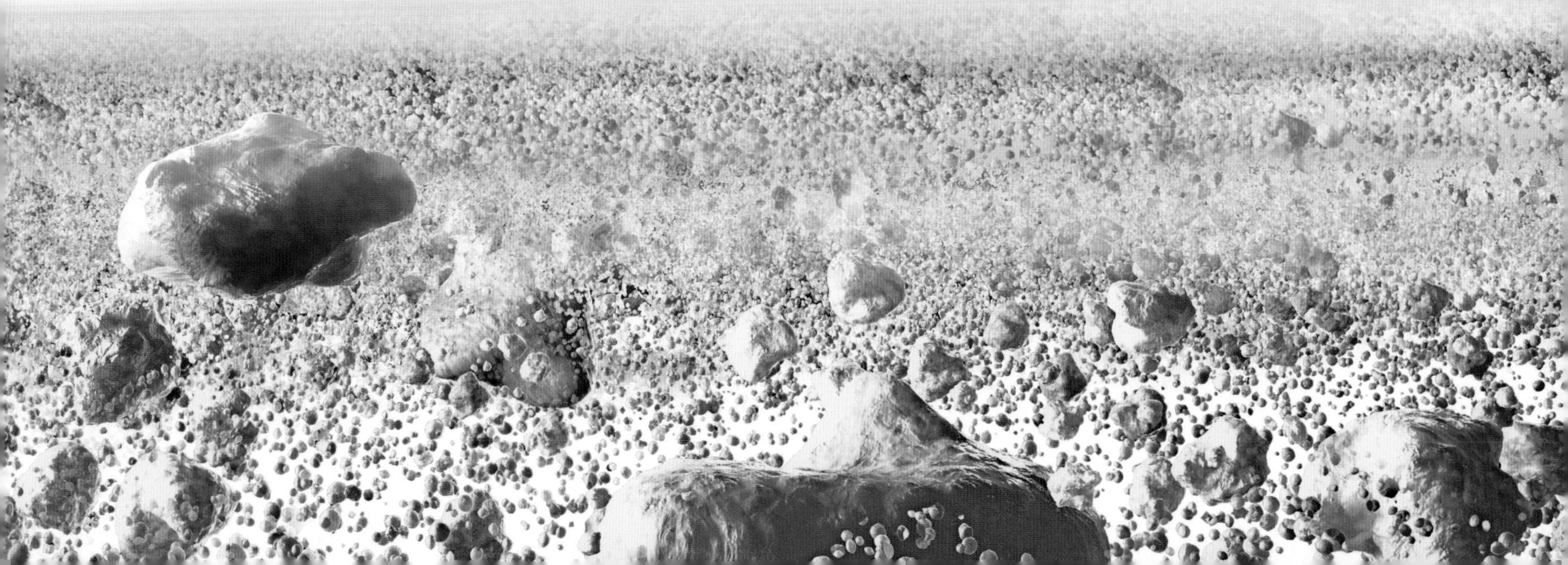

DK | Penguin Random House

DK London
Senior editor Ben Morgan
Senior art editor Smiljka Surla
Editor Steve Setford
Designer Jacqui Swan
Contributors Robert Dinwiddie, John Farndon, Geraint Jones, Ian Ridpath, Giles Sparrow, Carole Stott
Scientific consultant Jacqueline Mitton
Illustrators Peter Bull, Jason Harding, Arran Lewis
Jacket design development manager Sophia MTT
Jacket designer Laura Brim
Jacket editor Claire Gell
Producer, pre-production Nikoleta Parasaki
Producer Nancy-Jane Maun
Managing editor Paula Regan
Managing art editor Owen Peyton Jones
Publisher Andrew Macintyre
Associate publishing director Liz Wheeler
Art director Karen Self
Design director Stuart Jackman
Publishing director Jonathan Metcalf

DK Delhi
Senior editor Bharti Bedi
Senior art editor Nishesh Batnagar
Project editor Priyanka Kharbanda
Art editors Heena Sharma, Supriya Mahajan
Assistant editor Sheryl Sadana
DTP designer Nityanand Kumar
Senior DTP designers Shanker Prasad, Harish Aggarwal
Picture researcher Deepak Negi
Jacket designer Dhirendra Singh
Managing jackets editor Saloni Singh
Managing editor Kingshuk Ghoshal
Managing art editor Govind Mittal
Pre-production manager Balwant Singh
Production manager Pankaj Sharma

First published in Great Britain in 2015
by Dorling Kindersley Limited
80 Strand, London WC2R 0RL

A Penguin Random House Company
10 9 8 7 6 5 4 3
003 - 264881 - September/2015

A CIP catalogue record for this
book is available from the British Library.

ISBN: 978-0-2412-9264-8

Printed in China

A WORLD OF IDEAS:
SEE ALL THERE IS TO KNOW

www.dk.com

CONTENTS

THE SOLAR SYSTEM

STARS

GALAXIES

EXPLORING SPACE

THE NIGHT SKY

REFERENCE

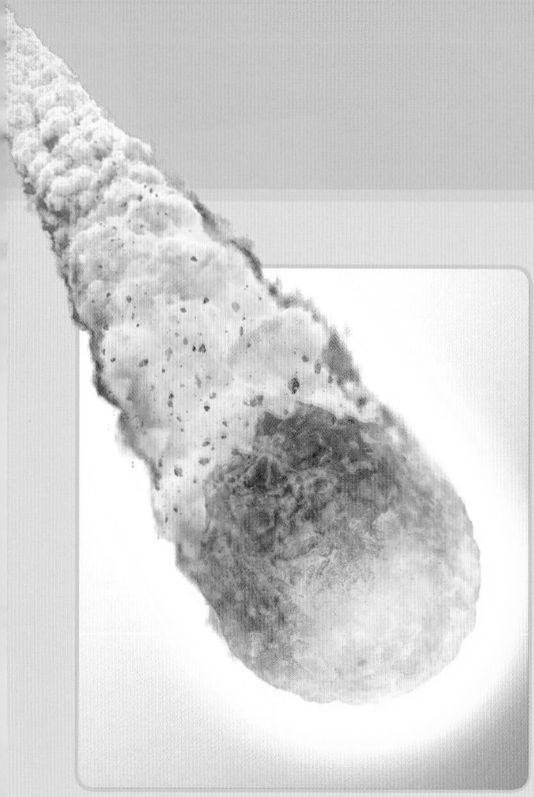

THE SOLAR SYSTEM

Our local neighbourhood in space is called the Solar System. At its heart is the Sun, an ordinary star that is so close it floods our planet with light. Trapped in its orbit by gravity are Earth and seven other planets, their many moons, and millions of comets and asteroids.

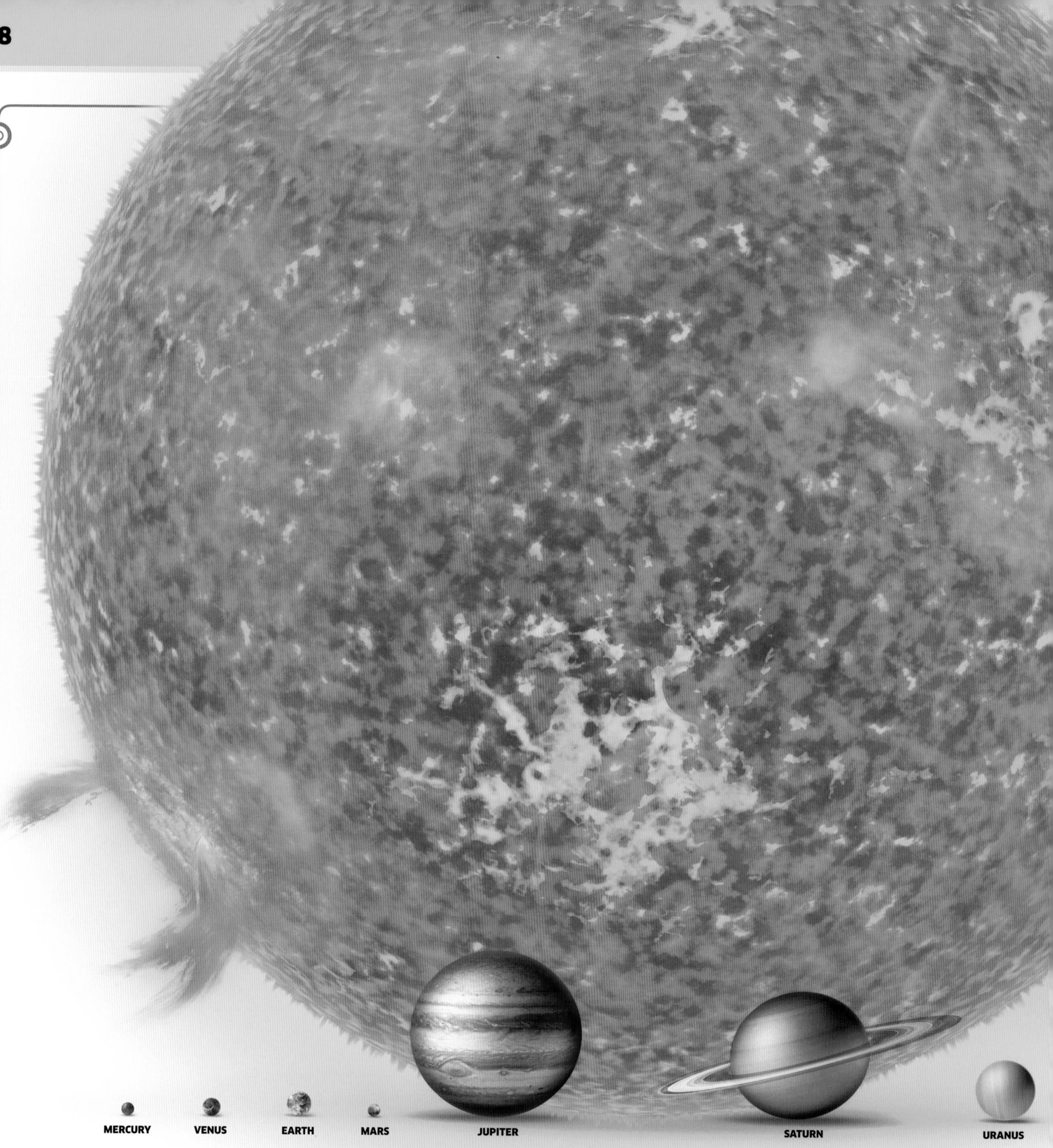
MERCURY
VENUS
EARTH
MARS
JUPITER
SATURN
URANUS

THE SUN AND PLANETS

The Sun is huge compared to even the biggest of the planets, Jupiter, and it contains 99.8 per cent of the Solar System's entire mass. At nearly 1.4 million km (870,000 miles) wide, the Sun is ten times wider than Jupiter and over 1,000 times more massive. Yet even Jupiter is gigantic compared to Earth. The Solar System's eight planets form two distinct groups. The inner planets – Mercury, Venus, Earth, and Mars – are solid balls of rock and metal. In contrast, the outer planets are gas giants – enormous, swirling globes made mostly of hydrogen and helium.

1.3 million – the number of times Earth's volume could fit inside the Sun.

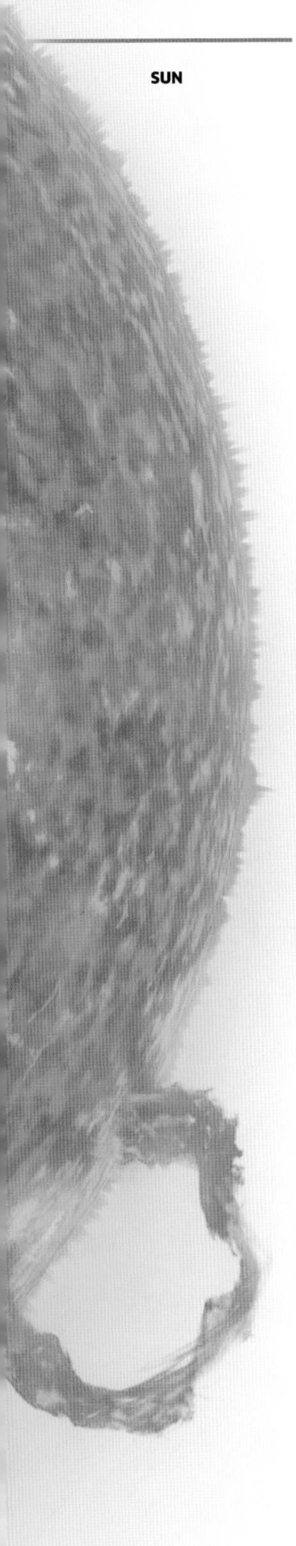

SUN

The Sun's family

The Solar System is a vast disc of material over 30 billion km (19 billion miles) across, with the Sun at its centre. Most of it is empty space, but scattered throughout are countless solid objects bound to the Sun by gravity and orbiting (travelling around) it, mostly in the same direction. The biggest objects are almost perfectly round and are called planets. There are eight of them, ranging from the small rocky planet Mercury to gigantic Jupiter. The Solar System also has hundreds of moons and dwarf planets, millions of asteroids, and possibly millions or billions of comets.

NEPTUNE

ORBITAL PLANE

The orbits of the planets and most asteroids around the Sun are aligned, making a flat shape known as a plane. This means they rarely bump into each other. Comets, though, can be in orbits at any angle.

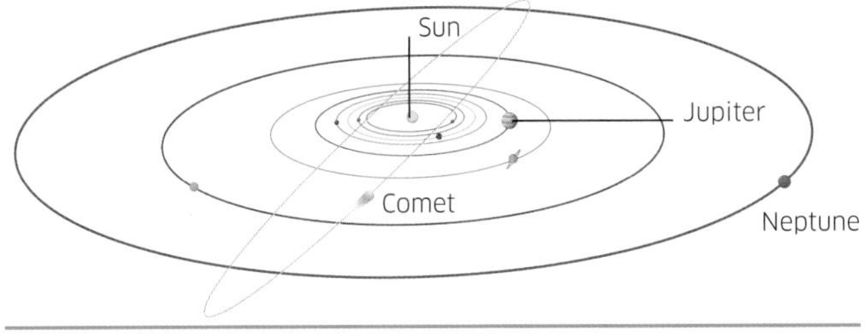
Sun
Jupiter
Comet
Neptune

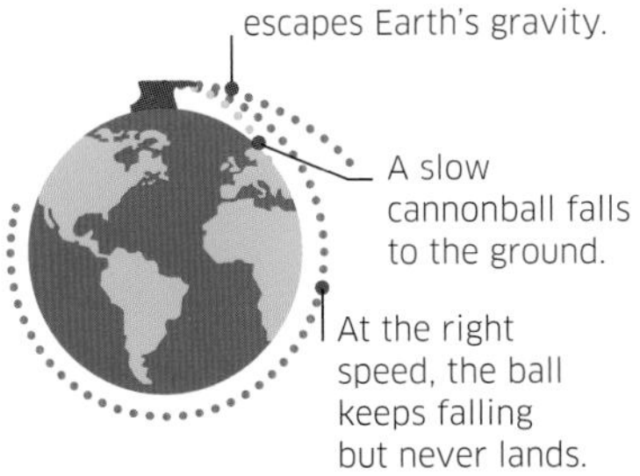
A fast cannonball escapes Earth's gravity.
A slow cannonball falls to the ground.
At the right speed, the ball keeps falling but never lands.

How orbits work

To understand how orbits work, English scientist Isaac Newton imagined cannonballs being fired into space. If a cannonball flies so fast that the curvature of its fall matches Earth's curvature, it will keep flying forever, orbiting the planet.

MINOR BODIES

Besides the planets, there are so many other bodies in the Solar System that astronomers have not been able to identify them all. Bodies more than 200 km (125 miles) or so wide, such as dwarf planets and large moons, are round. Smaller objects are lumpy in shape.

Asteroids
There are millions of these rocky lumps, most of which circle the Sun in an area between Mars and Jupiter: the Asteroid Belt. A few asteroids have orbits that take them perilously close to Earth or other planets.

Comets
Comets are icy bodies that travel in from the outer Solar System, forming a bright tail as they come close enough to the Sun for the ice to evaporate. Many comets are thought to come from a vast cloud called the Oort Cloud, far beyond the planets.

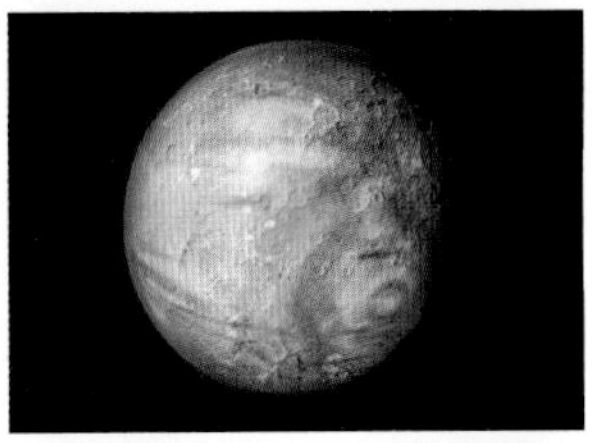

Dwarf planets
The force of gravity pulls large objects into a spherical shape over time. Dwarf planets have enough gravity to become spherical but not enough to sweep the area around their orbits clear of other objects. The total number of dwarf planets is unknown.

Moons
Most of the planets and many of the other objects in the Solar System have moons – natural satellites that orbit them, in the same way that the planets orbit the Sun. Nineteen of these moons are large enough to be round, and two of them are larger than the planet Mercury.

STRUCTURE

The Solar System has no clear outer edge and is so big that distances are measured not in kilometres but in astronomical units (AU). One astronomical unit is the average distance from Earth to the Sun.

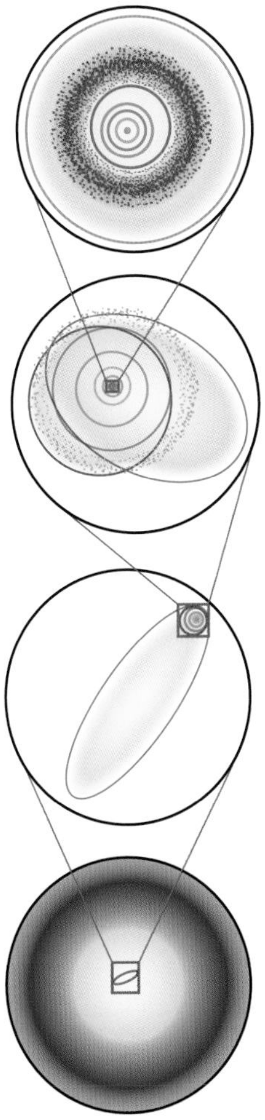

Inner Solar System
Circling nearest to the Sun are the four inner planets: Mercury, Venus, Earth, and Mars. Beyond Mars lies the Asteroid Belt, and beyond the Asteroid Belt is Jupiter (orbit in orange) at 5 AU from the Sun.

Outer Solar System
Beyond the orbits of Jupiter, Saturn, Uranus, and Neptune is a ring of icy bodies known as the Kuiper Belt, some 30–50 AU from the Sun. Two of the largest objects in the Kuiper Belt are Pluto (orbit in purple) and Eris (orbit in red).

Beyond Pluto
One of the most distant Solar System objects known is Sedna, a minor body whose elongated orbit takes it as far from the Sun as 937 AU. Sedna's journey around the Sun takes 11,400 years to complete. The Sun would look so tiny from Sedna that you could blot it out with a pin.

Oort Cloud
Far beyond Sedna's orbit is the Oort Cloud – a vast ball of icy bodies reaching 100,000 AU from the Sun. Some comets are thought to come from the Oort Cloud. The Sun's gravity is so weak here that objects in the cloud can be dislodged by the gravity of other stars.

800,000 kph (500,000 mph) – the speed at which the whole Solar System is moving around our galaxy.

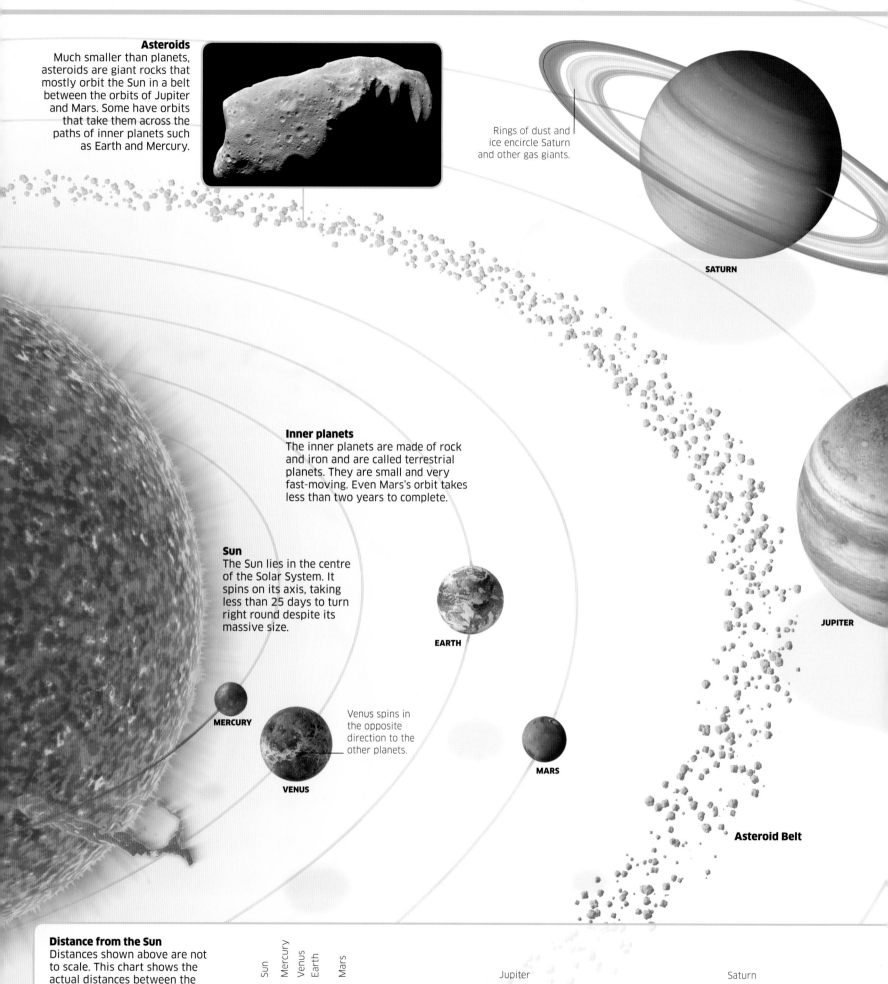

Asteroids
Much smaller than planets, asteroids are giant rocks that mostly orbit the Sun in a belt between the orbits of Jupiter and Mars. Some have orbits that take them across the paths of inner planets such as Earth and Mercury.

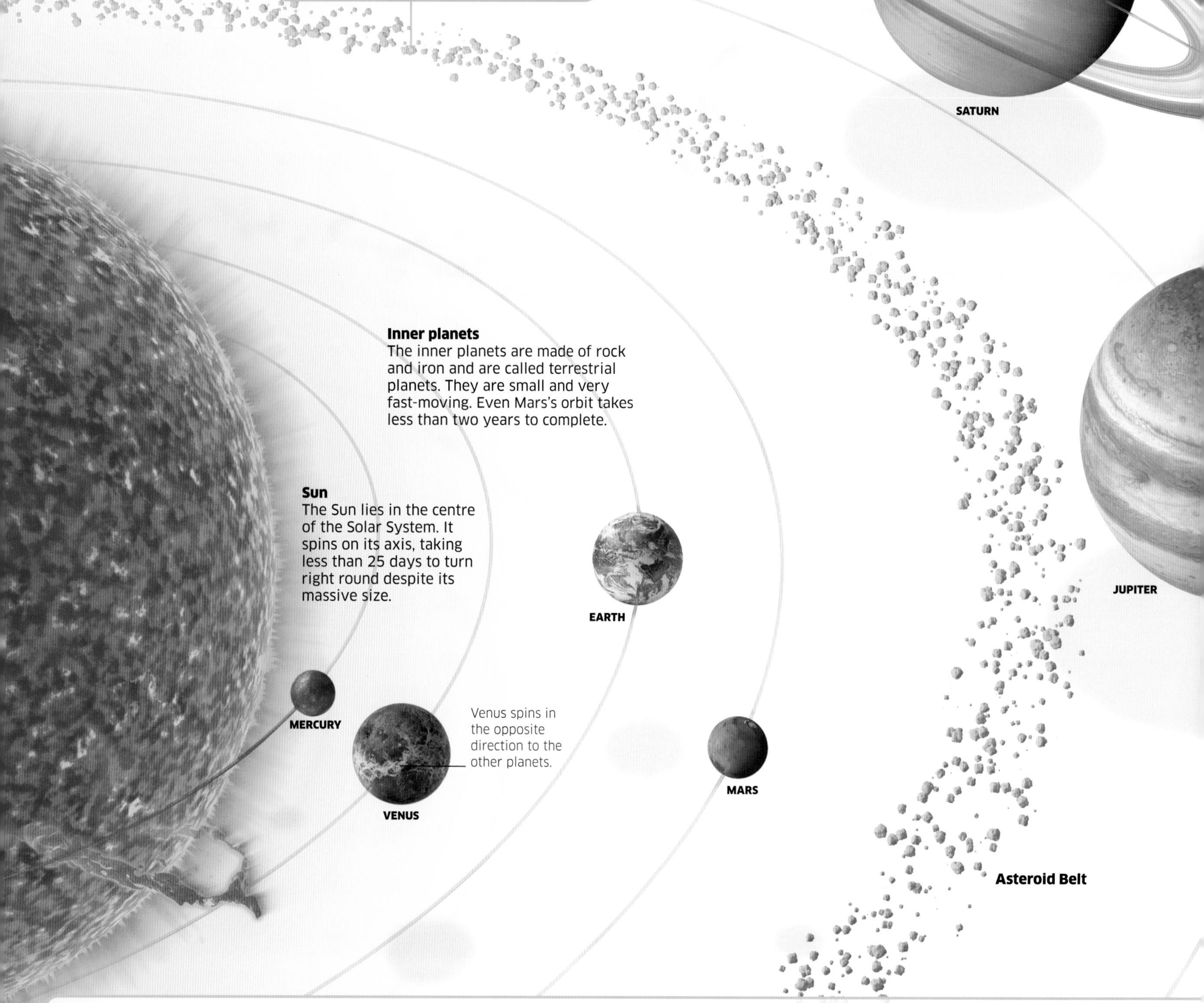
Rings of dust and ice encircle Saturn and other gas giants.
SATURN
JUPITER
EARTH
MERCURY
VENUS
MARS
Venus spins in the opposite direction to the other planets.
Asteroid Belt

Inner planets
The inner planets are made of rock and iron and are called terrestrial planets. They are small and very fast-moving. Even Mars's orbit takes less than two years to complete.

Sun
The Sun lies in the centre of the Solar System. It spins on its axis, taking less than 25 days to turn right round despite its massive size.

Distance from the Sun
Distances shown above are not to scale. This chart shows the actual distances between the planets. Distances are shown in astronomical units (AU). One AU is the distance from Earth to the Sun.

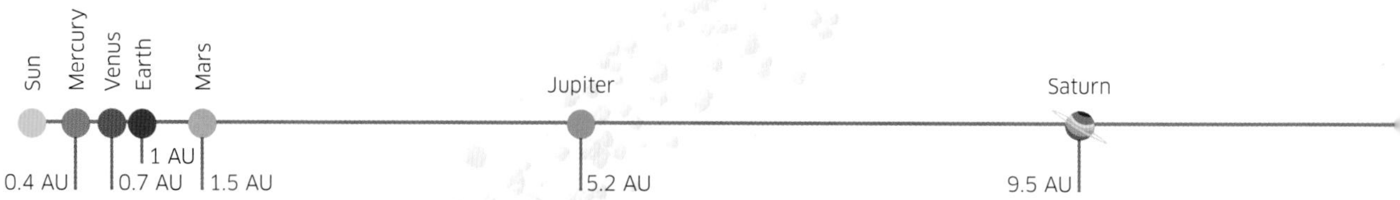
Sun
Mercury
Venus
Earth
Mars
Jupiter
Saturn
0.4 AU
0.7 AU
1 AU
1.5 AU
5.2 AU
9.5 AU

Comets
Comets are giant lumps of ice and dust that have highly elliptical orbits. They can spend centuries in the outer reaches of the Solar System before swooping close to the Sun and developing tails as they warm up.

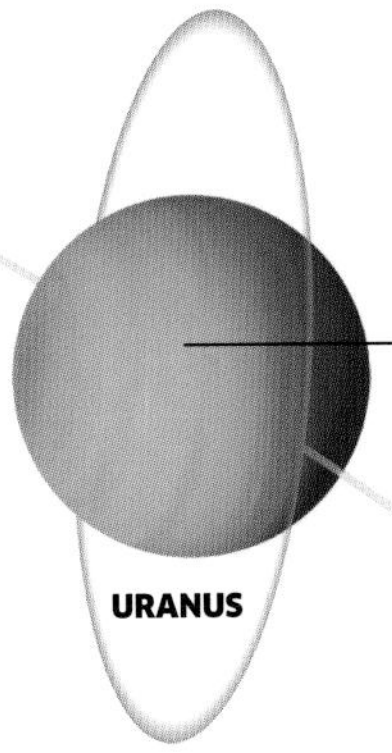
URANUS

Uranus, unlike the other planets, spins on its side, rolling round on its orbit.

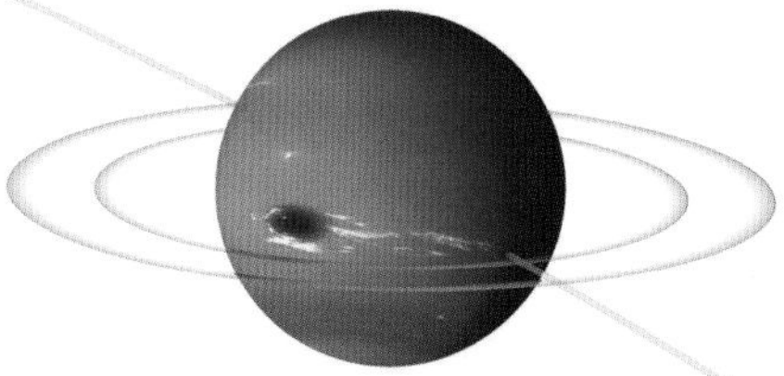
NEPTUNE

Kuiper Belt
Beyond the planets is a belt of icy bodies, some of which are large enough to be classed as dwarf planets. These objects are so far from the Sun that they can take hundreds of years to complete one orbit.

Gas giants
The outer planets are all much bigger than the inner planets. They are called gas giants because they are made mostly of hydrogen and helium. These substances are gases on Earth, but in the gas giants they are mostly in liquid form.

Jupiter spins round faster than any other planet, completing one rotation in under ten hours. The speed of movement at its equator is 43,000 kph (27,000 mph).

Around the Sun

Trapped by the Sun's gravity, the eight planets of the Solar System travel around the central star on nearly circular paths, spinning like tops as they go.

The farther a planet is from the Sun, the longer its orbit takes and the slower it travels. The farthest planet, Neptune, takes 165 years to get round the Sun and moves at just over 5 km (3 miles) per second. Earth, meanwhile, bowls through space nearly six times as fast, and Mercury, the planet nearest the Sun, whizzes around it in just 88 days at a speedy 50 km (30 miles) per second. The planets' orbits are not circular. Instead, they follow slightly oval paths, known as ellipses, that take them closer to the Sun at one point. Mercury's orbit is the most elliptical: its farthest point from the Sun is more than 50 per cent farther than its nearest point.

Every object in space is spinning round, from planets and moons to stars, black holes, and galaxies.

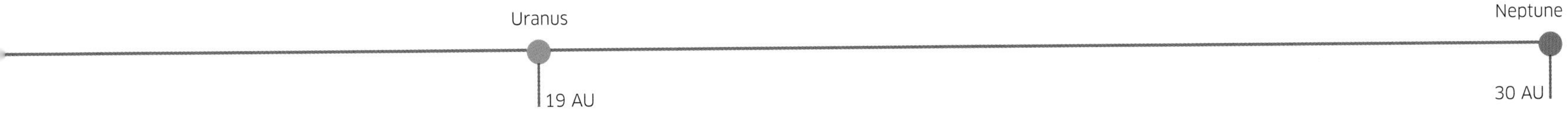
Uranus
19 AU
Neptune
30 AU

New Sun
The Sun contains 99.8 per cent of the material now in the Solar System.

Rocky planets
Grains of rock and metal collected in the inner part of the young Solar System, which was much hotter than the outer zone. This material would form the inner planets –Mercury, Venus, Earth, and Mars – which have rocky outer layers and cores of iron.

Birth of the Solar System

The planets of the Solar System formed from gas and grains of dust and ice surrounding the newly formed Sun.

The Solar System was born inside a vast, dark cloud of gas and dust. About 5 billion years ago, something triggered a burst of star formation in the cloud – perhaps a nearby star exploded, sending a shock wave rippling through the cloud. Hundreds of pockets of gas were squeezed into clumps. Their gravity pulled in more and more gas, making the clumps larger and denser. This made them heat up inside and start to glow. Eventually, the cores of the clumps got so hot and dense that nuclear reactions began and they became stars. One of those stars was our Sun.

Oldest rocks
Meteorites are space rocks that fall onto Earth. They include the oldest rocks known to science. Many are leftovers from the cloud of debris that formed the planets.

Solar nebula

When the Sun formed inside a vast cloud of gas and dust, it was rotating, and a swirling disc of material collected in a flat plane around it. This disc is called the solar nebula.

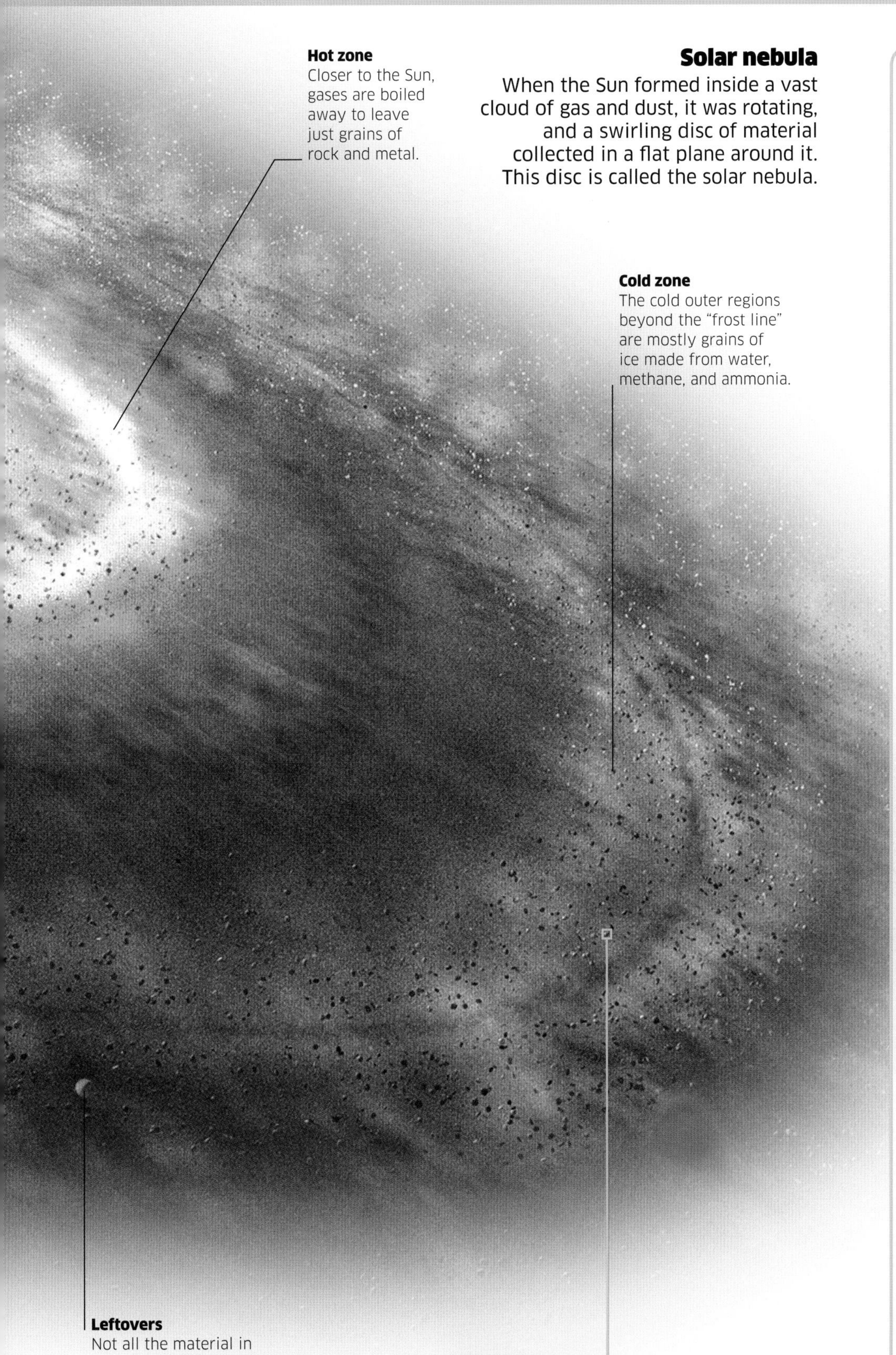
Hot zone
Closer to the Sun, gases are boiled away to leave just grains of rock and metal.
Cold zone
The cold outer regions beyond the "frost line" are mostly grains of ice made from water, methane, and ammonia.
Leftovers
Not all the material in the solar nebula formed planets – the leftovers formed moons, asteroids, comets, and dwarf planets.

Birth of the giants
Vast amounts of icy debris collected in the cold outer part of the Solar System. This material drew together to form planets so large that they had enough gravity to pull in gases such as hydrogen and helium. These planets would become the gas giants: Jupiter, Saturn, Uranus, and Neptune.

The Solar System forms

The Solar System formed 4.6 billion years ago when a clump of gas and dust was pulled together by its own gravity inside a giant cloud. The collapsing mass gave birth to our Sun, surrounded by a flattened spinning disc (the solar nebula) from which the planets formed.

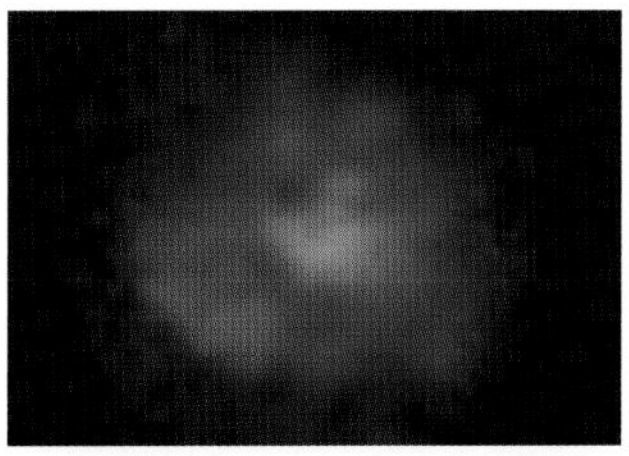

Collapsing clump
Within the giant cloud, a pocket of gas began to shrink, perhaps because a shock wave from a supernova (exploding star) disturbed the cloud.

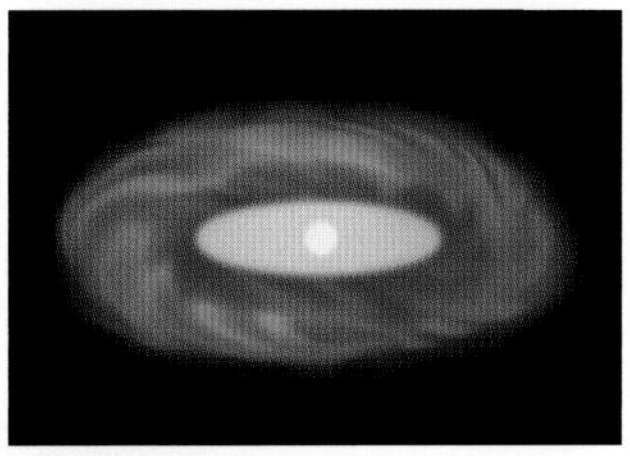

Spinning disc
As the clump shrank it began spinning, turning faster and faster until it formed a disc. Its centre began to heat up.

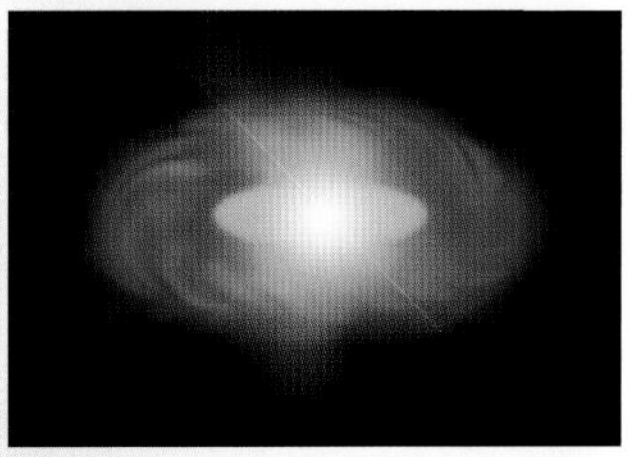

The Sun is born
Nuclear reactions began in the dense centre, which began to shine as a star. The leftover matter formed a disc called a solar nebula.

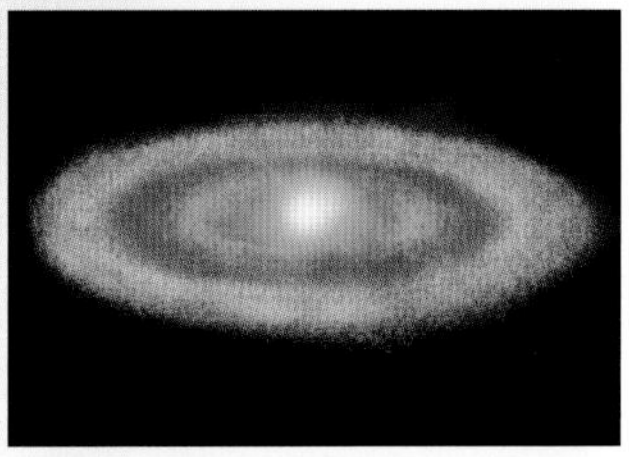

Planetesimals
Gravity caused the particles in the disc to clump together, forming billions of tiny planets, or planetesimals.

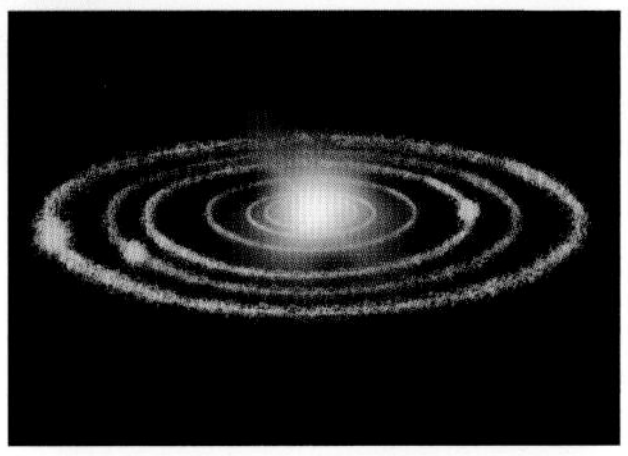

Planets form
The planetesimals crashed into each other, sticking together and growing into fewer, larger planets.

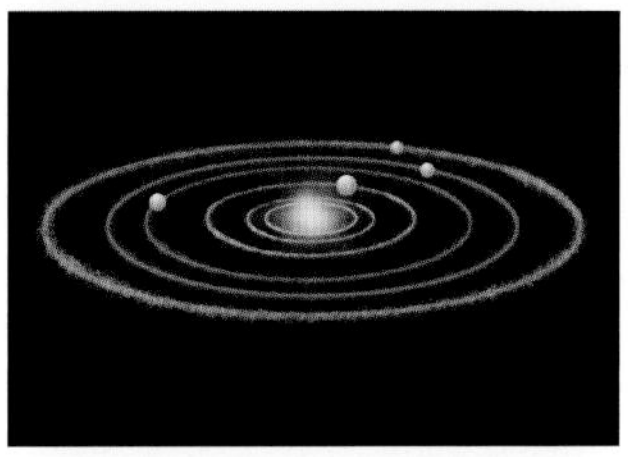

Migration
The orbits of the giant planets changed. Neptune and Uranus moved farther out, pushing smaller icy bodies into even more distant orbits.

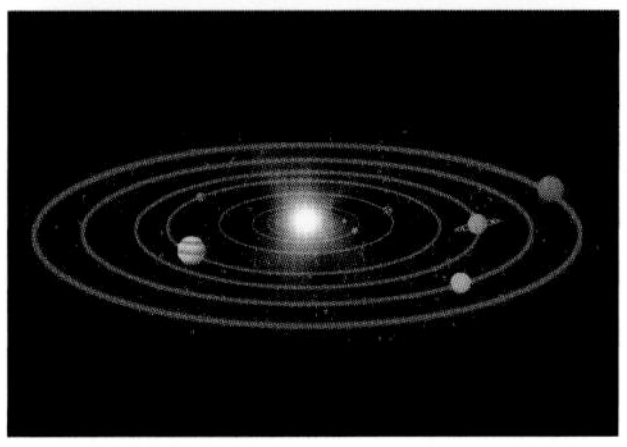

The Solar System today
By about 3.9 billion years ago, the Solar System had settled down into its present pattern of planets.

The Sun

Our Sun is a typical star – a vast, glowing ball made mostly of superhot hydrogen and helium gas.

The Sun has been shining for nearly 5 billion years and will probably continue to shine for another 5 billion. More than a million times larger in volume than Earth, it contains over 99 per cent of the Solar System's mass. The tremendous force of gravity generated by this mass keeps the planets of the Solar System trapped in orbit around it. The Sun's source of power lies buried deep in its core, where temperatures soar to 15 million °C (27 million °F). The intense heat and pressure in the core trigger nuclear fusion reactions, turning 4 million tonnes of matter into pure energy every second. This energy spreads upwards to the seething surface of the Sun, where it floods out into space as light and other forms of radiation.

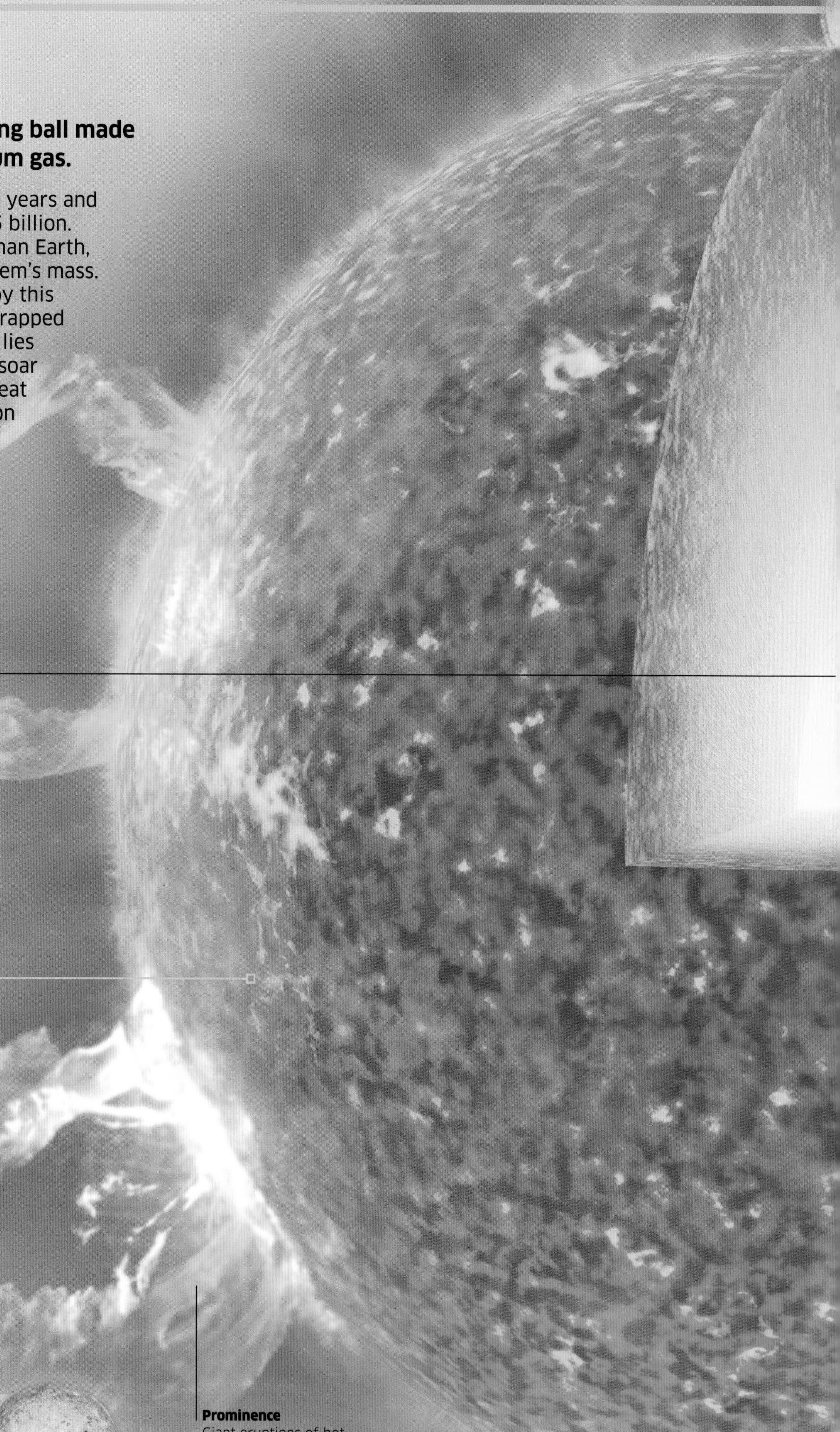

Core
The Sun's core is like a nuclear reactor. The nuclei (centres) of hydrogen atoms are forced together to form helium nuclei – a process called nuclear fusion.

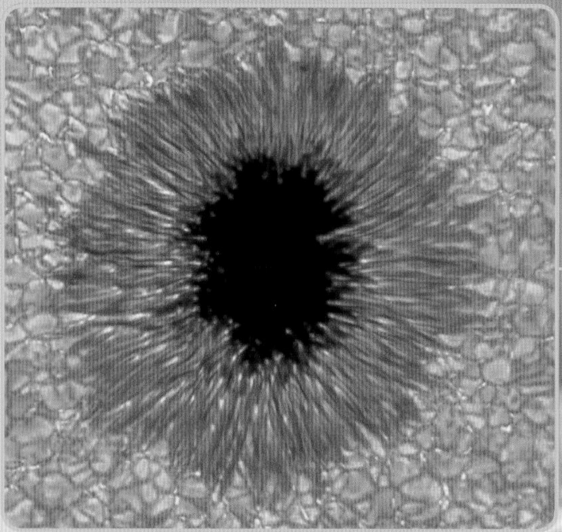

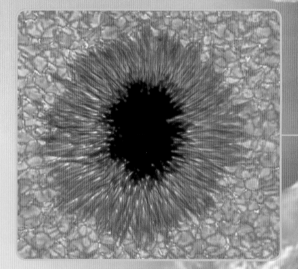

Sunspots
Sometimes dark patches appear on the Sun, often in groups. Called sunspots, they look darker because they are about 2,000°C (3,500°F) cooler than the rest of the surface. They last only a few weeks and are caused by the Sun's magnetic field.

Prominence
Giant eruptions of hot gas sometimes burst out from the Sun. Called prominences, they follow loops in the Sun's invisible magnetic field.

FAST FACTS

Diameter: 1,392,684 km (865,374 miles)

Mass (Earth = 1): 333,000

Surface temperature: 5,500°C (9,930°F)

Core temperature: 15 million °C (27 million °F)

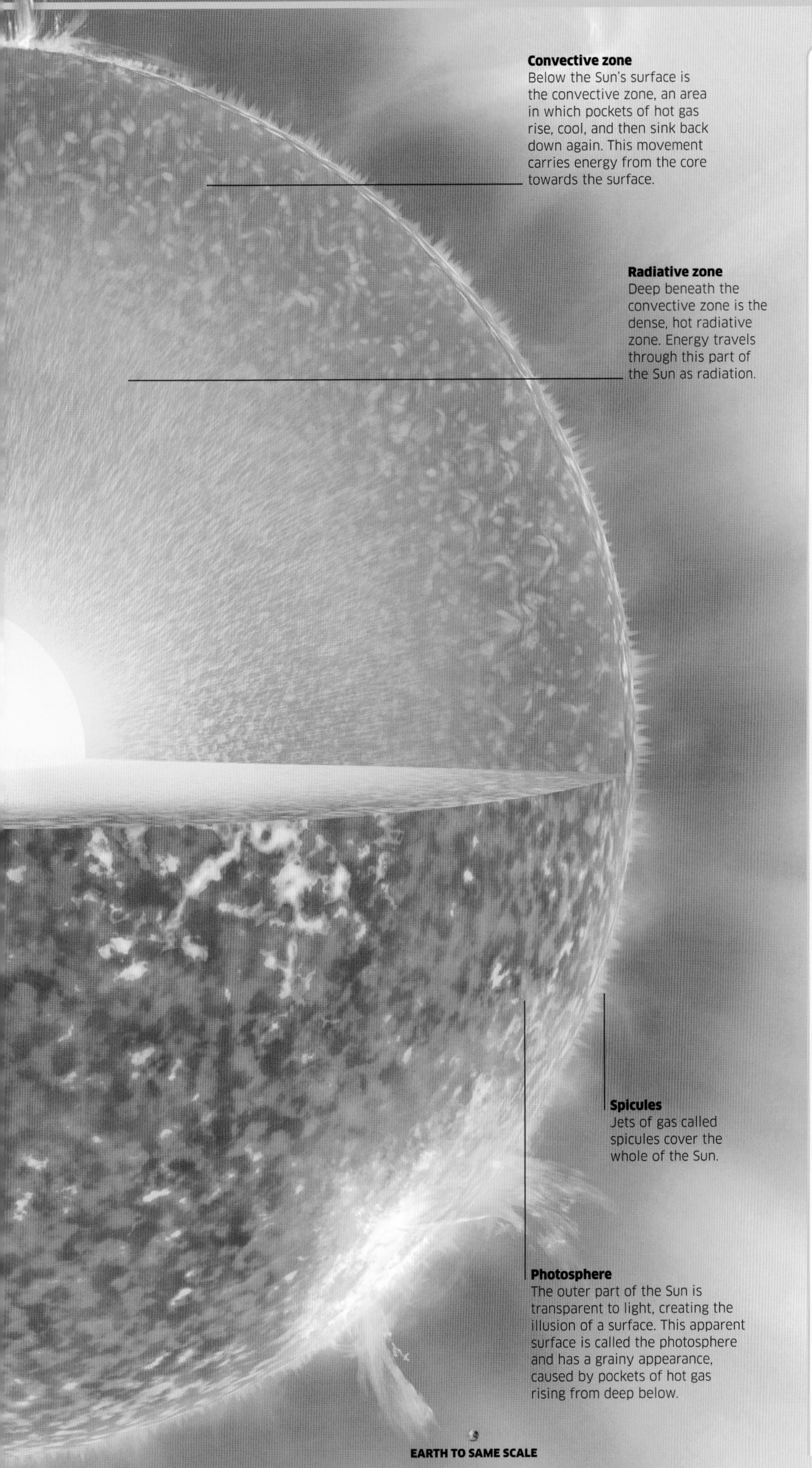
Convective zone
Below the Sun's surface is the convective zone, an area in which pockets of hot gas rise, cool, and then sink back down again. This movement carries energy from the core towards the surface.
Radiative zone
Deep beneath the convective zone is the dense, hot radiative zone. Energy travels through this part of the Sun as radiation.
Spicules
Jets of gas called spicules cover the whole of the Sun.
Photosphere
The outer part of the Sun is transparent to light, creating the illusion of a surface. This apparent surface is called the photosphere and has a grainy appearance, caused by pockets of hot gas rising from deep below.
EARTH TO SAME SCALE

Speed of light

Travelling at the speed of light, it takes a mere eight minutes for the Sun's energy to travel across space to reach Earth. However, it can take up to 100,000 years for energy to travel through the star's dense interior to reach its surface.

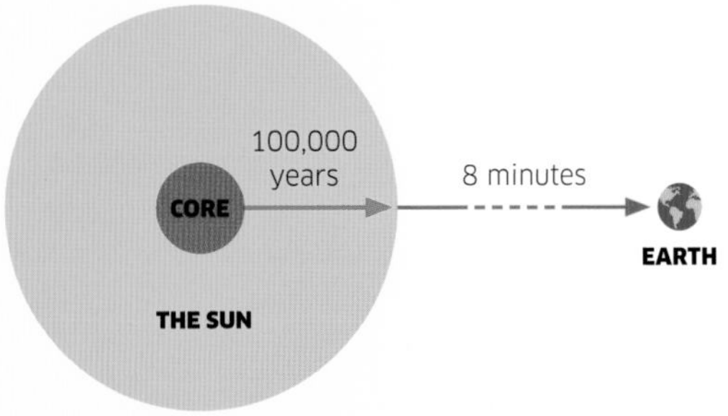
100,000 years
8 minutes
CORE
EARTH
THE SUN

Northern lights

As well as producing heat and light, the Sun flings out streams of deadly high-energy particles, forming the "solar wind". Earth's magnetic field protects us from these particles like an elastic cage, but when a strong blast of them disturbs the magnetic field, trapped particles cascade down into the atmosphere. They set off brilliant light displays near the poles, called auroras or the northern and southern lights.

Solar cycle

The number of sunspots on the Sun varies in a regular cycle, reaching a peak every 11 years or so before dying down again. This happens because of the way the Sun rotates. The star's equator spins 20 per cent faster than its poles, causing the Sun's magnetic field to get tangled up. Every 11 years it gets so tangled that it breaks down, before forming afresh.

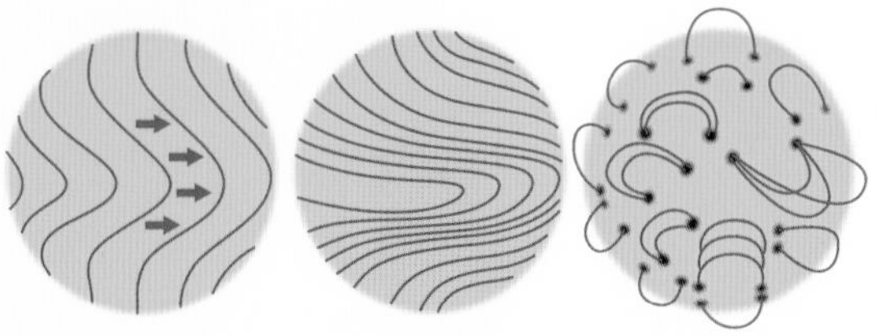

The Sun spins much faster at its equator than at its poles.

The difference in speeds twists magnetic field lines out of shape.

The twisted field lines burst in loops from the surface, creating sunspots.

176 Earth days – the **length of a day** on Mercury from sunrise to sunrise.

Mercury

The planet Mercury is a giant ball of iron covered in a shallow layer of rock. It is the smallest planet and the one closest to the Sun.

Mercury is the speedster of the planets, completing its journey around the Sun in just 88 Earth days at the brisk pace of 173,000 kph (108,000 mph), which is faster than any other planet. Scorched by the Sun's heat, Mercury's dusty, moon-like surface is hotter than an oven by day but freezing at night. Deep under the surface, a giant core of iron almost fills the planet's interior. The outsized core suggests Mercury was once struck with such violence that most of its rocky outer layers were blasted away into space.

Mercury's cliffs
Among Mercury's most distinctive features are long, winding cliffs called rupes, shown in this artist's impression. They probably formed at least 3 billion years ago when the young planet was cooling and shrinking, which made its surface wrinkle.

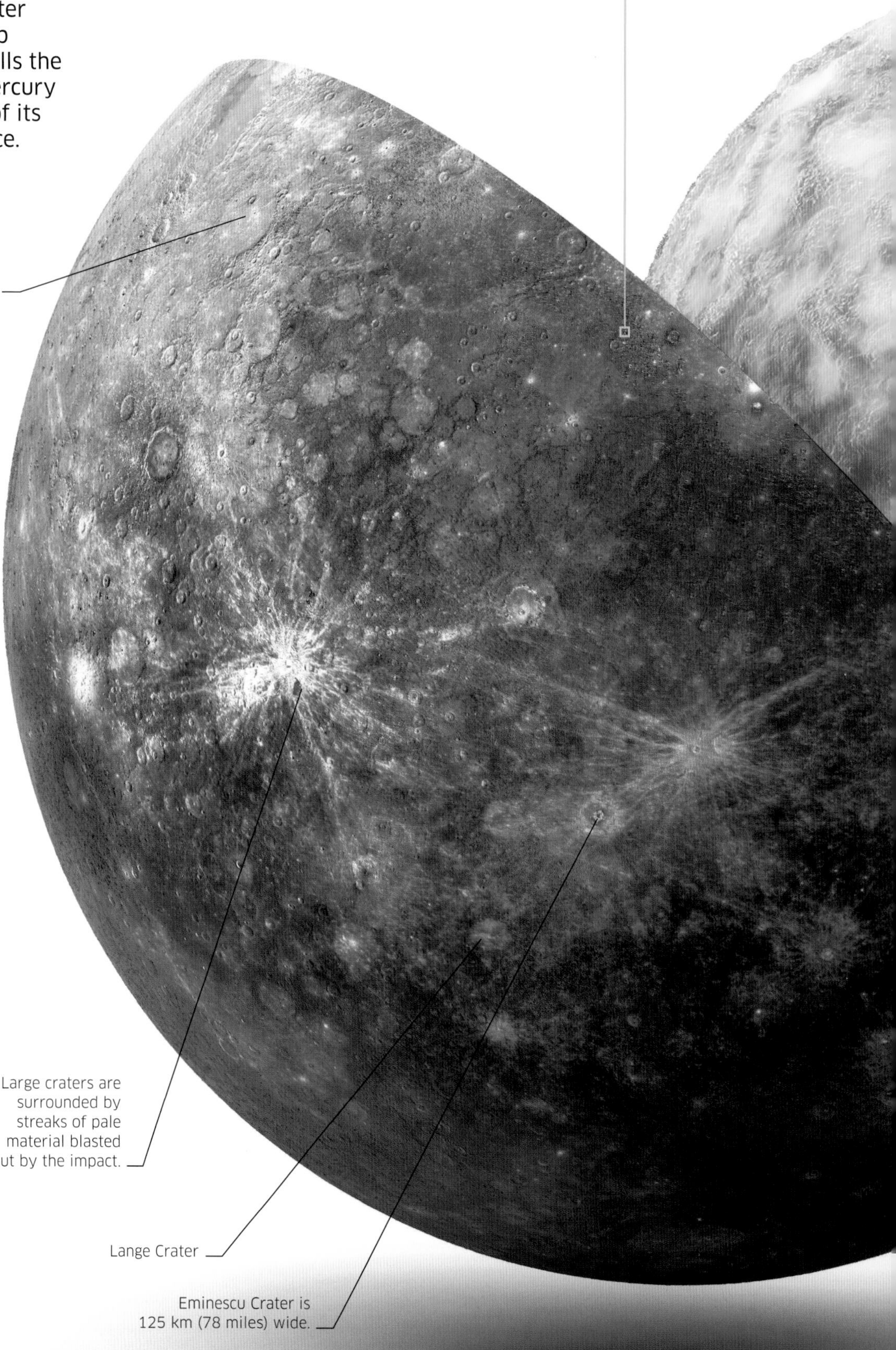
Craters on Mercury, such as the Mendelssohn Crater, are named after writers, artists, and composers.
Large craters are surrounded by streaks of pale material blasted out by the impact.
Lange Crater
Eminescu Crater is 125 km (78 miles) wide.

Around the Sun

Mercury takes 88 Earth days to orbit the Sun. As it travels, its shape as seen through a telescope appears to change because we see different parts of the planet lit by sunlight.

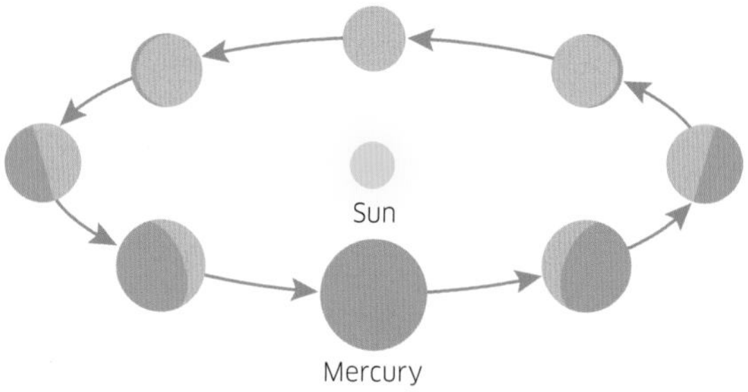
Sun
Mercury

Deep impact

The Caloris Basin, seen here in false colour, is one of the biggest impact craters in the Solar System. The crater is 1,550 km (960 miles) wide, but the collision that produced it was so violent that debris was flung more than 1,000 km (620 miles) beyond the crater rim.

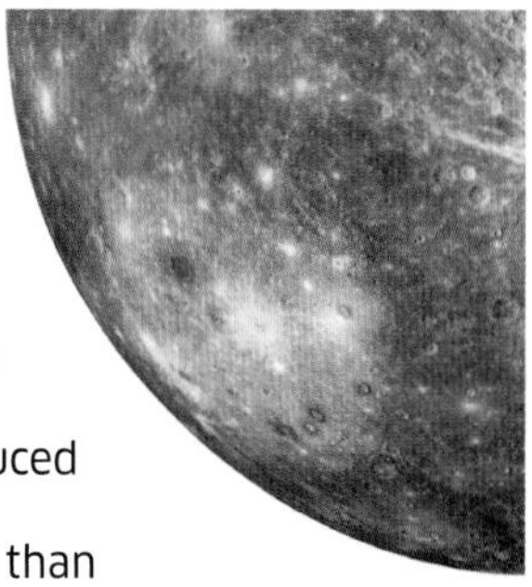
Caloris Basin

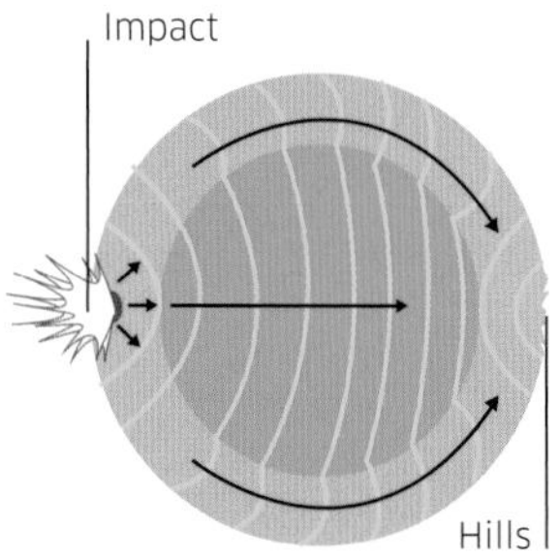
Impact
Hills

Cracked planet
On the opposite side of Mercury from the Caloris Basin is a strange area of jumbled hills. Scientists think shock waves from the giant impact travelled all the way through Mercury and converged here, cracking the ground.

FAST FACTS

Surface gravity (Earth = 1): 0.38

Time to rotate once: 59 Earth days

Year: 88 Earth days

Moons: 0

Core
Mercury's gigantic core is made of iron. Because of the way Mercury wobbles a little as it rotates, scientists think the outer part of the core might be liquid.
Mantle
At only 600 km (370 miles) deep, Mercury's mantle is remarkably thin. Like Earth's mantle, it's made of silicate rock.
Crust
Unlike Earth's crust, which is broken into plates, Mercury's crust is a single solid shell of rock.
Atmosphere
Because Mercury's gravity is weak and its surface is blasted by solar radiation, its atmosphere is thin and contains only a trace of gas.
Scar face
Impacts billions of years ago have left Mercury thoroughly pitted by craters. Because the planet is small, it doesn't have enough gravity to hold on to a thick atmosphere, and there's no air to stop meteorites crashing into it.
At the base of the mantle is a solid layer of iron sulphide. On Earth this mineral forms shiny rocks known as "fool's gold".

1966 The year in which the Russian Venera 7 became **the first space probe to land on Venus.**

Venus rotates in the **opposite direction** to other planets.

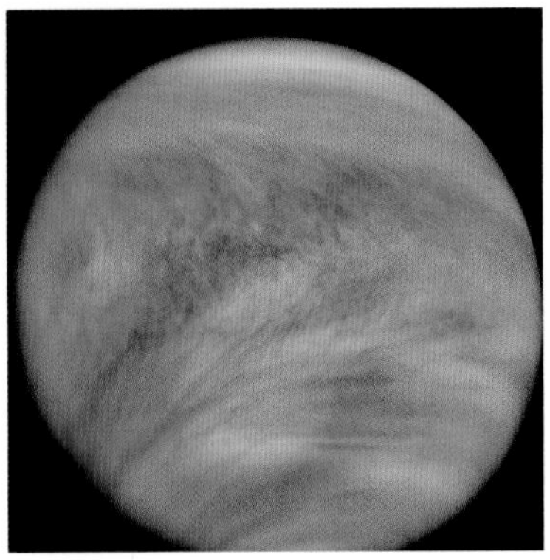

Deadly clouds

Venus's dense atmosphere is about 97 per cent carbon dioxide. A thick layer of cloud, about 60 km (35 miles) above the surface, hides the planet's surface entirely. These clouds are made of drops of sulphuric acid.

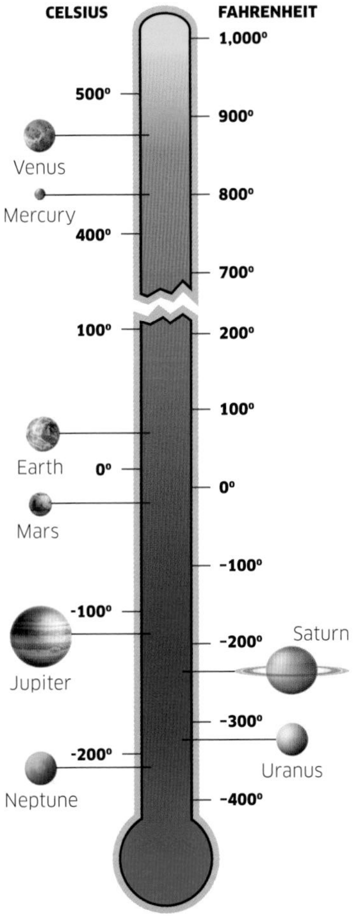
CELSIUS
FAHRENHEIT
1,000°
500°
900°
Venus
800°
Mercury
400°
700°
100°
200°
100°
Earth
0°
0°
Mars
-100°
-100°
-200°
Saturn
Jupiter
-300°
-200°
Uranus
Neptune
-400°
SURFACE TEMPERATURE OF THE PLANETS

Hot planet

Venus is hot not just because it is close to the Sun but also because its air contains so much carbon dioxide. Like glass in a greenhouse, carbon dioxide traps the Sun's heat. This greenhouse effect warms Earth too, because of the water vapour and carbon dioxide in the air, but it is much weaker than on Venus.

Venus

Our nearest neighbour in space, Venus is very similar to Earth in size. However, the furnace-like surface of this rocky planet bears little resemblance to our world.

Venus is cloaked in swirls of yellowish clouds. Unlike Earth's clouds, which contain life-giving water, these clouds are made of deadly sulphuric acid. The atmosphere is so thick that pressure on the planet's surface is 92 times that on Earth – enough to crush a car flat. At 460°C (860°F), the surface is also hotter than that of any other planet in the Solar System.

Volcanoes

Venus has more volcanoes than any other planet in the Solar System. Half a billion years ago, the entire surface of the planet was remade by volcanic eruptions. We can't see if any of the volcanoes are active as Venus's thick clouds hide them from view. However, scientists have detected unusual heat from the largest volcano, Maat Mons (below), which suggests it might be erupting.

Many craters on the surface, called coronas, were made not by impacts but by collapsing volcanoes.

Blank areas in the model of Venus are regions that the Magellan spacecraft did not survey.

The Dali Chasma is a 2,000 km (1,243 mile) long network of canyons and valleys.

FAST FACTS

Surface gravity (Earth = 1): 0.91

Moons: 0

Year: 225 Earth days

Time to rotate once: 243 Earth days

Pancake domes
Unlike volcanoes on Earth, those on Venus rarely erupt explosively. Instead, they ooze lava slowly. In some places, thick lava has piled up on the surface to form squat, rounded volcanoes called pancake domes.

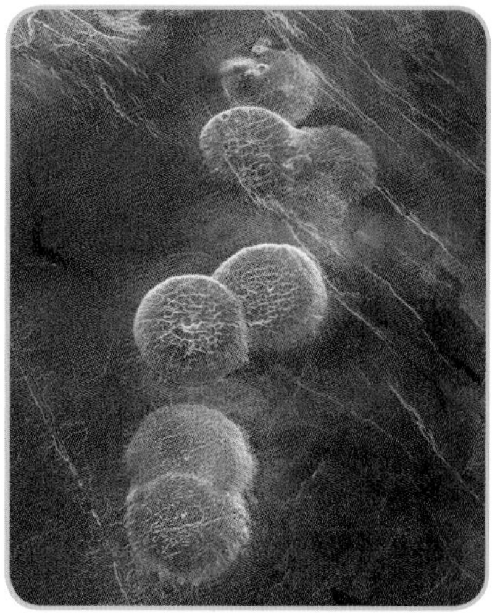

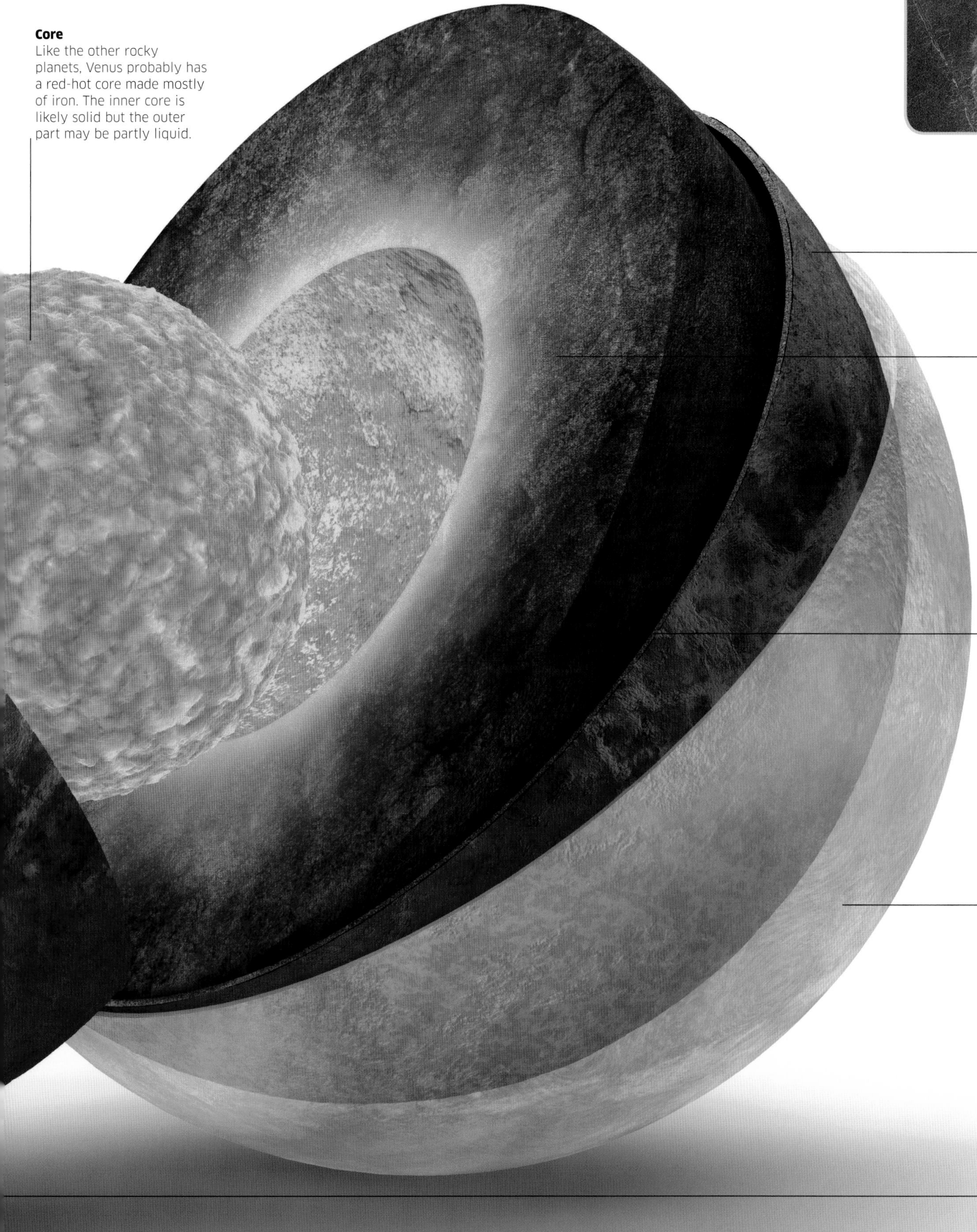

Core
Like the other rocky planets, Venus probably has a red-hot core made mostly of iron. The inner core is likely solid but the outer part may be partly liquid.

The surface consists of bare rock and is so hot that an astronaut would be burnt to a cinder in just a few minutes.

Mantle
Venus's mantle of rock is kept slightly soft by heat from the core. Over millions of years, the soft rock slowly churns about.

Crust
Unlike Earth's crust, that of Venus is quite thick and rarely moves, merely bulging up in places every now and then.

Atmosphere
Venus has the thickest, densest atmosphere of all the rocky planets, with a permanent blanket of cloud that covers the entire planet. The cloud-free view on the left side of this 3-D model was created from radar data sent to Earth by the Magellan spacecraft.

107,000 kph (67,000 mph) – the average speed at which Earth orbits the Sun.

Earth

Of all the planets known to science, ours is the only one known to harbour life and to have vast oceans of liquid water on the surface.

Earth's distance from the Sun and its moderately thick atmosphere mean it never gets very hot or very cold at the surface. In fact, it is always just the right temperature for water to stay liquid, making life as we know it possible. That is very different from scorching Venus, where all water boils away, and icy Mars, where any water seems to be frozen. Life on Earth began around 3.8 billion years ago, soon after the newly formed planet cooled down, allowing water to form oceans. Since then, living organisms have slowly transformed the planet's surface, colouring the land green and adding oxygen to the atmosphere, which makes our air breathable.

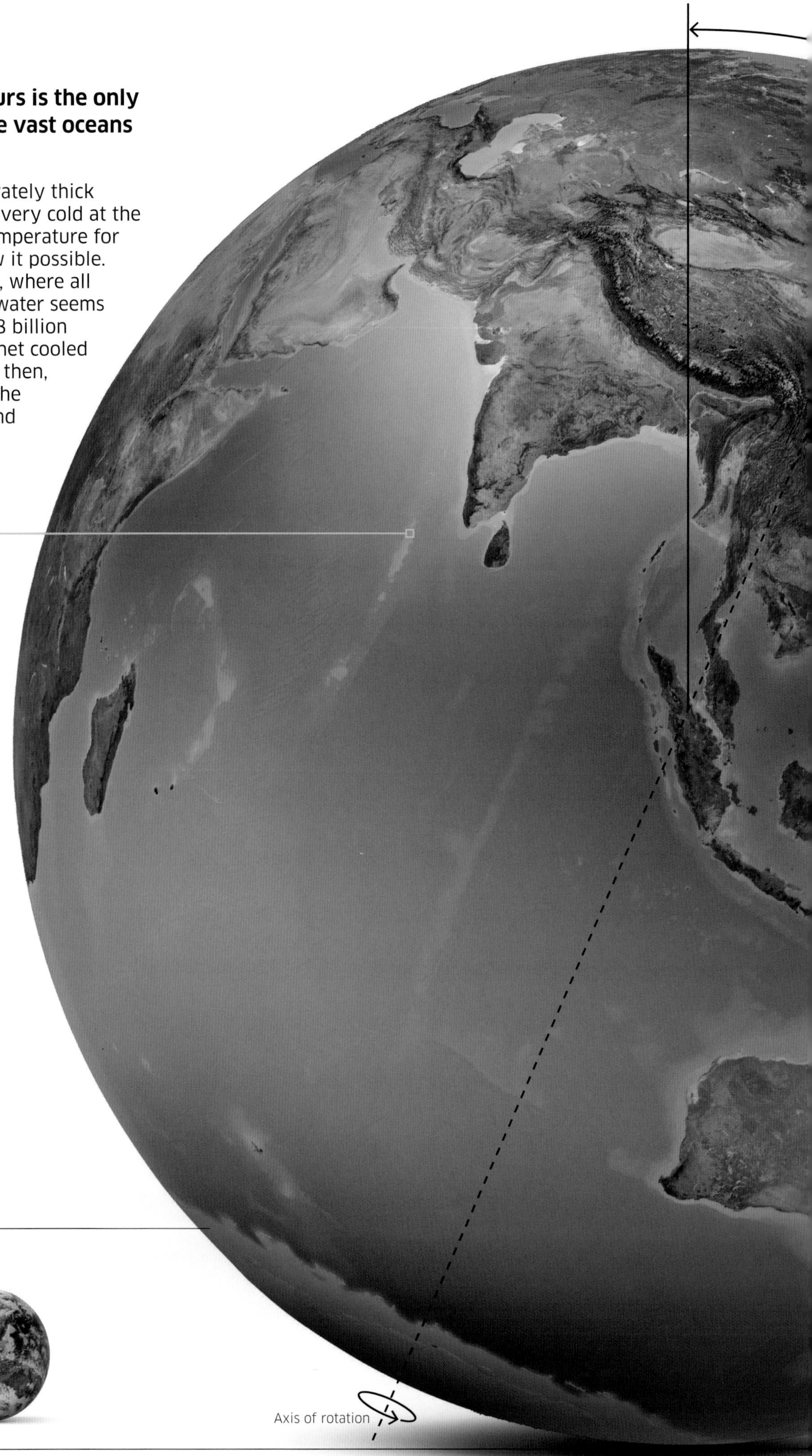
Axis of rotation

Life in water
Water is essential to all forms of life on Earth because the chemical reactions that keep organisms alive happen in water. Most scientists think life began in water, perhaps at the bottom of the sea, where volcanic chimneys might have provided essential warmth and nutrients. Today, oceans contain some of the most diverse natural habitats on the planet, such as the coral reefs of tropical seas.

Polar ice
Because Earth's poles receive so little warmth from the Sun, they are permanently cold and are covered in ice. An icy continent sits over Earth's South Pole, but an icy ocean sits at the North Pole.

FAST FACTS

Time to rotate once: 23.9 hours

Year: 365.26 days

Moons: 1

Average temperature: 16°C (61°F)

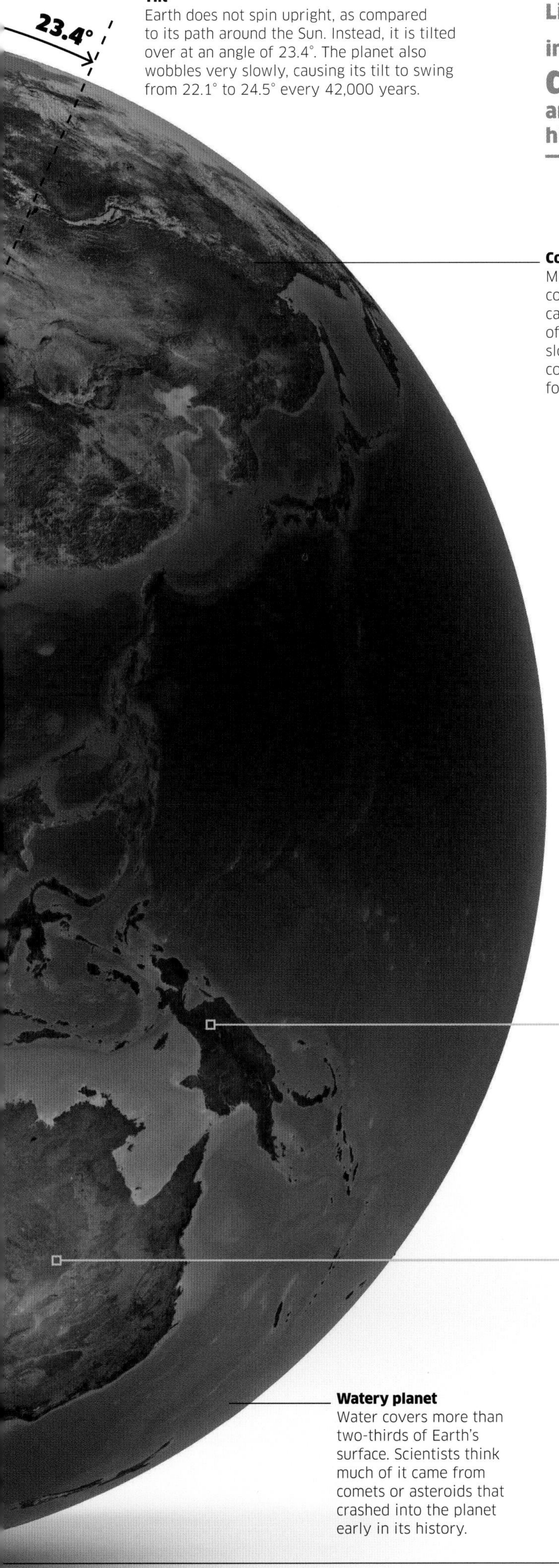
23.4°

Tilt
Earth does not spin upright, as compared to its path around the Sun. Instead, it is tilted over at an angle of 23.4°. The planet also wobbles very slowly, causing its tilt to swing from 22.1° to 24.5° every 42,000 years.

Living organisms have been found in rock 5 km (3 miles) deep underground and in the air 16 km (10 miles) high in the atmosphere.

Continents
Most of Earth's land is concentrated in large masses called continents. Over millions of years, the continents very slowly move around the planet, colliding and breaking up to form new patterns.

Life on land
For billions of years life existed only in water. Then, 475 million years ago, tiny plants inched their way out of swamps and onto land. From this small beginning, life spread over the continents, covering the wettest places with dense forests.

Watery planet
Water covers more than two-thirds of Earth's surface. Scientists think much of it came from comets or asteroids that crashed into the planet early in its history.

Orbit and seasons

Earth's tilt causes different parts of the planet to lean towards the Sun or away from it during the year, creating seasons. When the northern hemisphere leans towards the Sun, the weather is warmer and days are longer, causing the season of summer. When it leans away from the Sun, the weather is colder and nights are longer, causing winter.

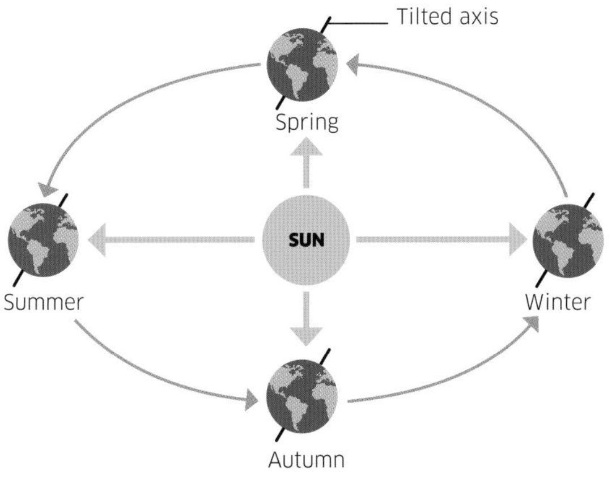
Tilted axis
Spring
SUN
Summer
Winter
Autumn

Human influence

In recent centuries, our species has changed Earth's surface so much that our influence is visible from space. As well as lighting up the planet's night side with electricity, we have changed the atmosphere and climate and have replaced large areas of natural ecosystems with farmland and cities.

Deserts
Not all of Earth's surface is covered by life. Deserts don't have enough water to sustain lush forests, and only special kinds of plants and animals can survive in them. Some of Earth's deserts resemble landscapes of other planets. The deserts of central Australia even have the same reddish colour as Martian deserts, thanks to iron oxide in the soil – the chemical that gives Mars its colour.

4.5 billion years – the age of planet Earth.

Inside Earth

If you could pull Earth apart with your hands, you'd discover it's made of distinct layers that fit together like the layers of an onion.

Earth is made almost entirely of rock and metal. When the young planet was forming and its interior was largely molten, heavy materials like metal sank all the way to the centre, while lighter materials such as rock settled on top. Today, Earth's interior is mostly solid, but it is still very hot, with temperatures rising to 6,000°C (10,800°F) in the core, which is hotter than the surface of the Sun. This powerful inner heat keeps the planet's interior slowly moving.

Volcanic action
Most of the rock in Earth's crust and mantle is solid. However, pockets of molten rock form where plates collide or in hotspots where heat wells up from Earth's core. In such places, molten rock may erupt from the surface, forming volcanoes.

Stormy skies
Water from the oceans creates clouds in the lower part of Earth's atmosphere. The layer of clouds gives us rain, snow, and storms such as this hurricane over Florida, USA.

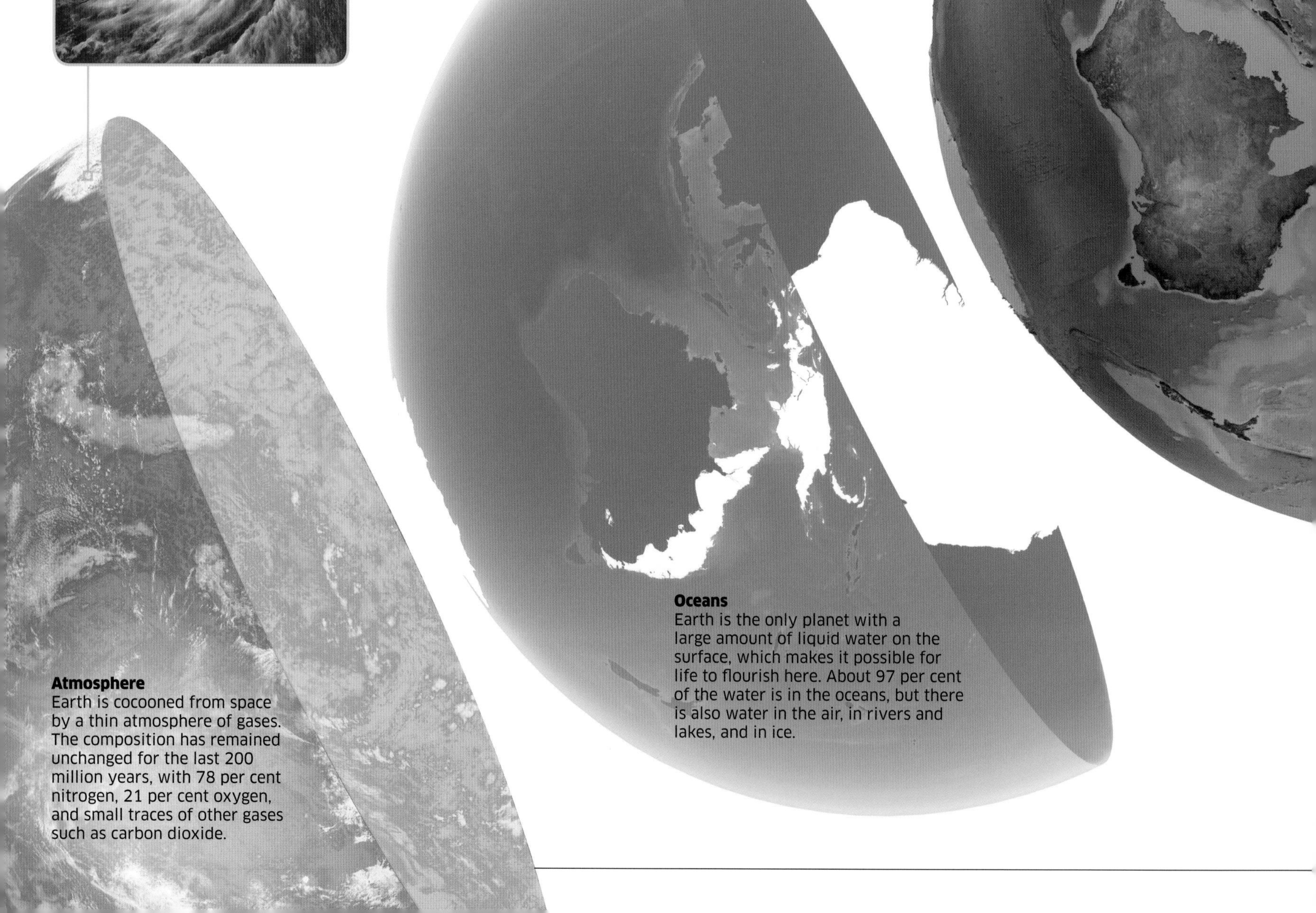

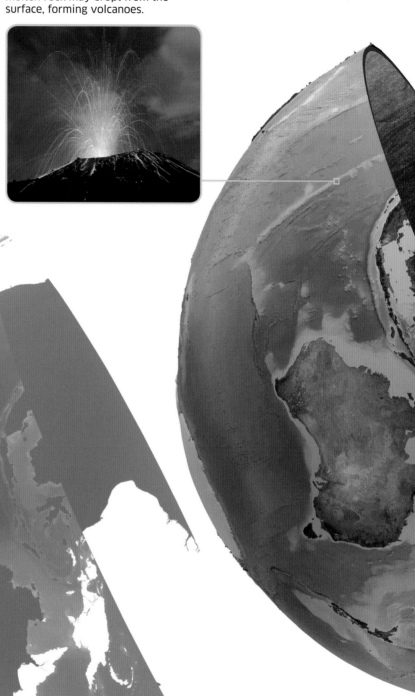

Oceans
Earth is the only planet with a large amount of liquid water on the surface, which makes it possible for life to flourish here. About 97 per cent of the water is in the oceans, but there is also water in the air, in rivers and lakes, and in ice.

Atmosphere
Earth is cocooned from space by a thin atmosphere of gases. The composition has remained unchanged for the last 200 million years, with 78 per cent nitrogen, 21 per cent oxygen, and small traces of other gases such as carbon dioxide.

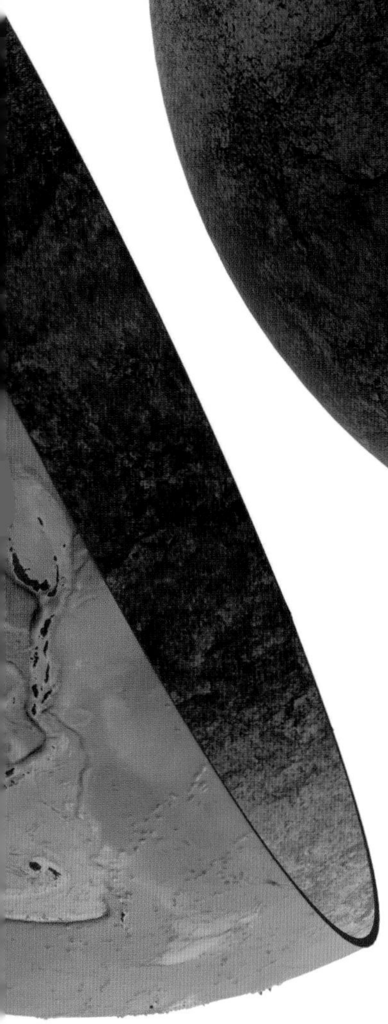

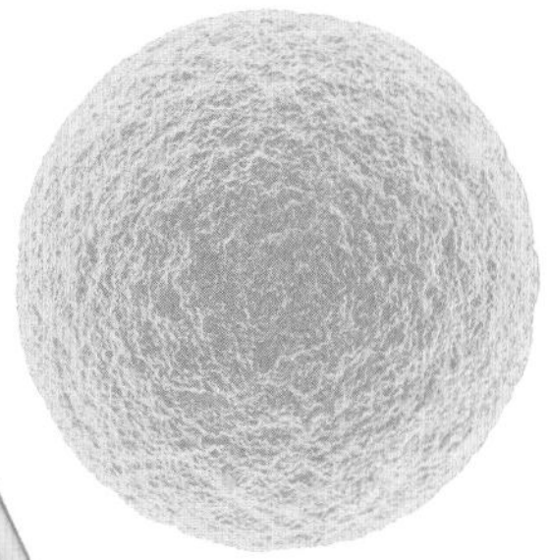

Inner core
The inner part of the core is solid metal. The pressure here is so high that the iron and nickel are solid despite the intense heat. The temperature is about 6,000°C (10,800°F).

Outer core
Around 3,000 km (1,850 miles) below Earth's surface is the planet's core, which is made of white-hot iron and nickel. The core is so hot that its outer layer is molten and swirls about. The swirling motion generates Earth's magnetic field.

Mantle
Beneath the crust is a 2,900 km (1,800 mile) thick layer of rock called the mantle. Heat from the core makes the rock in the mantle slightly soft. Over millions of years, it churns about slowly like thick treacle, and this motion moves the rigid crust on top.

Crust
The outermost part of Earth's solid surface is the crust, which is only a few dozen kilometres deep. Thick areas of crust form continents, while thin areas form the floors of oceans.

Tectonic plates

Earth's brittle outer crust is broken into giant slabs called tectonic plates. There are seven or eight major plates and dozens of small ones. The plates move across Earth's surface at about the speed that fingernails grow, carrying the continents with them.

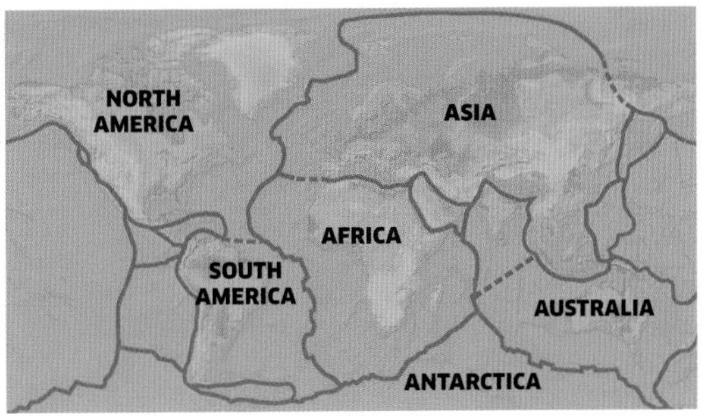
NORTH AMERICA
ASIA
AFRICA
SOUTH AMERICA
AUSTRALIA
ANTARCTICA

Atmosphere

Earth's atmosphere has five layers, but only the bottom layer contains clouds and breathable air. Airliners fly above the clouds in the clear air of the stratosphere. The atmosphere has no upper edge as it fades gradually, but the boundary between the atmosphere and space is defined as 100 km (62 miles) high, which is in the thermosphere.

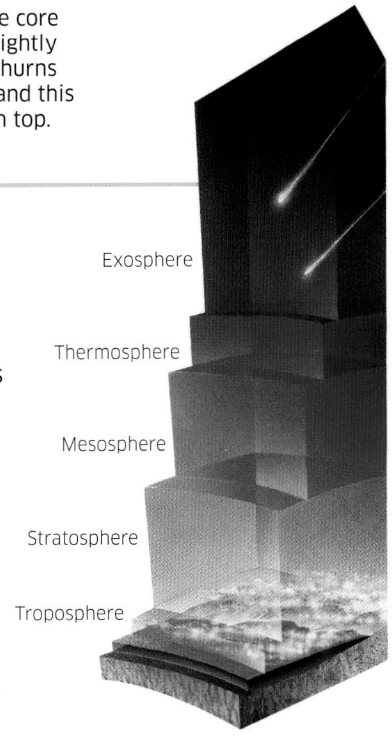
Exosphere
Thermosphere
Mesosphere
Stratosphere
Troposphere

380 kg (838 lb) – the amount of Moon rock brought to Earth by Apollo astronauts.

How the Moon formed

Scientists have various theories about how the Moon formed. Most think it formed when a small planet smashed into the young Earth around 4.5 billion years ago. The impact destroyed the small planet and tipped over Earth's axis of rotation. Debris was flung into space to form a cloud. Over time, the debris particles stuck together to become the Moon.

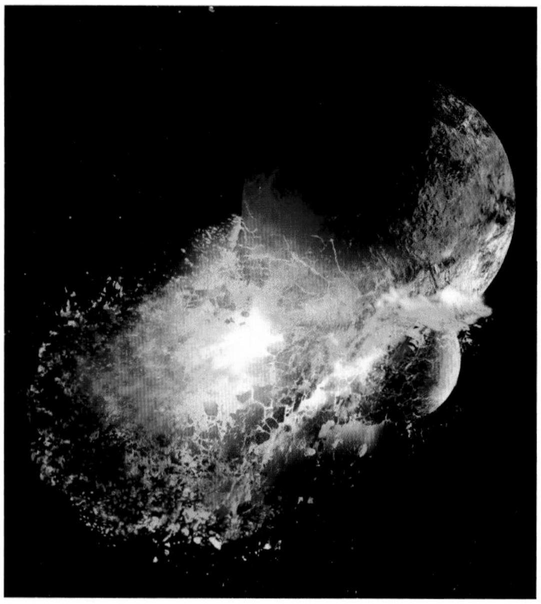

Weak gravity

The force of gravity, which pulls things to the ground, is much weaker on the Moon than on Earth because the Moon has less mass. Astronauts weigh one-sixth of their Earth weight on the Moon and would be able to jump six times higher if they didn't have heavy spacesuits.

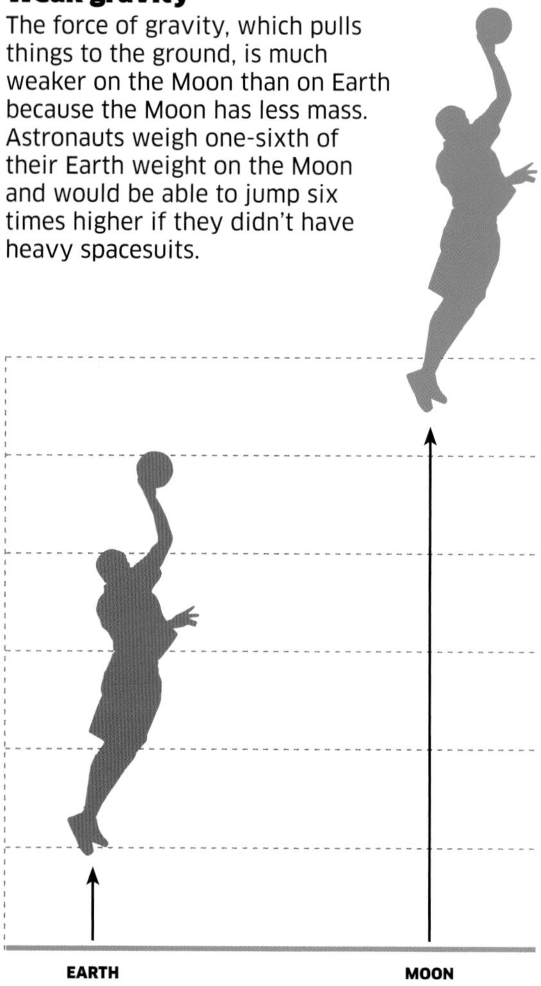
EARTH
MOON

Inner core
In the centre of the Moon is a ball of incredibly hot but solid iron about 500 km (300 miles) wide. Its temperature is about 1,300°C (2,400°F).
Outer core
Surrounding the inner core is a layer of iron that may have melted, thanks to lower pressure. This outer core is about 700 km (430 miles) wide.
Lower mantle
Heat from the core has probably melted the bottom of the mantle, which is made of rock.

The Moon

So large and bright that we can see it even in daytime, the Moon is the only object in space whose surface features are visible to the naked eye.

The Moon is a quarter as wide as Earth, making it the largest moon relative to its parent planet in the Solar System. It is also the largest and brightest object in the night sky by far, and its fascinating surface – scarred with hundreds of thousands of impact craters – is a spectacular sight through binoculars or telescopes. The Moon formed about 4.5 billion years ago, shortly after Earth, but unlike Earth its surface has hardly changed in billions of years. The dark "seas", or maria, on its near side are flat plains formed by giant floods of lava that erupted about 3 billion years ago. Surrounding these are the lunar highlands, their ancient hills and valleys littered with the debris of countless meteorite impacts.

FAST FACTS

Time to orbit Earth: 27.32 Earth days

Mass (Earth = 1): 0.167

Distance from Earth: 385,000 km (239,227 miles)

Average diameter: 3,474 km (2,159 miles) wide

The far side
Because the Moon rotates exactly once each time it orbits Earth, we always see the same face: the near side. The Moon's far side, seen here from an Apollo spacecraft, can only be viewed from space. It is covered with large craters and has fewer of the dark seas that are common on the near side.

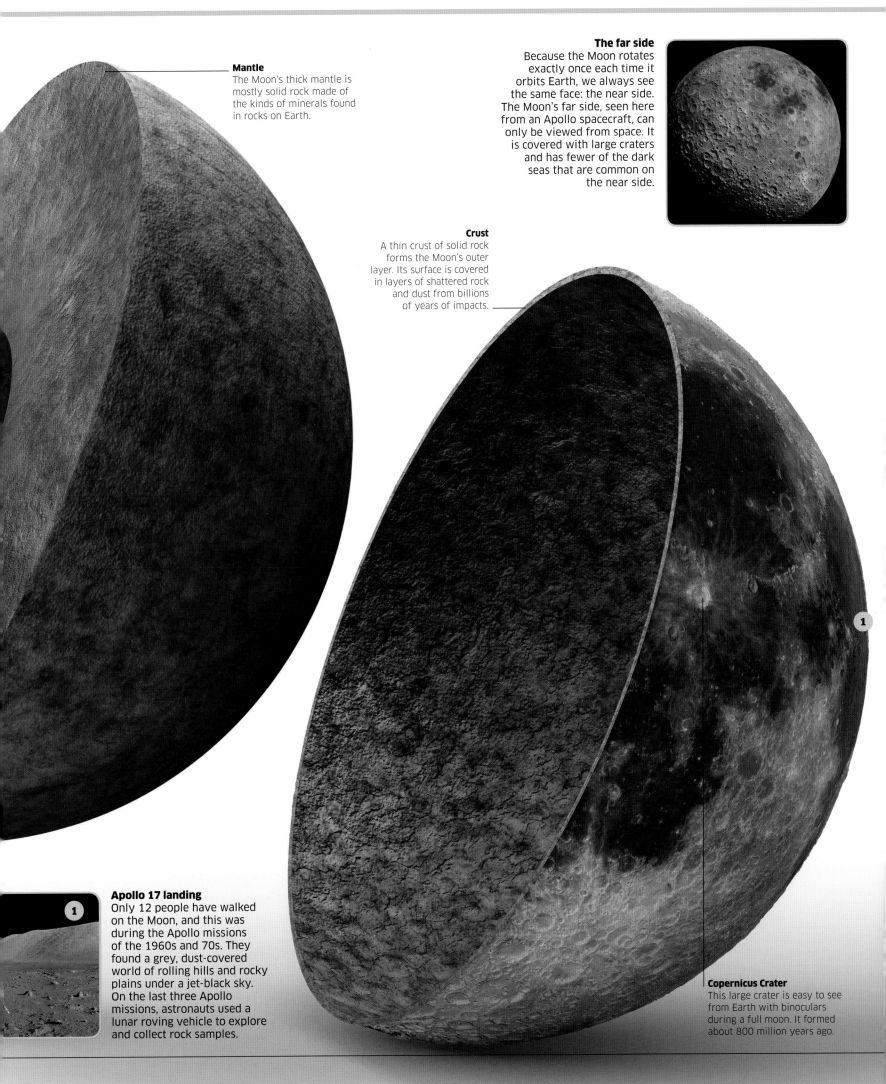

Mantle
The Moon's thick mantle is mostly solid rock made of the kinds of minerals found in rocks on Earth.

Crust
A thin crust of solid rock forms the Moon's outer layer. Its surface is covered in layers of shattered rock and dust from billions of years of impacts.

Copernicus Crater
This large crater is easy to see from Earth with binoculars during a full moon. It formed about 800 million years ago.

Apollo 17 landing
Only 12 people have walked on the Moon, and this was during the Apollo missions of the 1960s and 70s. They found a grey, dust-covered world of rolling hills and rocky plains under a jet-black sky. On the last three Apollo missions, astronauts used a lunar roving vehicle to explore and collect rock samples.

Key

Failed

Successful

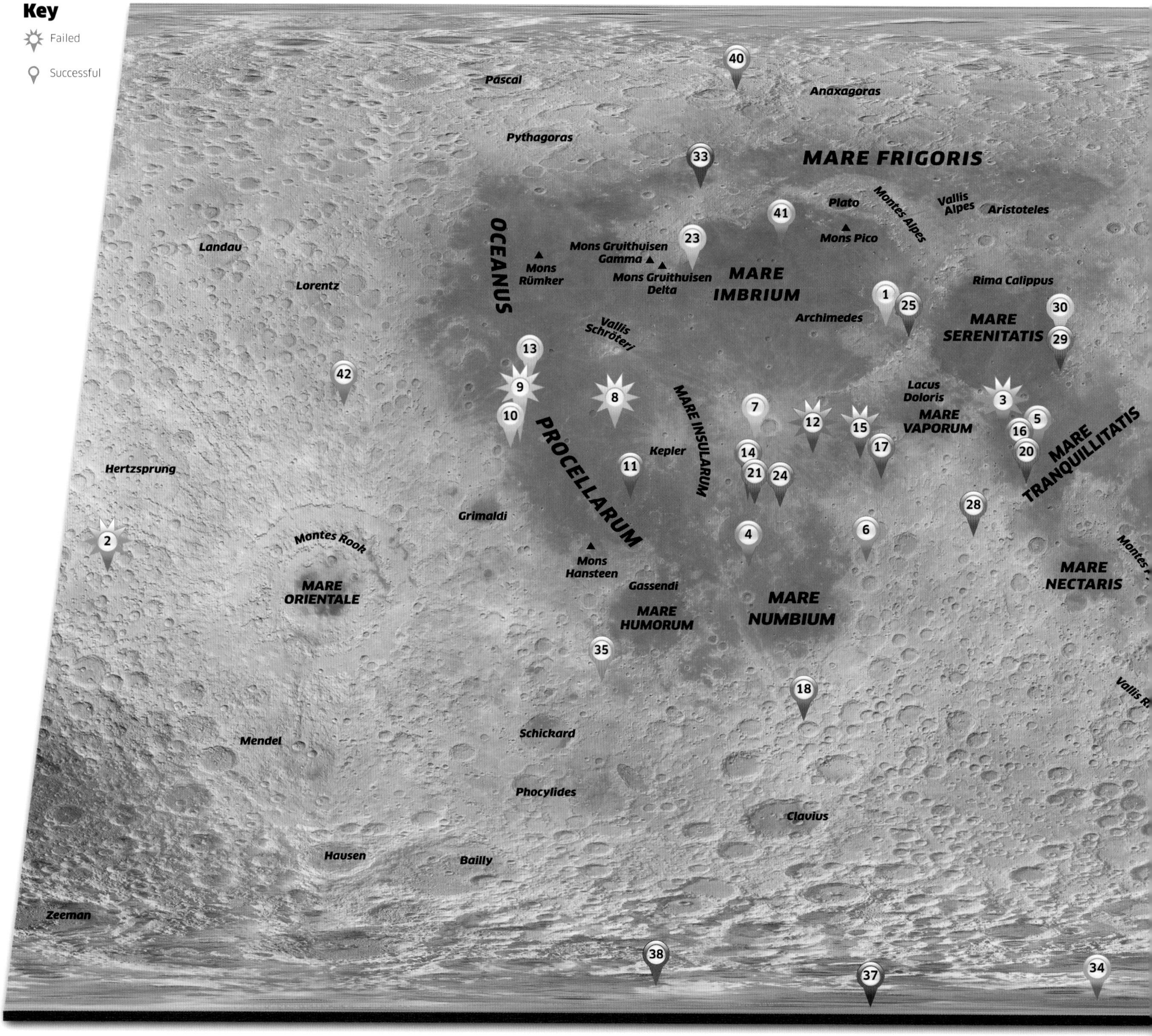

Pascal
Anaxagoras
Pythagoras
MARE FRIGORIS
Plato
Montes Alpes
Vallis Alpes
Aristoteles
Mons Pico
OCEANUS
Landau
Mons Rümker
Mons Gruithuisen Gamma
Mons Gruithuisen Delta
MARE IMBRIUM
Lorentz
Rima Calippus
Archimedes
MARE SERENITATIS
Vallis Schröteri
Lacus Doloris
MARE VAPORUM
MARE INSULARUM
PROCELLARUM
Kepler
MARE TRANQUILLITATIS
Hertzsprung
Grimaldi
Montes Rook
Mons Hansteen
MARE ORIENTALE
Gassendi
MARE HUMORUM
MARE NUMBIUM
MARE NECTARIS
Schickard
Mendel
Phocylides
Clavius
Hausen
Bailly
Zeeman

Landmark missions

Most lunar spacecraft were launched as part of a series of similar missions. The USA's Ranger Programme, for example, included nine missions, only three of which were successful. The first 20 or so years of Moon missions were driven by rivalry between the US and USSR, who saw conquering space as a sign of military might or political strength.

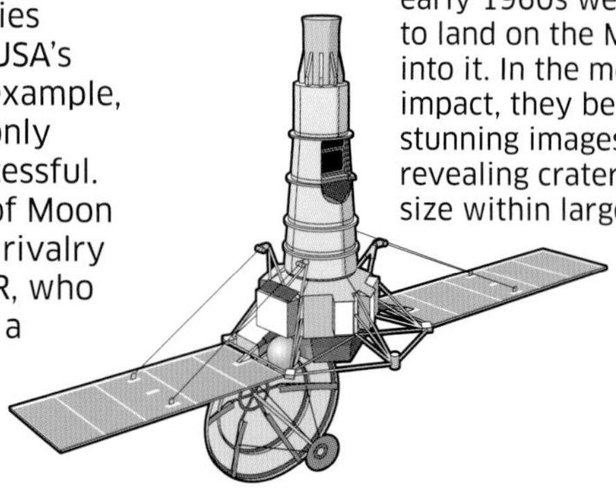

Ranger programme

The US Ranger spacecraft of the early 1960s were designed not to land on the Moon but to crash into it. In the moments before impact, they beamed back stunning images of the surface, revealing craters of ever smaller size within larger craters.

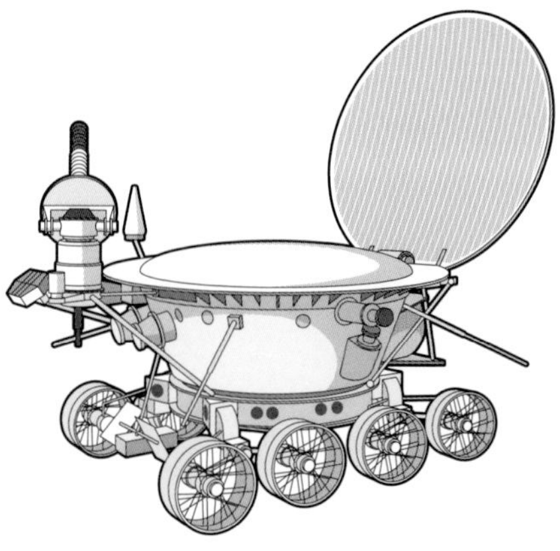

Lunokhod

Russia's Lunokhod ("moonwalker") rovers looked like bathtubs on wheels but were a great success. Lunokhod 1 was the first rover to explore another world. It travelled nearly 11 km (7 miles) in 1970–71 and took thousands of pictures. Powered by solar panels, it hibernated at night.

Exploring the Moon

Spacecraft have paid more visits to Earth's neighbour than any other body in the Solar System, and the Moon remains the only world beyond Earth that people have set foot on.

It takes only four days for a spacecraft to reach the Moon, which makes it an obvious target for robotic explorers. More than 100 missions to the Moon have been attempted, and more than 40 spacecraft have landed on it; their landing sites are shown on this map. Making a controlled, soft touchdown on the Moon is difficult, so most landers have performed "hard landings", crashing into the lunar surface at speed. The first hard landing was in 1959, and the first soft landing took place in 1966. Remarkably, just three years later, the US Apollo 11 mission placed two men on the Moon and returned them safely to Earth.

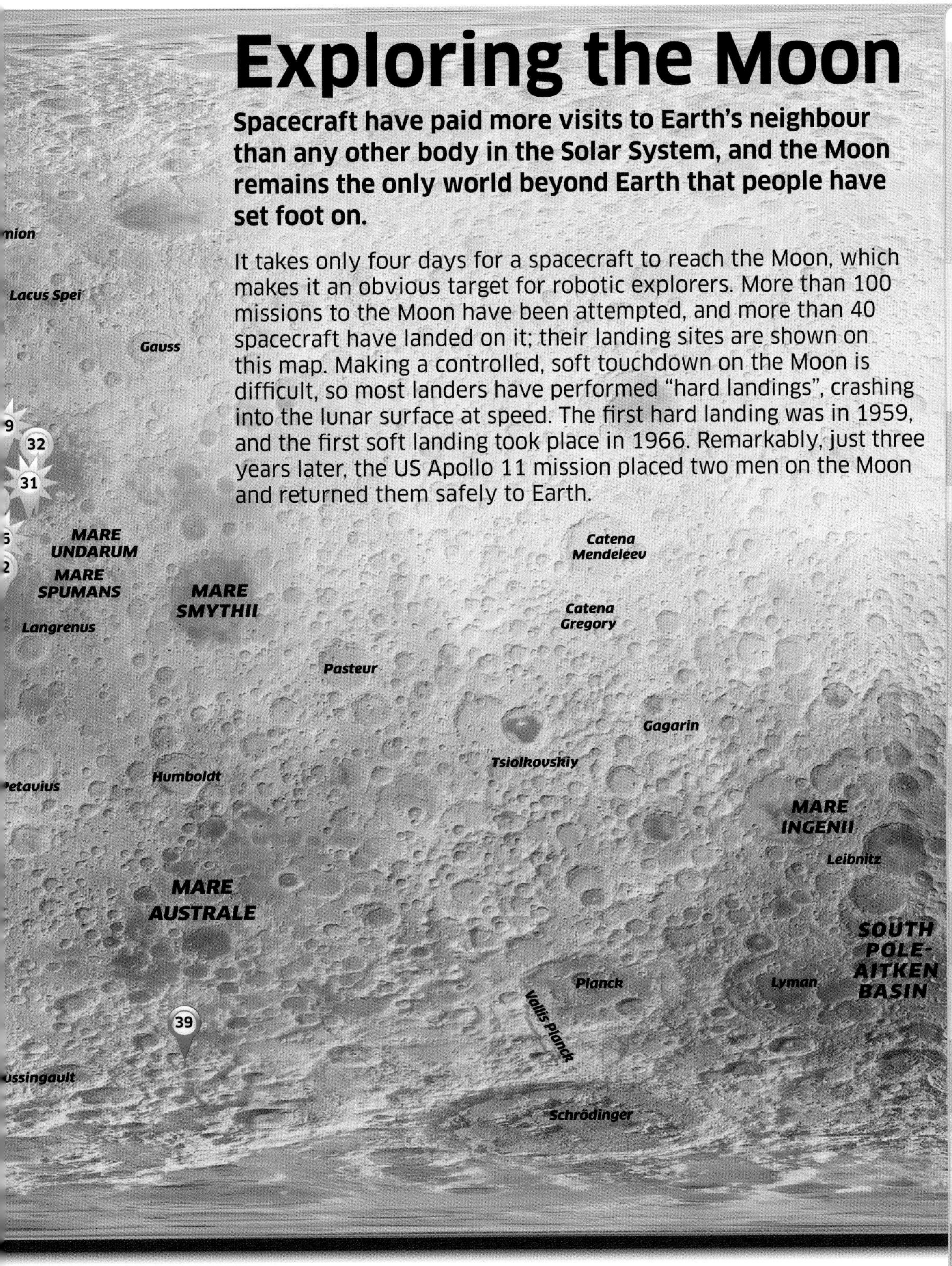
mion
Lacus Spei
Gauss
9
32
31
MARE UNDARUM
MARE SPUMANS
MARE SMYTHII
Langrenus
Catena Mendeleev
Catena Gregory
Pasteur
Gagarin
Tsiolkovskiy
Humboldt
etavius
MARE INGENII
Leibnitz
MARE AUSTRALE
SOUTH POLE-AITKEN BASIN
Planck
Vallis Planck
Lyman
39
ussingault
Schrödinger

	Name	Year	Country
1	Luna 2	1959	USSR
2	Ranger 4	1962	USA
3	Ranger 6	1964	USA
4	Ranger 7	1964	USA
5	Ranger 8	1965	USA
6	Ranger 9	1965	USA
7	Luna 5	1965	USSR
8	Luna 7	1965	USSR
9	Luna 8	1965	USSR
10	Luna 9	1966	USSR
11	Surveyor 1	1966	USA
12	Surveyor 2	1966	USA
13	Luna 13	1966	USSR
14	Surveyor 3	1967	USA
15	Surveyor 4	1967	USA
16	Surveyor 5	1967	USA
17	Surveyor 6	1967	USA
18	Surveyor 7	1978	USA
19	Luna 15	1969	USSR
20	Apollo 11	1969	USA
21	Apollo 12	1969	USA
22	Luna 16	1970	USSR
23	Luna 17/Lunokhod 1	1970	USSR
24	Apollo 14	1971	USA
25	Apollo 15	1971	USA
26	Luna 18	1971	USSR
27	Luna 20	1972	USSR
28	Apollo 16	1972	USA
29	Apollo 17	1972	USA
30	Luna 21/Lunokhod 2	1973	USSR
31	Luna 23	1974	USSR
32	Luna 24	1976	USSR
33	Hiten*	1993	Japan
34	Lunar prospector*	1999	USA
35	SMART-1*	2006	esa
36	Chang'e 1*	2007	China
37	Chandrayaan 1*	2008	India
38	LCROSS	2009	USA
39	SELENE*	2009	Japan
40	GRAIL*	2012	USA
41	Chang'e 3/Yutu	2013	China
42	LADEE*	2014	USA

*Lunar orbiters that impacted at the end of their missions.

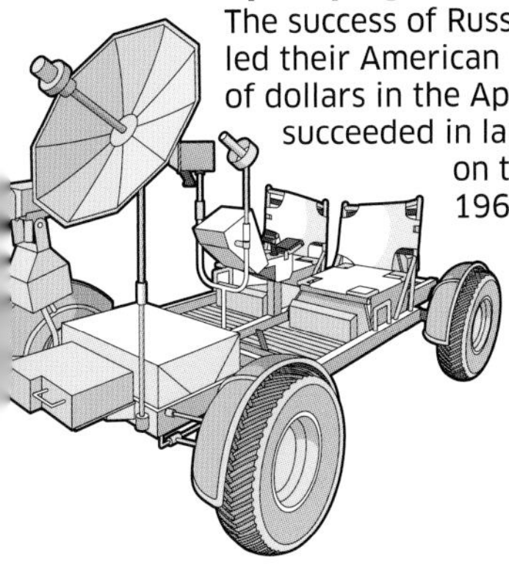

Apollo programme
The success of Russia's Luna Programme led their American rivals to invest billions of dollars in the Apollo programme, which succeeded in landing six manned craft on the Moon between 1969 and 1972. Later Apollo missions took a kind of car, the Lunar Roving Vehicle (LRV).

Yutu rover
China's Yutu rover arrived on the Moon in 2013, the first lunar rover since Lunokhod 2 in 1973. Although successful at first, it became unable to fold up its solar panels in preparation for the freezing lunar nights and was damaged by the cold. It drove a short distance after landing with the Chang'e 3 spacecraft.

3,300 km (2,050 miles) – the diameter of the **largest impact crater** in the Solar System: Utopia Planitia on Mars.

Impact craters

Asteroids, comets, and meteorites fly through space at such terrific speeds that they release devastating energy when they collide with planets and moons, vaporizing solid rock in an instant. The scars they leave behind are called impact craters.

Meteorite impacts have scarred the rocky planets and moons with countless craters. Our Moon is covered with craters, but Earth has far fewer – on Earth, craters are destroyed by erosion and other forces, while those on the Moon remain preserved for billions of years. Many of the Moon's craters formed early in the Solar System's history, when the inner planets were bombarded by asteroids. Collisions are much more rare today, but they still pose a deadly risk to Earth.

Lunar impact

The explosive force of a meteorite impact comes not just from the object's size but also from its speed. A typical meteorite is travelling at about 70,000 kph (45,000 mph) when it collides with a body such as the Moon, as shown here. This means it has 1,000 times as much kinetic energy as an equal-sized rock travelling at the speed of a car. When the meteorite collides, much of this kinetic energy turns into heat, causing rock in the ground to melt or even vaporize (turn to gas).

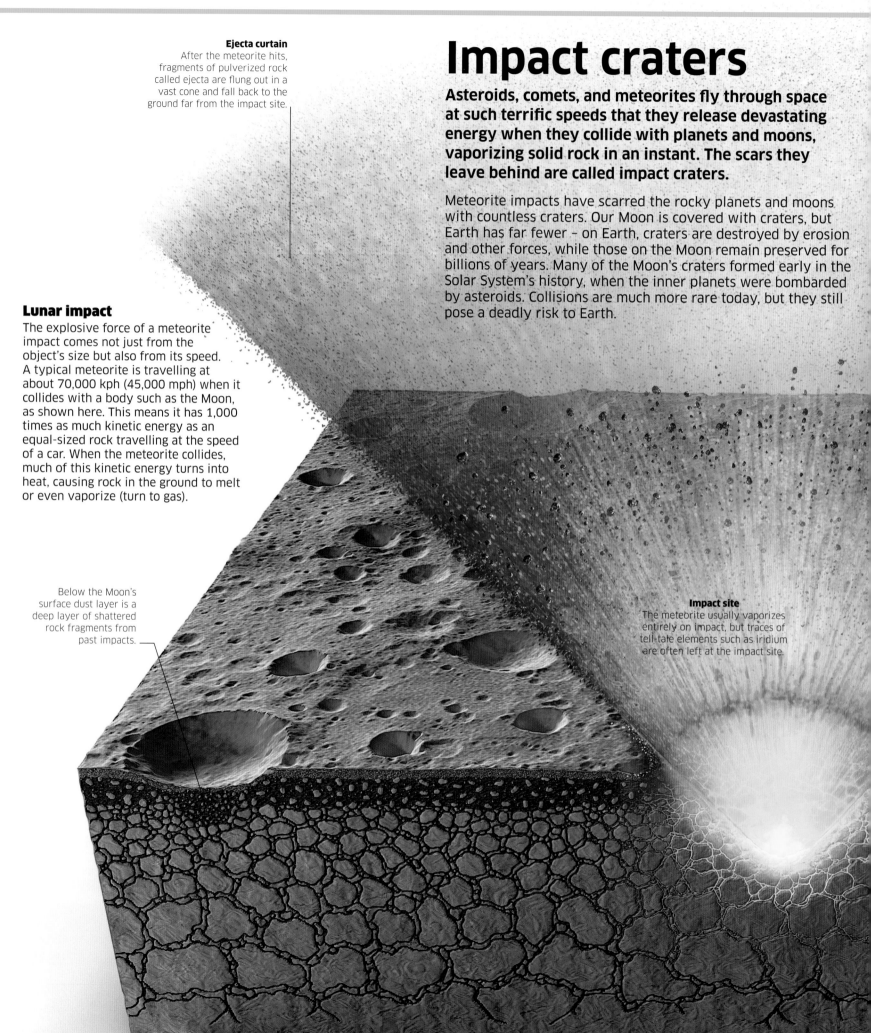

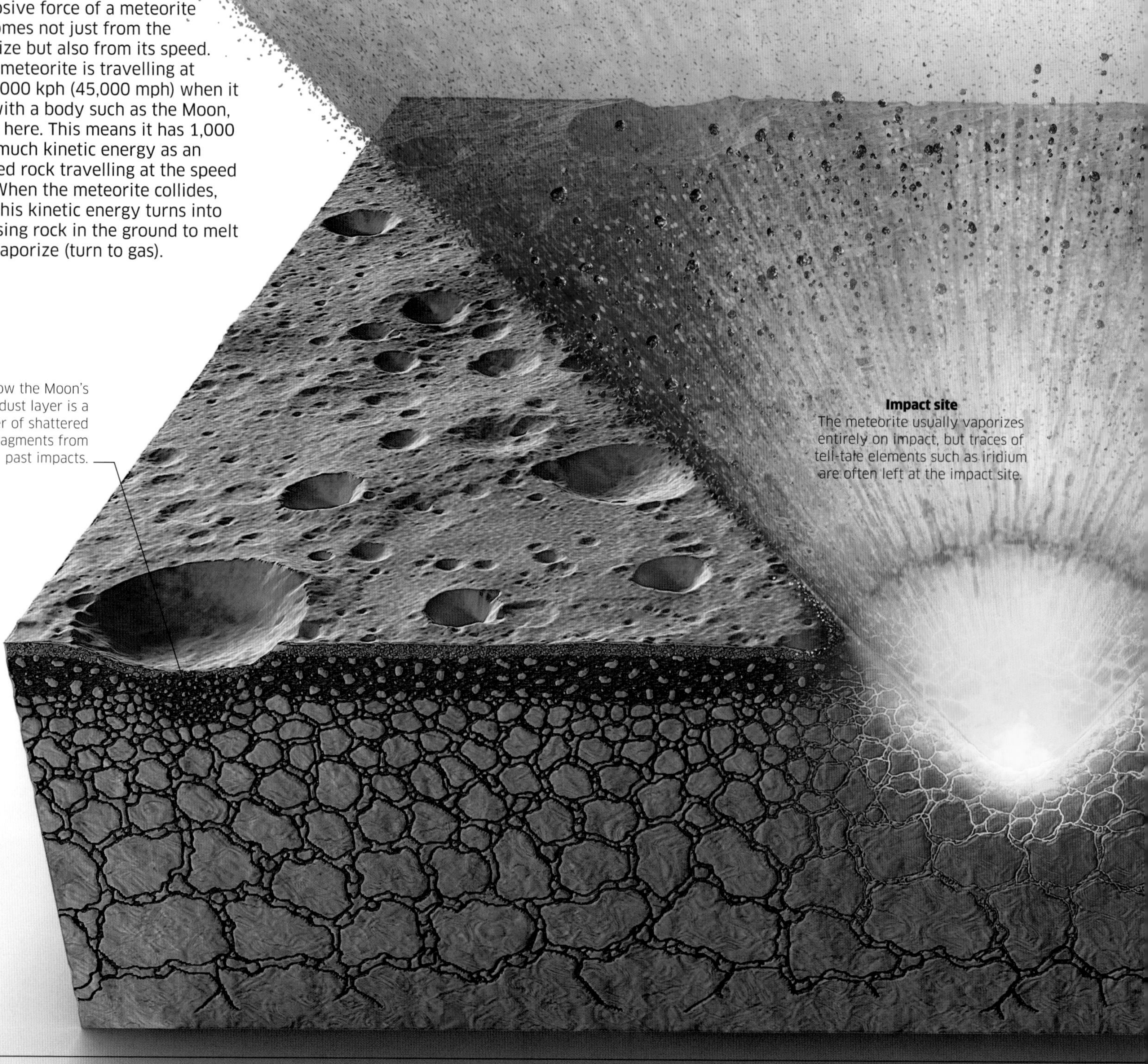
Ejecta curtain
After the meteorite hits, fragments of pulverized rock called ejecta are flung out in a vast cone and fall back to the ground far from the impact site.
Below the Moon's surface dust layer is a deep layer of shattered rock fragments from past impacts.
Impact site
The meteorite usually vaporizes entirely on impact, but traces of tell-tale elements such as iridium are often left at the impact site.

Vredefort crater in South Africa – the largest crater on Earth – is around **2 billion years old**.

The Aitken Basin impact crater on the Moon's south pole is **2,500 km (1,550 miles)** wide.

Barringer Crater

Barringer Crater (also known as Meteor Crater) in Arizona, USA, was the first site on Earth to be identified as an impact crater. Measuring just over 1 km (0.7 miles) wide, it formed some 50,000 years ago when a nickel-iron meteorite only 50 m (160 ft) or so wide struck the ground at around 50,000 kph (30,000 mph). The collision unleashed a thousand times more energy than the Hiroshima atomic bomb.

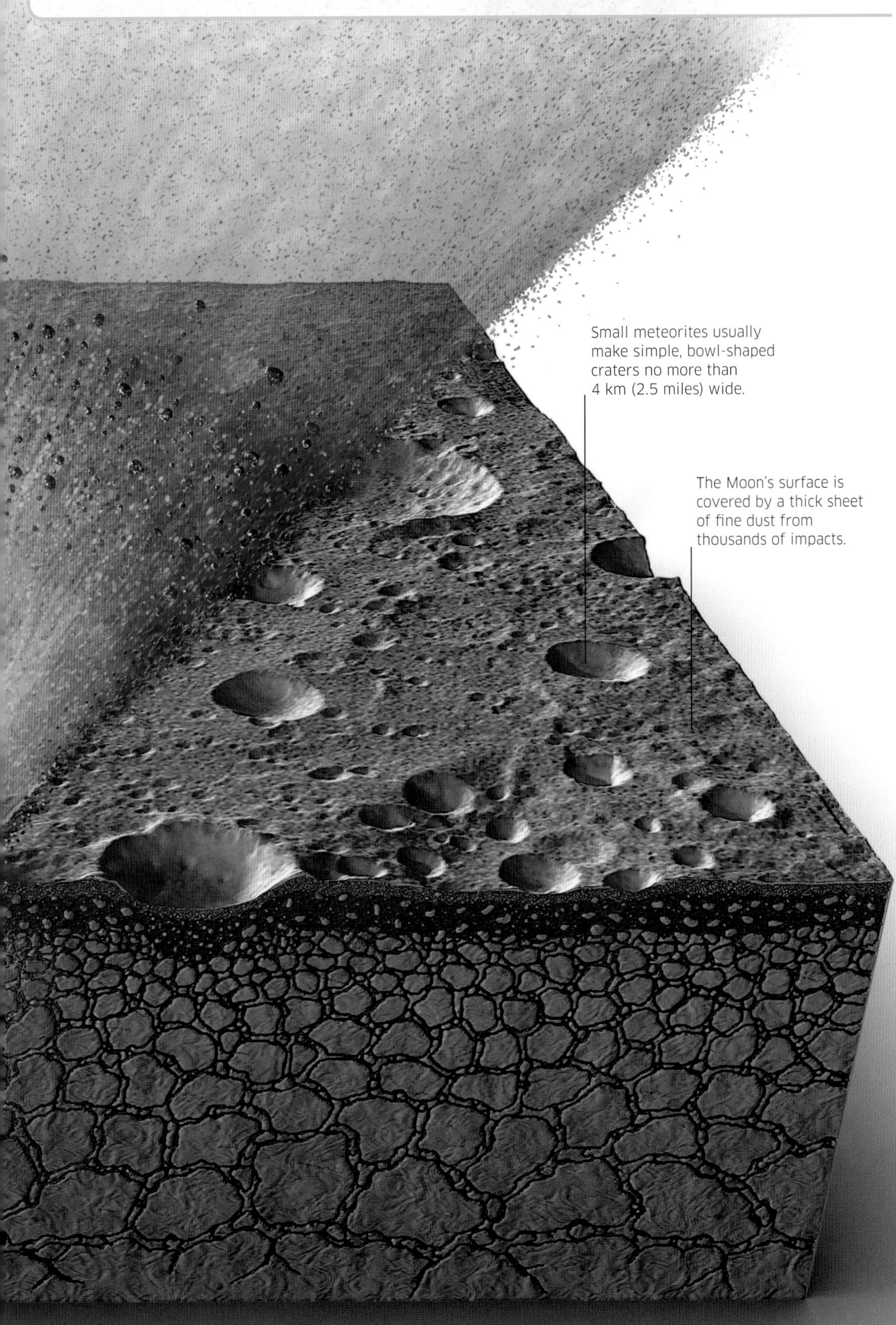
Small meteorites usually make simple, bowl-shaped craters no more than 4 km (2.5 miles) wide.
The Moon's surface is covered by a thick sheet of fine dust from thousands of impacts.

How craters form

It takes a mere ten minutes for an impact crater to fully form, but most of the action happens in the split second after impact, when the release of kinetic energy causes an effect like a nuclear explosion. Small impacts leave bowl-shaped pits, but larger impacts create more complex craters with central hills or terraces.

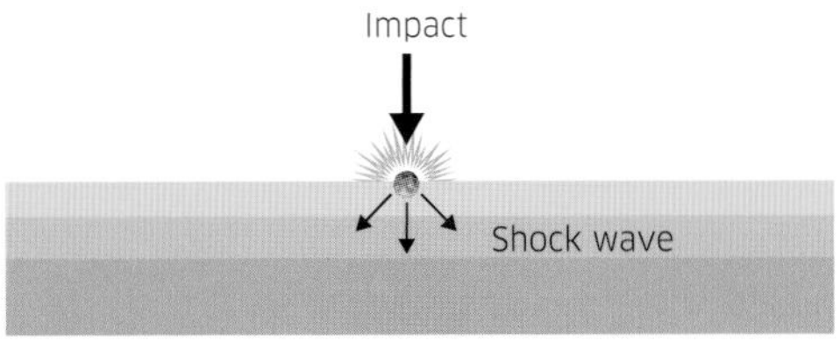
Impact
Shock wave

1 Contact
The meteorite smashes into the Moon, compressing the surface dramatically and sending a devastating shock wave through the ground, pulverizing lunar rock.

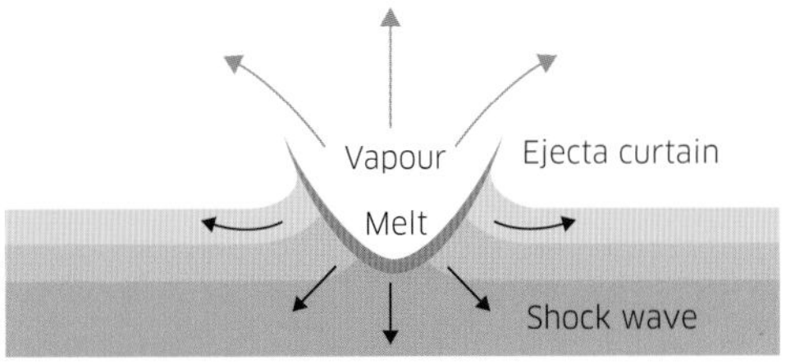
Vapour
Ejecta curtain
Melt
Shock wave

2 Transient crater forms
Energy released by the impact vaporizes the meteorite and much of the surface rock. Debris is thrown out in an ejecta curtain, forming a deep but transient crater.

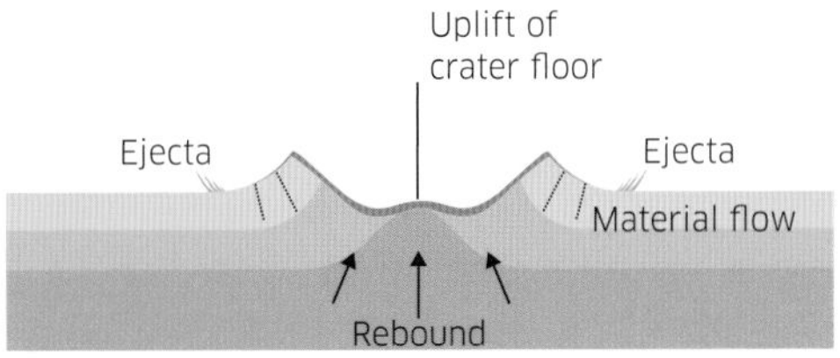
Uplift of crater floor
Ejecta
Ejecta
Material flow
Rebound

3 Collapse and rebound
The force of a large impact is so great that the pulverized ground flows like a liquid. The sides of the transient crater collapse, and the crater floor rebounds like water splashing, creating a central hill.

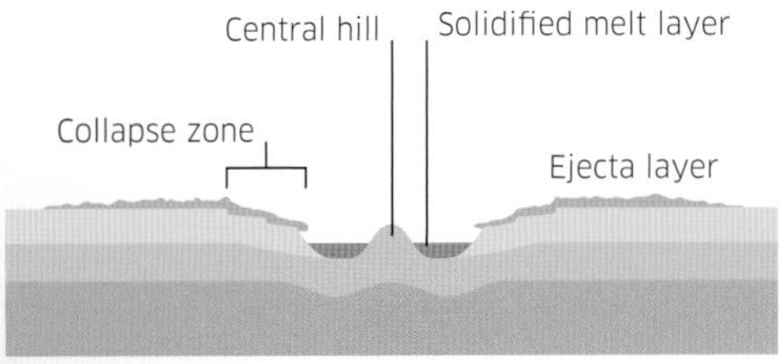
Central hill
Solidified melt layer
Collapse zone
Ejecta layer

4 Final crater
After a crater forms, its shape may remain unchanged for a long time, unless altered by volcanic or other geological activity. On the Moon, old craters frequently have younger craters within them.

2,000 kph (1,250 mph) – the **speed** at which the **Moon's shadow** crosses Earth during a solar eclipse.

Eclipses

A total solar eclipse is an amazing event. For a few minutes, the Sun disappears behind the Moon and day turns suddenly to night.

Eclipses happen when Earth and the Moon line up with the Sun and cast shadows on each other. When the Moon casts a shadow on Earth, our view of the Sun is blocked and we see a solar eclipse. When the Moon swings behind Earth and passes through Earth's shadow, we see a lunar eclipse – the Moon darkens and turns an unusual reddish colour.

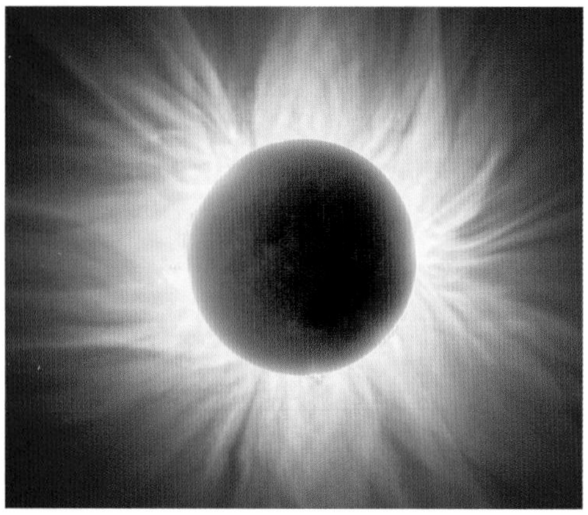

The corona

During a total solar eclipse, the Sun's spectacular outer atmosphere, which is normally impossible to see, becomes visible. Called the corona, it consists of billowing streams of hazy gas surrounding the Sun like a glowing white halo.

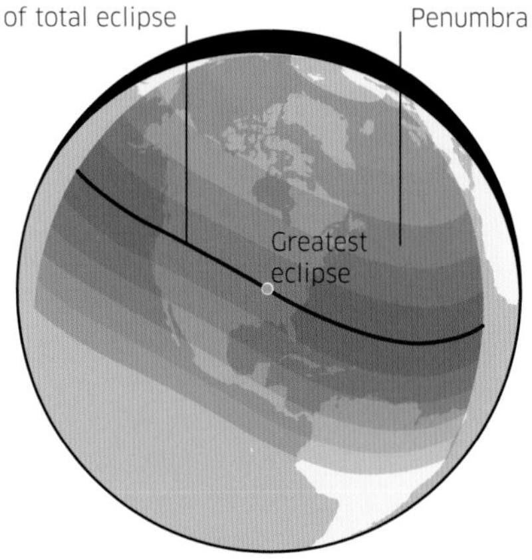
Path of total eclipse
Penumbra
Greatest eclipse

TOTAL SOLAR ECLIPSE OF 21 AUGUST 2017

Eclipse path

Astronomers can predict eclipses years in advance. This diagram shows where the total solar eclipse of 2017 will be visible. It will pass across North America from Portland, Oregon, at 5:15 pm (universal time) to Charleston, South Carolina, at 6:45 pm.

Solar eclipse

On most of its monthly orbits around Earth, the Moon does not line up directly with the Sun. When the Moon's main shadow (umbra) does sweep across Earth, it is only a few kilometres wide, so a total eclipse is visible only from a narrow strip across the globe. People viewing from the outer part of the shadow (the penumbra) barely notice the eclipse as the Sun is not completely covered. Because Earth is rotating, the umbra sweeps across the planet's surface quickly, giving viewers in any one spot only a couple of minutes to see it.

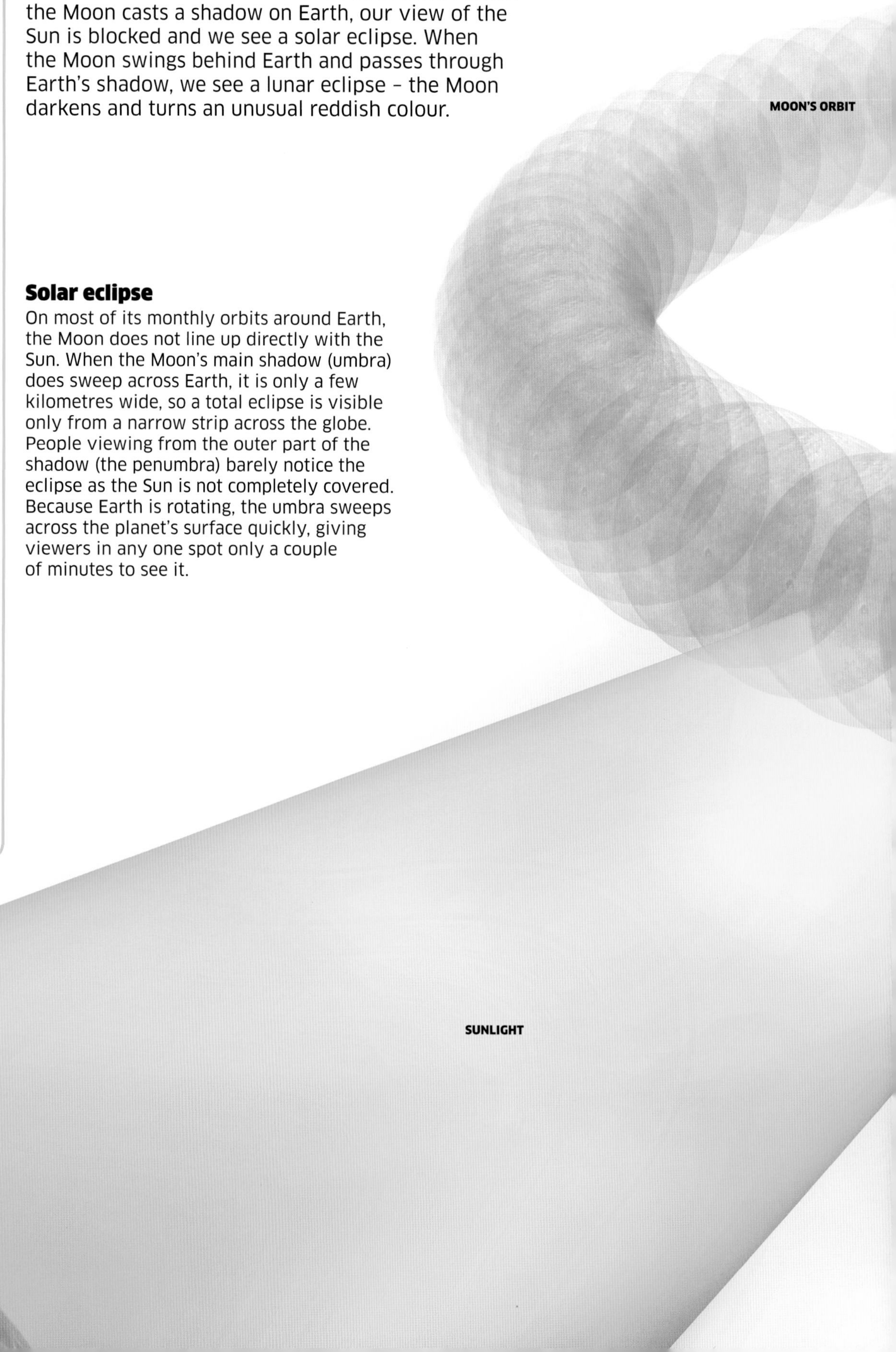
MOON'S ORBIT
SUNLIGHT
SUN

Lunar eclipse

In a total lunar eclipse, Earth's shadow covers the entire Moon. The Moon doesn't disappear from the night sky altogether, though, because some sunlight is deflected by Earth's atmosphere. This weak light is reddish like the light from a sunset and so it changes the Moon's colour.

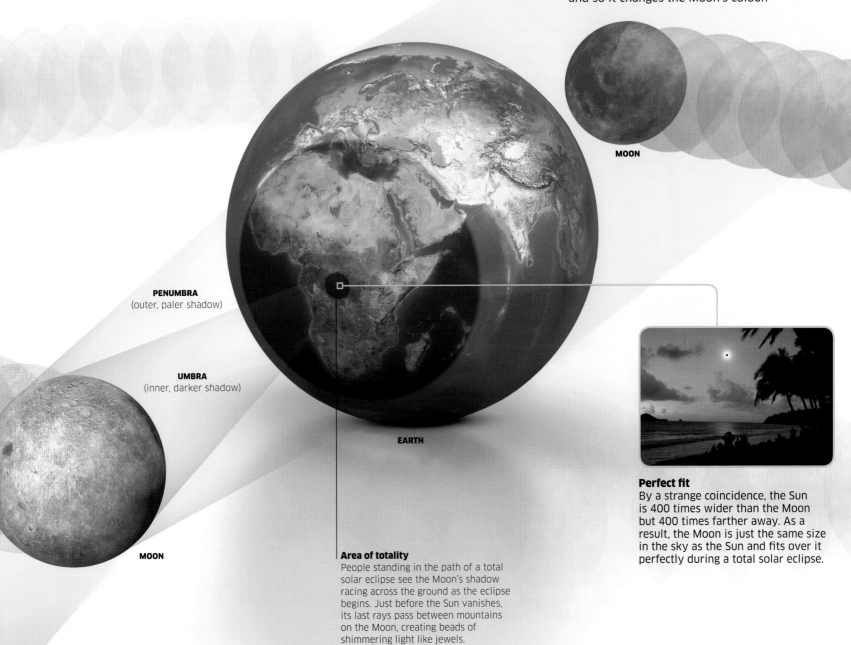

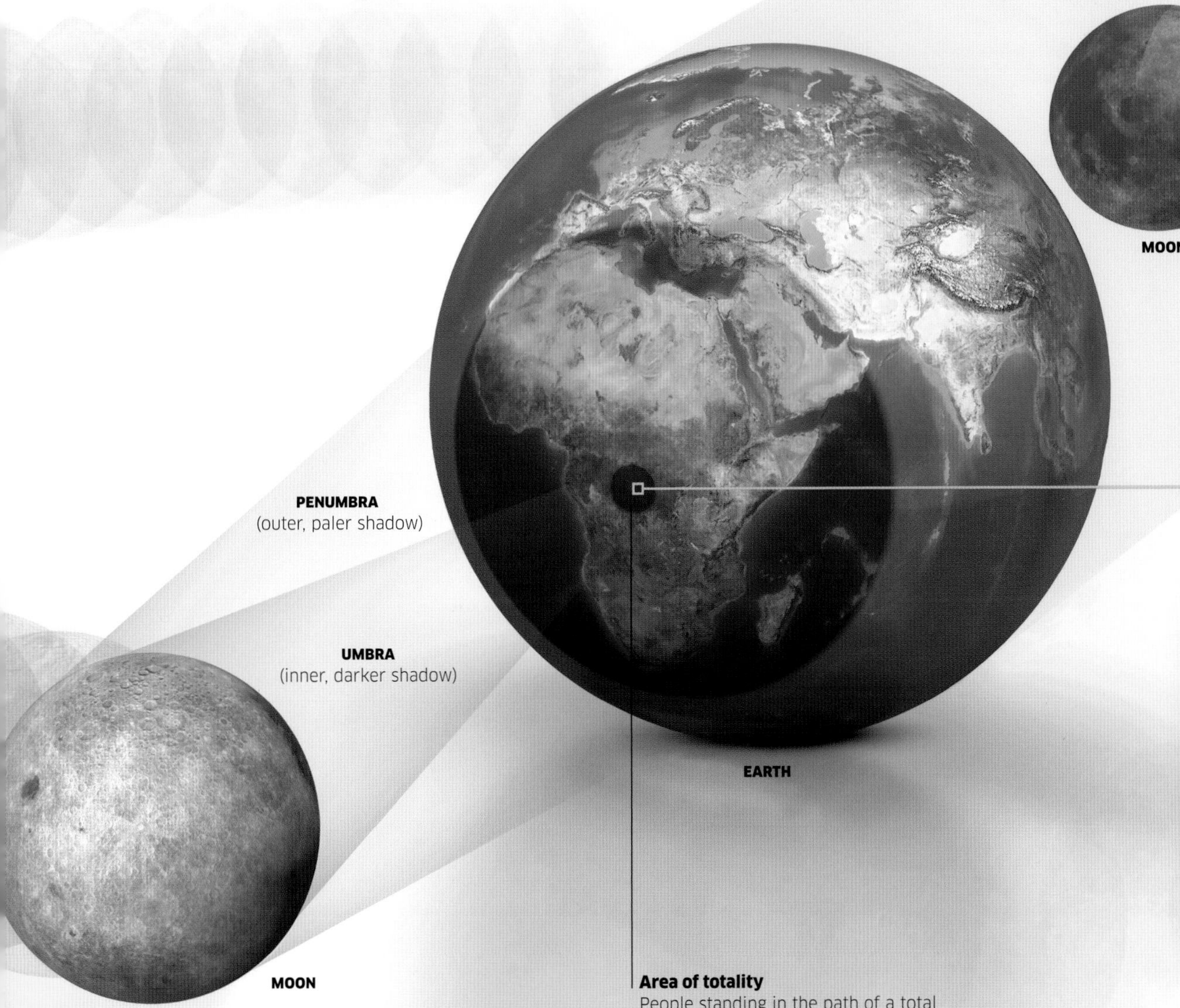
MOON
PENUMBRA
(outer, paler shadow)
UMBRA
(inner, darker shadow)
EARTH
MOON

Area of totality
People standing in the path of a total solar eclipse see the Moon's shadow racing across the ground as the eclipse begins. Just before the Sun vanishes, its last rays pass between mountains on the Moon, creating beads of shimmering light like jewels.

Perfect fit
By a strange coincidence, the Sun is 400 times wider than the Moon but 400 times farther away. As a result, the Moon is just the same size in the sky as the Sun and fits over it perfectly during a total solar eclipse.

Red Moon

Total lunar eclipses happen on average about once a year and are easy to see because anyone on Earth's night side can watch. Over several hours, Earth's shadow slowly creeps across the Moon's face, giving the remaining bright part of the Moon a peculiar shape. The period of totality, when the Moon turns red, can last nearly two hours.

Surface temperatures on Mars can plunge to **–143°C (–225°F).**

The most recent volcanic eruption on Mars happened 2 million years ago.

Mars

Earth's second nearest neighbour in space is Mars – a freezing desert world that may once have harboured life.

Mars is half Earth's size and much colder, but its arid surface looks oddly familiar, with rocky plains, rolling hills, and sand dunes much like those on Earth. The dusty ground is tinged brownish red by rust (iron oxide) and makes Mars look reddish from Earth, which is why the ancient Greeks and Romans named the planet after their god of war. Mars may have been warmer and wetter in the past, and there are signs that water once flowed across its surface, carving out gullies and laying down sedimentary rock. There may even be fossils of alien life forms hidden in the ground.

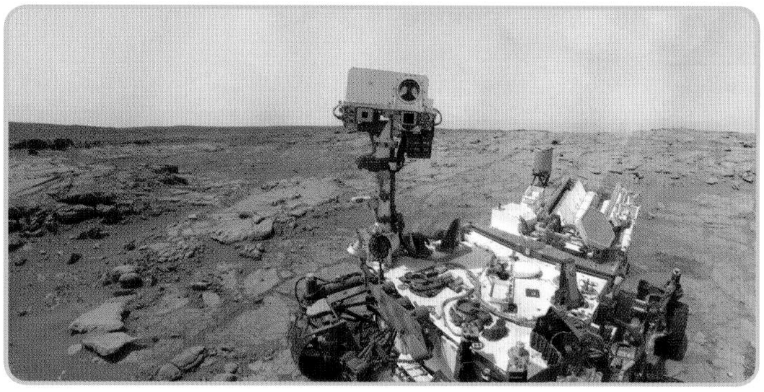

On the surface
The first soft landing on Mars was made by the Soviet probe Mars 3 in 1971. More than 20 spacecraft have successfully flown close to, orbited, or landed on Mars. Seven of these were landers that successfully returned data. Many missions to Mars have ended in failure, but some successful missions have placed robotic rovers on the planet, such as the car-sized rover Curiosity (above), which arrived in 2012.

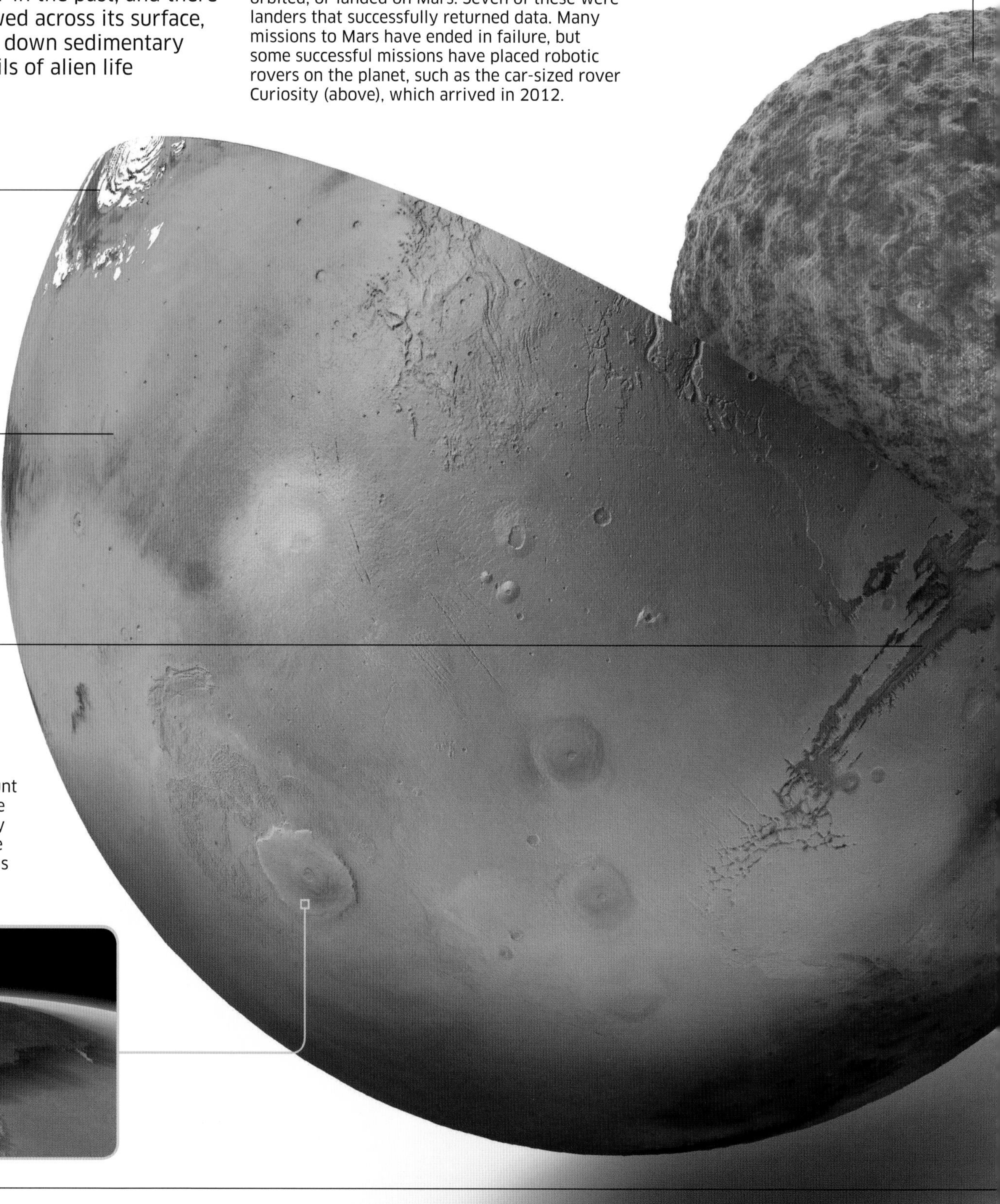

Core
Mars's small, hot core is mostly iron, but unlike Earth's core it is largely solid. Only the outer layer is partially molten.

Like Earth, Mars has permanent caps of ice at the poles.

Surface
The desert-like surface is made of rocky plains and valleys, rolling hills, mountains, and canyons. Sandy areas are pale; areas of bare rock look darker.

Valles Marineris
A gigantic canyon system called Valles Marineris is etched deep in the planet's surface near its equator.

Olympus Mons
Mars is home to the largest volcano in the Solar System: Olympus Mons. Its summit is 22 km (14 miles) high, making it three times taller than Mount Everest, though its slopes are so wide and gentle that a visitor would barely see it. Unlike Earth's volcanoes, those on Mars can keep growing for millions of years because the planet's crust doesn't move about.

Crust
The crust is made mostly of volcanic rock, covered in dust. Unlike Earth's crust, which is broken into moving plates, the Martian crust is a solid shell.

Mantle
Under the crust is Mars's mantle: a deep layer of silicate rock. In the past, the planet's internal heat kept the mantle soft enough to move like treacle, warping the crust and creating volcanoes.

Atmosphere
Mars has a thin atmosphere made mostly of carbon dioxide gas. Strong winds sometimes whip up clouds of dust from the arid ground.

Billions of years ago, vast rivers flowed on the Martian surface, carving out giant valleys.

FAST FACTS

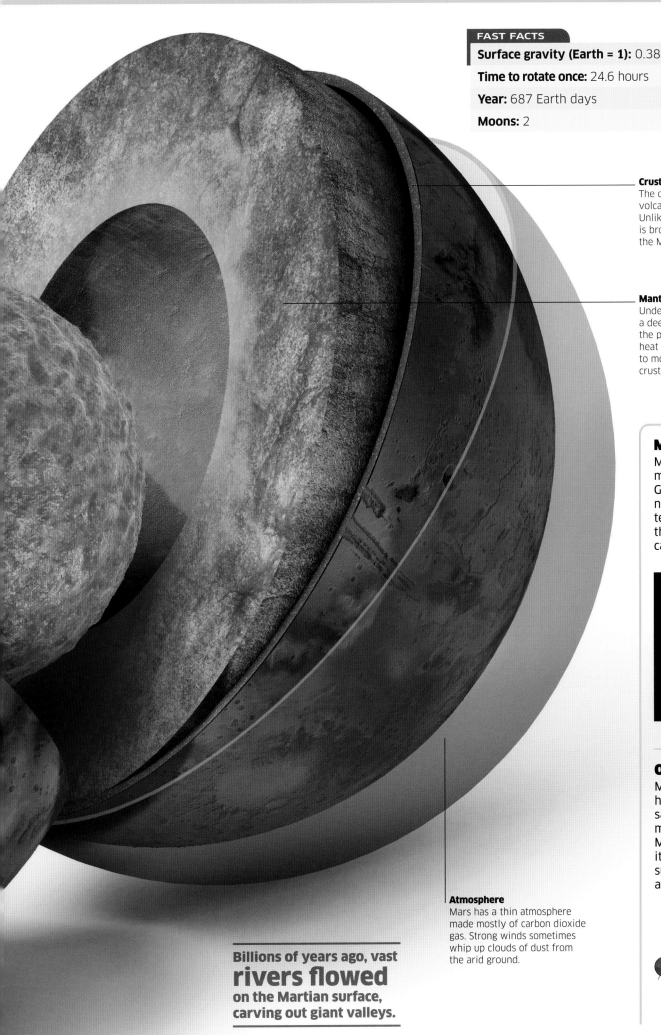

Surface gravity (Earth = 1): 0.38

Time to rotate once: 24.6 hours

Year: 687 Earth days

Moons: 2

Moons

Mars has two small, potato-shaped moons: Phobos, named after the Greek god of fear; and Deimos, named after the Greek god of terror. The moons may be asteroids that flew close to Mars and were captured by the planet's gravity.

PHOBOS **DEIMOS**

Orbit and seasons

Mars rotates in just under 25 hours, making its day much the same as Earth's. Its year, though, is much longer, lasting 687 days. As Mars is tilted on its axis, like Earth, it has four seasons – winter, spring, summer, and autumn – but they are all freezing cold and bone dry.

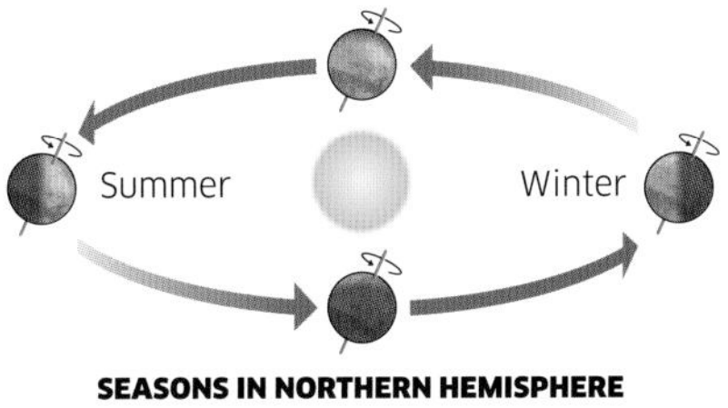
Summer
Winter

SEASONS IN NORTHERN HEMISPHERE

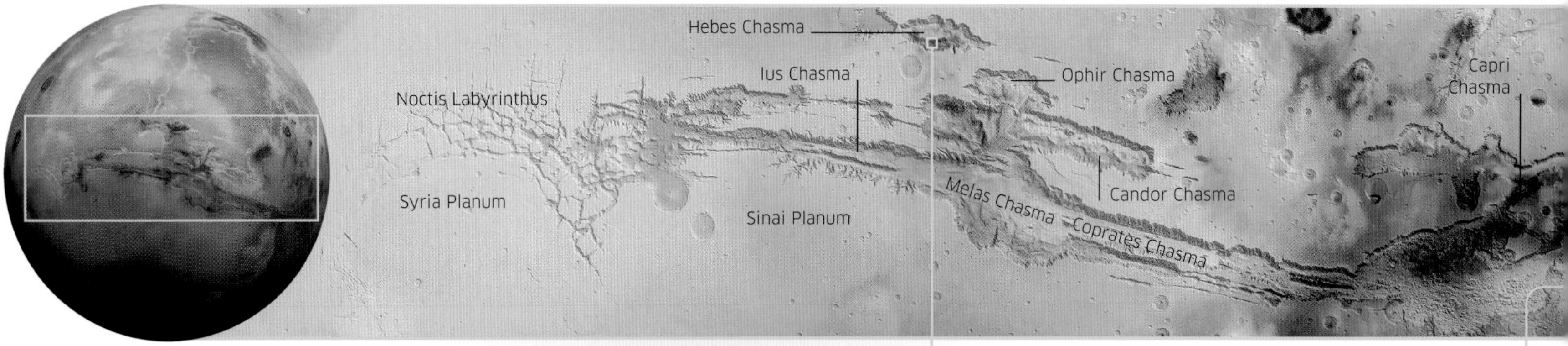
Hebes Chasma
Ius Chasma
Ophir Chasma
Capri Chasma
Noctis Labyrinthus
Syria Planum
Sinai Planum
Candor Chasma
Melas Chasma
Coprates Chasma

Sand dunes
Windblown sand collects on the floor of the Valles Marineris, forming huge dunes. In this false-colour photo from the Mars Reconnaissance Orbiter, the reddish Martian sand appears blue. The patterns are continually changing as the dunes slowly migrate, blown by the wind.

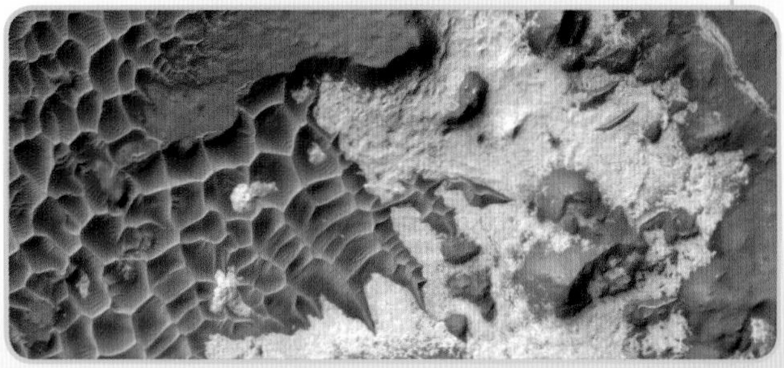

Flood channels
In and around Valles Marineris are smaller valleys called outflow channels. These might have formed when ice suddenly melted, triggering floods, or they might have been created by volcanic eruptions.

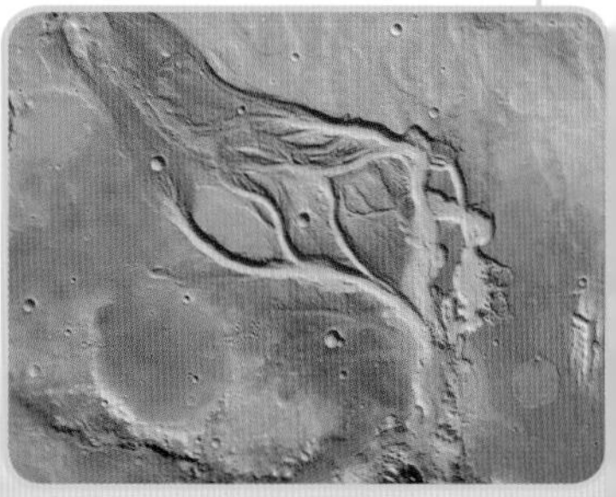

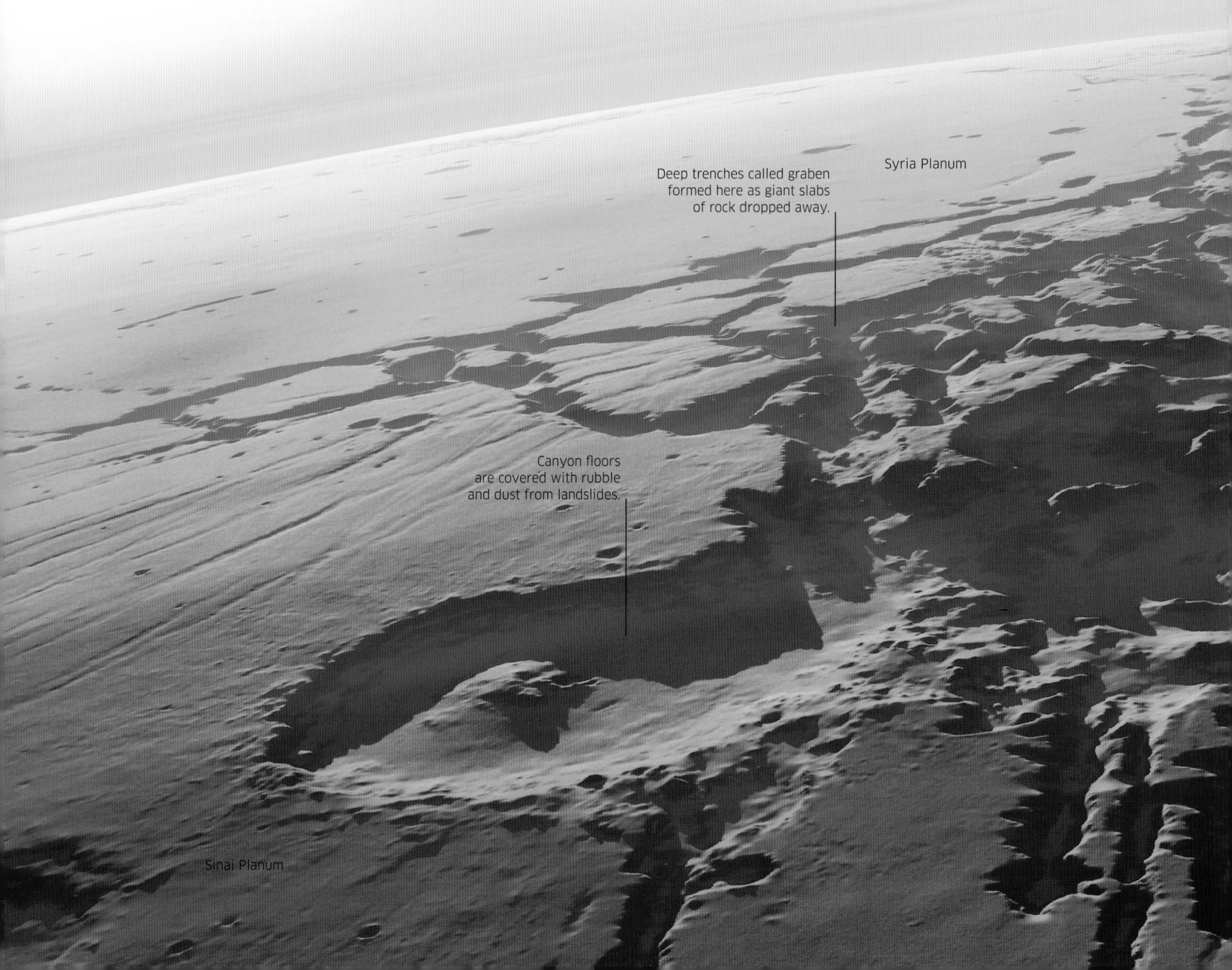
Syria Planum
Deep trenches called graben formed here as giant slabs of rock dropped away.
Canyon floors are covered with rubble and dust from landslides.
Sinai Planum

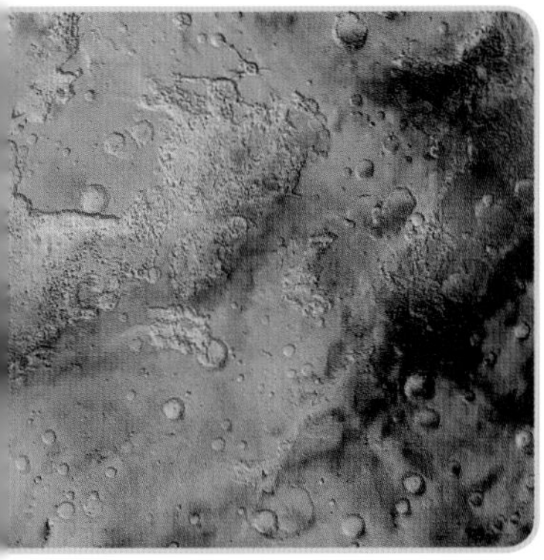

Valles Marineris

Five times as long and almost four times as deep as Earth's Grand Canyon, the massive Valles Marineris canyon system on Mars is one of the wonders of the Solar System.

Named after the Mariner 9 spacecraft that discovered it in 1972, Valles Marineris is a gigantic crack that first ripped open early in Mars's history as nearby volcanoes made the planet's crust bulge. Today it stretches a fifth of the way round Mars and resembles a vast slash in the planet's face. Over billions of years, floods have gouged out deeper channels and landslides have destroyed valley walls, creating an amazingly varied landscape of canyons, cliffs, and dunes.

Maze of the night

At its western end, the Valles Marineris splits into a maze of steep-walled canyons known as Noctis Labyrinthus, or "maze of the night". The valleys here have more water-related minerals than any other place on Mars. Two billion years ago, when the rest of Mars was dry, they may have been moist enough to harbour life.

A chain of giant volcanoes lies to the west of Valles Marineris.
Some of the canyons in Noctis Labyrinthus are over 5,000 m (16,400 ft) deep.

Formation

Valles Marineris began to form around 3.5 billion years ago when volcanic activity made a nearby region of the Martian crust bulge and split. Powerful forces pulled the crust apart, causing a central section to drop and form a deep valley. The valley grew wider over time as its walls eroded.

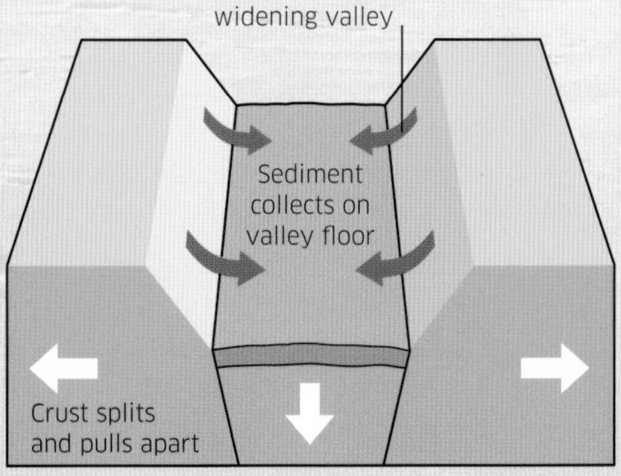
Cliffs collapse in landslides, widening valley
Sediment collects on valley floor
Crust splits and pulls apart
Valley floor sinks

Size

The immense Valles Marineris is more than 4,000 km (2,500 miles) long and up to 7 km (4.3 miles) deep. It dwarfs the Grand Canyon in Arizona, USA, which is about 800 km (500 miles) long and 1.6 km (1 mile) deep.

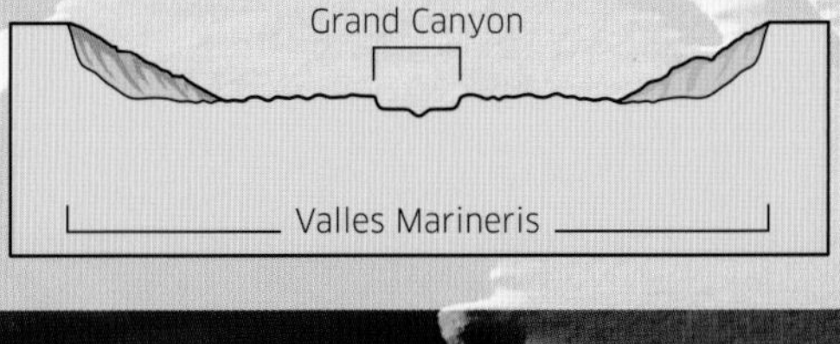
Grand Canyon
Valles Marineris

150–300 days – the time taken for a spacecraft to reach Mars.

Name	Year	Country
1 Mars 2	1971	USSR
2 Mars 3	1971	USSR
3 Mars 6	1974	USSR
4 Viking 1	1976	USA
5 Viking 2	1976	USA
6 Sojourner	1997	USA
7 Mars Polar Lander	1999	USA
8 Beagle 2	2003	UK
9 Spirit	2004	USA
10 Opportunity	2004	USA
11 Phoenix	2007	USA
12 Curiosity	2012	USA

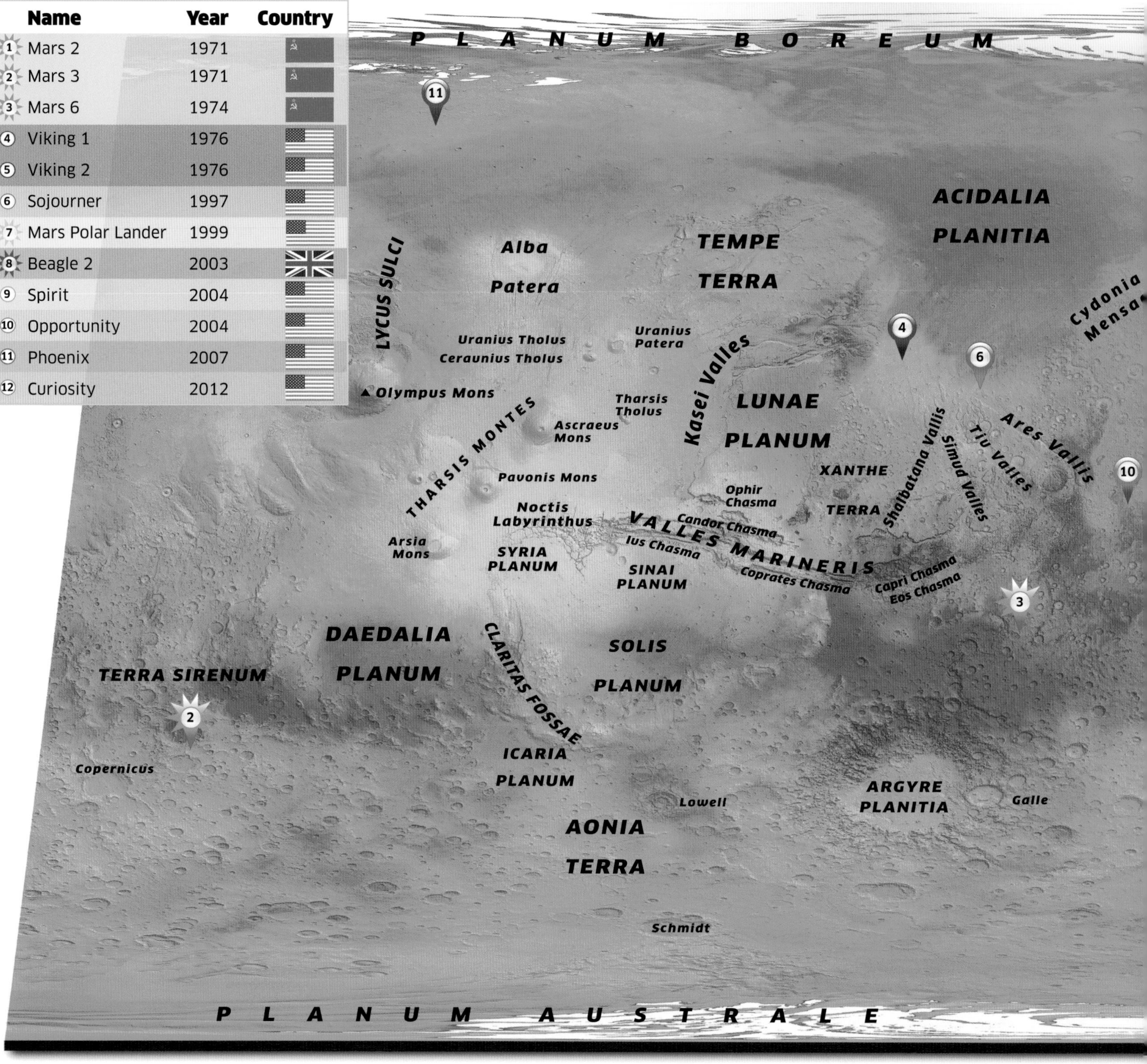
PLANUM BOREUM
ACIDALIA PLANITIA
Alba Patera
TEMPE TERRA
LYCUS SULCI
Cydonia Mensa
Uranius Tholus
Ceraunius Tholus
Uranius Patera
Kasei Valles
Olympus Mons
Tharsis Tholus
LUNAE PLANUM
THARSIS MONTES
Ascraeus Mons
Ares Vallis
Tiu Valles
Simud Valles
Shalbatana Vallis
XANTHE TERRA
Pavonis Mons
Ophir Chasma
Noctis Labyrinthus
Candor Chasma
VALLES MARINERIS
Ius Chasma
Arsia Mons
SYRIA PLANUM
SINAI PLANUM
Coprates Chasma
Capri Chasma
Eos Chasma
DAEDALIA PLANUM
CLARITAS FOSSAE
SOLIS PLANUM
TERRA SIRENUM
ICARIA PLANUM
Copernicus
Lowell
ARGYRE PLANITIA
Galle
AONIA TERRA
Schmidt
PLANUM AUSTRALE
1
2
3
4
6
10
11

Viking invaders

In July 1976, Viking 1 became the first spacecraft to land on Mars, followed in September by Viking 2 (above). The landers tested the Martian soil for biological activity but found no evidence of life.

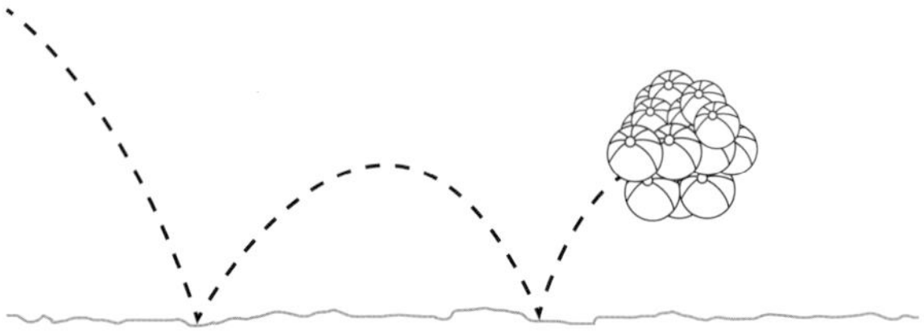

Bounce-down on Mars

The Pathfinder spacecraft used airbags to land safely on Mars in 1997. It bounced five times before coming to a stop. The airbags then deflated and the spacecraft's side panels folded open like petals to allow a small rover to drive out.

Exploring Mars

The Earth-like surface of Mars has made this desert world the target of more space probes than any other planet. More than 40 missions to Mars have been attempted, and 12 spacecraft have landed on the planet; their landing sites are shown on this map.

Mars has been called a spacecraft graveyard because so many of the probes sent there have met a sticky end. Some missed their small target and sailed past into space. Others smashed into it because they failed to brake their speed before landing. Some made it all the way but then simply didn't work. After a string of failures, however, Vikings 1 and 2 finally succeeded in landing on Mars in 1976 and relayed the first tantalizing images of the surface. It was another 20 years before the next successful mission, when NASA succeeded in putting a rover on Mars. Bigger and better rovers soon followed, and a manned mission may eventually be planned.

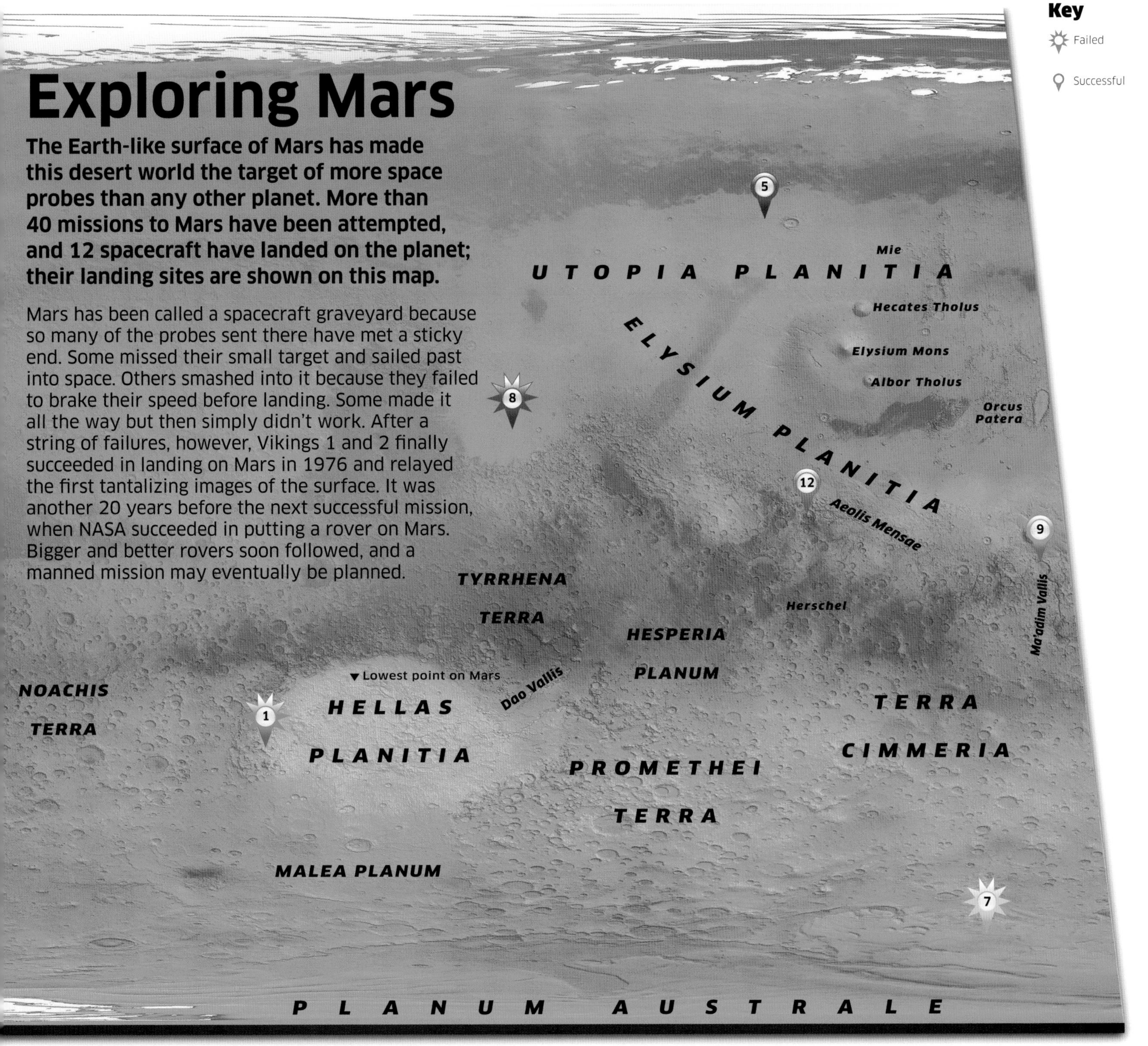
Key
Failed
Successful
5
Mie
UTOPIA PLANITIA
Hecates Tholus
ELYSIUM PLANITIA
Elysium Mons
Albor Tholus
8
Orcus Patera
12
Aeolis Mensae
9
TYRRHENA TERRA
Herschel
Ma'adim Vallis
HESPERIA PLANUM
▼Lowest point on Mars
Dao Vallis
NOACHIS TERRA
1
HELLAS PLANITIA
TERRA CIMMERIA
PROMETHEI TERRA
MALEA PLANUM
7
PLANUM AUSTRALE

Missing in action

In 2003 the Beagle 2 lander from the Mars Express mission began its descent to the Martian surface. Then it went silent. Everyone assumed it had crashed, but in 2014 it was spotted intact on the Mars surface by another probe. It seems that the solar panels had simply failed to open.

Curiosity rover

The Curiosity rover is the most successful Martian visitor so far and has sent back a huge amount of data. On 6 August 2013, Curiosity marked the anniversary of its landing by playing "Happy Birthday" out loud – the first time music has been played on another planet.

Red planet

The rust-coloured landscapes of Mars remind us of sandy deserts on Earth, but the temperature here is as cold as Earth's South Pole in midwinter.

Mars would be deadly to humans without spacesuits, but conditions are ideal for robotic rovers. NASA's car-sized Curiosity rover took this photo of its tracks on 9 February 2014 – day 538 of its tour of Mars. The distant hills form part of the rim of a 155 km (96 mile) wide crater that Curiosity is searching for signs that Mars may once have been suitable for life.

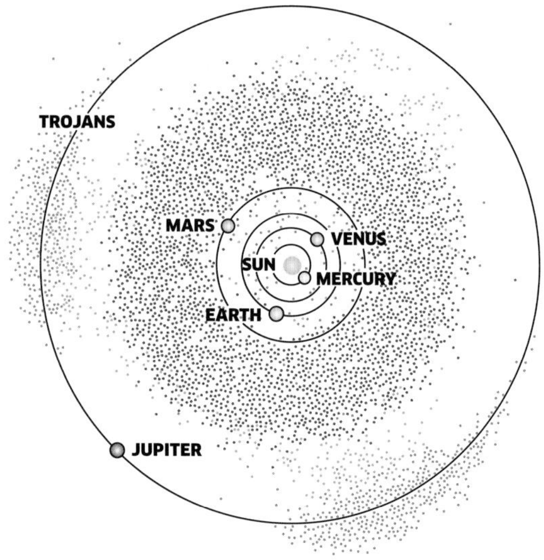
TROJANS
MARS
VENUS
SUN
MERCURY
EARTH
JUPITER

Asteroid Belt

Most asteroids are in a doughnut-shaped belt between the orbits of Mars and Jupiter, but there are also scattered asteroids among the inner planets and large groups of asteroids in the same orbit as Jupiter, known as "Trojans". The belt often looks crowded in illustrations, but in reality the asteroids are so far apart that passengers on a spacecraft flying through the belt probably wouldn't see a single one. The total mass of all the asteroids in the belt is only 4 per cent of the Moon's mass.

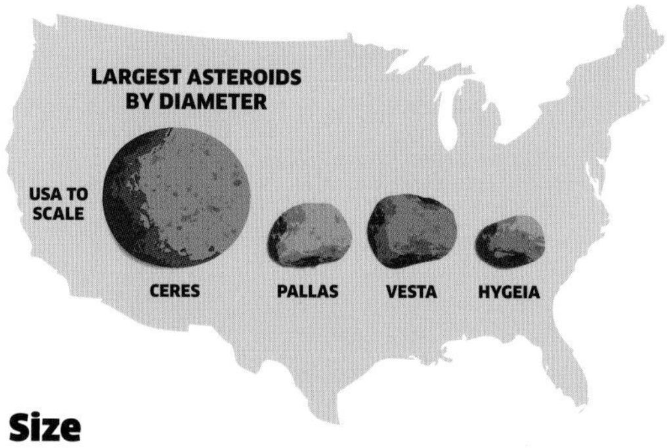
LARGEST ASTEROIDS BY DIAMETER
USA TO SCALE
CERES
PALLAS
VESTA
HYGEIA

Size

Large asteroids are very rare – only 26 asteroids are known to be more than 200 km (125 miles) wide. However, there are hundreds of thousands of asteroids wider than 1 km (0.6 miles) and millions of smaller ones.

Asteroids

Millions of rocks known as asteroids hurtle around the inner Solar System, most of them in a belt between the orbits of Mars and Jupiter. They range in size from pebbles to monsters hundreds of miles wide.

Asteroids are leftovers from the cloud of rubble that gave birth to the planets. Most of the rubble in the inner Solar System collected together to become the rocky planets, but the rocks near Jupiter were disturbed by the giant planet's gravity and failed to build up. The Asteroid Belt is what remains today of that debris. Asteroids follow their own orbits around the Sun, spinning as they go, like planets. They are also called minor planets, and the largest asteroid of all – Ceres – is classed as a dwarf planet. Asteroids occasionally collide, forming craters or even smashing each other. Less often, they crash into moons and planets.

Head and body
The shape of Toutatis suggests it might have formed from two asteroids that stuck together, a small asteroid forming the "head" (left) and a larger one forming the "body". Most asteroids have an irregular shape, but the very largest ones pull themselves into a sphere through their own gravity.

Because of its potato shape, Toutatis spins around two axes. As a result, it tumbles through space like **a badly thrown rugby ball.**

Near-Earth asteroids

In the past, asteroids have hit Earth with devastating effect, wiping out huge numbers of animals, including the dinosaurs. Today, astronomers keep a close eye on asteroids that wander close to our planet. About 12,000 near-Earth asteroids have been found, of which about 1,000 are more than 1 km (0.6 miles) wide – large enough to make a crater the size of a big city.

Craters
Asteroids are pockmarked with craters caused by collisions with smaller asteroids.

Toutatis

In 1989 French astronomer Christian Pollas discovered the 5 km (3 mile) wide asteroid 4179 Toutatis, shown in the artist's impression above. Toutatis is a near-Earth asteroid, which means its orbit sometimes brings it close to Earth. When it passed Earth in 2004, it was just four times farther away than the Moon. Asteroids as big as Toutatis hit Earth about once every 20 million years but have the potential to wipe out the entire world population.

Shooting stars and meteorites

The shooting stars we sometimes see streaking across the night sky are not stars at all, but tiny flecks of space rock. Millions of these rock fragments, called meteoroids, hurtle into Earth's atmosphere every year.

Most meteoroids come from the Asteroid Belt or from comets, but a few are chipped off the Moon or Mars by meteorite impacts. They are usually no bigger than a grain of sand, but even tiny grains hit the atmosphere so hard and fast – at up to 71 km (44 miles) per second – that they make the air glow brightly as they ram into it, causing the streak of light we call a meteor or shooting star. Most meteoroids burn up entirely in the atmosphere, but a few really big ones survive to crash into the ground as meteorites.

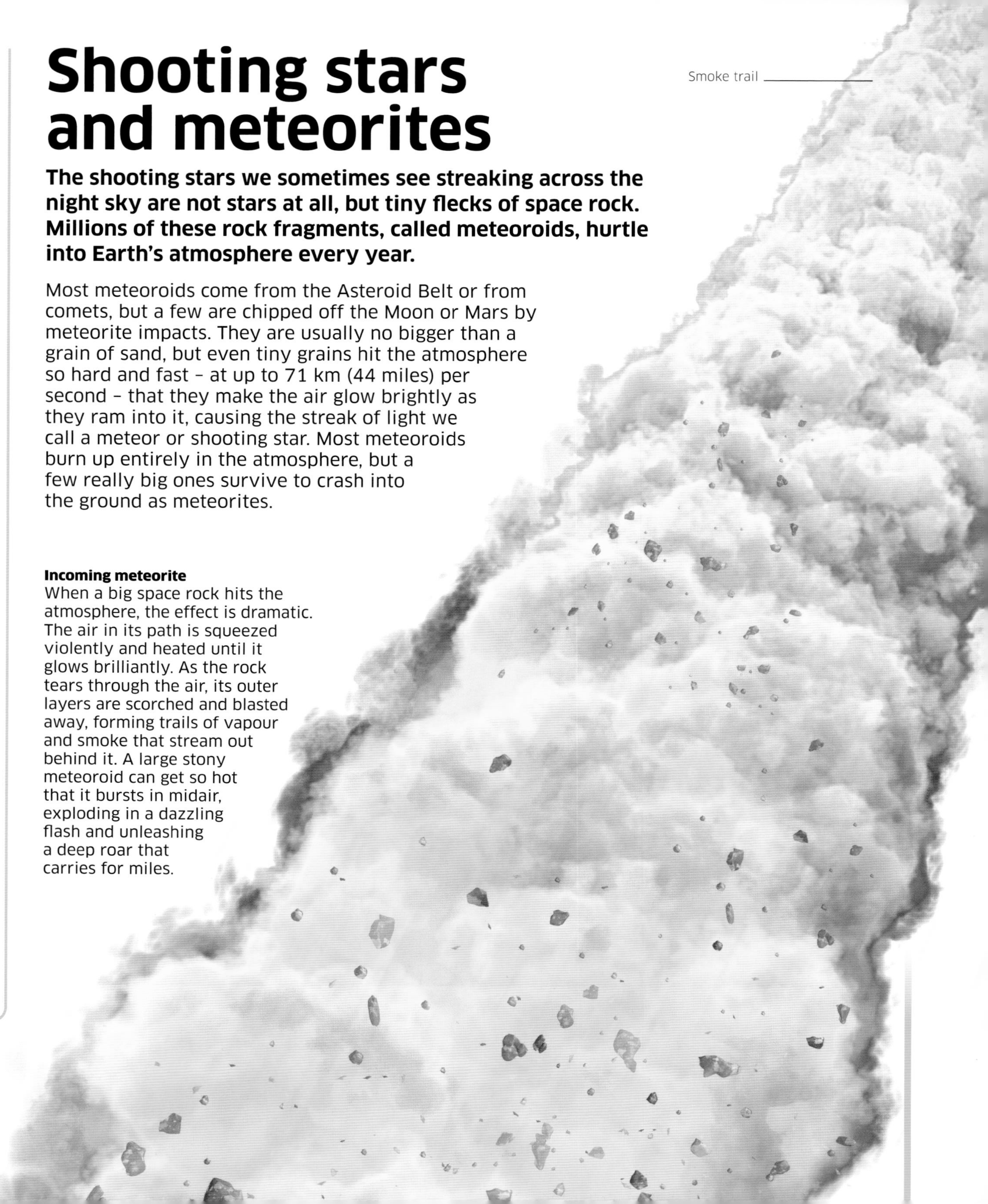
Smoke trail

Incoming meteorite
When a big space rock hits the atmosphere, the effect is dramatic. The air in its path is squeezed violently and heated until it glows brilliantly. As the rock tears through the air, its outer layers are scorched and blasted away, forming trails of vapour and smoke that stream out behind it. A large stony meteoroid can get so hot that it bursts in midair, exploding in a dazzling flash and unleashing a deep roar that carries for miles.

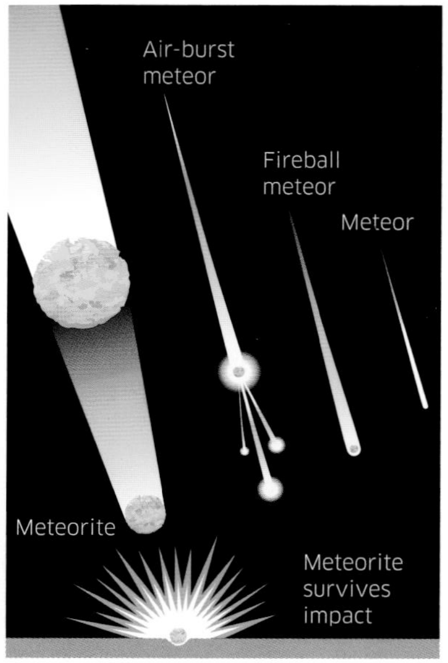
Air-burst meteor
Fireball meteor
Meteor
Meteorite
Meteorite survives impact

Rocks in the sky

Meteoroids the size of sand grains become meteors (shooting stars), which are only visible at night. Those as big as footballs can create brilliant "fireballs" that are visible even by day and may leave a trail of smoke. Some big stony meteoroids hit the atmosphere with such force they explode in midair. The blast from these "air-burst meteors" can flatten trees. Meteoroids that reach the ground and survive are called meteorites.

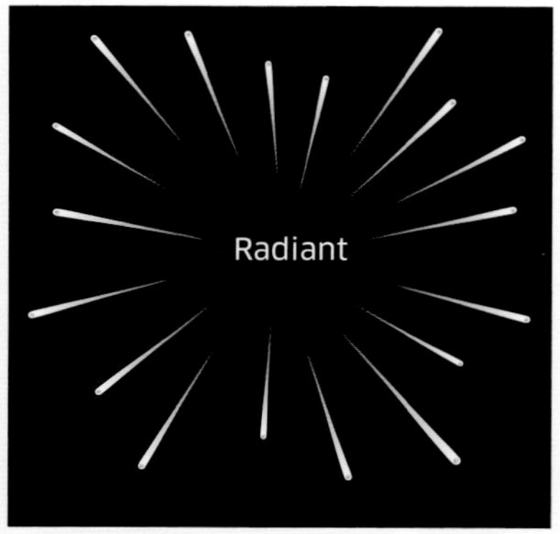
Radiant

Meteor showers

At certain times of year, Earth passes through the trail of dust left in space by a comet, causing over 100 visible meteors an hour. They all appear to come from the same point, called the radiant. Impressive meteor showers include the Perseids in August and the Geminids in December.

WILLAMETTE METEORITE, 1939

Big hitters

The largest meteorite in North America is the Willamette meteorite in the American Museum of Natural History. This 15 tonne lump of iron and nickel is so heavy it has its own foundations to stop it falling through the museum floor.

Every year more than **30,000 meteorites** larger than a strawberry collide with Earth.

In 1908 a **meteor airburst over Siberia** flattened 2,000 square km (770 square miles) of trees.

4.55 billion years – the **age of most meteoroids.**

100 tonnes of meteors and meteorites collide with Earth every day – about the same weight as 20 elephants.

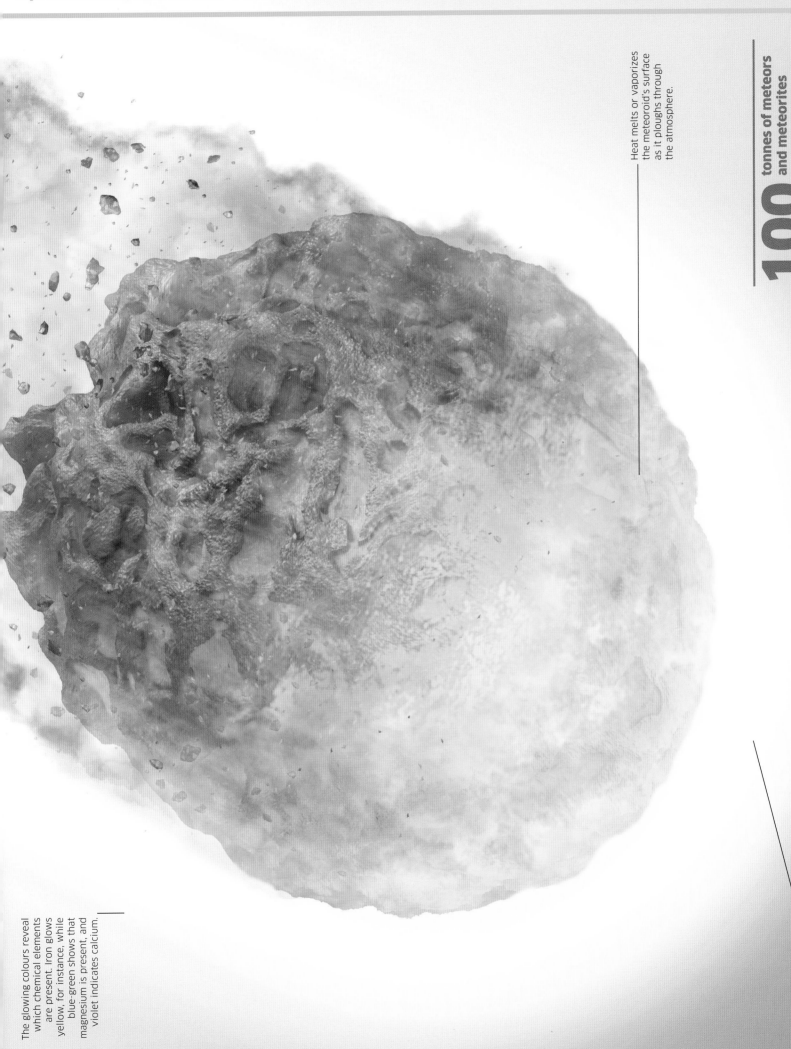

Heat melts or vaporizes the meteoroid's surface as it ploughs through the atmosphere.
Ahead of the meteorite, air is compressed with such force that it becomes white-hot and glows.
The glowing colours reveal which chemical elements are present. Iron glows yellow, for instance, while blue-green shows that magnesium is present, and violet indicates calcium.

Comets and asteroids have been observed **crashing into Jupiter.**

–148°C (–234°F) – the **temperature** of Jupiter's cloud tops.

Jupiter

The largest planet of all, Jupiter is more than twice as massive as all the other planets combined. Unlike rocky worlds, such as Earth or Mars, Jupiter is a gas giant – a vast, spinning globe of gas and liquid with no solid surface.

Jupiter is 1,300 times greater in volume than Earth, and the pull of its gravity is so great that it bends the paths of comets and asteroids flying through the Solar System. Despite the planet's great size, it spins quickly, giving it a day less than ten hours long. The rapid rotation makes Jupiter bulge visibly at its equator and whips its colourful clouds into horizontal stripes and swirling storms. The largest storm – the Great Red Spot – is bigger than Earth. Lightning storms flicker through the blackness on Jupiter's night side, and the whole planet is surrounded by belts of lethal radiation that would make a manned mission extremely dangerous.

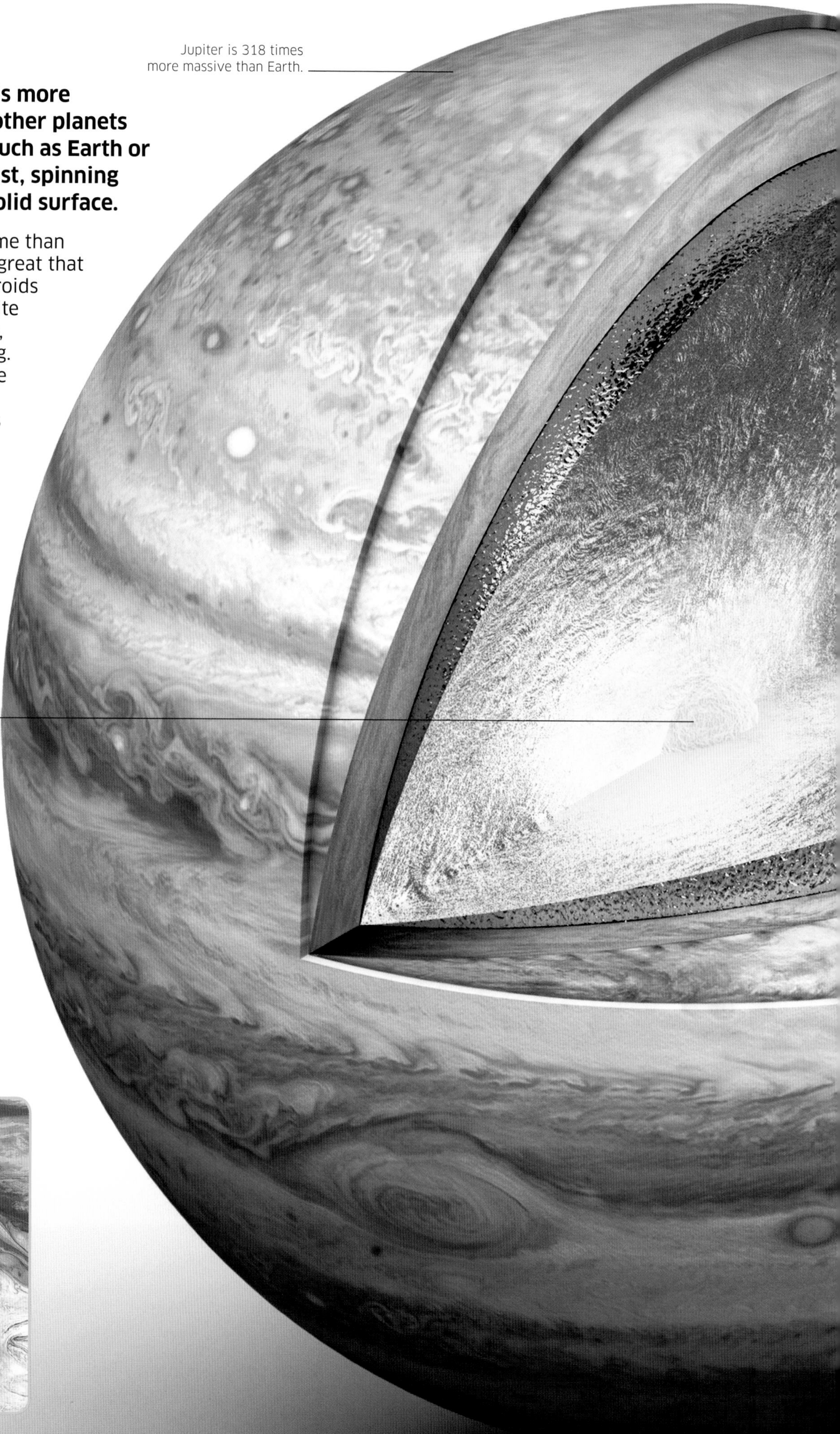

Jupiter is 318 times more massive than Earth.

Core
At Jupiter's centre is a rock core that's hotter than the surface of the Sun. It makes up about 10 per cent of the planet's mass.

Storm spots
Storms in Jupiter's atmosphere form ovals of different colours. The 12,000 km (7,450 mile) wide Great Red Spot has been raging for several hundred years. Its red colour is probably caused by sunlight breaking up chemicals in the tops of the highest clouds.

360 kph (225 mph) – **typical wind speed** on Jupiter.

46 km (29 miles) per second – the **speed at which the Galileo probe** entered Jupiter's atmosphere.

Jupiter gives out **1.6 times more energy** than falls on it, due to **internal heating** of the planet.

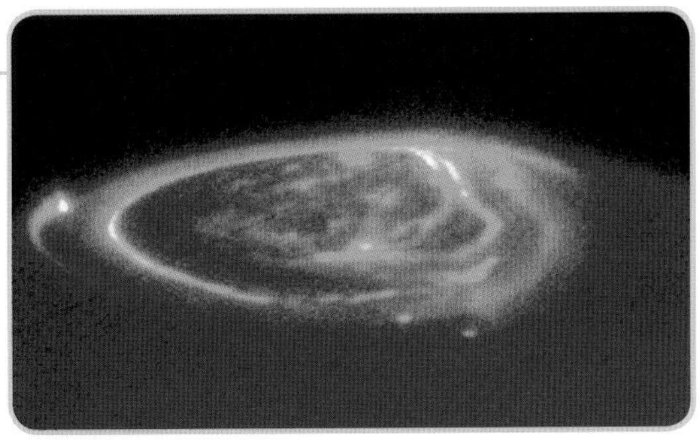

Polar lights
Spectacular light displays called auroras (seen here in ultraviolet light) sometimes occur at Jupiter's poles. Like Earth's northern and southern lights, they are caused by charged particles from space that crash into the atmosphere and make the gas atoms glow. The auroras on Jupiter are up to 100 times brighter than those on Earth.

Liquid metallic layer
Under huge pressure, the hydrogen deep inside Jupiter behaves like a liquid metal. Helium and neon are probably also present in this layer.

Liquid layer
Above the metallic layer is a vast sea of liquid hydrogen. This sea has no surface; instead, it gradually thins out at the top, merging with the gas in Jupiter's atmosphere.

Atmosphere
Hydrogen gas makes up 90 per cent of Jupiter's atmosphere. The rest is mostly helium, with small amounts of other elements.

Winds blow in opposite directions in neighbouring cloud bands, causing swirling patterns at the boundaries.

Cloud layer
The cloud layer is only 50 km (30 miles) thick. Most of the clouds are thought to consist of frozen ammonia crystals.

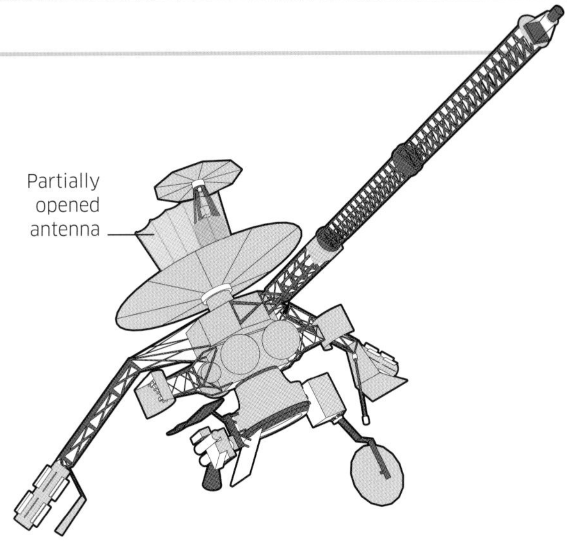
Partially opened antenna

Galileo spacecraft
Although hampered by a partially opened communications dish, this NASA spacecraft made many important discoveries about Jupiter and its moons after its arrival in 1995. It released a probe that dived into Jupiter's clouds and then opened a parachute, allowing it to analyse the chemicals. Galileo orbited Jupiter until 2003.

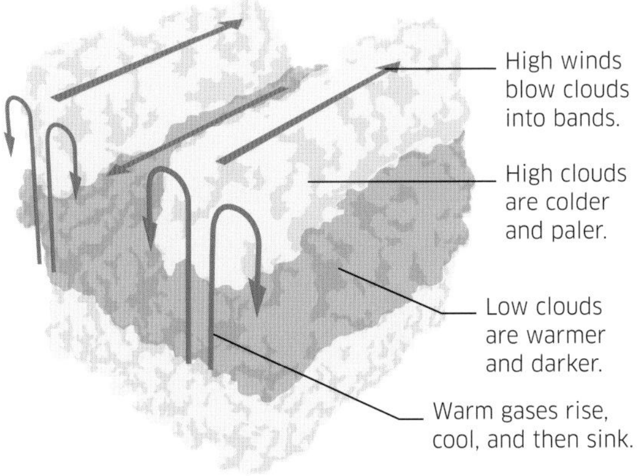
High winds blow clouds into bands.
High clouds are colder and paler.
Low clouds are warmer and darker.
Warm gases rise, cool, and then sink.

Cloud bands
Jupiter's colourful bands are made up of clouds at different heights. In the paler bands, gases are rising and forming high icy clouds. Gaps between these bands of high clouds allow us to see down to the warmer cloud layers below, which are darker in colour.

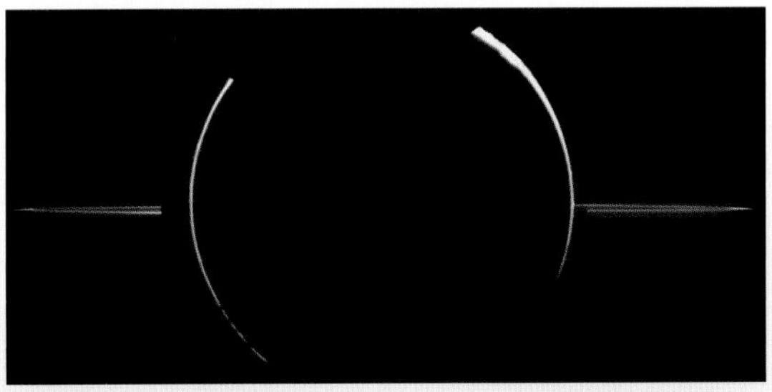

Tenuous rings
Jupiter's faint rings were first seen in 1979 in images taken by Voyager 1. They have since been detected from Earth by viewing the planet in infrared light. The rings consist mainly of dust from Jupiter's smaller moons.

FAST FACTS

Surface gravity (Earth = 1): 2.36

Time to rotate once: 9.9 hours

Year: 12 Earth years

Moons: At least 67

In 2009 a comet hit Jupiter and made a black scar the **size of the Pacific Ocean**.

JUPITER
AMALTHEA
ADRASTEA
METIS
THEBE

Europa
Europa's icy surface is covered in strange grooves and cracks. Just as Earth's crust of rock is broken into colliding fragments, so Europa's crust of ice is broken into sheets that push and pull in opposite directions. Water from a salty ocean deep underground erupts from the cracks and freezes, creating new ground.

Io
Caught in a tug-of-war between the gravity of Jupiter and the other Galilean moons, Io is torn by powerful forces that have melted its insides. Molten rock, rich in colourful sulphur chemicals, erupts all over its surface from giant volcanoes.

Ganymede
This large moon is nearly 10 per cent wider than Mercury and would be called a planet if it orbited the Sun rather than Jupiter. Its surface is a jigsaw of ancient dark areas with lots of craters, and younger paler areas with few craters. Eruptions of slushy ice from underground have resurfaced the younger areas.

Moons of Jupiter

Jupiter's massive size makes the pull of its gravity strong. As a result, the giant planet has trapped nearly 70 known moons in orbit around it. Some are probably asteroids or comets that flew too close to Jupiter and were captured by its gravity. Others are as large as planets.

Jupiter's four largest moons are called the Galilean moons because they were discovered by the great Italian astronomer Galileo Galilei, in 1610. These four worlds are very different. The innermost moon, Io, has hundreds of active volcanoes. Next is Europa, which is covered in ice, though a hidden ocean may lie below – one of the few places in the Solar System that might harbour life. Ganymede is the Solar System's largest moon and the only one with a magnetic field. Callisto is covered in craters. Its surface is considered the oldest of any moon or planet in the Solar System.

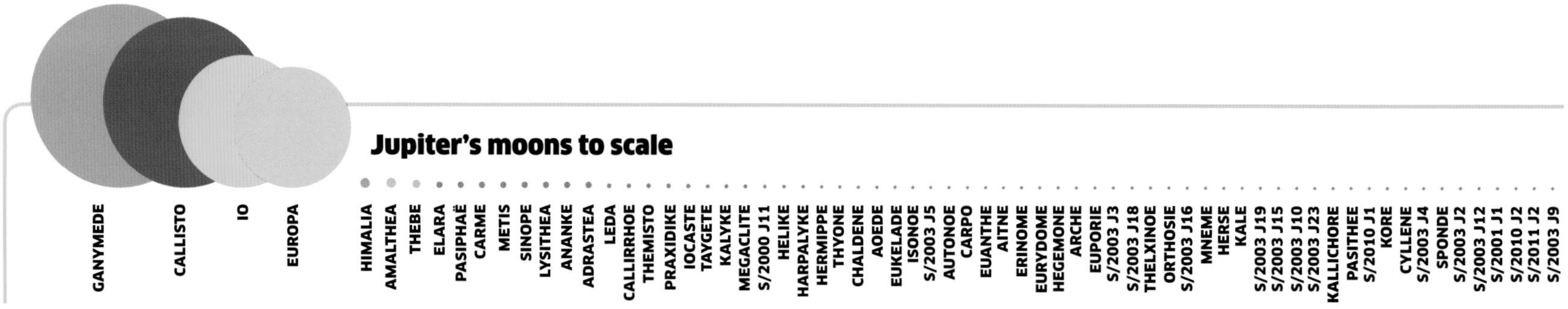
Jupiter's moons to scale
GANYMEDE
CALLISTO
IO
EUROPA
HIMALIA
AMALTHEA
THEBE
ELARA
PASIPHAË
CARME
METIS
SINOPE
LYSITHEA
ANANKE
ADRASTEA
LEDA
CALLIRRHOE
THEMISTO
PRAXIDIKE
IOCASTE
TAYGETE
KALYKE
MEGACLITE
S/2000 J11
HELIKE
HARPALYKE
HERMIPPE
THYONE
CHALDENE
AOEDE
EUKELADE
ISONOE
S/2003 J5
AUTONOE
CARPO
EUANTHE
AITNE
ERINOME
EURYDOME
HEGEMONE
ARCHE
EUPORIE
S/2003 J3
S/2003 J18
THELXINOE
ORTHOSIE
S/2003 J16
MNEME
HERSE
KALE
S/2003 J19
S/2003 J15
S/2003 J10
S/2003 J23
KALLICHORE
PASITHEE
S/2010 J1
KORE
CYLLENE
S/2003 J4
SPONDE
S/2003 J2
S/2003 J12
S/2001 J1
S/2010 J2
S/2011 J2
S/2003 J9

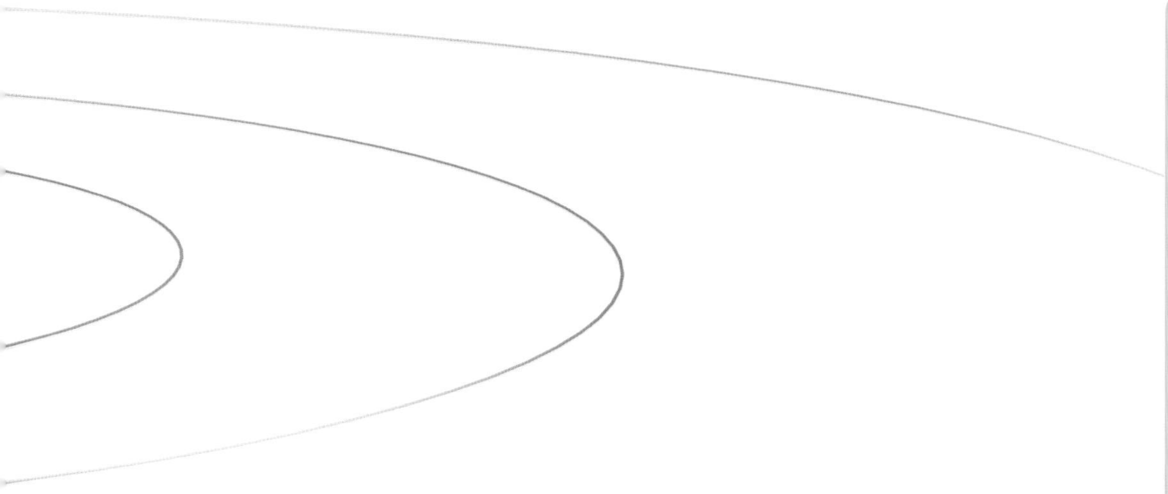

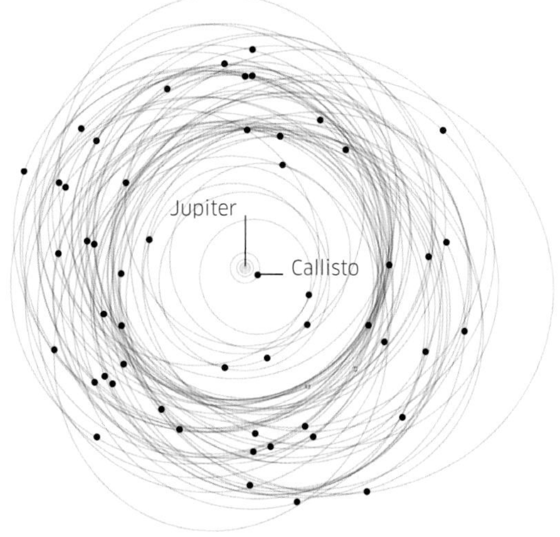
Jupiter
Callisto

Callisto

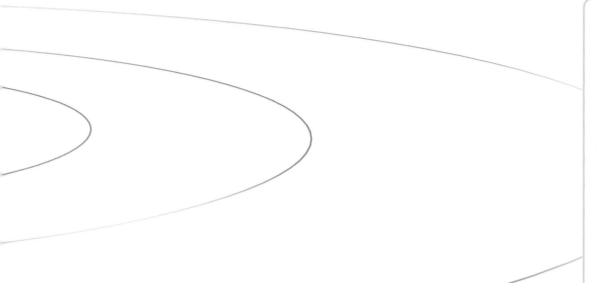

The Solar System's most heavily cratered object, Callisto is peppered with meteorite scars. The large number of craters shows that its surface is very old. Oddly, there are very few small craters on Callisto. Scientists think small craters gradually fade away as the ice in their rims evaporates into space, leaving small hills.

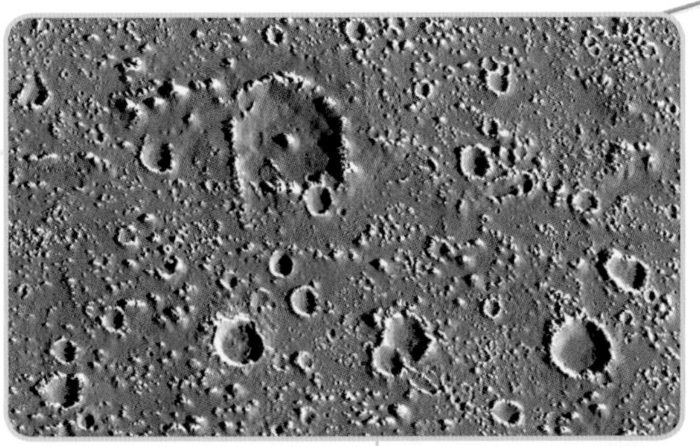

Outer moons

Jupiter's 60 or so outer moons are only a few miles wide and orbit the planet in a messy cloud. The inner moons travel in the same direction as Jupiter's rotation, and their circular orbits line up neatly with Jupiter's equator. In contrast, the outer moons orbit in both directions and their orbits are often wildly tilted or oval. This pattern suggests that most of them are captured objects.

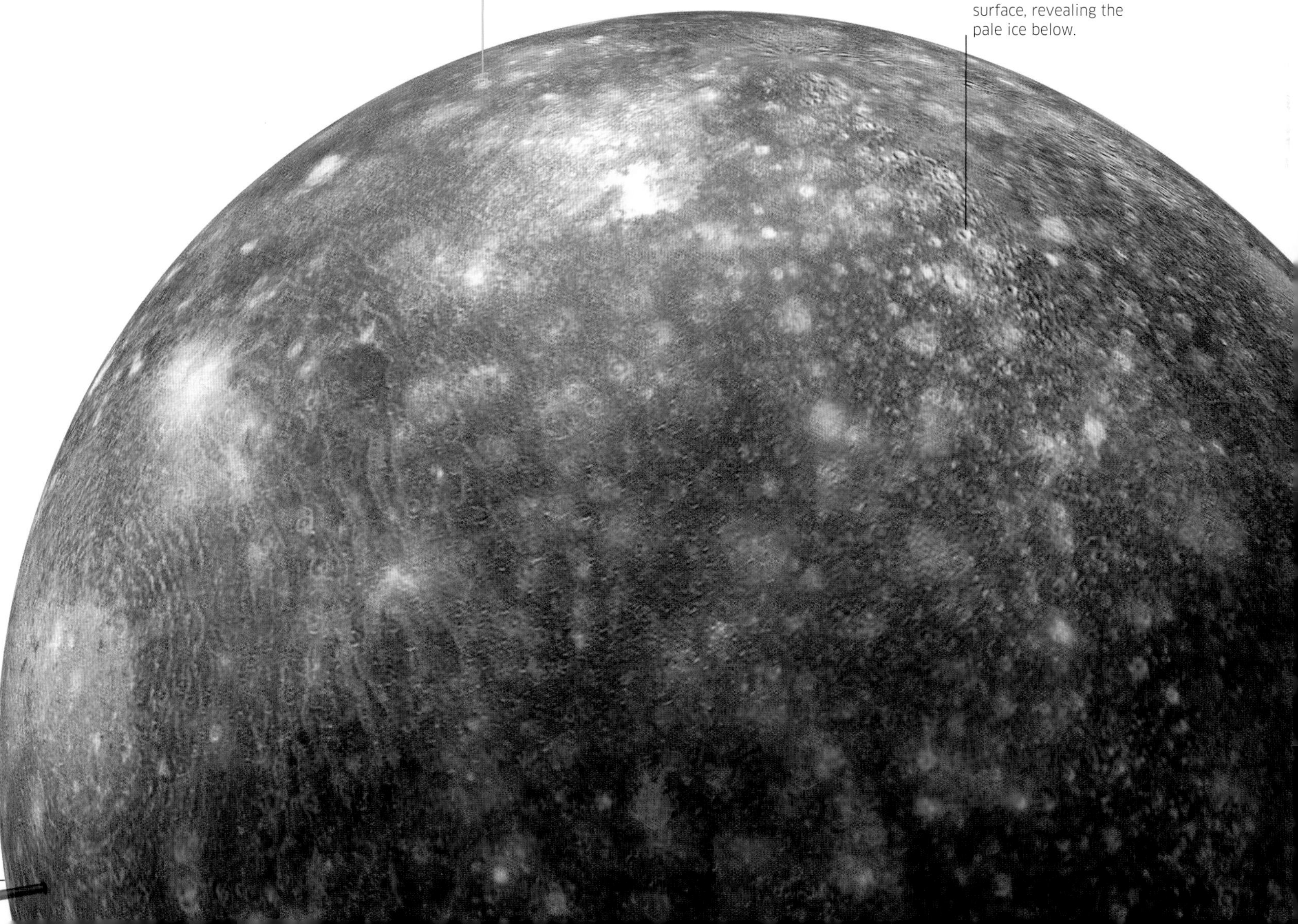

Meteorites have blasted holes in Callisto's dark surface, revealing the pale ice below.

1610 **The year in which Italian astronomer Galileo Galilei discovered Io.**

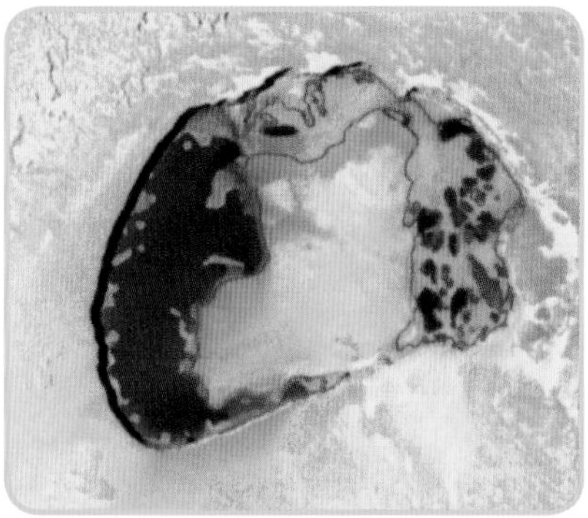

Volcanic crater
The volcanic crater Tupan Patera, bounded by steep walls, displays a wide range of colours that are caused by lava mixing with materials rich in sulphur.

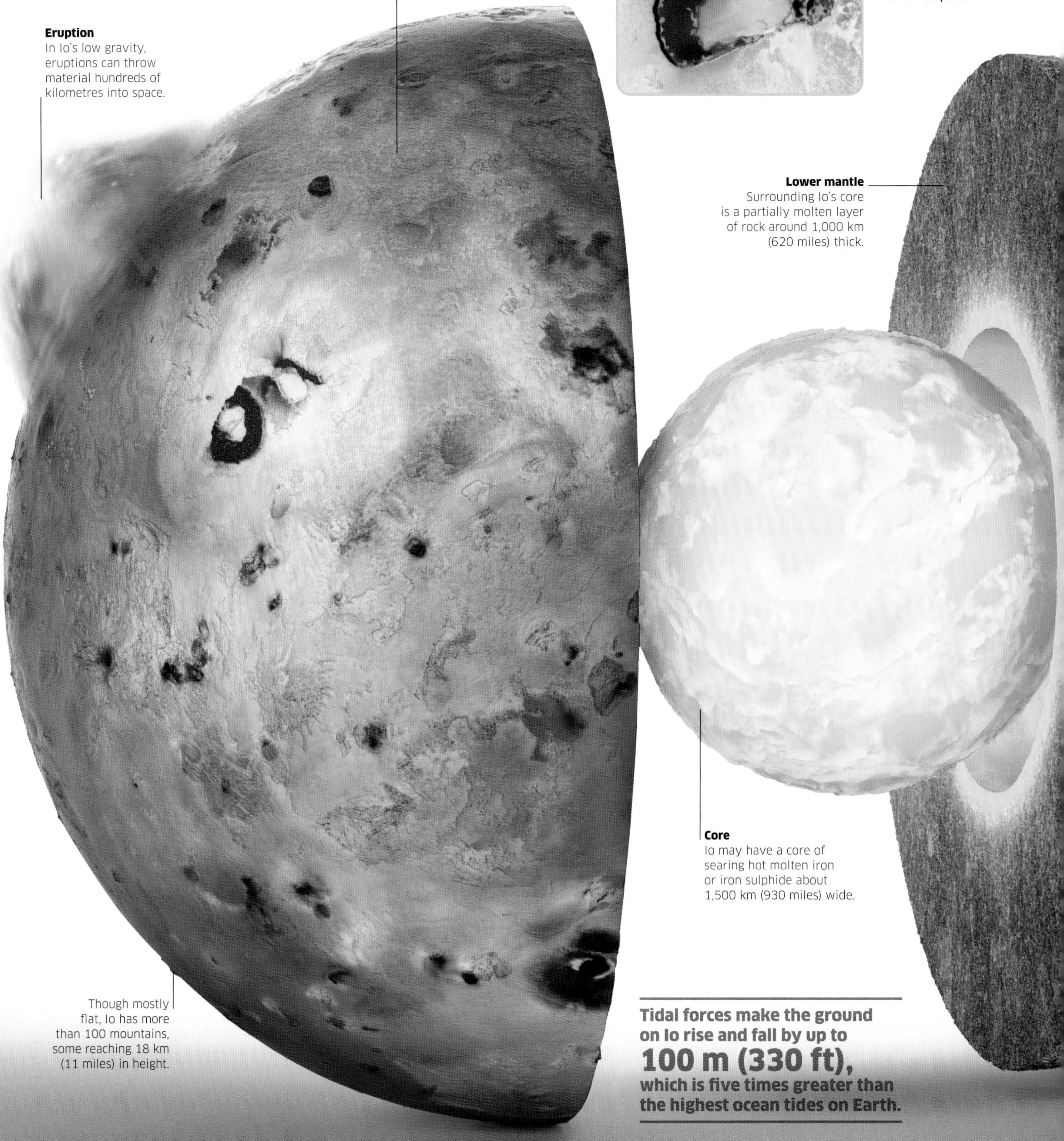
No impact craters have been found on Io's surface. Lava and ash quickly hide the scars of any impacts.
Eruption
In Io's low gravity, eruptions can throw material hundreds of kilometres into space.
Lower mantle
Surrounding Io's core is a partially molten layer of rock around 1,000 km (620 miles) thick.
Core
Io may have a core of searing hot molten iron or iron sulphide about 1,500 km (930 miles) wide.
Though mostly flat, Io has more than 100 mountains, some reaching 18 km (11 miles) in height.

Tidal forces make the ground on Io rise and fall by up to

100 m (330 ft),

which is five times greater than the highest ocean tides on Earth.

FAST FACTS

Time to orbit Jupiter: 1.77 Earth days

Mass (Earth = 1): 0.015

Surface temperature: –163°C (–262°F)

Diameter: 3,643 km (2,262 miles)

IO
THE MOON

Io

The most volcanically active body in the Solar System, Jupiter's moon Io is constantly spewing matter into space from its eruptions. Its blotchy, lava-covered face is a world away from the icy terrain of Jupiter's other moons.

This moon's volcanic eruptions don't just affect Io itself. They pump huge amounts of material into space, forming a vast, doughnut-shaped ring of charged particles around Jupiter, called a plasma torus. The plasma torus allows electric currents to flow through space between Jupiter and Io, triggering lightning storms in Jupiter and causing gases around Io to glow. The existence of Io's volcanoes was predicted by scientists before the Voyager 1 spacecraft made a close encounter with the moon in 1979. The incredible images Voyager took confirmed the scientists' predictions: Io erupts so frequently that the moon is literally turning itself inside out.

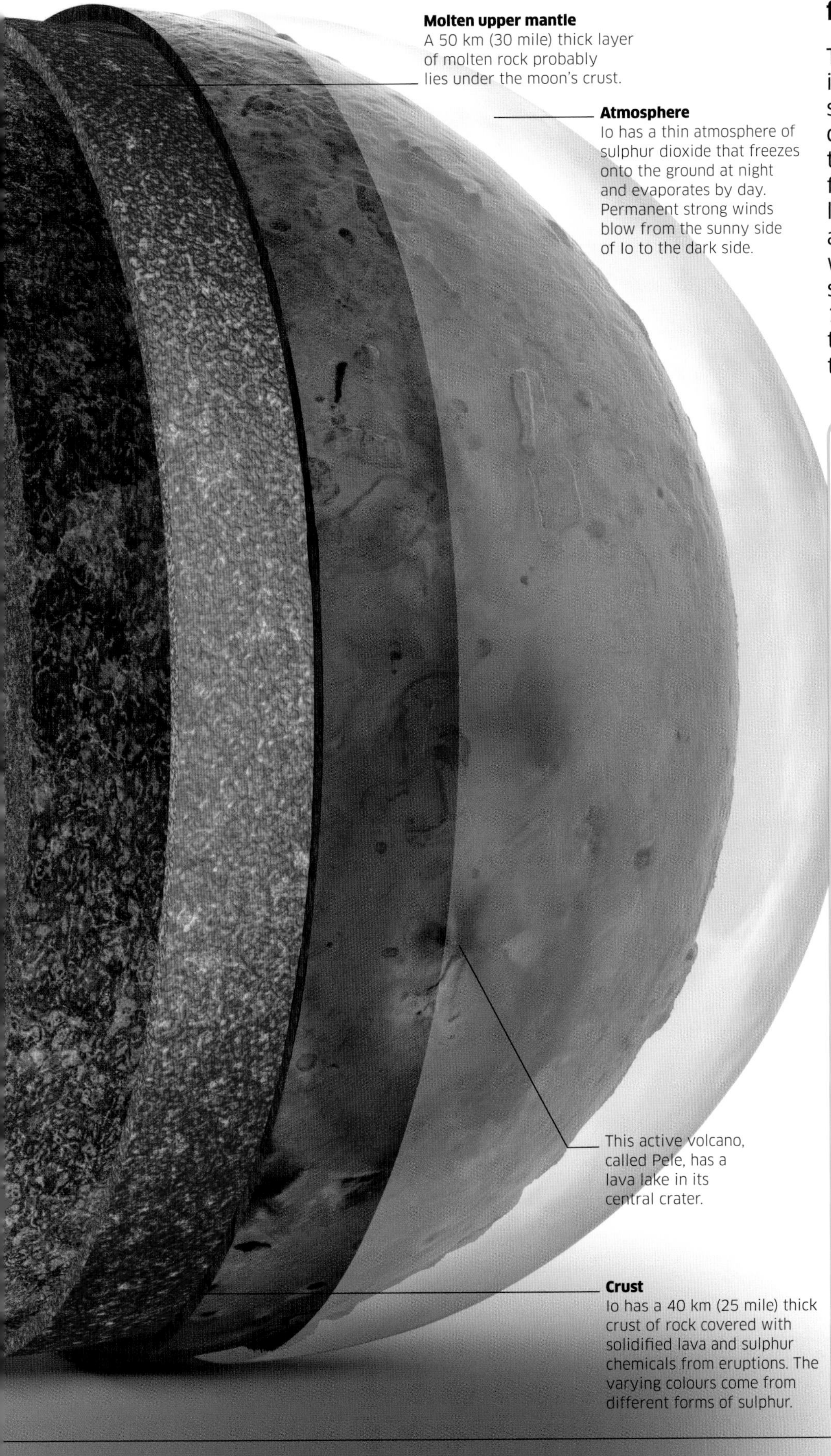
Molten upper mantle
A 50 km (30 mile) thick layer of molten rock probably lies under the moon's crust.
Atmosphere
Io has a thin atmosphere of sulphur dioxide that freezes onto the ground at night and evaporates by day. Permanent strong winds blow from the sunny side of Io to the dark side.
This active volcano, called Pele, has a lava lake in its central crater.
Crust
Io has a 40 km (25 mile) thick crust of rock covered with solidified lava and sulphur chemicals from eruptions. The varying colours come from different forms of sulphur.

Tidal heating

The cause of Io's volcanic activity is gravity. As it orbits Jupiter, Io is stretched in different directions by the gravitational pull of Jupiter and the other moons. These tidal forces keep changing Io's shape, causing friction that heats up and melts its interior.

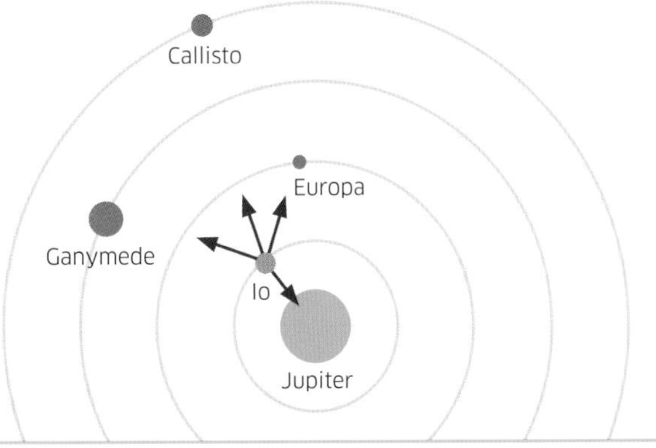
Callisto
Europa
Ganymede
Io
Jupiter

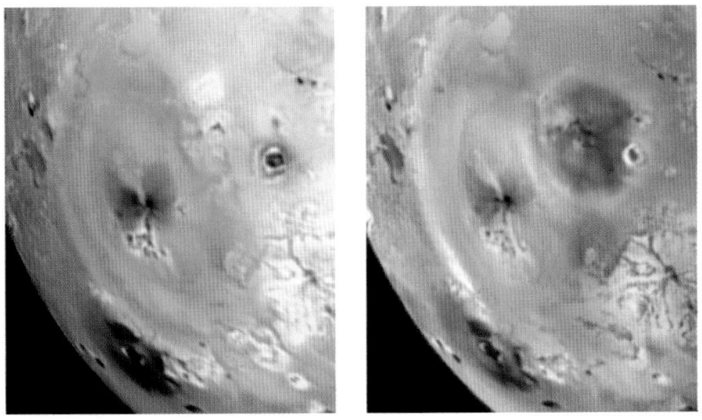

Changing face

Io's appearance can change quickly because of its frequent eruptions. These two images taken five months apart show how fallout from an eruption blanketed a 400 km (250 mile) wide area with black material. The red ring is fallout from another volcano, called Pele.

764 The number of times Earth's volume could **fit inside Saturn.**

Saturn

The spectacular rings around this giant planet make it one of the wonders of our Solar System. Saturn is the second-biggest planet after Jupiter, and like Jupiter it has a huge family of moons.

Saturn is a gas giant – a vast, spinning globe made of chemicals that exist as gases on Earth, such as hydrogen. Saturn is 96 per cent hydrogen, but only the outer layers are gas. Deep inside the planet, the hydrogen is compressed into a liquid by the weight of the gas above it. Saturn is almost as wide as Jupiter but has less than a third of its mass, making Saturn far less dense. In fact, it is the least dense planet of all. It is also the least spherical: Saturn spins so fast that it bulges at the waist, making it wider than it is tall. Like Jupiter, it has a stormy outer atmosphere lashed by powerful winds that sweep its clouds into horizontal bands.

Saturn's poles turn blue in winter, an effect caused by sunlight being scattered by relatively cloud-free air.
Atmosphere
Saturn's atmosphere is mostly hydrogen and helium, with clouds of ammonia ice and water ice on top. Horizontal winds sweep the creamy coloured clouds into bands like those on Jupiter, but with fewer large eddies and storms.
Liquid hydrogen layer
The huge weight of Saturn's atmosphere squeezes the hydrogen underneath into a liquid, forming a vast internal ocean. This sea of liquid hydrogen has no surface – instead, it gradually merges into the gas layer above it.
Rings
Saturn's rings are made of fragments of dirty ice orbiting the planet in an almost perfectly flat plane. The ice reflects the Sun's light, often making the rings look very bright.

FAST FACTS

Surface gravity (Earth = 1): 1.02

Time to rotate once: 10.7 hours

Year: 29 Earth years

Moons: At least 62

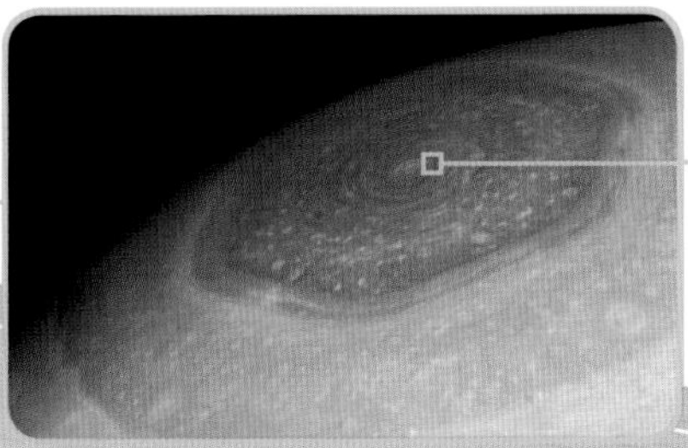

POLAR HEXAGON

POLAR HURRICANE

Polar hexagon

Around the north pole, clouds form a mysterious hexagonal pattern that has persisted for decades. Each side of the hexagon is wider than Earth. It may be a long-lived wave, but no such pattern is seen at the south pole. In its centre is a raging hurricane, shown here in false colour, in which wind speeds reach 530 kph (330 mph) – five times faster than in a hurricane on Earth.

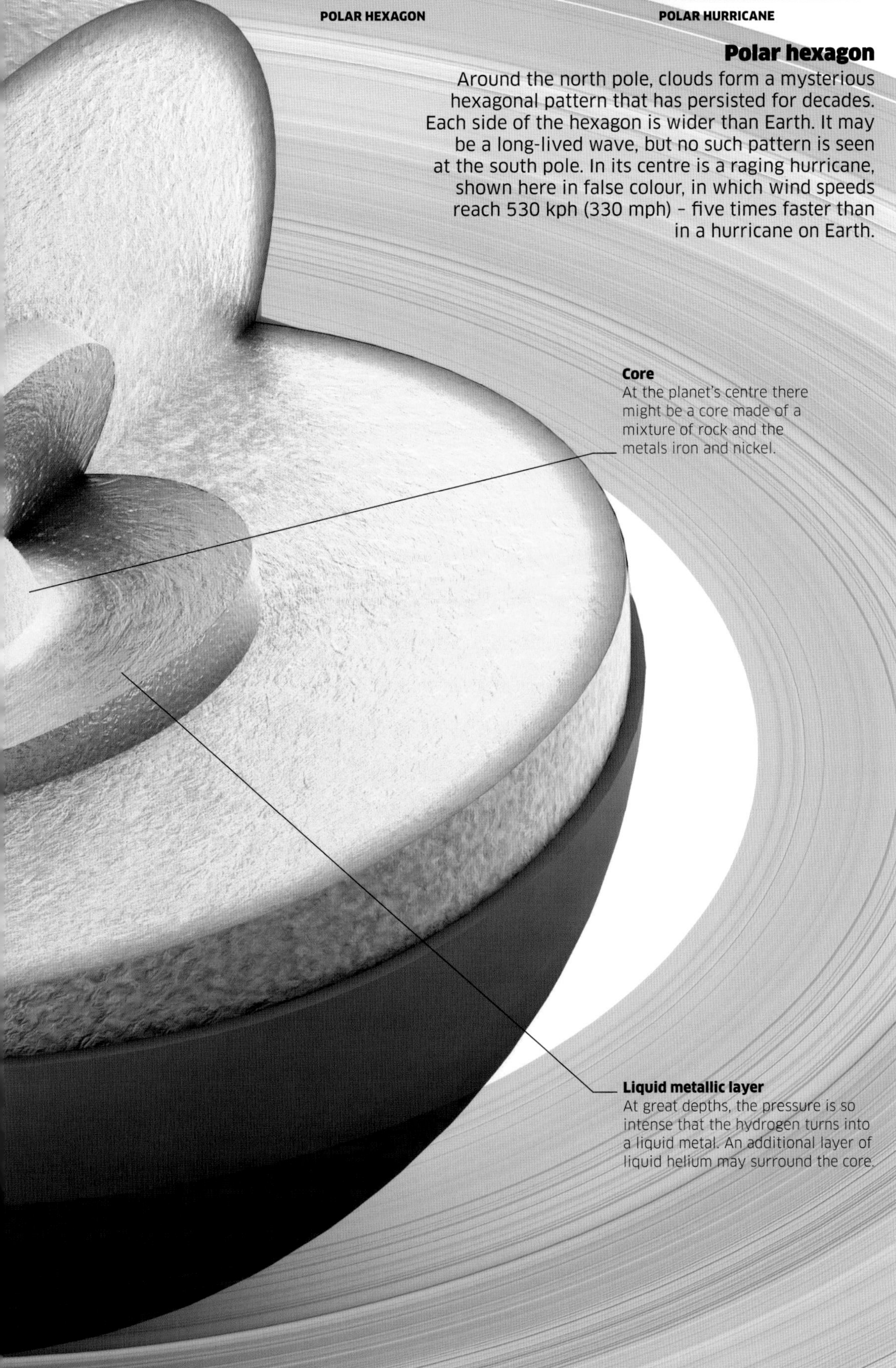
Core
At the planet's centre there might be a core made of a mixture of rock and the metals iron and nickel.
Liquid metallic layer
At great depths, the pressure is so intense that the hydrogen turns into a liquid metal. An additional layer of liquid helium may surround the core.

Changing view

Saturn is tilted on its axis, so our view of the rings from Earth changes greatly as Saturn orbits the Sun. When the rings are side-on, they are almost invisible. It takes around 15 years for the rings to go from full view to almost invisible and back again.

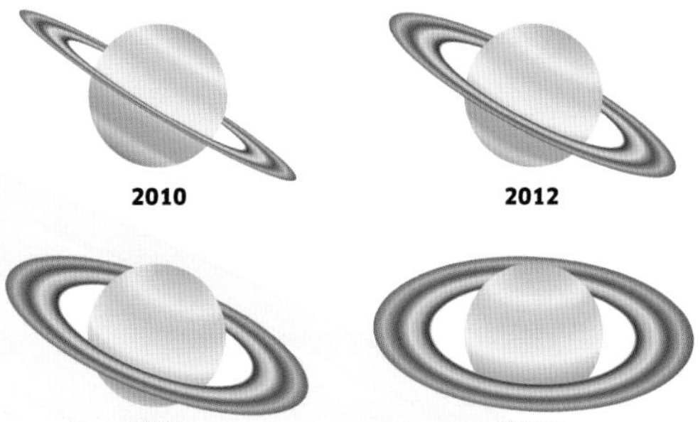
2010
2012
2014
2017

Elongated storm

In 2011 a huge storm broke through Saturn's hazy surface and quickly spread eastwards. After a few months, it had spread all the way around the planet, stirring up the clouds into swirls and ripples (shown here in false colour).

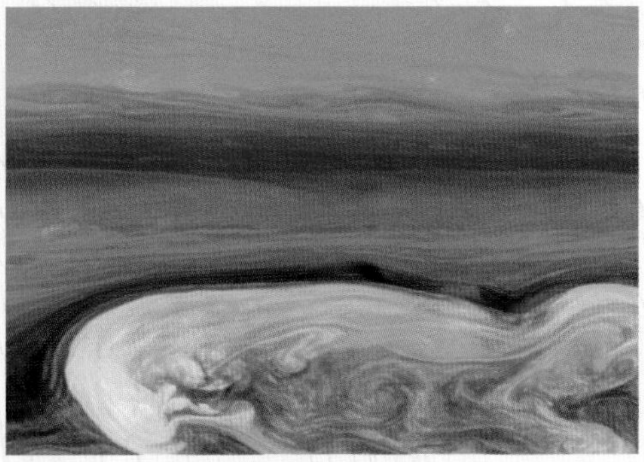

Mission to Saturn

In 2004 the nuclear-powered Cassini spacecraft arrived at Saturn, packed with scientific instruments to study the planet and its rings and moons. The data and images it has since sent back have transformed our understanding of Saturn. Cassini released a separate probe, Huygens, that parachuted onto the surface of Saturn's biggest moon, Titan.

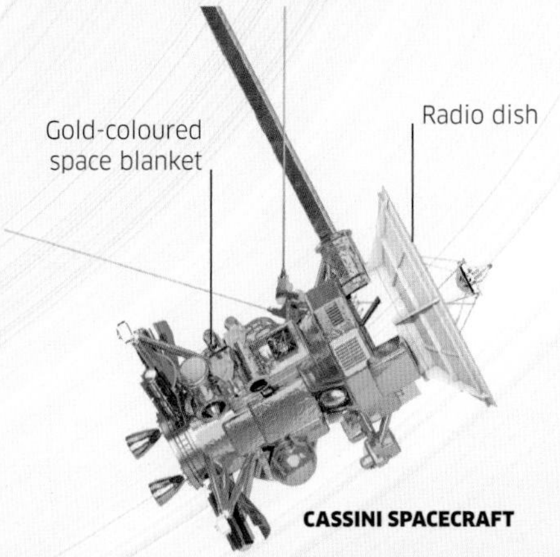
Gold-coloured space blanket
Radio dish

CASSINI SPACECRAFT

1610 The year **Saturn's rings were discovered by Italian astronomer Galileo Galilei.**

Saturn's rings

The vast circle of icy debris orbiting Saturn may be the remains of a moon that broke apart in the past. Visible even in small telescopes, Saturn's rings are thousands of miles in diameter but but only a few metres thick.

Each particle in Saturn's rings is in orbit about the planet, trapped by the gas giant's gravity. The floating chunks of ice also attract each other through gravity, and they are pulled by the gravity of Saturn's moons. All these forces combine to make the material in the rings bunch up at certain distances from Saturn and thin out at others, forming a series of distinct rings and gaps. All the gas giants have ring systems, but those of Jupiter, Uranus, and Neptune are much fainter than Saturn's.

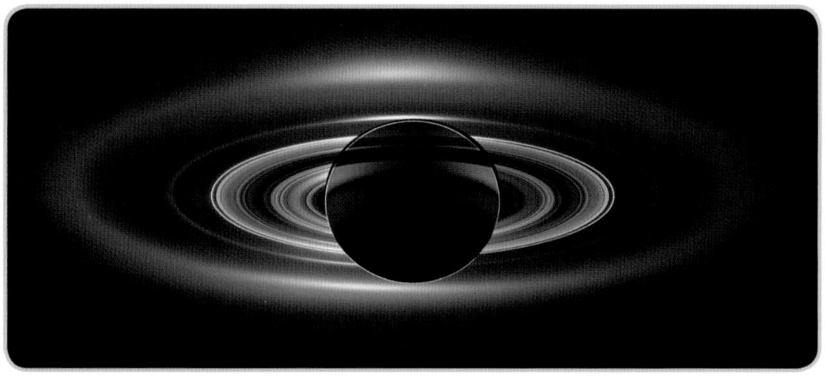

Through Cassini's eyes
The Cassini spacecraft has studied the rings in detail since it arrived at Saturn in 2004. In July 2013, Cassini slipped into Saturn's shadow and captured incredible pictures of its rings lit from behind by the Sun. The images reveal hazy, blue outer rings that are not normally visible. The largest of these – the E ring – is a cloud of microscopic ice grains from geysers erupting on Saturn's moon Enceladus.

Ring system

The main parts of Saturn's rings are given letters, and the gaps within them are named after famous astronomers. The gravitational tug of Saturn's moon Mimas creates the biggest gap, known as the Cassini Division.

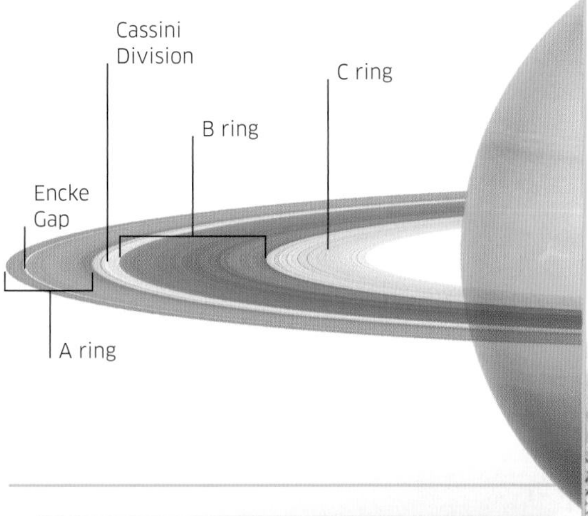
Cassini Division
C ring
B ring
Encke Gap
A ring

Shepherd moons

Some of Saturn's moons orbit the planet within the rings. The gravity of these "shepherd moons" sweeps their orbits clear, herding the icy debris elsewhere. Saturn's moon Daphnis (above) also kicks up waves in the rings as it hurtles around the planet.

Main rings

The artist's impression below shows the most densely packed part of Saturn's main rings: the B ring. Fragments of ice here occasionally collide and break. The newly exposed icy surfaces capture the sunlight, making Saturn's rings much brighter than the dark, dusty rings of other gas giants.

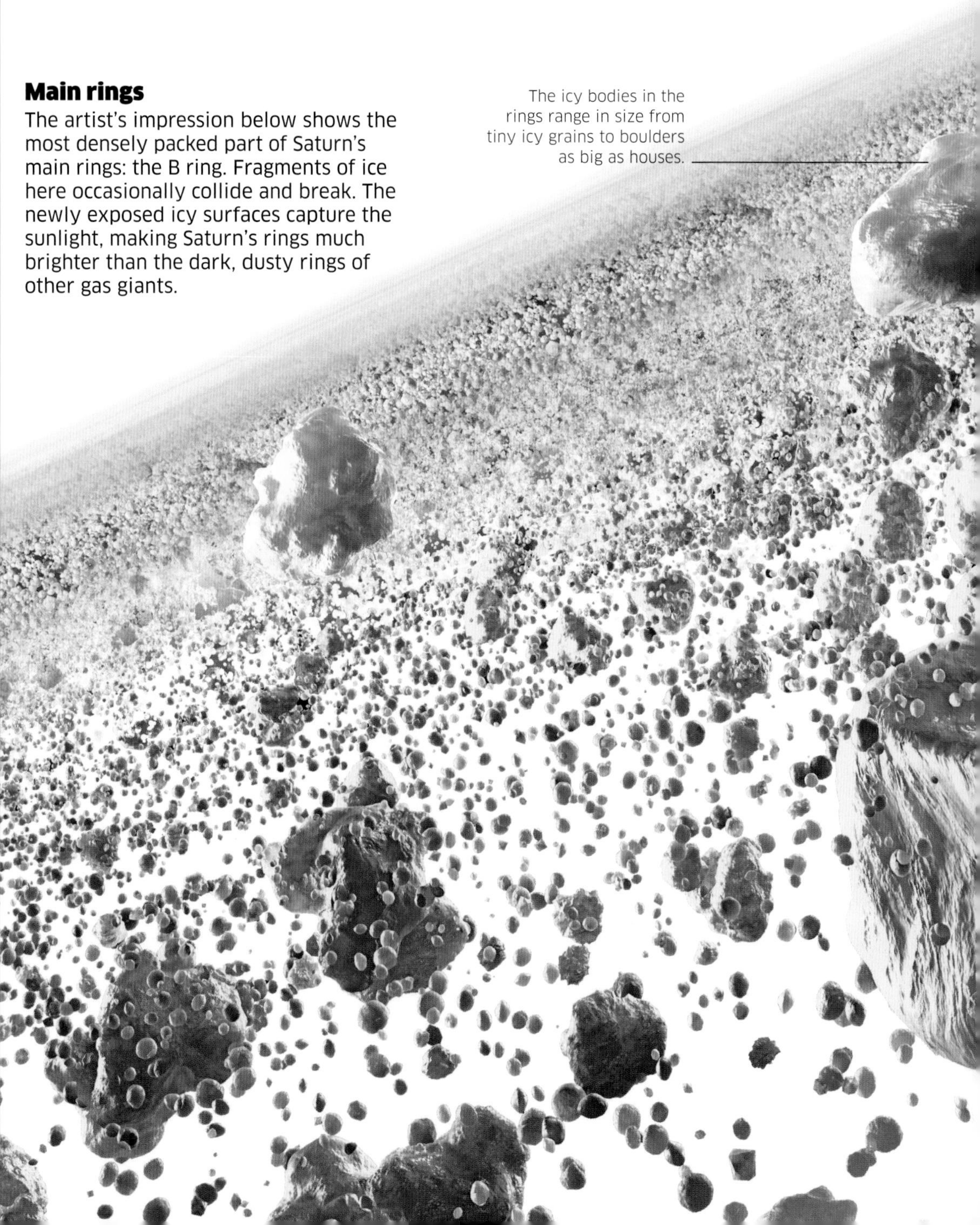
The icy bodies in the rings range in size from tiny icy grains to boulders as big as houses.

A comet or asteroid hit Saturn's D ring in 1983, causing wobbles in the ring material that lasted for over 30 years.

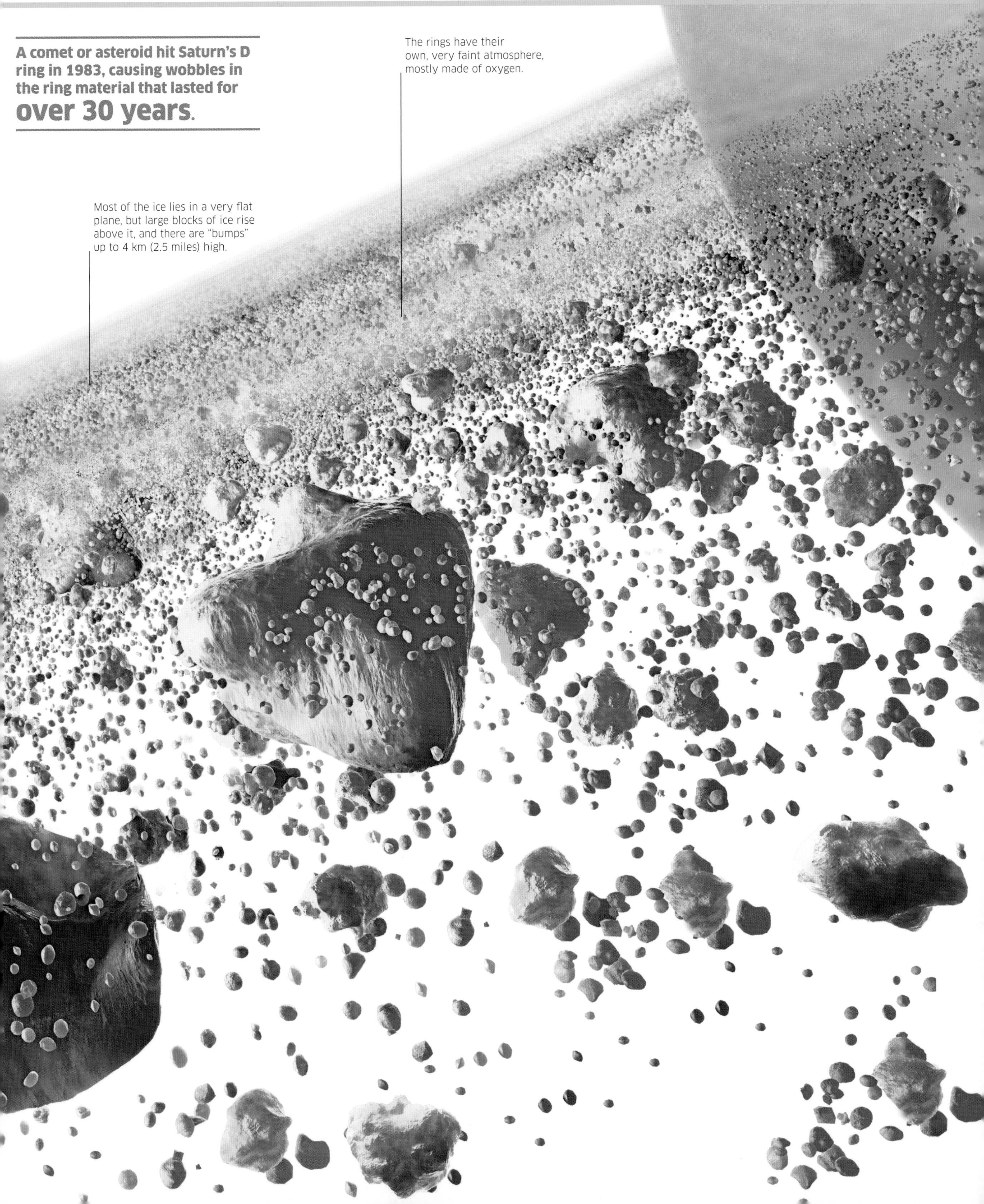
The rings have their own, very faint atmosphere, mostly made of oxygen.
Most of the ice lies in a very flat plane, but large blocks of ice rise above it, and there are "bumps" up to 4 km (2.5 miles) high.

Ring world

Saturn's breathtaking rings are made of billions of sparkling fragments of ice that range in size from snowflakes to icebergs.

The first person to see the rings was the Italian astronomer Galileo, who called them "ears". Since then, telescopes and spacecraft have revealed ever more detail in the rings, which are made up of thousands of individual ringlets. This image is a mosaic of 126 photos captured by the Cassini spacecraft in 2004. Gravity has pulled the material in the rings into a plane so incredibly thin that a disc of paper made to the same scale would be about 1.4 km (0.9 miles) in diameter.

150 The **number of moonlets** so far detected in Saturn's rings.

Moons of Saturn

There are so many moons orbiting the planet Saturn that they form what looks like a miniature version of the Solar System.

Saturn has at least 62 known moons, but the true number may be far greater. The innermost moons are part of Saturn's ring system, and some of these have gathered so much dust around their equators that they look like flying saucers. Beyond the rings are Saturn's largest moons, which are hundreds of kilometres wide and mostly have icy crusts. Largest of all is Titan, which is bigger than the planet Mercury. The inner moons and the large moons all move in the same direction as Saturn's rotation, which suggests they formed at the same time as the planet. Farther out, however, is a chaotic cloud of tiny moons that orbit at wild angles.

Most large moons of Saturn are tidally locked, which means they always keep the same side facing Saturn.

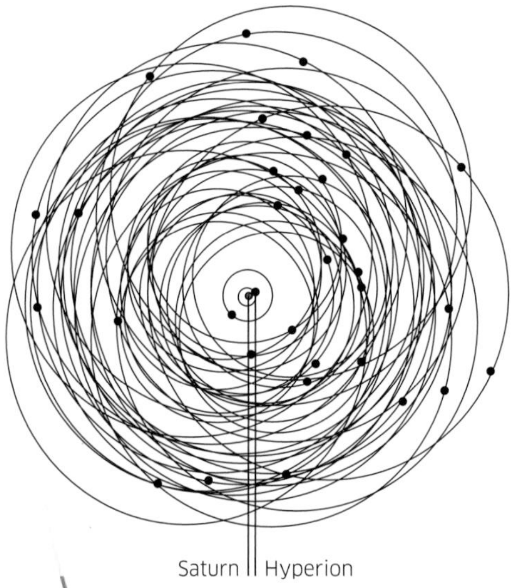
Saturn
Hyperion

Orbits of the outer moons

Far from Saturn are dozens of small moons in tilted, noncircular orbits. Many of these orbit in the opposite direction to the main moons. This suggests they formed elsewhere and were captured by Saturn's gravity.

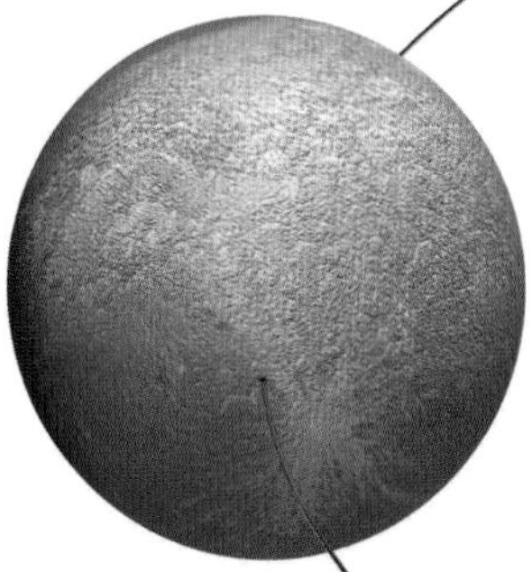

Rhea
Saturn's second-largest moon has an icy surface with intriguing discoloured patches around the equator, which suggest it may once have had rings.

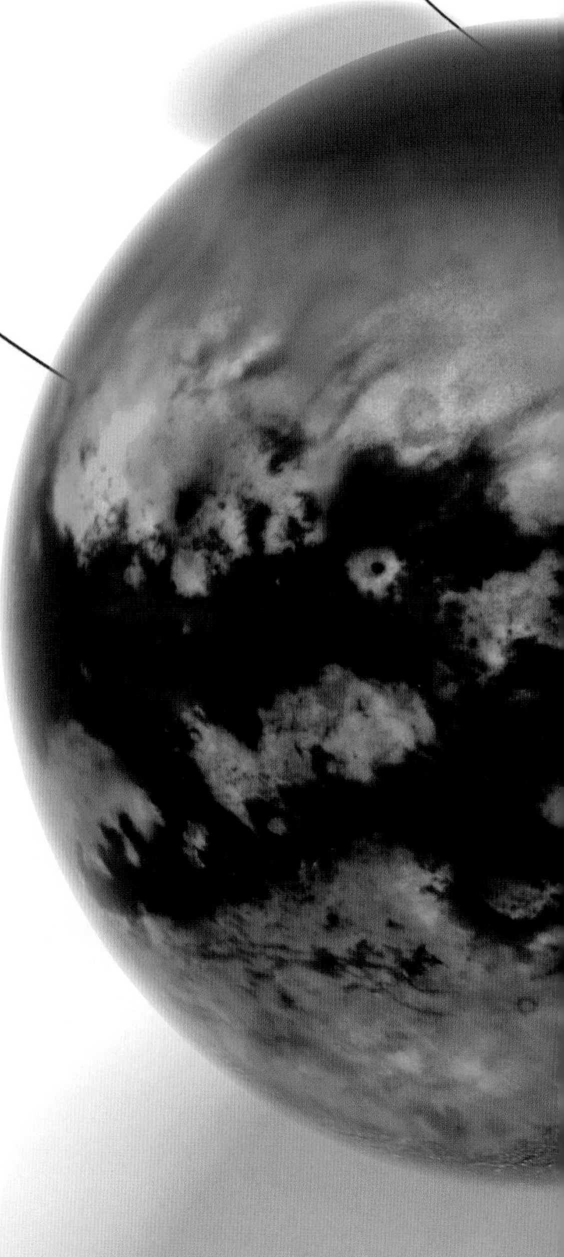

Titan
This is Saturn's largest moon and the second-largest moon in the Solar System. It has a thick, hazy atmosphere that hides the surface from view.

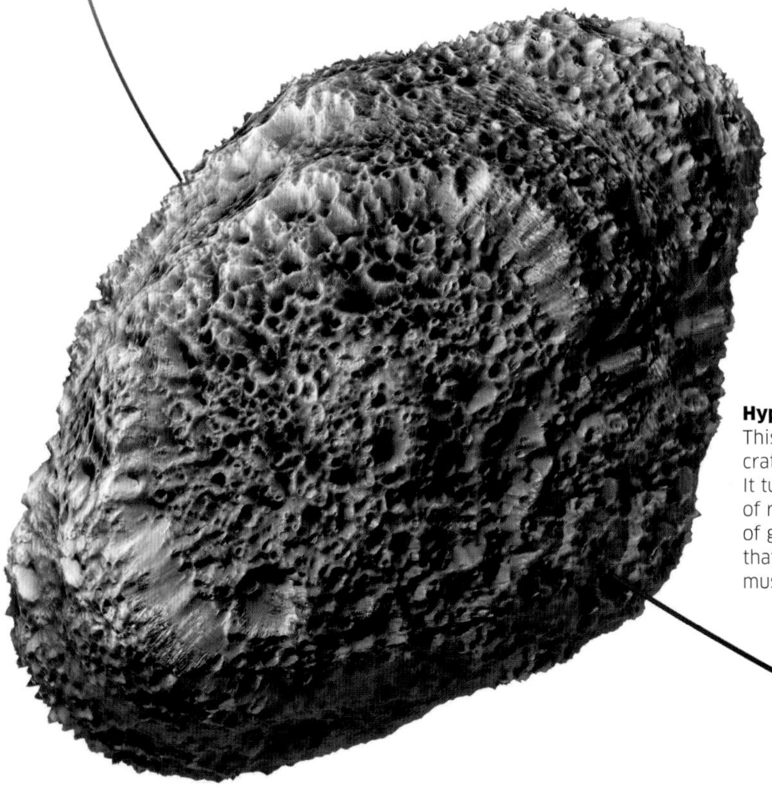

Hyperion
This peculiar moon has so many deep craters that it looks like a bath sponge. It tumbles as it flies through space, its axis of rotation wobbling due largely to the pull of gravity from Titan. Measurements show that Hyperion is partly empty; large hollows must exist under its surface.

Prometheus
Atlas
Polydeuces
Dione
Daphnis
Telesto
Mimas
Tethys
Pandora
Calypso
Pan
Epimetheus
Enceladus
Janus
Pallene
Methone
Helene

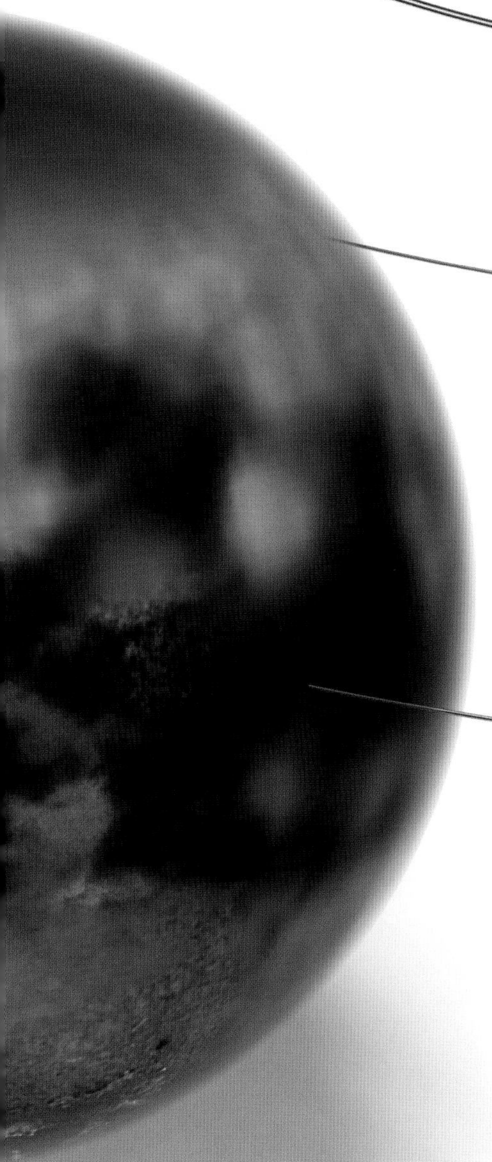

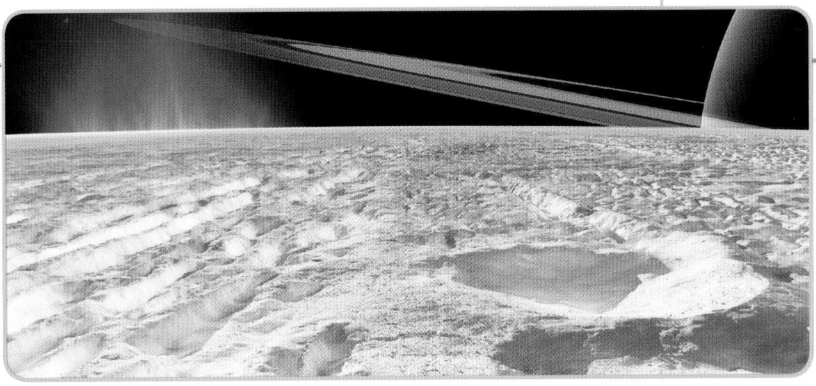

Ice world
Enceladus's icy exterior is the most reflective surface of any body in the Solar System. Although the snow-white ground is frozen solid, an ocean of liquid water may lie hidden underneath. Near the south pole, jets of gas and ice grains erupt from ice volcanoes. Much of the ice falls back to the surface, coating Enceladus with volcanic snow.

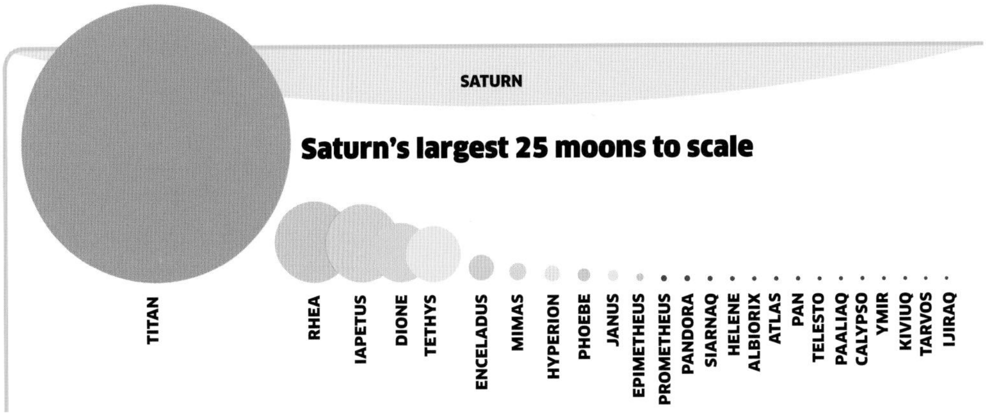
SATURN
Saturn's largest 25 moons to scale
TITAN
RHEA
IAPETUS
DIONE
TETHYS
ENCELADUS
MIMAS
HYPERION
PHOEBE
JANUS
EPIMETHEUS
PROMETHEUS
PANDORA
SIARNAQ
HELENE
ALBIORIX
ATLAS
PAN
TELESTO
PAALIAQ
CALYPSO
YMIR
KIVIUQ
TARVOS
IJIRAQ

1655 The year Titan was **discovered** by Dutchman **Christiaan Huygens**.

Titan

Saturn's largest moon, Titan, has some tantalizing similarities with Earth. It has nitrogen-rich air, cloudy skies, mountains, rivers, and lakes. However, this chilly world is far too cold for life as we know it.

In 1980, when the Voyager 1 spacecraft returned the first close-up images of Titan, the scientists back on Earth were disappointed. A thick, orange haze covered the Moon, hiding the surface from view. However, the haze turned out to be a fascinating mix of the kind of carbon chemicals that existed on Earth billions of years ago, before life began. In the distant future, when the Sun brightens and Titan warms up, conditions on the surface may become just right for life.

Crust
As hard as solid rock, water ice probably makes up most of Titan's outer crust.

Seeing through the clouds

A layer of haze surrounds Titan, making it impossible to photograph the surface from space. However, the Cassini spacecraft has a radar system that can "see" through the haze by bouncing radio waves off the ground.

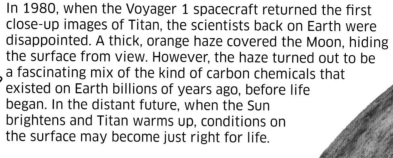

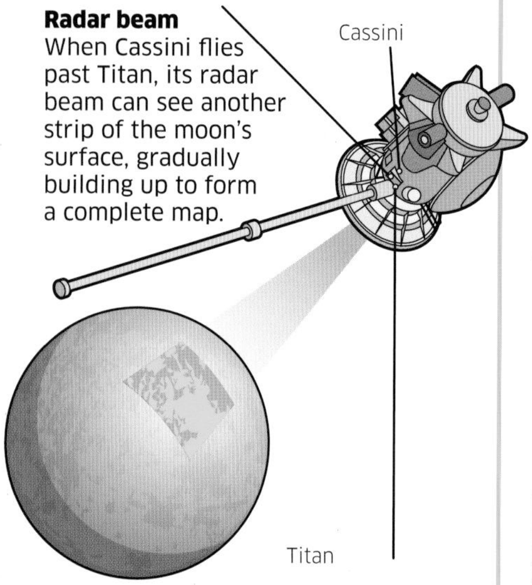
Radar beam
When Cassini flies past Titan, its radar beam can see another strip of the moon's surface, gradually building up to form a complete map.
Cassini
Titan

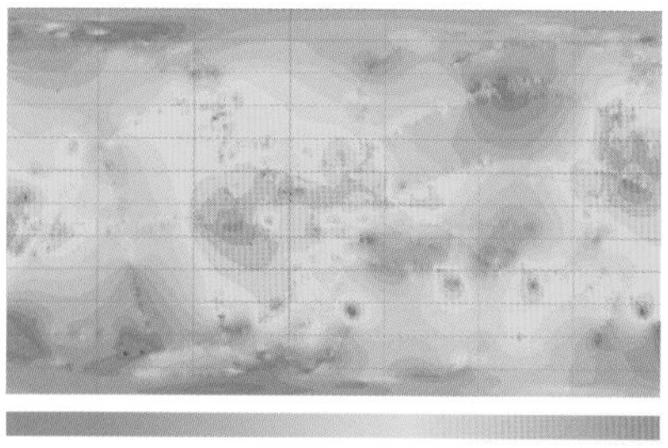
-1,800 M (-5,900 FT)
600 M (2,000 FT)

Mapping Titan
Cassini's map of Titan shows the height of the ground in colour. The mountain peaks are red. Some of the mountains may be ice volcanoes, from which water rather than lava erupts. As the water flows down the sides it freezes, making the volcano grow.

Distant shores

This Cassini radar view has been colour-coded to show low-lying, smooth areas as blue, and higher, rougher areas as orange. The colours reveal Titan's lakes and rivers. These contain not water but carbon chemicals such as ethane.

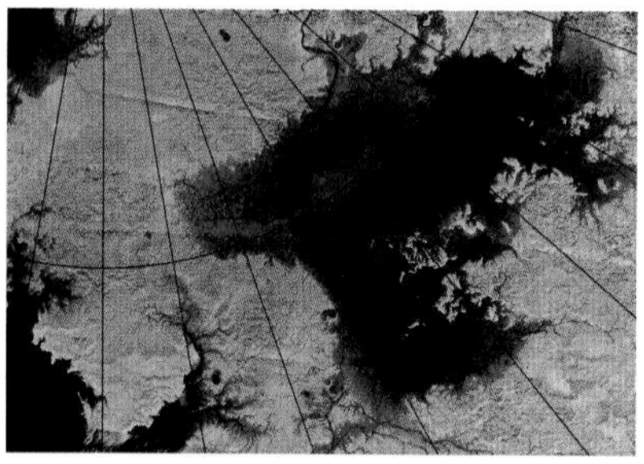

Surface view
In January 2005 the European Space Agency's Huygens space probe landed on Titan's surface. Once released from the orbiting Cassini spacecraft, Huygens took three weeks to reach Titan and then parachute down to the surface to return the first images of the hidden world below. This photo shows "rocks" of ice littering the bed of what was once a lake. The smoggy orange sky casts a gloomy light across the whole landscape.

FAST FACTS

Distance from Saturn: 1.4 billion km (900 million miles)

Mass (Earth = 1): 0.002

Time to rotate once: 16 Earth days

Size: 5,150 km (3,200 miles) wide

95% The amount of **nitrogen** in Titan's **atmosphere**.

The **same side** of Titan always faces its parent planet, Saturn.

Titan is the **second-largest moon in the Solar System**, after Jupiter's moon Ganymede.

Polar lakes
On Earth, clouds, rain, and lakes are made of water; on Titan, they are made of chemicals called ethane and methane. Both are invisible gases on Earth, but Titan is so cold that there they turn into a liquid. They form droplets in the air that fall as rain, feeding lakes near the north pole, like the one in this artist's impression.

Atmosphere
Titan's air is mostly nitrogen, like Earth's air. The nitrogen may have been delivered to Titan by comets crashing into it.

Core
Titan's core could be either solid rock or a mixture of ice and rock all the way to the centre.

Mantle
The top of Titan's mantle might be made of liquid water, forming a hidden ocean. Deeper down, the mantle consists of ice.

The lower part of the mantle is thought to consist of a special kind of ice that forms under high pressure.

42 years – the **length of one night** at **Uranus's north and south poles.**

Uranian moons

Uranus has 27 known moons. The largest, Titania, is 1,577 km (980 miles) wide. The smallest are Trinculo and Cupid, which are only about 18 km (11 miles) wide. All the moons are named after characters from the works of William Shakespeare and the poet Alexander Pope.

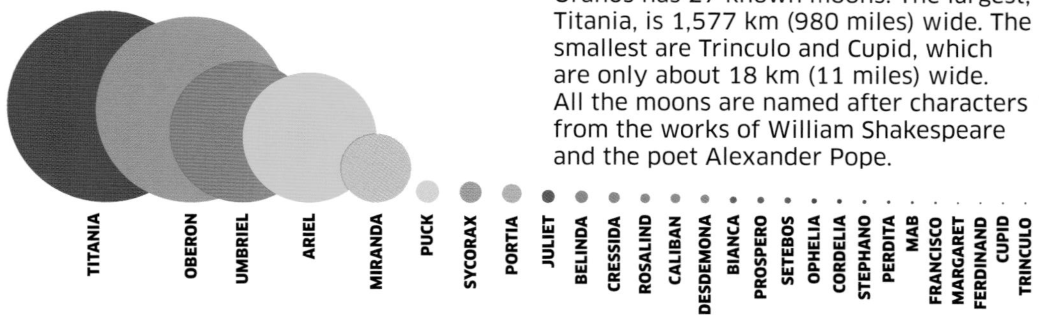
TITANIA
OBERON
UMBRIEL
ARIEL
MIRANDA
PUCK
SYCORAX
PORTIA
JULIET
BELINDA
CRESSIDA
ROSALIND
CALIBAN
DESDEMONA
BIANCA
PROSPERO
SETEBOS
OPHELIA
CORDELIA
STEPHANO
PERDITA
MAB
FRANCISCO
MARGARET
FERDINAND
CUPID
TRINCULO

Rocky moons

Uranus's moon Miranda looks as though it was smashed by an impact and then rebuilt, but with the pieces falling in the wrong places. As a result, vast cracks formed as its crust resettled, creating the highest cliff in the Solar System: Verona Rupes, which is well over 5 km (3 miles) tall.

ARTIST'S IMPRESSION OF VERONA RUPES

Uranus

In 1781 the astronomer William Herschel peered through the telescope in his garden in England and saw what he thought was a comet. It turned out to be something much more exciting: a new planet.

Uranus is an ice giant much like Neptune, but tipped on its side. For two centuries after Herschel discovered Uranus, very little was learnt about it, except that it has moons, rings, and an unusual tilt. Only one spacecraft – Voyager 2 – has ever visited the planet, and the pictures it sent back in 1986 revealed a disappointingly boring, pale blue globe with a few faint wisps of cloud. Unlike the other giant planets, Uranus gives off relatively little heat. It does, however, have a strong but lopsided magnetic field.

FAST FACTS

Surface gravity (Earth = 1): 0.89

Time to rotate once: 17.2 hours

Year: 84 Earth years

Moons: At least 27

Rings
Uranus is surrounded by a set of narrow rings, most of which were discovered in 1977 when they passed in front of a star. More rings, sharing orbits with small moons, were found later.

Atmosphere
Hydrogen and helium are the main gases in Uranus's atmosphere, but there is also plenty of methane, which gives the planet its pale blue colour.

Mantle
Water, methane, and ammonia combine to form a slushy mixture of ice and liquid in Uranus's mantle. At the base of the mantle there may be a sea of diamond.

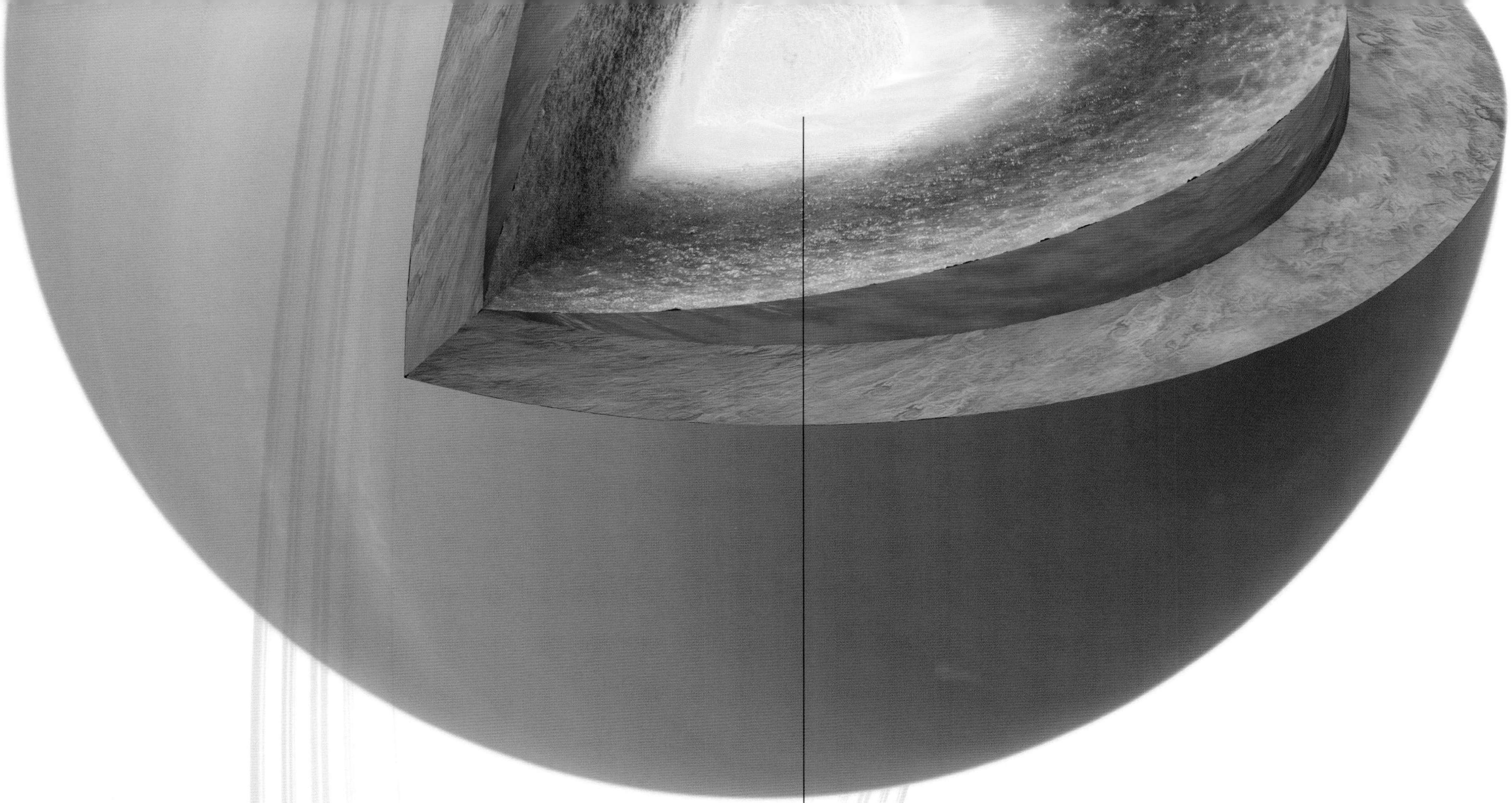

Core
At the planet's centre is a core of possibly molten rock, iron, and nickel, with a temperature of more than 5,000°C (9,000°F).

Storm clouds
Uranus looked featureless when Voyager visited because its south pole was facing the Sun. When its equator faces the Sun, however, the atmosphere springs to life. Recent images from telescopes reveal horizontal cloud bands like those on Jupiter, violent storms, and giant polar hurricanes.

On a roll
Most planets rotate upright like spinning tops, but Uranus's axis of rotation is tipped over on its side. This gives the planet and its moons extreme seasons. In the winter hemisphere, the pole is in constant darkness for 42 years, while the summer pole is in constant sunlight.

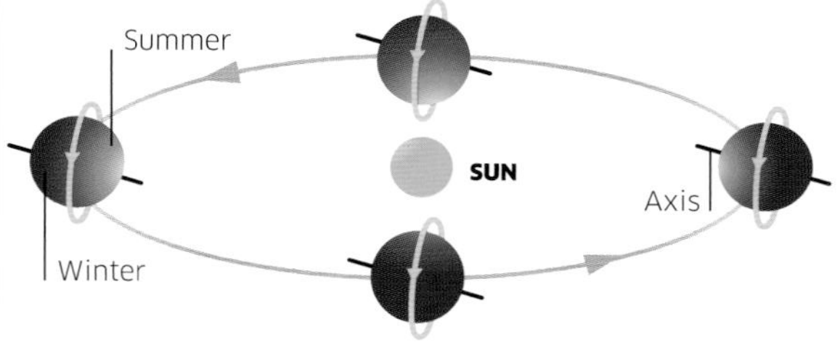
Summer
Winter
SUN
Axis

Neptune is 30 times farther away from the Sun than Earth is.

Neptune

The Solar System's outermost and coldest planet has a striking blue colour like Earth. Similar in size and structure to Uranus, Neptune is an ice giant: a vast ball of gas, liquid, and ice.

Neptune was the last planet to be discovered and was found thanks to maths. Astronomers had noticed that Uranus wandered off its predicted path as though pulled by the gravity of a hidden planet. When they calculated where the mystery world should be and looked through a telescope, they saw Neptune. Just 17 days later, in October 1846, they also saw Neptune's icy moon Triton. Only Voyager 2 has visited Neptune. It flew past the planet in 1989 and sent back pictures of white clouds in Neptune's sky, blown into streaks by furious winds, and faint rings around the gas giant. Triton turned out to be a fascinating world of erupting geysers and frozen nitrogen lakes, surrounded by a thin atmosphere.

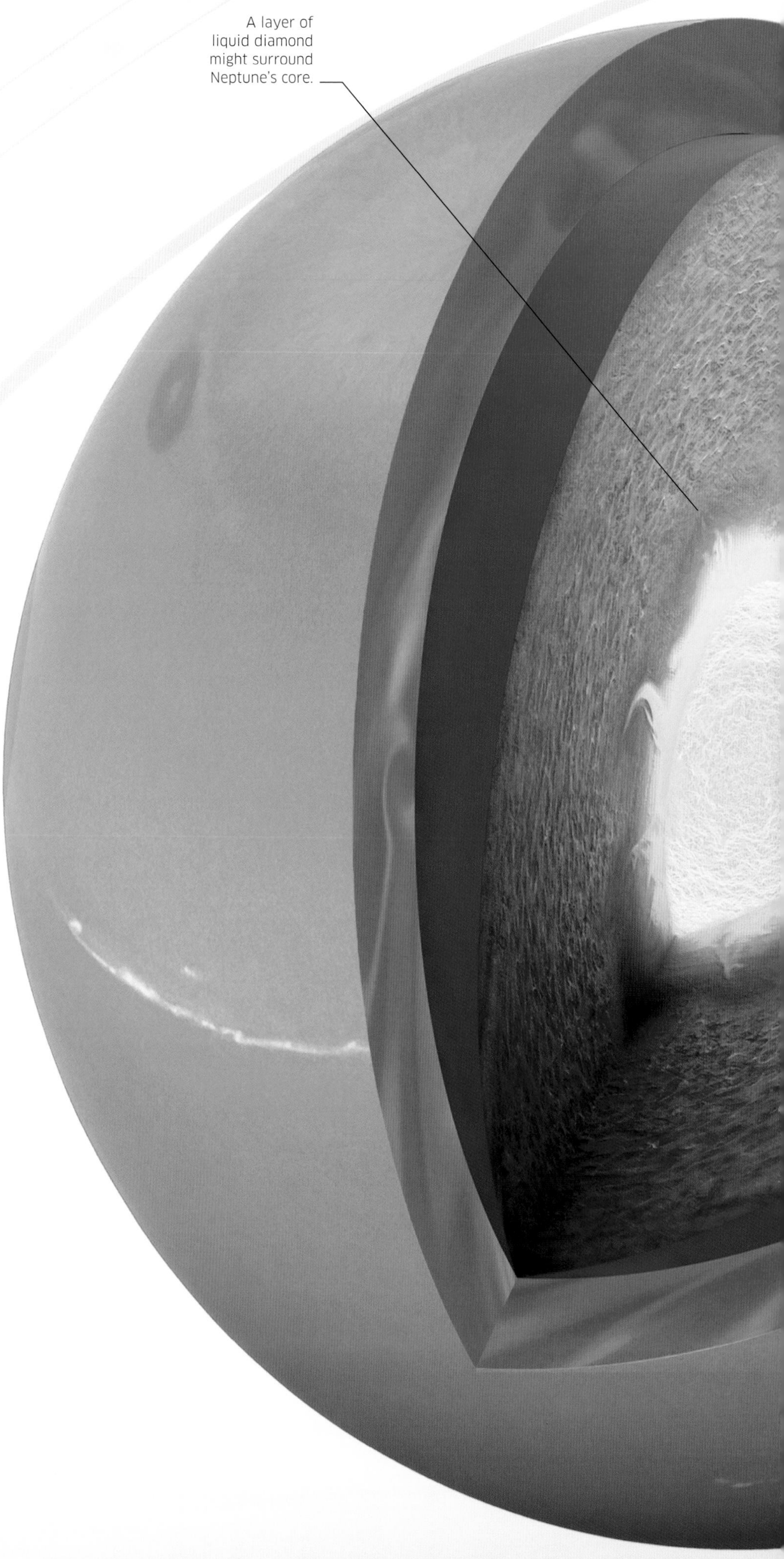
A layer of liquid diamond might surround Neptune's core.
Rings
Neptune is surrounded by several thin, faint rings made mostly of dust.

Dust rings

Neptune's rings are made of dark dust that's hard to see, but Voyager 2 took this photo when they were lit from behind by the Sun. The rings have thick and thin sections, making them uneven.

Neptune's moons

For over a century, Triton was Neptune's only known moon, but 14 others have now been discovered. After Triton, the next largest moon is Proteus, at 420 km (260 miles) wide. Nereid has a highly stretched orbit: it swoops close to Neptune before flying seven times farther out.

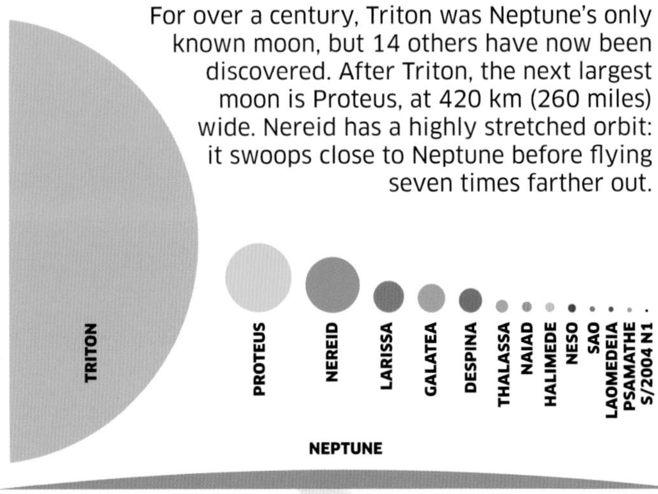
TRITON
PROTEUS
NEREID
LARISSA
GALATEA
DESPINA
THALASSA
NAIAD
HALIMEDE
NESO
SAO
LAOMEDEIA
PSAMATHE
S/2004 N1
NEPTUNE

The astronomer Galileo Galilei saw Neptune 234 years before its discovery but didn't realize it was a planet.

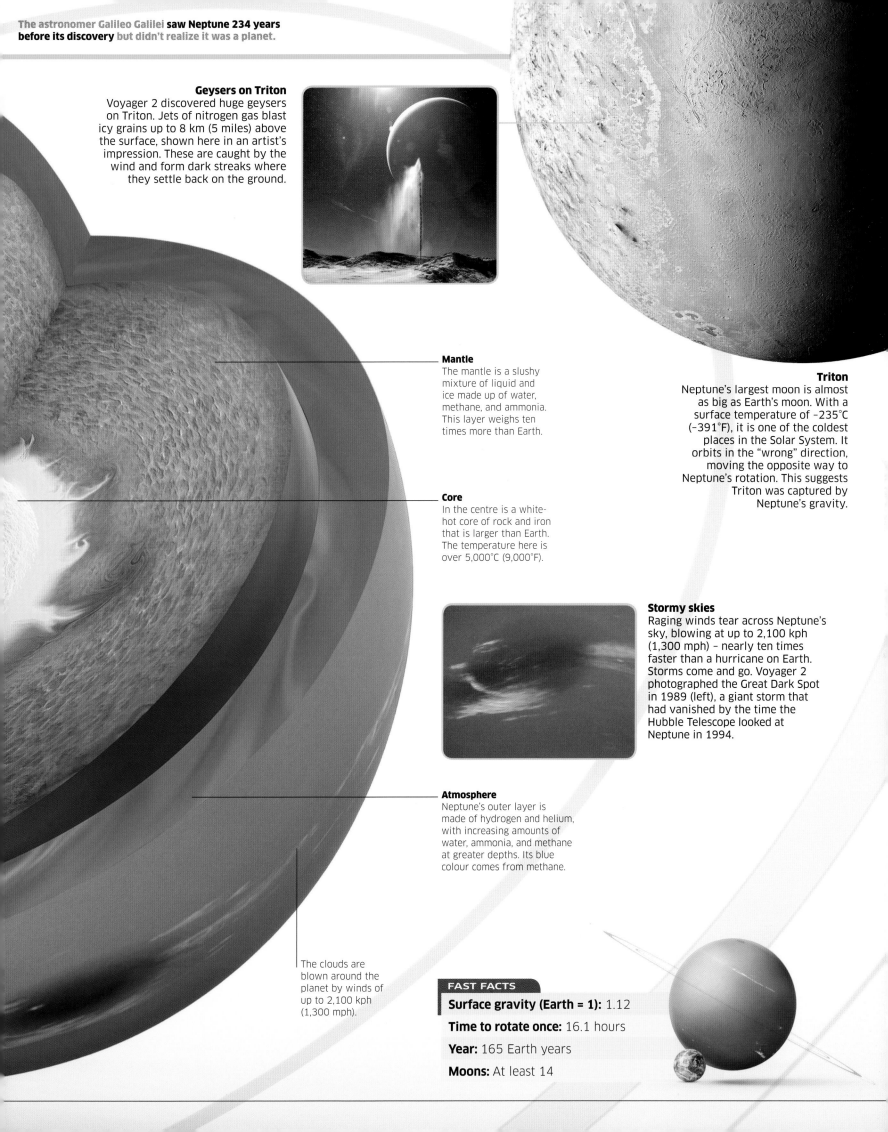

Geysers on Triton
Voyager 2 discovered huge geysers on Triton. Jets of nitrogen gas blast icy grains up to 8 km (5 miles) above the surface, shown here in an artist's impression. These are caught by the wind and form dark streaks where they settle back on the ground.

Triton
Neptune's largest moon is almost as big as Earth's moon. With a surface temperature of –235°C (–391°F), it is one of the coldest places in the Solar System. It orbits in the "wrong" direction, moving the opposite way to Neptune's rotation. This suggests Triton was captured by Neptune's gravity.

Mantle
The mantle is a slushy mixture of liquid and ice made up of water, methane, and ammonia. This layer weighs ten times more than Earth.

Core
In the centre is a white-hot core of rock and iron that is larger than Earth. The temperature here is over 5,000°C (9,000°F).

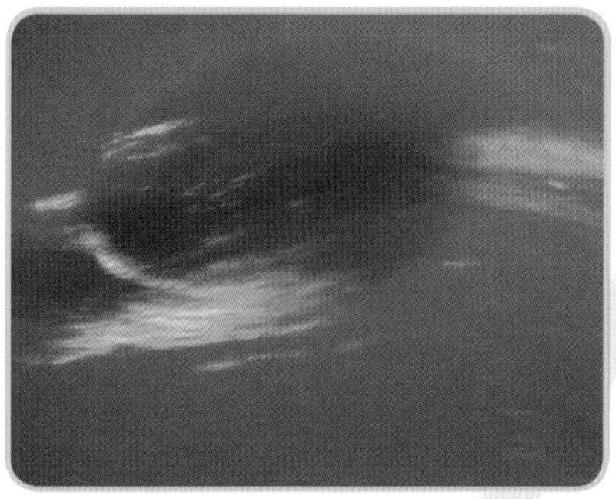

Stormy skies
Raging winds tear across Neptune's sky, blowing at up to 2,100 kph (1,300 mph) – nearly ten times faster than a hurricane on Earth. Storms come and go. Voyager 2 photographed the Great Dark Spot in 1989 (left), a giant storm that had vanished by the time the Hubble Telescope looked at Neptune in 1994.

Atmosphere
Neptune's outer layer is made of hydrogen and helium, with increasing amounts of water, ammonia, and methane at greater depths. Its blue colour comes from methane.

The clouds are blown around the planet by winds of up to 2,100 kph (1,300 mph).

FAST FACTS

Surface gravity (Earth = 1): 1.12

Time to rotate once: 16.1 hours

Year: 165 Earth years

Moons: At least 14

The Oort Cloud may contain **over a trillion bodies** larger than 1 km (0.6 mile) wide.

Minor planets

Billions of rocky and icy objects orbit the Sun, some weaving paths between the planets but most orbiting further out. Called "minor planets", they are leftovers from the Solar System's formation, and many are fascinating worlds in their own right.

There are minor planets scattered throughout the Solar System, but most fall into groups that share similar orbits. Nearest the Sun are the asteroids, which are mostly made of rock. Further out, the minor planets tend to be icy. Some minor planets have their own moons and rings, and the very largest are roundish in shape and classed as dwarf planets. The most famous of these is Pluto, which was once considered a planet.

Haumea
The dwarf planet Haumea is egg-shaped rather than round. Its shape is too small to see with a telescope but astronomers figured it out by studying how it reflects different amounts of light as it rotates. Haumea has two moons, Hi'aka and Namaka, shown in this artist's impression.

Eris
The dwarf planet Eris was discovered in 2005 and is larger than Pluto. It belongs to the scattered disc – a group of icy objects that travel far north and south of the Kuiper Belt disc.

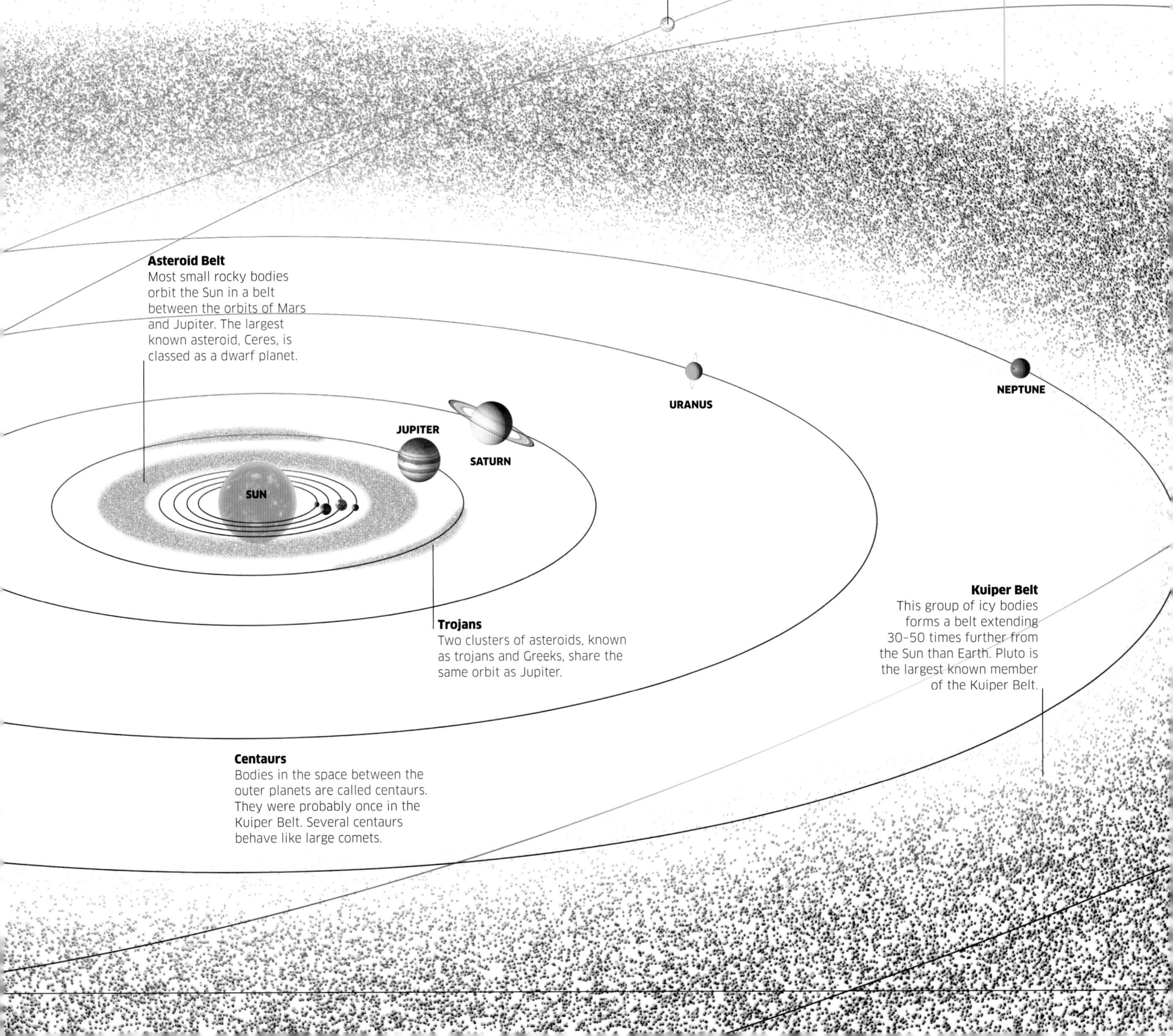
URANUS
NEPTUNE
JUPITER
SATURN
SUN

Asteroid Belt
Most small rocky bodies orbit the Sun in a belt between the orbits of Mars and Jupiter. The largest known asteroid, Ceres, is classed as a dwarf planet.

Trojans
Two clusters of asteroids, known as trojans and Greeks, share the same orbit as Jupiter.

Kuiper Belt
This group of icy bodies forms a belt extending 30–50 times further from the Sun than Earth. Pluto is the largest known member of the Kuiper Belt.

Centaurs
Bodies in the space between the outer planets are called centaurs. They were probably once in the Kuiper Belt. Several centaurs behave like large comets.

ARTIST'S IMPRESSION OF PLUTO

Pluto's surface
Since Pluto is so far from the Sun, most substances that are gases on Earth are solids on Pluto. The very thin atmosphere on this dwarf planet probably freezes and evaporates with Pluto's changing seasons.

Ceres
Ceres, the largest asteroid, is so big that scientists consider it a dwarf planet. This 950 km (590 mile) wide body is a battered, rocky world, but it has icy patches on its surface and sometimes releases water vapour into space. In 2015 NASA's Dawn spacecraft became the first one ever to visit Ceres.

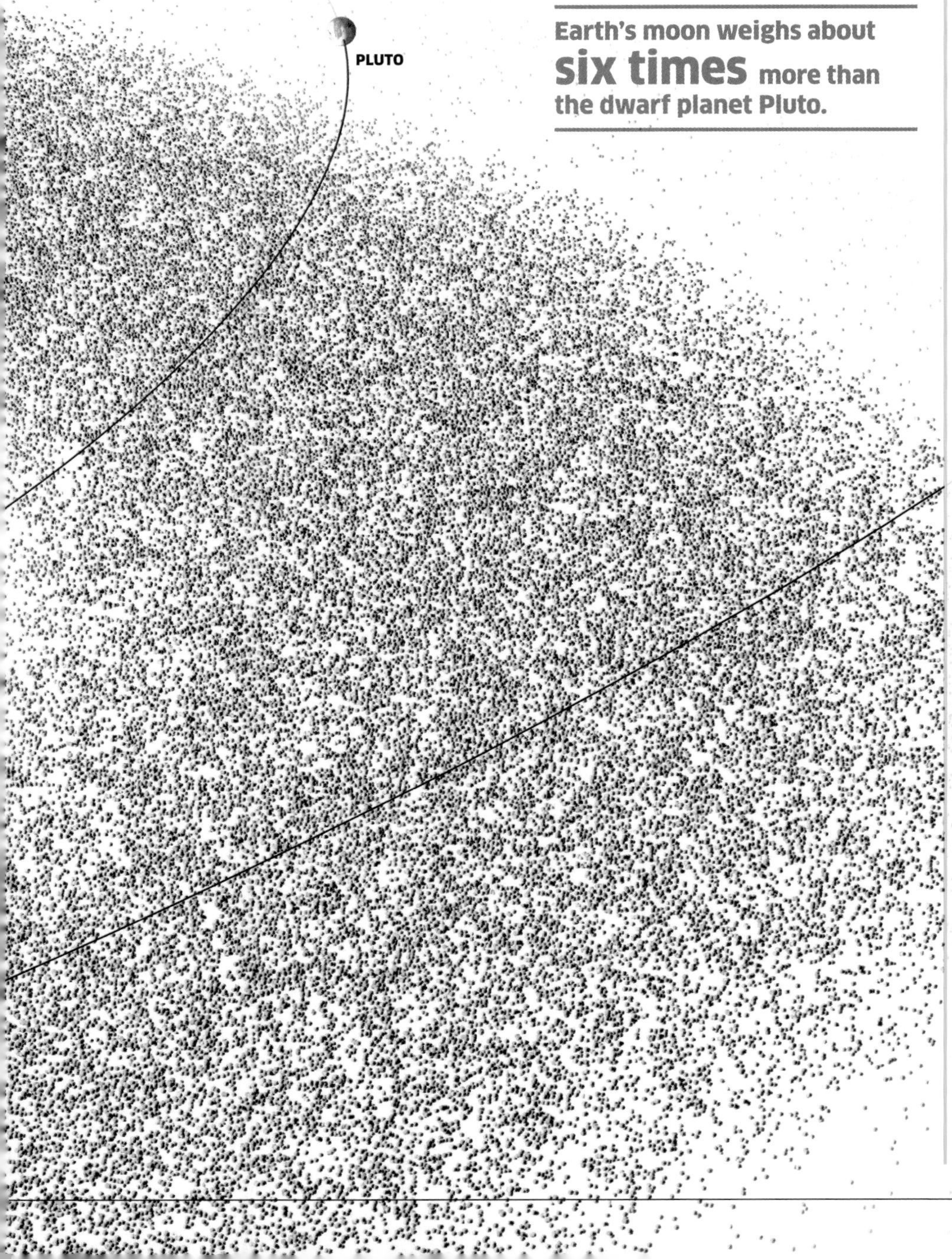
PLUTO

Earth's moon weighs about six times more than the dwarf planet Pluto.

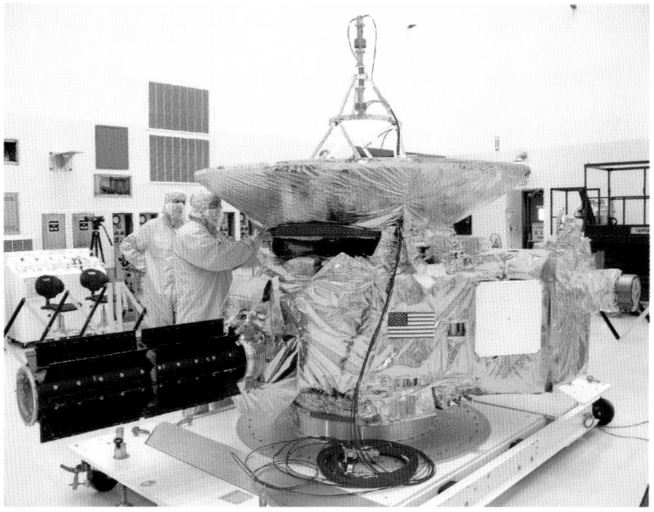

New Horizons mission
NASA's nuclear-powered New Horizons spacecraft visited the dwarf planet Pluto and its five moons in 2015. After its encounter, the 400 kg (880 lb) craft set off towards other Kuiper Belt objects to improve our knowledge of these dim and distant worlds.

LARGEST KNOWN MINOR PLANETS

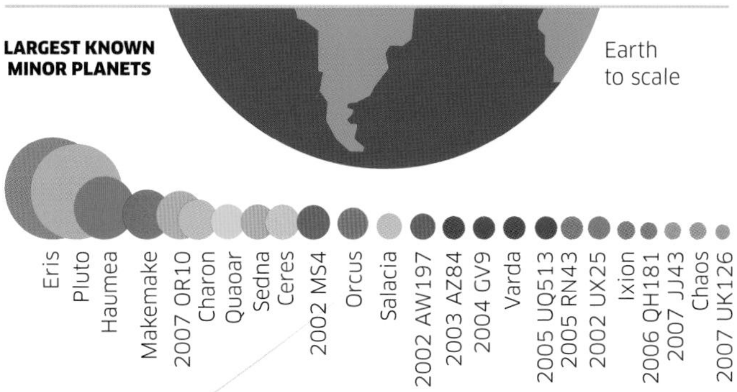
Earth to scale
Eris
Pluto
Haumea
Makemake
2007 OR10
Charon
Quaoar
Sedna
Ceres
2002 MS4
Orcus
Salacia
2002 AW197
2003 AZ84
2004 GV9
Varda
2005 UQ513
2005 RN43
2002 UX25
Ixion
2006 QH181
2007 JJ43
Chaos
2007 UK126

Size
Though small relative to Earth, minor planets rival the Solar System's moons in size. Five are recognized as dwarf planets: Eris, Pluto, Haumea, Makemake, and Ceres. However, there may be hundreds of objects beyond Neptune that could qualify as dwarf planets.

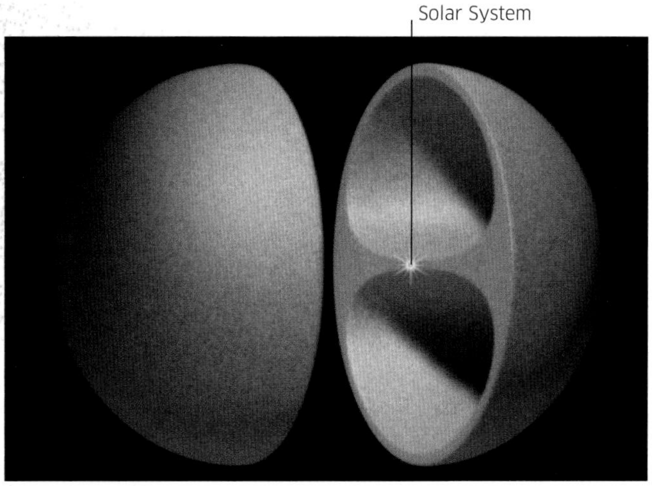
Solar System

Oort Cloud
Beyond the Kuiper Belt lies a roughly spherical cloud of icy bodies that probably stretches a quarter of the way to the nearest star. Many comets are likely to originate from this planetary deep freeze.

4.6 billion years – the **average age of comets.**

Comets

Comets are strange but beautiful sights, like stars with glowing tails. From time to time they swoop into the inner Solar System and appear in the night sky, only to shoot back out to space and vanish.

For thousands of years, people were puzzled by comets or even frightened by them, seeing their unexpected appearance as bad omens. We now know these visitors from the outer Solar System are simply ancient lumps of ice and dust – leftovers from the cloud of rubble from which the planets formed, billions of years ago. When comets venture close to the Sun, the ice warms up and releases gas and dust into a gigantic cloud and tails. Comets have changed little since they first formed, which makes them a prime target for space scientists who want to learn more about the early Solar System.

Structure of a comet

The cloud of gas and dust that surrounds the nucleus is called the coma. The coma's largest part, visible in ultraviolet light, is made of hydrogen. Both tails follow the comet's motion around the Sun.

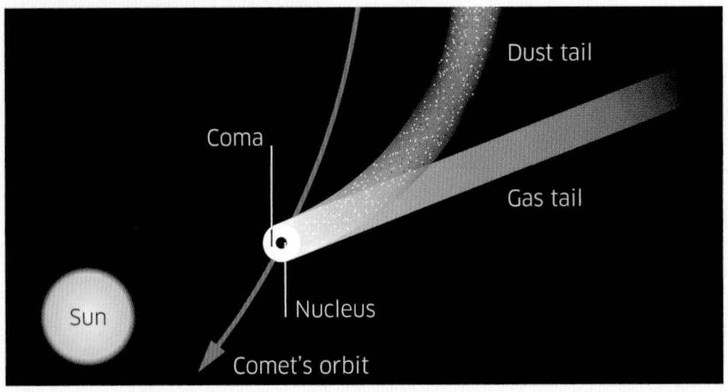
Dust tail
Coma
Gas tail
Sun
Nucleus
Comet's orbit

Around the Sun

The orbits of comets are typically elliptical (oval). Only when comets come close to the Sun do their tails develop. The time taken to make one orbit varies enormously – Comet Encke, a short-period comet, takes only three years to orbit the Sun, but long-period comets can take millions of years.

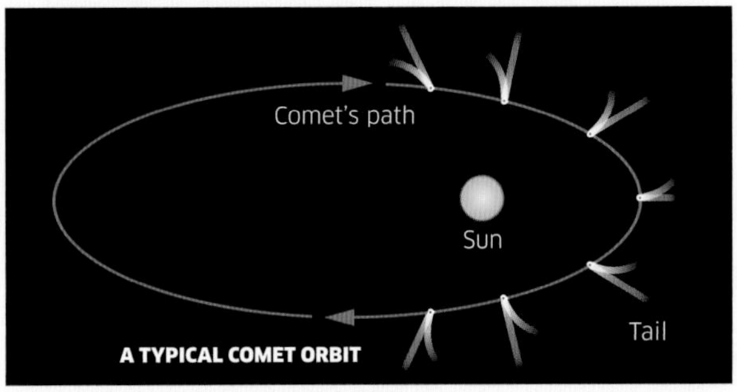
Comet's path
Sun
Tail
A TYPICAL COMET ORBIT

SIZE OF COMET 67P RELATIVE TO A CITY

Comet 67P

The best-studied comet in history is the 5 km (3 mile) wide Comet 67P, which was explored by the European spacecraft Rosetta that arrived at it in 2014. Rosetta released a separate probe called Philae to make the first soft landing (as opposed to a violent impact) on a comet nucleus. The harpoon meant to anchor Philae to the comet failed to fire on landing, causing Philae to bounce hundreds of metres into space. It bounced twice before settling.

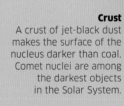

Crust
A crust of jet-black dust makes the surface of the nucleus darker than coal. Comet nuclei are among the darkest objects in the Solar System.

Tall tails
Comets look as though they are streaking through space with their tails stretched out behind them, but that's just an illusion. In reality, the tails always point away from the Sun, whichever way a comet is travelling. There are two main tails: a gas tail (blue in the photo of Comet Hale-Bopp on left) and a dust tail (white). The gas tail points almost directly away from the Sun, but the dust tail bends back towards the comet's path.

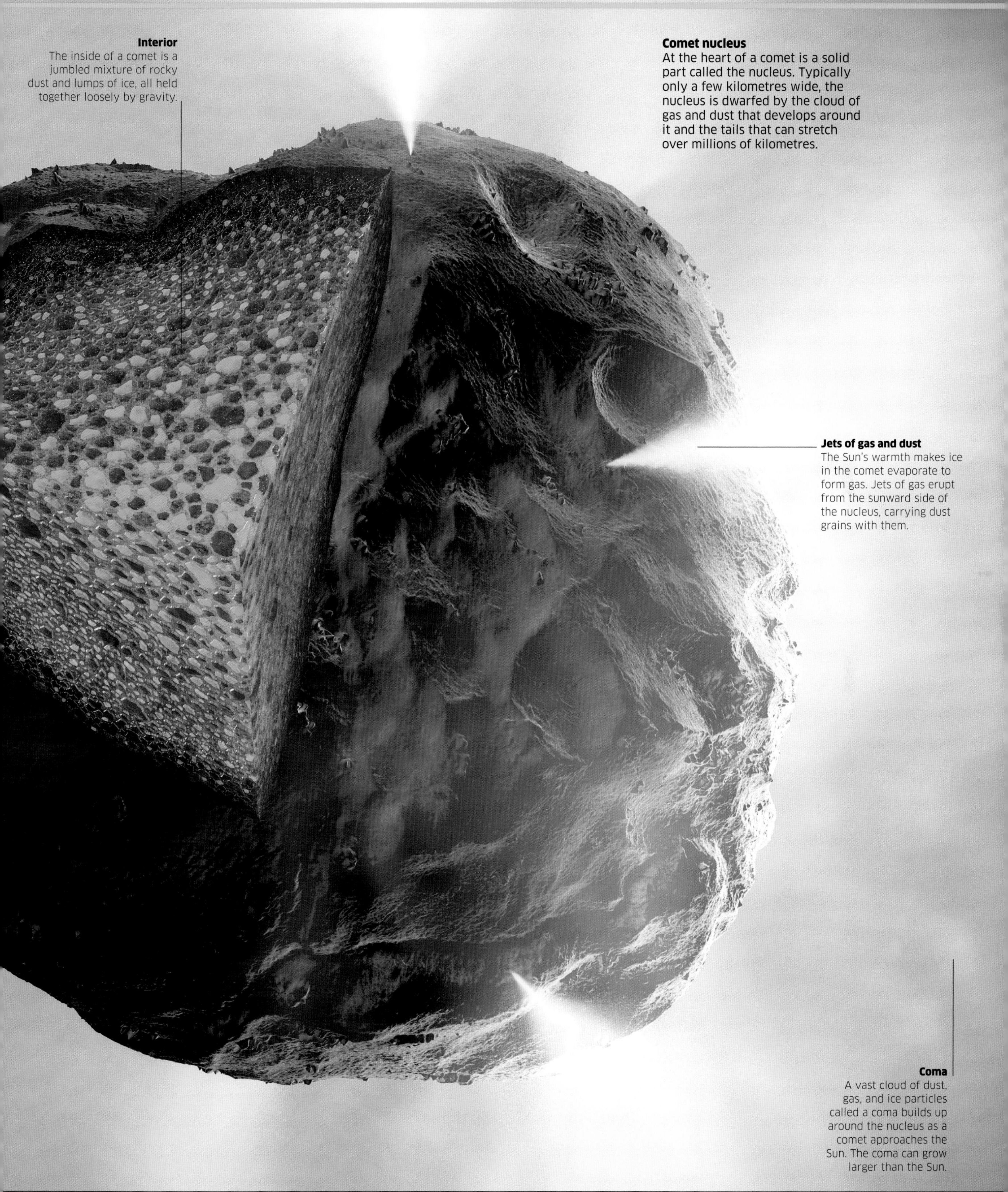
Interior
The inside of a comet is a jumbled mixture of rocky dust and lumps of ice, all held together loosely by gravity.
Comet nucleus
At the heart of a comet is a solid part called the nucleus. Typically only a few kilometres wide, the nucleus is dwarfed by the cloud of gas and dust that develops around it and the tails that can stretch over millions of kilometres.
Jets of gas and dust
The Sun's warmth makes ice in the comet evaporate to form gas. Jets of gas erupt from the sunward side of the nucleus, carrying dust grains with them.
Coma
A vast cloud of dust, gas, and ice particles called a coma builds up around the nucleus as a comet approaches the Sun. The coma can grow larger than the Sun.

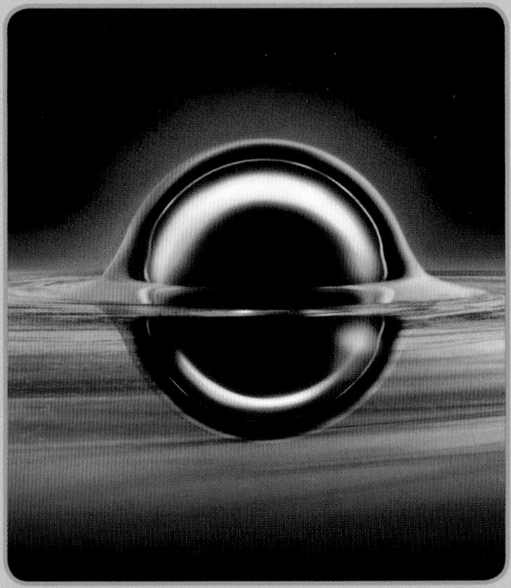

STARS

On a dark night you can see thousands of stars twinkling in the sky, but there are countless trillions more scattered across the fathomless depths of space. Like our Sun, all stars are dazzling balls of hot gas that can shine for billions of years, powered by nuclear fusion.

How stars work

A star is a brilliant, shining ball of extremely hot gas, mainly hydrogen, that generates fantastic amounts of energy in its core. This energy travels out through the star until it reaches the surface, where it escapes into space as light, heat, and other types of radiation invisible to our eyes. Stars are bright and hot because of the vast quantity of energy they generate.

PARTS OF A STAR

Stars vary tremendously in their size, but all of them have the same parts. Every star has an extremely hot central region, or core, that produces energy; one or more layers of gas through which this energy travels outwards; a very hot surface; and an atmosphere.

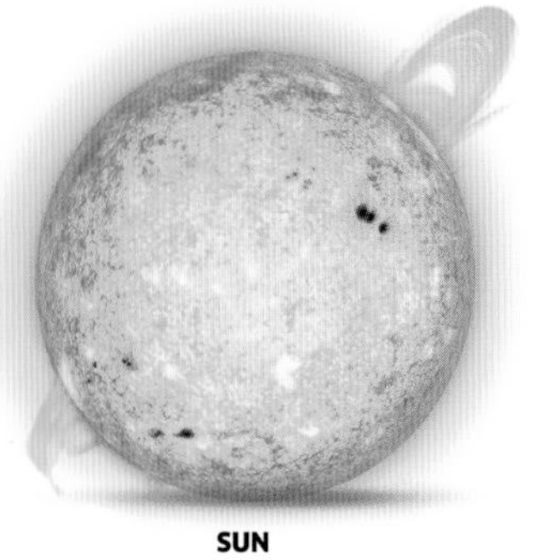

SUN

An average star

Our Sun is an ordinary star that looks huge to us because it's so close. Sun-sized stars have two layers through which energy moves outwards from the core: an inner layer where it travels by radiation, and an outer layer that carries it by convection (rising and falling currents). In larger stars, these two layers are the other way round, while some smaller stars have only a convection layer. Like all stars, the Sun has a brilliant surface that emits light and heat.

How stars shine

The energy produced by a star is released by nuclear fusion in its core. This process involves the nuclei (central parts) of atoms joining together to make more massive nuclei. Fusion can only occur at the extremely high temperatures present in star cores.

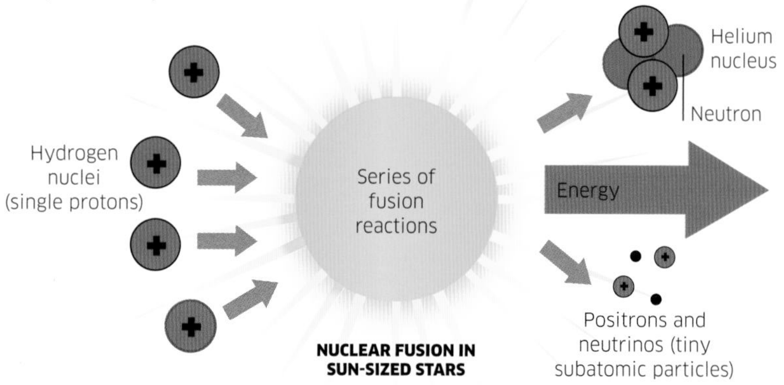
Hydrogen nuclei (single protons)
Series of fusion reactions
Energy
Helium nucleus
Neutron
Positrons and neutrinos (tiny subatomic particles)

NUCLEAR FUSION IN SUN-SIZED STARS

Forces in stars

Most stars exist in a stable state through a delicate balance between two forces: gravity, which pushes matter inwards; and pressure, generated by energy released from the core, which pushes matter outwards.

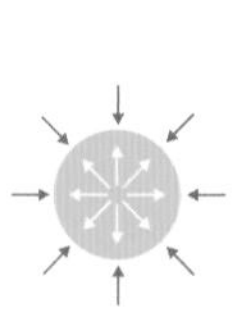

Forces in balance
In a normal star, the inward push of gravity balances the outward pressure.

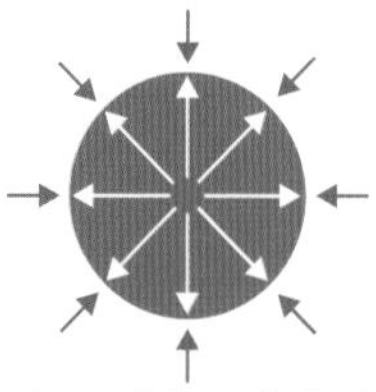

Star turns into red giant
The cores of old stars heat up. The extra heat boosts the outward pressure, so the star swells.

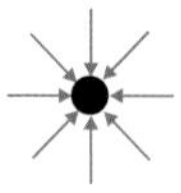

Collapse to black hole
When a particularly large star dies, gravity may cause its core to collapse to form a black hole.

STARLIGHT

As well as visible light, stars emit invisible types of radiation, such as ultraviolet rays and microwaves, all of which travel as waves. The whole range of these different radiations, including light, is called the electromagnetic (EM) spectrum. Stars are too distant for us to visit them to study, but we can tell a lot about them from the light and other radiation they emit.

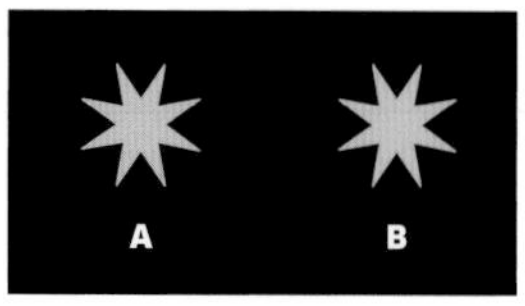
A
B

These two stars look equally bright in the night sky, but in reality, star A is brighter but farther away.

Star brightness

A star's brightness, or magnitude, can be stated either as how bright it looks or how bright it really is. These differ, as stars vary in their distance from Earth, which affects how bright they appear. Oddly, a star's brightness is measured on a scale in which a small number denotes a bright star and a big number indicates a dim star.

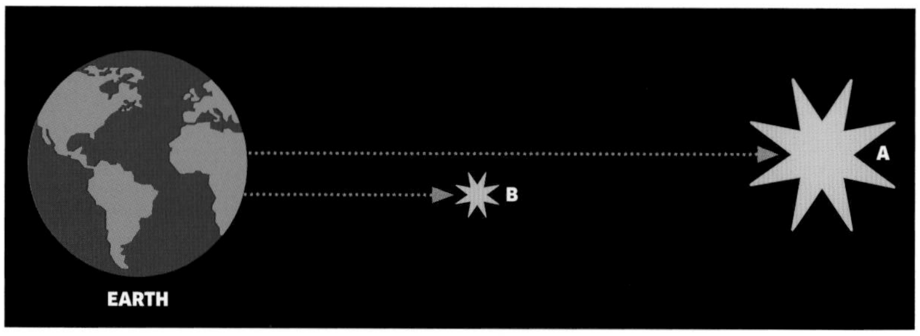
A
B
EARTH

The electromagnetic spectrum

Light travels as a wave, and we see light waves of different lengths as colours: red light, for example, has longer waves than blue. Stars produce energy in a huge range of wavelengths, most of which are invisible to our eyes. Many astronomers study stars by using wavelengths we cannot see.

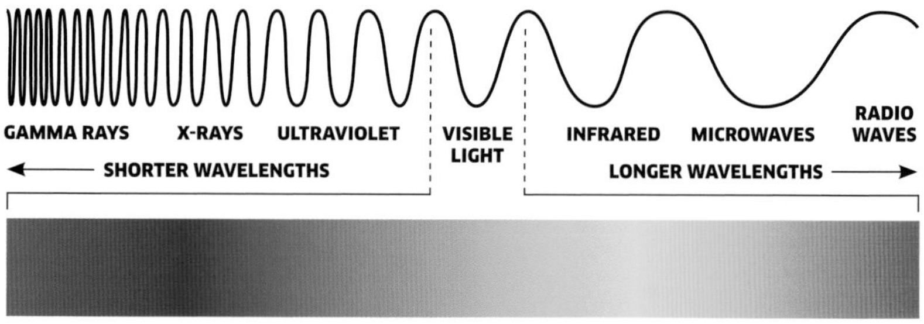
GAMMA RAYS
X-RAYS
ULTRAVIOLET
VISIBLE LIGHT
INFRARED
MICROWAVES
RADIO WAVES
SHORTER WAVELENGTHS
LONGER WAVELENGTHS

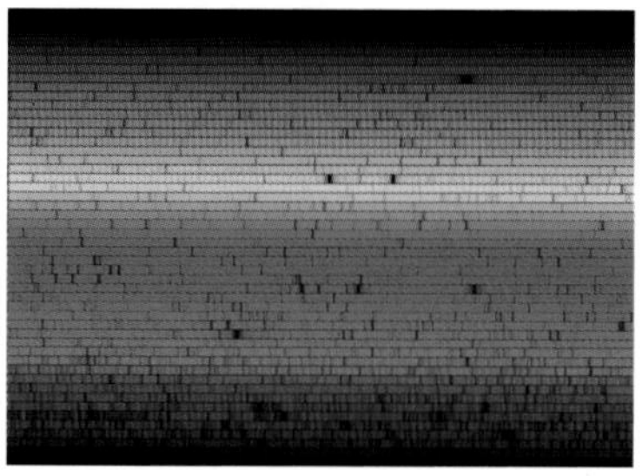

Studying stars

By studying the spectrum of a star, astronomers can figure out many of the chemical elements it contains. Each chemical element in the star's atmosphere absorbs particular wavelengths in the spectrum of radiation from the hotter gas beneath, producing a unique pattern, like a fingerprint. The dark gaps in the spectrum of light from our Sun (above) are caused by 67 different elements.

Variable stars

Some stars regularly vary in both size and brightness. These stars are constantly trying to reach an equilibrium between the inward-pulling gravitational force and the outward-pushing pressure. They swell and shrink in regular cycles, varying from a few hours to a few years – being brightest (and hottest) when smallest, and dimmest (and coolest) when biggest.

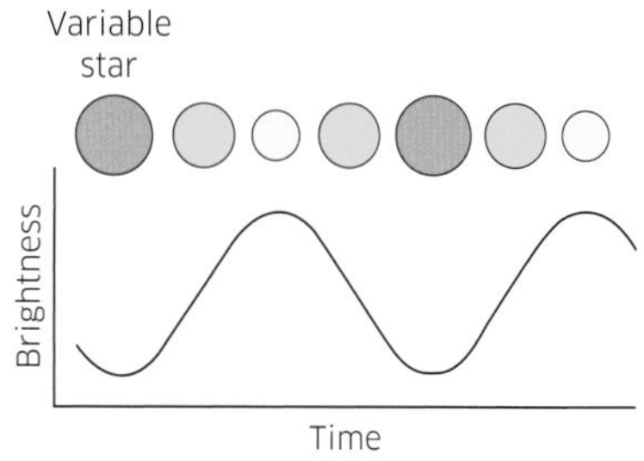
Variable star
Brightness
Time

HOW FAR ARE THE STARS?

All stars other than the Sun are situated at incredible distances from Earth, which is why they appear as just pinpricks of light in the night sky. They are so far away that a special unit is needed to express their distance. This unit is the light year, which is the distance light travels in a year. A light year is about 9.5 trillion km (6 trillion miles).

Nearby stars

There are 32 stars lying within 12.5 light years of the Sun, some of which belong to multiple star systems containing two or three stars (binary or trinary systems). Many of these nearby stars are small, dim ones called red dwarfs, but a few are larger, dazzling yellow, orange, and white stars. The diagram below shows their positions in space, relative to the Sun at the centre.

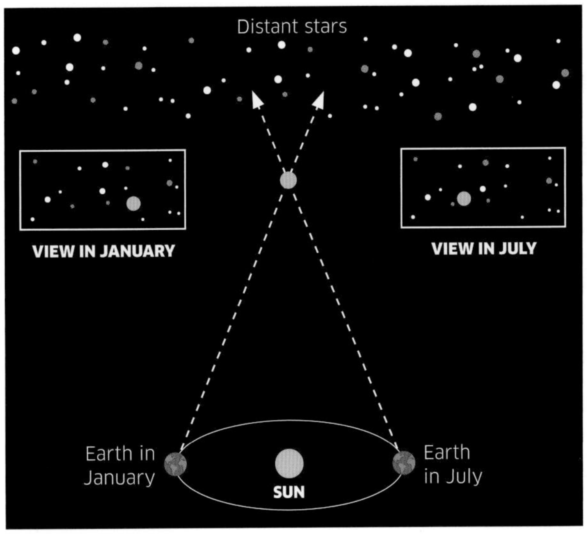

Distant stars
VIEW IN JANUARY
VIEW IN JULY
Earth in January
SUN
Earth in July

Measuring distance

There are various ways of measuring how far away stars are. One clever technique is to view the same star at two distinct times of year, when Earth is at opposite sides of its orbit around the Sun. If a star is nearby, its position relative to more distant stars appears to shift between these two points of view (an effect known as parallax). The amount of shift can be used to calculate exactly how far away it is. Using this method, astronomers have worked out that Proxima Centauri – the star closest to the Sun – is about 4.2 light years away.

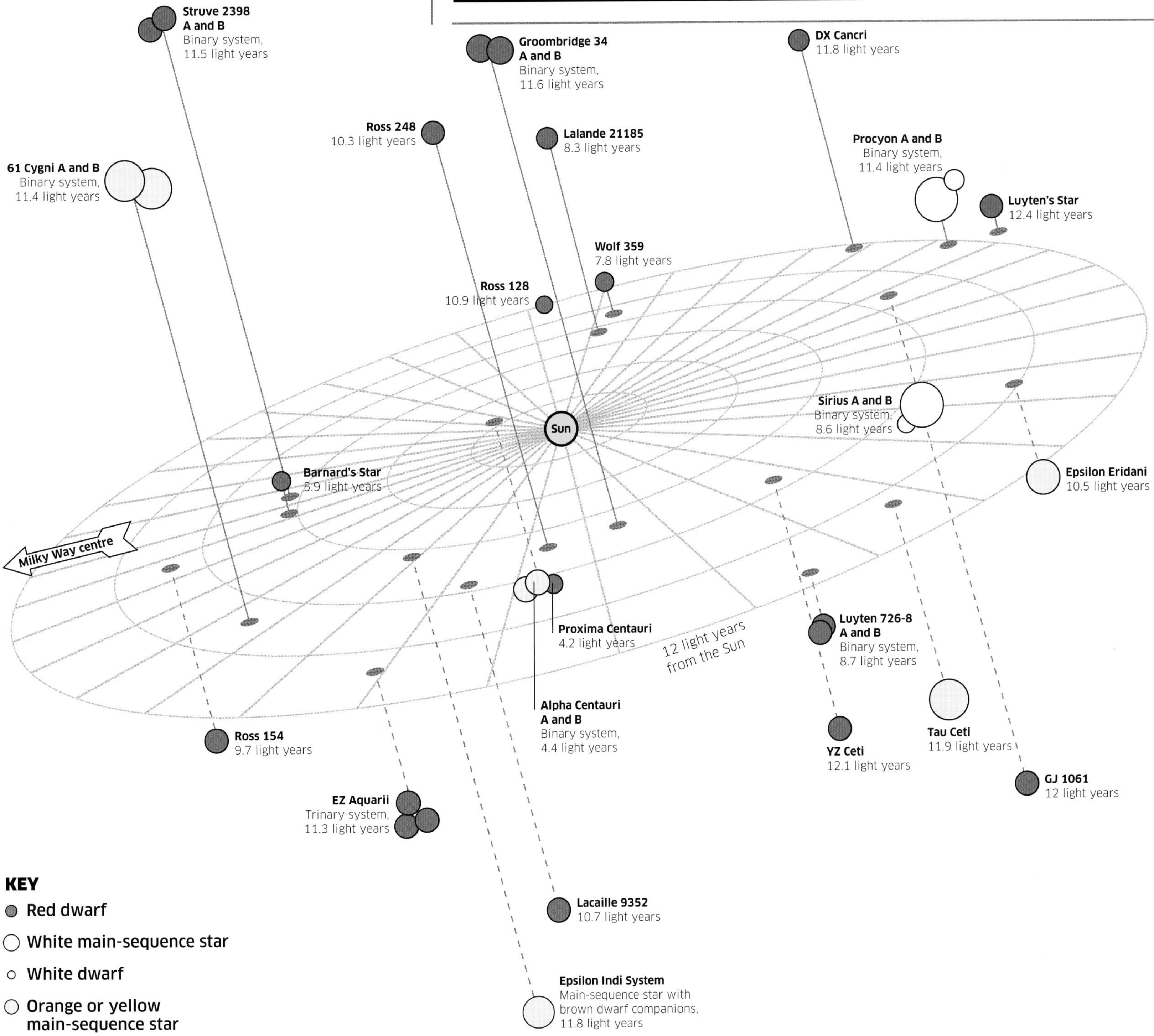

Struve 2398 A and B
Binary system, 11.5 light years
Groombridge 34 A and B
Binary system, 11.6 light years
DX Cancri
11.8 light years
Ross 248
10.3 light years
Lalande 21185
8.3 light years
Procyon A and B
Binary system, 11.4 light years
61 Cygni A and B
Binary system, 11.4 light years
Luyten's Star
12.4 light years
Wolf 359
7.8 light years
Ross 128
10.9 light years
Sun
Sirius A and B
Binary system, 8.6 light years
Barnard's Star
5.9 light years
Epsilon Eridani
10.5 light years
Milky Way centre
Proxima Centauri
4.2 light years
12 light years from the Sun
Luyten 726-8 A and B
Binary system, 8.7 light years
Alpha Centauri A and B
Binary system, 4.4 light years
Ross 154
9.7 light years
Tau Ceti
11.9 light years
YZ Ceti
12.1 light years
GJ 1061
12 light years
EZ Aquarii
Trinary system, 11.3 light years
KEY
Red dwarf
White main-sequence star
White dwarf
Orange or yellow main-sequence star
Lacaille 9352
10.7 light years
Epsilon Indi System
Main-sequence star with brown dwarf companions, 11.8 light years

Types of star

In the night sky, all stars look like tiny pinpricks of light. However, stars differ greatly in size, colour, brightness, and lifespan.

The smallest are tiny dwarf stars less than a thousandth of the Sun's volume. The largest are 8 billion times greater in volume than the Sun. The largest stars are also billions of times brighter than the smallest stars. The characteristics of a star depend mainly on how much matter it contains – its mass. The more massive a star is, the hotter and brighter it will be, but the shorter its lifespan. This is because big stars burn through their nuclear fuel much faster. Astronomers use the colour, size, and brightness of stars to classify them into a number of groups.

Giant stars

The largest stars are ageing stars that have swelled and brightened enormously towards the end of their lives. Giant stars are up to about 200 times wider than the Sun and can be thousands of times more luminous. Supergiants and hypergiants are up to 2,000 times wider than the Sun and up to a billion times brighter.

Dwarf stars

Dwarf stars make up the majority of stars and are relatively small and dim. They include stars about the size of the Sun or somewhat larger and many smaller stars called red dwarfs. They also include white dwarfs – the tiny, dense remnants of giant stars that have lost their outer layers.

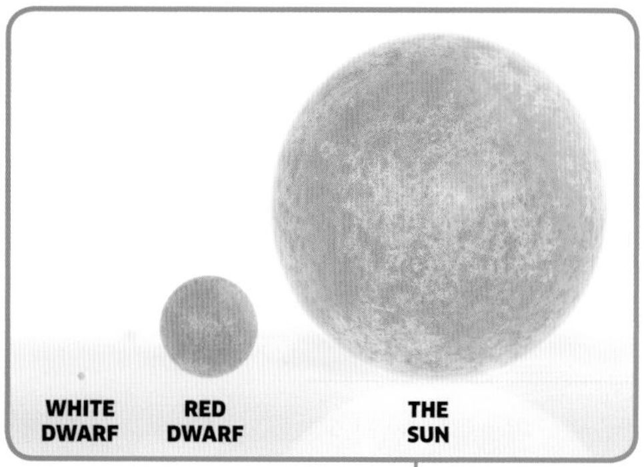
WHITE DWARF
RED DWARF
THE SUN

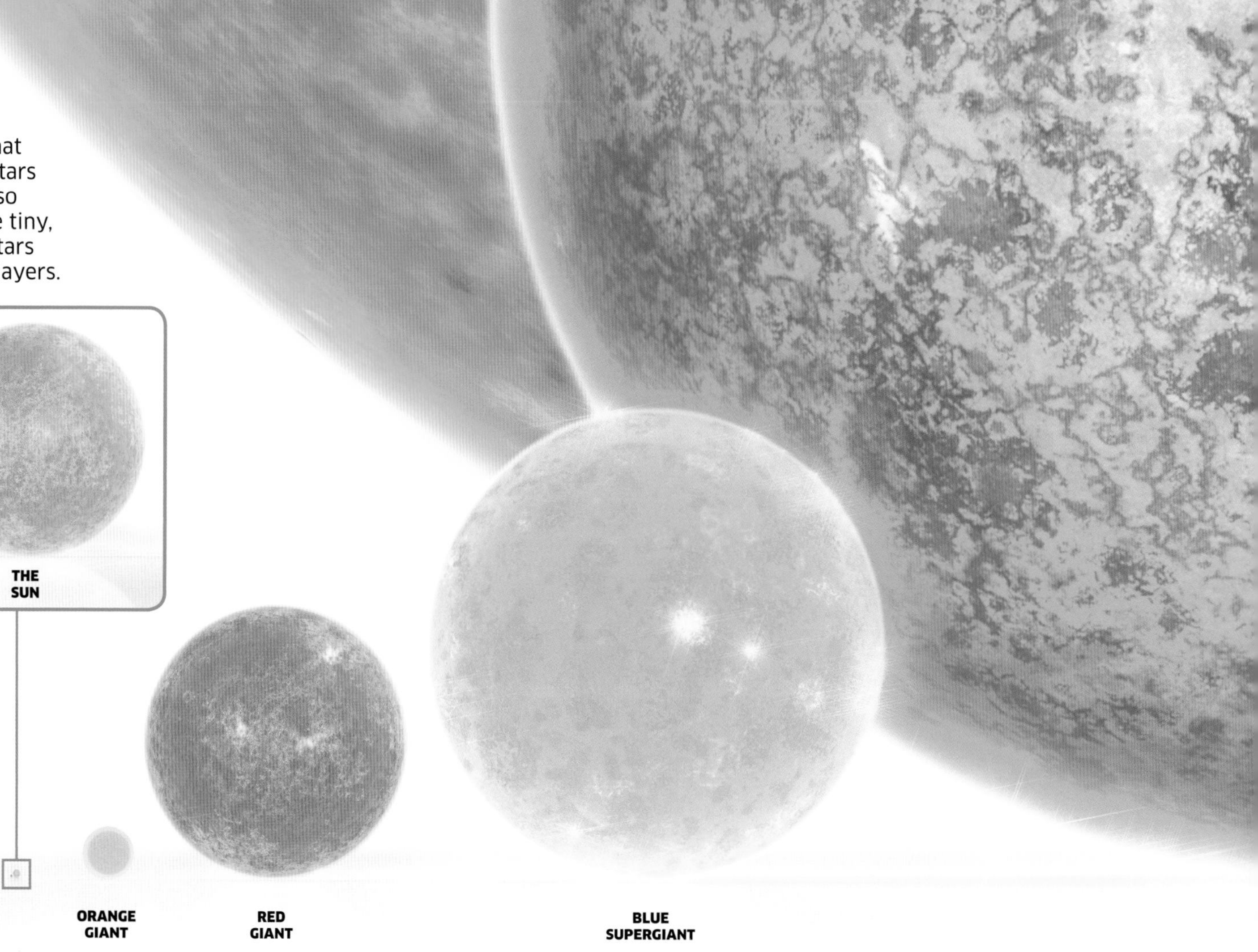
ORANGE GIANT
RED GIANT
BLUE SUPERGIANT

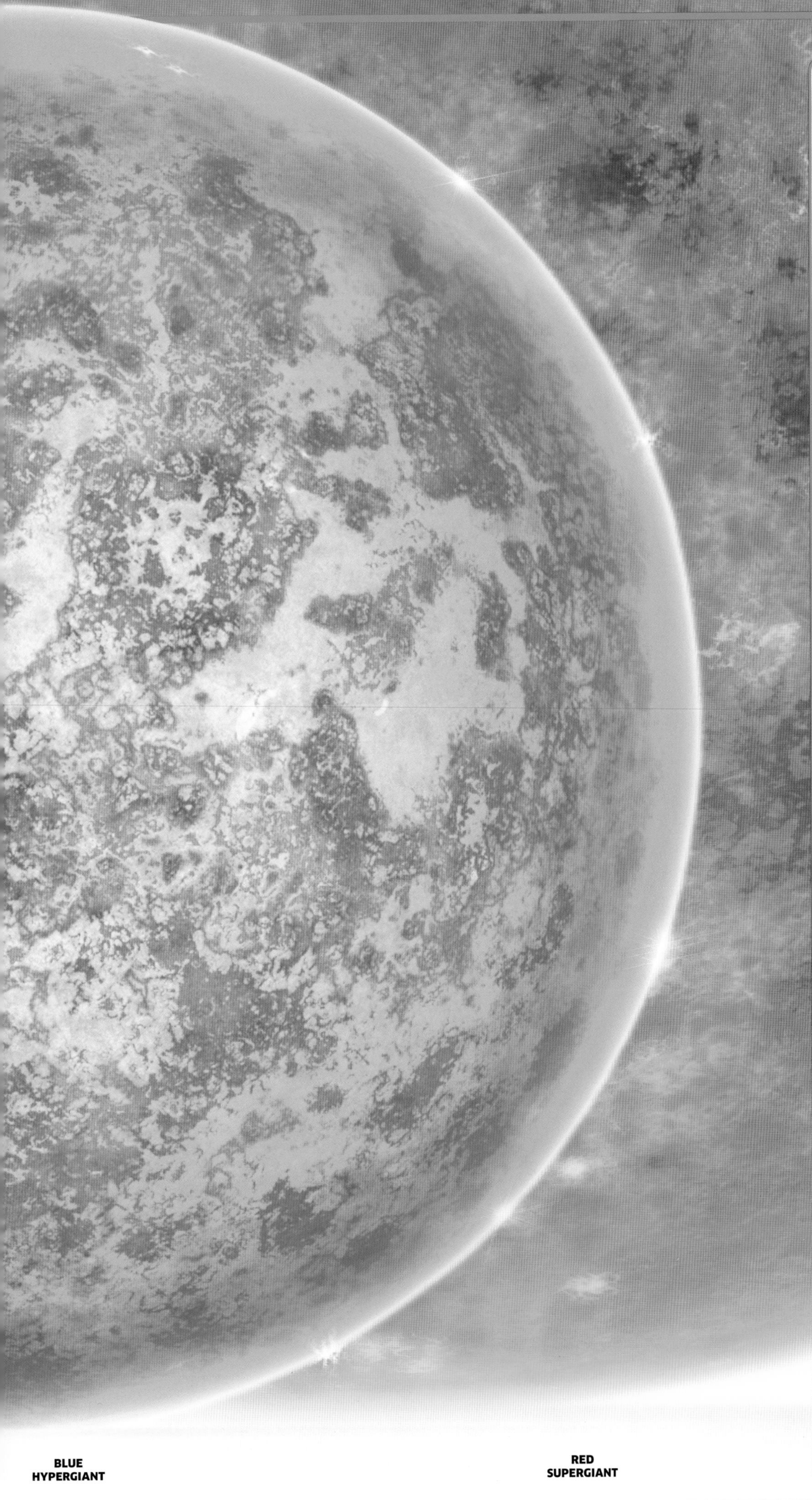

BLUE HYPERGIANT

RED SUPERGIANT

Colours

A star's colour depends on how hot its surface is. The hottest stars produce a bluish light, while cooler stars are an orangish red. You can see these colours on a clear night by using binoculars to look closely at different stars.

Colour	Temperature
Blue	45,000°C (80,000°F)
Bluish white	30,000°C (55,000°F)
White	12,000°C (22,000°F)
Yellowish white	8,000°C (14,000°F)
Yellow	6,500°C (12,000°F)
Orange	5,000°C (9,000°F)
Red	3,500°C (6,500°F)

Star chart

About 100 years ago, two astronomers discovered an ingenious way of classifying stars that also shows the stage each star has reached in its life. The astronomers – Ejnar Hertzsprung and Henry Russell – did this by making a graph of stars with temperature along the bottom and brightness up the side. Most stars, including our Sun, fall into a band on the diagram called the main sequence; these are small to medium stars in a range of colours. The other stars, including giants and dwarfs, form separate groups. These are older stars that would have been in the main sequence millions of years ago.

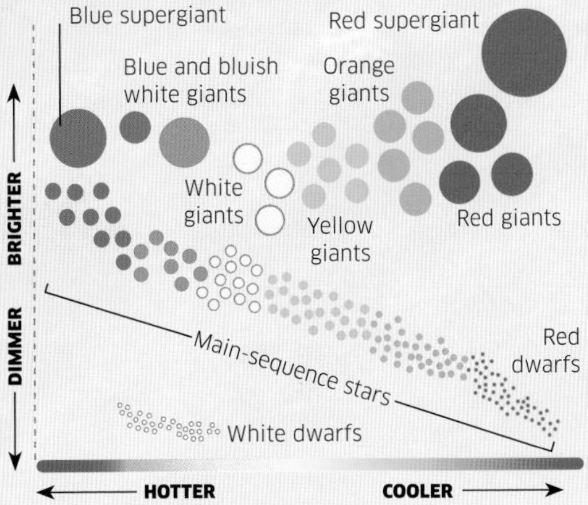
Blue supergiant
Red supergiant
Blue and bluish white giants
Orange giants
White giants
Yellow giants
Red giants
Main-sequence stars
Red dwarfs
White dwarfs
BRIGHTER
DIMMER
HOTTER
COOLER

Seeing stars

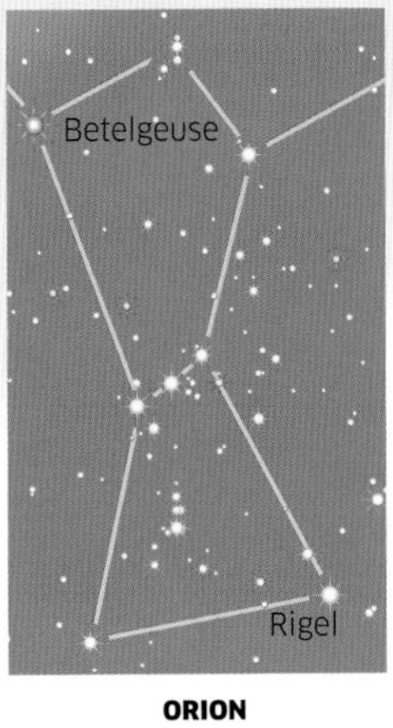
Betelgeuse
Rigel

ORION

Supergiant stars are easy to see if you look out for the famous constellation Orion, "the hunter". Orion's shoulder is a red supergiant called Betelgeuse, which is one of the largest stars in the northern sky. Orion's foot is a blue supergiant, Rigel.

The molecular clouds in which stars form can be **600 light years** wide.

Orion Nebula

At a distance of 1,500 light years from Earth, this colourful gas cloud is the closest star-forming region to Earth. The Orion Nebula contains massive young stars giving off enormous amounts of energy, which makes the surrounding gases glow brightly. You can see the Orion Nebula easily by using binoculars to look at the constellation of Orion, but the colours will be much fainter than shown here.

Trapezium stars
In the heart of the Orion Nebula is a cluster of very bright, newly formed stars called the Trapezium. These stars are up to 30 times more massive than our Sun, and their intense energy illuminates much of the surrounding cloud.

This gas cloud is separated from the main part of the nebula by dark dust lanes and is lit up by a young star at its centre.

Nair al Saif is the brightest star in Orion's sword.

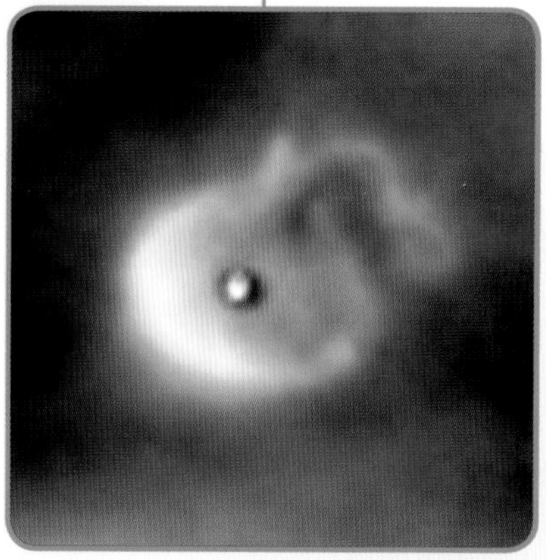

Star babies
The youngest stars in the Orion Nebula are still surrounded by dense discs of gas and dust. The Hubble Space Telescope has photographed 30 of these discs, which are also known as proplyds. Planets may eventually form from the gas and dust in them.

Star birth

New stars and planets are born in vast clouds of interstellar gas and dust in a process that can take millions of years.

The gas clouds that give birth to stars are known as molecular clouds and are made of hydrogen gas. While most of the hydrogen is spread out incredibly thinly across space, denser clumps can form if something disturbs the cloud. Once that happens, the clumps of gas may begin to shrink due to gravity and pull in more gas, concentrating it at their centres. Eventually, the core regions become so dense and hot that stars ignite. These brilliant newborn stars may illuminate the clouds in which they formed, creating a dazzling display of light and colour.

Intense ultraviolet radiation from young stars makes atoms in the gas clouds emit light. Each element emits a characteristic colour. Hydrogen, for instance, glows red. The colours in this photograph are enhanced.
Bubble-shaped region containing hot gas
Fierce stellar winds from massive newborn stars create arcs of gas and dust.
Wisps of hydrogen gas and dust
The dark areas are dust clouds that block light.

How a star forms

Star formation begins when a gas and dust cloud in deep space is subjected to a trigger event, such as a nearby supernova or an encounter with a nearby star. Once the cloud starts to collapse, gravity does the rest of the work to form a star.

Clumps form
Pockets of dense gas form in a molecular cloud (a huge cloud of cold, dark gas and dust).

Clump contracts
The force of gravity makes a gas clump shrink and pull in more gas from around it.

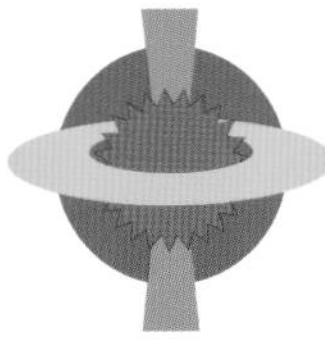

Spinning disc
The clump shrinks to form a hot, dense core surrounded by a spinning disc of matter. Jets of gas shoot out from its poles.

Star ignites
When the centre is hot enough, nuclear fusion begins and a star is born. A disc of matter still orbits the young star.

Disc disperses
The leftover material is either dispersed into space or clumps together to form planets, moons, and other objects.

Stellar nurseries

Our galaxy contains many star-birth regions. The Horsehead Nebula looks like a silhouette of a horse's head in ordinary light but is pink in the infrared image below. The Carina Nebula, four times larger than the Orion Nebula, is famous for a gargantuan dust-gas pillar known as Mystic Mountain.

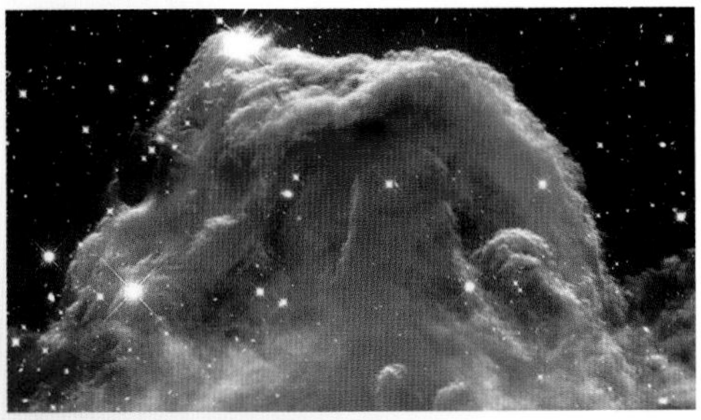

HORSEHEAD NEBULA

MYSTIC MOUNTAIN IN THE CARINA NEBULA

1584 The year in which Italian scholar **Giordano Bruno** predicted the existence of exoplanets.

Exoplanets

The first exoplanet – a planet outside our Solar System orbiting an ordinary star – was discovered in 1995. Since then, astronomers have found more than 1,000 of these alien worlds, some of which are similar to Earth and may even harbour life.

Until the 1990s, the only planets known to science were the eight planets that orbit our Sun. People suspected that planets might orbit other stars, but such worlds were impossible to detect because of the vast distances separating them from us. However, as telescopes became more advanced, astronomers began to notice faint changes in the colour or intensity of light from distant stars, which suggested planets were passing in front of them. Careful studies followed, and the first exoplanet was confirmed in 1995. Hundreds of extrasolar systems have now been discovered, some with as many as seven planets. These range from small, probably rocky worlds like Earth to giants with rings 200 times wider than Saturn's. There may be hundreds of billions of exoplanets in our galaxy.

Astronomers reckon there could be 11 billion Earth-like habitable exoplanets in our galaxy.

The Kepler-62 system

In 2013 the Kepler space telescope discovered five exoplanets orbiting the star Kepler-62, which lies 11 million billion km (7 million billion miles) from Earth. The picture below is an artist's impression of the planets, which are too far away to photograph. Two of them orbit in the star's "habitable zone" where the temperature is right for life. Like all newly discovered exoplanets, the planets in Kepler-62 have catalogue names but may receive proper names in the future.

Dense clouds may cover Kepler-62d, which is likely to have a thick atmosphere.

Sun-scorched
The planet Kepler-62b orbits very close to the star, zipping around it every six days. Its surface temperature is 475°C (887°F) – probably too hot for life.

Mars-sized
Kepler-62c is about the size of Mars. It is fiercely hot, with a surface temperature of 300°C (572°F).

Largest planet
Kepler-62d's size suggests it has enough gravity to hold on to a thick atmosphere. Its surface is hotter than boiling water.

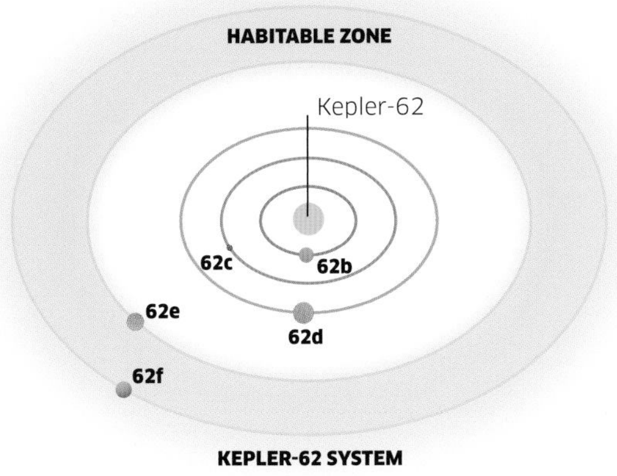
HABITABLE ZONE
Kepler-62
62c
62b
62e
62d
62f
KEPLER-62 SYSTEM

Habitable zone

Two of the planets in the Kepler-62 system orbit in an area known as the habitable zone (or "Goldilocks zone"), where temperatures are just right for water to exist as a liquid on a planet's surface. Many scientists think liquid water is essential for life to flourish.

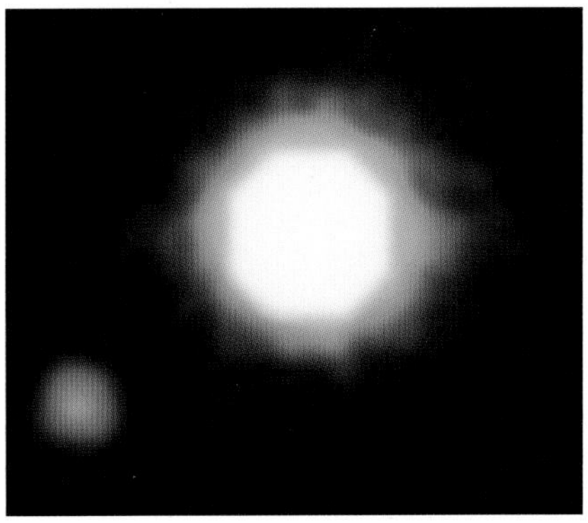

First photo of an exoplanet

This blurry image, taken in 2004, is the first photo of an exoplanet, which appears as a brown blob next to its brighter parent star. The planet is a type known as a "hot Jupiter" – a boiling-hot gas giant. It lies about 2 million billion km (1 million billion miles) from Earth.

Worlds beyond

This artist's impression shows how the Kepler-62 system might look from the planet 62f. Planet 62e looms in the sky nearby, while the other three planets and the Kepler-62 star are visible in the background.

Kepler-62e is likely to be a rocky planet with a thick atmosphere and possibly oceans or ice on its surface.

Earth-like
Kepler-62e is one of the most Earth-like planets known. Its surface temperature is 0°C (32°F), which means it may have liquid water, a cloudy atmosphere, and even life.

Cold Earth
Kepler-62f is similar to 62e but colder. It may have surface water and ice. Its year is 267 days long, and its surface gravity is probably stronger than Earth's.

The atmosphere contains significant amounts of water vapour.

Orange star

The orange dwarf star HD 189733 A has only one known exoplanet – the hot Jupiter HD 189733 b, which orbits its parent star every 2.2 days. The planet was detected from a slight dimming it causes in the star's light each time it passes between the star and Earth.

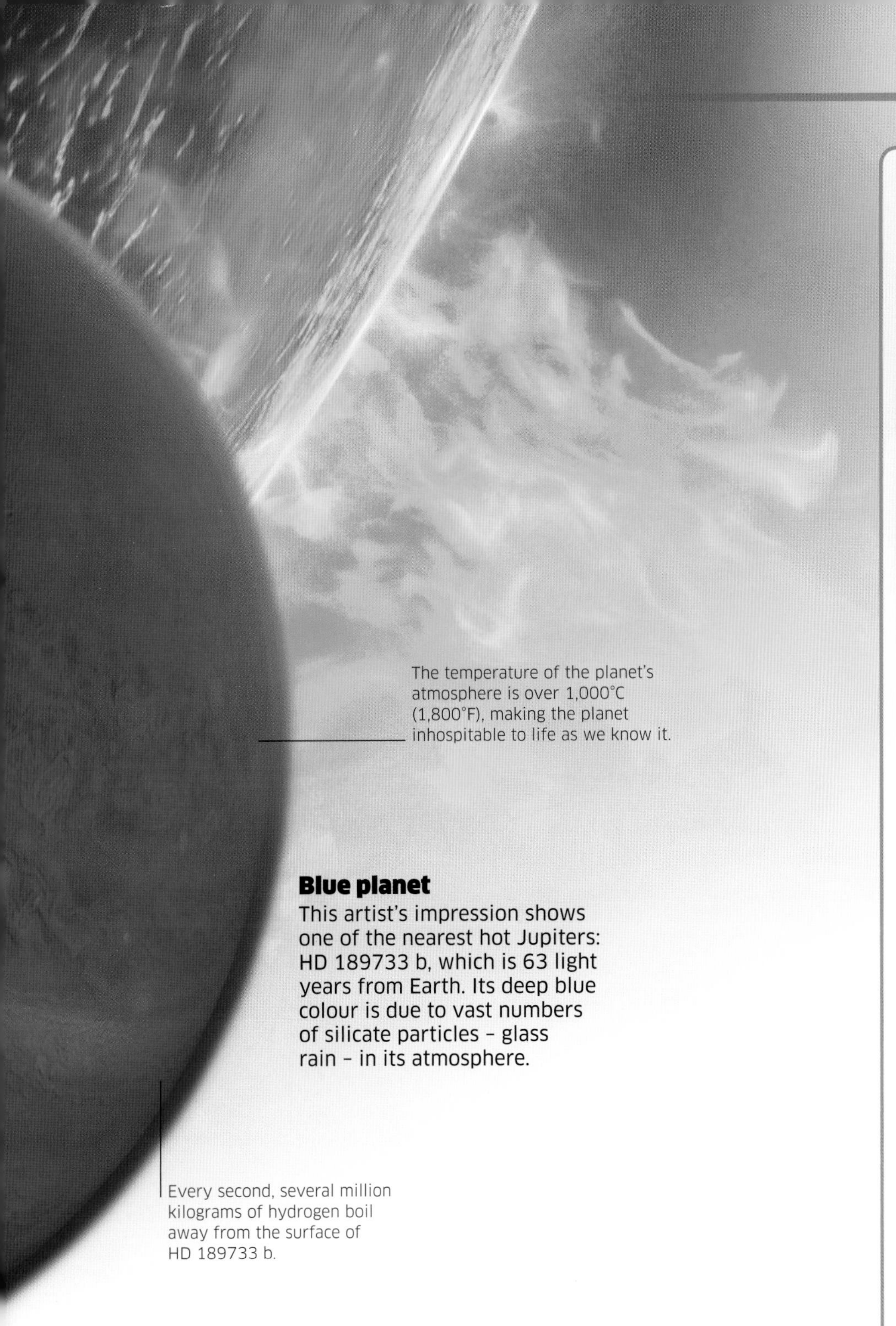
The temperature of the planet's atmosphere is over 1,000°C (1,800°F), making the planet inhospitable to life as we know it.
Every second, several million kilograms of hydrogen boil away from the surface of HD 189733 b.

Blue planet
This artist's impression shows one of the nearest hot Jupiters: HD 189733 b, which is 63 light years from Earth. Its deep blue colour is due to vast numbers of silicate particles – glass rain – in its atmosphere.

Hot Jupiters

Many of the planets that have been detected outside our own Solar System are of a type called "hot Jupiters" – weird, exotic gas giants that are about the size of Jupiter or larger, but much hotter because they orbit close to their stars.

Hot Jupiters orbit at a distance of 2–75 million km (1–46 million miles) from their stars – much closer than Jupiter, which orbits hundreds of million kilometres from the Sun. These star-snuggling worlds are scorched by their stars, producing extreme weather conditions in their atmospheres, including howling winds, temperatures high enough to melt steel, and molten-glass rain. Scientists think that hot Jupiters must have originated farther away from their stars and then migrated towards them, as there would not have been enough material so close to a star for such huge planets to form there.

Death of hot Jupiters

Hot Jupiters often have violent deaths. Some spiral in towards their parent star and are consumed. Others boil away into space, leaving behind just a rocky or metallic core.

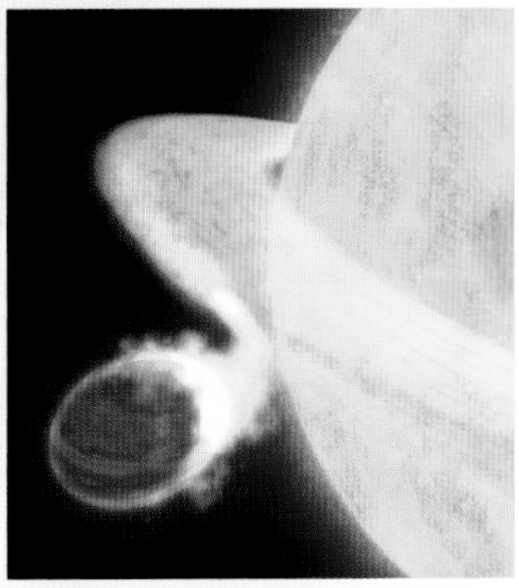

Pulled in by gravity
The hot Jupiter WASP-12 orbits so close to its star that gravity is distorting it and ripping off its atmosphere.

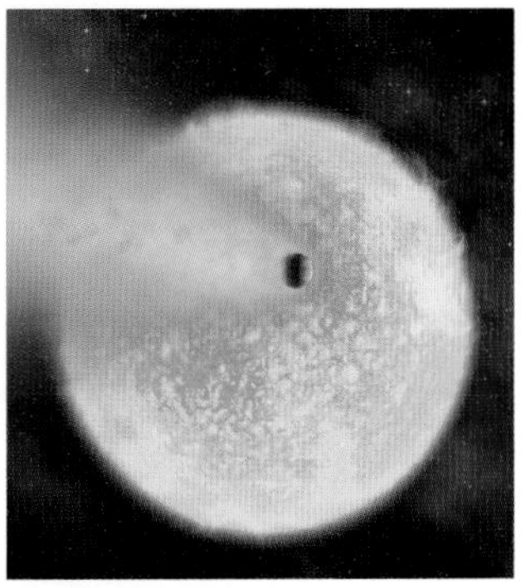

Loss of atmosphere
The atmosphere of HD 209458 b is boiling away into space at a rate of thousands of tonnes per second, forming a long tail of hydrogen.

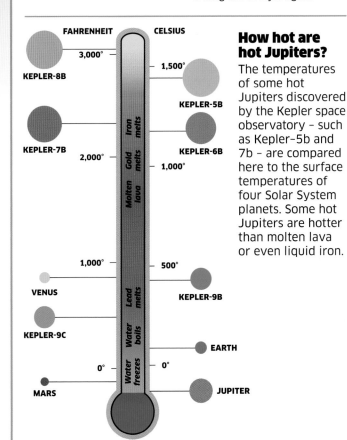

How hot are hot Jupiters?

The temperatures of some hot Jupiters discovered by the Kepler space observatory – such as Kepler-5b and 7b – are compared here to the surface temperatures of four Solar System planets. Some hot Jupiters are hotter than molten lava or even liquid iron.

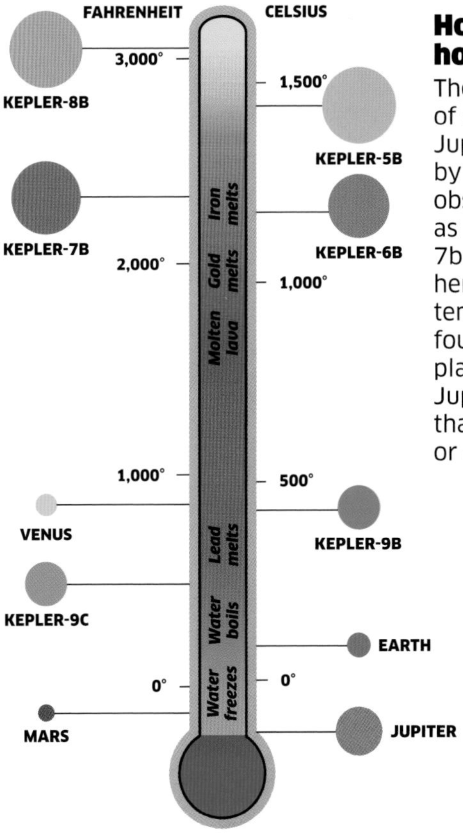
FAHRENHEIT
CELSIUS
3,000°
2,000°
1,000°
0°
1,500°
1,000°
500°
0°
KEPLER-8B
KEPLER-7B
VENUS
KEPLER-9C
MARS
KEPLER-5B
KEPLER-6B
KEPLER-9B
EARTH
JUPITER
Iron melts
Gold melts
Molten lava
Lead melts
Water boils
Water freezes

Wild orbits

Upsilon Andromedae b was one of the first hot Jupiters to be detected. It is one of four planets orbiting a star 44 light years away. Shown here are three of the planets' orbits, which are tilted at wildly different angles.

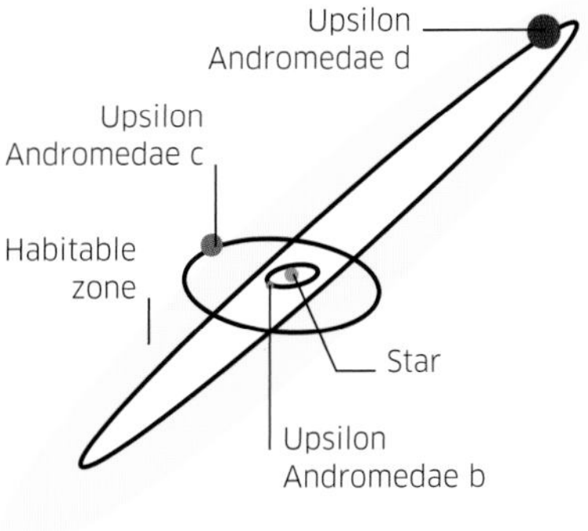
Upsilon Andromedae d
Upsilon Andromedae c
Habitable zone
Star
Upsilon Andromedae b

A supernova occurs somewhere in the observable Universe about **once a second**.

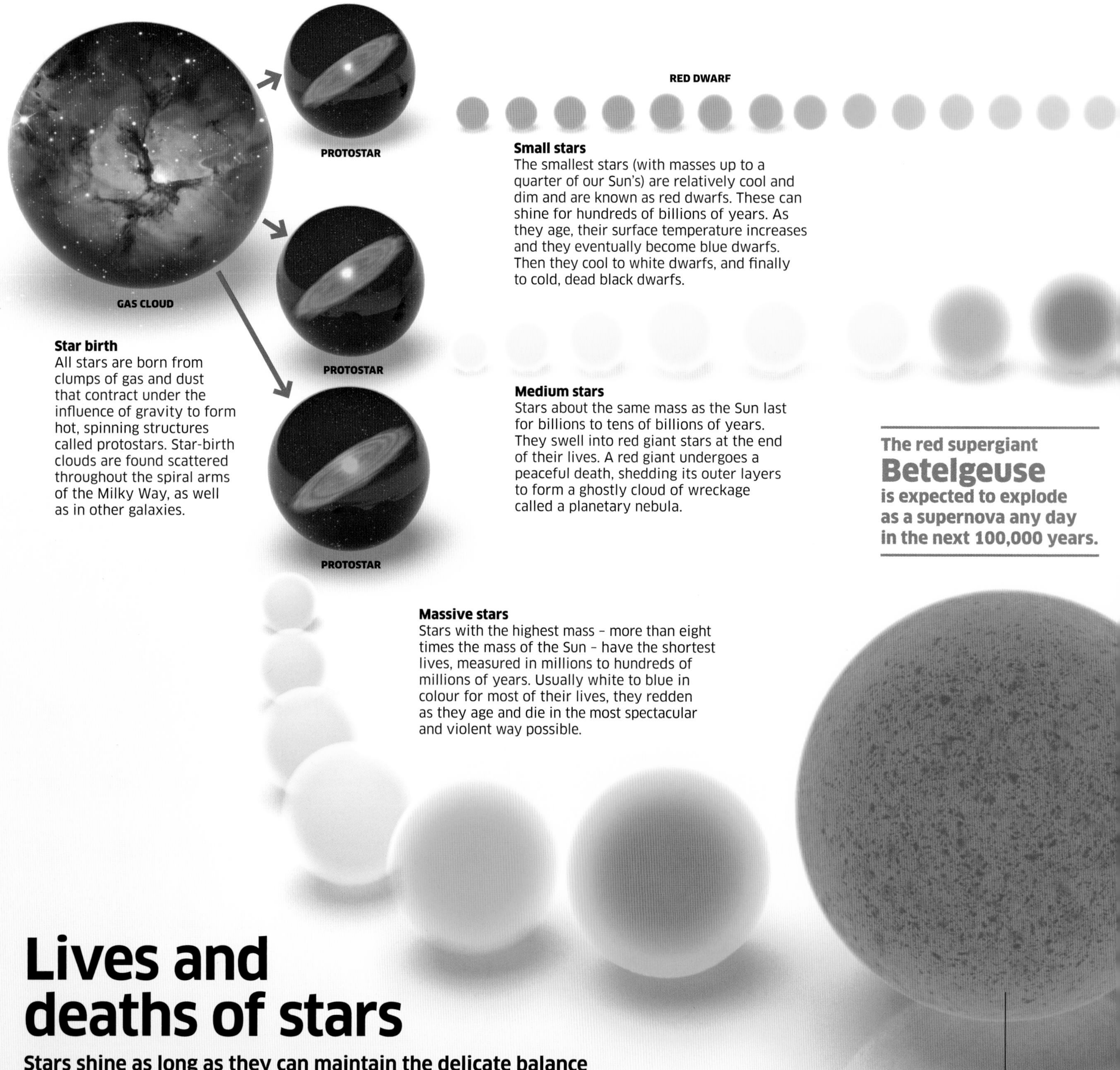
GAS CLOUD
PROTOSTAR
PROTOSTAR
PROTOSTAR
RED DWARF

Star birth
All stars are born from clumps of gas and dust that contract under the influence of gravity to form hot, spinning structures called protostars. Star-birth clouds are found scattered throughout the spiral arms of the Milky Way, as well as in other galaxies.

Small stars
The smallest stars (with masses up to a quarter of our Sun's) are relatively cool and dim and are known as red dwarfs. These can shine for hundreds of billions of years. As they age, their surface temperature increases and they eventually become blue dwarfs. Then they cool to white dwarfs, and finally to cold, dead black dwarfs.

Medium stars
Stars about the same mass as the Sun last for billions to tens of billions of years. They swell into red giant stars at the end of their lives. A red giant undergoes a peaceful death, shedding its outer layers to form a ghostly cloud of wreckage called a planetary nebula.

The red supergiant Betelgeuse is expected to explode as a supernova any day in the next 100,000 years.

Massive stars
Stars with the highest mass – more than eight times the mass of the Sun – have the shortest lives, measured in millions to hundreds of millions of years. Usually white to blue in colour for most of their lives, they redden as they age and die in the most spectacular and violent way possible.

Lives and deaths of stars

Stars shine as long as they can maintain the delicate balance between the inward pull of their own gravity and the outward pressure of energy from the core. How long this lasts depends on how much matter a star starts off with.

Massive stars have relatively short lives because they use up their hydrogen fuel in nuclear reactions quickly. The most massive stars die in stupendous explosions called supernovas. Small stars have less fuel but they use it slowly and can last for hundreds of billions of years before they gradually fade away. Medium-mass stars, like the Sun, evolve along an intermediate path and end up as beautiful objects called planetary nebulas when they die.

Red supergiant
When a massive star has fused all the hydrogen fuel in its core, it starts producing energy by fusing together helium atoms. Eventually the core runs out of helium, but it continues to force together atoms to form heavier and heavier elements until iron atoms are formed. At the same time, the star swells into a red supergiant. When the core turns into iron, it can no longer produce enough energy to withstand the inward pull of the star's gravity and the star collapses violently and then explodes in a supernova.

Life stories

Contrasted here are the life stories of the three main types of star: low-mass stars (top row); medium-mass stars like the Sun (middle row); and massive stars (bottom row). Small stars have the longest lives. In fact, they live for so long that no red dwarf in the Universe has yet evolved to the blue dwarf or black dwarf stage.

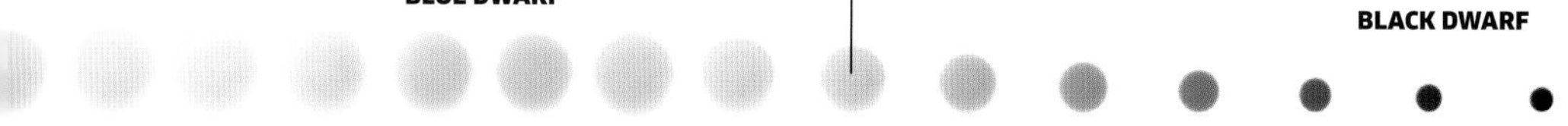
Star's light begins to dim
BLUE DWARF
BLACK DWARF

BLACK DWARF

White dwarf
Left at the heart of a planetary nebula is all that remains of the red giant's core: a small, brilliant star called a white dwarf. This causes the surrounding cloud to shine. Over a long period of time it cools to a black dwarf.

Red giant
A red giant forms when a medium-mass star runs out of hydrogen in its core. The core begins to use helium as a fuel, while hydrogen is "burnt" as a fuel in a shell surrounding the core. At the same time, the star expands to a giant size.

When all its fuel is used up, the outer layers of a red giant are shed.

Planetary nebula
A planetary nebula is a glowing cloud of material shed by a red giant, often with a beautiful and complex shape. Planetary nebulas last for only a few tens of thousands of years.

Supernova
When it can produce no more energy by nuclear fusion reactions, a red supergiant disintegrates in a supernova explosion. The star's outer layers dissipate into space while its core continues to collapse on itself. Depending on its mass, the core of the star implodes to form either a neutron star or a black hole.

Neutron star
If the remaining core has between 1.4 and 3 times as much mass as our Sun, it collapses to about the size of a city and becomes a neutron star – an incredibly compact object made of neutrons that spins round at a furious rate. Neutron stars are so dense that a single teaspoonful of their matter has a mass of about 10 million tonnes.

Black hole
If the remaining core is more than three times more massive than the Sun, it shrinks until it is infinitely smaller than an atom and forms a black hole – a region of space from which nothing (not even light) can escape.

Supernova remnant
Supernovas leave behind clouds of wreckage that slowly disperse into space. The material in the cloud may eventually form new stars, repeating the cycle of star birth and death.

Butterfly Nebula

When stars like our Sun die, they cast off their outer layers into glowing clouds of wreckage. These ghostly remains are known as planetary nebulas.

Planetary nebulas were so named because the first to be noticed were round in shape, like planets. Others, however, fling their gas in two directions to form wings or a figure-of-eight shape. The Butterfly Nebula, captured here by the Hubble Space Telescope, is about 500 times wider than our Solar System, and the gas in its wings is hurtling through space at 950,000 kph (590,000 mph). Hidden in its heart is all that remains of the original star's core – a tiny, feeble star called a white dwarf.

100 billion °C (180 billion °F) – the temperature of a supergiant's core just before a **supernova explosion**.

Red supergiants

The largest stars in the Universe are red supergiants. These are massive stars that have swollen to a vast size as they have grown old.

All stars produce energy by the process of nuclear fusion. Inside the star's core, the temperature and pressure are so high that hydrogen atoms are forced together, fusing them into helium atoms – a process that releases colossal amounts of energy. Massive stars use up the fuel in the core quickly and then begin to balloon in size as nuclear fusion spreads out from the core. The outer layers of the most massive stars expand into an immense sphere of glowing gas, forming a red supergiant. Eventually, the star disintegrates in a sudden and violent explosion called a supernova, leaving behind either a tiny neutron star or a black hole.

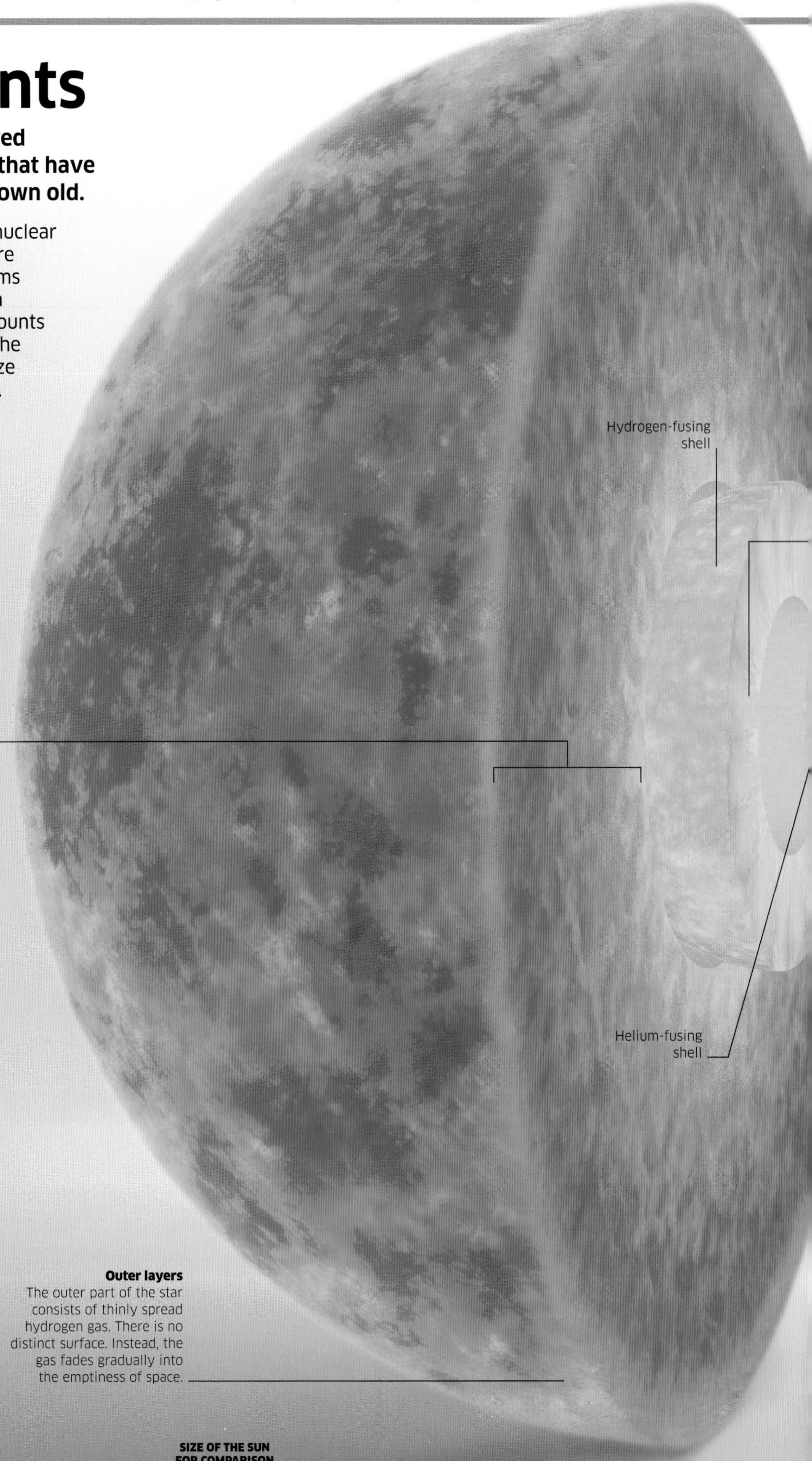
Hydrogen-fusing shell
Helium-fusing shell
SIZE OF THE SUN FOR COMPARISON

Convective layer
Pockets of hot gas rise within the convective layer, before cooling and sinking back down. This process of rising and falling is called convection.

Structure
This model reveals the inner structure of a red supergiant in the last moment of its life, before a supernova explosion destroys it. The size of the core, which is minuscule relative to the supergiant's full extent, is exaggerated in our model. After hydrogen runs out, the core fuses a succession of heavier elements, forming a series of shells in the star's centre. The heaviest element a star can fuse is silicon, which powers the star for about a day, causing iron to build up. When the star attempts to fuse iron, it explodes.

Outer layers
The outer part of the star consists of thinly spread hydrogen gas. There is no distinct surface. Instead, the gas fades gradually into the emptiness of space.

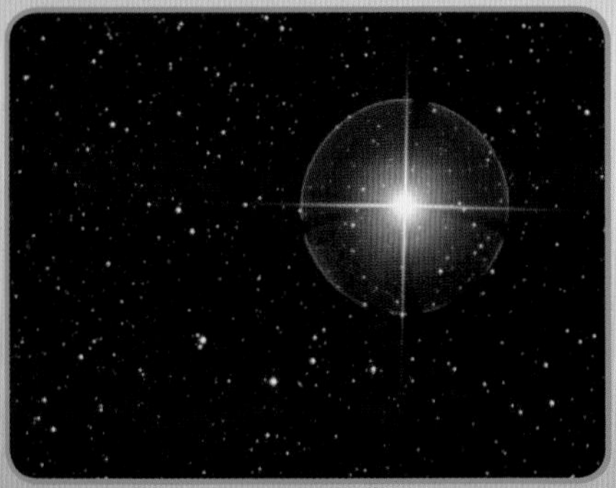

Our local red supergiant
The red supergiant closest to Earth is a star called Antares, which is 880 times wider than our Sun. Although 550 light years away, Antares is easily visible in the night sky. It could explode in a supernova at any point in the next million years or so, but it poses no threat to Earth.

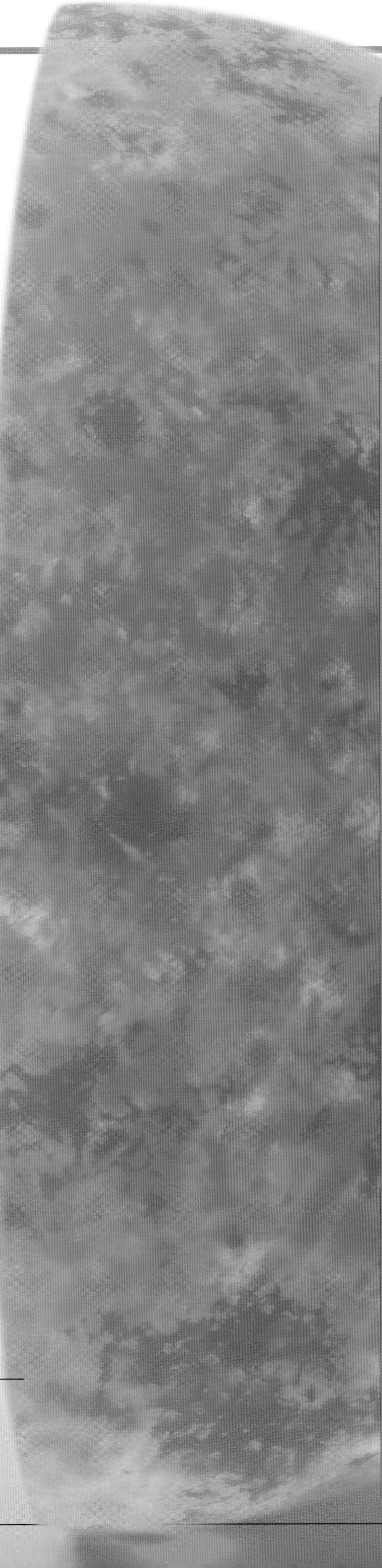

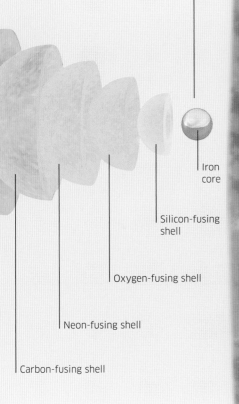

Core
Nuclear fusion takes place only in the core, where elements such as hydrogen are fused to make heavier elements.

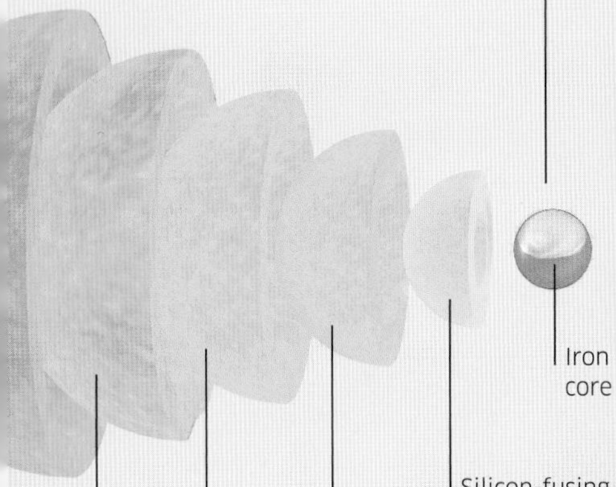
Iron core
Silicon-fusing shell
Oxygen-fusing shell
Neon-fusing shell
Carbon-fusing shell

Warm colour
The outer layer of a red supergiant has a temperature of about 3,800°C (6,900°F), which is much lower than the surface temperature of a Sun-like star. The cooler surface gives the star its reddish colour.

Life and death of a supergiant

Two powerful forces govern the life of a star: gravity, which pulls matter in the star inwards; and pressure, which pushes matter outwards. Normally balanced, these forces can become unbalanced at the end of a star's life.

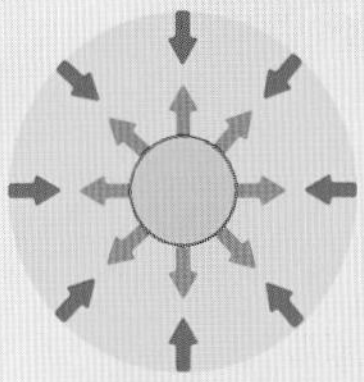

1 HYDROGEN BURNING
For most of a star's life, its core turns hydrogen into helium by nuclear fusion. The energy this releases maintains pressure that pushes the star's matter outwards, balancing the inward pull of gravity.

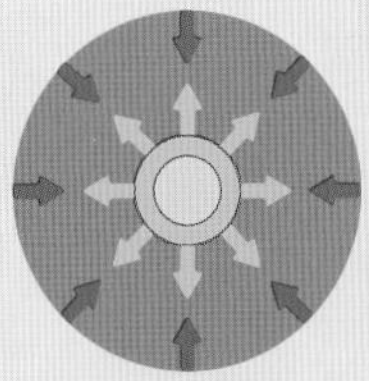

2 HELIUM BURNING
When hydrogen in the core runs out, massive stars begin to fuse helium. Hydrogen burning spreads to a shell outside the inner core, causing the star's outer layers to expand.

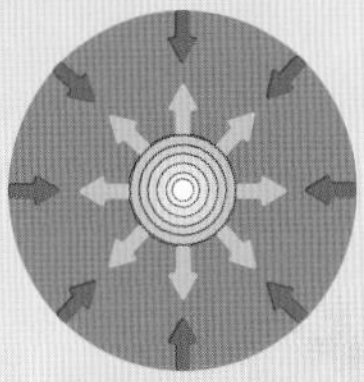

3 MULTILAYER CORE
When helium in the core runs out, the star starts to fuse carbon to form neon. Next it fuses neon into oxygen. A series of shells forms in the core region, fusing different elements.

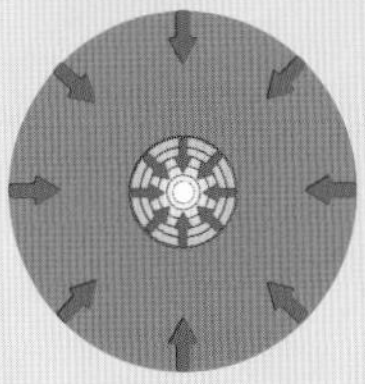

4 COLLAPSE
When the core finally tries to fuse iron, disaster ensues. Iron fusion cannot maintain outward pressure, so gravity overwhelms the core. It collapses to the size of a city in a split second, rushing inwards at a quarter of the speed of light.

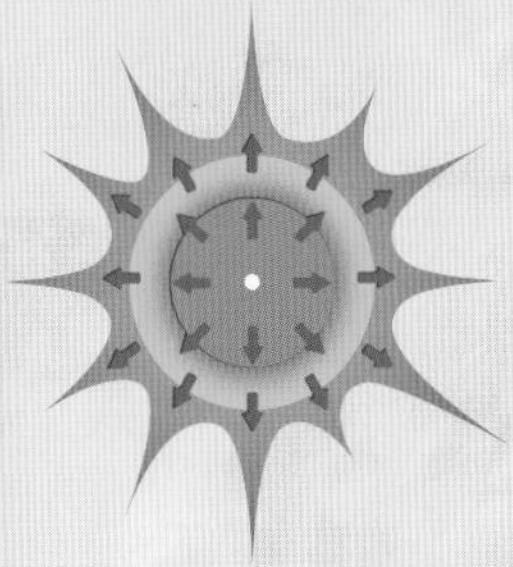

5 EXPLOSION
As temperatures in the core soar, a flood of particles called neutrinos is released. The star's collapsing outer layers rebound off this flood, causing a catastrophic explosion brighter than a billion Suns: a supernova.

Supersize stars

If a typical red supergiant were placed in the centre of our Solar System, it would extend out to between the orbits of Mars and Jupiter. In contrast, a large red giant would reach out only to about Earth's orbit.

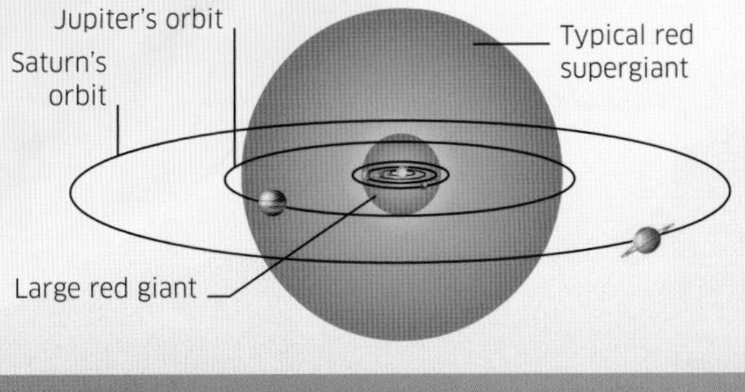
Jupiter's orbit
Saturn's orbit
Typical red supergiant
Large red giant

Neutron stars

When a huge star self-destructs in a supernova explosion, one of two things may happen. The core of a particularly massive star, crushed by its own stupendous gravity, shrinks until it is tinier than an atom and becomes a black hole. The core of a smaller star, however, shrinks to the size of a city to become a neutron star.

Neutron stars are the tiniest, densest stars known and can pack the mass of the whole Sun into an area smaller than London. They are so compact that a mere pinhead of matter has more than twice the mass of the largest supertanker on Earth. All neutron stars spin round at a furious rate, some rotating as fast as 700 times a second. We know this because neutron stars send out beams of radiation that sweep round the sky as they spin, making them appear to flash on and off if they sweep across Earth. Neutron stars that flash like this are called pulsars.

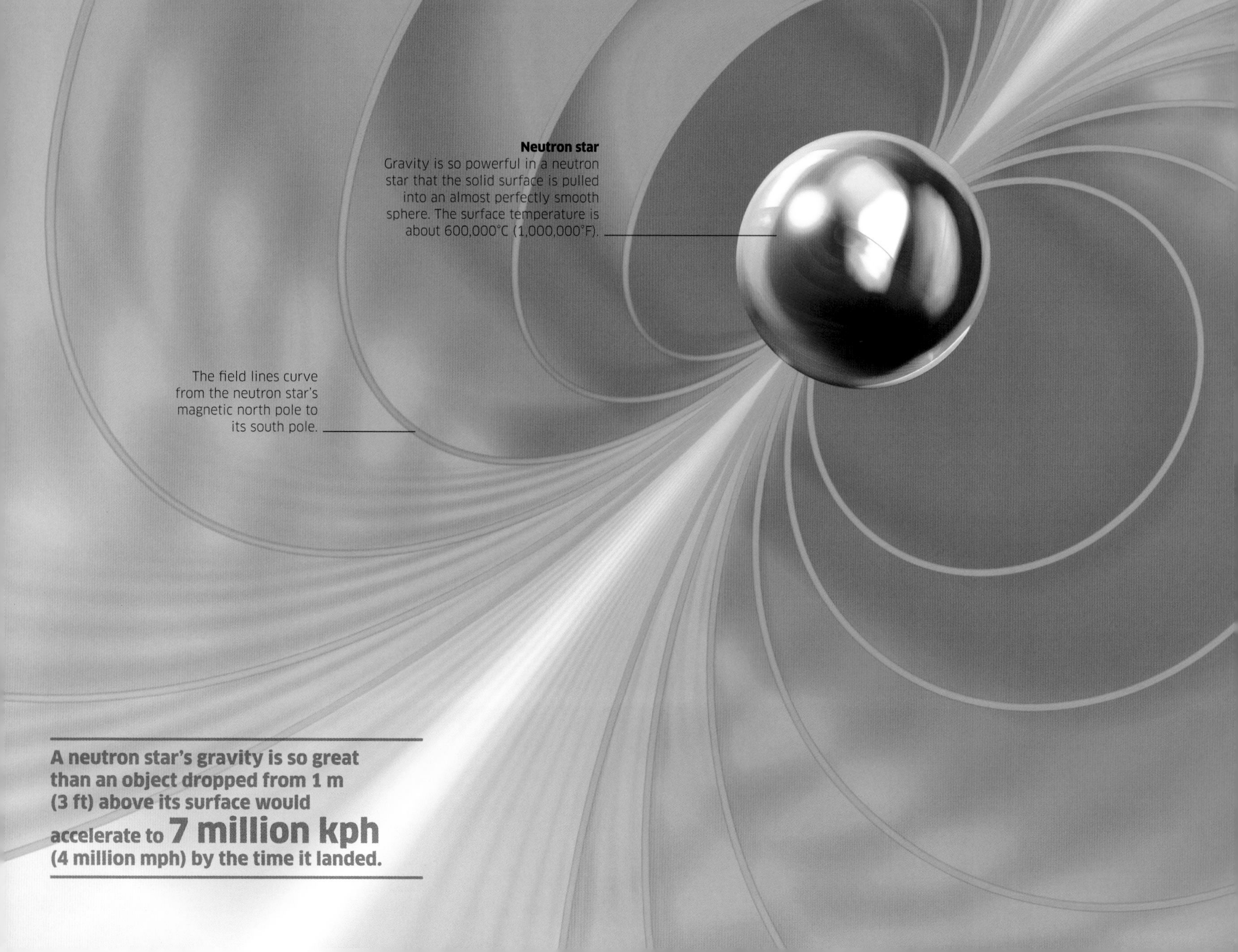
Neutron star
Gravity is so powerful in a neutron star that the solid surface is pulled into an almost perfectly smooth sphere. The surface temperature is about 600,000°C (1,000,000°F).
The field lines curve from the neutron star's magnetic north pole to its south pole.

A neutron star's gravity is so great than an object dropped from 1 m (3 ft) above its surface would accelerate to 7 million kph (4 million mph) by the time it landed.

Pulsars

Astronomers have discovered around 2,000 pulsars (flashing neutron stars) since the first one was spotted in 1967. These neutron stars have powerful magnetic fields and produce beams of radio waves from their magnetic poles. As the star spins about its axis of rotation, the two radio beams sweep out cone shapes across the sky, causing them to pulse where they sweep across Earth. The slowest pulsars send out about five pulses of radio waves a second. The fastest send out 716 pulses a second.

Radiation beam
A neutron star emits beams of radiation from its magnetic poles. The radiation may take the form of radio waves, X-rays, gamma rays, or even visible light.
Magnetic field
The magnetic field of a neutron star can be a quadrillion times more powerful than Earth's magnetic field. It rotates at the same speed as the star.

Inside a neutron star

Most stars are made of gas, but a neutron star has a crust of solid iron about 1 km (0.6 miles) thick. Beneath this is a sea of subatomic particles called neutrons, crammed together by powerful gravity, forming a kind of liquid that doesn't exist on Earth.

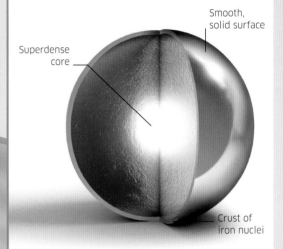

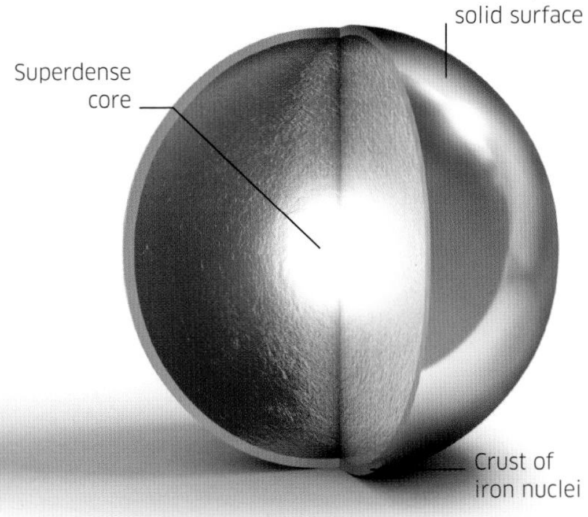
Smooth, solid surface
Superdense core
Crust of iron nuclei

Size

At 15–25 km (9–15 miles) wide, neutron stars are about as big as a city. Compared to other stars, however, they are tiny. Their density produces incredibly powerful gravity at the surface – an average man on a neutron star would weigh 7 billion tonnes.

NEUTRON STAR COMPARED TO VANCOUVER, CANADA

Density

The material that makes up a neutron star is so dense that a single teaspoonful brought to Earth would weigh more than the entire world population. A football made from neutron star matter would weigh 5 trillion tonnes – about the same as Mount Everest.

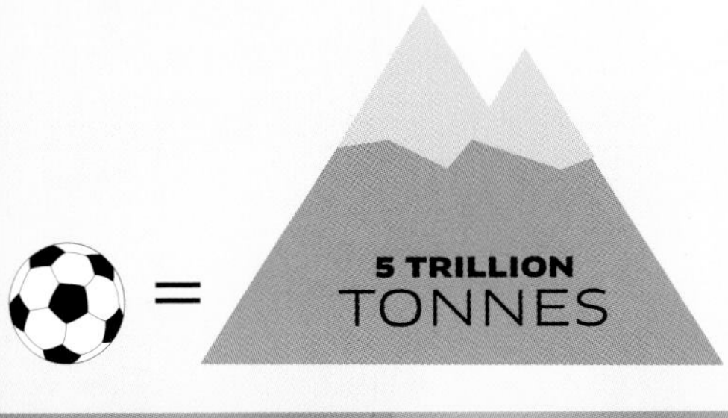
=
5 TRILLION TONNES

Black holes

Black holes are among the strangest objects in the Universe. The pull of their gravity is so great that nothing can escape from them – not even light.

Most black holes form when massive stars run out of fuel and die in an explosion. The dead star's core – unable to resist the crushing force of its own gravity – collapses, shrinking in milliseconds until it is infinitely smaller than an atom. The core becomes what scientists call a singularity: an object so impossibly small that it has zero size but infinite density. Anything straying within a certain distance of the singularity is doomed to get pulled in by gravity and disappear forever. The point of no return forms a spherical boundary around the singularity called an event horizon, which marks how close you can safely get.

Event horizon
Anything that crosses this boundary from the outside can never escape.

Types of black hole
Two main types of black hole exist: stellar and supermassive. Stellar black holes form when enormous stars explode as supernovas at the ends of their lives. Supermassive black holes are bigger and are found at the centres of galaxies, often surrounded by a whirlpool of intensely hot, glowing matter

Lensing
Black holes bend light. In this artist's impression, light from the accretion disc is bent to form a glowing halo around the black hole.
Singularity
Hidden in the black hole's centre is a singularity, where matter has been squeezed into a point of infinite density.
Accretion disc
Gas, dust, and disintegrated stars spiral around some black holes in a disc. The material in the disc is not doomed – it may stay in orbit, just as planets orbit stars.

Spaghettification

The gravitational pull of a black hole rises so steeply nearby that an astronaut falling into one would be stretched like spaghetti and torn apart.

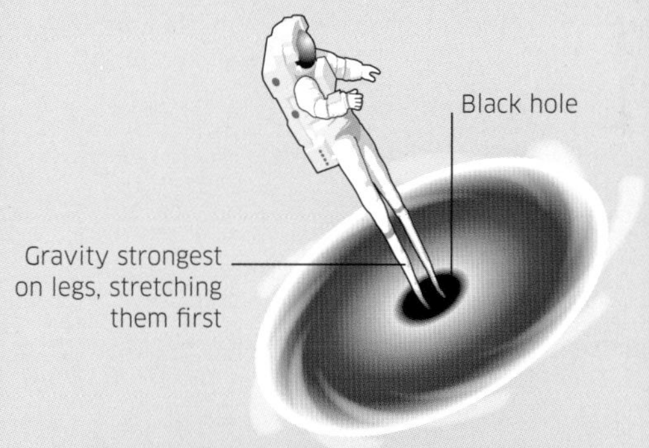
Black hole
Gravity strongest on legs, stretching them first

Bending light and stretching time

Black holes have such powerful gravity that they bend light like giant lenses. If Earth orbited a black hole, an observer would see a highly distorted image of the planet, like the one above. According to Albert Einstein's theory of relativity, black holes also slow down time. If an astronaut spent only an hour or so near a black hole, he might return to Earth to find that many years had passed.

Wormholes

Einstein's theory of relativity says that massive objects bend the four combined dimensions of space and time (space-time). Some experts have speculated that black holes might warp space-time so much that they could create shortcuts, called wormholes, between different parts of the Universe or different times. There is no direct evidence that wormholes exist.

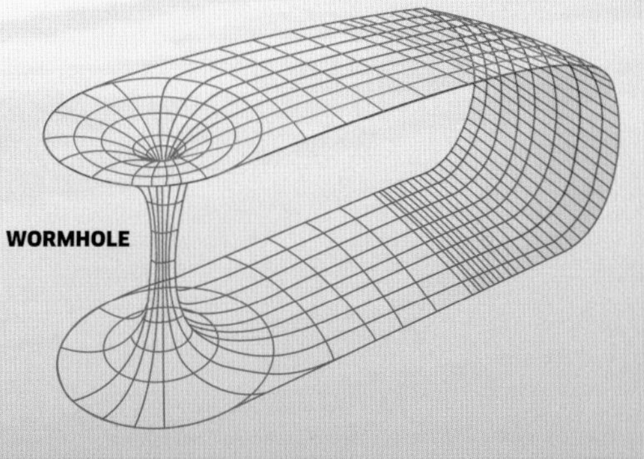
WORMHOLE

The pole star, **Polaris**, is actually a **triple star system**.

Some star pairs take **millions of years** to orbit each other.

Star clusters

Large groups of stars are called clusters. These can contain anything from a few dozen to several million stars. There are two main types of star cluster: globular and open. The Milky Way galaxy contains many examples of both.

Globular cluster
These are roughly spherical collections of up to several million ancient stars that formed at the same time. The example above is the Great Globular Cluster in Hercules.

Open cluster
Open clusters are loosely bound collections of young stars that formed around the same time from the same cloud of gas. The example here is the Butterfly Cluster in the constellation Scorpius.

Multiple stars

Unlike many other stars, our Sun is a loner with no companions. Most of the stars we can see in the night sky belong to multiple star systems – that is, two or more stars orbiting each other, held together by gravity.

Pairs of stars that simply orbit each other are called binary systems, but there are also systems of three, four, or more stars, with complicated orbital patterns. Some pairs of stars are so close together that material flows between them. These stars are called interacting binaries. As the stars age, the system can develop in a variety of dramatic ways. For example, in an X-ray binary, material flows from a normal or giant star to an extremely dense companion – a neutron star or a black hole – and gives off powerful X-rays as it spirals inwards. Alternatively, material spilling from a normal or giant star onto a white dwarf may cause the dwarf to produce occasional brilliant blasts of light called novas.

One side of the donor star becomes distorted as gas is pulled towards the white dwarf by gravity.
The gas forms a funnel shape as it is pulled off the giant star.
Accretion disc
Gravity causes the material in this disc to spiral in towards the star at the centre. As it does so, vast amounts of energy are released as heat and radiation.
White dwarf
A white dwarf star is the remains of a previous giant star that lost its outer layers. It is extremely dense: one teaspoon of white dwarf material weighs about 15 tonnes.

Interacting binary

Here, gas flows from a red giant to a nearby white dwarf, forming a swirling disc as it spirals in towards the dwarf star. The white dwarf becomes unstable as its mass increases, causing nuclear explosions at its surface. From Earth, these outbursts of light look like new stars appearing, which is why they are called novas, from the Latin word *nova*, meaning new.

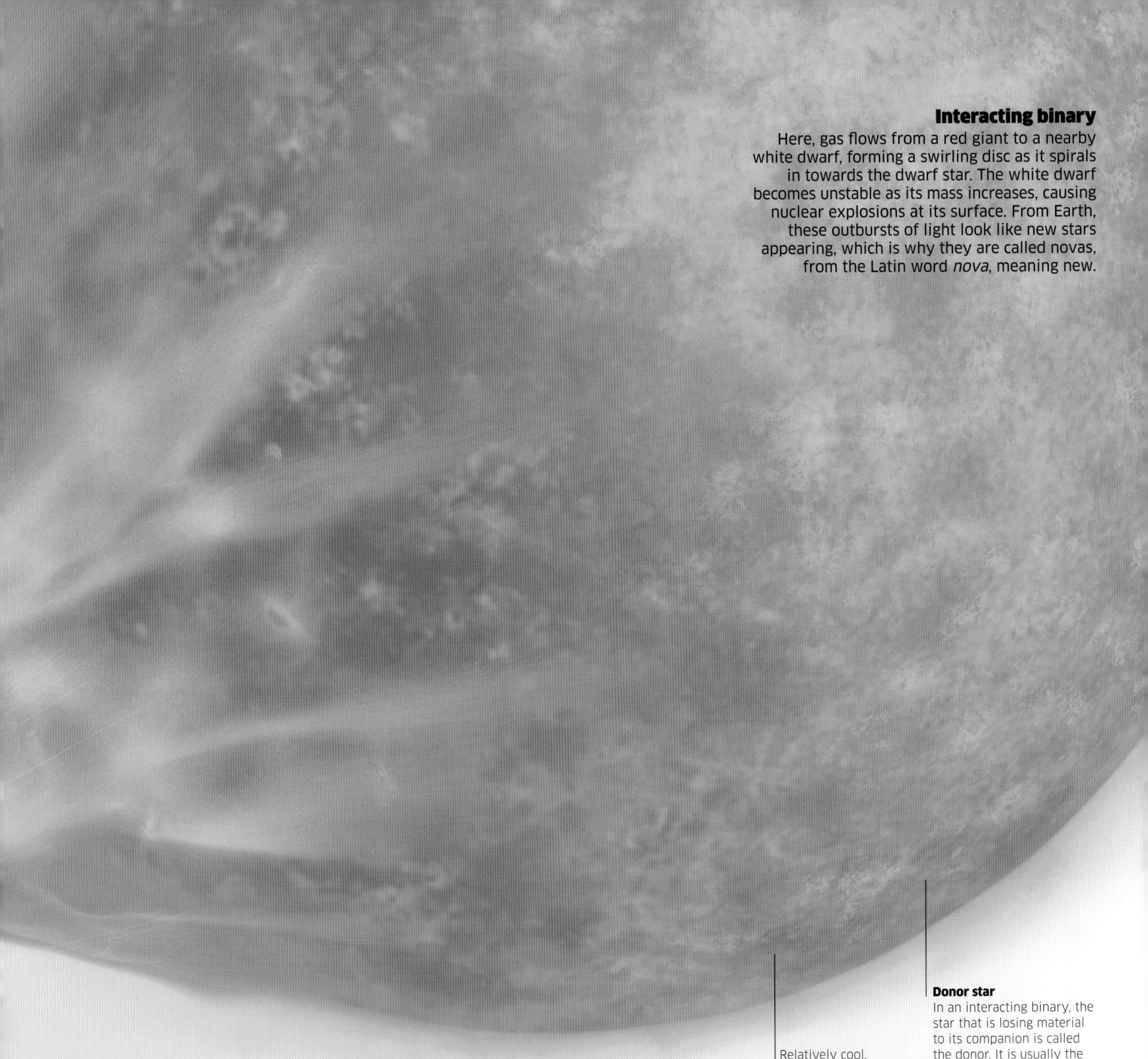

Relatively cool, low-density hydrogen gas

Donor star
In an interacting binary, the star that is losing material to its companion is called the donor. It is usually the larger star in a pair – in this case, a red giant.

Type 1a supernova

The transfer of gas onto a white dwarf star can lead not just to nova outbursts but eventually, scientists think, to a cataclysmic explosion called a Type 1a supernova. This happens because the mass lost by the white dwarf during each nova blast is less than the mass it gains between outbursts, so it slowly grows. Finally, it becomes so massive that it is totally destabilized, triggering a supernova.

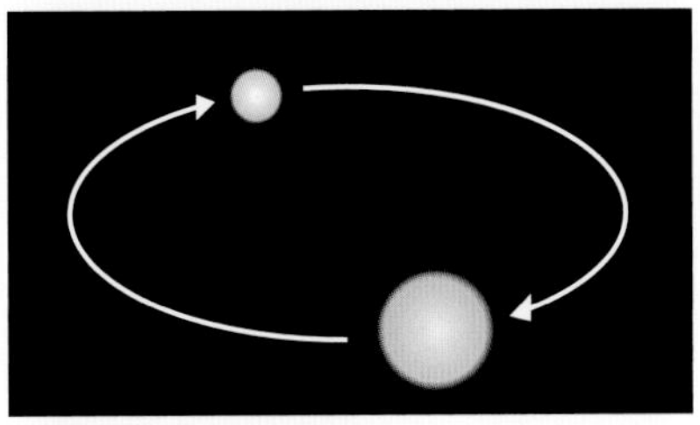

1 PAIR OF ORBITING STARS
Two interacting binary stars are orbiting relatively close to each other. One is a yellow star like our own Sun. Its smaller, denser companion is a white dwarf star.

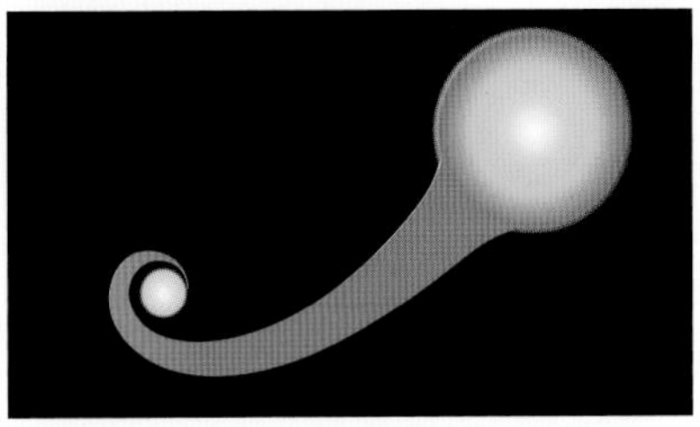

2 MATTER TRANSFER
As the Sun-like star ages, it swells to become a red giant. Some of its gas spills onto the smaller white dwarf star. This can lead to a series of surface outbursts, or novas.

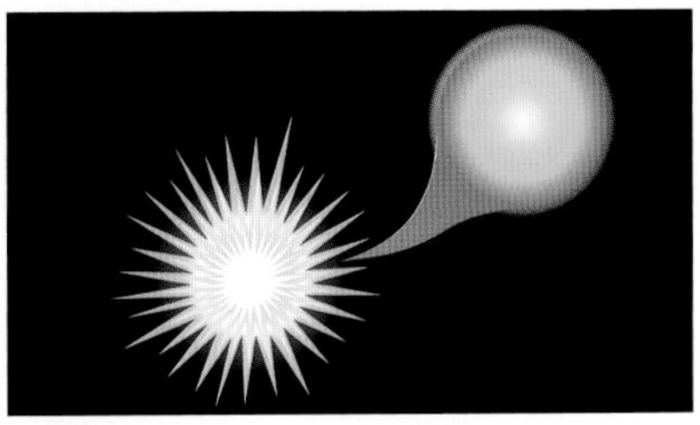

3 WHITE DWARF EXPLODES
The white dwarf's mass increases until it becomes unstable and explodes as a Type 1a supernova. The explosion may cause the red giant star to be blown away.

Star cloud

Every single tiny dot in this image of our galaxy's centre is a star, possibly with a family of planets.

Our eyes can make out about 6,000 stars in the whole of the night sky, but that's only a ten-millionth of the total number of stars in our galaxy. Most are hidden behind clouds of dust, but the telescope that created this image used infrared light to see them. The image shows an area of sky about the size of your fist held at arm's length. The bright patch is the centre of the Milky Way, where a supermassive black hole lies hidden.

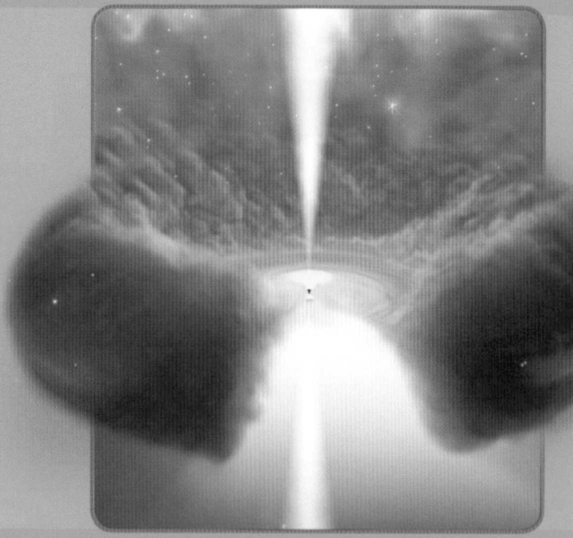

GALAXIES

Our Sun is just one of perhaps 200 billion stars that are held together in space by gravity to form a galaxy – a vast, swirling collection of stars, dust, gas, and invisible matter. There are billions of galaxies in the Universe, stretching as far as we can see in every direction.

The cosmos

The cosmos, or Universe, is everything that exists – not just on Earth or in the Solar System, but also across the mind-bogglingly vast expanses of space. The cosmos includes the galaxy of stars to which our Sun belongs, countless billions of other galaxies, and unfathomable stretches of emptiness between the galaxies. Scientists who study the cosmos are called cosmologists. While astronomers study the stars and galaxies, cosmologists try to find out how and when the Universe began, why it has changed over time, and what its eventual fate will be.

WHAT'S THE UNIVERSE MADE OF?

The Universe is made of matter and energy. Matter includes visible objects such as stars, but also a mysterious invisible substance called dark matter, which we can only detect through its gravity. Energy includes radiation, such as light, and dark energy. Almost nothing is known of dark energy, except that it is causing the Universe to expand faster and faster.

Mass-energy

Scientists have found that matter and energy are interchangeable forms of the same thing, called mass-energy. This pie chart shows how the total mass-energy of the Universe divides up into ordinary matter, dark matter, and dark energy.

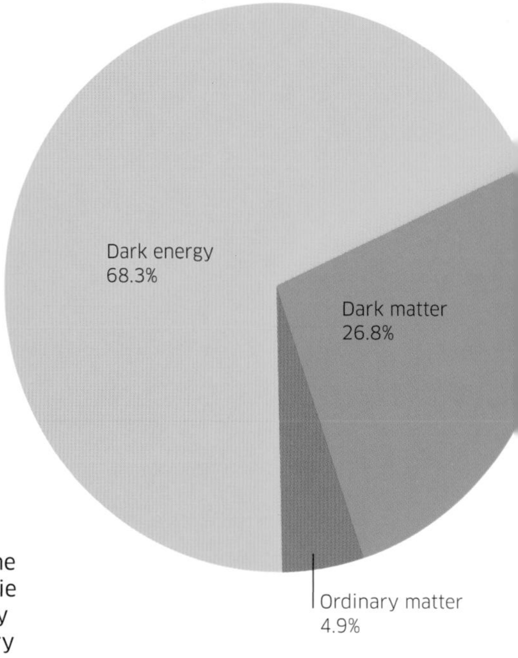

Dark energy
68.3%
Dark matter
26.8%
Ordinary matter
4.9%

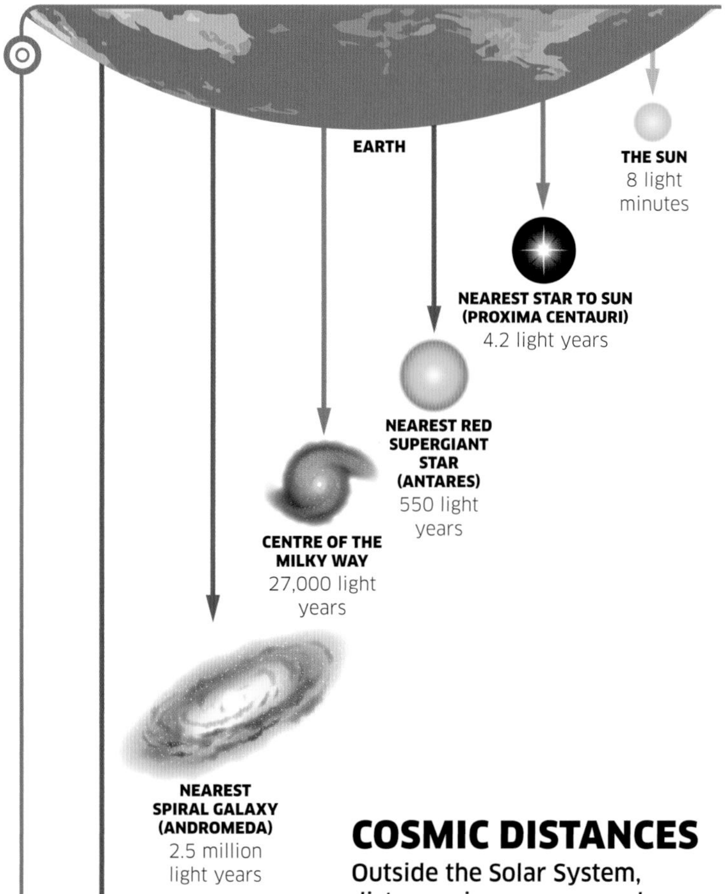

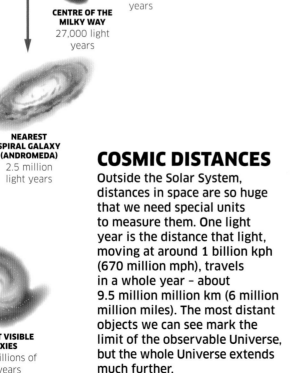

EARTH
THE SUN
8 light minutes
NEAREST STAR TO SUN (PROXIMA CENTAURI)
4.2 light years
NEAREST RED SUPERGIANT STAR (ANTARES)
550 light years
CENTRE OF THE MILKY WAY
27,000 light years
NEAREST SPIRAL GALAXY (ANDROMEDA)
2.5 million light years

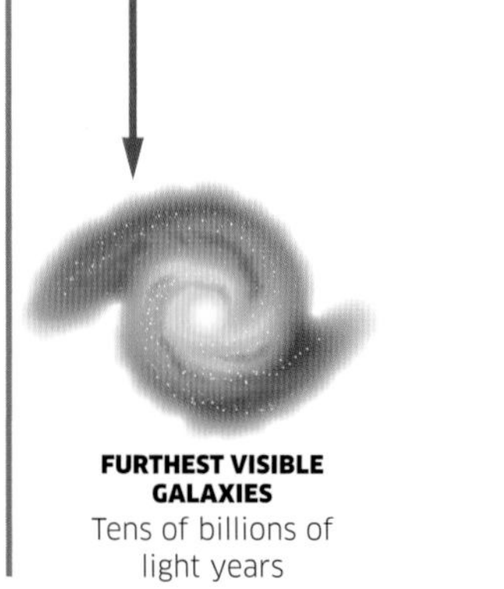

FURTHEST VISIBLE GALAXIES
Tens of billions of light years

COSMIC DISTANCES

Outside the Solar System, distances in space are so huge that we need special units to measure them. One light year is the distance that light, moving at around 1 billion kph (670 million mph), travels in a whole year – about 9.5 million million km (6 million million miles). The most distant objects we can see mark the limit of the observable Universe, but the whole Universe extends much further.

THE EXPANDING UNIVERSE

About 90 years ago, astronomers discovered that distant galaxies are rushing away from us at great speed. This isn't just because they are flying through space – it's because space itself is expanding, making the furthest galaxies rush away the fastest. The discovery meant the Universe must once have been much smaller and perhaps began with a sudden, dramatic expansion from a single point. This idea, known as the big bang theory, is the best explanation for how the Universe began. More recently, scientists have discovered that the expansion is getting faster.

Expanding space

Although the Universe is expanding, it isn't expanding *into* anything. Instead, space itself is expanding. One way to visualize this tricky idea is to imagine a two-dimensional universe on the surface of a balloon. As the balloon inflates, the galaxies get further apart.

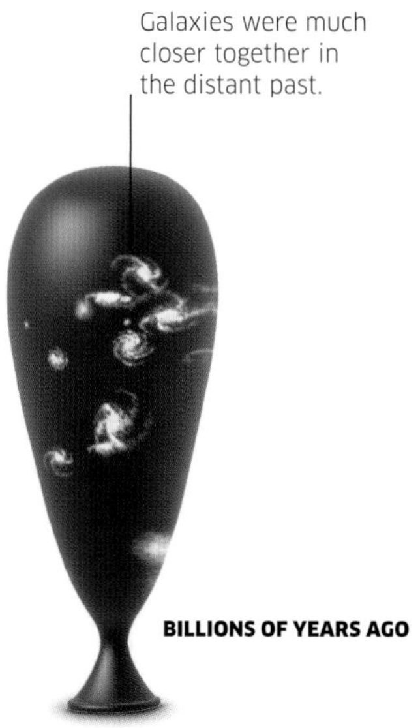

Galaxies were much closer together in the distant past.
BILLIONS OF YEARS AGO

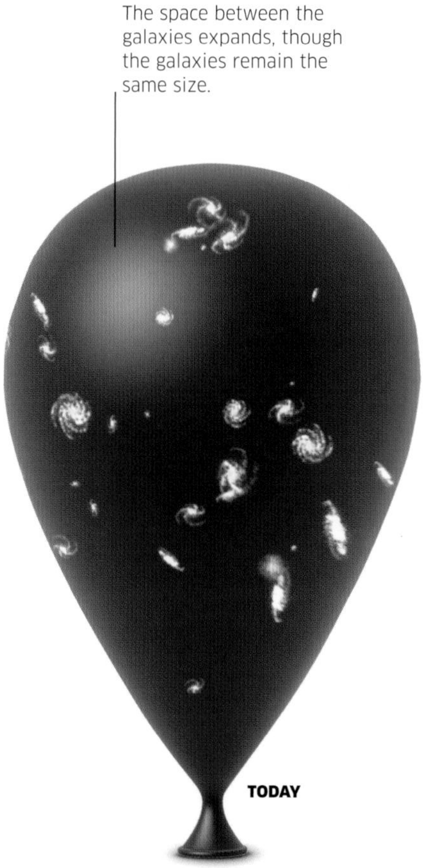

The space between the galaxies expands, though the galaxies remain the same size.
TODAY

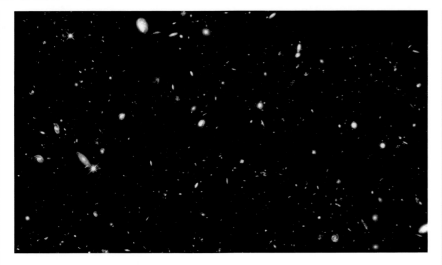

Ordinary matter

Everything we can see or touch – from our own bodies to Earth, the planets, and stars – is made up of what astronomers call ordinary matter. Ordinary matter is made of atoms, and most of the ordinary matter in the Universe is concentrated in galaxies, such as those dotted throughout the Hubble Space Telescope image above.

Dark matter

Most of the matter in the Universe is not ordinary matter but dark matter, which is impossible to see and isn't made up of atoms. Dark matter can only be detected by the gravity it exerts. In the picture above, which shows a cluster of many galaxies, the area coloured blue shows where astronomers think dark matter lies, based on their calculations.

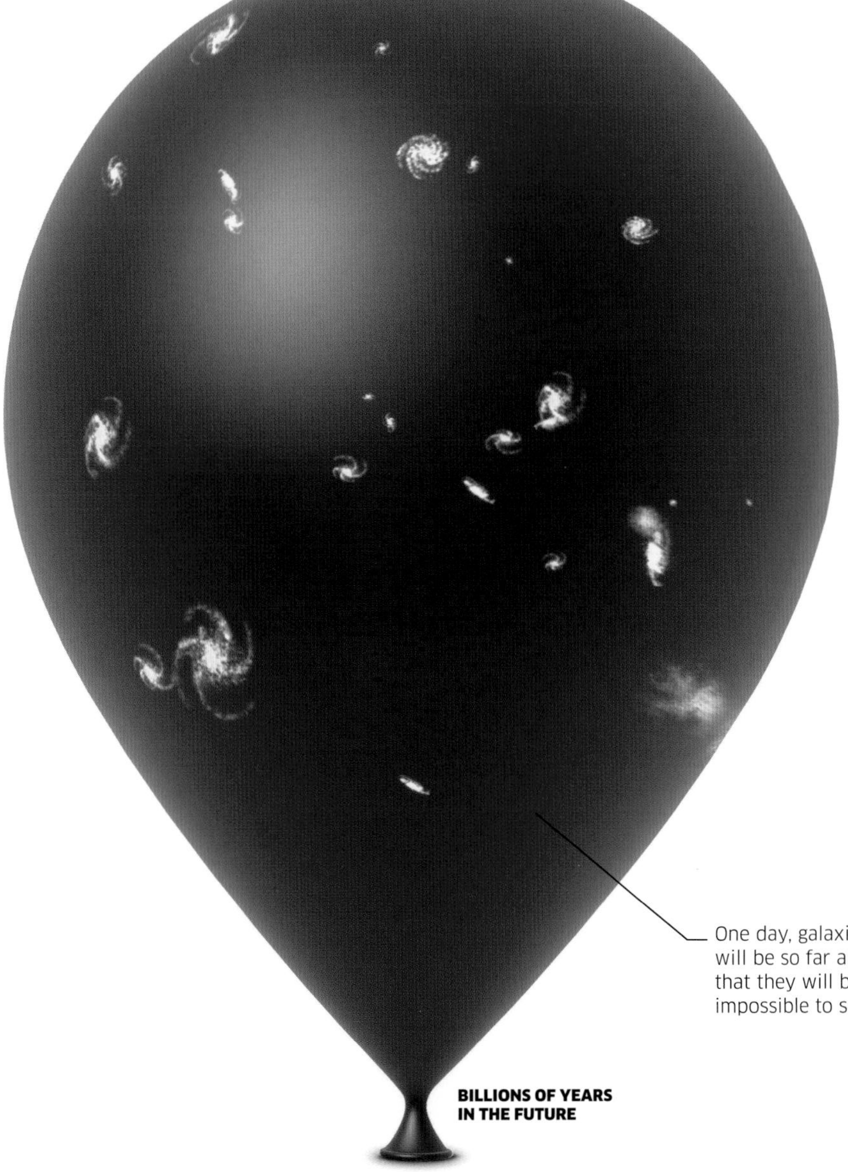

One day, galaxies will be so far apart that they will be impossible to see.

BILLIONS OF YEARS IN THE FUTURE

GRAVITY

The force of gravity is the most important force at large scales in the Universe. It is gravity that holds planets together in the Solar System, keeps stars together in galaxies, and groups galaxies together into galaxy clusters.

Law of gravity

The English scientist Isaac Newton discovered how gravity works more than 300 years ago. He was the first person to realize that the force of gravity keeps the Moon in orbit around Earth and keeps the planets in orbit around the Sun.

MODEL OF INNER SOLAR SYSTEM

Space-time

Newton's law of gravity allowed scientists to predict the motion of planets with great accuracy, but it wasn't perfect. In 1915 German scientist Albert Einstein published an even more accurate theory. Einstein said that gravity happens because massive objects bend the fabric of space and time, a bit like a heavy ball in a rubber sheet. A star, for instance, creates a kind of dent in space-time that causes planets to circle around it.

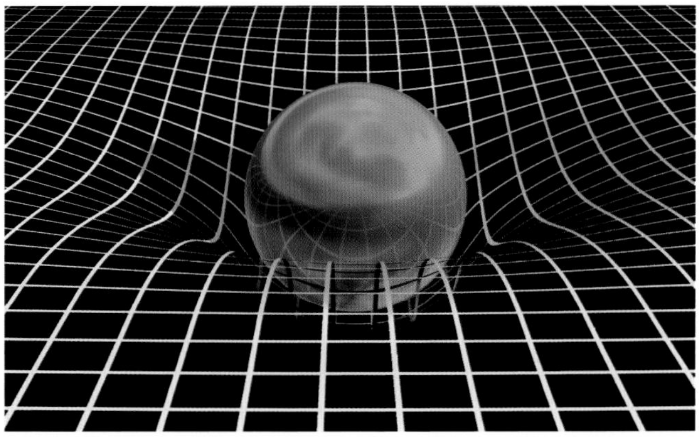

Milky Way

Seen from the southern hemisphere in winter, the Milky Way's central area forms a spectacular band of light stretching across the night sky.

Although the Milky Way is a spiral galaxy, we see its disc as a plane because we are inside it. The bright cloud on the right marks the star-packed heart of the galaxy. The dark lanes are vast, interstellar dust clouds that block the light of the stars behind. Here, photographers at Castlepoint beach in New Zealand try to capture the galaxy in all its midwinter glory.

1923 The year in which **astronomers** first realized that there are galaxies beyond our own.

12–13 billion years – the **age of the Milky Way** galaxy.

Galaxies

Like nearly all stars, the Sun belongs to a huge collection of stars held together by gravity: a galaxy. Our galaxy is just one of hundreds of billions of galaxies floating in the vastness of the Universe.

On very clear, dark nights you can sometimes see a band of milky light across the sky. The light comes from stars in the main part of our own galaxy, the Milky Way. The Milky Way is disc-shaped, but because we are inside it, we see its light as a band. It is so huge that its size defies imagination. It would take 150 billion years to cross the Milky Way at the speed of an airliner, and even the nearest star would take 6 million years to reach. Almost everything the naked eye can see in the sky belongs to the Milky Way. Beyond it, countless other galaxies stretch in all directions as far as telescopes can see.

The Milky Way contains about 200 billion stars.

Barred spiral The Milky Way is classed as a barred spiral galaxy because the central bulge is bar-shaped.
Scutum-Centaurus Arm This is one of the two main spiral arms of the galaxy. The area where it joins the central bar is rich in star-forming clouds.
Dark lane formed by dust
Norma Arm

Milky Way

The Milky Way is shaped like two fried eggs back-to-back. In the centre is a bulge containing most of the galaxy's stars, and around this is a flat disc. The disc is made up of spiral arms that curve out from the centre. There are two major spiral arms and several minor ones. In the heart of the central bulge is a black hole 4 million times more massive than the Sun.

1

Eagle Nebula
Glowing clouds of gas and dust occur throughout our galaxy. The dark pillars in this image of the Eagle Nebula are clouds of dust and hydrogen thousands of times larger than the Solar System. Inside these clouds new stars are forming.

2

Galactic centre
The bright white region seen here marks the centre of our galaxy. This is an extremely active place. At its heart, matter spirals into a gigantic black hole. The reddish areas next to the centre are large arcs of glowing gas.

3

Solar System
Our Solar System orbits the galactic centre once every 225 million years, travelling at about 200 km (120 miles) per second. So far, it has completed only 23 orbits.

Orion Arm
Our Solar System is located close to the inner edge of this small arm, which is about 10,000 light years long. Many of the brightest stars in the night sky can be found in this arm.

Carina–Sagittarius Arm
Situated inside the Orion Arm, this minor spiral arm is rich in bright nebulas and star clusters.

Nebula
Outer Arm
3
1
2

Perseus Arm
A major arm of the Milky Way, this is around 100,000 light years long and curves around the outside of the Orion Arm, which includes our Solar System. Numerous star clusters and nebulas dot the Perseus Arm.

Galaxy shapes

Galaxies come in various shapes and sizes, from fuzzy clouds with no clear shape to beautiful spirals with graceful, curving arms. The main types of galaxy shape are shown below. Whatever the shape, all galaxies spin – though their individual stars do not all orbit the centre at the same speed. As the stars in a galaxy orbit, they may pass in and out of crowded areas, like cars passing through traffic jams. These crowded areas appear to us as spiral arms.

Spiral
These galaxies consist of a central hub of stars surrounded by a flat rotating disc containing stars, gas, and dust. The material in the disc is concentrated into two or more spiral arms, which curve outwards. The spiral galaxy here, known as Bode's Galaxy, is relatively close to our own, at 12 million light years away.

Barred spiral
This type is similar to a spiral except that a straight bar of stars, dust, and gas runs across the centre, connecting curved or spiral arms. Our own galaxy, the Milky Way, is a barred spiral, as is NGC 1365 (left). At 200,000 light years across, NGC 1365 is one of the largest galaxies known.

Elliptical
These galaxies can be spherical, rugby-ball shaped, or even cigar-shaped, with no clear internal structure. They contain mostly very old red stars, which give the galaxy an orange or reddish hue, but little gas and dust. Their stars follow a variety of orbits. M60, shown here, is quite a large elliptical galaxy.

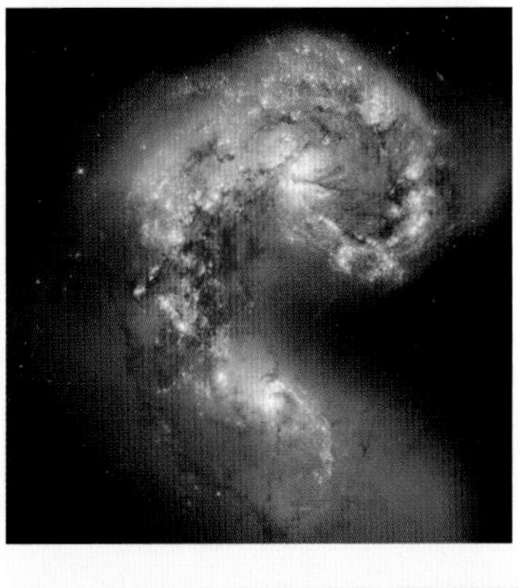

Irregular
Galaxies of this type have no particular shape or symmetry. Some are made by collisions between two galaxies. For example, the Antennae Galaxies (left) were separate spirals until 1.2 billion years ago, when they started merging.

2.5 billion Suns – the **mass of the black hole in the centre of radio galaxy Hercules A.**

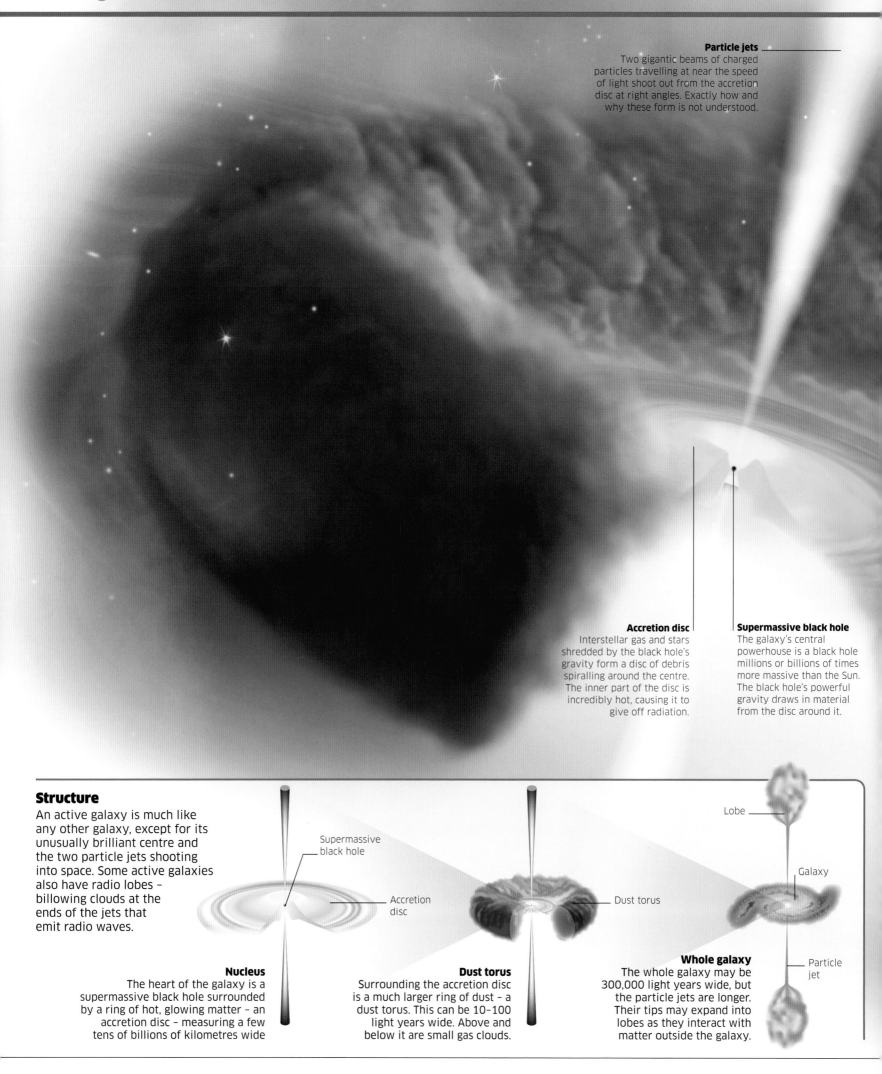

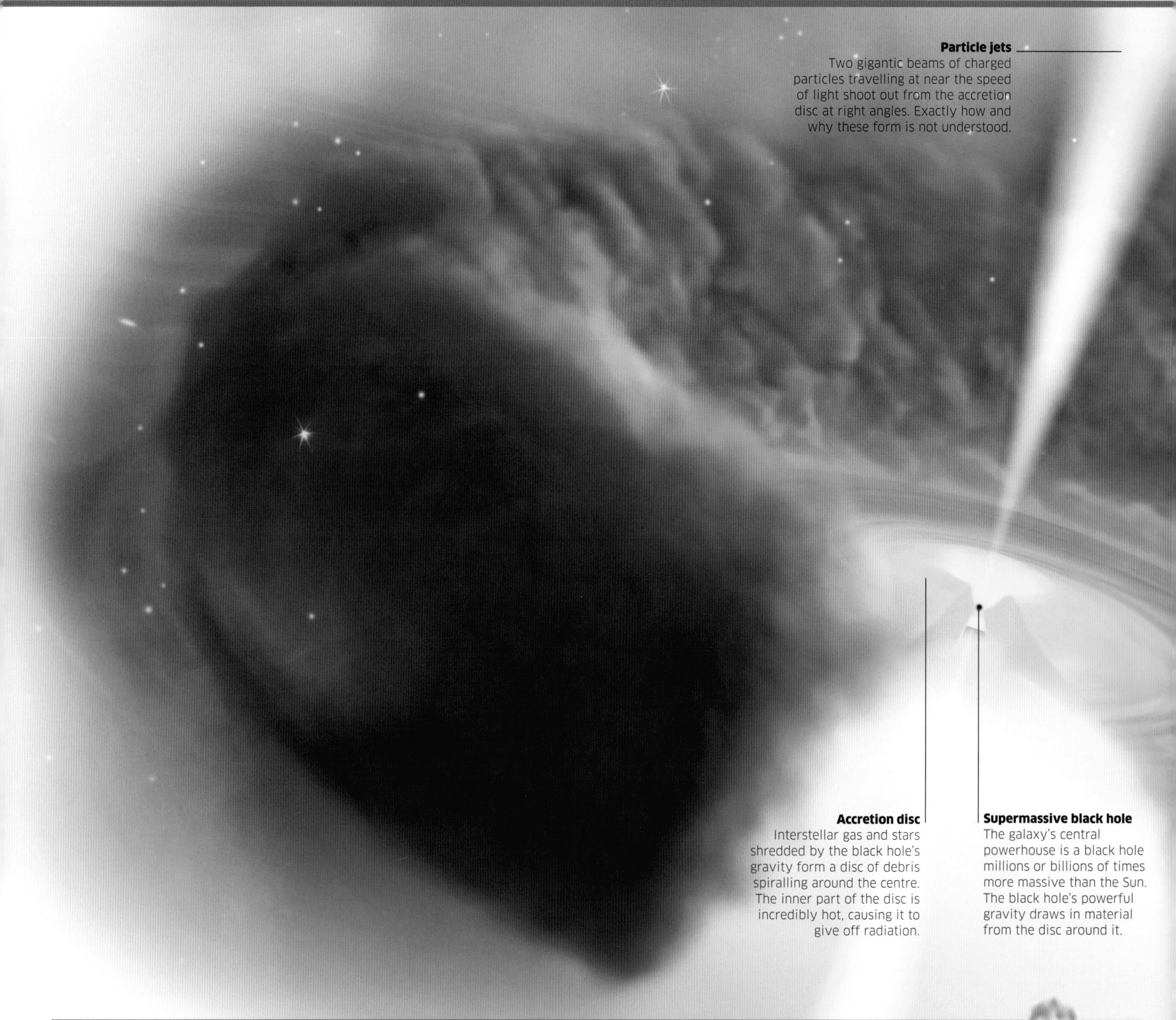
Particle jets
Two gigantic beams of charged particles travelling at near the speed of light shoot out from the accretion disc at right angles. Exactly how and why these form is not understood.
Accretion disc
Interstellar gas and stars shredded by the black hole's gravity form a disc of debris spiralling around the centre. The inner part of the disc is incredibly hot, causing it to give off radiation.
Supermassive black hole
The galaxy's central powerhouse is a black hole millions or billions of times more massive than the Sun. The black hole's powerful gravity draws in material from the disc around it.

Structure

An active galaxy is much like any other galaxy, except for its unusually brilliant centre and the two particle jets shooting into space. Some active galaxies also have radio lobes – billowing clouds at the ends of the jets that emit radio waves.

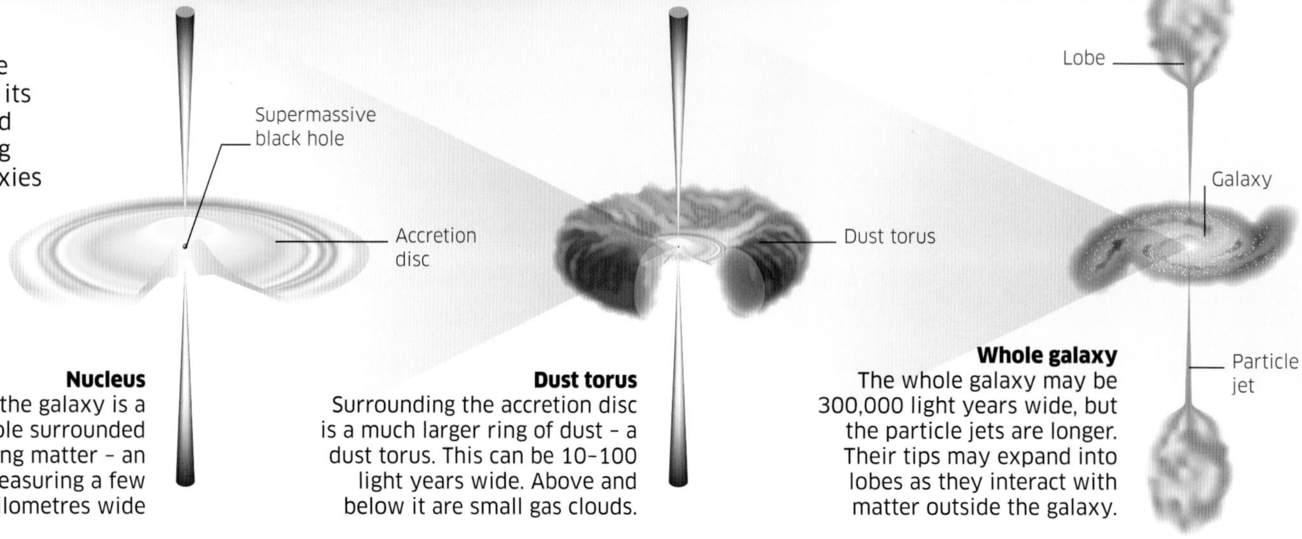
Supermassive black hole
Accretion disc
Dust torus
Lobe
Galaxy
Particle jet

Nucleus
The heart of the galaxy is a supermassive black hole surrounded by a ring of hot, glowing matter – an accretion disc – measuring a few tens of billions of kilometres wide

Dust torus
Surrounding the accretion disc is a much larger ring of dust – a dust torus. This can be 10–100 light years wide. Above and below it are small gas clouds.

Whole galaxy
The whole galaxy may be 300,000 light years wide, but the particle jets are longer. Their tips may expand into lobes as they interact with matter outside the galaxy.

Active galaxies

Galaxies glow in the darkness of space thanks to the light from their stars. A few galaxies, however, also blast out vast amounts of light and other types of radiation from their cores. These are active galaxies.

The centre, or nucleus, of an active galaxy emits a staggeringly large amount of electromagnetic radiation. This energy floods out into space not only as visible light but also as radio waves, X-rays, ultraviolet radiation, and gamma rays. The radiation comes from an intensely hot and dense disc of matter spiralling around and into a black hole perhaps a billion times the mass of the Sun – a supermassive black hole. Active galaxies also fling out jets of particles that penetrate deep into intergalactic space. These strange galaxies include some of the most distant objects we can see, such as quasars – objects so astonishingly far away that their light has taken billions of years to reach us, meaning they probably no longer exist.

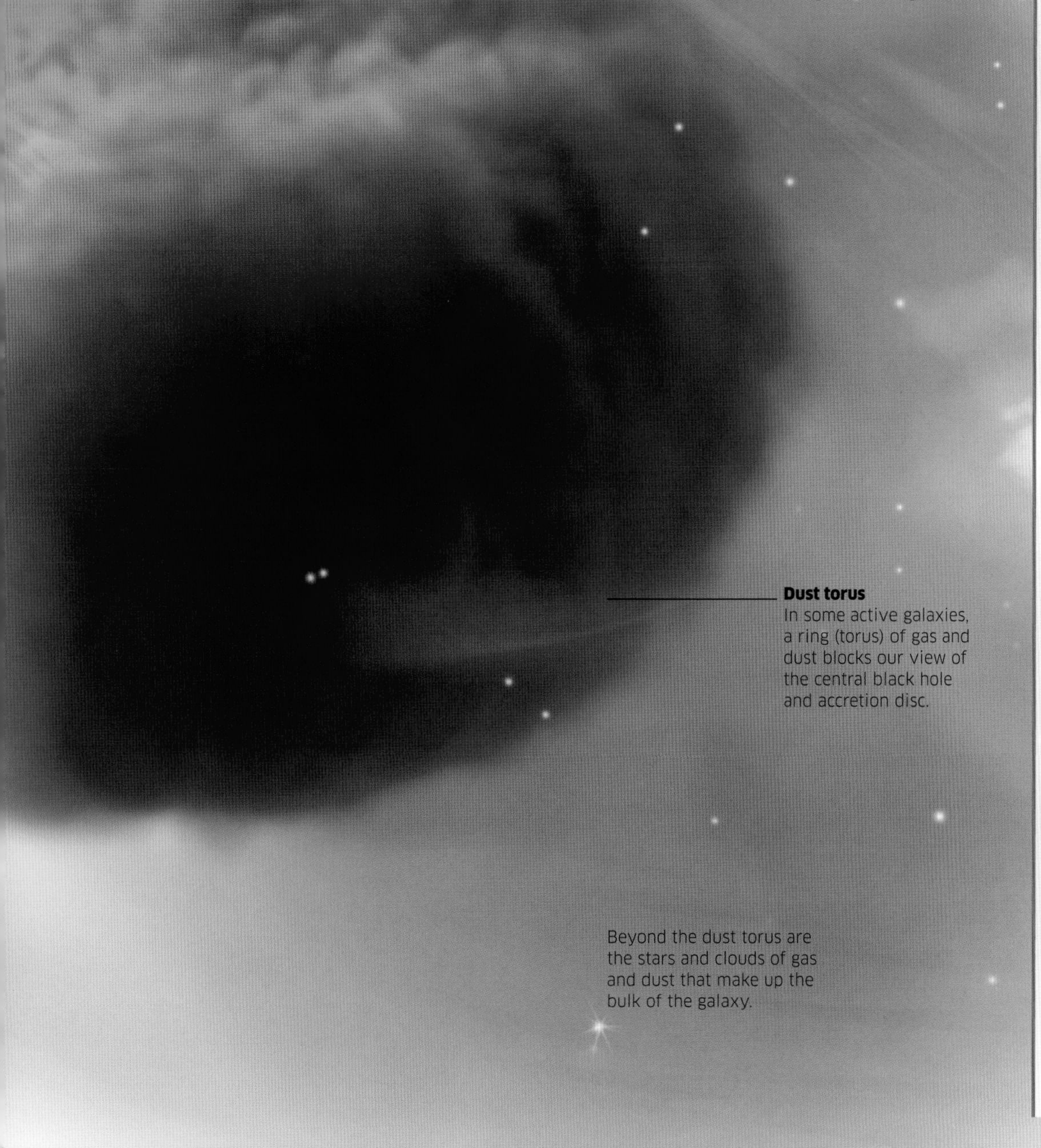
Dust torus
In some active galaxies, a ring (torus) of gas and dust blocks our view of the central black hole and accretion disc.
Beyond the dust torus are the stars and clouds of gas and dust that make up the bulk of the galaxy.

Types of active galaxy

Active galaxies seen from different angles or distances can look very different. As a result, astronomers have distinct names for what look like different objects but are actually part of the same family.

Radio galaxies
When seen with a radio telescope, radio galaxies are flanked by gigantic, billowing clouds called lobes. Those on Hercules A (above) are nearly ten times longer than our Milky Way galaxy.

Seyfert galaxies
These galaxies have much brighter centres than normal galaxies. Most, such as NGC 1566 above, are spiral in shape.

Quasars
The brightest objects in the Universe are quasars, which are active galactic nuclei billions of light years away. Studying them allows astronomers to look back in time billions of years.

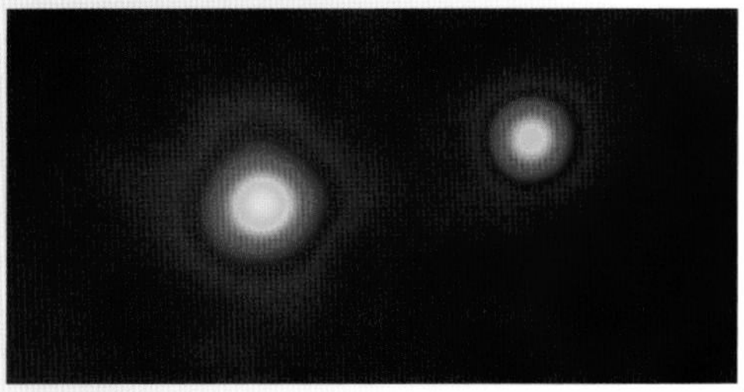

Blazars
When the particle jet of an active galaxy points directly towards Earth, we see a blazar. These are active galactic nuclei, usually in elliptical galaxies.

Colliding galaxies

Neighbouring galaxies sometimes drift close enough for the force of gravity to make them collide. Flying into each other at millions of miles an hour, they crash in a blaze of fireworks as colliding gas clouds give birth to thousands of new stars.

Because the stars in a galaxy are so far apart, galaxies can collide without any of their stars crashing into one another. In fact, during a collision, two galaxies can pass right through each other. Nevertheless, the gravitational tug of war wreaks havoc on the galaxies' shapes, tearing spiral arms apart and flinging billions of stars into space. Often the collision slows down the movement of the galaxies so much that a second or third pass-through happens. In time, the two galaxies may merge to form one larger galaxy.

The Whirlpool Galaxy has two very clear spiral arms. It was the first galaxy to be described as a spiral.
The dark stripes are "lanes" of dust that block the light from the stars behind them.
The Whirlpool Galaxy has a very bright centre because it is what astronomers call an active galaxy – one in which huge amounts of light are being released by gas and dust spiralling into a central black hole.
Clusters of hundreds of thousands of hot, newborn stars blaze with a bluish light.

Whirlpool Galaxy

About 300 million years ago, the Whirlpool Galaxy was struck by a dwarf galaxy that now appears to dangle from one of the larger galaxy's spiral arms. The dwarf galaxy, called NGC 5195, may already have passed through the Whirlpool Galaxy twice. The gravity of the dwarf galaxy has stirred up gas clouds inside the Whirlpool, triggering a burst of star formation. On a dark night, you can see this galactic collision through a small telescope in the constellation of Canes Venatici.

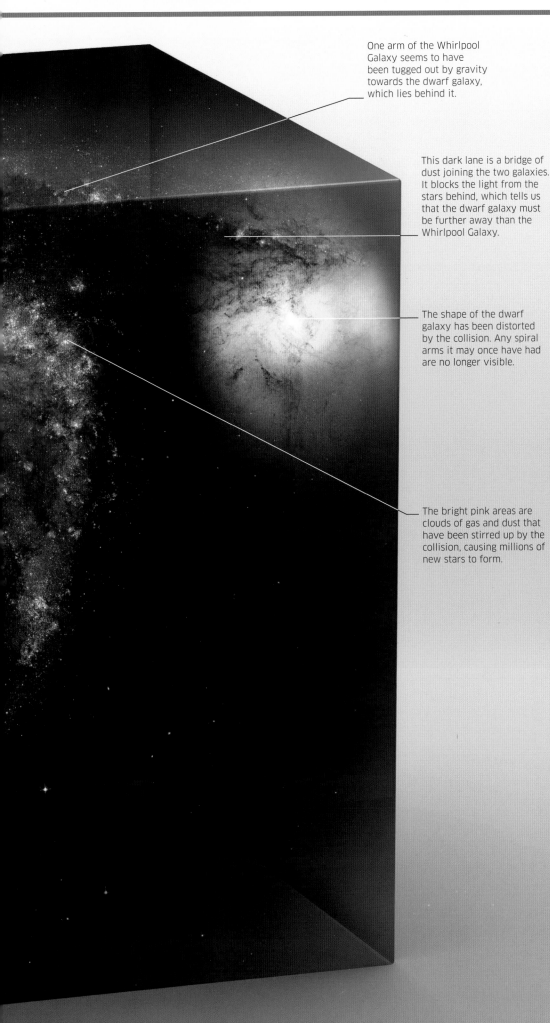

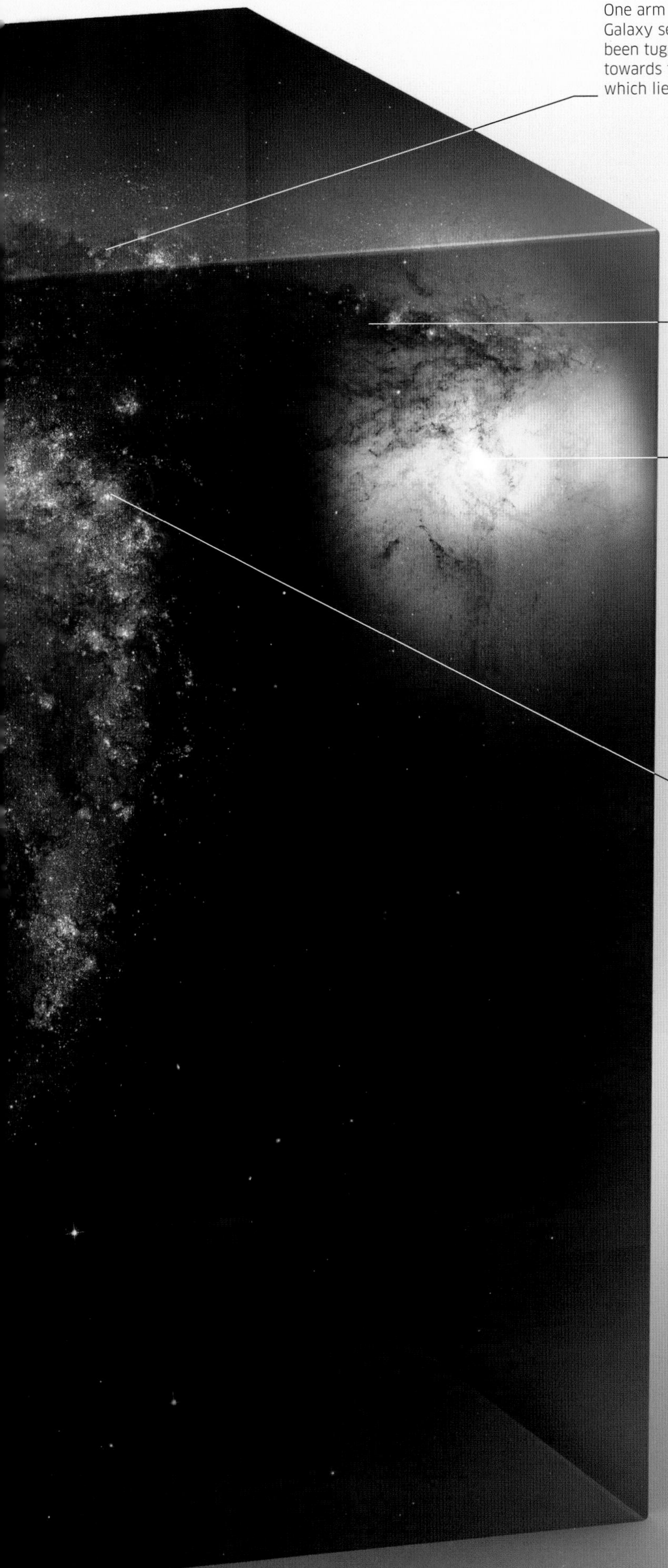
One arm of the Whirlpool Galaxy seems to have been tugged out by gravity towards the dwarf galaxy, which lies behind it.
This dark lane is a bridge of dust joining the two galaxies. It blocks the light from the stars behind, which tells us that the dwarf galaxy must be further away than the Whirlpool Galaxy.
The shape of the dwarf galaxy has been distorted by the collision. Any spiral arms it may once have had are no longer visible.
The bright pink areas are clouds of gas and dust that have been stirred up by the collision, causing millions of new stars to form.

Oddball galaxies

The Universe contains many strange-looking galaxies that do not seem to fit into the usual galaxy classification system. Astronomers reckon many of these oddities are the result of collisions, mergers, or other interactions between two or more galaxies.

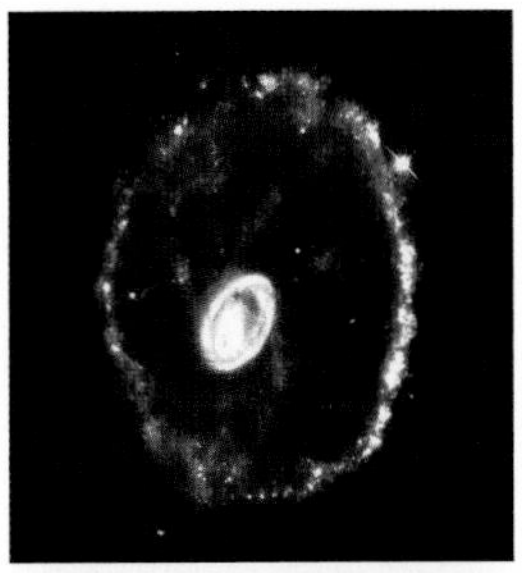

Cartwheel Galaxy
This bizarre object formed when a spiral galaxy bumped into a smaller companion 200 million years ago. The shock wave it produced rearranged the galaxies into a bluish ring and central bright portion.

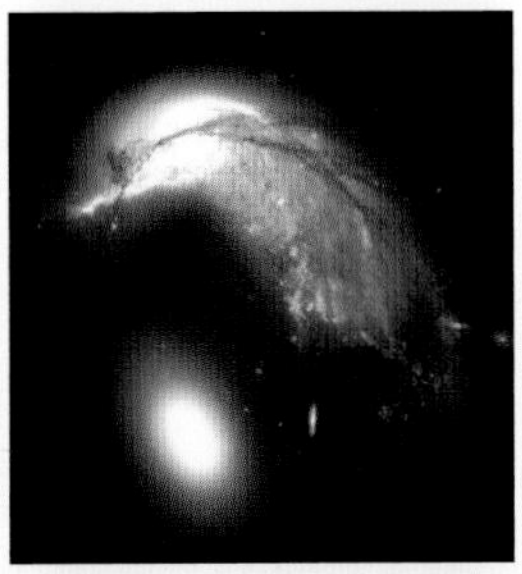

The Porpoise
Here, what was once a spiral galaxy is being reshaped by the gravity of a galaxy below it. The end result looks like a porpoise leaping over a fuzzy oval ball. A burst of newly formed blue stars forms the porpoise's nose.

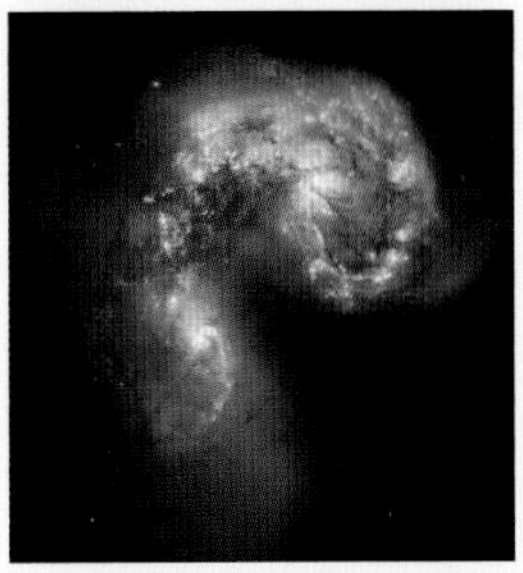

Antennae Galaxies
These intertwined spiral galaxies are going through a "starburst" phase. Clouds of dust and gas are compressing each other, causing stars to form rapidly. The areas of star formation glow with brilliant pink and blue colours.

Future galactic merger

Our own galaxy – the Milky Way – is hurtling towards the neighbouring Andromeda Galaxy at 400,000 kph (250,000 mph). Billions of years from now, they will collide and eventually merge. Above is an artist's idea of how the collision might look from Earth around the time it starts, with the Andromeda Galaxy (left) grown to an enormous size in the night sky.

10,000 The number of galaxies in the richest galaxy clusters.

Nearby clusters

Spread out in many directions from the Local Group are other galaxy clusters, a few of which are shown below. Clusters are grouped into even bigger structures called superclusters.

Abell 1689
This buzzing hive of galaxies is one of the biggest clusters known.

Virgo cluster
Two elliptical galaxies resembling eyes lie near the centre of this cluster.

Leo cluster
The Leo cluster is part of a huge sheet of galaxies known as the Great Wall.

Abell 1185
This cluster contains an odd-looking galaxy called the Guitar (left).

Gravitational lensing

Galaxy clusters contain so much matter that their gravity can bend light rays passing close by. As a result, they act like giant lenses in space and can distort the shapes of more distant galaxies as viewed from Earth. This effect is known as gravitational lensing.

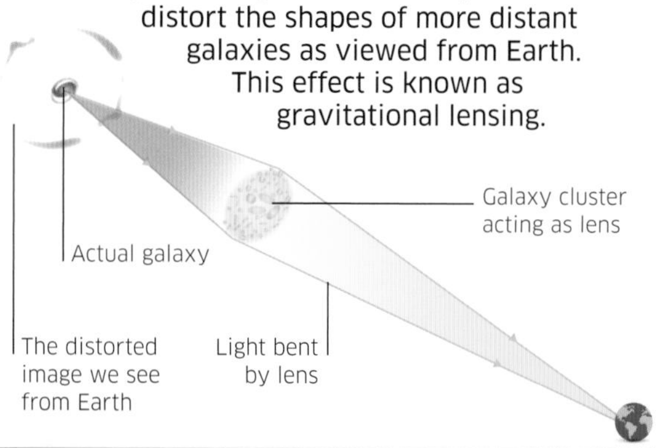
Galaxy cluster acting as lens
Actual galaxy
The distorted image we see from Earth
Light bent by lens

Space bananas
The banana-shaped arcs in the lower left of this image of galaxy cluster Abell 2218 are galaxies beyond the cluster. Their appearance has been warped by gravitational lensing.

Local Group

Our home galaxy belongs to a cluster called the Local Group. The Local Group has three large spiral or barred spiral galaxies (the Milky Way, Andromeda, and Triangulum) and more than 50 smaller dwarf and irregular galaxies. They are spread out over a region roughly 10 million light years across. Many of the smaller galaxies are clustered around the two largest spirals.

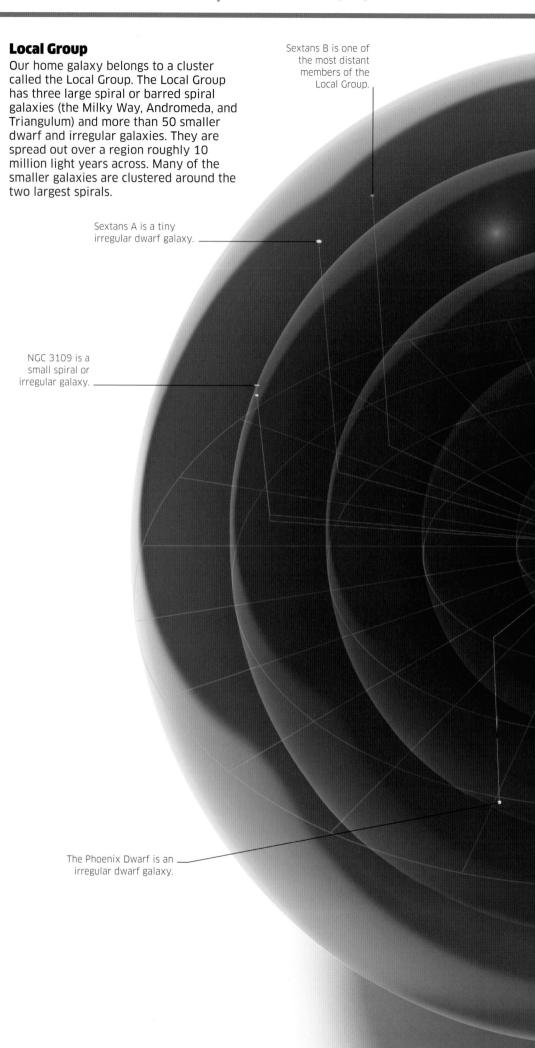

Sextans B is one of the most distant members of the Local Group.
Sextans A is a tiny irregular dwarf galaxy.
NGC 3109 is a small spiral or irregular galaxy.
The Phoenix Dwarf is an irregular dwarf galaxy.

Galaxy clusters

Galaxies are held together in clusters by gravity, sometimes orbiting each other and often colliding. These clusters typically measure a few million light years across.

Some galaxy clusters are quite sparse and contain only a few galaxies. The cluster that our own Milky Way galaxy belongs to is one of these. Other clusters are much denser and contain hundreds or even thousands of galaxies, often arranged chaotically but sometimes forming a neat, spherical pattern. A giant elliptical galaxy usually lies at the centre of these dense clusters. Galaxy clusters don't just contain galaxies. They also contain large amounts of thin, hot gas and mysterious dark matter, which we can't see.

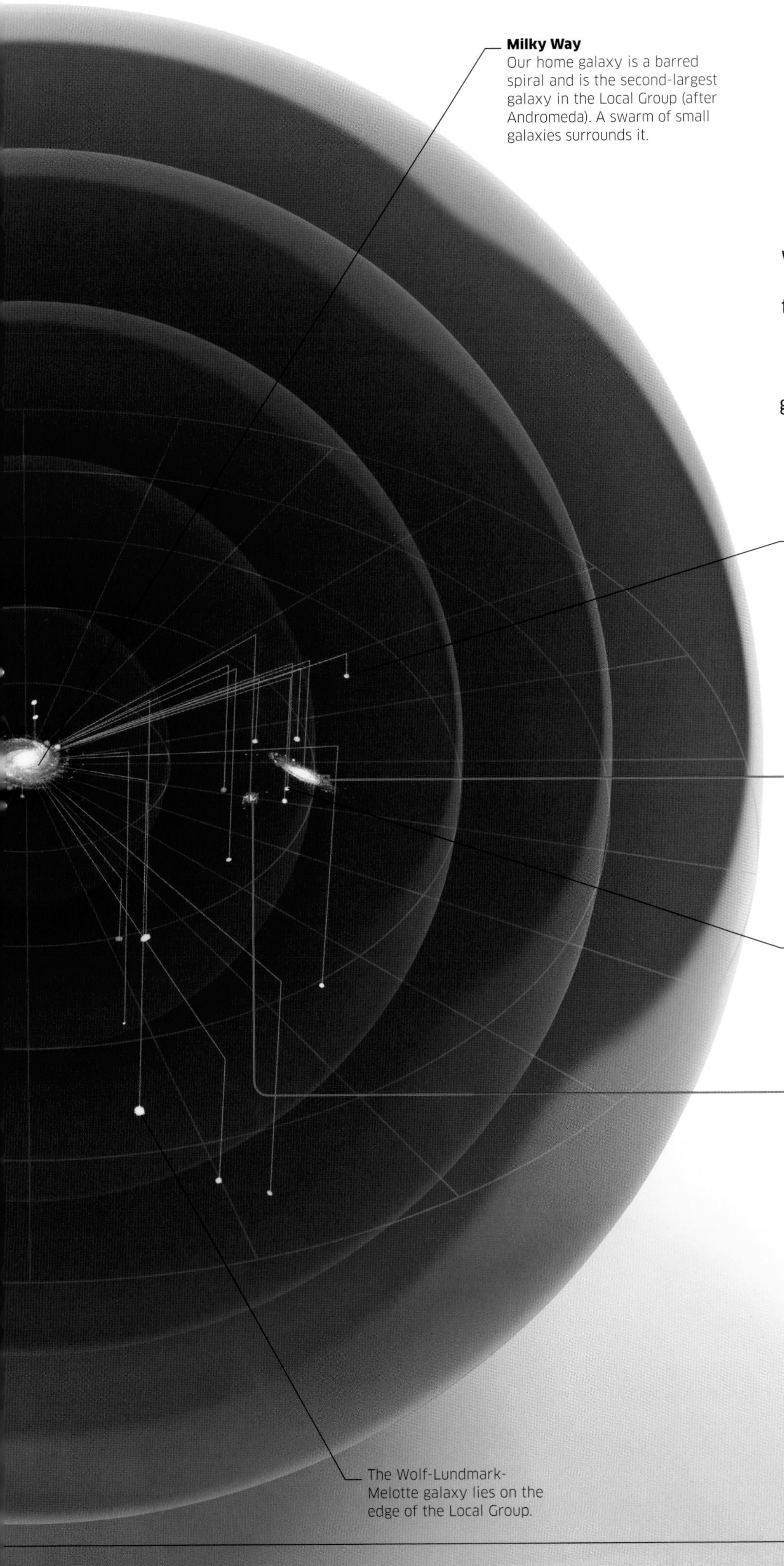

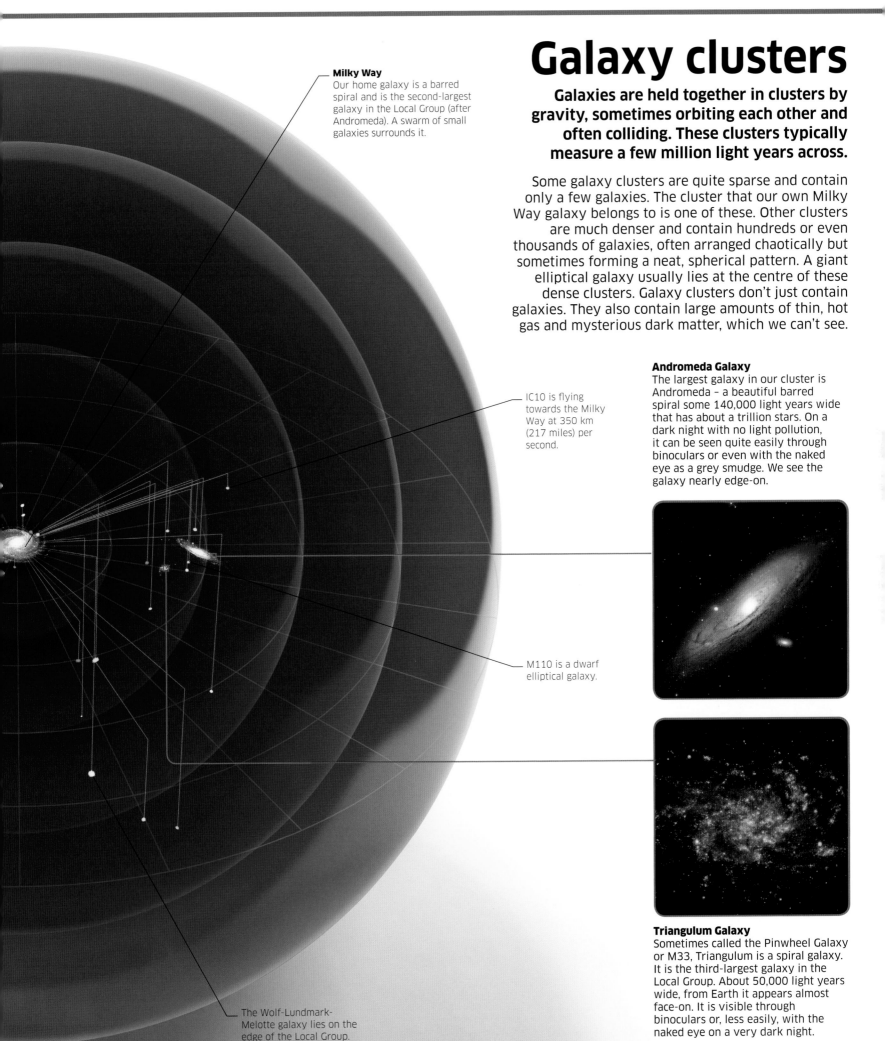

Milky Way
Our home galaxy is a barred spiral and is the second-largest galaxy in the Local Group (after Andromeda). A swarm of small galaxies surrounds it.

IC10 is flying towards the Milky Way at 350 km (217 miles) per second.

M110 is a dwarf elliptical galaxy.

The Wolf-Lundmark-Melotte galaxy lies on the edge of the Local Group.

Andromeda Galaxy
The largest galaxy in our cluster is Andromeda – a beautiful barred spiral some 140,000 light years wide that has about a trillion stars. On a dark night with no light pollution, it can be seen quite easily through binoculars or even with the naked eye as a grey smudge. We see the galaxy nearly edge-on.

Triangulum Galaxy
Sometimes called the Pinwheel Galaxy or M33, Triangulum is a spiral galaxy. It is the third-largest galaxy in the Local Group. About 50,000 light years wide, from Earth it appears almost face-on. It is visible through binoculars or, less easily, with the naked eye on a very dark night.

The shape of space

The three dimensions of space are “bent” by the gravitational pull of all the matter in the Universe into a fourth dimension, which we cannot see. Since this is hard to visualize, scientists use the metaphor of a two-dimensional rubber sheet to explain the idea. Scientists used to think that the rubber sheet might be bent in any of three ways, depending on how densely packed with matter the Universe is. We now know that the observable Universe has a “flat” shape.

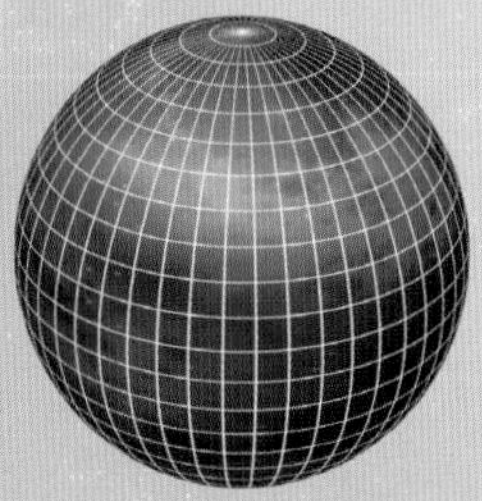

Closed
A dense Universe would bend itself into a closed shape. In such a Universe, travelling in a straight line would eventually bring you back to your starting point.

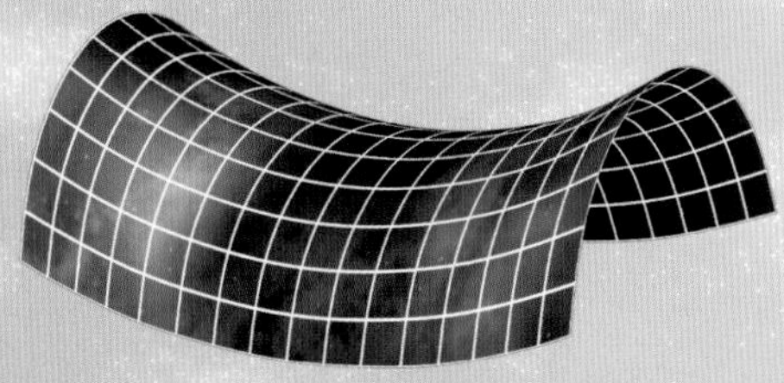

Open
If the Universe is of low density, it might extend into an “open” shape. In this case, it would be infinite in size and have no outer edge.

Flat
Our Universe appears to have just the right concentration of matter to have a “flat” shape. This suggests it will keep expanding forever, and like an open Universe it might be infinite in size.

6
2
1

1 Earth
Our home world is a small, rocky planet floating in the enormous emptiness of space. Our nearest neighbouring planet, Venus, is about a 15-minute journey away at the speed of light.

2 Solar System
Earth belongs to a family of planets and other objects that orbit the Sun. The farthest planet, Neptune, is 4.5 hours away at the speed of light, but the whole Solar System is over 3 light years wide.

3 Local stars
The nearest star to the Sun is about 4 light years away. Within 16 light years of the Sun, there are 43 star systems containing 60 stars. Some of these star systems may have families of planets too.

4 Milky Way
The Sun and its neighbouring stars occupy a tiny fraction of the Milky Way galaxy – a vast, swirling disc containing 200 billion stars and enormous clouds of gas and dust. It is over 100,000 light years wide.

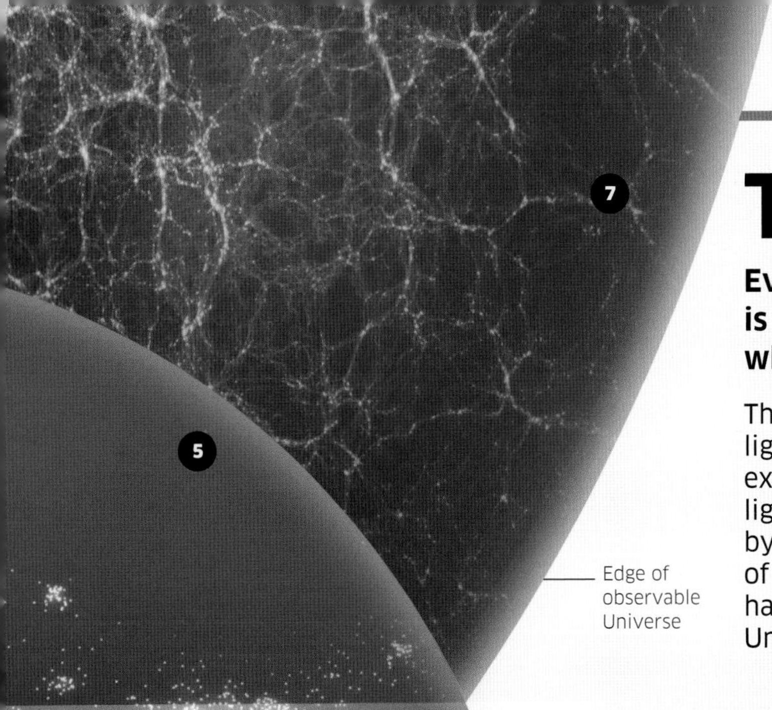
7
5
Edge of observable Universe

The Universe

Everything in the Universe is a part of something bigger. Earth is part of the Solar System, which lies in the Milky Way galaxy, which is just a tiny bit of the whole Universe.

The scale of the Universe defies the imagination. Astronomers use light as a yardstick to measure distance because nothing can cross the vast expanses of interstellar space faster. Yet even one light year – the distance light travels in a whole year, or 10 trillion km (6 trillion miles) – is dwarfed by the largest structures observed in the known Universe. Only a fraction of the Universe is visible to us: the part of the Universe from which light has had time to reach Earth since the big bang. The true extent of the Universe is unknown; it may even be infinite in size.

Orion arm of the Milky Way
4
3

5 Virgo supercluster
Our galaxy is just one of tens of thousands of galaxies that are clustered together in a group called the Virgo supercluster. This vast array of galaxies is more than 100 million light years across.

6 Supercluster filaments
Superclusters form a web of massive, thread-like structures called filaments, which occupy about 5 per cent of the visible Universe. Between these are immense, bubble-like voids.

7 Observable Universe
The part of the Universe we can see is about 93 billion light years across, with Earth at the centre. It contains millions of superclusters, forming a vast, foam-like structure. What lies beyond is unknown.

The Milky Way and nearby galaxies are being drawn towards a mysterious concentration of mass in intergalactic space called the Great Attractor.

1 **billionth of a trillionth of a trillionth of a second** – the time the Universe took to expand from nothing to the size of a football field.

Afterglow of the big bang

A faint afterglow of the big bang exists throughout space. This radiation was released when the Universe was about 380,000 years old and still extremely hot. The image on the right is a map of the radiation across the whole sky. The variations in intensity, shown in colour, are due to minute variations in density in the early Universe. Gravity, working on these tiny variations, created the uneven distribution of matter we can see in the Universe today, with clusters of galaxies separated by immense voids.

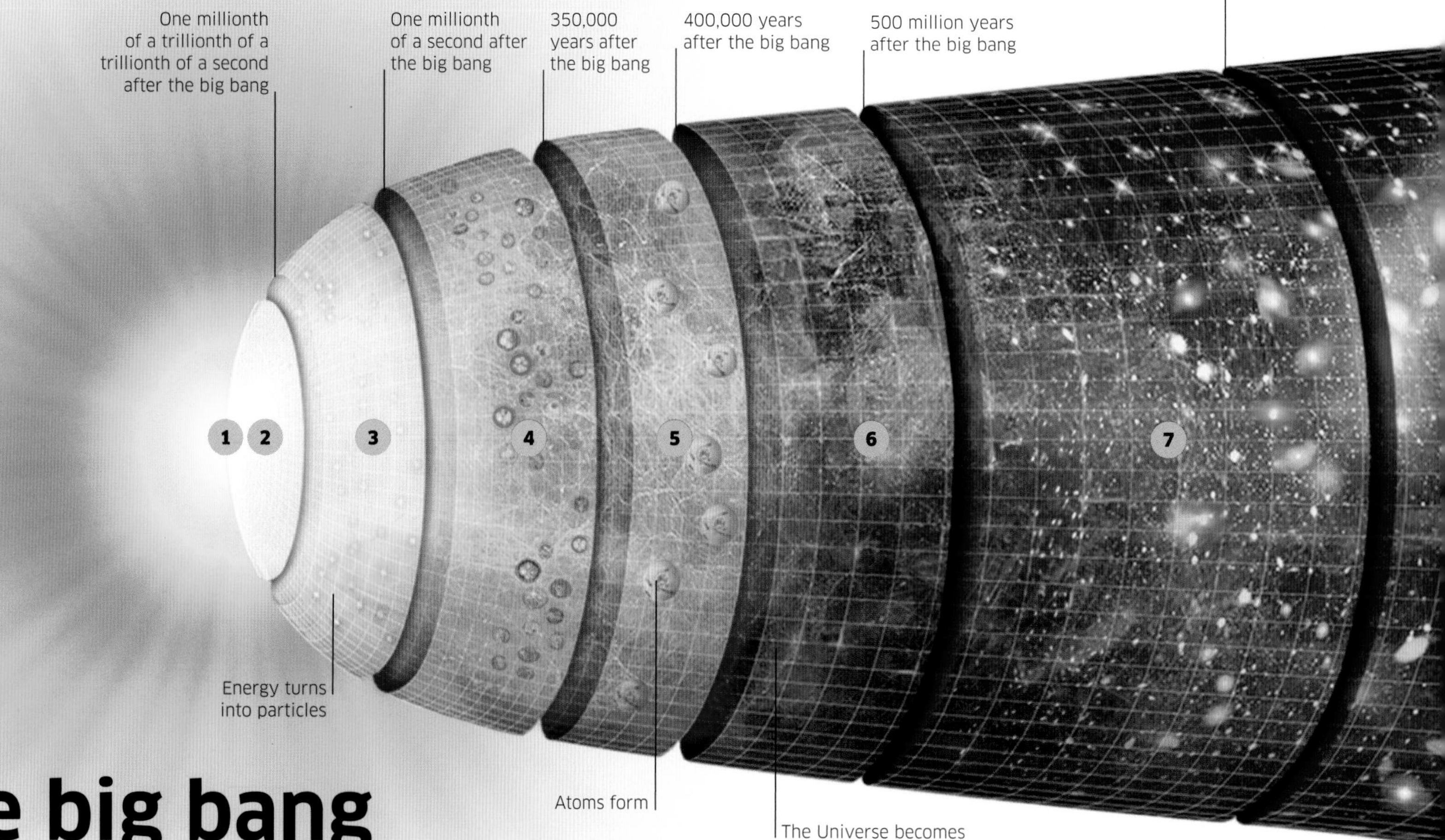
One millionth of a trillionth of a trillionth of a second after the big bang
One millionth of a second after the big bang
350,000 years after the big bang
400,000 years after the big bang
500 million years after the big bang
3 billion years after the big bang
1
2
3
4
5
6
7
Energy turns into particles
Atoms form
The Universe becomes transparent as light begins to pass freely through space.

The big bang

About 14 billion years ago, the Universe suddenly appeared from nowhere as a tiny concentration of pure energy. It then expanded trillions of trillions of times in an instant – an event known as the big bang.

In the first millisecond of existence, the intense energy of the newborn Universe produced a vast number of subatomic particles (particles smaller than atoms). Some of these joined together to form the nuclei (centres) of atoms – the building blocks of all the matter we see in the Universe today. But it wasn't until the Universe was about 380,000 years old that actual atoms formed, and it wasn't until hundreds of millions of years later that galaxies and stars appeared. As well as producing energy and matter, the big bang also gave rise to four basic forces that govern the way everything in the Universe works, from the force of gravity to the forces that hold atoms together. Ever since the big bang, the Universe has continued to expand and cool down, and it will probably continue doing so forever.

1 The Universe starts as an unimaginably hot point of energy, infinitely smaller than a single atom.

2 In a tiny fraction of a second it expands to the size of a city, and the rate of inflation then slows. This was not an explosion of matter into space, but an expansion of space itself.

3 So far, the Universe is just energy. But soon, a seething mass of tiny particles and antiparticles (the same as their corresponding particles, but with the opposite electric charge) form from this energy. Most of these cancel out, turning back into energy, but some are left over.

4 The leftover matter begins to form protons and neutrons. By now, the Universe is about a millionth of a second old. Within a few minutes, the neutrons and many of the protons join to form atomic nuclei.

5 About 380,000 years later, the Universe has cooled enough for atomic nuclei to combine with electrons to make hydrogen and helium atoms.

6 The Universe is now a vast cloud of hydrogen and helium atoms. Light can pass more easily through space, so the Universe becomes transparent. Gravity acts on tiny variations in the gas cloud, pulling the gas into clumps that will eventually become galaxies.

7 Around 550 million years after the big bang, the first stars ignite within the densest parts of these gas clumps. By 600 million years after the big bang,

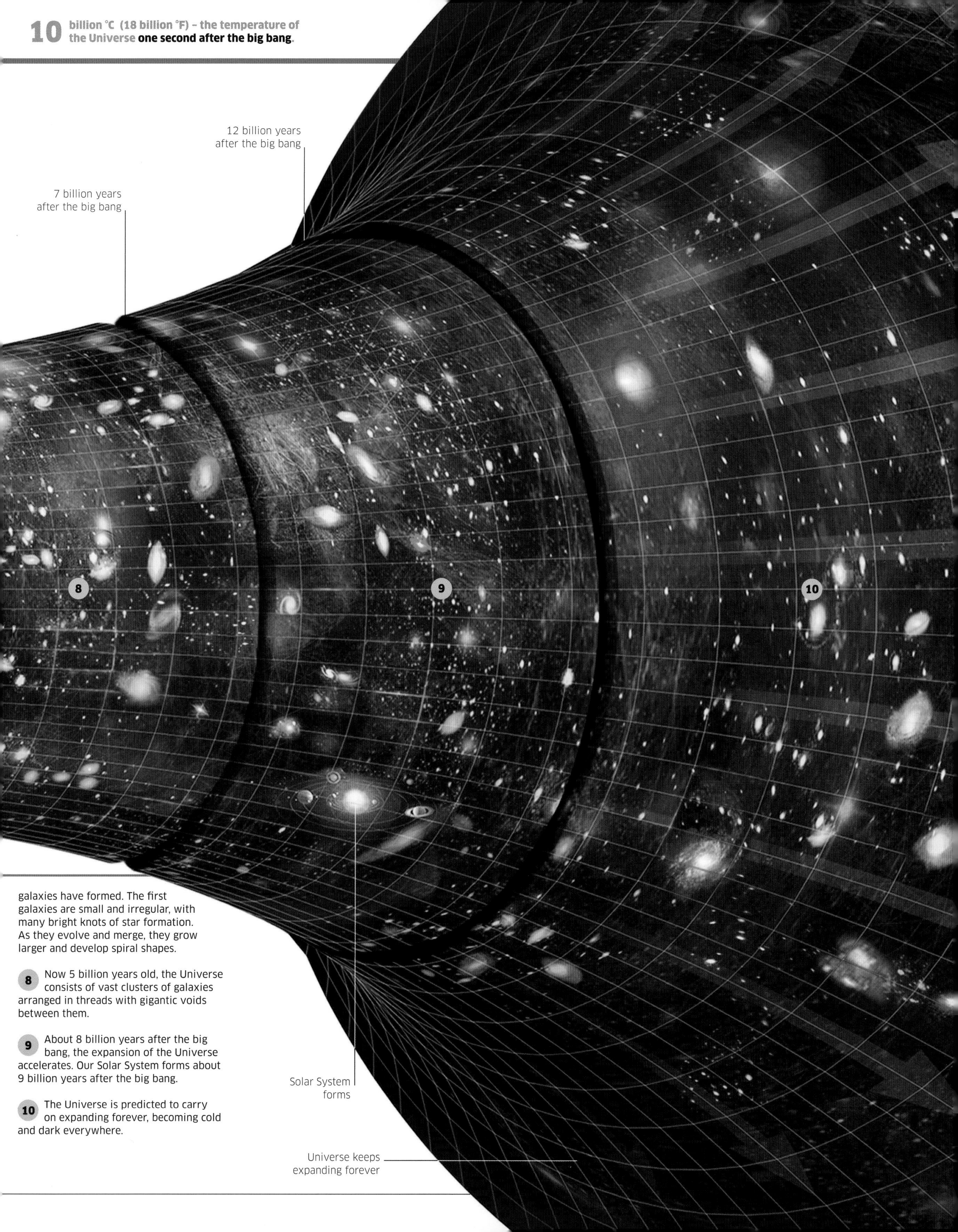
12 billion years after the big bang
7 billion years after the big bang
8
9
10
Solar System forms
Universe keeps expanding forever

galaxies have formed. The first galaxies are small and irregular, with many bright knots of star formation. As they evolve and merge, they grow larger and develop spiral shapes.

8 Now 5 billion years old, the Universe consists of vast clusters of galaxies arranged in threads with gigantic voids between them.

9 About 8 billion years after the big bang, the expansion of the Universe accelerates. Our Solar System forms about 9 billion years after the big bang.

10 The Universe is predicted to carry on expanding forever, becoming cold and dark everywhere.

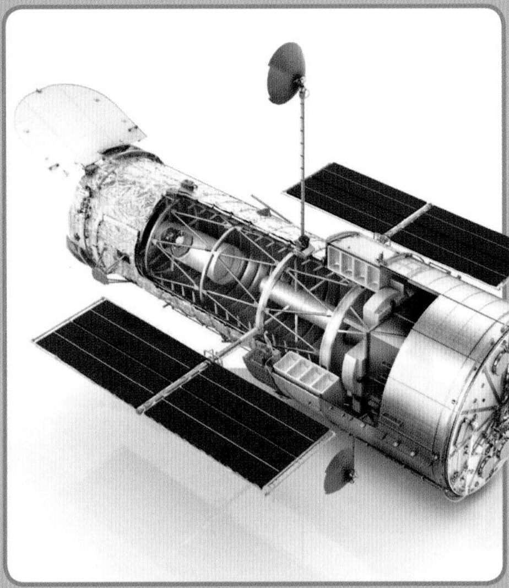

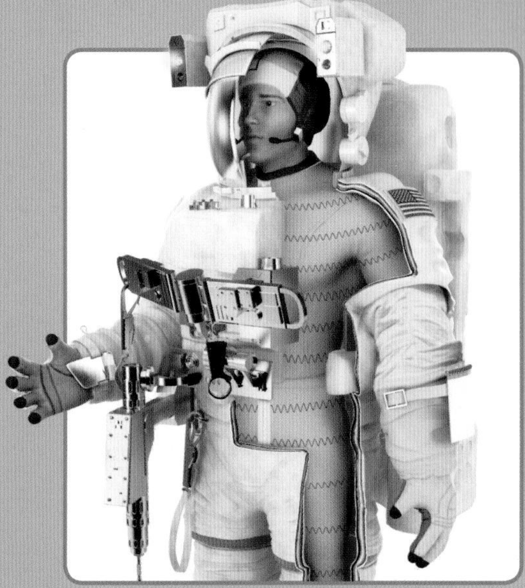

EXPLORING SPACE

People have studied the stars and planets for centuries, but it wasn't until 1957 that the first man-made object went into orbit, marking the beginning of the Space Age. Since then, thousands of rockets have been launched, hundreds of people have become astronauts, and 12 men have walked on the Moon.

Space exploration

Space starts a mere 100 km (60 miles) above our heads. It is a short journey away – less than ten minutes by rocket – but it is a dangerous and difficult one. We've been sending spacecraft to explore the Solar System for only 60 years or so, but we've been using telescopes to explore the skies for more than 400 years, and our curiosity about the cosmos goes back millennia. The more we discover, the more we want to explore.

SPACE TAXIS

The space shuttle is the only reusable spacecraft that has ever been to space. After taking off vertically like a rocket, it landed back on Earth like a plane. Five different shuttles operated between 1981 and the shuttle's retirement in 2011. Many of the missions were for building the International Space Station (ISS).

United States
Atlantis

The main part of the shuttle system was called the orbiter.

Booster rockets fell back to Earth after launch, to be collected and reused.

ATLANTIS LIFTING OFF FROM KENNEDY SPACE CENTER, USA

Soyuz
Russia's Soyuz craft have been operating since the 1960s and are now used to ferry astronauts to the ISS.

Orion
For future trips to the Moon, asteroids, and Mars, Orion will be launched by the USA's Space Launch System (SLS) rocket.

Dragon
Dragon became the first privately built craft to visit the International Space Station (ISS) when it docked in 2012.

Boeing CST-100
This future craft, designed to be reused ten times, will ferry crews of up to seven to the International Space Station.

LAUNCH SITES

There are about 30 launch sites on Earth, nine of which are shown below. The best place to launch from is near the equator, where a rocket gets an extra push from Earth's spin. The largest launch site is Baikonur, which sends spacecraft to the International Space Station.

YASNY, RUSSIA
VANDENBERG, USA
JIUQUAN, CHINA
BAIKONUR, KAZAKHSTAN
CAPE CANAVERAL/ KENNEDY SPACE CENTER, USA
TANEGASHIMA, JAPAN
XICHANG, CHINA
SRIHARIKOTA, INDIA
KOUROU, FRENCH GUIANA

LAUNCH VEHICLES

Rockets are built not to explore space themselves but to launch other smaller vehicles into orbit, such as satellites or planetary spacecraft. The smaller vehicle usually travels in the rocket's nose. Built to make the journey only once, rockets are destroyed as they fall back to Earth and burn up. The larger the rocket, the heavier and more complicated the cargo it can carry. Most rockets carrying spacecraft are launched by the USA, Russia, and Europe.

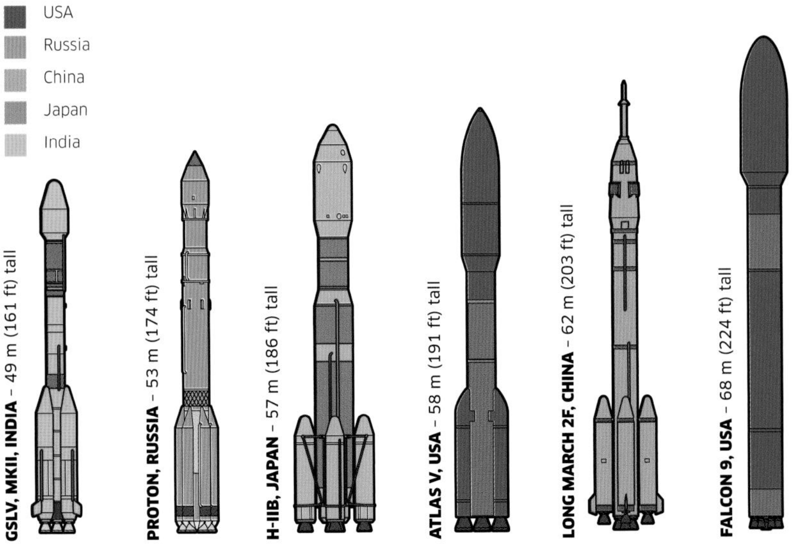

USA
Russia
China
Japan
India
GSLV, MKII, INDIA – 49 m (161 ft) tall
PROTON, RUSSIA – 53 m (174 ft) tall
H-IIB, JAPAN – 57 m (186 ft) tall
ATLAS V, USA – 58 m (191 ft) tall
LONG MARCH 2F, CHINA – 62 m (203 ft) tall
FALCON 9, USA – 68 m (224 ft) tall

SPACE EXPLORERS

Over 130 spacecraft have successfully left Earth to explore the Solar System. All have been robotic, except for the manned Apollo craft that went to the Moon. Powered by the Sun or by radioactive chemicals, robotic craft can work for years, peering down onto planets from orbit or landing to explore the surface. They send data and often spectacular images back to Earth.

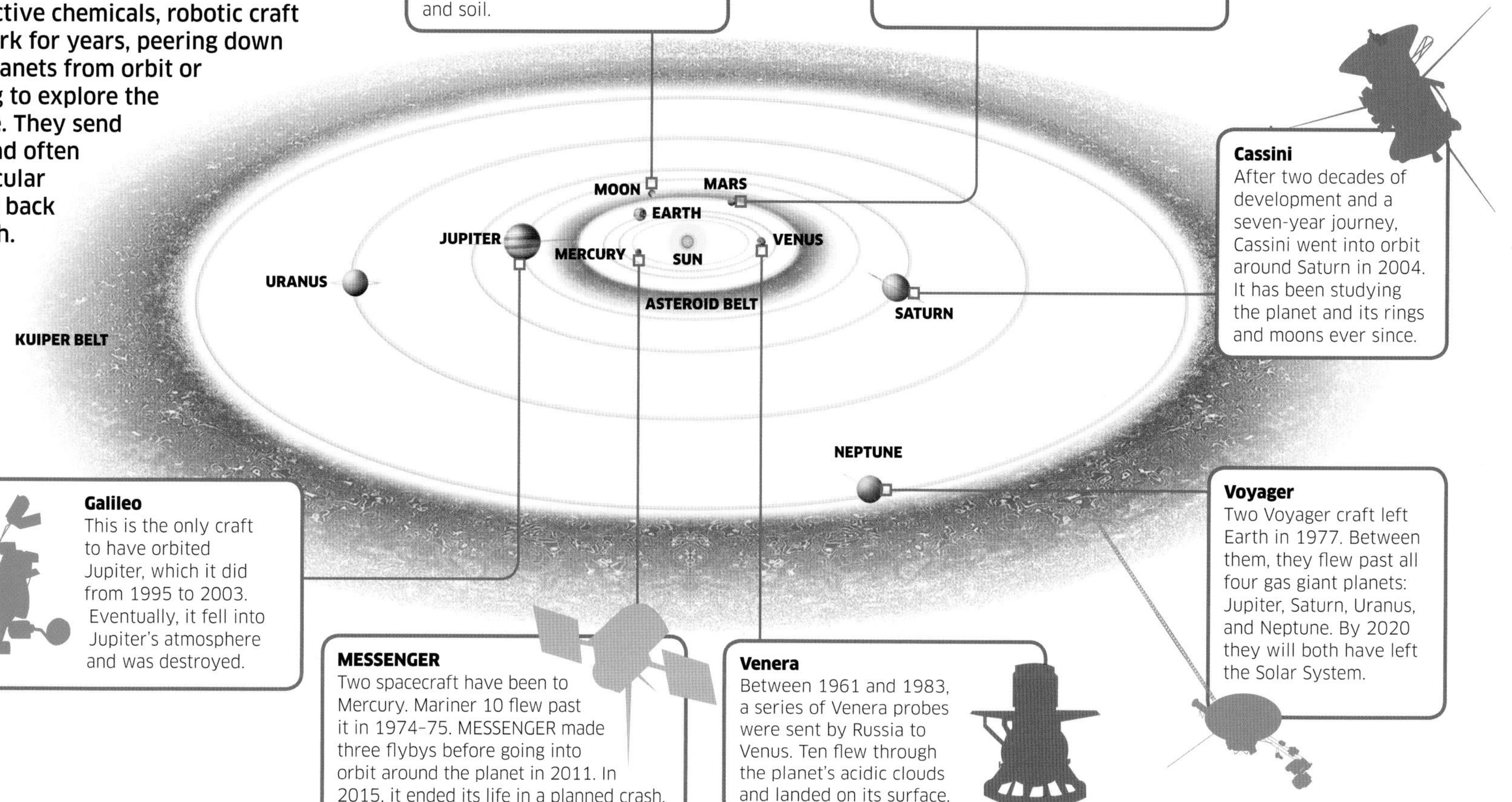
MOON
MARS
EARTH
JUPITER
MERCURY
SUN
VENUS
URANUS
ASTEROID BELT
SATURN
KUIPER BELT
NEPTUNE

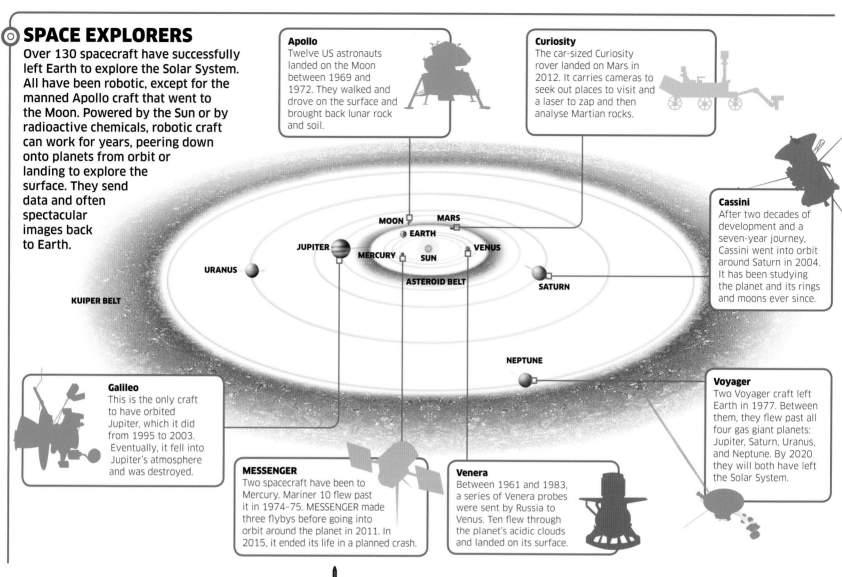

Apollo
Twelve US astronauts landed on the Moon between 1969 and 1972. They walked and drove on the surface and brought back lunar rock and soil.

Curiosity
The car-sized Curiosity rover landed on Mars in 2012. It carries cameras to seek out places to visit and a laser to zap and then analyse Martian rocks.

Cassini
After two decades of development and a seven-year journey, Cassini went into orbit around Saturn in 2004. It has been studying the planet and its rings and moons ever since.

Galileo
This is the only craft to have orbited Jupiter, which it did from 1995 to 2003. Eventually, it fell into Jupiter's atmosphere and was destroyed.

Voyager
Two Voyager craft left Earth in 1977. Between them, they flew past all four gas giant planets: Jupiter, Saturn, Uranus, and Neptune. By 2020 they will both have left the Solar System.

MESSENGER
Two spacecraft have been to Mercury. Mariner 10 flew past it in 1974–75. MESSENGER made three flybys before going into orbit around the planet in 2011. In 2015, it ended its life in a planned crash.

Venera
Between 1961 and 1983, a series of Venera probes were sent by Russia to Venus. Ten flew through the planet's acidic clouds and landed on its surface.

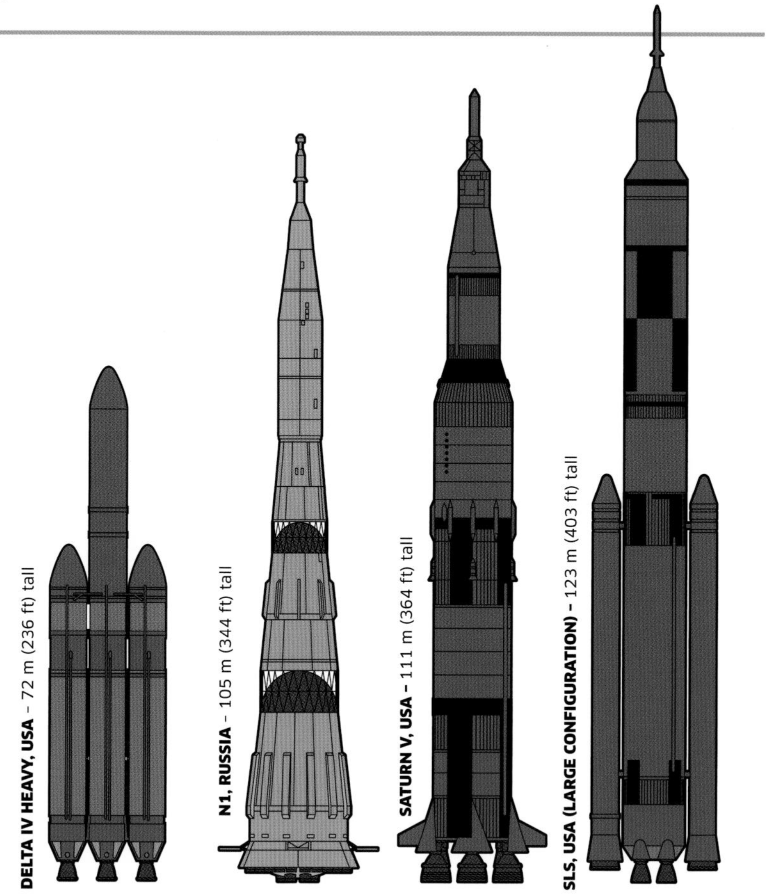
DELTA IV HEAVY, USA – 72 m (236 ft) tall
N1, RUSSIA – 105 m (344 ft) tall
SATURN V, USA – 111 m (364 ft) tall
SLS, USA (LARGE CONFIGURATION) – 123 m (403 ft) tall

SEEING THE INVISIBLE

As well as producing light that our eyes can see, objects in space produce other kinds of radiation that are invisible to us. All types of radiation travel as waves. Astronomers use special telescopes to capture waves of different lengths, from radio waves, which have long wavelengths, to gamma rays, which are very short.

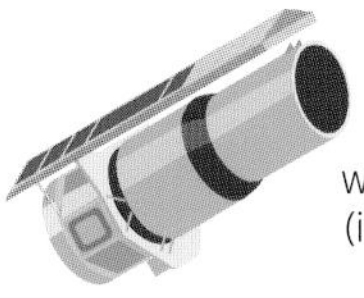

Infrared telescope
Star-forming nebulas are easy to see with infrared telescopes, which capture the heat (infrared rays) that the nebulas produce.

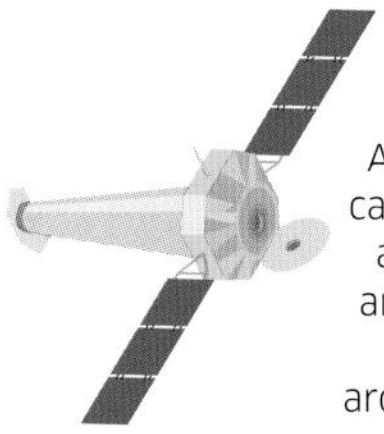

X-ray telescope
An X-ray telescope can see objects that are releasing huge amounts of energy, such as the area around a black hole.

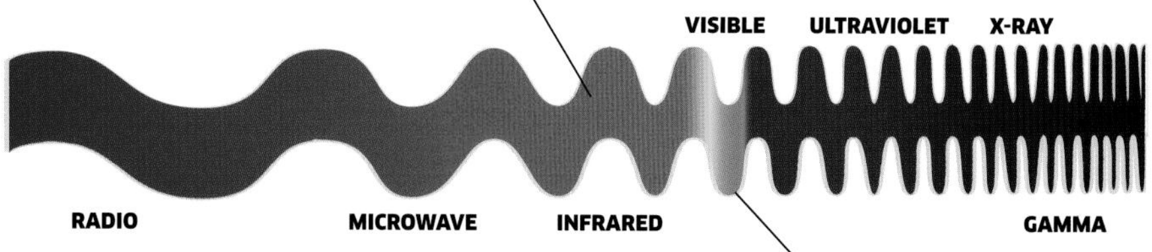
VISIBLE
ULTRAVIOLET
X-RAY
RADIO
MICROWAVE
INFRARED
GAMMA

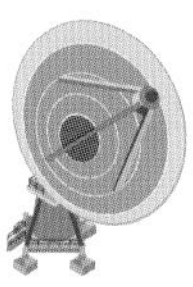

Radio telescope
Radio waves are the longest. They have revealed galaxies that would otherwise remain unseen.

Microwave telescope
Telescopes that capture microwaves allow us to see the afterglow of the big bang.

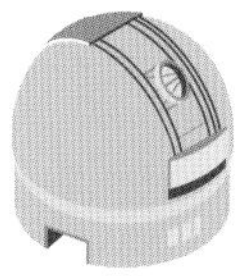

Optical telescope
Optical telescopes use visible light but magnify the image, letting us see further than the naked eye.

20,000 years ago
In Africa people mark pieces of bone with what may be the first record of Moon phases. Farmers follow the cycles of the Sun and Moon to plan their crops.

5,000–1,000 years ago
For ancient peoples, astronomy is part of religion. Many sacred monuments, such as Stonehenge in England, are built to align with the Sun or constellations.

Discovering space

The history of astronomy and the study of the heavens spans thousands of years, linking ancient religious sites with high-tech 21st-century observatories and spacecraft.

Since the dawn of history, people have looked into the night sky and wondered what the countless points of light were. It wasn't until fairly recently that we realized the stars are suns like ours, but incredibly far away. Just as early seafarers explored the world in search of new lands, modern explorers have sailed into space on voyages of discovery. Only a few people have visited another world, but scores of robotic probes have ventured to the planets on our behalf.

GODDARD WITH ROCKET

1926: Rocket science
American engineer Robert Goddard successfully fires the first liquid-fuelled rocket. It rises 12 m (41 ft) into the air before fizzling out. Over the next 15 years, he launches another 34 rockets, some of which soar to heights of more than 2 km (1.2 miles).

FRUIT FLY

1947: First animals in space
The US adapts captured German V2 rockets, used as deadly weapons in World War II, to send the first living creatures into space. The earliest astro-animals are fruit flies, followed by monkeys. The missions aim to see how animals' bodies respond to being in space.

SPACE SHUTTLE COLUMBIA

1976–77: Mars and beyond
Two American space robots, Viking 1 and 2, land on Mars, carry out soil tests, and send back colour images. In 1977, the space probe Voyager 2 blasts off, eventually flying by Jupiter, Saturn, Uranus, and Neptune.

1971–73: Living in space
Space stations allow astronauts to spend weeks in orbit. The first, in 1971, is the Russian Salyut 1. The US follows with its own, Skylab, in 1973.

SKYLAB SPACE STATION

1981: Shuttle launch
The 1980s see missions begin for the space shuttle, the first reusable manned orbiter. Shuttles will remain in service until 2011. In 1986 the Russians start to build the Mir space station.

1990: Hubble
The Hubble Space Telescope is placed in orbit. It reveals many distant wonders of space never seen before.

PILLAR AND JETS IN THE CARINA NEBULA

2009–12: Kepler Observatory
NASA launches the Kepler Observatory, which uses a special light-measuring device to search for planets orbiting distant stars.

ARTIST'S IMPRESSION OF KEPLER SPACECRAFT

STONEHENGE, ENGLAND

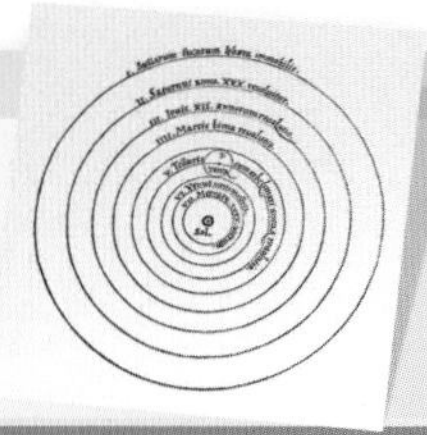

COPERNICUS'S DRAWING OF THE SOLAR SYSTEM

1540s: A shocking idea

Polish astronomer Nicolaus Copernicus writes a book about a shocking new idea. He suggests that the Sun, not Earth, is at the centre of the Solar System.

ISAAC NEWTON'S TELESCOPE

1600s: Telescopes

Italian astronomer Galileo Galilei greatly improves telescope design, and the Solar System can now be seen clearly. English scientist Isaac Newton explains how gravity holds the planets in orbit around the Sun.

THE WAR OF THE WORLDS
H.G. WELLS

1890s: Science fiction

The first science fiction novels hit the market. Books like *The War of the Worlds* and *The Time Machine*, both written by H.G. Wells, arouse public interest in space exploration and also inspire serious science projects.

1957: Sputnik

In Russia rocket scientists achieve two firsts this year. They send up the first artificial satellite, Sputnik 1, and a month later they launch Sputnik 2, which carries Laika, the first dog to go into orbit. As planned, Laika perishes at the end of the mission.

80
MONGOLIA·МОНГОЛ ШУУДАН

1961: First person in space

Russian cosmonaut Yuri Gagarin becomes the first person in space, orbiting Earth in a flight lasting just over 100 minutes. Later in the decade, the Russians achieve the first human spacewalk (1965) and the first soft landing on the Moon by a spacecraft (1966).

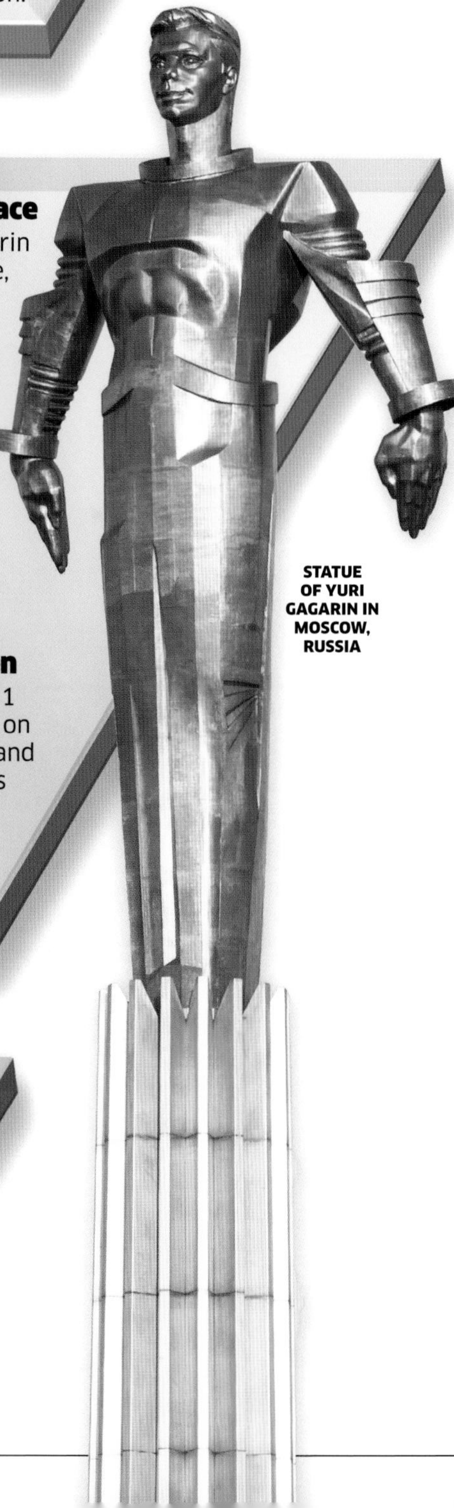

STATUE OF YURI GAGARIN IN MOSCOW, RUSSIA

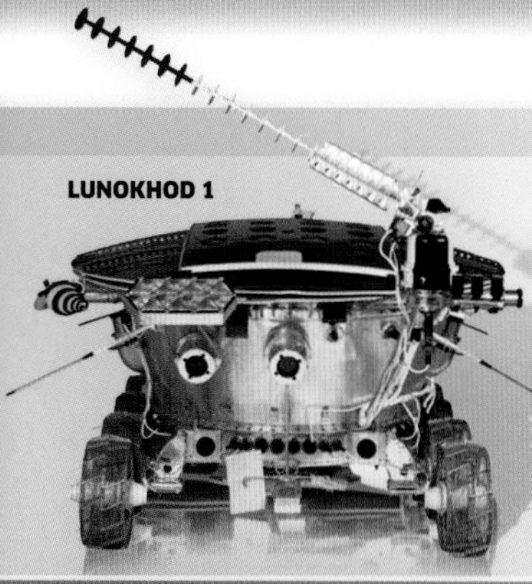

LUNOKHOD 1

1970: First rover

Russians launch the first lunar roving vehicle: Lunokhod 1, a remote-control, eight-wheeled buggy. It soft lands on the Moon and operates for 11 days, sending back pictures and taking soil samples.

1969: Men on the Moon

The United States' Apollo 11 craft lands the first people on the Moon: Neil Armstrong and Buzz Aldrin. The astronauts stay for nearly 24 hours, collecting Moon rocks and taking photographs of the lunar surface.

COMET 67P

2014: Comet landing

A robotic device detaches from the Rosetta space probe and makes the first soft landing on a comet, called 67P. It returns images and information about the comet's water content.

Into the future

Over the coming decades, a focus of space research will be the continuing hunt for distant planets that might harbour life. A manned mission to Mars by 2050 may be feasible.

Telescopes

The first telescopes were little more than hand-held wooden tubes, but they allowed astronomers to discover mountains on the Moon and moons around Jupiter. Today's giant telescopes let us see billions of light years into the far reaches of space.

Like eyes, telescopes collect light and focus it to create an image. Unlike our eyes, however, telescopes can train their sights on tiny targets and can add together the light they receive over a long period. The bigger a telescope is, the more light it can collect and the sharper the image. With a large telescope, we can zoom in on distant galaxies or volcanoes on Mars. The first telescopes used glass lenses, but big lenses bend under their own weight, so astronomers switched to mirrors to make telescopes bigger. In the largest telescopes, dozens of segments are arranged together to form one giant, curved mirror. Earth's atmosphere blurs our view of space, so large professional telescopes are built on mountains where the air is dry and still, or launched into space.

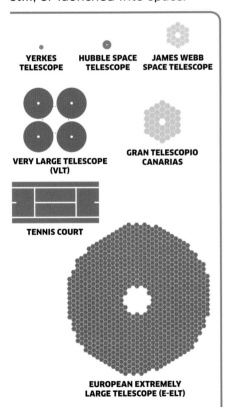

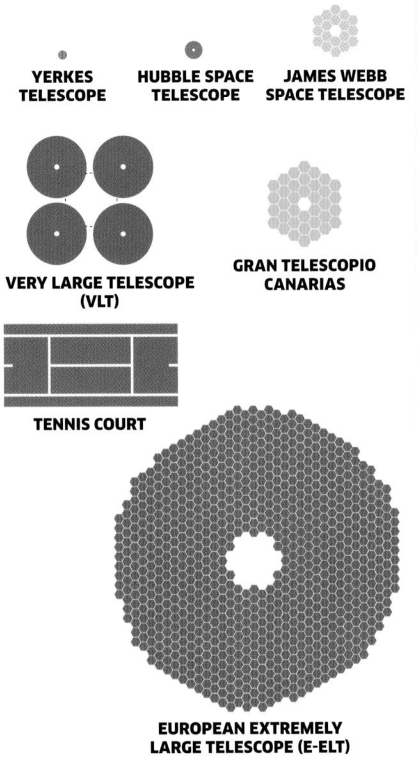
YERKES TELESCOPE
HUBBLE SPACE TELESCOPE
JAMES WEBB SPACE TELESCOPE
VERY LARGE TELESCOPE (VLT)
GRAN TELESCOPIO CANARIAS
TENNIS COURT
EUROPEAN EXTREMELY LARGE TELESCOPE (E-ELT)

Collecting light

A key part of a telescope is the mirror or lens that collects light. The world's largest telescope lens (in the Yerkes telescope, USA) is only 1 m (40 in) wide. Mirrors made of hexagonal segments in a honeycomb pattern can be far bigger. The E-ELT mirror will be nearly four times larger in area than a tennis court.

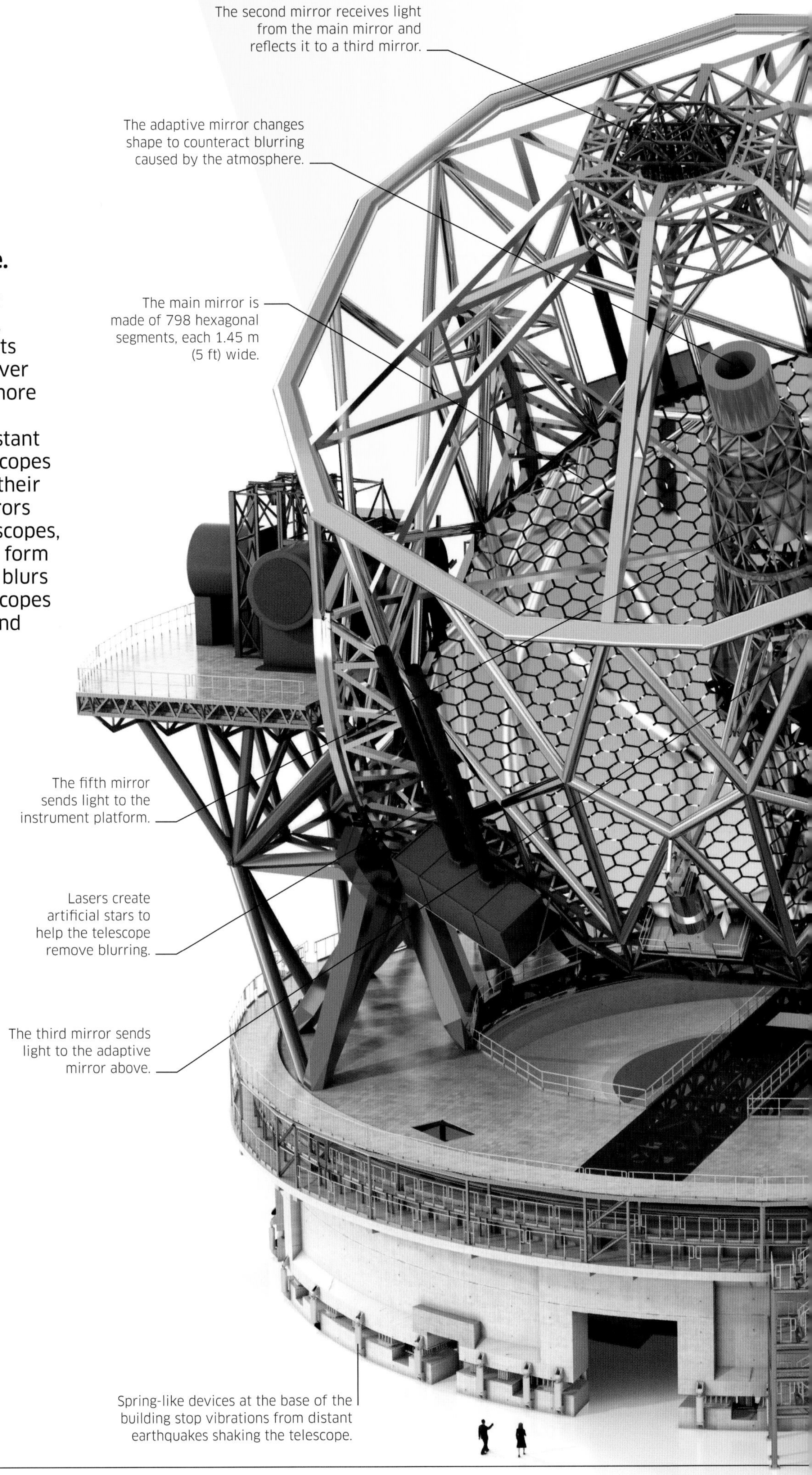
The second mirror receives light from the main mirror and reflects it to a third mirror.
The adaptive mirror changes shape to counteract blurring caused by the atmosphere.
The main mirror is made of 798 hexagonal segments, each 1.45 m (5 ft) wide.
The fifth mirror sends light to the instrument platform.
Lasers create artificial stars to help the telescope remove blurring.
The third mirror sends light to the adaptive mirror above.
Spring-like devices at the base of the building stop vibrations from distant earthquakes shaking the telescope.

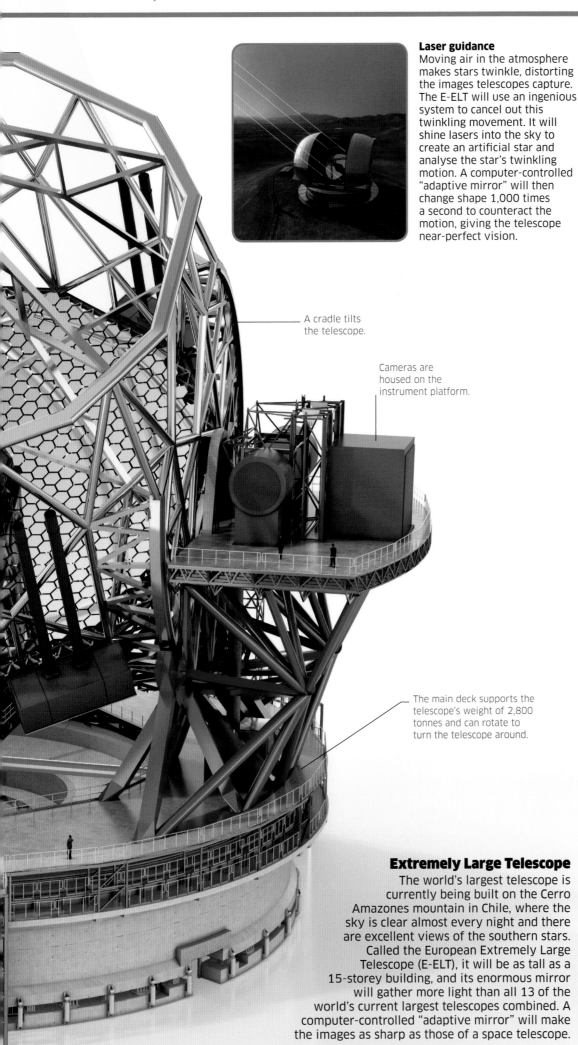

A cradle tilts the telescope.
Cameras are housed on the instrument platform.
The main deck supports the telescope's weight of 2,800 tonnes and can rotate to turn the telescope around.

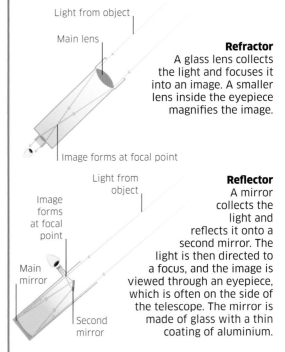

Laser guidance
Moving air in the atmosphere makes stars twinkle, distorting the images telescopes capture. The E-ELT will use an ingenious system to cancel out this twinkling movement. It will shine lasers into the sky to create an artificial star and analyse the star's twinkling motion. A computer-controlled "adaptive mirror" will then change shape 1,000 times a second to counteract the motion, giving the telescope near-perfect vision.

Extremely Large Telescope

The world's largest telescope is currently being built on the Cerro Amazones mountain in Chile, where the sky is clear almost every night and there are excellent views of the southern stars. Called the European Extremely Large Telescope (E-ELT), it will be as tall as a 15-storey building, and its enormous mirror will gather more light than all 13 of the world's current largest telescopes combined. A computer-controlled "adaptive mirror" will make the images as sharp as those of a space telescope.

How simple telescopes work

A telescope uses a lens or a mirror to collect light from distant objects and focus it to create an image. In simple telescopes, the image is viewed through an eyepiece lens that magnifies the image. Telescopes that use lenses to capture light are called refractors. Those that use mirrors are called reflectors.

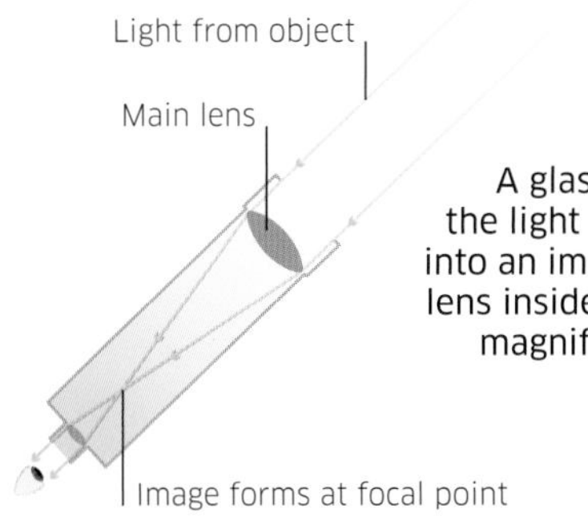
Light from object
Main lens
Image forms at focal point

Refractor
A glass lens collects the light and focuses it into an image. A smaller lens inside the eyepiece magnifies the image.

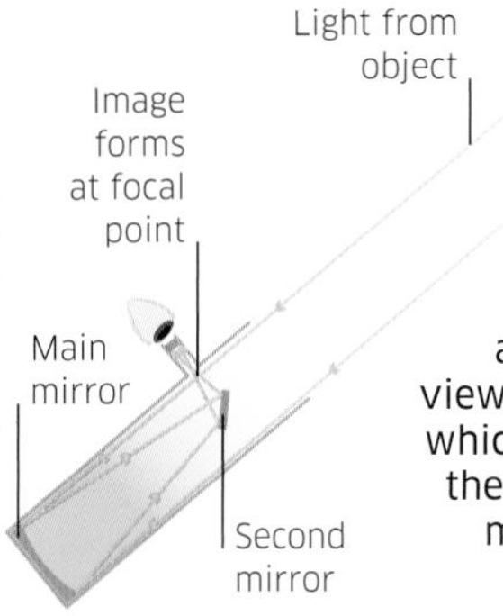
Light from object
Image forms at focal point
Main mirror
Second mirror

Reflector
A mirror collects the light and reflects it onto a second mirror. The light is then directed to a focus, and the image is viewed through an eyepiece, which is often on the side of the telescope. The mirror is made of glass with a thin coating of aluminium.

In a different light

Telescopes collect wavelengths of energy other than light. Each wavelength reveals different details in an object. A typical galaxy, such as the Andromeda Galaxy below, gives off energy in many wavelengths. X-rays, for instance, come from very hot areas, and radio waves come from colder areas.

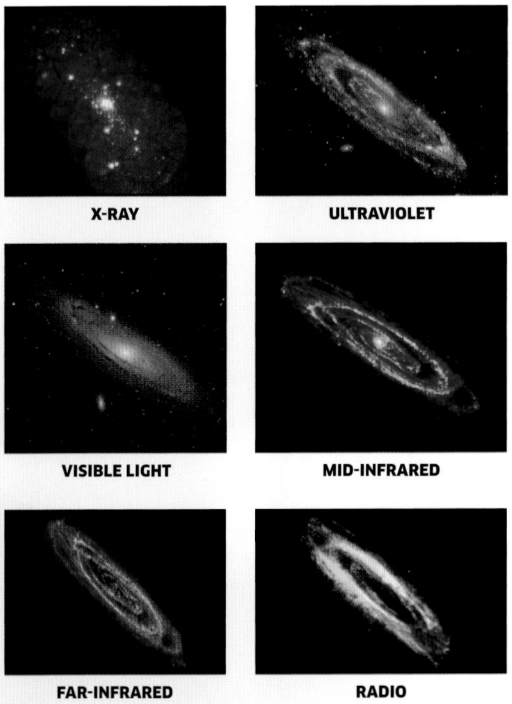
X-RAY
ULTRAVIOLET
VISIBLE LIGHT
MID-INFRARED
FAR-INFRARED
RADIO

13.2 m (43.5 ft) – the length of Hubble, about the size of a **tourist coach.**

40 million – the approximate **number of stars** Gaia looks at every day.

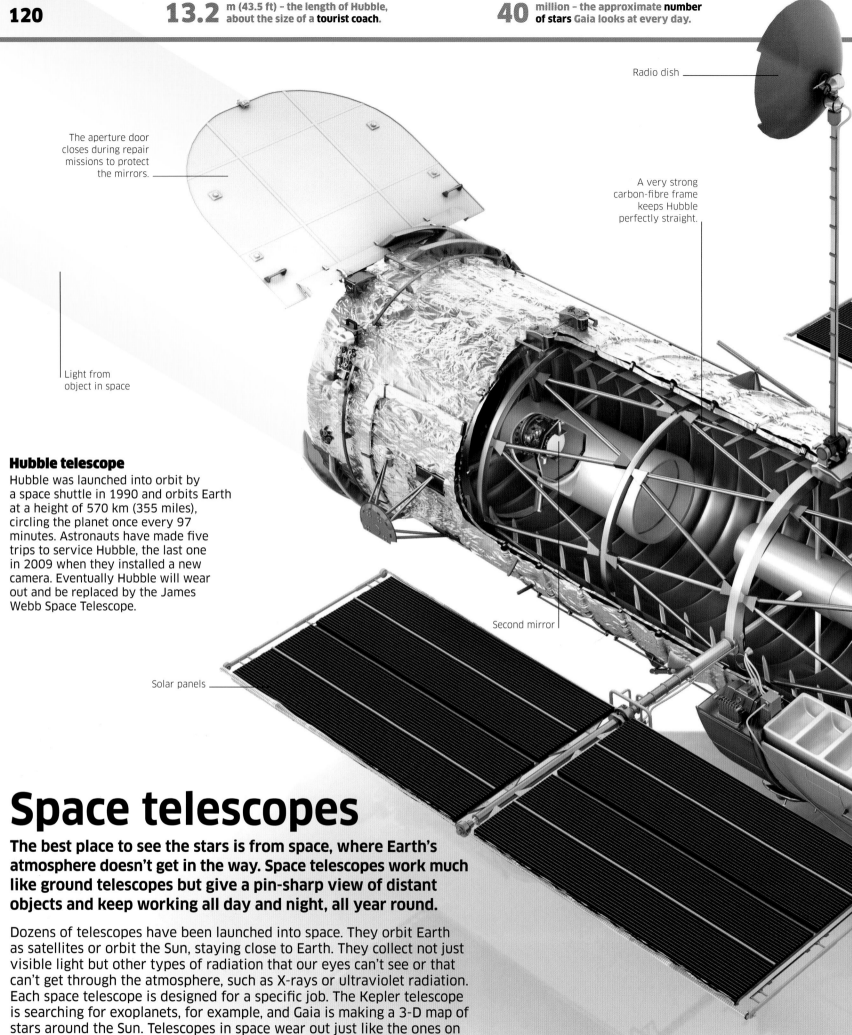

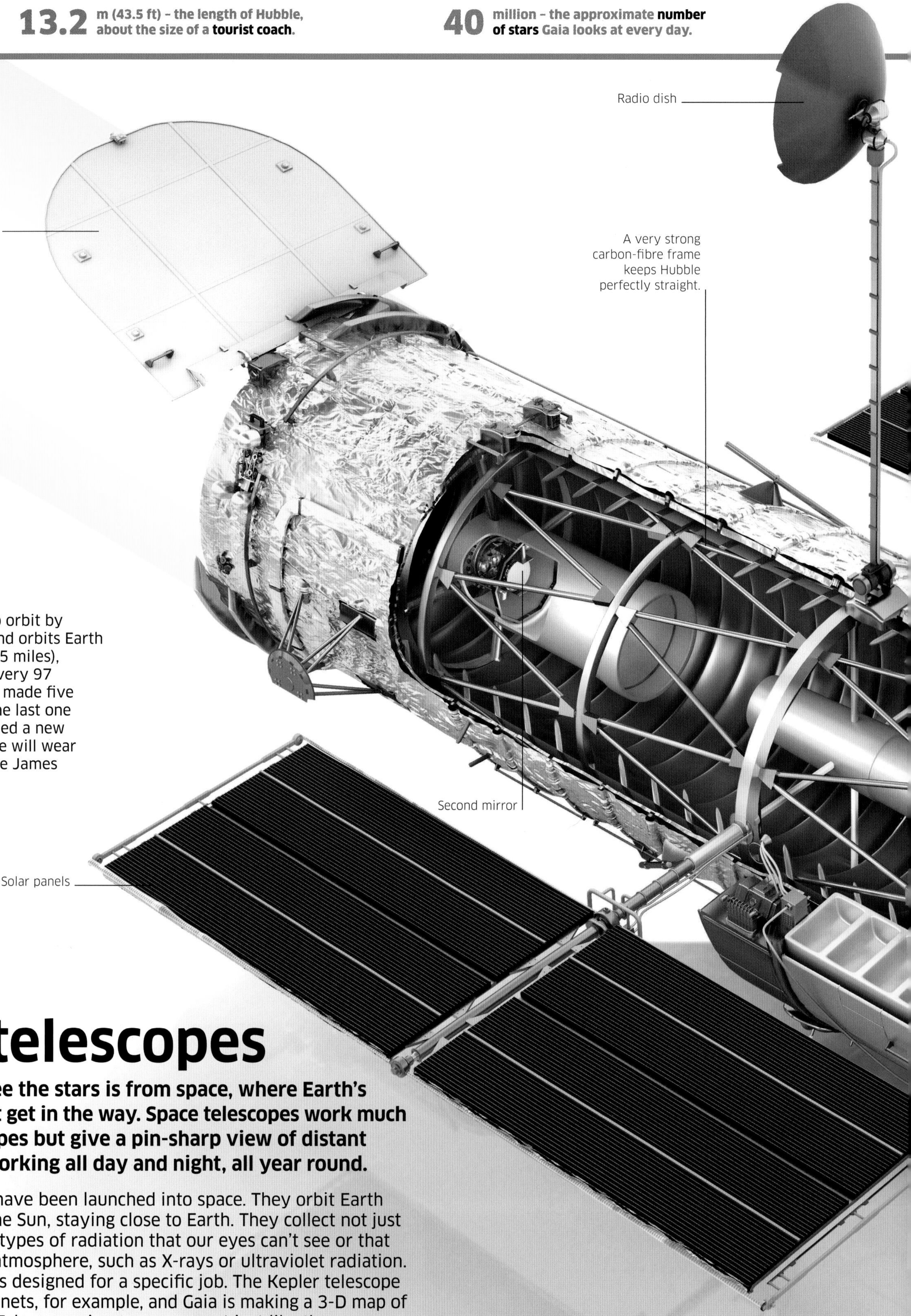
Radio dish
The aperture door closes during repair missions to protect the mirrors.
A very strong carbon-fibre frame keeps Hubble perfectly straight.
Light from object in space
Second mirror
Solar panels

Hubble telescope

Hubble was launched into orbit by a space shuttle in 1990 and orbits Earth at a height of 570 km (355 miles), circling the planet once every 97 minutes. Astronauts have made five trips to service Hubble, the last one in 2009 when they installed a new camera. Eventually Hubble will wear out and be replaced by the James Webb Space Telescope.

Space telescopes

The best place to see the stars is from space, where Earth's atmosphere doesn't get in the way. Space telescopes work much like ground telescopes but give a pin-sharp view of distant objects and keep working all day and night, all year round.

Dozens of telescopes have been launched into space. They orbit Earth as satellites or orbit the Sun, staying close to Earth. They collect not just visible light but other types of radiation that our eyes can't see or that can't get through the atmosphere, such as X-rays or ultraviolet radiation. Each space telescope is designed for a specific job. The Kepler telescope is searching for exoplanets, for example, and Gaia is making a 3-D map of stars around the Sun. Telescopes in space wear out just like the ones on Earth, but the repair man can't visit if things go wrong. Only the Hubble Space Telescope was designed to be serviced in space by astronauts.

Main mirror
The 2.4 m (7.87 ft) wide main mirror in the Hubble Space Telescope collects light and reflects it onto a second mirror. The second mirror reflects the beam back through a hole in the middle of the main mirror to a suite of cameras and scientific instruments. Hubble's main mirror is almost perfectly smooth. If it were scaled up to the size of Earth, the biggest bump on its surface would be just 15 cm (6 in) high.

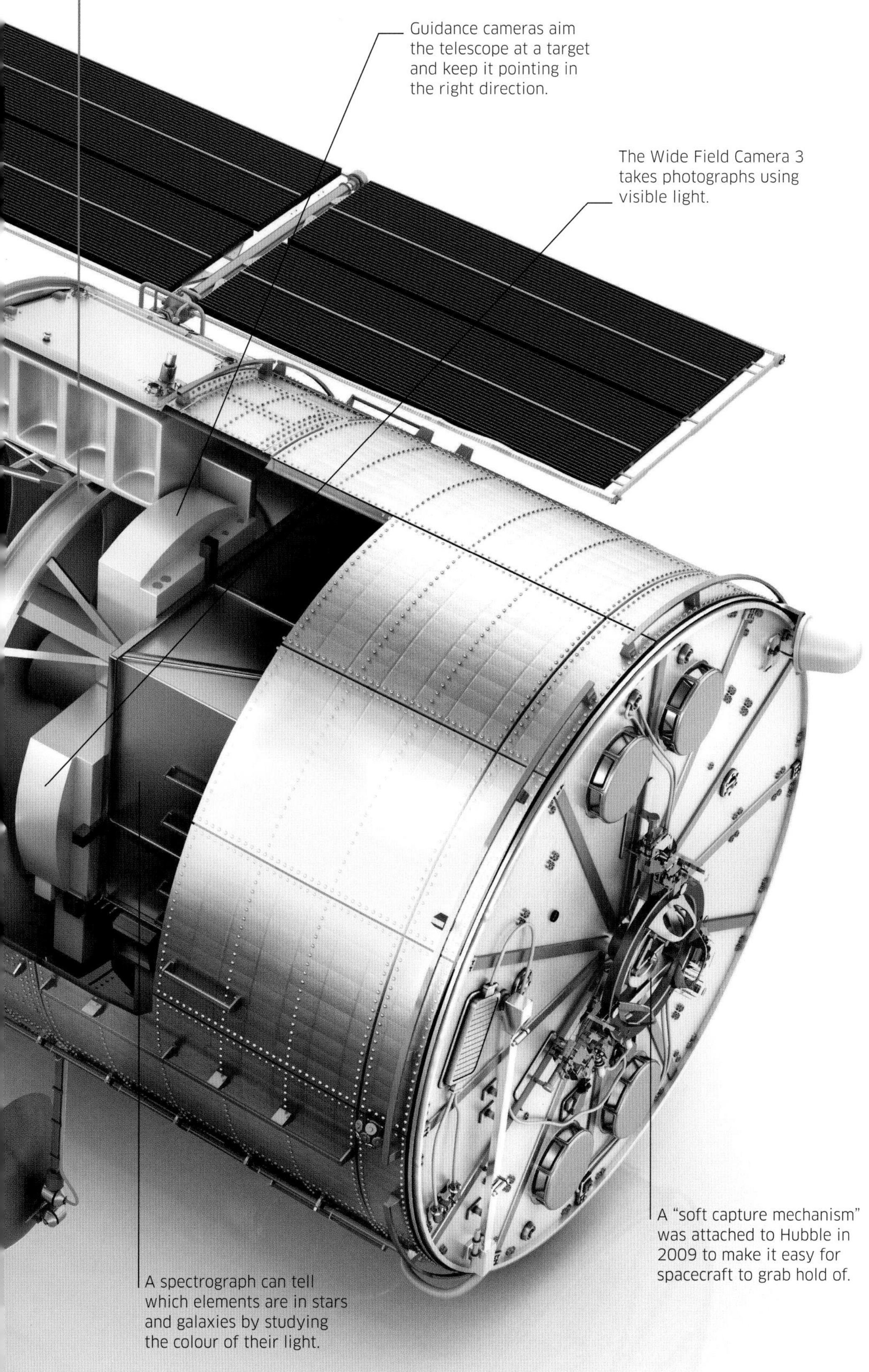
Guidance cameras aim the telescope at a target and keep it pointing in the right direction.
The Wide Field Camera 3 takes photographs using visible light.
A "soft capture mechanism" was attached to Hubble in 2009 to make it easy for spacecraft to grab hold of.
A spectrograph can tell which elements are in stars and galaxies by studying the colour of their light.

Looking deep

When we look into space we are looking back in time. Since its launch, Hubble has let us see deeper and deeper into space, revealing young galaxies in the early Universe. The James Webb Space Telescope will look even deeper to see newborn galaxies.

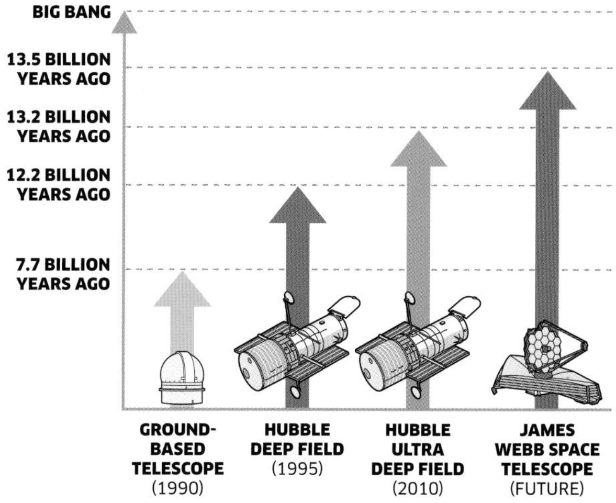
BIG BANG
13.5 BILLION YEARS AGO
13.2 BILLION YEARS AGO
12.2 BILLION YEARS AGO
7.7 BILLION YEARS AGO
GROUND-BASED TELESCOPE (1990)
HUBBLE DEEP FIELD (1995)
HUBBLE ULTRA DEEP FIELD (2010)
JAMES WEBB SPACE TELESCOPE (FUTURE)

Hubble hits

Astronomers have processed the data from Hubble to create many beautiful images, including galaxies, star-birth regions such as the Eagle Nebula, and dying stars such as the Cat's Eye Nebula.

SOMBRERO GALAXY

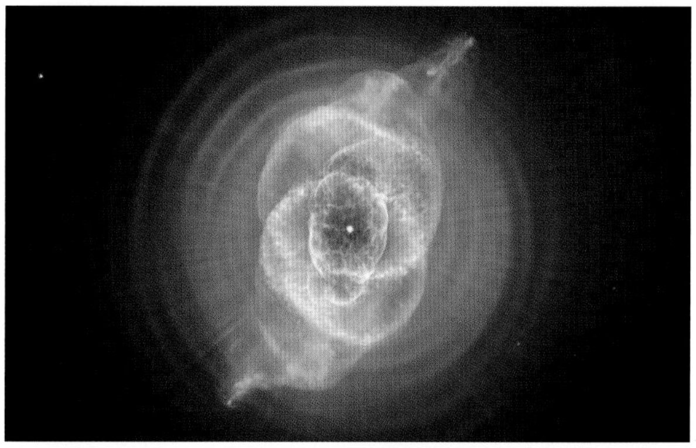

CAT'S EYE NEBULA

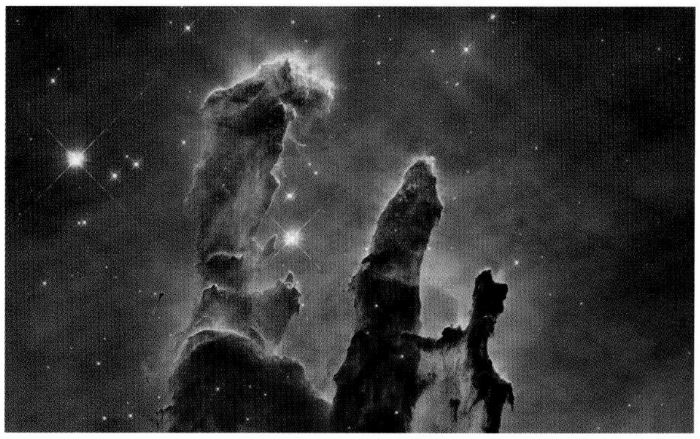

EAGLE NEBULA

Rockets

It takes a staggering amount of energy to break free from Earth's gravitational pull and fly into space. The only vehicles capable of doing this are rockets, which harness the explosive power of burning fuel to lift cargo such as satellites and spacecraft into orbit. Most of a rocket's weight is fuel, and nearly all of it is consumed in the first few minutes, burning at a rate of up to 15 tonnes every second.

People used rockets as weapons for hundreds of years before they became safe and powerful enough to reach space. Since the first spaceflight in 1944, rockets have got larger and more complicated. A modern rocket is really several rockets in one, with separate "stages" stacked cleverly together. When the lowest stage runs out of fuel, it drops off, making the remaining vehicle lighter. The stage above then ignites. The cargo is usually in the uppermost stage, under the rocket's nose. Most rockets are built to fly to space only once and are destroyed as their parts fall back to Earth.

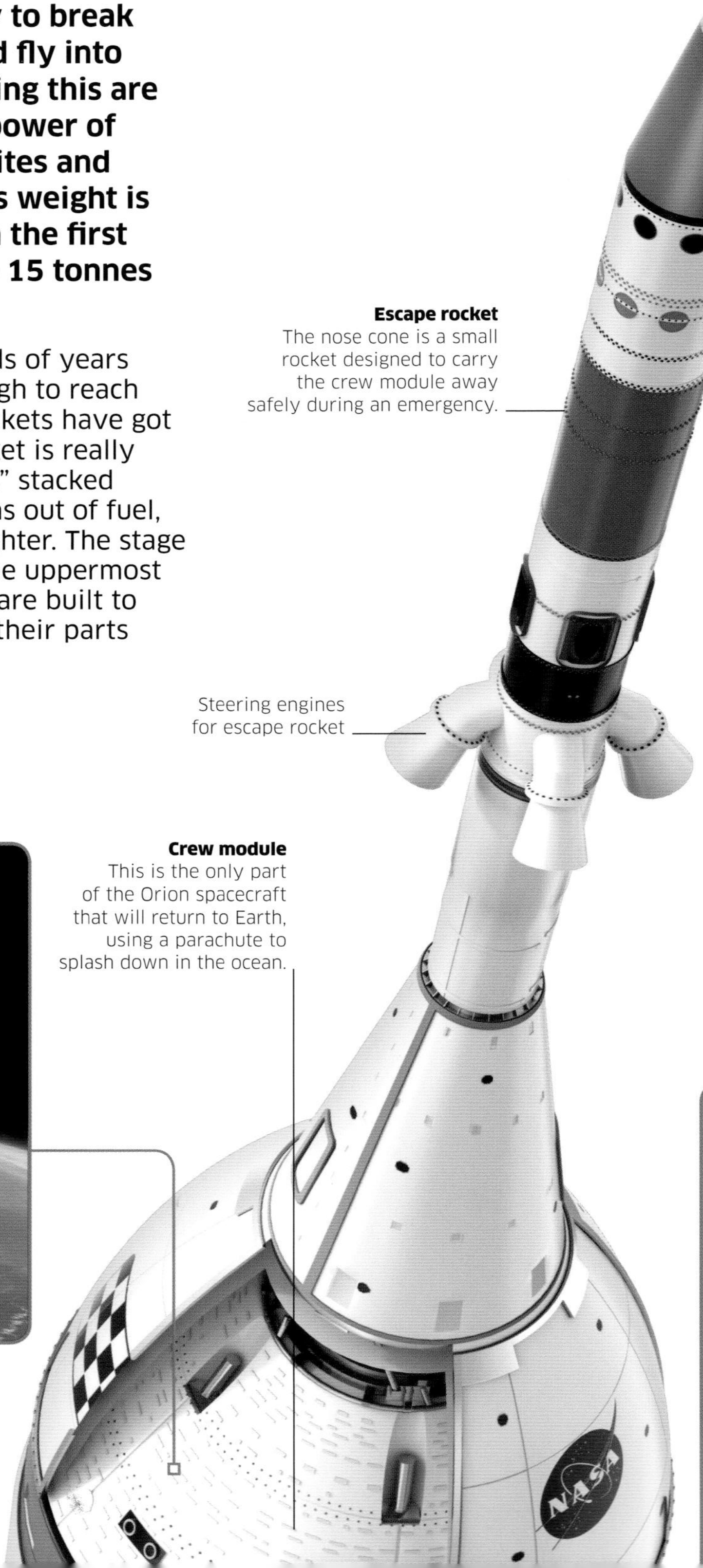
NASA

Escape rocket
The nose cone is a small rocket designed to carry the crew module away safely during an emergency.

Steering engines for escape rocket

Crew module
This is the only part of the Orion spacecraft that will return to Earth, using a parachute to splash down in the ocean.

Onwards to Mars
Powered by its own rocket engine, the Orion spacecraft will be able to carry astronauts further into space than ever before. The crew will live inside the conical section at the front, which is based on the command module used by astronauts during the Apollo Moon missions.

Launch pad
The SLS's space journey will start at the Kennedy Space Center in Florida, USA. Launch pad 39B was once used by the Apollo Moon missions and the Space Shuttle.

Space Launch System

Standing taller than the Statue of Liberty, the Space Launch System (SLS) is a giant new rocket being built by NASA for spaceflights in the 2020s. When complete, it could launch manned spacecraft to the Moon, near-Earth asteroids, and Mars. The configuration shown here has one main rocket stage and two booster rockets on the side. Inside the rocket's nose is the Orion spacecraft, with its own rocket engine. Taller configurations with an extra stage will allow the SLS to launch larger cargoes.

How rockets work

Most of the body of a rocket is taken up by huge tanks containing fuel and an oxidizer (a chemical needed to make fuel burn). Once ignited, these two chemicals react explosively to make hot gases, which rush out of the rear nozzle. The rush of hot gases creates the force of thrust that pushes the rocket forwards.

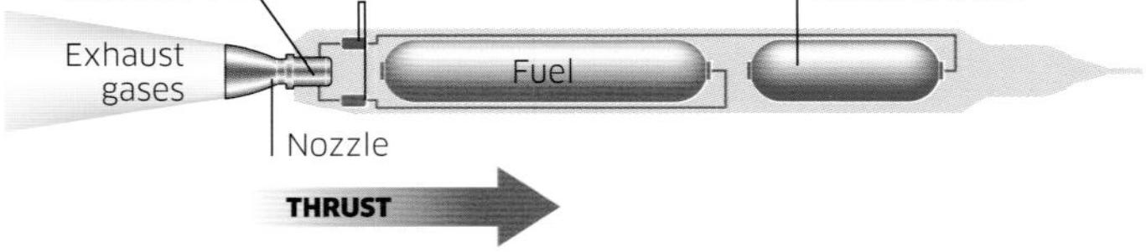
Combustion chamber
Pumps
Liquid oxygen
Exhaust gases
Fuel
Nozzle
THRUST

UNITED STATES

Service module
The central section of the Orion spacecraft carries fuel and other supplies.

Spacecraft engine
Orion's engine will be able to propel the craft to Mars in three to four months.

Boosters
Two booster rockets provide most of the thrust needed for liftoff. They produce enough power in two minutes to supply 92,000 homes for a whole day.

Cargo weight

The heavier a rocket's cargo, the more fuel is needed to lift it, which adds further to the weight. The Saturn V rocket used for the Apollo Moon missions carried a cargo as heavy as 24 elephants, but the whole rocket weighed as much as 400 elephants.

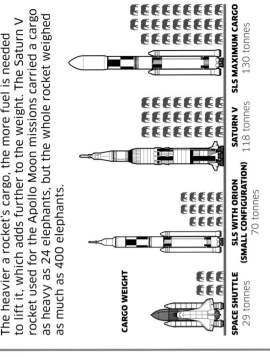

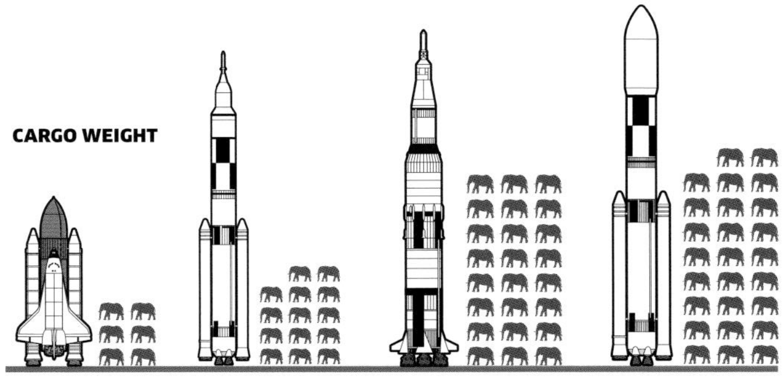
CARGO WEIGHT
SPACE SHUTTLE
29 tonnes
SLS WITH ORION
(SMALL CONFIGURATION)
70 tonnes
SATURN V
118 tonnes
SLS MAXIMUM CARGO
130 tonnes

Thrust

The force that pushes a rocket is called thrust. To reach low Earth orbit, a rocket must generate enough thrust to reach a speed of 29,000 kph (18,000 mph) – nine times faster than a bullet.

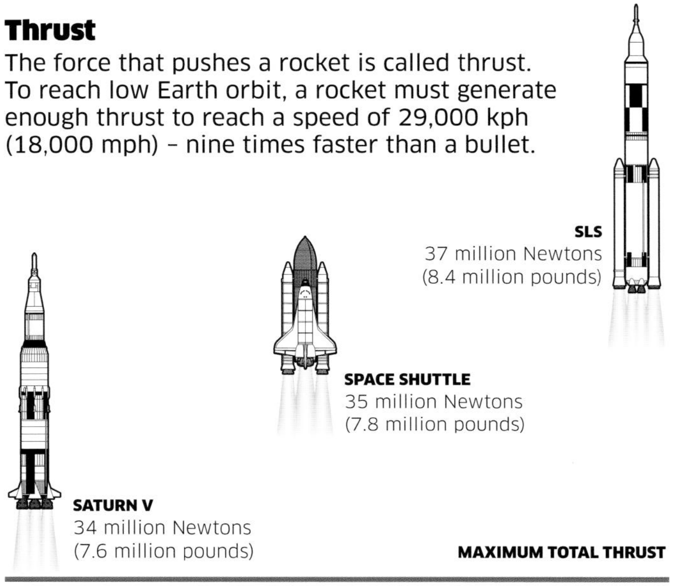
SLS
37 million Newtons
(8.4 million pounds)
SPACE SHUTTLE
35 million Newtons
(7.8 million pounds)
SATURN V
34 million Newtons
(7.6 million pounds)
MAXIMUM TOTAL THRUST

Main engines
At the base of the rocket are four RS-25 engines – the same kind of engine that was used to power space shuttles. Working together, the SLS's main engines and boosters produce as much power as 13,400 train engines.

6 **The number of manned spaceflights made in the Vostok spacecraft.**

First person in space

In 1961 Russian pilot Yuri Gagarin became the first person in space when he made a daredevil two-hour trip around Earth in a tiny spacecraft called Vostok 1. Since then, more than 500 people have been to space.

The race to put the first person in space began in October 1957 when Russia's unmanned Sputnik 1 became the first spacecraft to orbit the planet. Sputnik 2 followed later that year, carrying a dog called Laika – a stray from the streets of Moscow. The craft was not designed to return to Earth, so Laika died during the mission. About three years later, Yuri Gagarin made his historic trip, and within six weeks of his return the US pledged to put men on the Moon. The first space travellers were jet pilots who were used to dangerous, physically gruelling flights and had been trained to use ejector seats and parachutes. But even for experienced pilots, space travel was deadly. Of the 100 or so unmanned missions before Gagarin's flight, half ended in failure. And prior to Vostok 1, no one was certain that a human could travel to space and return alive to Earth.

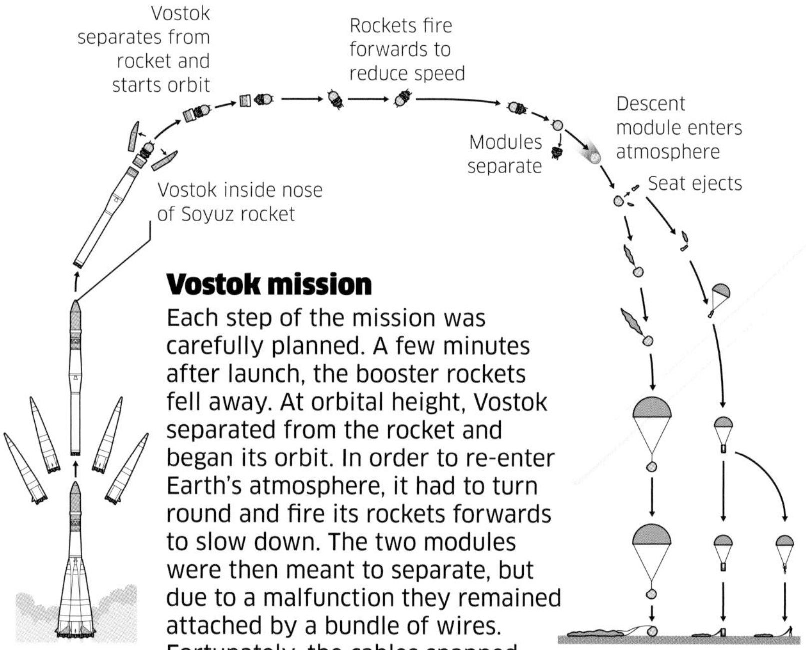
Vostok separates from rocket and starts orbit
Rockets fire forwards to reduce speed
Descent module enters atmosphere
Modules separate
Seat ejects
Vostok inside nose of Soyuz rocket
Gagarin separates from seat and lands

Vostok mission

Each step of the mission was carefully planned. A few minutes after launch, the booster rockets fell away. At orbital height, Vostok separated from the rocket and began its orbit. In order to re-enter Earth's atmosphere, it had to turn round and fire its rockets forwards to slow down. The two modules were then meant to separate, but due to a malfunction they remained attached by a bundle of wires. Fortunately, the cables snapped as the craft began re-entry, which caused it to shake violently.

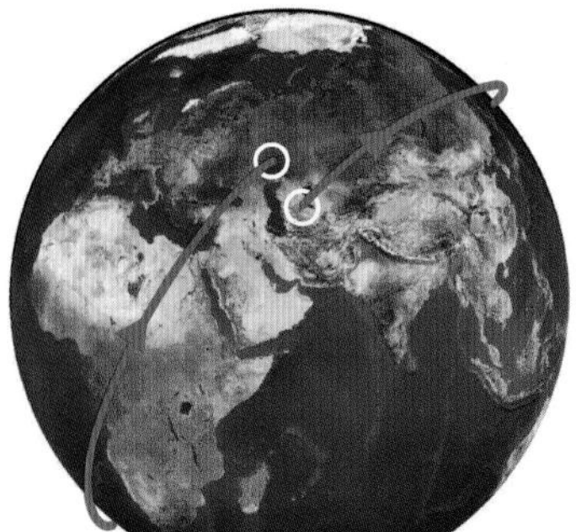

Around the world
Gagarin took off from the Baikonur Cosmodrome (space centre) in Kazakhstan and travelled east around the planet, taking 108 minutes to complete a single orbit. Vostok's modules separated when he was over Africa, and Gagarin landed shortly afterwards in a grassy field near the Russian town of Engels.

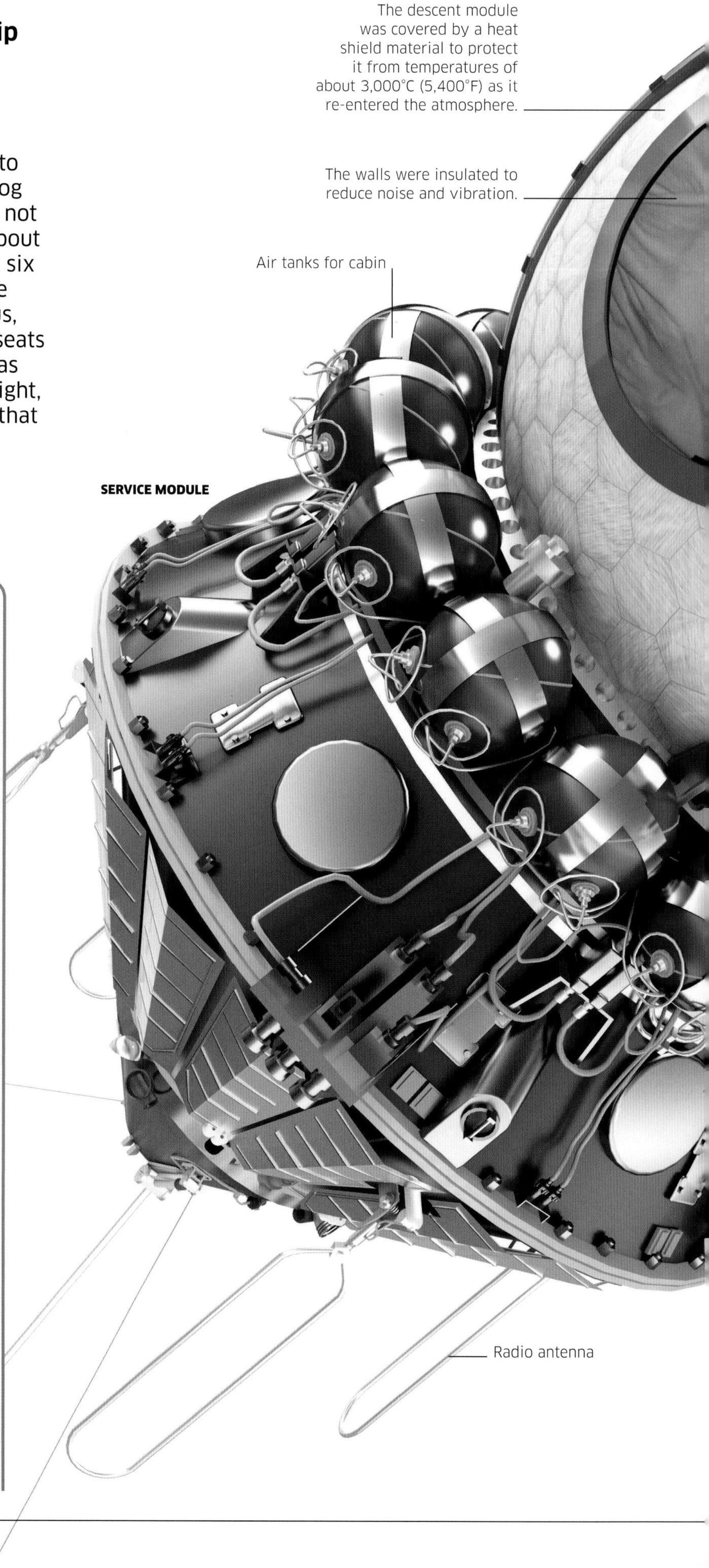
The descent module was covered by a heat shield material to protect it from temperatures of about 3,000°C (5,400°F) as it re-entered the atmosphere.
The walls were insulated to reduce noise and vibration.
Air tanks for cabin
SERVICE MODULE
Radio antenna

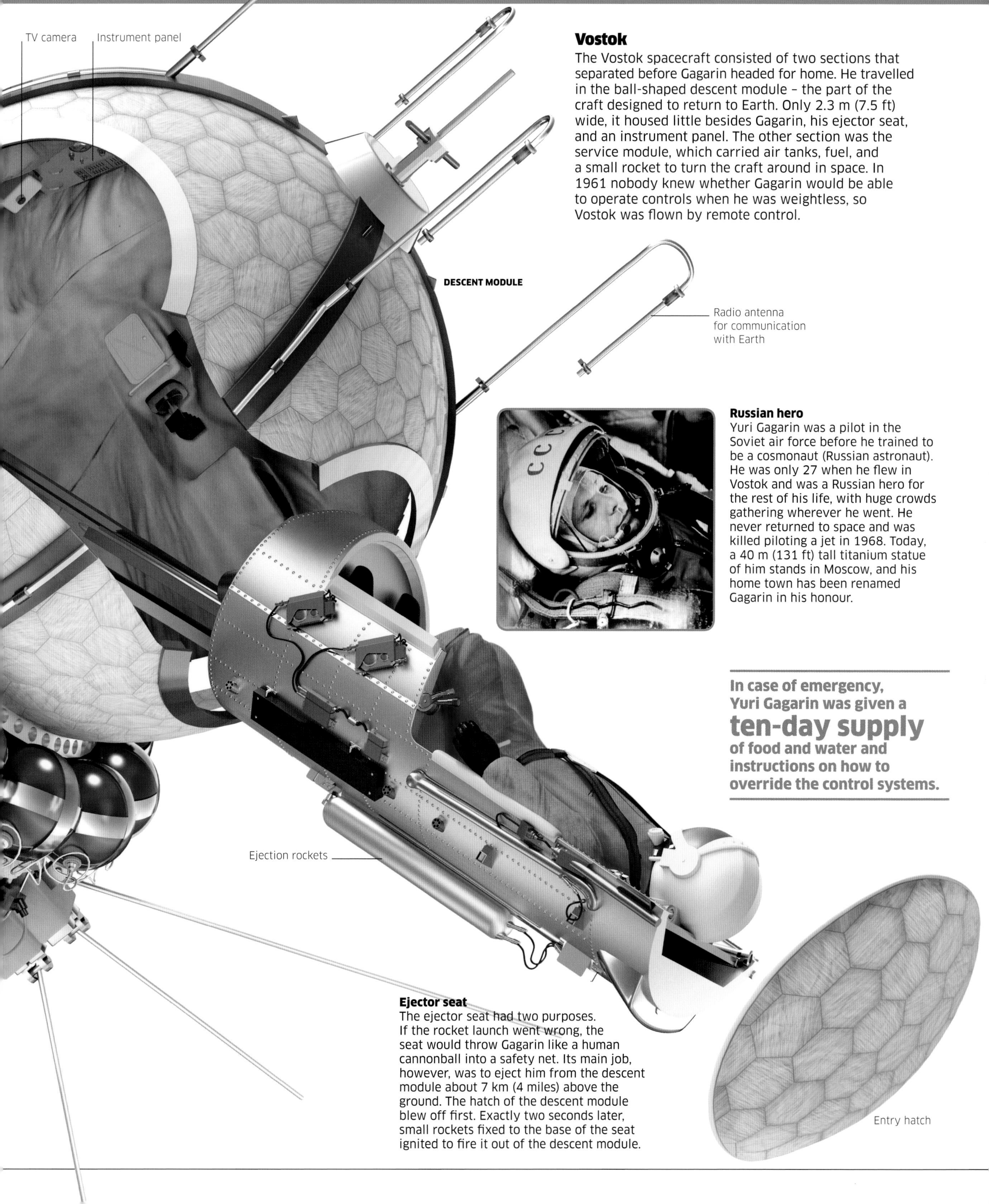
TV camera
Instrument panel
DESCENT MODULE
Radio antenna for communication with Earth
Ejection rockets
Entry hatch

Vostok

The Vostok spacecraft consisted of two sections that separated before Gagarin headed for home. He travelled in the ball-shaped descent module – the part of the craft designed to return to Earth. Only 2.3 m (7.5 ft) wide, it housed little besides Gagarin, his ejector seat, and an instrument panel. The other section was the service module, which carried air tanks, fuel, and a small rocket to turn the craft around in space. In 1961 nobody knew whether Gagarin would be able to operate controls when he was weightless, so Vostok was flown by remote control.

Russian hero
Yuri Gagarin was a pilot in the Soviet air force before he trained to be a cosmonaut (Russian astronaut). He was only 27 when he flew in Vostok and was a Russian hero for the rest of his life, with huge crowds gathering wherever he went. He never returned to space and was killed piloting a jet in 1968. Today, a 40 m (131 ft) tall titanium statue of him stands in Moscow, and his home town has been renamed Gagarin in his honour.

In case of emergency, Yuri Gagarin was given a ten-day supply of food and water and instructions on how to override the control systems.

Ejector seat
The ejector seat had two purposes. If the rocket launch went wrong, the seat would throw Gagarin like a human cannonball into a safety net. Its main job, however, was to eject him from the descent module about 7 km (4 miles) above the ground. The hatch of the descent module blew off first. Exactly two seconds later, small rockets fixed to the base of the seat ignited to fire it out of the descent module.

Types of spacecraft

Most spacecraft simply fly past or orbit their target, but some attempt to land. Landers may stay put on the surface or rove around. Probes such as Huygens are released by an orbiter to enter a planet's or moon's atmosphere. All types have power, communication systems, and scientific instruments onboard.

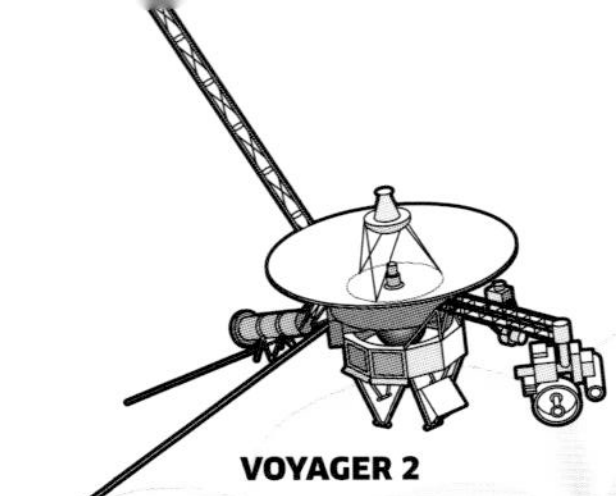
VOYAGER 2

Flyby
Voyager 2, launched in 1977, flew past Jupiter, Saturn, Uranus, and Neptune. The only craft to have visited the outer two planets, it is now heading out into deep space.

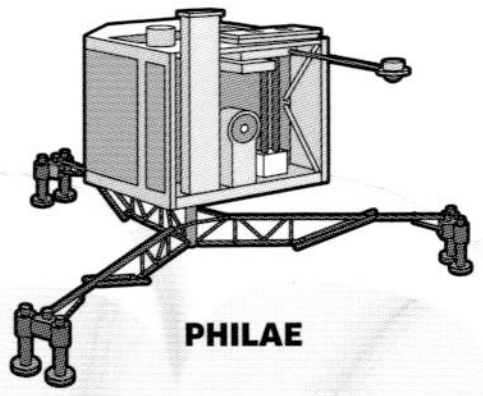
PHILAE

Lander
Released by the Rosetta spacecraft, this fridge-sized lander touched down on the nucleus of a comet in late 2014. Philae took the first images from a comet.

GALILEO

Orbiter and probe
From 1995 to 2003, Galileo orbited Jupiter and flew close to its larger moons. It released a probe to study the top 160 km (100 miles) of Jupiter's atmosphere.

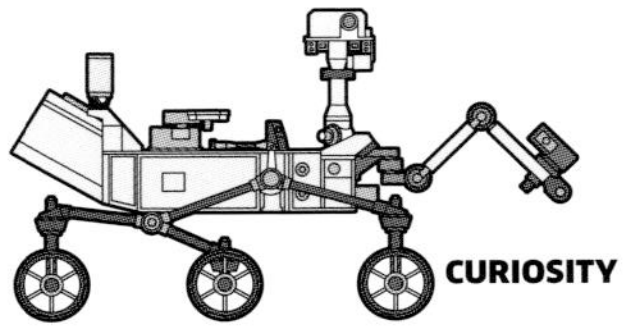
CURIOSITY

Rover
Four rovers have travelled across Mars, the most recent arrival being Curiosity in August 2012. Its task is to investigate whether Mars is, or was, suitable for life.

DEEP IMPACT

Flyby and impactor
As Deep Impact flew by the comet Tempel 1 in July 2005, it released an impactor that "bombed" the comet's surface, releasing gas and dust.

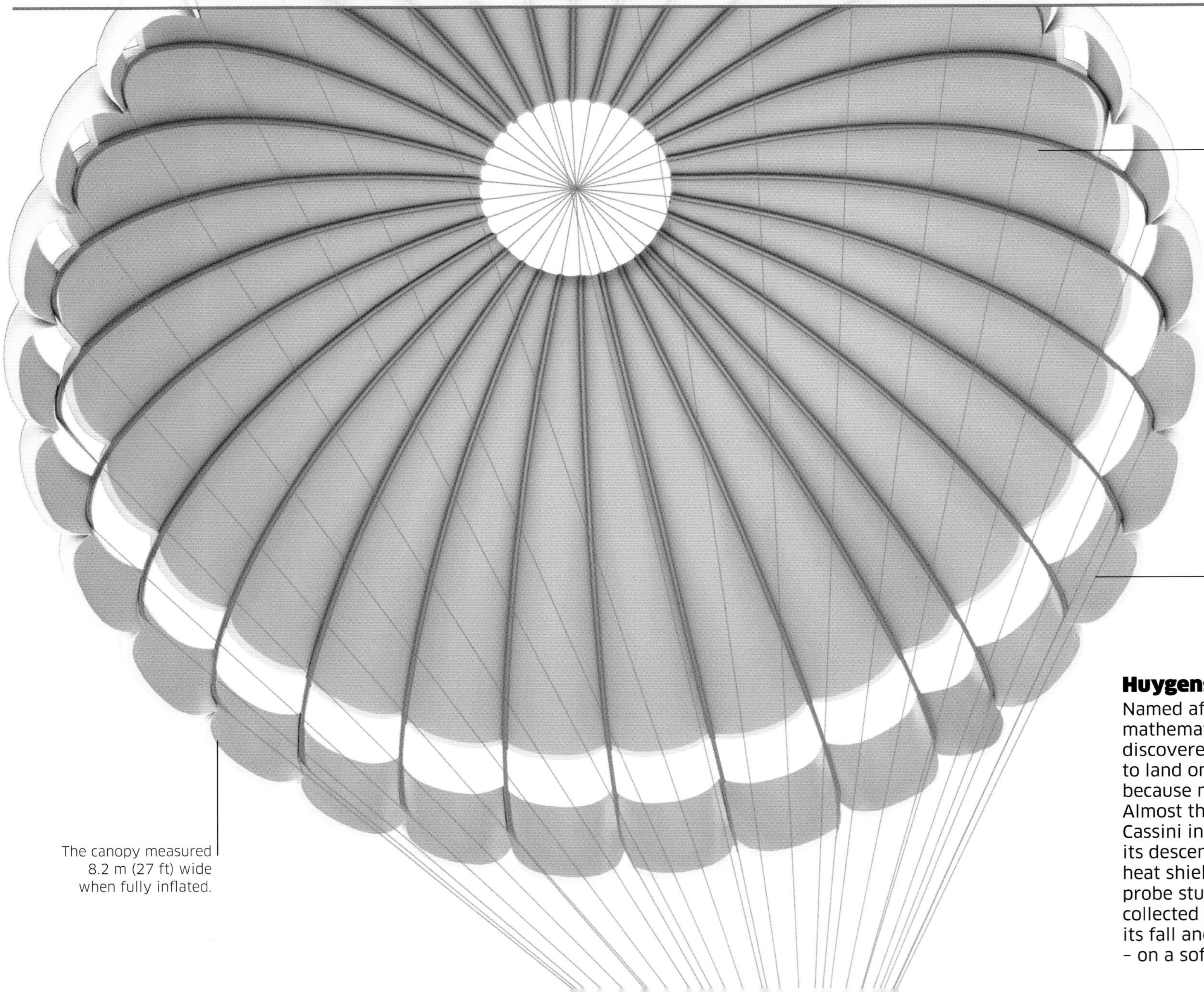

Main parachute
Made of nylon fabric, the main parachute opened about 165 km (100 miles) above the surface, when the probe was travelling at 290 kph (180 mph). It was jettisoned after 15 minutes, and a smaller parachute took over for the last 125 km (78 miles) of the descent.

Kevlar suspension lines, about 24 m (79 ft) long, secured the probe to the parachute canopy.

The canopy measured 8.2 m (27 ft) wide when fully inflated.

Huygens probe

Named after Dutch scientist and mathematician Christiaan Huygens (the discoverer of Titan), this probe was designed to land on either solid ground or liquid, because no-one knew what Titan was like. Almost three weeks after being released by Cassini in December 2004, Huygens began its descent to Titan's surface. Protected by a heat shield as it fell, instruments inside the probe studied Titan's atmosphere. Huygens collected and transmitted data throughout its fall and for about 1.5 hours after landing – on a soft but solid surface.

Space probes

Robotic spacecraft can work for years at a time in remote locations and in harsh conditions that humans could never endure.

Each craft is designed for a specific mission. It could be orbiting Mars, which is what Mars Express does, or travelling with a comet as it flies round the Sun, like Rosetta. Once these craft have reached their destinations, their onboard instruments test and record conditions on these faraway worlds. Some craft, such as Cassini–Huygens, are two in one. Cassini, the bigger of the two, left Earth for Saturn in 1997 with Huygens attached to its side. After a seven-year journey, the pair arrived at the planet. Then Huygens started its own mission, parachuting down onto Titan, the largest of Saturn's many moons.

Getting there

On its way to Saturn, Cassini-Huygens got help from Venus twice, and Earth and Jupiter once each. Too heavy to fly direct, it flew by these planets and was boosted by their gravity, giving the craft the speed needed to reach Saturn.

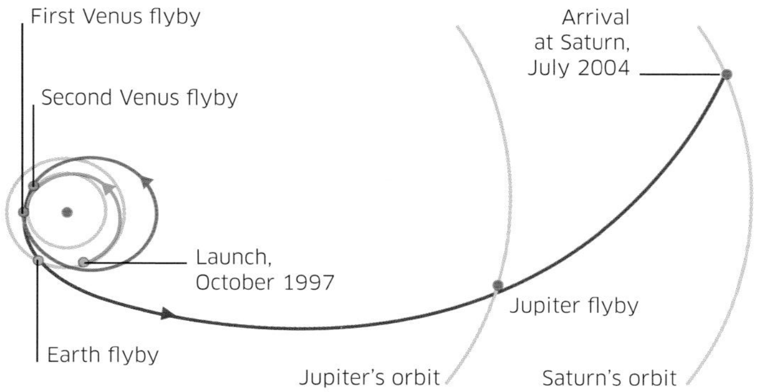
First Venus flyby
Second Venus flyby
Launch, October 1997
Earth flyby
Jupiter's orbit
Jupiter flyby
Saturn's orbit
Arrival at Saturn, July 2004

Cassini spacecraft

Cassini is the fourth craft to visit Saturn and the first to orbit it. About the size of a small bus, it has 12 instruments to study the planet, its rings, and its moons. It is so far away that messages between Cassini and Earth take over an hour.

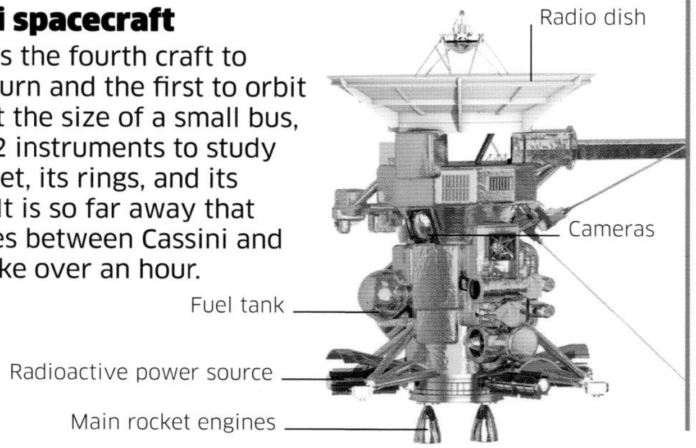
Radio dish
Cameras
Fuel tank
Radioactive power source
Main rocket engines

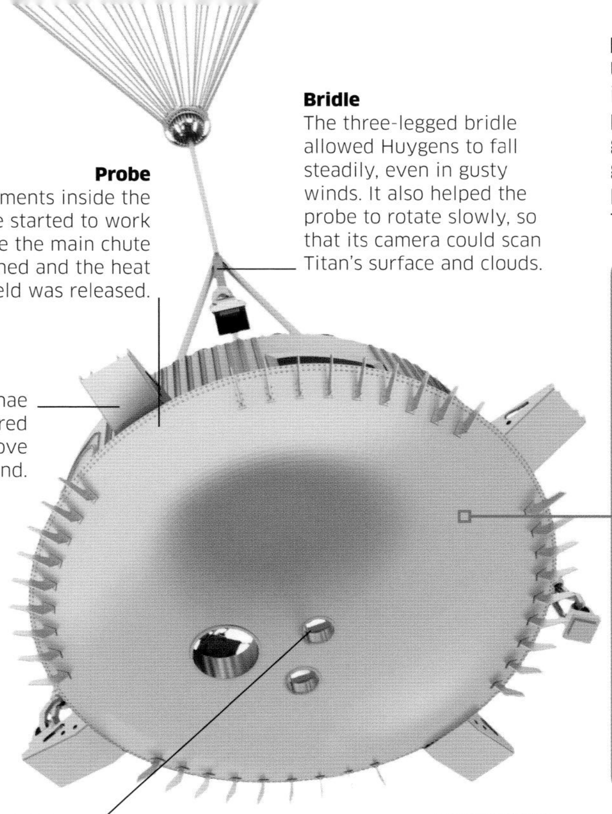
Probe
Instruments inside the probe started to work once the main chute opened and the heat shield was released.
Bridle
The three-legged bridle allowed Huygens to fall steadily, even in gusty winds. It also helped the probe to rotate slowly, so that its camera could scan Titan's surface and clouds.
Four radar antennae on the probe measured the height above ground.
Atmospheric gases entered the probe through holes in the cover.

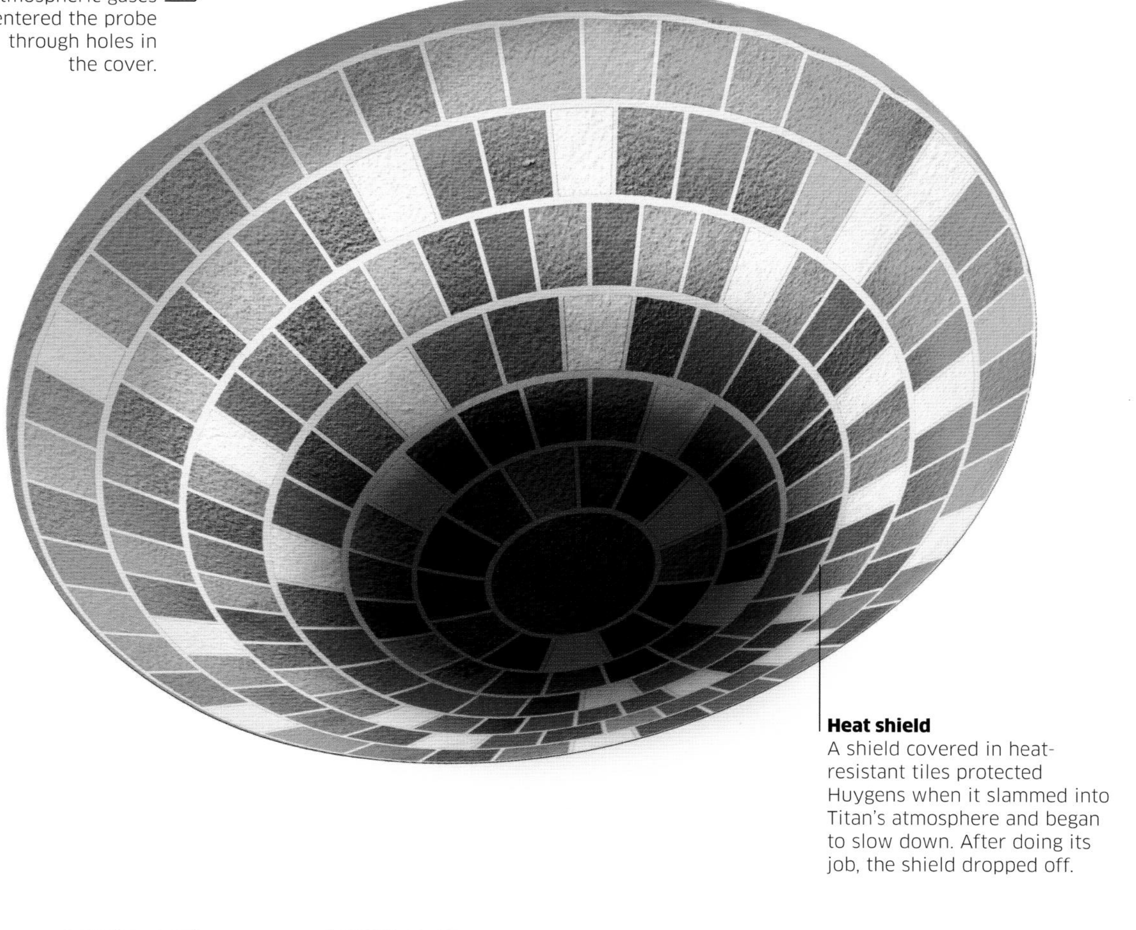
Heat shield
A shield covered in heat-resistant tiles protected Huygens when it slammed into Titan's atmosphere and began to slow down. After doing its job, the shield dropped off.

Inside Huygens
Under Huygens's covers was a platform of instruments. Fixed to the lower side of this platform were instruments that analysed the gases in Titan's air and the materials on the ground. Another instrument measured the probe's landing speed and determined what the landing site was like.

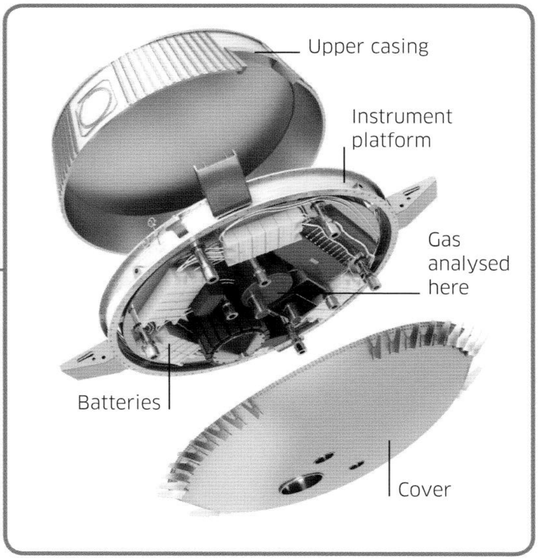
Upper casing
Instrument platform
Gas analysed here
Batteries
Cover

100,000 The approximate **number of TV pictures** captured by Russia's Lunokhod rovers on the Moon.

Rovers

Most spacecraft that touch down on other worlds have to stay put where they land. Rovers, however, are built to explore. These sophisticated robots are sent commands by radio signal from Earth but are programmed to find their own way around.

The smallest rovers are the size of a microwave oven; the largest are as big as a car. Solar panels provide power, and an internal computer serves as a rover's "brain". Rovers are packed with scientific instruments, from special cameras to onboard chemical laboratories. They use radio antennae to send their data and discoveries back to a control centre on Earth.

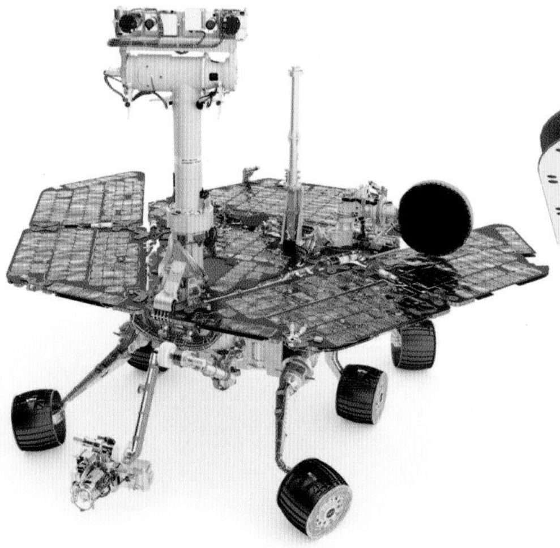

Spirit rover
The rover Spirit, shown here, was one of a pair of identical rovers that landed on opposite sides of Mars in 2004. Spirit lost power in 2010 but its twin, Opportunity, is still working. It receives commands from Earth in the morning and sends back data in the afternoon, once it has finished travelling, taking pictures, and testing rock.

Rock drill
Opportunity uses a drill to grind the surface off rocks so it can obtain deeper samples for chemical analysis. The rock shown here, nicknamed "Marquette Island", is about the size of a basketball and is unlike any of the rocks around it. It may have been thrown out of an impact crater some distance away.

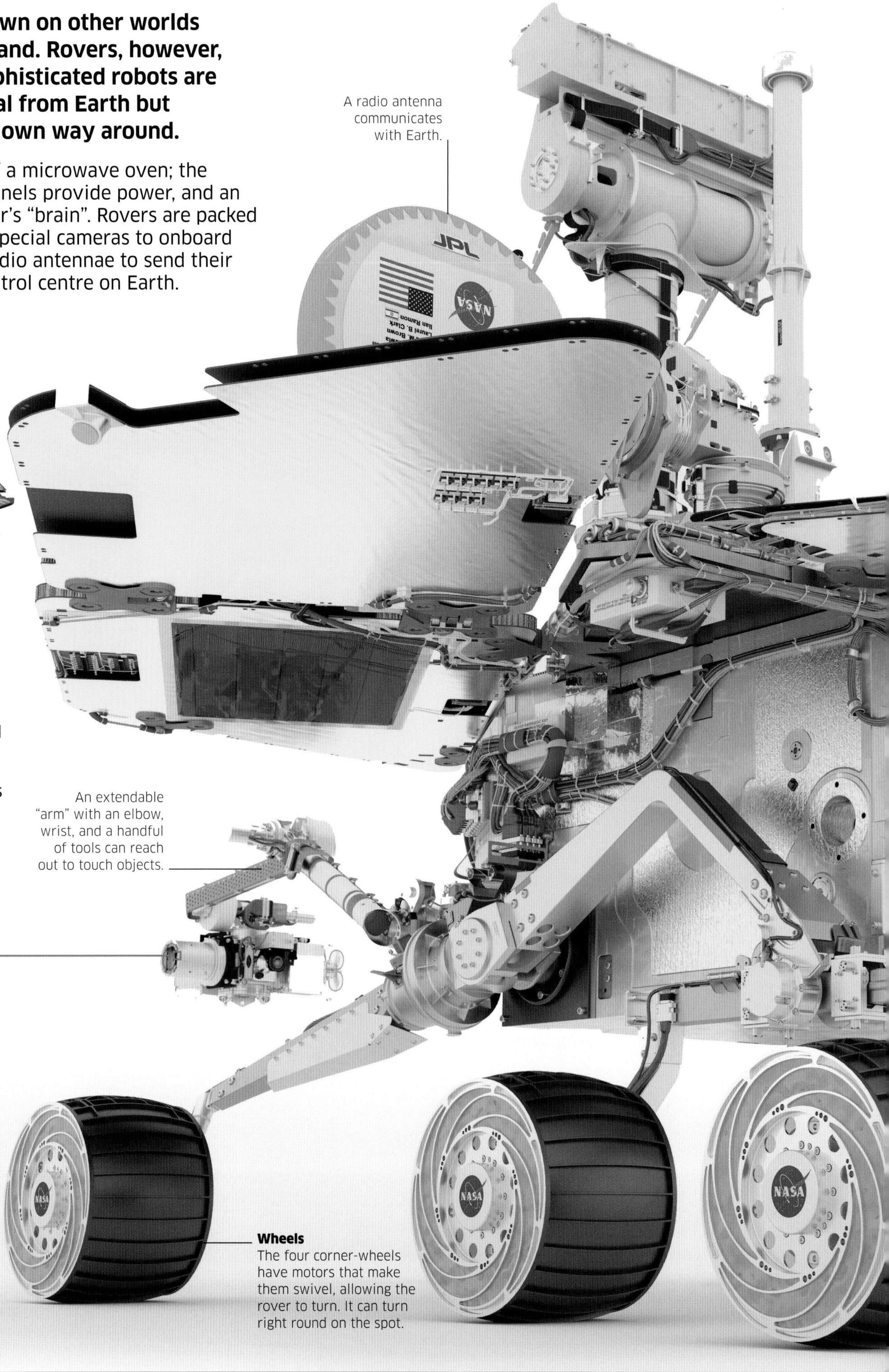
A radio antenna communicates with Earth.
JPL
NASA
An extendable "arm" with an elbow, wrist, and a handful of tools can reach out to touch objects.
NASA
NASA

Wheels
The four corner-wheels have motors that make them swivel, allowing the rover to turn. It can turn right round on the spot.

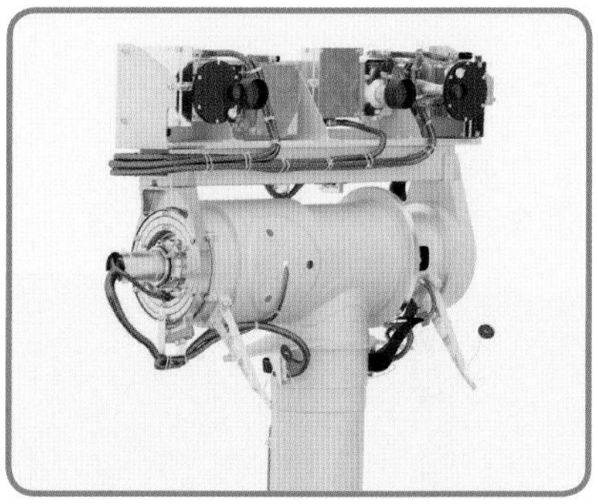

Panoramic camera
Four cameras held on a mast at head height serve as the rover's eyes. Two "pancams" take colour photos of the Martian landscape, helping scientists choose places to visit. Two "navcams" take 3-D images of the ground, helping the rover plan its route.

Finding the way
Rovers are given destinations but they find their own way there, using their cameras and onboard computers to calculate the safest path. They travel only a few centimetres a second and stop every few seconds to reassess the route. Opportunity's top speed is 0.18 kph (0.11 mph) but its average speed is a fifth of this.

TRACKS LEFT BY OPPORTUNITY

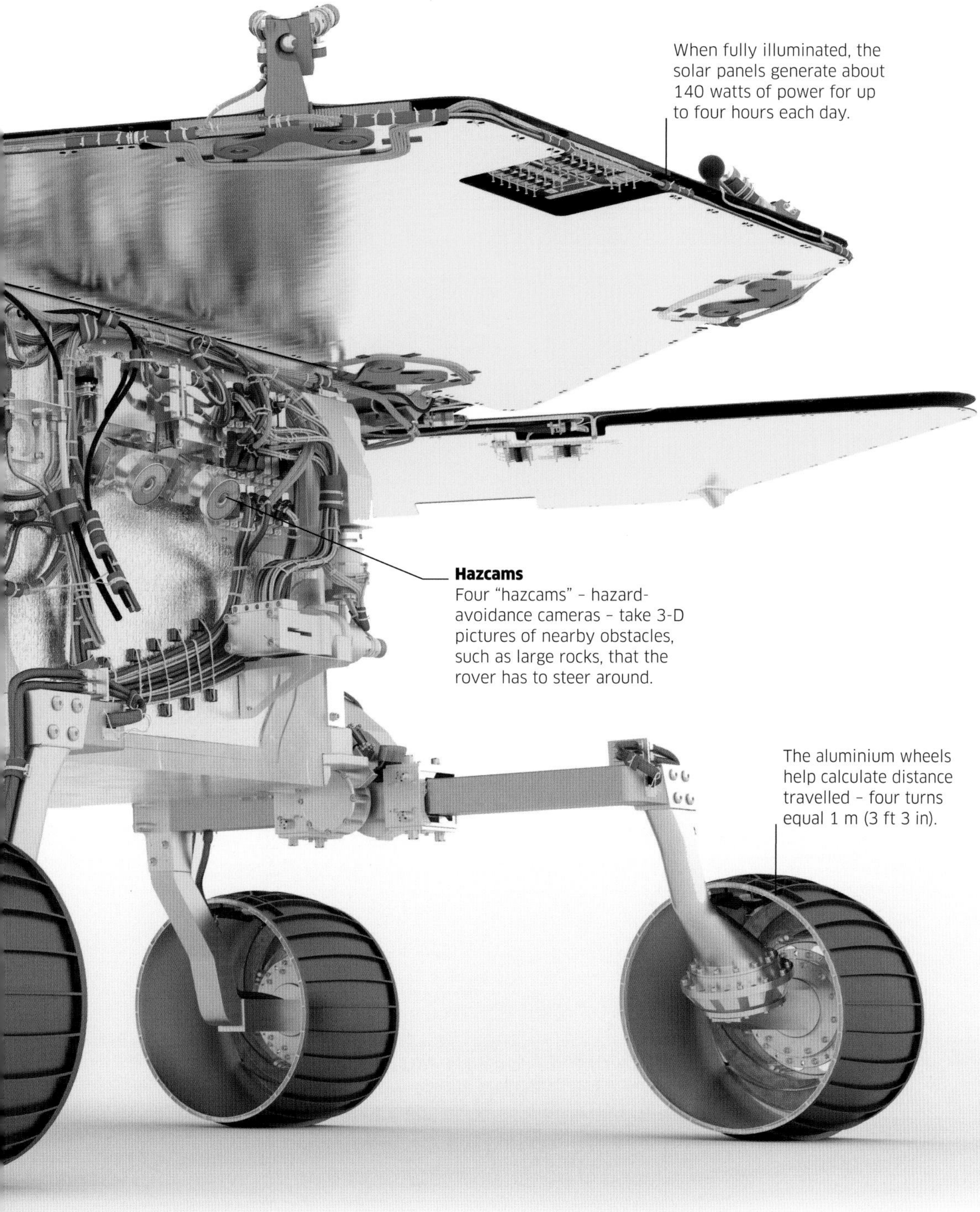
When fully illuminated, the solar panels generate about 140 watts of power for up to four hours each day.
Hazcams
Four "hazcams" – hazard-avoidance cameras – take 3-D pictures of nearby obstacles, such as large rocks, that the rover has to steer around.
The aluminium wheels help calculate distance travelled – four turns equal 1 m (3 ft 3 in).

Rover records

Opportunity holds the record for the greatest distance travelled by a rover. The first rover to visit another world was Russia's Lunokhod 1, which landed on the Moon in 1970. The "lunar roving vehicles" that explored the Moon during NASA's Apollo missions were not robotic rovers but manned vehicles designed to carry astronauts and equipment.

OPPORTUNITY 2004–15 – **41.4 KM (25.7 MILES)**

LUNOKHOD 2 1973 – **39 KM (24.2 MILES)**

APOLLO 17 LUNAR ROVING VEHICLE (LRV) 1972 – **35.74 KM (22.2 MILES)**

APOLLO 15 LRV 1971 – **27.8 KM (17.3 MILES)**

APOLLO 16 LRV 1972 – **27.1 KM (16.8 MILES)**

LUNOKHOD 1 1970–71 – **10.5 KM (6.5 MILES)**

CURIOSITY 2012–15 – **8.8 KM (5.5 MILES)**

SPIRIT 2004–10 – **7.7 KM (4.8 MILES)**

SOJOURNER 1997 – **0.1 KM (0.06 MILES)**

YUTU 2013–14 – **0.1 KM (0.06 MILES)**

ON MARS
ON THE MOON

Balancing act
The wheels are attached to the body by an arrangement called a rocker-bogie suspension. This clever system of levers allows the wheels to ride over bumpy ground while the rover's body stays level.

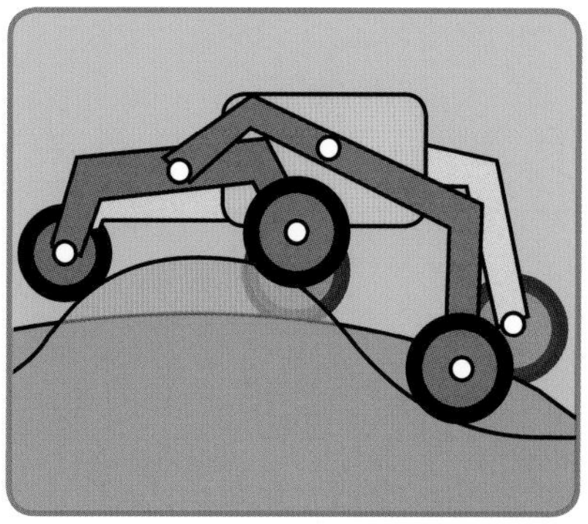

1 month – the length of time life-support systems on Soyuz can **keep the crew alive.**

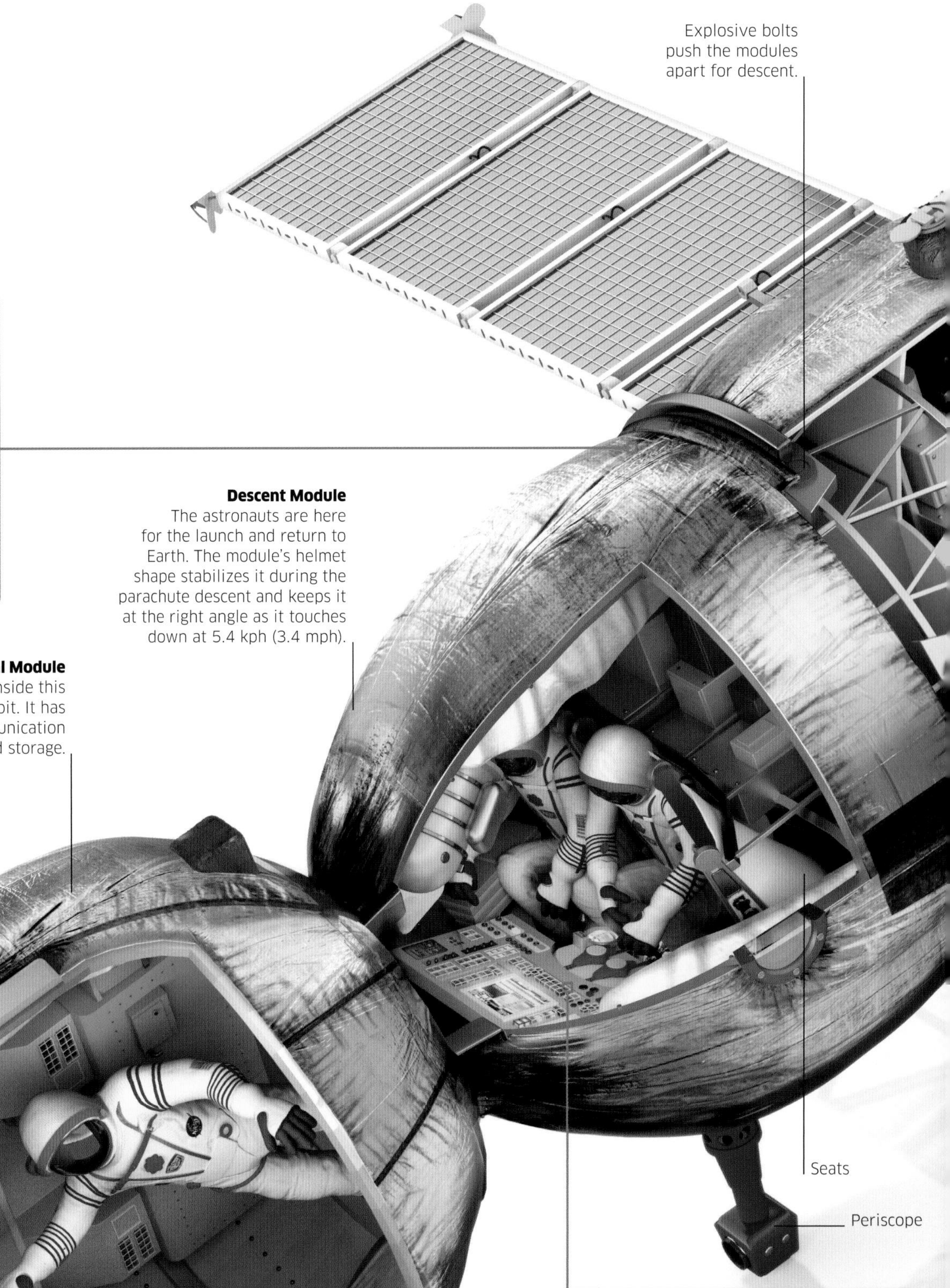

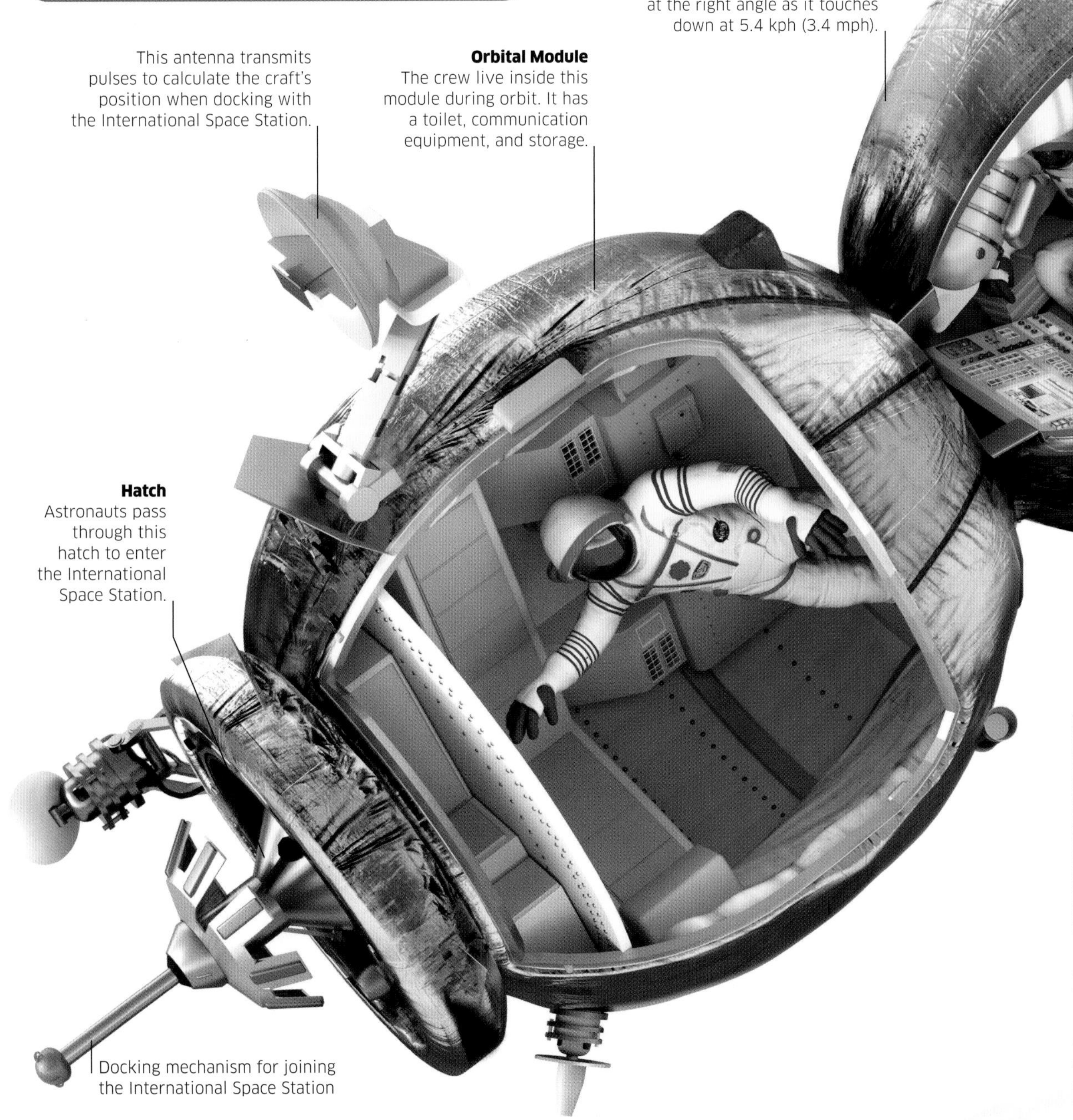
Explosive bolts push the modules apart for descent.
Descent Module
The astronauts are here for the launch and return to Earth. The module's helmet shape stabilizes it during the parachute descent and keeps it at the right angle as it touches down at 5.4 kph (3.4 mph).
This antenna transmits pulses to calculate the craft's position when docking with the International Space Station.
Orbital Module
The crew live inside this module during orbit. It has a toilet, communication equipment, and storage.
Hatch
Astronauts pass through this hatch to enter the International Space Station.
Seats
Periscope
Docking mechanism for joining the International Space Station

Back to Earth
Only the Descent Module returns to Earth – the other two modules are jettisoned and burn up in Earth's atmosphere. The Descent Module's thrusters control its return before it is slowed by a series of parachutes. Three and a half hours after leaving the International Space Station, it lands in open country in Kazakhstan. The crew are helped out and flown away by helicopter.

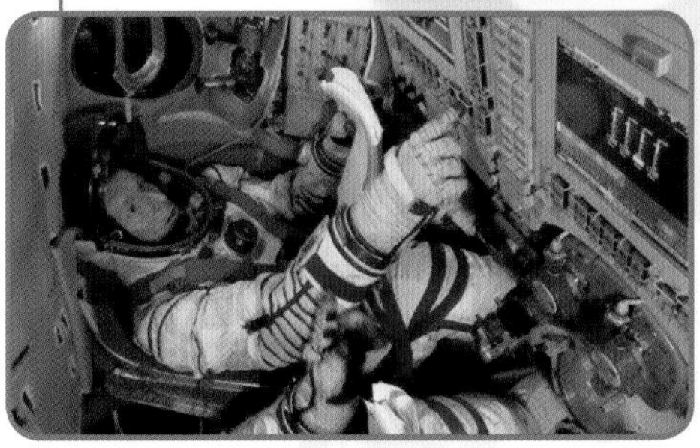

Cockpit
The crew of three sit elbow to elbow for launch and return. In front of them is the control desk with guidance and navigation controls to manoeuvre the craft. Above the desk is the hatch into the Orbital Module.

Manned spacecraft

People first went into orbit around Earth in the 1960s. Only 24 have gone further – to the Moon. Astronauts come from many countries, but they have been launched into space by just three nations.

Russia and the US have been launching manned missions for around 50 years; China launched its first manned spacecraft in 2003. The first vehicles carried one astronaut, then two, and later three – always in cramped conditions. Today's Soyuz is a three-person craft that is used only once. For 30 years, the space shuttle was the alternative ride. It carried more crew in greater comfort and returned intact. More reusable spacecraft are now in development, including spacecraft that will ferry ticket-carrying tourists to space.

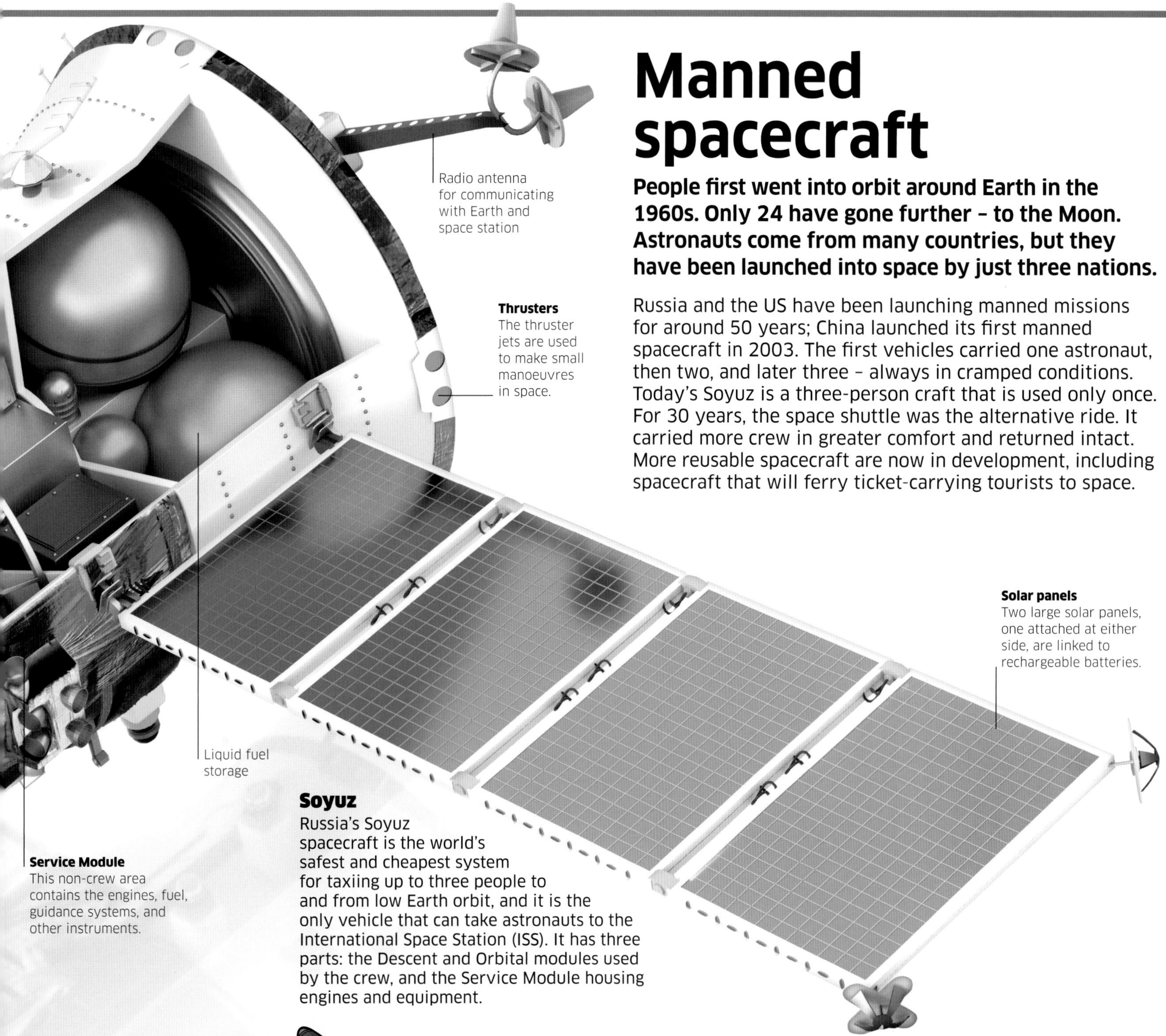
Radio antenna for communicating with Earth and space station
Thrusters The thruster jets are used to make small manoeuvres in space.
Solar panels Two large solar panels, one attached at either side, are linked to rechargeable batteries.
Liquid fuel storage
Service Module This non-crew area contains the engines, fuel, guidance systems, and other instruments.

Soyuz
Russia's Soyuz spacecraft is the world's safest and cheapest system for taxiing up to three people to and from low Earth orbit, and it is the only vehicle that can take astronauts to the International Space Station (ISS). It has three parts: the Descent and Orbital modules used by the crew, and the Service Module housing engines and equipment.

Space vehicles

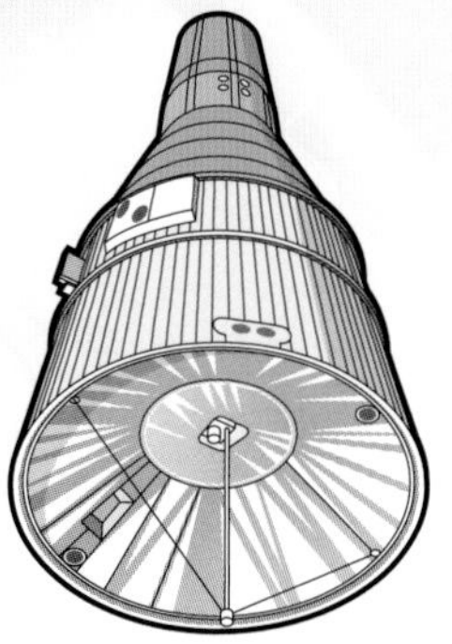

Gemini
One of the first US manned spacecraft was Gemini, which took ten two-man crews into orbit in 1965–1966. There they made America's first spacewalk.

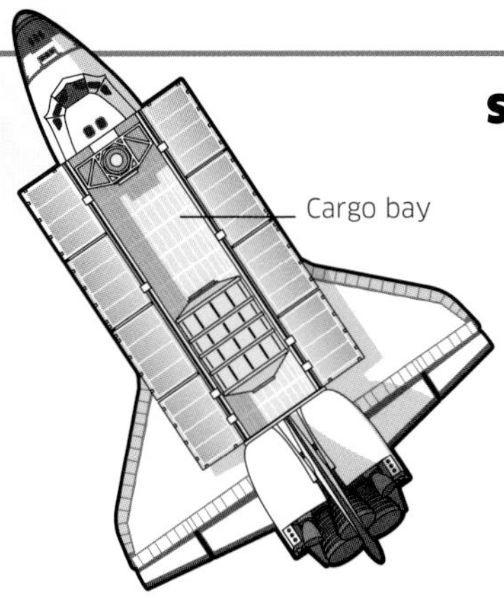
Cargo bay

Space shuttle
The five space shuttles flew crews of up to eight into space between 1981 and 2011. In total, the reusable shuttle fleet completed 21,030 orbits of Earth.

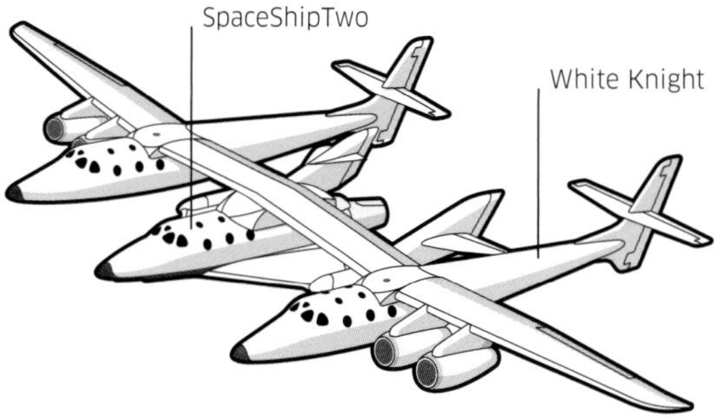
SpaceShipTwo
White Knight

SpaceShipTwo
The privately owned SpaceShipTwo is designed for future space tourism. Released above Earth by the White Knight aircraft, it uses a rocket to climb to the edge of space.

Dragon V2
This reusable craft, able to make at least ten flights, will carry future crews to the ISS and back. Launched by a Falcon 9 rocket, it will touch down back home on its landing legs.

Atlantis
RESCUE

Space shuttle

The space shuttle was the world's first reusable spacecraft, designed to carry a crew of 2–8 astronauts to space and back.

NASA's fleet of five shuttles operated for 30 years, launching 135 times and spending a total of 3.6 years in flight. Launched with the aid of two disposable solid-fuel rockets, they reached orbit in only 8 minutes, accelerating from 0 to 25,000 kph (16,000 mph). The shuttle programme ended in 2011, having lasted twice the 15-year lifespan it was originally designed for.

195 hours 18 minutes – the **total length** of the **first Apollo mission** to the Moon.

Apollo programme

The Apollo missions of the 1960s and 70s are the only space missions that have put people on another world. Reaching the Moon required an extraordinary three-part spacecraft and the largest rockets that have ever been launched.

Between 1969 and 1972, NASA launched six successful Apollo missions and put 12 astronauts on the Moon. Each mission took a crew of three men a total of 1.5 million km (950,000 miles) through space on a looping, figure-of-eight journey to the Moon and back. Launched by the gigantic Saturn V rocket – which had to be built anew for each trip – the astronauts travelled in an Apollo spacecraft made of three parts that could separate. The spider-like Lunar Module carried two men down to the lunar surface. The remaining crew member stayed in the cone-shaped, silvery Command Module, which also carried the crew home. Attached to this was the cylindrical Service Module, housing the spacecraft's rocket engine, fuel, and supplies.

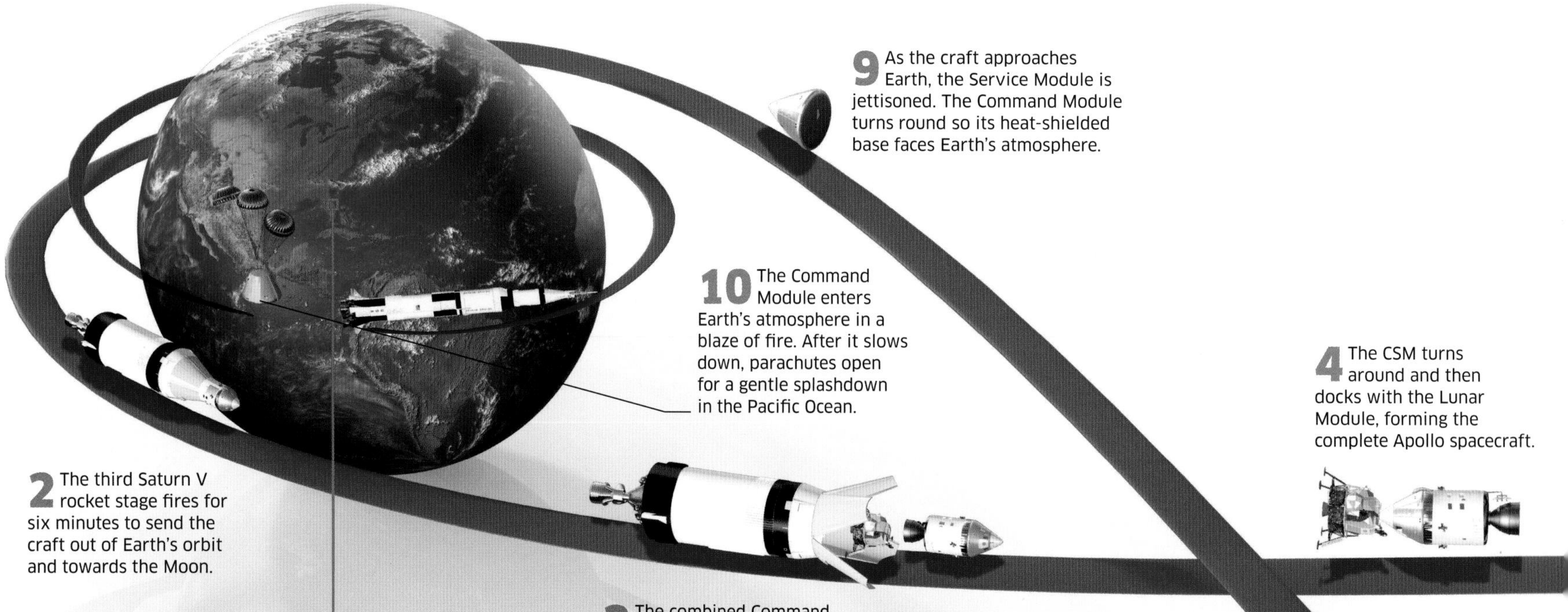

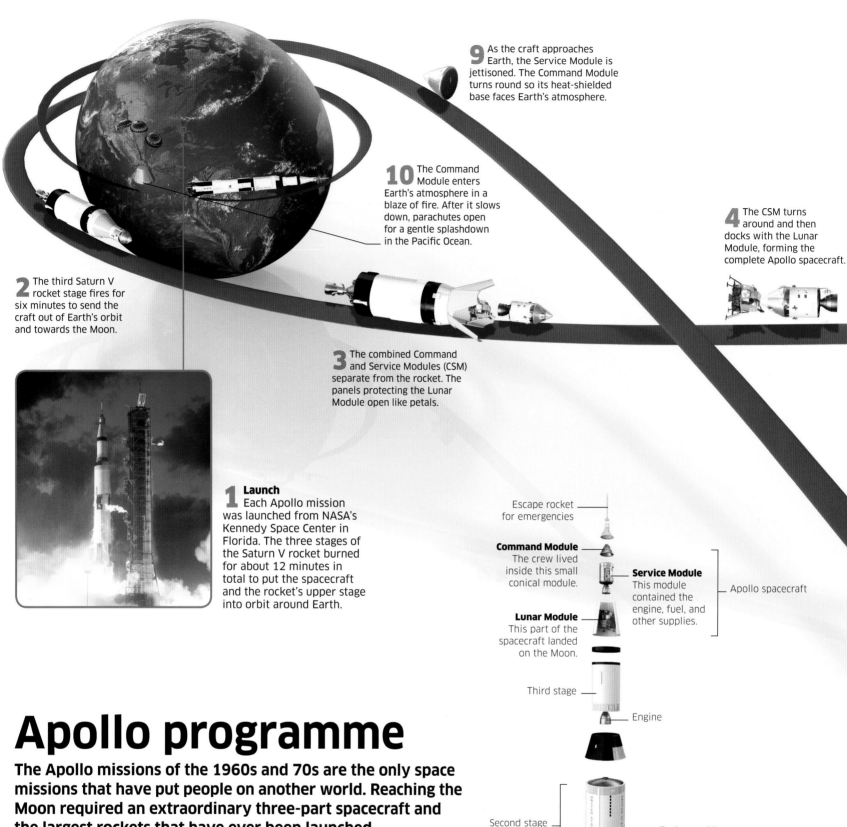

9 As the craft approaches Earth, the Service Module is jettisoned. The Command Module turns round so its heat-shielded base faces Earth's atmosphere.

10 The Command Module enters Earth's atmosphere in a blaze of fire. After it slows down, parachutes open for a gentle splashdown in the Pacific Ocean.

4 The CSM turns around and then docks with the Lunar Module, forming the complete Apollo spacecraft.

2 The third Saturn V rocket stage fires for six minutes to send the craft out of Earth's orbit and towards the Moon.

3 The combined Command and Service Modules (CSM) separate from the rocket. The panels protecting the Lunar Module open like petals.

1 Launch
Each Apollo mission was launched from NASA's Kennedy Space Center in Florida. The three stages of the Saturn V rocket burned for about 12 minutes in total to put the spacecraft and the rocket's upper stage into orbit around Earth.

Escape rocket for emergencies
Command Module The crew lived inside this small conical module.
Service Module This module contained the engine, fuel, and other supplies.
Apollo spacecraft
Lunar Module This part of the spacecraft landed on the Moon.
Third stage
Engine
Second stage
First stage
Engines

Saturn V
Standing 111 m (364 ft) high, the Saturn V launch vehicle was taller than New York's Statue of Liberty. The main body was made of three different rockets, or "stages", stacked together. The Apollo spacecraft, tiny by comparison, was on top. The main rockets fired in sequence, each stage propelling the sections above to greater speeds and heights before running out of fuel and falling back to Earth.

15 tonnes – the quantity of fuel **burned every second** during launch.

300 The **total number of hours** Apollo astronauts spent on the Moon.

In 1970 Apollo 13 was **damaged by an explosion** on the way to the Moon and had to return to Earth.

Command and Service Modules
The Command and Service Modules flew as a single unit (the CSM) for most of each mission. Astronauts lived in the Command Module – the conical front part – which had five triple-glazed windows for viewing the Moon, Earth, and docking manoeuvres. The living quarters were cramped and had very basic facilities, with no toilet. Instead, astronauts used plastic bags or a special hose connected to the vacuum of space.

Mission control

The nerve centre of each Apollo mission was the control room at Johnson Space Center in Houston, USA. Here, scientists and engineers kept a round-the-clock watch over the spacecraft and talked to the crew via radio. The crew remained in continual radio contact with mission control, except when the spacecraft travelled behind the Moon.

The Apollo programme cost $24 billion and employed 400,000 people at its peak.

5 The Apollo spacecraft sails to the Moon, a journey of about three days. It slows down to enter lunar orbit.

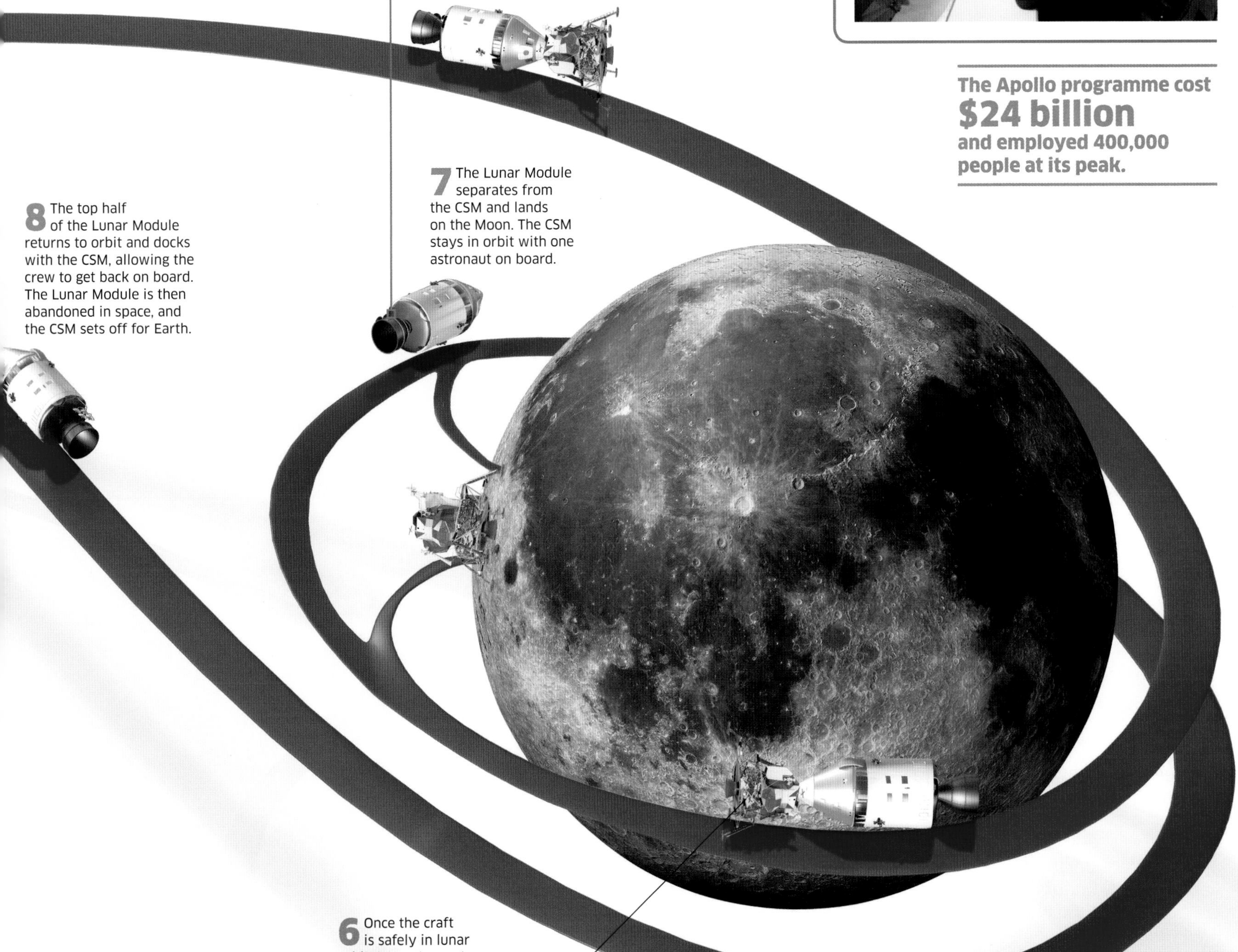

7 The Lunar Module separates from the CSM and lands on the Moon. The CSM stays in orbit with one astronaut on board.

8 The top half of the Lunar Module returns to orbit and docks with the CSM, allowing the crew to get back on board. The Lunar Module is then abandoned in space, and the CSM sets off for Earth.

6 Once the craft is safely in lunar orbit, two astronauts go through a hatch into the Lunar Module, ready for their descent to the Moon.

Lunar lander

In the greatest adventure that humans have ever been part of, six Apollo spacecraft touched down on the Moon between 1969 and 1972. The 12 men who landed explored the lunar surface and returned with bags of precious rock samples.

The race to reach the Moon was won on 20 July 1969, when US astronaut Neil Armstrong became the first person to set foot on it. Armstrong flew to the lunar surface with colleague Buzz Aldrin in the Apollo 11 Lunar Module, nicknamed Eagle, while their colleague Michael Collins remained in orbit in the Apollo Command Module. Armstrong had to take manual control of the Eagle in the last minutes of a hair-raising descent after realizing the planned landing site was unsafe. He touched down with only 30 seconds's fuel left and then made his famous announcement to the whole world: "Tranquility Base here. The Eagle has landed."

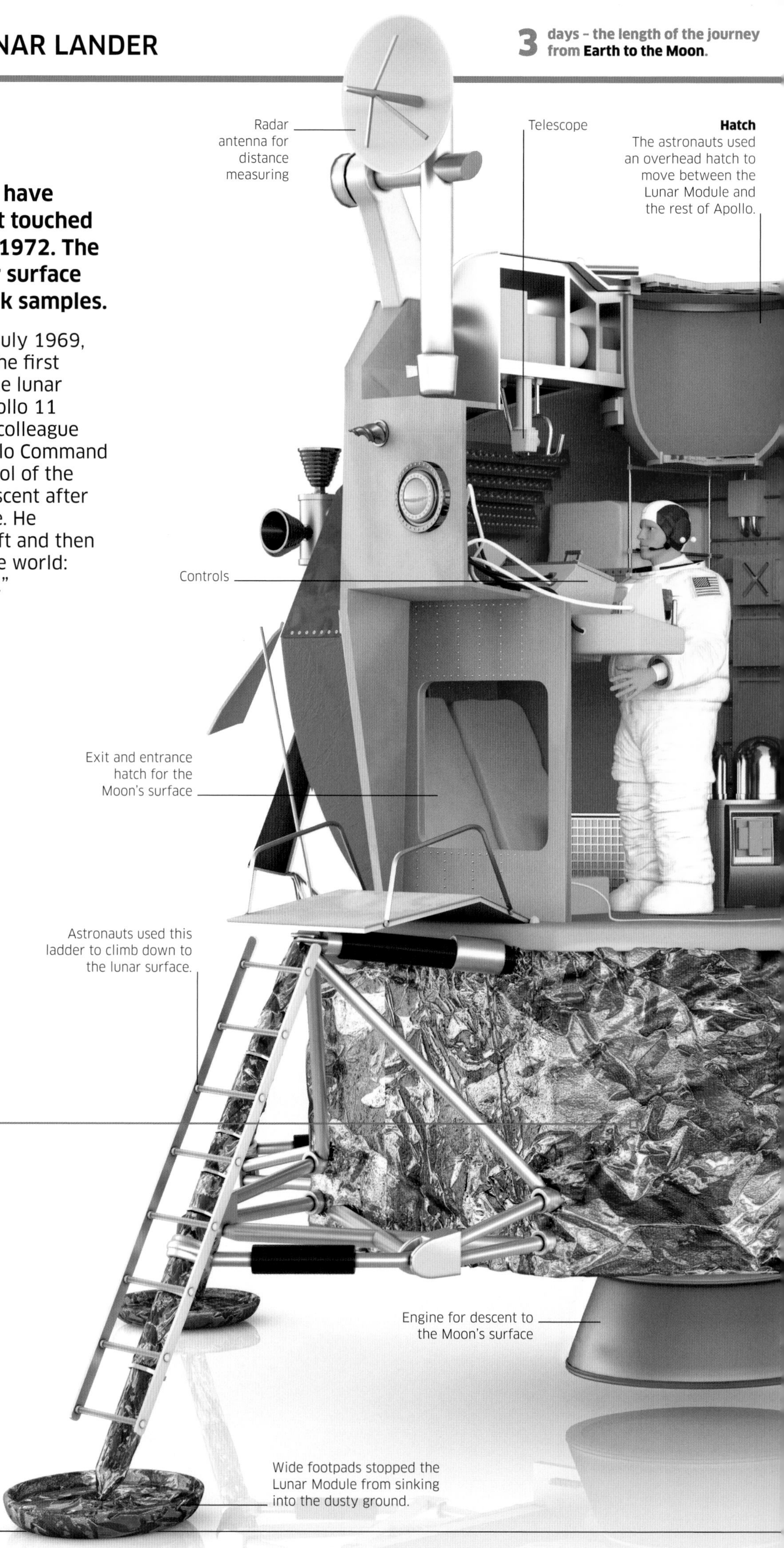
Radar antenna for distance measuring
Telescope
Hatch
The astronauts used an overhead hatch to move between the Lunar Module and the rest of Apollo.
Controls
Exit and entrance hatch for the Moon's surface
Astronauts used this ladder to climb down to the lunar surface.
Engine for descent to the Moon's surface
Wide footpads stopped the Lunar Module from sinking into the dusty ground.

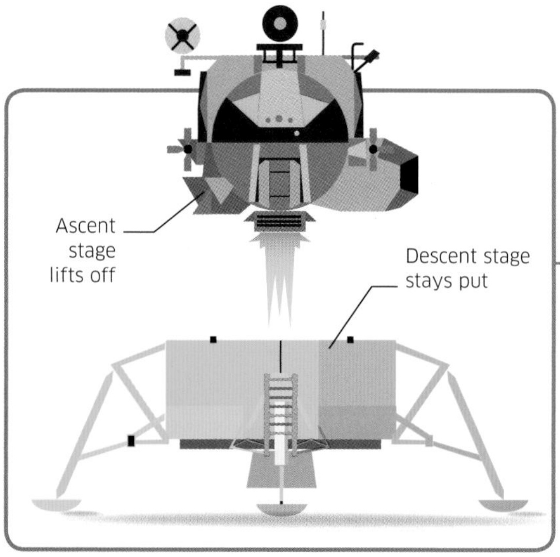
Ascent stage lifts off
Descent stage stays put

Lift off
When it was time to leave, the ascent engine fired. It lifted the ascent stage back into lunar orbit, where the craft docked with the Command and Service Modules. The two lunar astronauts moved back into the Command Module, stowing their rock samples and cameras. The ascent stage was then jettisoned to crash back into the lunar surface.

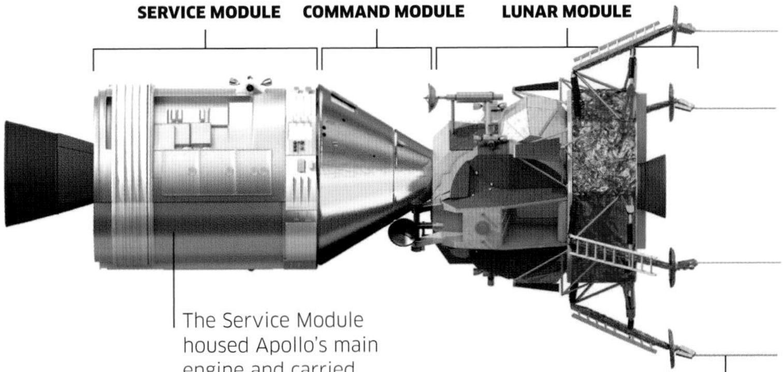
SERVICE MODULE
COMMAND MODULE
LUNAR MODULE

The Service Module housed Apollo's main engine and carried air, water, and fuel.

Probes detected the ground just before landing.

Apollo spacecraft

There were three parts to the Apollo craft. The crew travelled in the Command Module. Once at the Moon, two astronauts transferred to the Lunar Module for the descent to the surface. The third stayed in the combined Command and Service Modules, orbiting the Moon while awaiting their return. The Command Module was the only part of Apollo to return to Earth.

More than 500 million people watched Neil Armstrong on live TV when he left the Lunar Module and stepped onto the Moon.

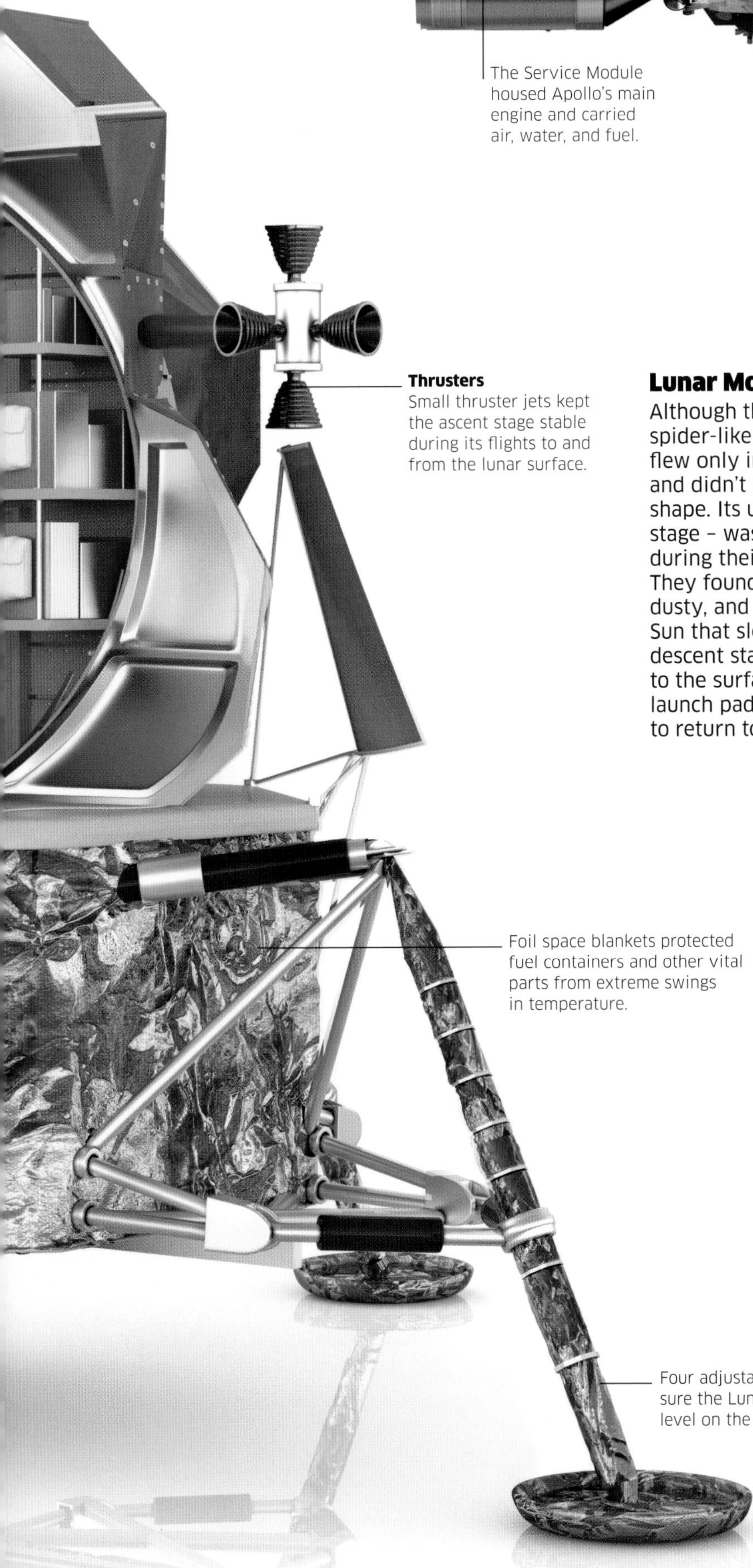

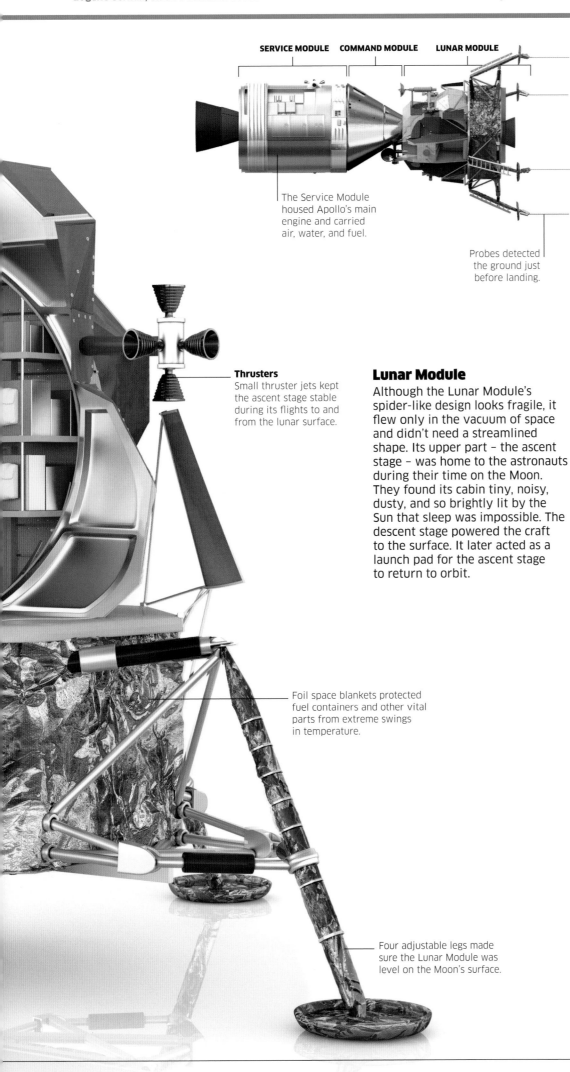

Thrusters
Small thruster jets kept the ascent stage stable during its flights to and from the lunar surface.

Foil space blankets protected fuel containers and other vital parts from extreme swings in temperature.

Four adjustable legs made sure the Lunar Module was level on the Moon's surface.

Lunar Module

Although the Lunar Module's spider-like design looks fragile, it flew only in the vacuum of space and didn't need a streamlined shape. Its upper part – the ascent stage – was home to the astronauts during their time on the Moon. They found its cabin tiny, noisy, dusty, and so brightly lit by the Sun that sleep was impossible. The descent stage powered the craft to the surface. It later acted as a launch pad for the ascent stage to return to orbit.

Lunar gravity

Gravity on the Moon is only one-sixth as strong as gravity on Earth. Not only do all things on the Moon weigh one-sixth of their Earth weight, but lunar hills are also six times easier to climb. And, as Apollo 16's commander John Young found out, you can jump six times higher on the Moon's surface.

Memento

Apollo craft and equipment, including six descent stages and three Moon buggies, are still on the Moon. David Scott and James Irwin of Apollo 15 left other mementos in the dusty soil: a list of 14 American and Russian astronauts who lost their lives, and a small figure representing a fallen astronaut.

$38 million – the **cost** of the **first lunar rover**.

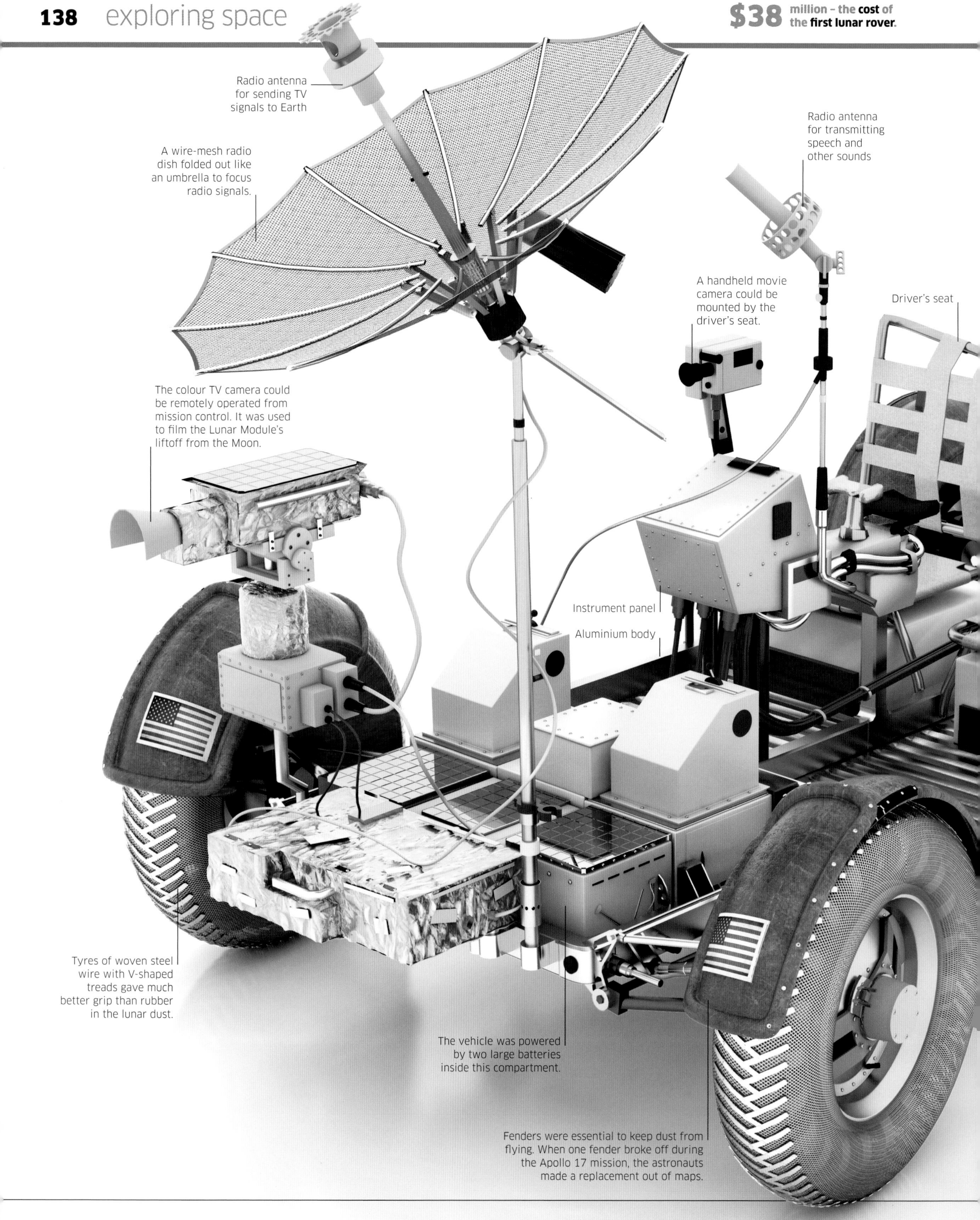
Radio antenna for sending TV signals to Earth
A wire-mesh radio dish folded out like an umbrella to focus radio signals.
Radio antenna for transmitting speech and other sounds
A handheld movie camera could be mounted by the driver's seat.
Driver's seat
The colour TV camera could be remotely operated from mission control. It was used to film the Lunar Module's liftoff from the Moon.
Instrument panel
Aluminium body
Tyres of woven steel wire with V-shaped treads gave much better grip than rubber in the lunar dust.
The vehicle was powered by two large batteries inside this compartment.
Fenders were essential to keep dust from flying. When one fender broke off during the Apollo 17 mission, the astronauts made a replacement out of maps.

90 km (56 miles) – the **total distance travelled** by all three lunar rovers.

19 kph (12 mph) – the **top speed** achieved by the LRV on the Moon.

7.6 km (4.7 miles) – the **greatest distance** a rover travelled from the landing site.

Moon buggy

The first Apollo astronauts had to explore the Moon on foot. On the last three missions, astronauts took a Lunar Roving Vehicle (LRV) – a battery-powered buggy that allowed them to travel for miles.

Built from the lightest materials possible, the LRV weighed a mere 35 kg (77 lb) in the Moon's low gravity – about twice the weight of a mountain bike on Earth. Four sturdy metal wheels, each equipped with its own motor, steering, and brake, enabled the LRV to ride safely over craters and rocks while maintaining grip in the loose lunar dust. Apollo 11 astronauts could walk only 100 m (330 ft) or so from the landing site in their bulky suits, but with the LRV to carry them, the crew of Apollo 17 travelled a total of 36 km (22 miles) as they explored and collected samples. Three LRVs were sent to the Moon, and all remain there today. Their last job was to use an onboard camera to film their drivers lifting off for the return to Earth.

The tool caddy at the back carried equipment for collecting samples, including brushes, a hammer, a scoop, and a rake.
The seats were made of aluminium tubing with nylon webbing and had Velcro seatbelts.
Handhold
Under-seat storage allowed astronauts to collect up to 27 kg (60 lb) of rock samples.

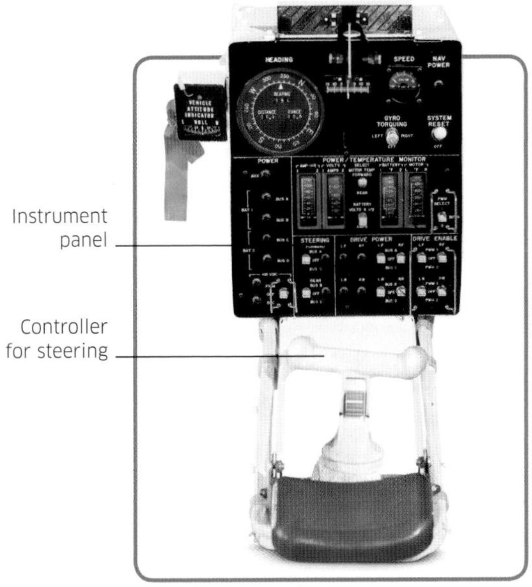

Instrument panel
Controller for steering

Controls
The instrument panel showed speed, direction, tilt, battery power, and temperature. The LRV had no steering wheel. Instead, the driver used a T-shaped controller to steer, accelerate, and brake. The LRV also had a map holder and storage space for tools and rock samples.

Unpacking the LRV

The LRV was designed to fold flat so it could travel to the Moon attached to the side of the Lunar Module. One astronaut had to climb the ladder and undo the clips that held the LRV securely in place so it could be pulled down.

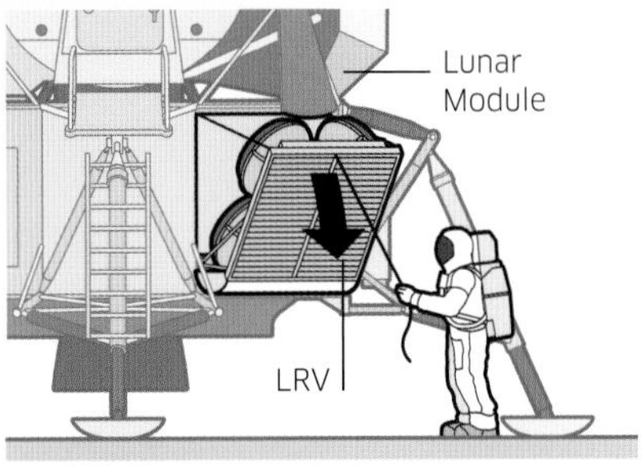

Lunar Module
LRV

1 LOWERING THE LRV Getting the LRV down to the ground required both astronauts to pull on a series of straps in careful sequence. Pulleys took care of the rest.

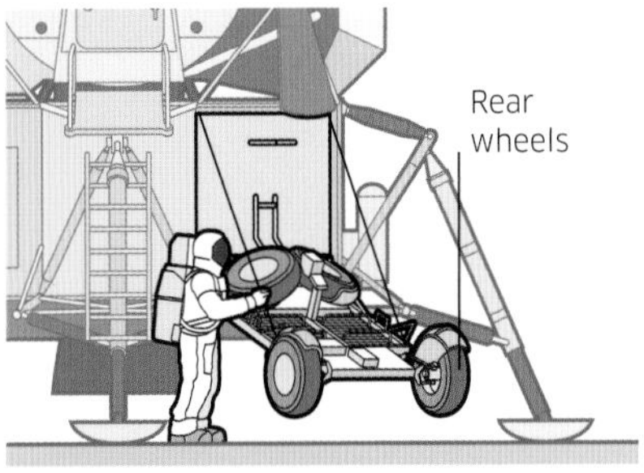

Rear wheels

2 CHASSIS UNFOLDS Lowering the LRV caused the rear wheels to fold out and lock into place automatically. The rover's seats were now facing upwards.

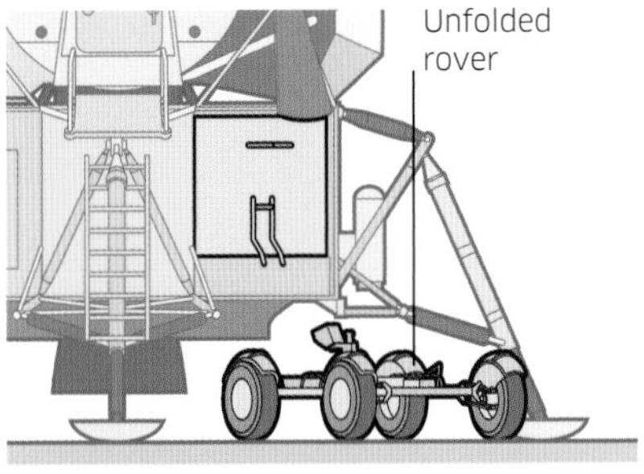

Unfolded rover

3 LRV DISCONNECTED The front wheels also unfolded and locked in place automatically. Finally, the astronauts raised the seats and other parts by hand.

Spacesuit

A modern spacesuit is far more than just protective clothing. It serves as a wearable spacecraft, creating a safe, Earth-like environment for the human body.

In the early days of space travel, a spacesuit was made in one piece, tailored to fit the astronaut who would wear it. Today, astronauts working outside the International Space Station wear a one-size-fits-all suit made of many parts. A semi-rigid top fits onto trousers, and a helmet, gloves, boots, and life-support backpack all go on top. Beneath the suit is a comfortable, one-piece garment containing tubes of flowing water to keep the body cool. On the outside of the suit are controls, tethers that attach the astronaut to the space station, and tools for the jobs to be done.

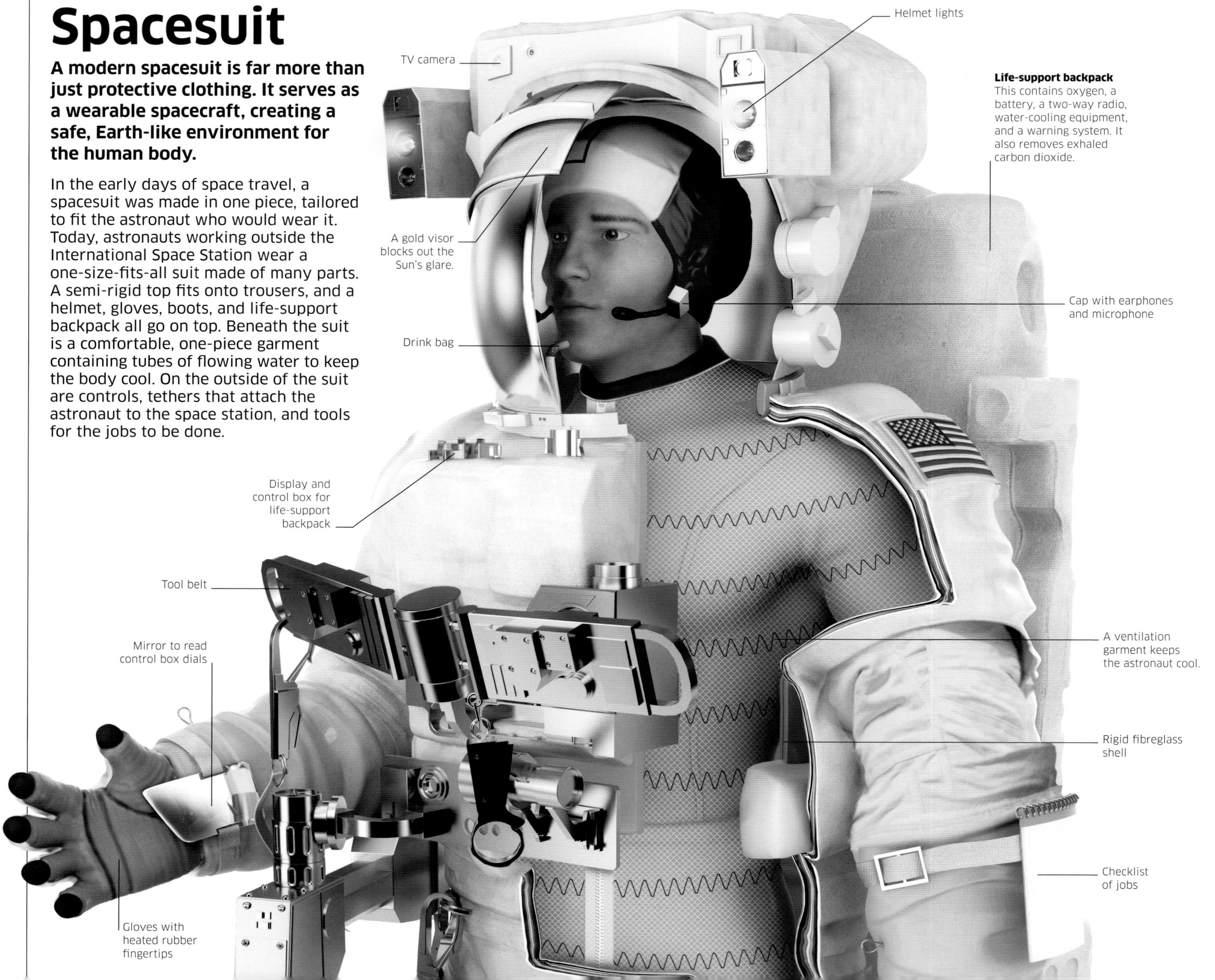
TV camera
Helmet lights
Life-support backpack This contains oxygen, a battery, a two-way radio, water-cooling equipment, and a warning system. It also removes exhaled carbon dioxide.
A gold visor blocks out the Sun's glare.
Cap with earphones and microphone
Drink bag
Display and control box for life-support backpack
Tool belt
Mirror to read control box dials
A ventilation garment keeps the astronaut cool.
Rigid fibreglass shell
Checklist of jobs
Gloves with heated rubber fingertips

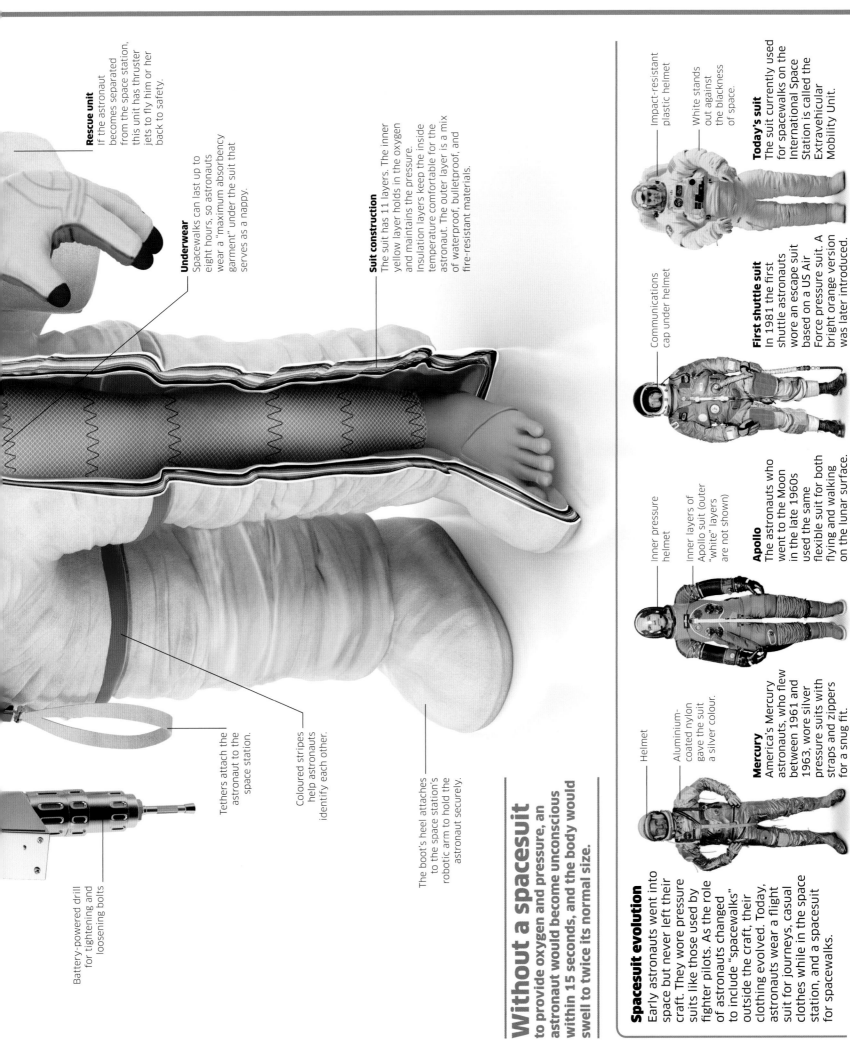

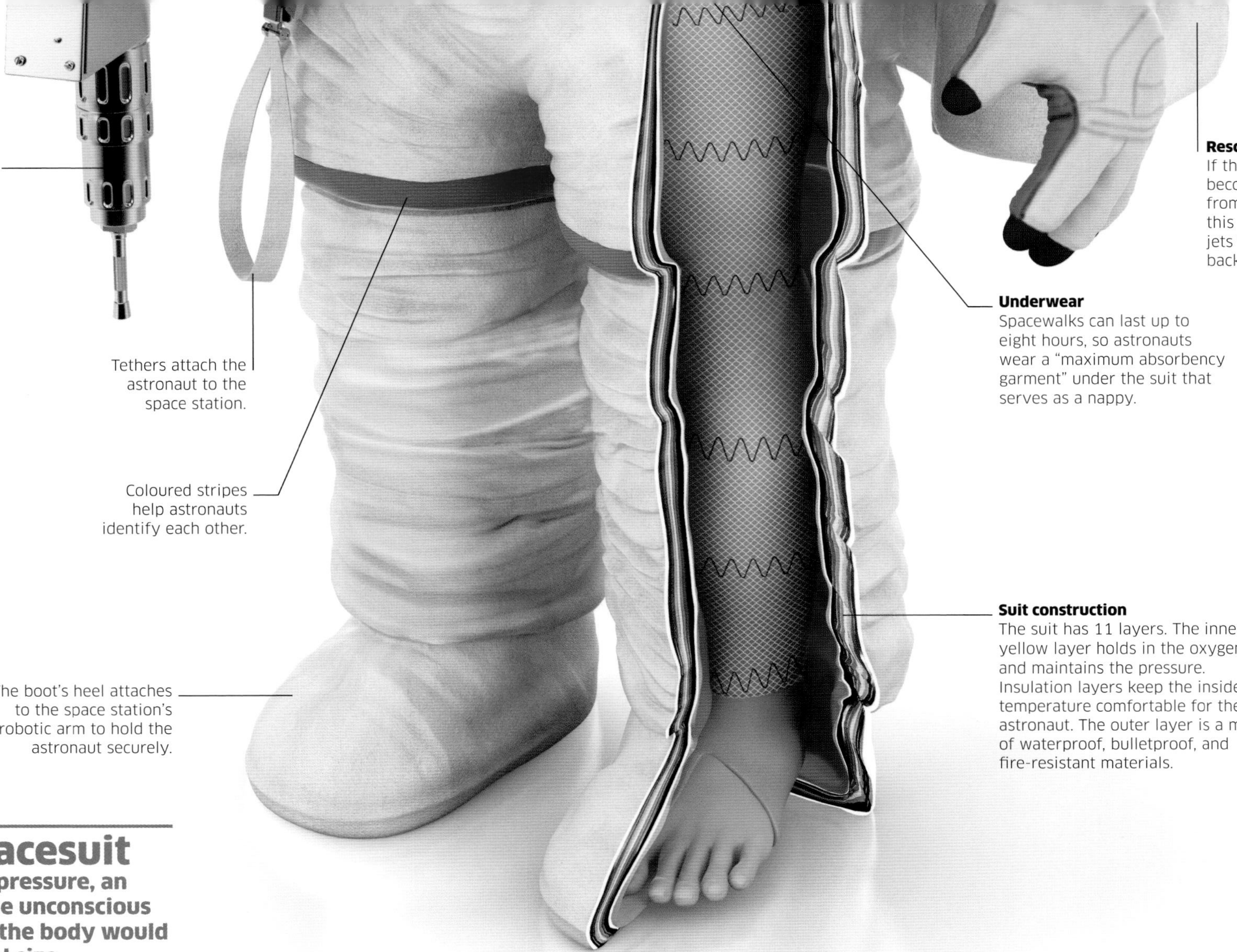
Battery-powered drill for tightening and loosening bolts
Tethers attach the astronaut to the space station.
Coloured stripes help astronauts identify each other.
The boot's heel attaches to the space station's robotic arm to hold the astronaut securely.
Rescue unit
If the astronaut becomes separated from the space station, this unit has thruster jets to fly him or her back to safety.
Underwear
Spacewalks can last up to eight hours, so astronauts wear a "maximum absorbency garment" under the suit that serves as a nappy.
Suit construction
The suit has 11 layers. The inner yellow layer holds in the oxygen and maintains the pressure. Insulation layers keep the inside temperature comfortable for the astronaut. The outer layer is a mix of waterproof, bulletproof, and fire-resistant materials.

Without a spacesuit

to provide oxygen and pressure, an astronaut would become unconscious within 15 seconds, and the body would swell to twice its normal size.

Spacesuit evolution

Early astronauts went into space but never left their craft. They wore pressure suits like those used by fighter pilots. As the role of astronauts changed to include "spacewalks" outside the craft, their clothing evolved. Today, astronauts wear a flight suit for journeys, casual clothes while in the space station, and a spacesuit for spacewalks.

Helmet
Aluminium-coated nylon gave the suit a silver colour.

Mercury
America's Mercury astronauts, who flew between 1961 and 1963, wore silver pressure suits with straps and zippers for a snug fit.

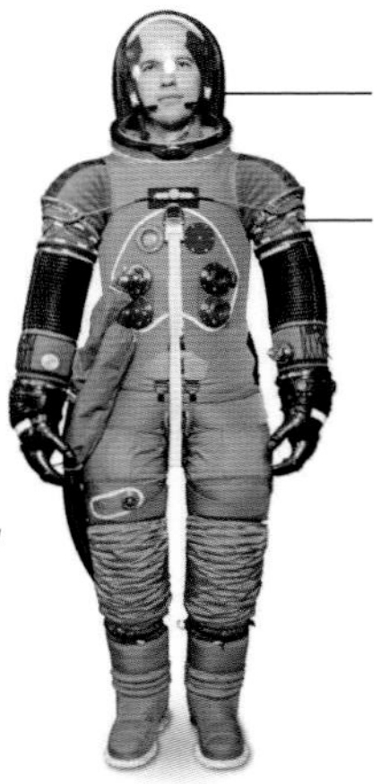
Inner pressure helmet
Inner layers of Apollo suit (outer "white" layers are not shown)

Apollo
The astronauts who went to the Moon in the late 1960s used the same flexible suit for both flying and walking on the lunar surface.

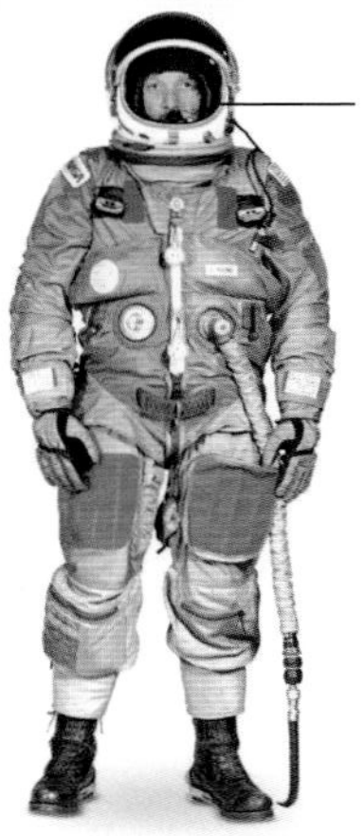
Communications cap under helmet

First shuttle suit
In 1981 the first shuttle astronauts wore an escape suit based on a US Air Force pressure suit. A bright orange version was later introduced.

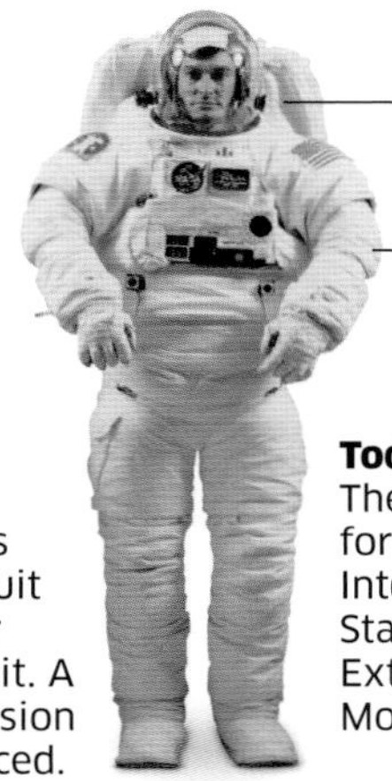
Impact-resistant plastic helmet
White stands out against the blackness of space.

Today's suit
The suit currently used for spacewalks on the International Space Station is called the Extravehicular Mobility Unit.

РОСКОСМОС

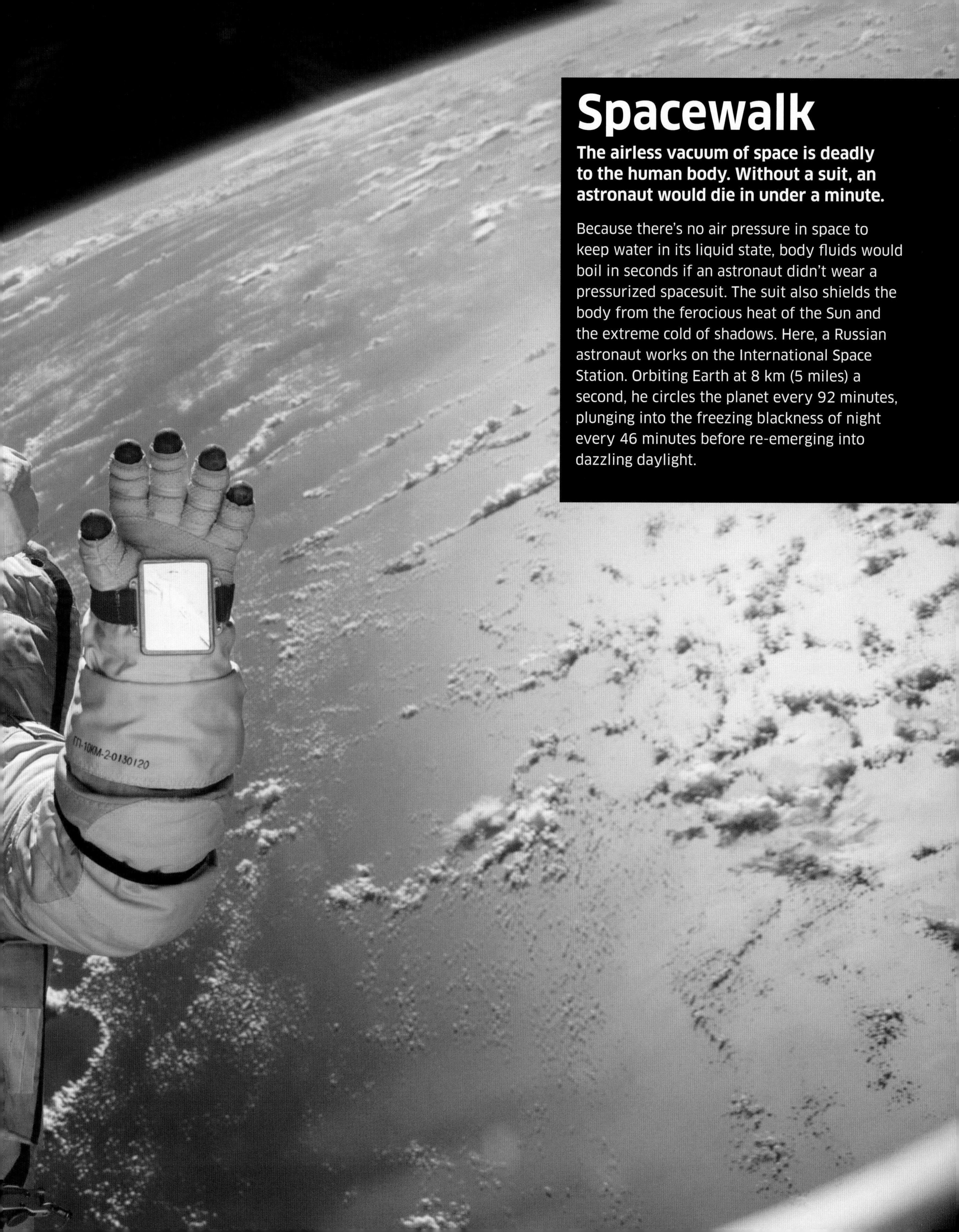
ГП-10КМ-2-0130120

Spacewalk

The airless vacuum of space is deadly to the human body. Without a suit, an astronaut would die in under a minute.

Because there's no air pressure in space to keep water in its liquid state, body fluids would boil in seconds if an astronaut didn't wear a pressurized spacesuit. The suit also shields the body from the ferocious heat of the Sun and the extreme cold of shadows. Here, a Russian astronaut works on the International Space Station. Orbiting Earth at 8 km (5 miles) a second, he circles the planet every 92 minutes, plunging into the freezing blackness of night every 46 minutes before re-emerging into dazzling daylight.

437.7 days – the **longest single stay in space**, by Valerie Poliakov on the Mir space station.

Space stations

Only three people have spent more than a year continuously in space, all of them on board a space station. These giant, orbiting spacecraft allow astronauts to spend long periods living and working off the planet.

A total of ten manned space stations have orbited Earth since 1971. The first one, Salyut 1, was small enough to be launched in one piece but had room for three people. Larger space stations are built in orbit by joining room-like parts called modules, which are constructed on Earth and launched separately. Astronauts used this method to build the International Space Station (ISS), fixing the first parts together in 1998. It is the largest man-made object ever to orbit Earth and is easily visible to the naked eye, looking like a bright star that sweeps across the sky in just a few minutes. The ISS is used for scientific research, but space stations may one day be used as staging posts for manned missions to the planets.

International Space Station

Inside, the ISS is as spacious as a six-bedroom house. Most of the space is taken up by work areas such as laboratories. The crew of six work nine hours a day, five days a week, performing experiments and exercising to keep fit.

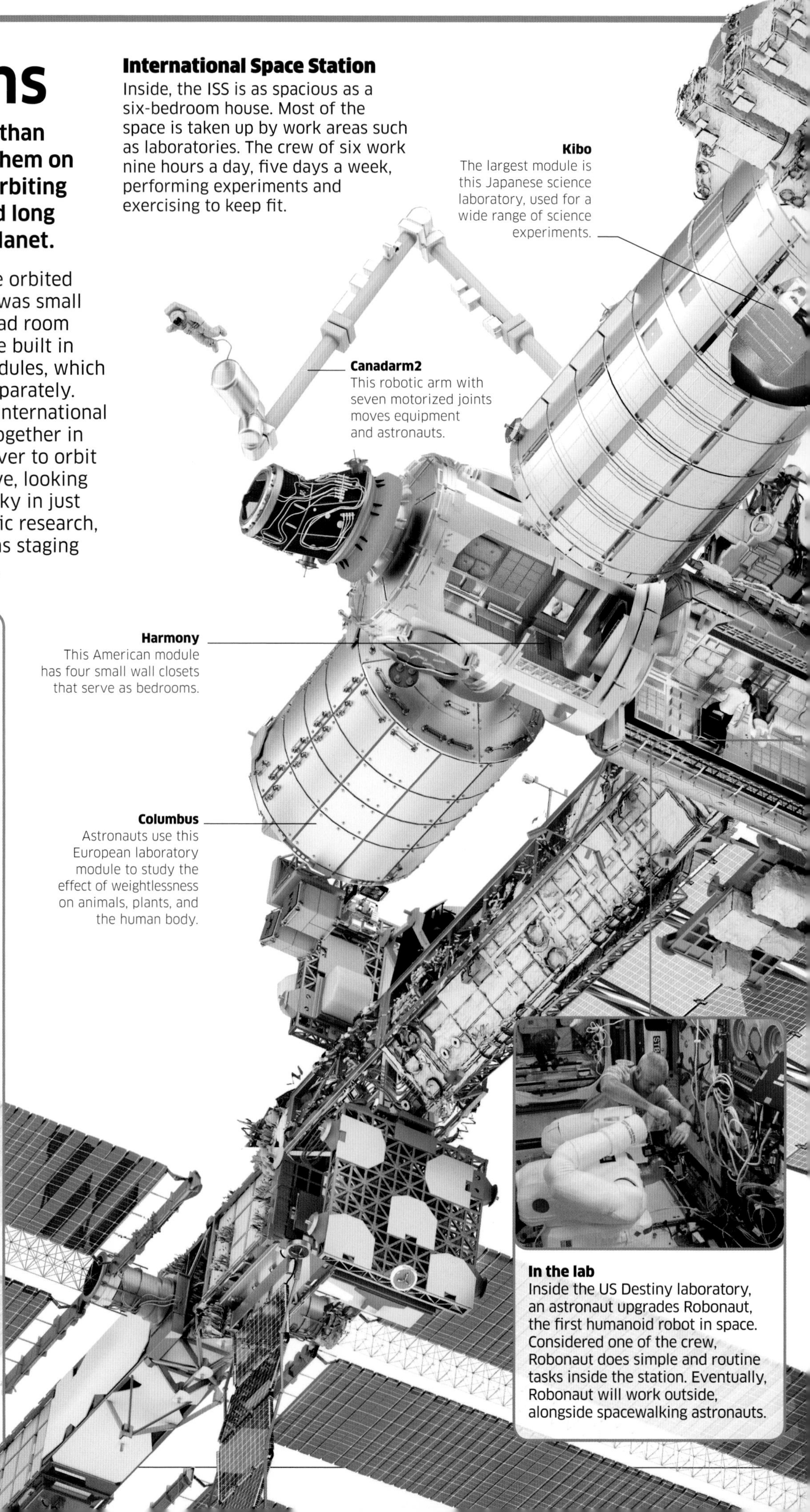

Kibo
The largest module is this Japanese science laboratory, used for a wide range of science experiments.

Canadarm2
This robotic arm with seven motorized joints moves equipment and astronauts.

Harmony
This American module has four small wall closets that serve as bedrooms.

Columbus
Astronauts use this European laboratory module to study the effect of weightlessness on animals, plants, and the human body.

How big is it?

The ISS is about the size of a football pitch and is more than 50 per cent longer than a Boeing 747 (the world's longest passenger aircraft). It weighs about 450 tonnes, which is about as much as 375 average cars.

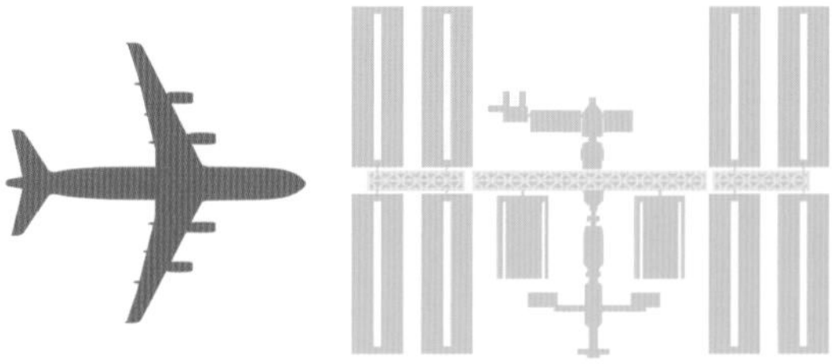

BOEING 747
71 m (233 ft) long

INTERNATIONAL SPACE STATION
109 m (357 ft) long

Orbit

Travelling at 27,600 kph (17,100 mph), the ISS circles Earth once every 90 minutes or so, crossing from the southern to northern hemisphere and back again on each orbit. Because Earth rotates, the ISS passes over a different part of the planet on each pass, tracing out the blue line below.

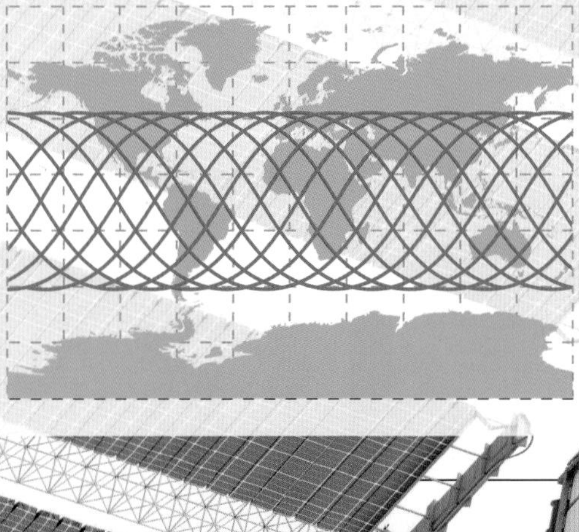

In the lab
Inside the US Destiny laboratory, an astronaut upgrades Robonaut, the first humanoid robot in space. Considered one of the crew, Robonaut does simple and routine tasks inside the station. Eventually, Robonaut will work outside, alongside spacewalking astronauts.

48 days (1,152 hours) of spacewalks were needed to build the ISS.

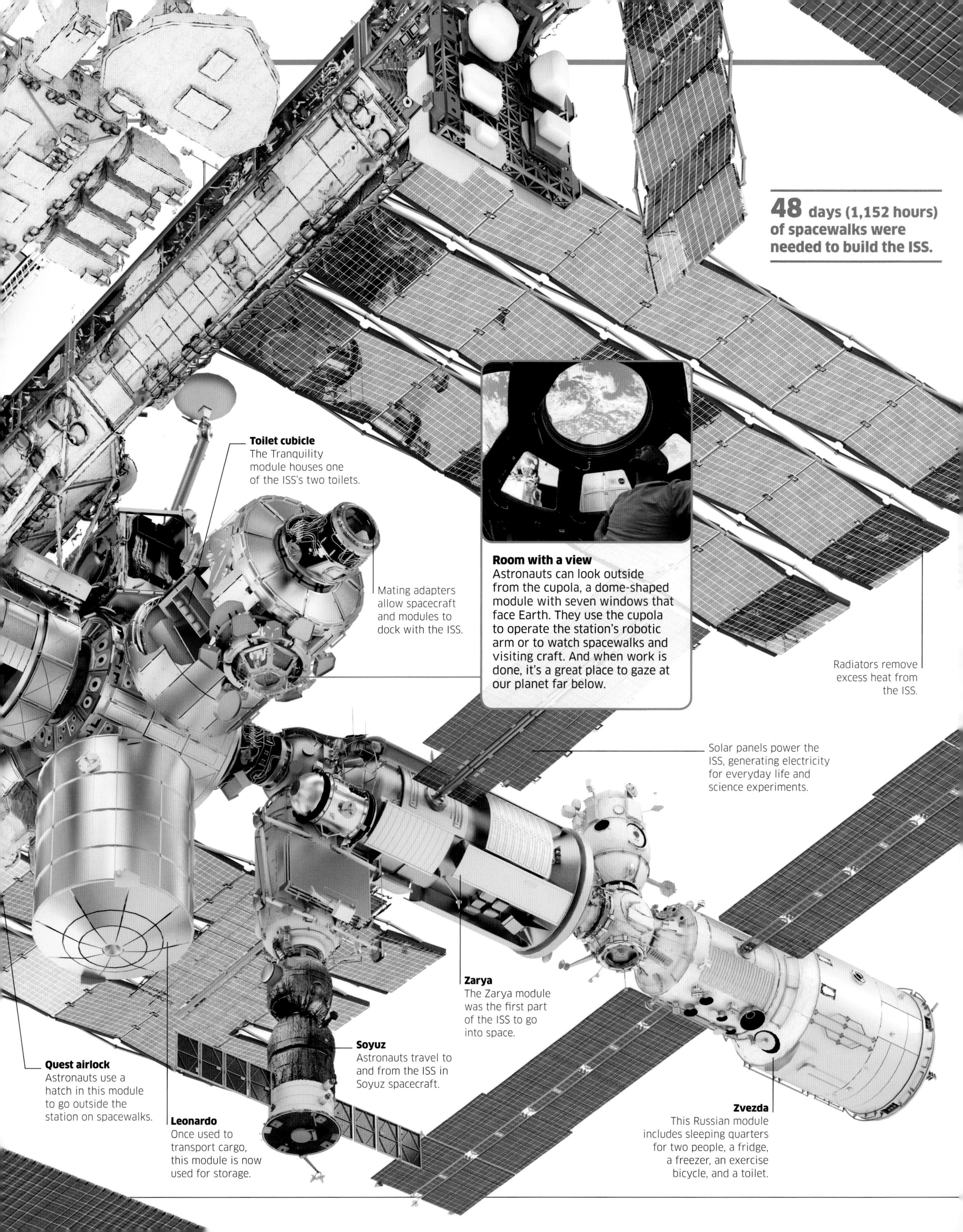
Toilet cubicle
The Tranquility module houses one of the ISS's two toilets.
Mating adapters allow spacecraft and modules to dock with the ISS.
Radiators remove excess heat from the ISS.
Solar panels power the ISS, generating electricity for everyday life and science experiments.
Zarya
The Zarya module was the first part of the ISS to go into space.
Soyuz
Astronauts travel to and from the ISS in Soyuz spacecraft.
Quest airlock
Astronauts use a hatch in this module to go outside the station on spacewalks.
Leonardo
Once used to transport cargo, this module is now used for storage.
Zvezda
This Russian module includes sleeping quarters for two people, a fridge, a freezer, an exercise bicycle, and a toilet.

Room with a view
Astronauts can look outside from the cupola, a dome-shaped module with seven windows that face Earth. They use the cupola to operate the station's robotic arm or to watch spacewalks and visiting craft. And when work is done, it's a great place to gaze at our planet far below.

Humans on Mars would weigh just over **one-third of their Earth weight**.

Future exploration

Although no humans have left Earth orbit since the last Apollo Moon mission in 1972, many proposals have been made to send astronauts further afield, with Mars being the most ambitious target.

The US space agency NASA has no plans to send astronauts back to the Moon, but China and Russia both hope to launch manned lunar missions in coming decades. NASA hopes to land astronauts on an asteroid by 2025 and on Mars in later decades, but the costs, technical challenges, and risks involved in a human mission to Mars are enormous. In the meantime, robotic spacecraft and rovers are likely to continue exploring the Solar System, advancing our knowledge of the planets without the dangers or costs of manned expeditions.

Martian base

This artist's impression shows one proposed idea for a Mars base. The main building is constructed from a series of landers that arrive separately and are joined together by robotic rovers already on the ground. The technology needed to build a base of this sophistication may not exist for decades.

Because Mars has a thin atmosphere and a weak magnetic field, dangerous levels of radiation reach the surface. Living quarters would need to be heavily shielded or underground.
Landers bring supplies of air and water.
Martian soil contains ice that could be melted to produce drinkable water and oxygen.

Greenhouse
Long-term settlers on Mars would have to produce their own food in greenhouses. The plants would need a large supply of water, which would be difficult to provide, as well as warmth, air, and artificial light. Growing plants outdoors on Mars would be impossible as the temperature is too low and there is no liquid water.

Living quarters
Because buried dwellings would have no windows, settlers would use screens to see outside and to keep in touch with Earth. However, live conversations with Earth would not be possible as radio signals from Mars take about 40 minutes to get there and back.

Inflatable homes
Constructing large buildings on Mars would be impossible, so settlers would either have to live inside landers or bring cleverly packaged dwellings that could be erected simply. One solution might be to use inflatable dwellings. Because the air pressure on Mars is very low, any dwellings would need to withstand being filled with pressurized air.

Solar panels provide power. Although Mars is farther from the Sun than Earth, its thinner air lets more solar energy reach the ground.

Space tourism

Only a handful of people have paid to go into space as tourists, all of them spending time on the International Space Station. One enjoyed his stay so much he went back again. In years to come, private companies may offer new ways for people to visit space as tourists.

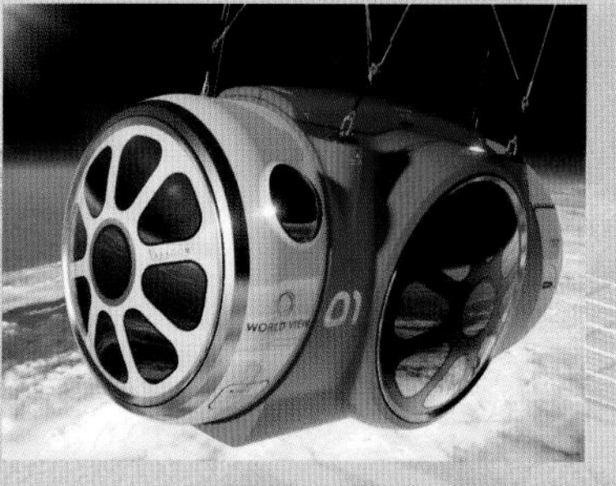

World-view balloon
This high-tech balloon ride will give six tourists a near-space experience. At 32 km (20 miles) above Earth, they'll see dark space above and our blue planet below.

SpaceShipTwo
A two-and-a-half-hour trip aboard SpaceShipTwo will take tourists just beyond the edge of space. They'll have six minutes to float around the cabin in weightlessness before returning.

The search for life

The Universe is a huge place. In our home galaxy, there may be as many as 100 billion stars with planets, yet our galaxy is just one of perhaps 200 billion galaxies. It seems unlikely, therefore, that Earth is the only place with life. Large telescopes all over the world are searching space for evidence that life could exist elsewhere. We probably won't come across any little green men – in fact, it may be hard to recognize life if we do find it. An unexplained radio signal, a hint of hidden water, a rock that might contain tiny fossils: these are the sorts of clues scientists are looking for.

IS ANYBODY OUT THERE?

In 1961 astronomer Frank Drake devised a method for estimating how many civilizations might be sending out radio signals in our galaxy. Known as the Drake Equation, this formula involves seven factors, written as symbols, which have to be multiplied together. The values of some of the factors can only be guessed at, so the equation gives only a very rough idea of our chances of finding extraterrestrials.

RADIO SIGNALS

If alien civilizations do exist somewhere, it's possible they have discovered how to use radio waves to send signals to each other, just as we do with phones, TV, and radio broadcasts. So one way of finding aliens is simply to search for their radio signals travelling through space. SETI (search for extraterrestrial intelligence) projects do this, using huge radio dishes to scan the skies for distinctive signals. We can also use radio telescopes to send out our own messages, aiming them at likely destinations in our galaxy. So far, neither approach has brought success.

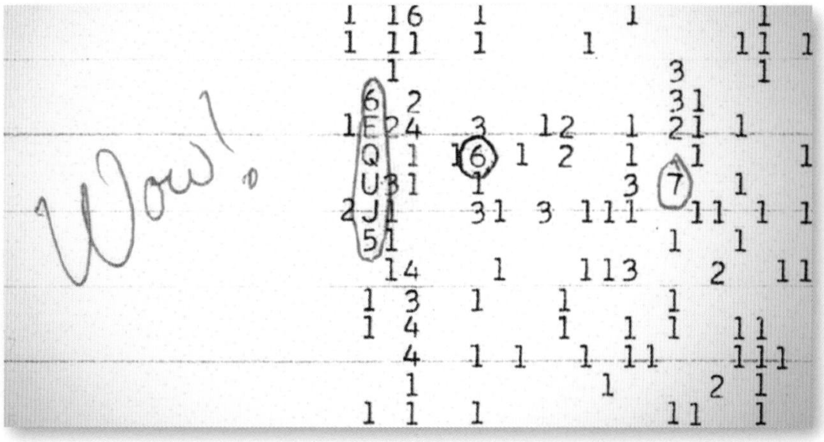
Wow!

The Wow! signal
In 1977 a scientist at an American radio observatory noticed that a signal from space was unusually strong. Thrilled that it might be a message from aliens, he wrote "Wow!" on a printout. Sadly, the Wow! signal was never detected again.

Searching the skies
The Arecibo radio telescope in Puerto Rico is the largest single-dish radio telescope ever built, measuring more than 300 m (1,000 ft) wide. This telescope sometimes searches for alien radio broadcasts at the same time as making regular astronomical observations.

$$N = R^{*} \times f_p \times n_e \times f_l \times f_i \times f_c \times L$$

- **N**: Number of alien civilizations that are sending out radio signals
- **R***: The rate at which new stars form in our galaxy each year
- **f_p**: The fraction of such stars that have a family of orbiting planets
- **n_e**: For each star, the number of planets that have the right conditions for life
- **f_l**: The fraction of such planets on which life appears
- **f_i**: The fraction of life-supporting planets on which intelligent life develops
- **f_c**: The fraction of civilizations that develop radio technology
- **L**: The lifespan of each civilization, judged by how long it continues to send messages

The Arecibo message

In 1974 astronomers used the Arecibo radio telescope to send a coded message towards a star cluster 25,000 light years away. The signal lasted three minutes and consisted of a stream of binary numbers that, when decoded, forms a simple picture telling aliens about life on Earth. Since the signal will take 25,000 years to reach its target – and any reply will take another 25,000 years to come back – the message was symbolic rather than a serious attempt to communicate.

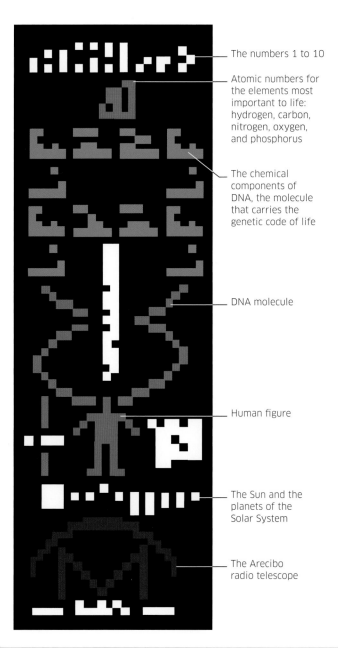

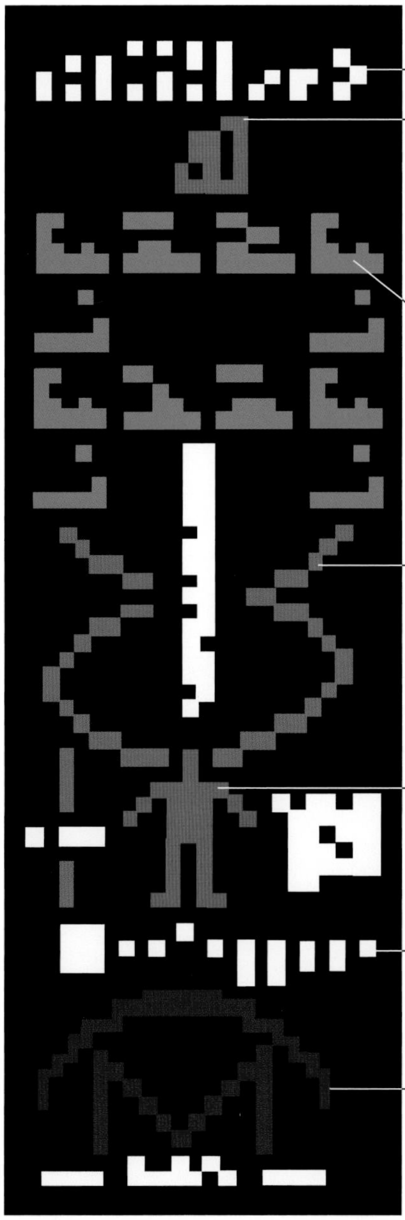
The numbers 1 to 10
Atomic numbers for the elements most important to life: hydrogen, carbon, nitrogen, oxygen, and phosphorus
The chemical components of DNA, the molecule that carries the genetic code of life
DNA molecule
Human figure
The Sun and the planets of the Solar System
The Arecibo radio telescope

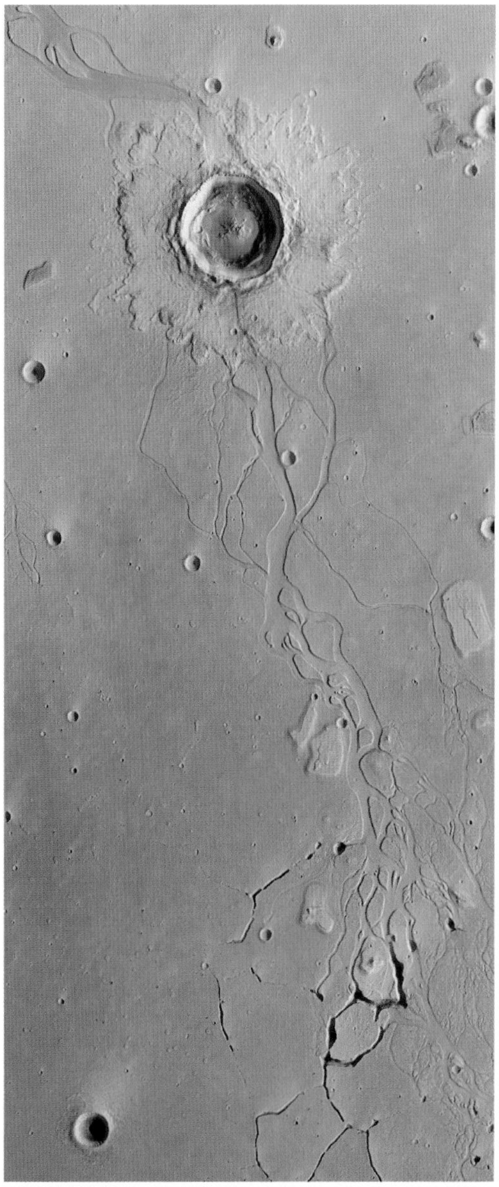

SEARCHING THE SOLAR SYSTEM

Although we have yet to find evidence of life in other parts of our Solar System, spacecraft have found evidence of liquid water, which is vital to life on Earth. Hidden oceans exist under the surface of some moons, and water almost certainly once flowed on Mars.

Mars

Photographs of Mars strongly suggest that water has flowed across its surface in the past, if only for brief periods. Long ago, Mars may have been warmer and wetter, allowing rivers and lakes to exist on the surface. Future Martian landers may try to find out whether there are any buried fossils from Mars's remote past.

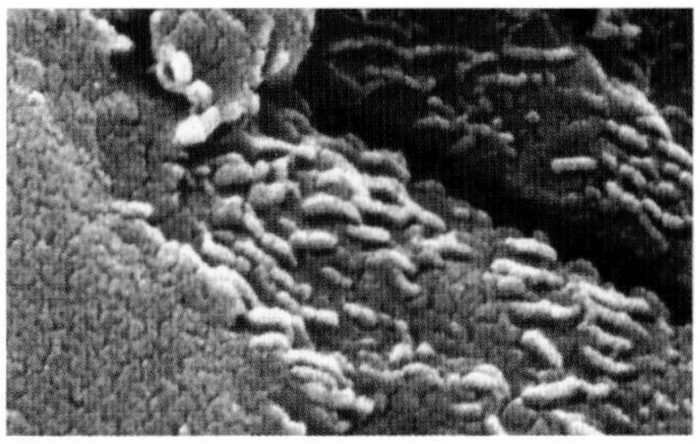

Martian meteorite
In 1996 scientists amazed the world when they announced the discovery of what looked like fossilized bacteria inside a Martian meteorite found in Antarctica. This evidence of extraterrestrial life seemed so strong that US president Bill Clinton made a televized statement about the discovery. Since then, scientists have argued about the structures inside meteorite ALH84001, which some claim are merely mineral deposits.

Under the ice

Hidden below the icy surface of Jupiter's moon Europa (left) there likely exists a huge salt-water ocean, warmed by strong tides. Since water and warmth are key to the development of life, Europa is high on scientists' list of Solar System locations to search for life. Saturn's moon Enceladus probably also has a liquid-water ocean beneath an ice covering, and this too might be a place that could harbour life.

THE NIGHT SKY

You don't need to board a rocket to see space – just walk outside on a clear night and look up. The constellations are easy to see with the naked eye, but with binoculars you can see more – from the moons of Jupiter to star-birth nebulas and even whole galaxies.

The celestial sphere

The celestial sphere is an imaginary sphere around Earth on which any object in the sky can be precisely mapped, just as locations on Earth can be mapped on a globe. Different parts of the sphere are visible from different areas of Earth, and because our planet is continually rotating, different areas of the sphere come into view over the course of a night. Stars and other distant objects stay fixed in more or less the same place on the celestial sphere for long periods of time, but objects in the Solar System, such as the Sun, Moon, and planets, are always moving.

THE SPINNING SKY

It's impossible to see the whole celestial sphere at once because Earth gets in the way. However, because Earth rotates and travels around the Sun, different parts of the celestial sphere come into view at different times. How much you can see, and how the stars move, depends on whereabouts on Earth you live.

Key to spheres

- Observer
- Observer's horizon
- Stars always visible
- Stars visible at some time
- Stars never visible

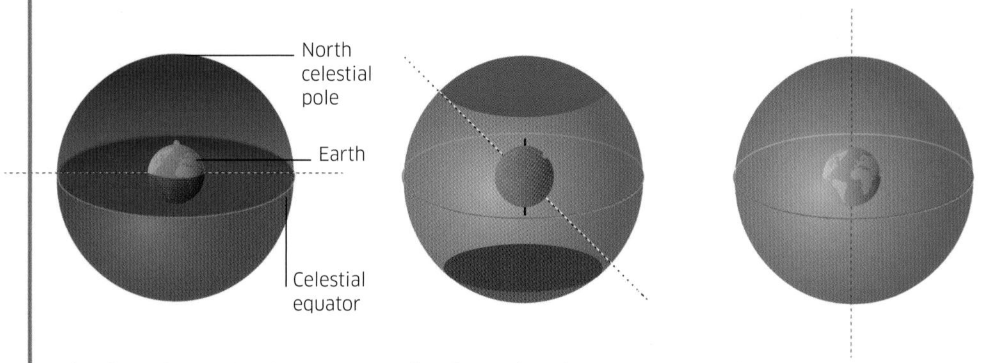
North celestial pole
Earth
Celestial equator

View from the North Pole
From here you can only see the northern half of the celestial sphere – the other half is never visible. As Earth rotates, the stars move in circles around the celestial pole, which is directly overhead.

View from mid-latitudes
From mid-latitude regions such as the US and Europe, you can always see the constellations around the celestial pole, but the other constellations change during the night and during the year.

View from the equator
From the equator, you can see the whole of the celestial sphere over the course of a year. The north and south celestial poles lie on the horizon, making polar constellations hard to see.

Through the year

Earth's night-side faces different parts of the celestial sphere over the course of the year as we orbit the Sun. Because of this, different constellations come in and out of view as the months pass. Stars are easiest to see in winter, because the nights are longer and the darkness is much deeper. In summer, nights are shorter and the sky doesn't get so dark, so stars look fainter.

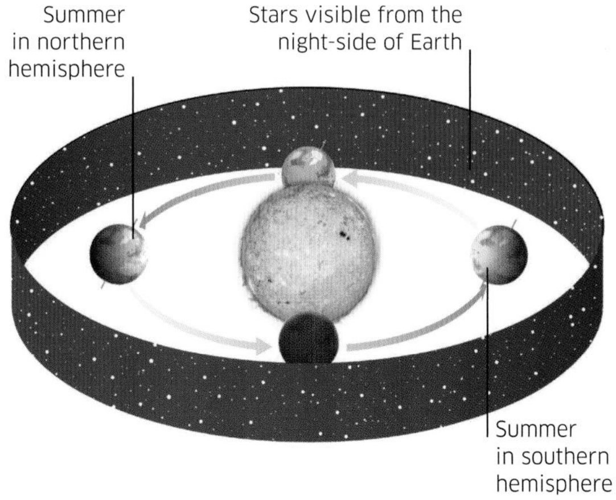
Summer in northern hemisphere
Stars visible from the night-side of Earth
Summer in southern hemisphere

WHAT IS THE CELESTIAL SPHERE?

Think of the celestial sphere as a giant glass ball around Earth with stars pinned to its surface. Because Earth rotates, the celestial sphere also appears to rotate. Like Earth, it has north and south poles and is divided into northern and southern hemispheres by an equator. We can pinpoint any location on Earth with measurements called latitude and longitude. The celestial sphere uses a similar system but the numbers are called declination and right ascension.

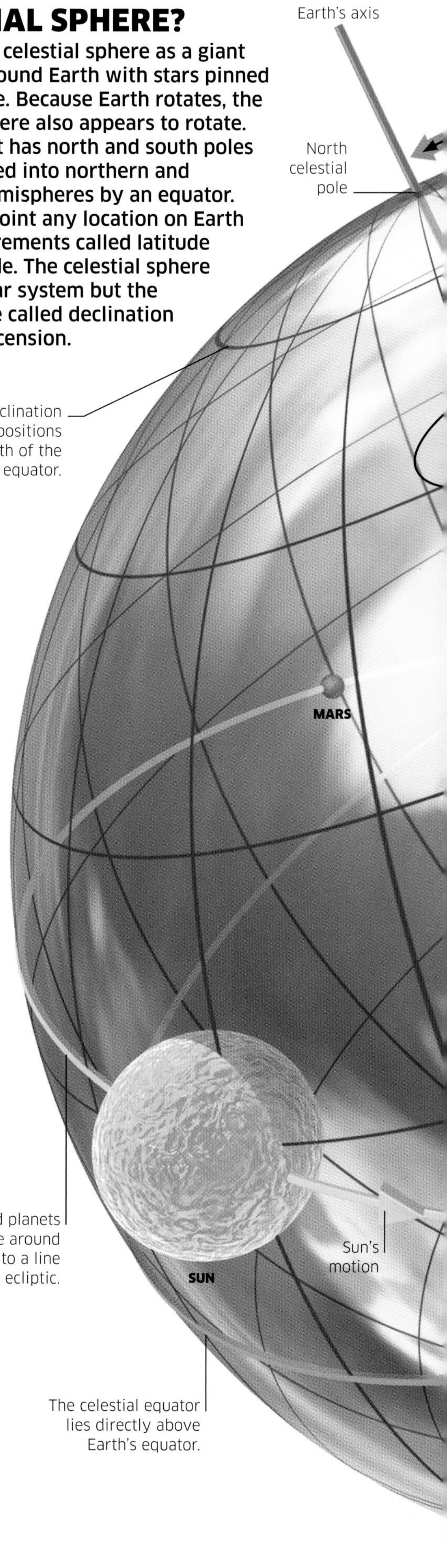
Earth's axis
North celestial pole
Lines of declination measure positions north or south of the celestial equator.
MARS
The Sun and planets appear to move around the sky close to a line called the ecliptic.
SUN
Sun's motion
The celestial equator lies directly above Earth's equator.

Earth's axis is
tilted by 23.4°
Lines of right ascension
are used to give east-west
positions on the celestial sphere.
The star patterns
don't change but the
whole sky seems to
turn in the opposite
direction to Earth's spin.
EARTH'S SPIN
JUPITER
SATURN
EARTH
Equator
VENUS
MERCURY
The south
celestial pole is
directly above
Earth's South Pole.

ORIGINS

In ancient times, people didn't know that Earth rotates, so they naturally thought that the Sun and stars were moving around us. Ancient stargazers thought Earth was the centre of the Universe, surrounded by a set of glass spheres – one for the stars and separate spheres for the Moon, each planet, and the Sun.

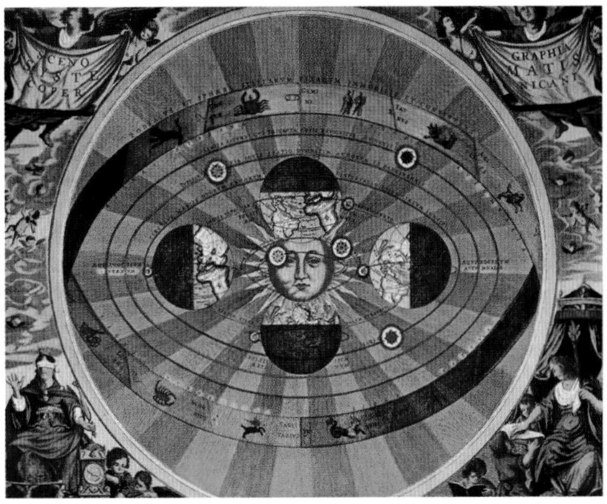

ILLUSTRATION OF THE COPERNICAN SYSTEM, 1661

Sun in the middle

About 500 years ago, Polish astronomer Nicolaus Copernicus realized he could predict the movements of the planets better by assuming the Sun was in the middle rather than Earth. His revolutionary theory showed that Earth was not the centre of creation.

The zodiac

The Sun's path along the ecliptic takes it through 13 constellations: 12, called the signs of the zodiac, have long been seen as having special significance. The 13th, Ophiuchus, is often overlooked.

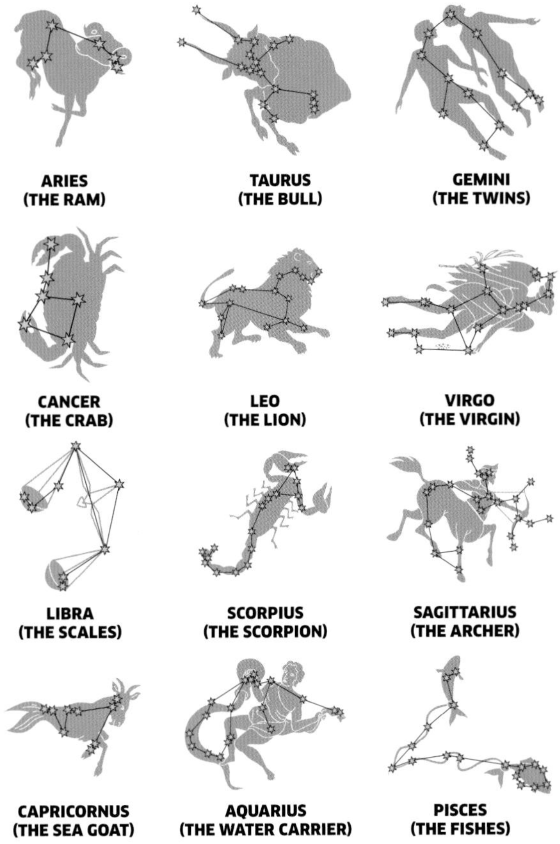
ARIES
(THE RAM)
TAURUS
(THE BULL)
GEMINI
(THE TWINS)
CANCER
(THE CRAB)
LEO
(THE LION)
VIRGO
(THE VIRGIN)
LIBRA
(THE SCALES)
SCORPIUS
(THE SCORPION)
SAGITTARIUS
(THE ARCHER)
CAPRICORNUS
(THE SEA GOAT)
AQUARIUS
(THE WATER CARRIER)
PISCES
(THE FISHES)

Practical stargazing

One of the things that makes astronomy such a great hobby is that everybody can join in. On a typical dark night, a person with good vision can see up to 3,000 stars, so there are plenty of interesting features to find with the naked eye and learn about. Before getting started, it's best to understand a few basics, such as the way the stars and other objects move across the sky and how astronomers keep track of them. Armed with this essential knowledge, anyone can go out and begin to identify the constellations or learn to spot red giants, star-birth nebulas, or even whole galaxies millions of light years from Earth.

BASIC EQUIPMENT

The essentials for a night's stargazing are warm clothes, a star chart of some sort, and a torch to see by. If you have a smartphone or tablet, you can download various apps that will show the night sky visible from your location at any time and date. However, many people prefer to use a circular chart called a planisphere.

Night vision
It takes about half an hour for your eyes to fully adjust to darkness so that you can see the faintest stars. Avoid bright light or you'll ruin your night vision. If you need to use a torch, a red one is best as it won't affect your ability to see in the dark.

SIZING UP THE SKY

Astronomers treat the sky as if it were a huge sphere surrounding Earth. Distances between objects are measured in degrees. There are 360 degrees in a circle, so the distance around the whole sky is 360 degrees. The Moon is about half a degree wide.

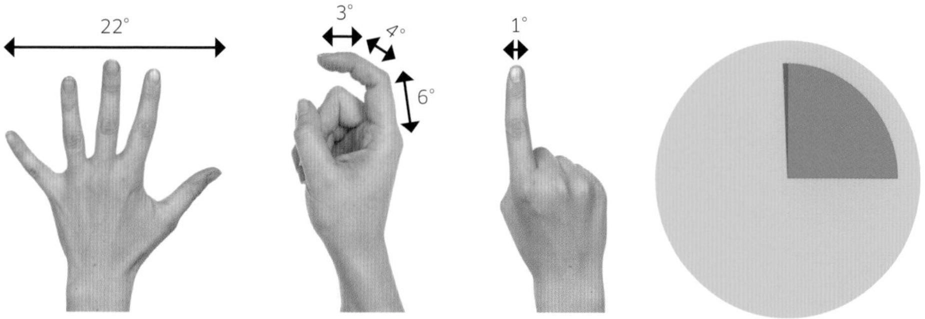
22°
3°
4°
6°
1°

Handspan
A hand held at arm's length with fingers spread widely covers an angle of about 22 degrees between the outstretched little finger and thumb.

Finger joints
The top part of an index finger is about 3 degrees wide. The middle part is 4 degrees wide, and the bottom part is 6 degrees wide.

Finger width
The tip of a finger pointing upwards at arm's length is about 1 degree wide and can completely cover a full moon.

1 degree
90 degrees
360 degrees

Mapping the stars

You can measure the exact position of a star at any moment with two numbers. One is altitude: the star's height above the horizon, measured in degrees. The other is azimuth: the angle from due north, measured in degrees clockwise. The star below, for example, has an altitude of 45 degrees and an azimuth of 25 degrees.

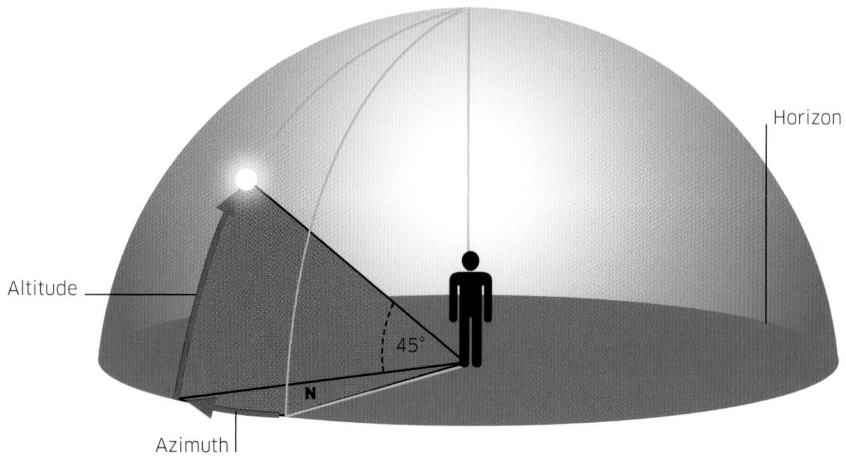
Horizon
Altitude
45°
N
Azimuth

UNDER DARK SKIES

The key to good stargazing is to find the darkest, clearest skies available. Professional observatories are often located on high mountaintops in remote areas, but the most important thing is simply to get away from city lights and the glow of "light pollution". Under a truly dark sky, the Milky Way is an unforgettable sight.

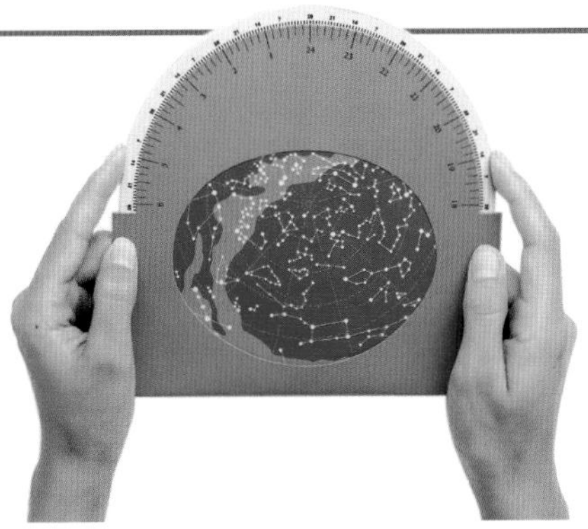

Planisphere
This astronomer's tool consists of a circular star chart and an overlay with an oval window. When the time and date marked around the edges of the two layers are correctly aligned, the stars shown in the window will mirror those in the sky above.

Optical Instruments

Binoculars and telescopes will boost your stargazing. Their big lenses or mirrors collect much more light than a human eye can, revealing very faint objects such as nebulas and galaxies. Their eyepieces, meanwhile, create a magnified image of a small part of the sky, allowing stargazers to separate closely spaced objects, such as double stars, and see more detail on the Moon and planets.

Binoculars
Binoculars have two large, light-collecting lenses and use prisms to direct light into magnifying eyepieces. Good binoculars will allow you to see Jupiter's moons, but you need steady hands to stop the image shaking.

Telescopes
A telescope has either an objective lens or a large primary mirror. It collects much more light than binoculars. The eyepiece gives a highly magnified image of a smaller area of sky. A tripod or other mount is used to steady the telescope and stop it wobbling about.

Milky Way
Our home galaxy is visible on clear, moonless nights as a wash of milky light across the sky. The best time to see it is late summer in the northern hemisphere and late winter in the southern hemisphere.

THE CHANGING SKY

Watch the sky for more than a few minutes and you'll notice that the stars move slowly around the sky, rising in the east and setting in the west. This is an illusion caused by Earth's rotation, and the pattern of movement varies between different parts of the world.

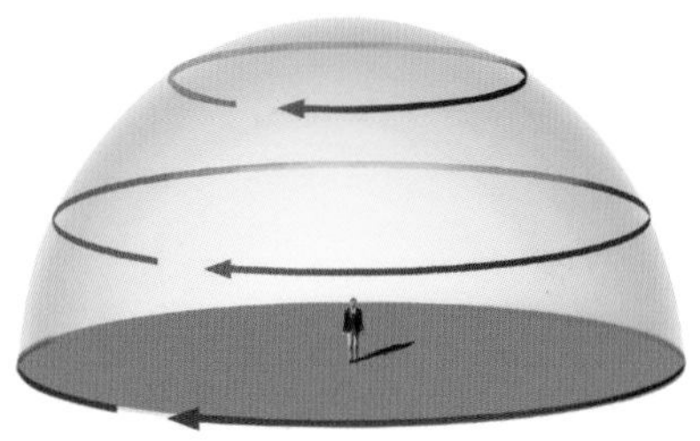

Motion at the North Pole
If you watched the sky from Earth's North Pole, no stars would ever rise or set. Instead, they would simply move in circles around the Pole Star, which never moves.

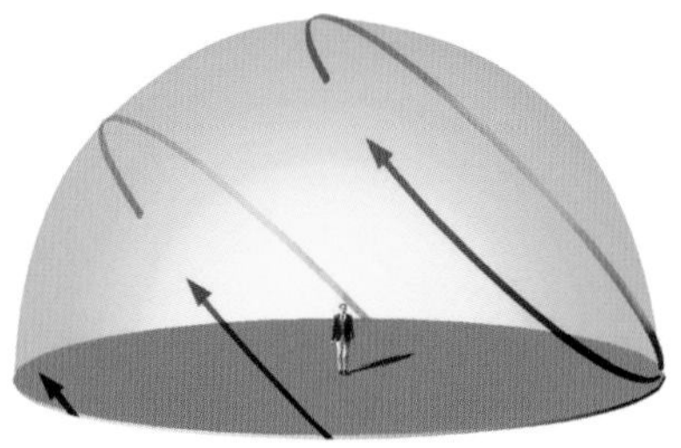

Motion at mid-latitudes
From most parts of the world, some stars stay visible throughout the night, travelling in a circle, while other stars rise and set.

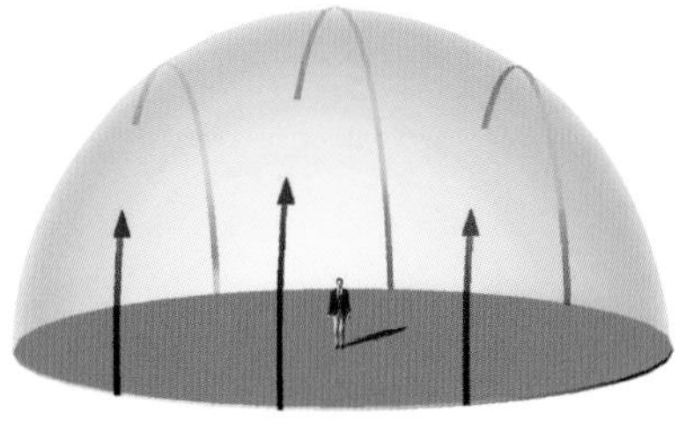

Motion at the equator
At the equator, all stars rise in the east, cross the sky, and then set in the west. The constellations visible by night change gradually over the course of a year.

Moving constellations

Earth's orbit around the Sun means that the positions of the constellations in the sky appear to change. You'll notice this if you view the same constellation at the same time over several weeks.

1 APRIL, 8 PM

8 APRIL, 8 PM

15 APRIL, 8 PM

Northern star hopping

To the untrained eye, the night sky can look like a bewildering mass of stars. A good way to make sense of it is to look for well-known landmarks and then trace imaginary lines from these to other constellations. This technique is called star hopping and is easy to do with the naked eye, though you can see more if you have binoculars or a telescope. The chart on this page shows how to star-hop around the north celestial pole, which is visible to people who live in Earth's northern hemisphere.

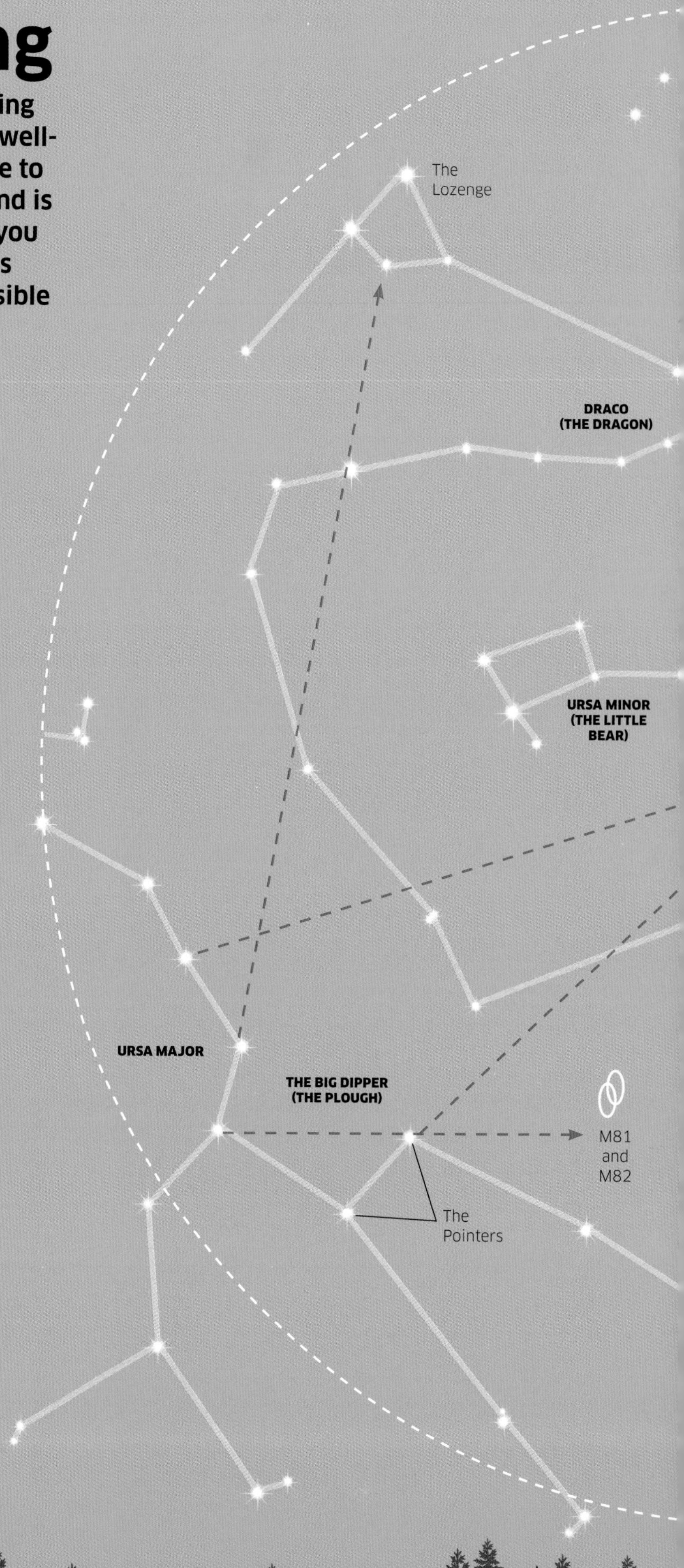
The Lozenge
DRACO (THE DRAGON)
URSA MINOR (THE LITTLE BEAR)
URSA MAJOR
THE BIG DIPPER (THE PLOUGH)
M81 and M82
The Pointers

FINDING THE WAY

This tour of the northern sky starts with a famous pattern of stars called the Plough or Big Dipper. You can use the Plough as a signpost to find the Pole Star and other sights nearby. Some are quite faint, so you will need a clear, dark night to see them all.

1 THE FIRST STEP is to find the Plough and locate the two stars farthest from its "handle", which are known as the Pointers. Draw an imaginary line through the Pointers and extend it to a bright star. This is the Pole Star and it is always due north.

2 EXTEND THE LINE from the Pointers past the Pole Star to reach the faint constellation Cepheus, which looks a bit like a lopsided house. Binoculars will reveal the bright red Garnet Star at the base of the house – the reddest star visible to the naked eye and one of the largest stars known.

3 NOW DRAW A LINE from the third star in the Plough's handle through the Pole Star to find the constellation Cassiopeia, which looks like a flattened "W". If you have binoculars, look for a star cluster just below the central peak of the "W".

4 THE LARGE BUT FAINT and shapeless constellation Draco (the Dragon) is best seen under very dark skies. A line from the fourth star in the Plough's handle cuts across the dragon's body and carries on to its head, a pattern of stars called the Lozenge.

5 TRACK DOWN one of the brightest galaxies in the sky with binoculars: follow a diagonal line across the Plough's rectangle of stars, and continue in the same direction looking for a pair of tiny fuzzy patches. These are the galaxies M81 and its fainter companion M82.

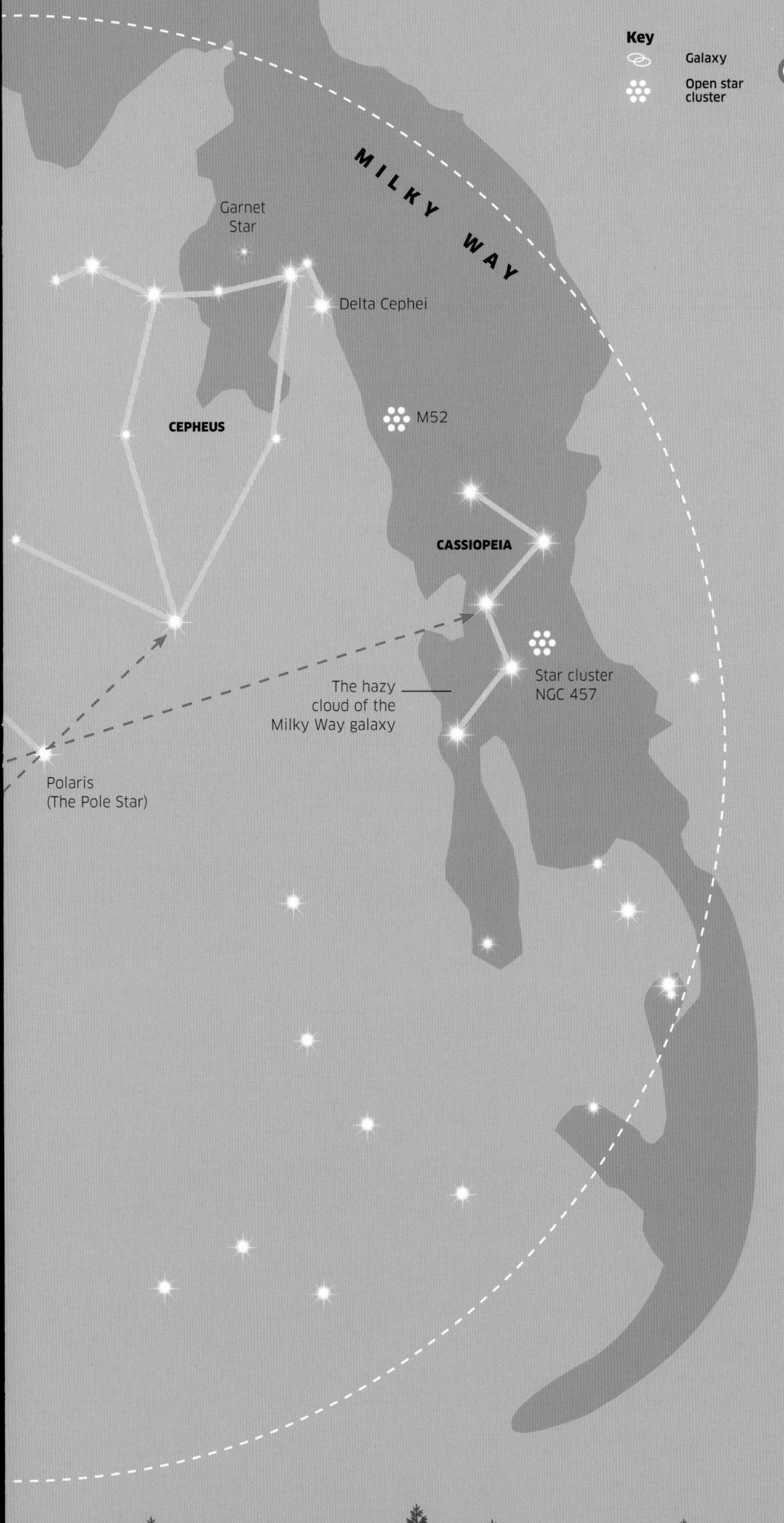

Key
Galaxy
Open star cluster
MILKY WAY
Garnet Star
Delta Cephei
CEPHEUS
M52
CASSIOPEIA
Star cluster NGC 457
The hazy cloud of the Milky Way galaxy
Polaris (The Pole Star)

WHAT TO SEE

Close to the band of the Milky Way, we can see densely packed stars, clusters, and nebulas. Away from it, we can only see a few relatively nearby stars, and some distant galaxies across the gulf of intergalactic space.

Big and Little bears
The brightest seven stars of the constellation Ursa Major, the Great Bear, form the familiar pattern known as the Plough or Big Dipper. Following the Pointers to the Pole Star reveals a similar pattern of seven stars called Ursa Minor, the Little Bear.

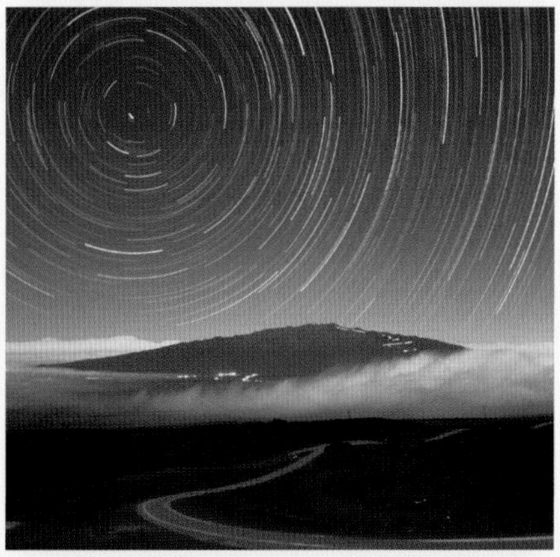

Pole Star
Because Earth rotates, stars move across the sky during the night, circling the north celestial pole. However, one star barely moves: the Pole Star, which lies in the tail of the Little Bear (Ursa Minor). Sailors used to use this guiding star to find north on clear nights.

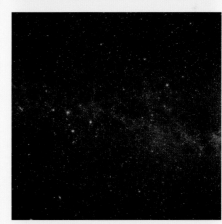

Cassiopeia and the Milky Way
The constellation of Cassiopeia lies embedded in the northern reaches of the Milky Way, the pale band of countless distant stars that wraps its way around the sky. This makes Cassiopeia a rich hunting ground for star clusters and other deep-sky objects.

M81 and M82
The bright spiral galaxy M81 (top), also called Bode's Galaxy, lies about 12 million light years from Earth. Nearby in the night sky is M82 (bottom), an irregular cloud of distant stars that is also known as the Cigar Galaxy.

Southern star hopping

This chart shows you how to star-hop your way around some of the top sights in the southern night sky, visible to people who live in Earth's southern hemisphere. The southern sky gives stargazers a fantastic view of our Milky Way galaxy and the bright constellations Carina, Centaurus, and the Southern Cross. There are many celestial wonders to spot, from colourful nebulas and star clusters to whole galaxies.

FINDING THE WAY

Southern stargazers don't have a pole star to guide them, and the constellations closest to the pole are faint and unremarkable. Fortunately, the Milky Way runs close by and is packed with bright stars and other landmarks. The Southern Cross (Crux) and the so-called Southern Pointers make good starting points for finding your way around the sky.

1 **FIRST IDENTIFY** the Southern Cross (not to be confused with the False Cross) and the Southern Pointer stars Alpha and Beta Centauri. Draw a line from Beta Centauri to the bottom of the Southern Cross and carry on for the same distance again to reach the famous Carina Nebula. This complex mix of a star-forming nebula and a massive star on the brink of explosion is well worth exploring with binoculars.

2 **TWO BEAUTIFUL STAR CLUSTERS** lie close to the Carina Nebula: NGC 3532 and the Southern Pleiades (IC 2602). This second cluster contains five or six naked-eye stars – see how many you can count (you'll see more by looking slightly to one side of it). Then use binoculars to view many more.

3 **NEXT FOLLOW A LINE** from the top of the Southern Cross, past the Carina Nebula, and onwards by the same distance again. Here you'll find the deceptive pattern of the False Cross, and just beyond it the star cluster IC 2391. This impressive jewel box of stars is best appreciated through binoculars.

4 **NOW FOLLOW THE** downward (longer) bar of the Southern Cross and cross an empty area of the sky to reach the Small Magellanic Cloud. This small galaxy orbits our own Milky Way galaxy and contains hundreds of millions of stars. Nearby is a impressive globular cluster of stars known as 47 Tucanae.

5 **FINALLY, RETURN** to the Southern Pointers and follow a line from Alpha Centauri to discover three bright stars that form a triangle shape – the unimaginatively named constellation Triangulum Australe.

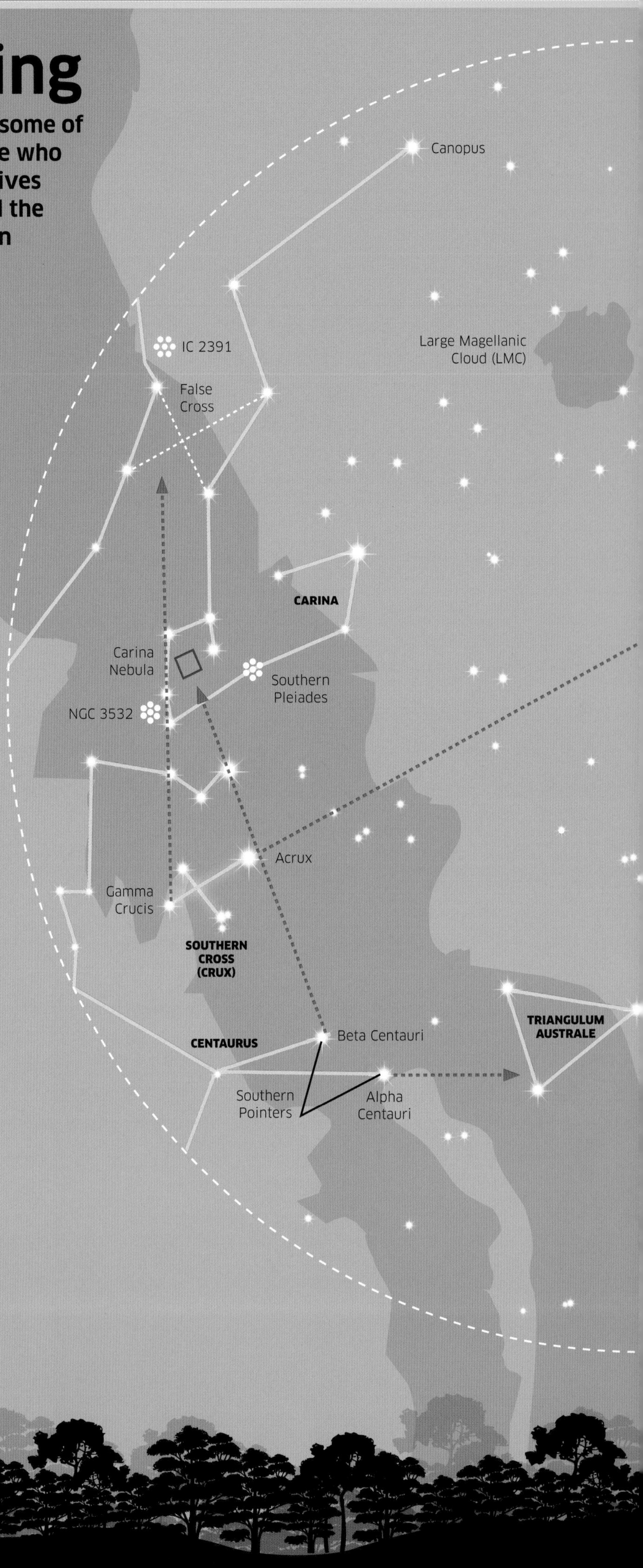
Canopus
IC 2391
False Cross
Large Magellanic Cloud (LMC)
CARINA
Carina Nebula
Southern Pleiades
NGC 3532
Acrux
Gamma Crucis
SOUTHERN CROSS (CRUX)
CENTAURUS
Beta Centauri
TRIANGULUM AUSTRALE
Southern Pointers
Alpha Centauri

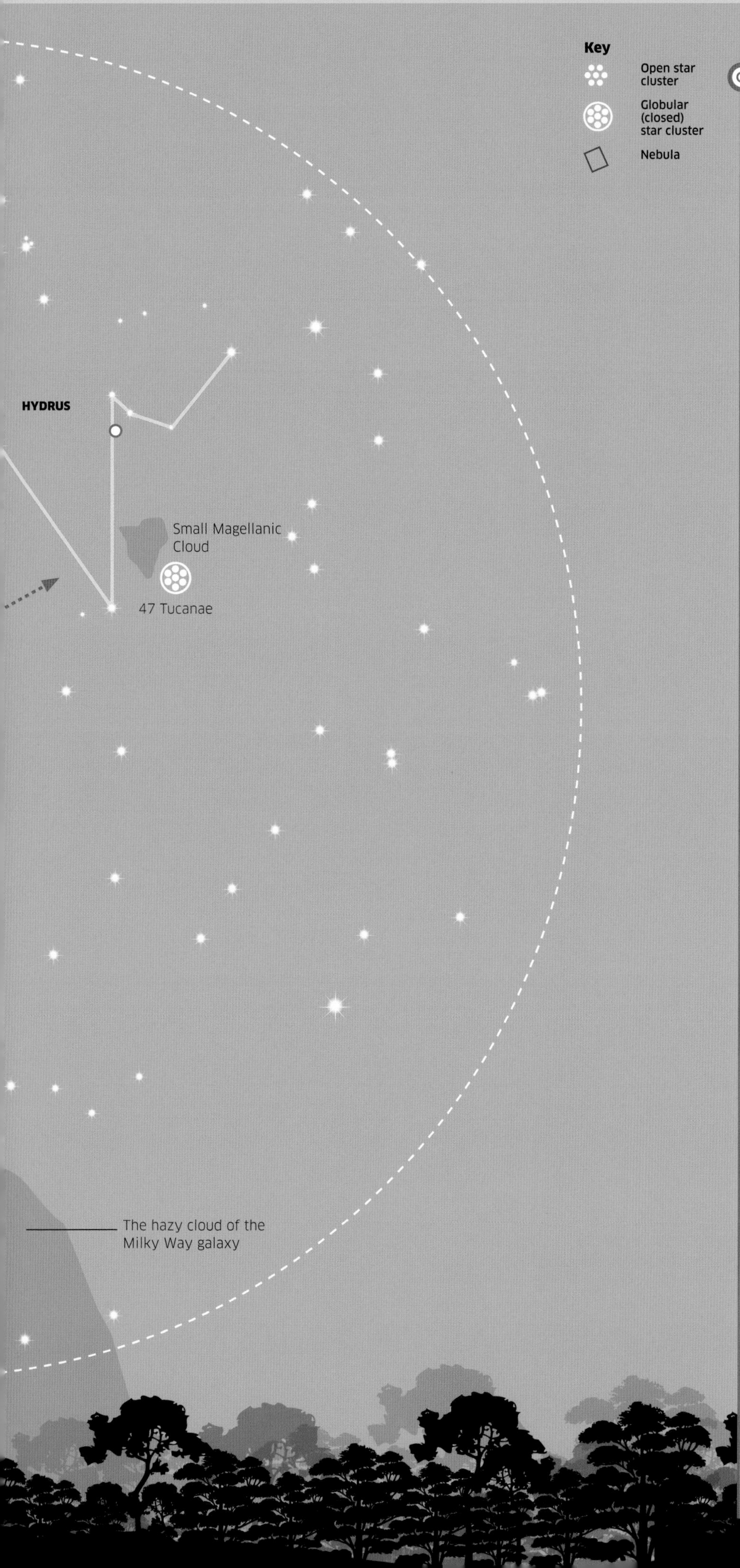
Key
Open star cluster
Globular (closed) star cluster
Nebula
HYDRUS
Small Magellanic Cloud
47 Tucanae
The hazy cloud of the Milky Way galaxy

WHAT TO SEE

The constellations directly around the south celestial pole may be faint, but there are many other interesting objects to see a little further afield. Most of these lie either within the band of the Milky Way or close to it.

FALSE CROSS
SOUTHERN CROSS

False Cross
The False Cross is made of bright stars from the constellations Carina and Vela. It mimics the shape of the true Southern Cross, which is why the two are often confused. However, the False Cross is slightly larger.

Carina Nebula
The Carina Nebula is a vast, star-forming gas cloud about 7,500 light years from Earth. Deep inside it is a massive star nearing the end of its life that will eventually explode in a supernova. Photographs capture the red colour of the Carina Nebula, but to the naked eye it appears white.

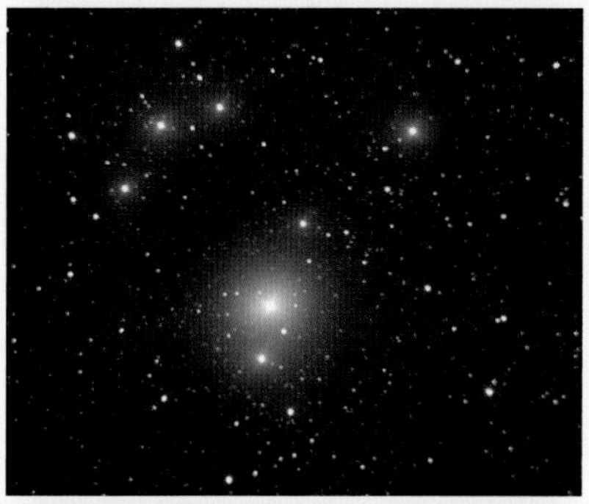

Southern Pleiades
The Southern Pleiades cluster (IC 2602) is an open cluster – a group of young stars that formed in the same gas cloud. It is visible to the naked eye, but binoculars will reveal more of the stars within it. There are around 60 stars in total.

Open cluster IC 2391
This bright open cluster likely originated from the same star-forming cloud as the Southern Pleiades, since it has a similar age (about 50 million years) and is a similar distance from Earth (500 light years).

Large and Small Magellanic clouds
These irregular galaxies are satellites of our own galaxy, the Milky Way. In southern skies they look like small, detached clumps of the Milky Way. The large cloud is about 160,000 light years from Earth, while the small cloud is around 210,000 light years away.

Star maps

From Earth about 6,000 stars are visible to the naked eye, though you can only see about half of these from any location at any one time.

Over a year you can see all the stars in either the north or south celestial hemisphere, depending on whether you are north or south of the equator, and some of the stars in the other celestial hemisphere too.

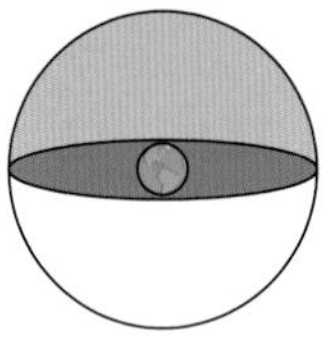

Northern sky

Most of the constellation names in the northern hemisphere come from the ancient Greeks. They are often linked to myths, such as the story of Perseus and Andromeda, but some of the fainter stars lie in more modern constellations.

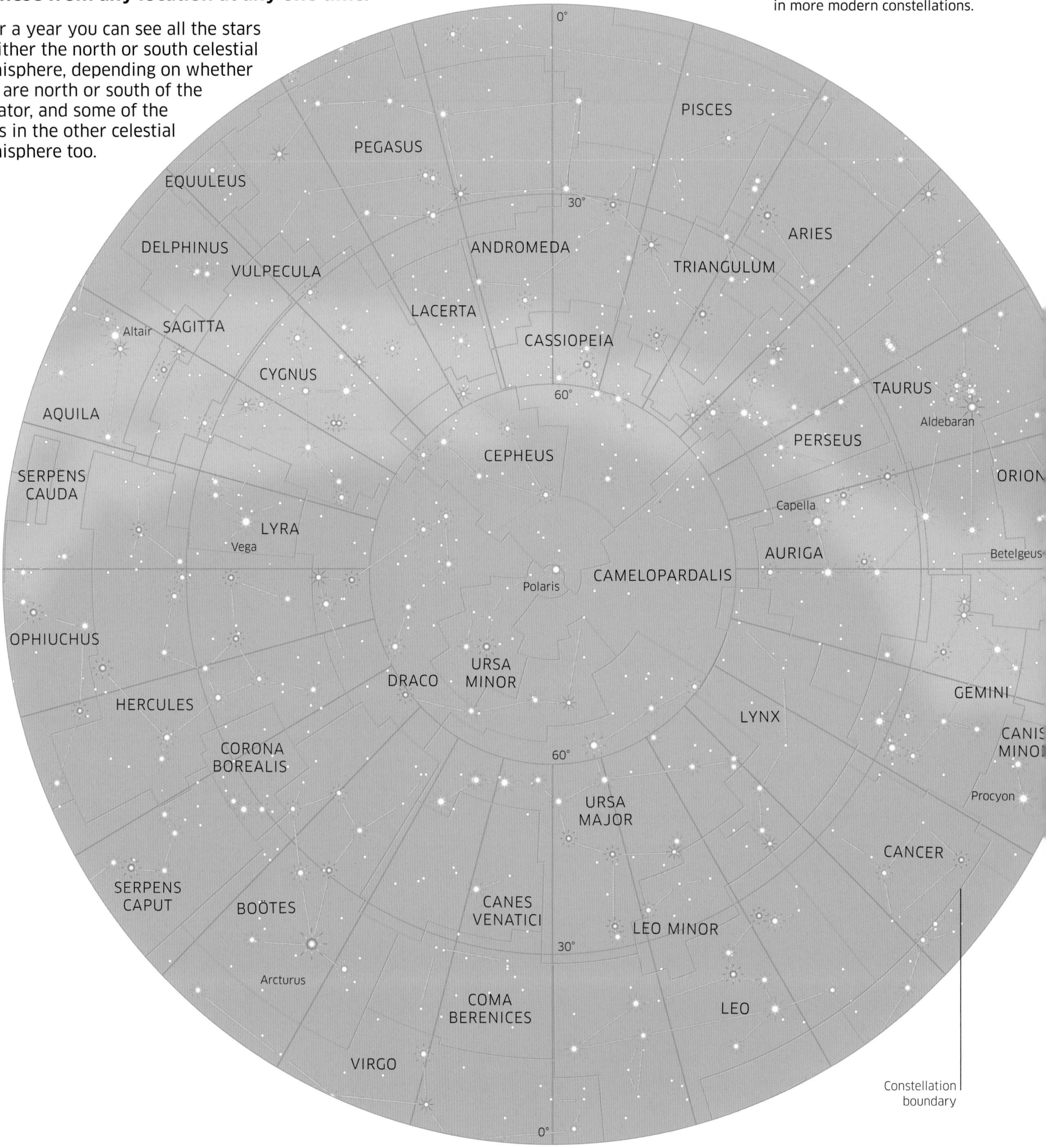

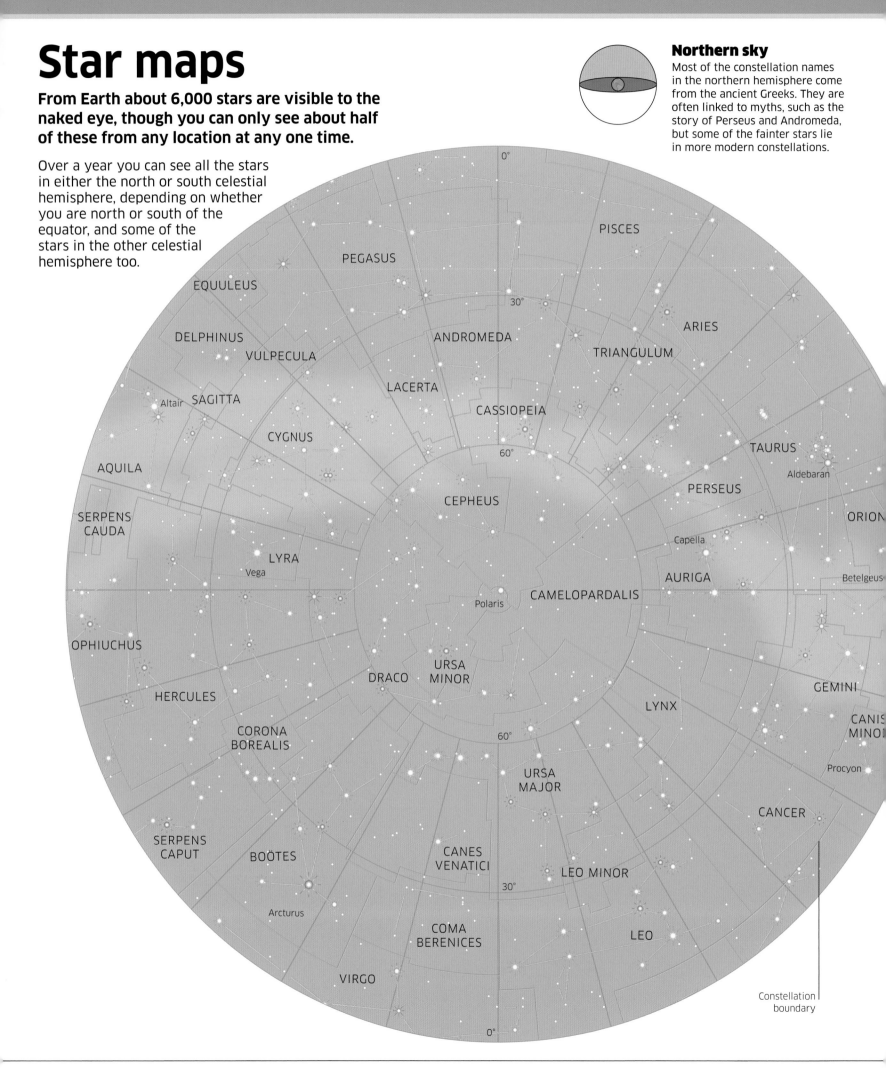

0°
30°
60°
PISCES
PEGASUS
EQUULEUS
ARIES
ANDROMEDA
DELPHINUS
VULPECULA
TRIANGULUM
LACERTA
Altair
SAGITTA
CASSIOPEIA
CYGNUS
TAURUS
AQUILA
Aldebaran
PERSEUS
CEPHEUS
SERPENS CAUDA
ORION
Capella
LYRA
Vega
AURIGA
Betelgeuse
Polaris
CAMELOPARDALIS
OPHIUCHUS
URSA MINOR
DRACO
GEMINI
HERCULES
LYNX
CORONA BOREALIS
CANIS MINOR
URSA MAJOR
Procyon
CANCER
SERPENS CAPUT
BOÖTES
CANES VENATICI
LEO MINOR
Arcturus
COMA BERENICES
LEO
VIRGO
Constellation boundary

Key

These maps show fairly bright stars, down to magnitude 5.0. There are many more faint stars visible to the naked eye.

- Yellow star
- Red star
- Orange star
- White star
- Blue star

- Magnitude brighter than 0.0
- Magnitude brighter than 1.0
- Magnitude brighter than 2.0
- Magnitude brighter than 3.0
- Magnitude brighter than 4.0
- Magnitude brighter than 5.0

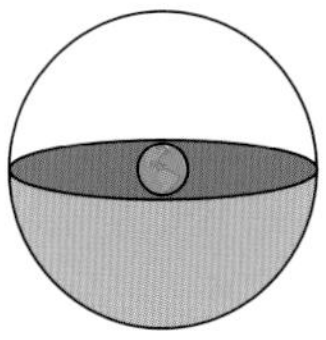

Southern sky

Southern-hemisphere stars close to the celestial equator (around the edges of the map) were visible to ancient Greek astronomers who grouped them into mythological constellations. Names for constellations around the south celestial pole were proposed by astronomers working from the late 16th century onwards.

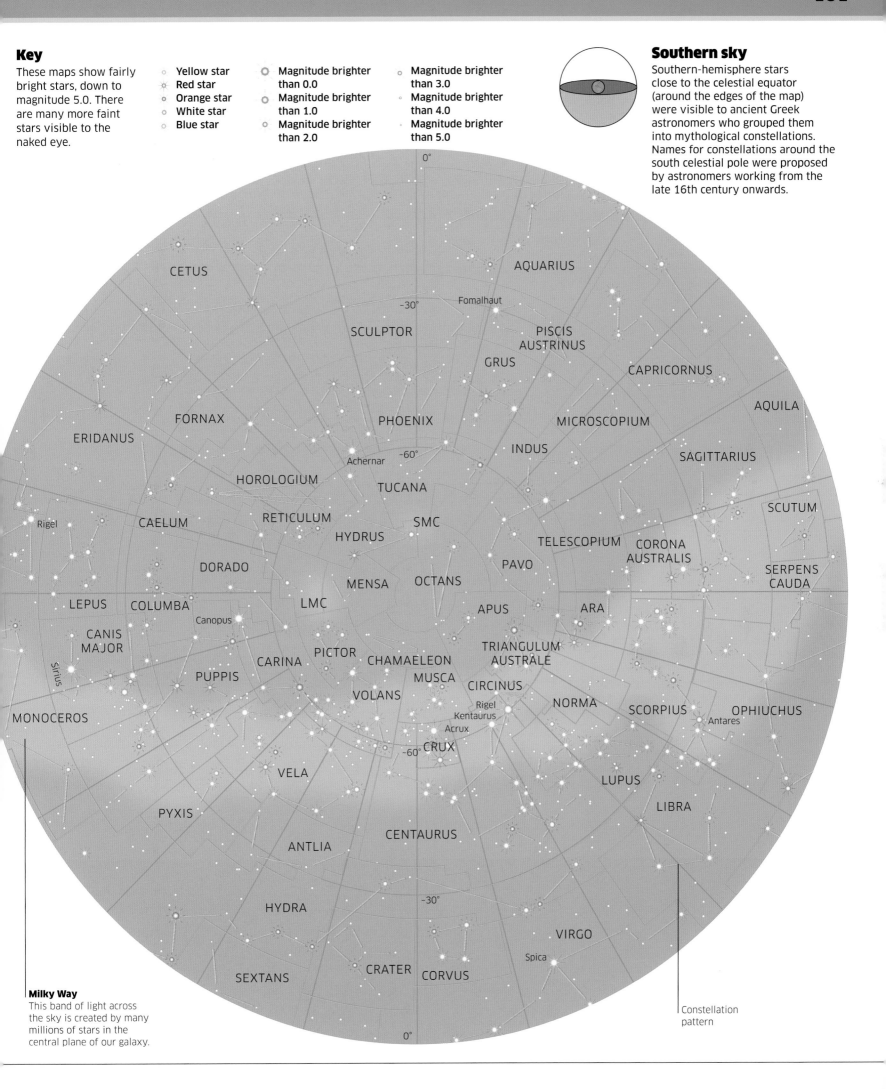

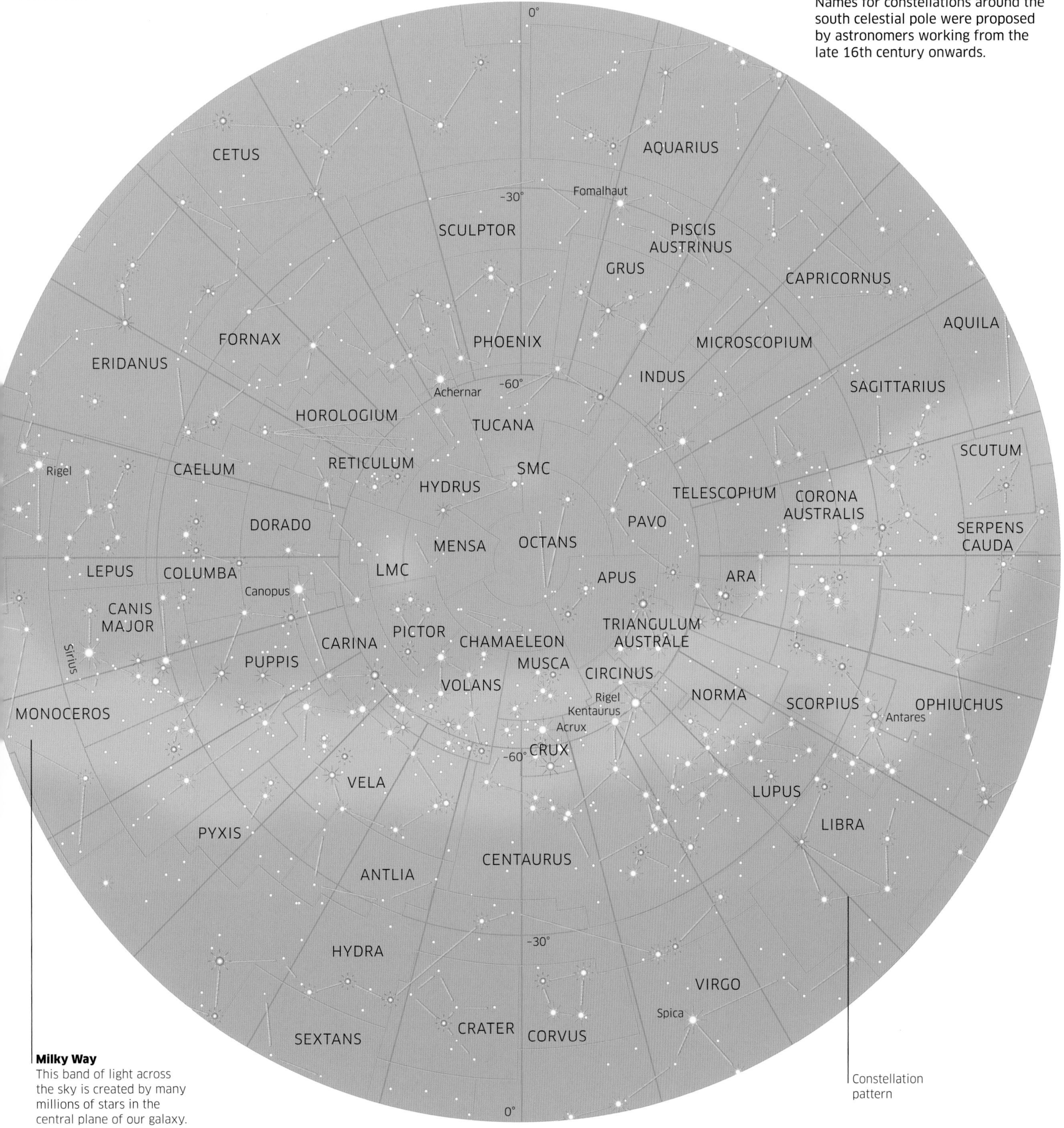
0°
CETUS
AQUARIUS
-30°
Fomalhaut
SCULPTOR
PISCIS AUSTRINUS
GRUS
CAPRICORNUS
FORNAX
PHOENIX
MICROSCOPIUM
AQUILA
ERIDANUS
-60°
Achernar
INDUS
SAGITTARIUS
HOROLOGIUM
TUCANA
SCUTUM
Rigel
CAELUM
RETICULUM
SMC
HYDRUS
TELESCOPIUM
CORONA AUSTRALIS
DORADO
PAVO
SERPENS CAUDA
MENSA
OCTANS
LEPUS
COLUMBA
LMC
APUS
ARA
Canopus
CANIS MAJOR
TRIANGULUM AUSTRALE
PICTOR
Sirius
CARINA
CHAMAELEON
PUPPIS
MUSCA
CIRCINUS
VOLANS
Rigel Kentaurus
NORMA
MONOCEROS
SCORPIUS
Antares
OPHIUCHUS
Acrux
-60°
CRUX
VELA
LUPUS
LIBRA
PYXIS
CENTAURUS
ANTLIA
-30°
HYDRA
VIRGO
Spica
CRATER
CORVUS
SEXTANS
0°

Milky Way
This band of light across the sky is created by many millions of stars in the central plane of our galaxy.

Constellation pattern

Constellations

Since the earliest times, people have looked for patterns in the stars. The people of ancient Greece knew 48 constellations, named after mythical beings, though the patterns bear little resemblance to the beings they are named after. Today scientists recognize 88 constellations. These modern constellations are not just patterns of stars – they are whole segments of the sky that fit together like a jigsaw to form a complete sphere.

KEY

Deep-sky objects

Galaxy | Globular cluster | Open cluster | Planetary nebula or supernova remnant | Black hole or X-ray binary | Other deep-sky object

Star magnitudes

-1.5-0 | 0-0.9 | 1.0-1.9 | 2.0-2.9 | 3.0-3.9 | 4.0-4.9 | 5.0-5.9 | 6.0-6.9

Constellation widths

Hand symbols are used to indicate a constellation's apparent size in the sky. A spread hand at arm's length spans about 22° of sky, while a closed hand covers about 10°. Combinations of these symbols are used to convey the full width and depth of the constellation.

CEPHEUS

The constellation Cepheus is named after a mythical king, the husband of Queen Cassiopeia. In Greek mythology, King Cepheus and Queen Cassiopeia were told by an oracle that they must sacrifice their daughter, Princess Andromeda, to a sea monster to stop it from destroying their coastline. In a dramatic rescue, Andromeda was saved from the monster's jaws by the warrior Perseus. All the characters from this myth have constellations named after them. The stars of Cepheus form a shape like a house with a pointed roof. The most famous of its stars is Delta Cephei.

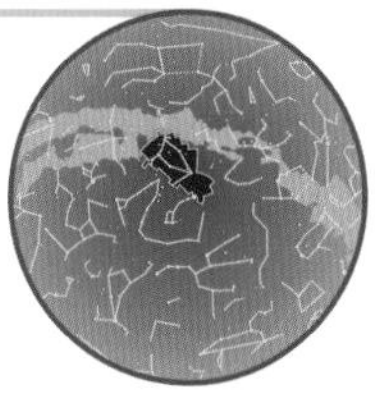

NORTHERN HEMISPHERE

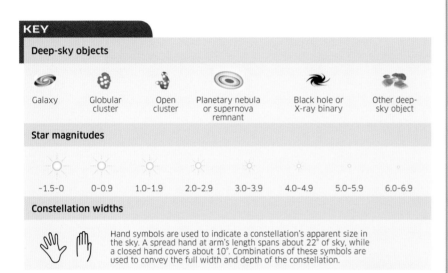

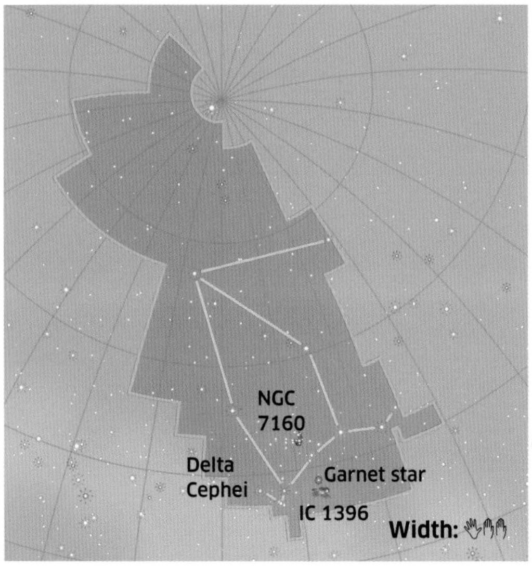
NGC 7160
Delta Cephei
Garnet star
IC 1396
Width:

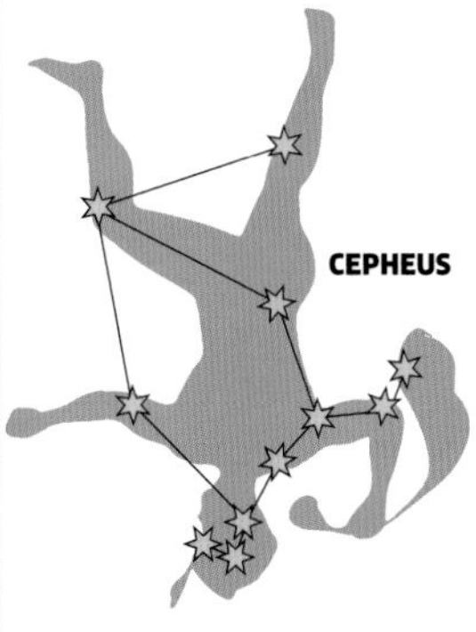

CEPHEUS

URSA MINOR

This constellation represents a small bear with a long tail. At the tip of its tail lies the Pole Star, called Polaris, which is the brightest star in the constellation. Ursa Minor is sometimes termed the Little Dipper because its main stars form a shape that looks like a smaller version of the Big Dipper in the constellation Ursa Major. It was one of the original constellations known to the ancient Greeks.

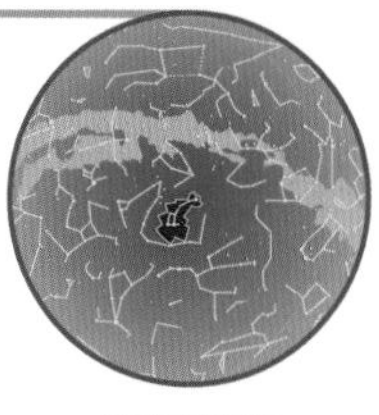

NORTHERN HEMISPHERE

Things to look for

Polaris
Most stars move around the sky but Polaris stays still and is always due north. Sailors have long used this star to find their way.

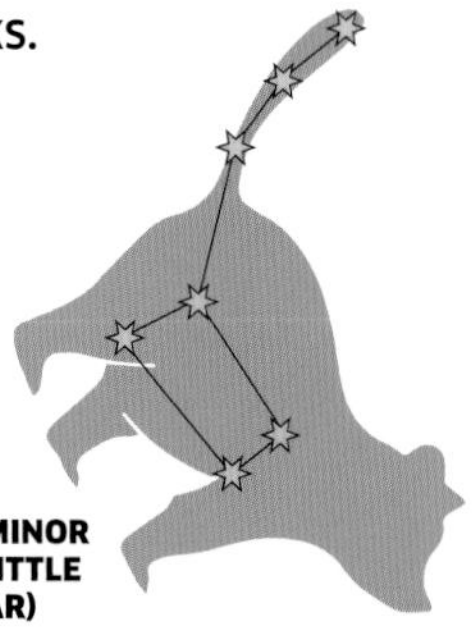

URSA MINOR (THE LITTLE BEAR)

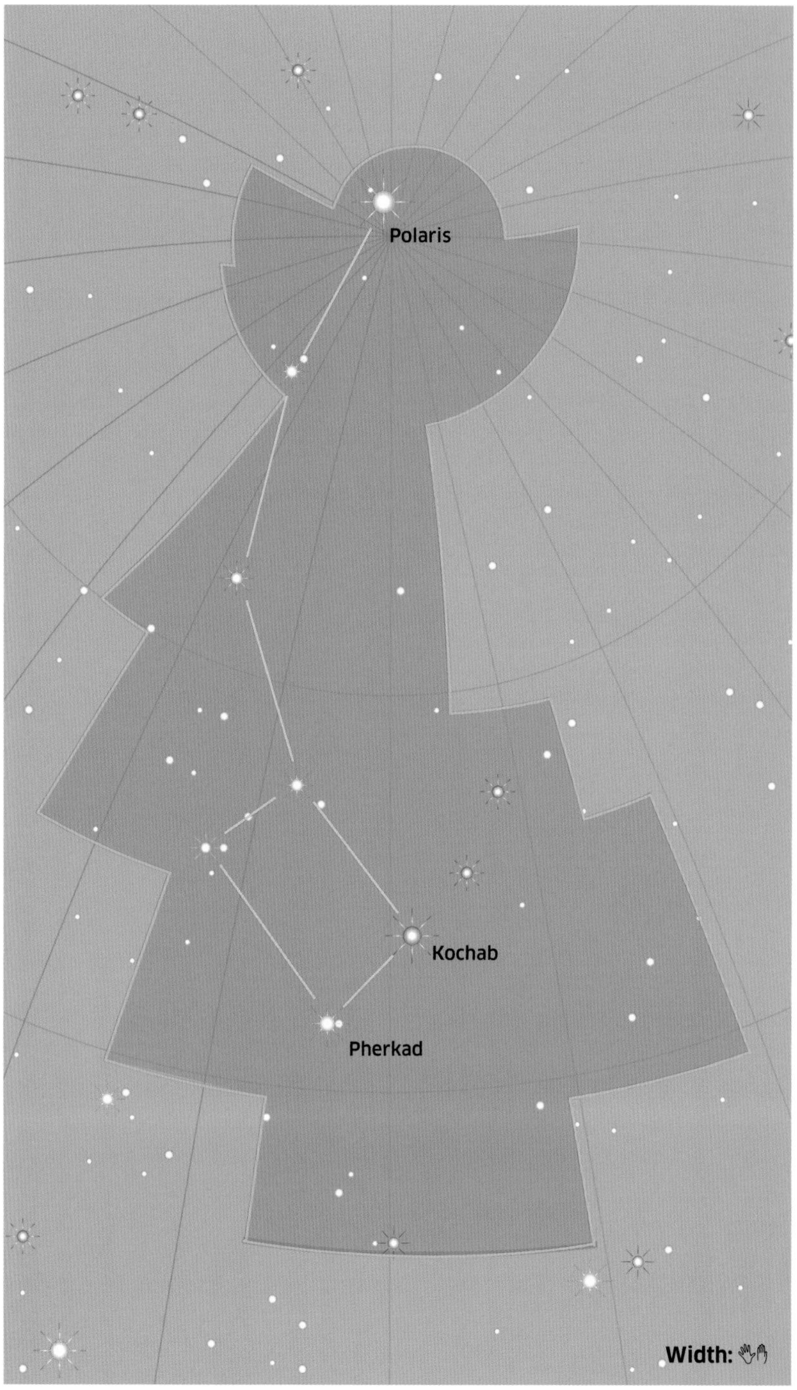
Polaris
Kochab
Pherkad
Width:

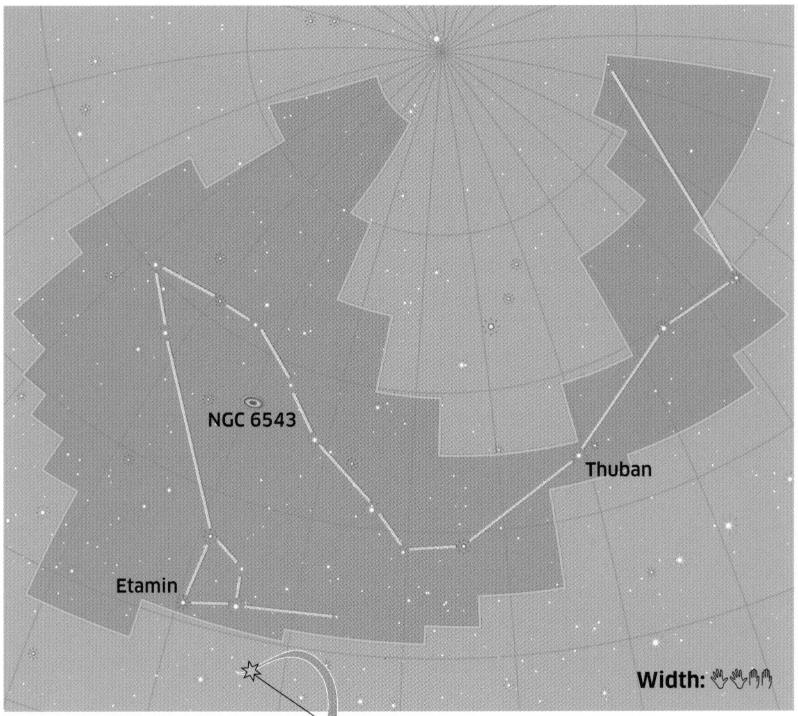
NGC 6543
Thuban
Etamin
Width:

DRACO

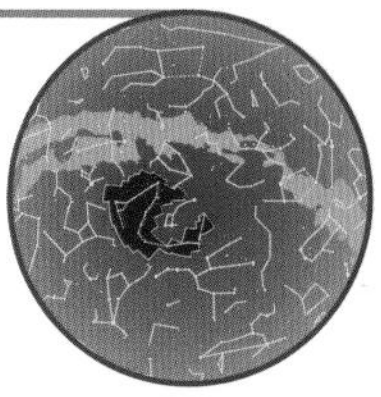

NORTHERN HEMISPHERE

Draco is a constellation representing a dragon. In Greek mythology, this was the dragon slain by the warrior Hercules, who is represented by a neighbouring constellation. The dragon's head is formed by four stars near the border with Hercules. The ancient Greeks visualized Hercules with one foot on the dragon's head. From the head, its body curls like a snake across the sky between Ursa Minor and Ursa Major. Draco's brightest star, Etamin, lies in the dragon's head.

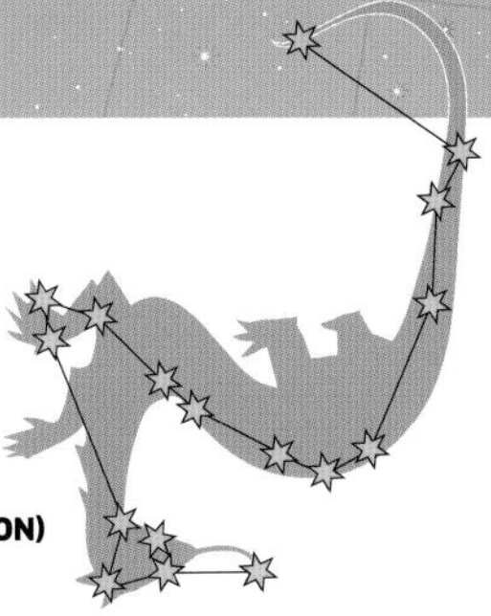

DRACO (THE DRAGON)

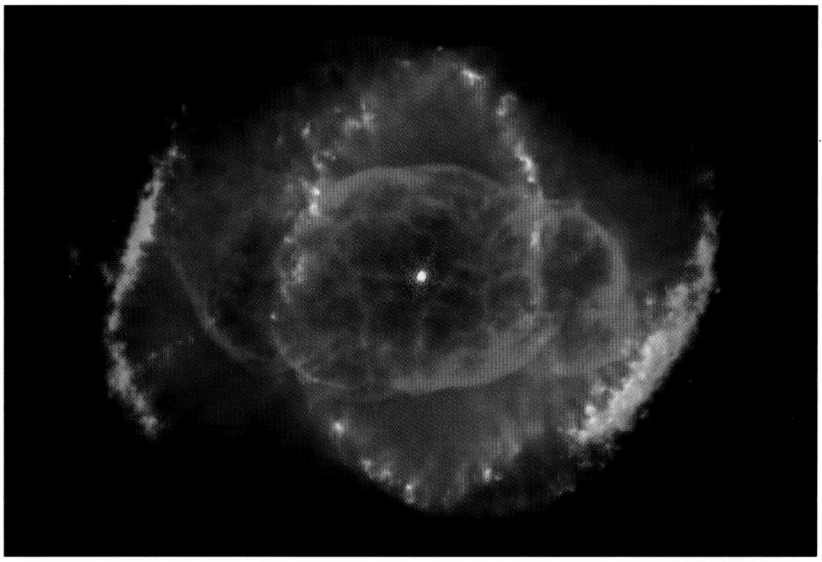

Cat's Eye Nebula (NGC 6543)
The fantastic Cat's Eye Nebula in Draco is seen here as pictured by the Hubble Space Telescope. The Cat's Eye is a type of object known as a planetary nebula, consisting of gas thrown off from a dying star. This nebula is also known by its catalogue number NGC 6543.

CASSIOPEIA

A mythical queen from ancient Greece – the wife of King Cepheus and the mother of Princess Andromeda – inspired the name of this constellation. On star maps she is depicted sitting in a chair and combing her hair. In the sky the main stars of Cassiopeia form a W-shape, which is easy to recognize but does not really look much like a person sitting in a chair. Cassiopeia contains several interesting clusters of stars. The brightest of them can be seen with binoculars and small telescopes.

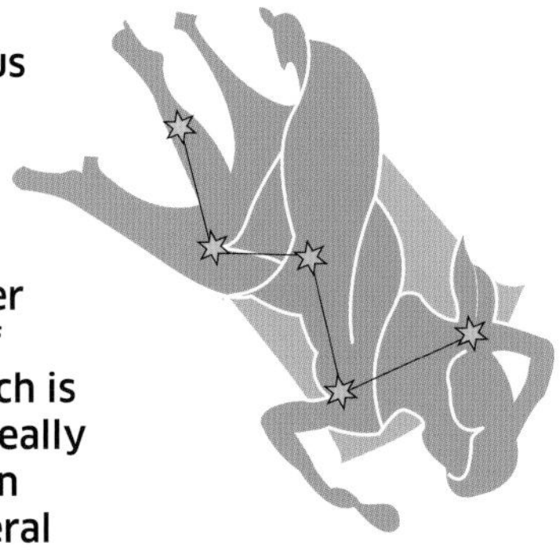

CASSIOPEIA

Star cluster M103
This star cluster in Cassiopeia is visible through small telescopes. Its three brightest stars form a line across the centre. The star at the top right actually lies closer to us than the others, so it is not really a member of the cluster at all.

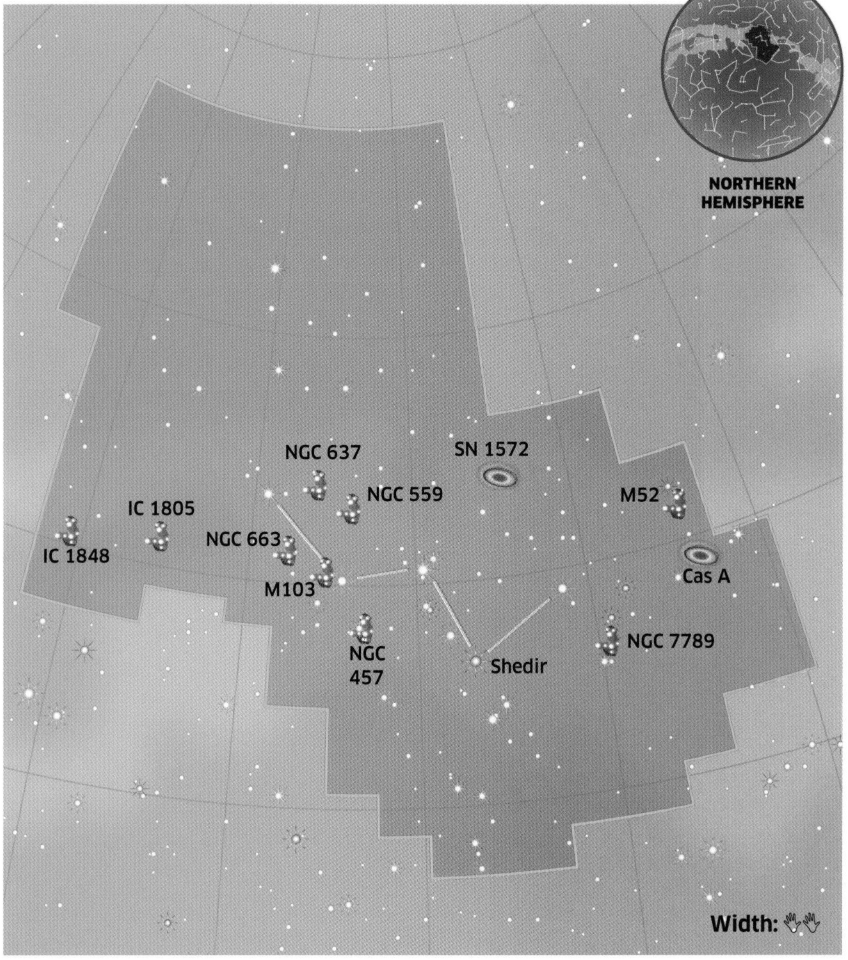
NGC 637
SN 1572
NGC 559
M52
IC 1805
NGC 663
IC 1848
M103
Cas A
NGC 7789
NGC 457
Shedir
Width:
NORTHERN HEMISPHERE

CAMELOPARDALIS

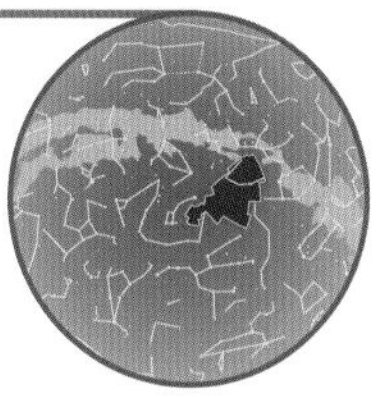

NORTHERN HEMISPHERE

Dutch astronomer Petrus Plancius devised this strangely named constellation in 1612. It represents a giraffe. The Greeks called giraffes "camel leopards" because of their long necks and spotted bodies, which is where Camelopardalis gets its name. It is difficult to spot because it contains only faint stars.

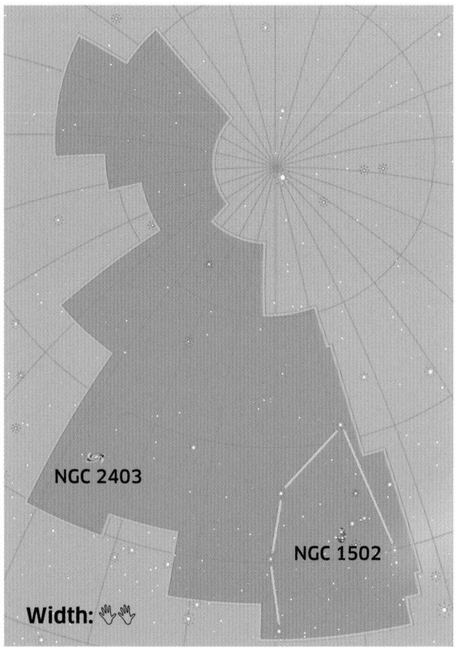
NGC 2403
NGC 1502
Width:

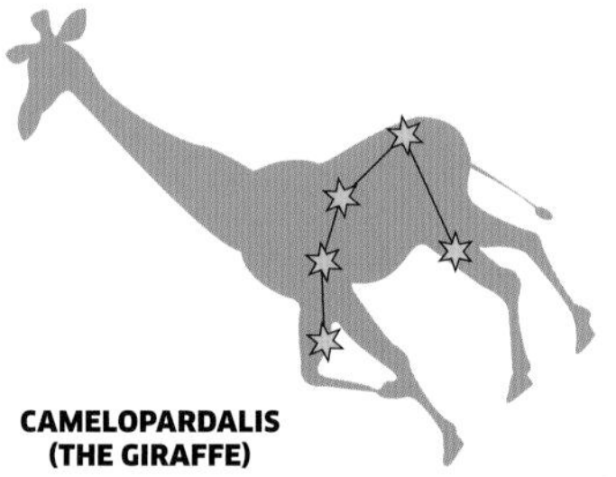

CAMELOPARDALIS (THE GIRAFFE)

LYNX

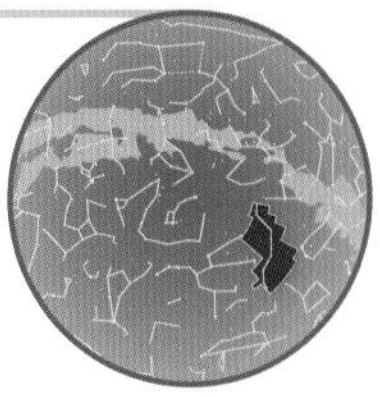

NORTHERN HEMISPHERE

This is a faint constellation squeezed in between the constellations Ursa Major and Auriga. Polish astronomer Johannes Hevelius created it in 1687. Hevelius had very sharp eyesight, and he named the constellation Lynx because, he said, you would have to be lynx-eyed to see it. It has a number of interesting double and triple stars, which can be studied with a small telescope.

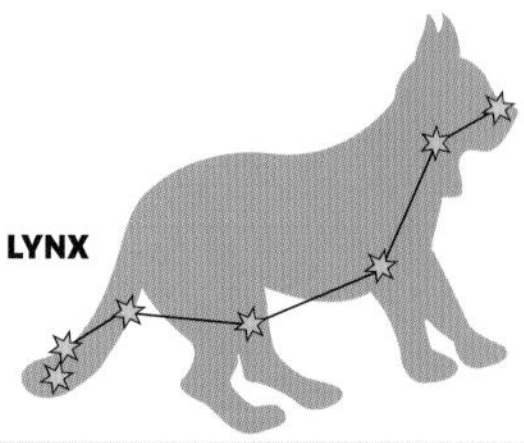

LYNX

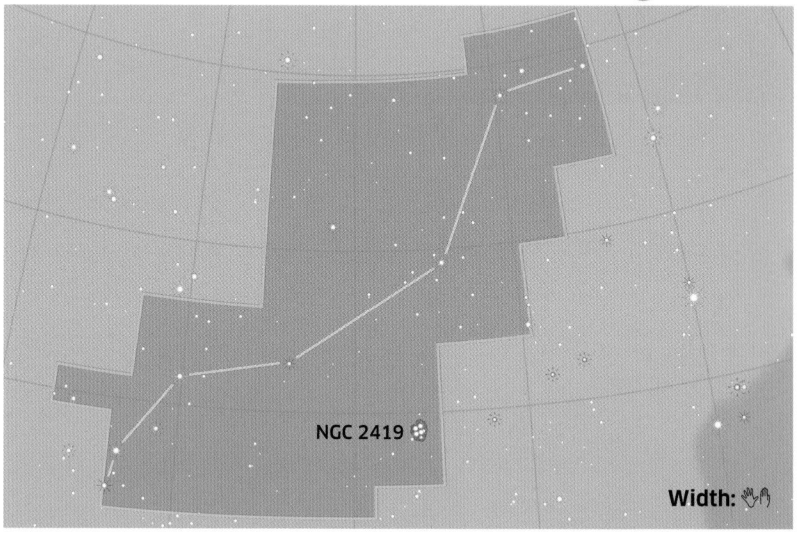
NGC 2419
Width:

AURIGA

The constellation Auriga is easy to find because it contains the star Capella, one of the brightest stars in the entire sky. To the ancient Greeks, the constellation represented a charioteer carrying a goat and two baby goats on his arm. Capella was the goat and the two fainter stars were the babies. Among the objects of interest in Auriga is a row of three star clusters, M36, M37, and M38, all visible through binoculars. The star that once marked the charioteer's right foot has now been transferred to Taurus the bull, which lies to the south.

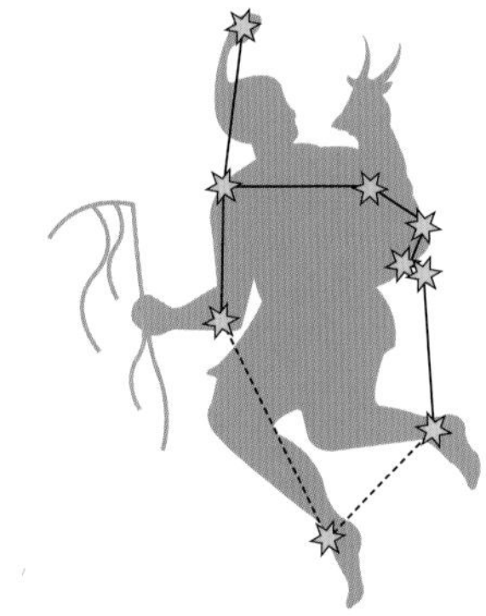

AURIGA (THE CHARIOTEER)

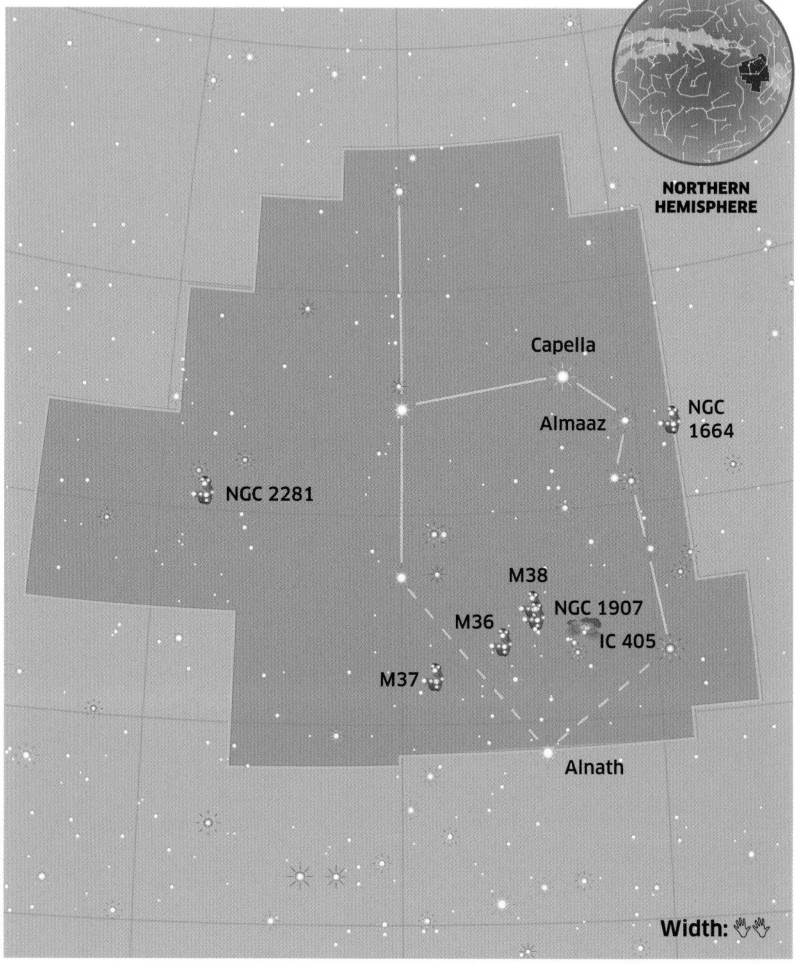
Capella
Almaaz
NGC 1664
NGC 2281
M38
NGC 1907
M36
IC 405
M37
Alnath
Width:

NORTHERN HEMISPHERE

Flaming Star Nebula
The Flaming Star Nebula (IC 405) is a giant cloud of gas lit up by a hot star called AE Aurigae. The nebula can only be seen through a large telescope.

URSA MAJOR

This large constellation's name is Latin for the Great Bear, which it represents. Seven of its brightest stars form a saucepan shape, popularly known as the Plough (or Big Dipper), which is one of the best-known features in the entire sky. The two stars in the bowl of the saucepan farthest from the handle, called Merak and Dubhe, are known as the Pointers because they point towards the Pole Star, Polaris. The curving handle of the saucepan points towards the bright star Arcturus in the nearby constellation Boötes.

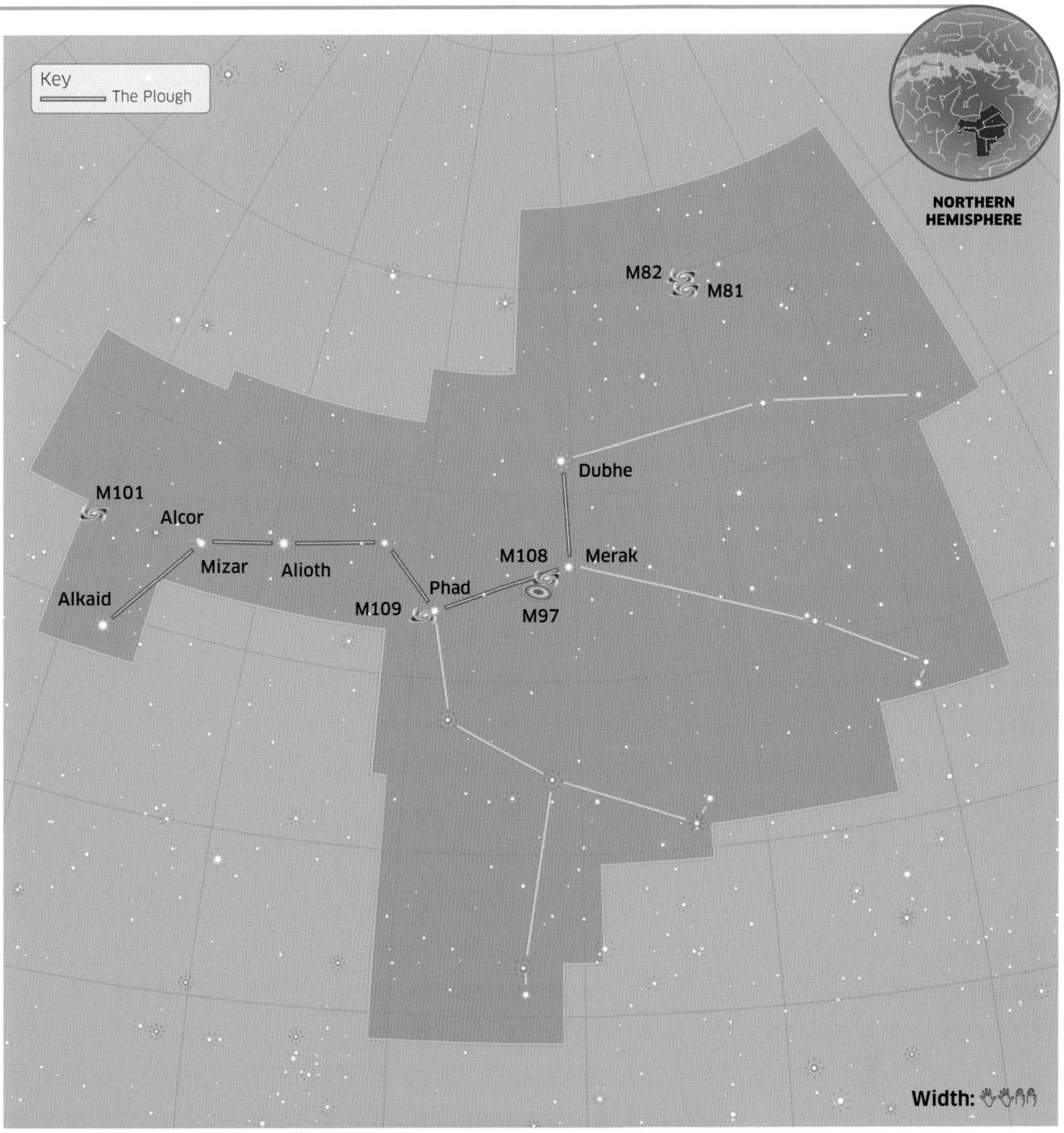
Key
The Plough
NORTHERN HEMISPHERE
M82
M81
Dubhe
M101
Alcor
Mizar
Alioth
M108
Merak
Phad
Alkaid
M109
M97
Width:

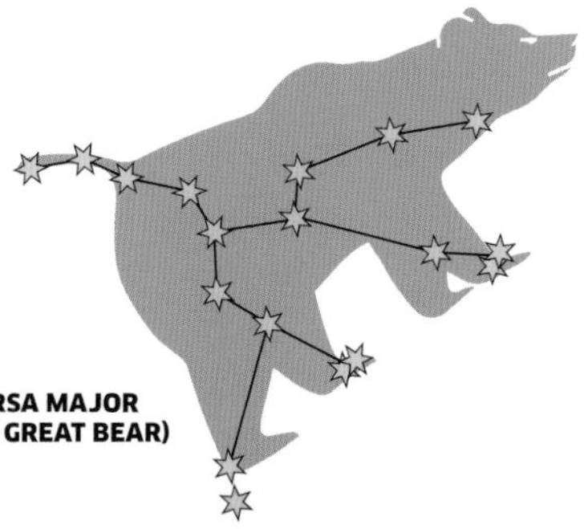
URSA MAJOR
(THE GREAT BEAR)

Spiral galaxy M81
In the northern part of Ursa Major lie two contrasting galaxies, known by their catalogue numbers M81 and M82. M81 is a beautiful spiral, shown in this Hubble Space Telescope image (above). M82 is irregular in shape. It is thought to be undergoing a burst of star formation resulting from an encounter with M81 millions of years ago. M81 and M82 both lie about 12 million light years away.

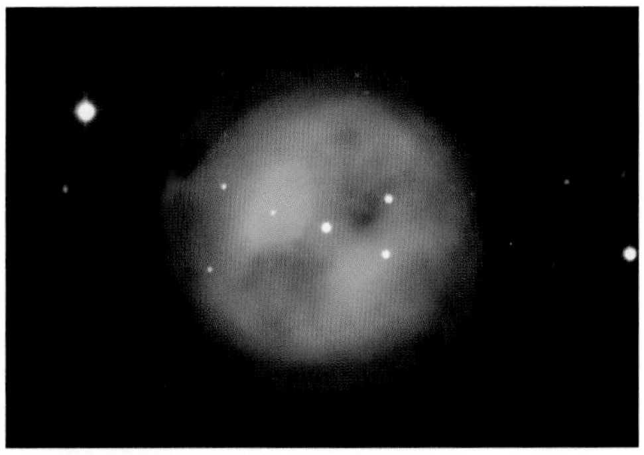

Owl Nebula
Just under the bowl of the Plough, a glowing cloud of gas called M97 can be seen through a telescope. It is also called the Owl Nebula because of the two darker spots that look like the eyes of an owl. It is a planetary nebula, made of gas thrown off from a dying star.

Spiral galaxy M101
Near the end of the handle of the Plough lies the spiral galaxy M101. Although it is too faint to see without binoculars or a telescope, its spiral arms show up clearly on photographs. It is sometimes called the Pinwheel Galaxy.

Things to look for

Mizar This is the second star in the handle of the Plough. Next to it is a fainter star called Alcor, which can also be seen with the naked eye.

CANES VENATICI

This constellation was named after a pair of hunting dogs by Polish astronomer Johannes Hevelius in 1687. There are only two stars of any note in the constellation, but it also contains many interesting galaxies. Most famous of these is the Whirlpool Galaxy. This can be seen through binoculars as a faint patch of light, but a large telescope is needed to make out its spiral shape. Another object of note is the globular star cluster M3 near the constellation's southern border.

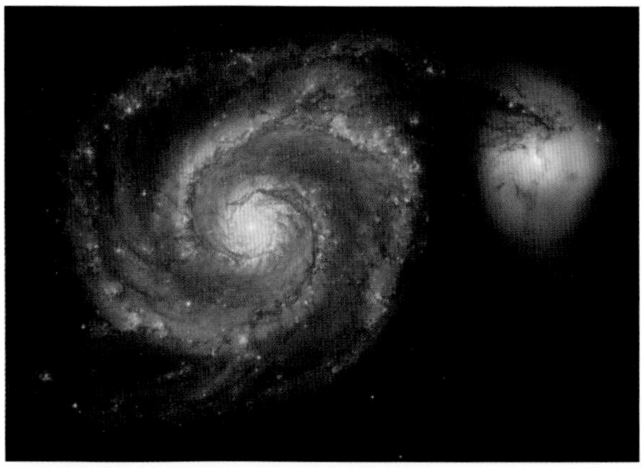

Whirlpool Galaxy
Seen here is a Hubble Space Telescope view of the Whirlpool Galaxy (M51), a vast spiral of stars some 30 million light years away. Behind it, near the end of one of its arms, is a smaller galaxy, which astronomers think will one day merge with it.

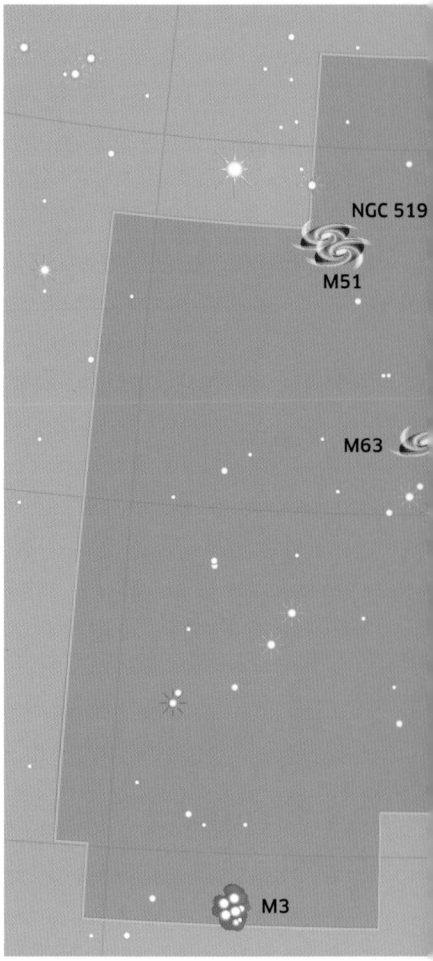
NGC 519
M51
M63
M3

Sunflower Galaxy
Another beautiful spiral galaxy in Canes Venatici is the Sunflower Galaxy (M63), seen here through a large telescope. The star on the right is not connected with the galaxy but is much closer to us.

BOÖTES

Boötes represents a man herding the Great Bear around the pole. He is sometimes referred to as the herdsman or bear driver. This constellation contains Arcturus, the brightest star in the northern half of the sky. It is a giant star and looks pale orange to the eye.

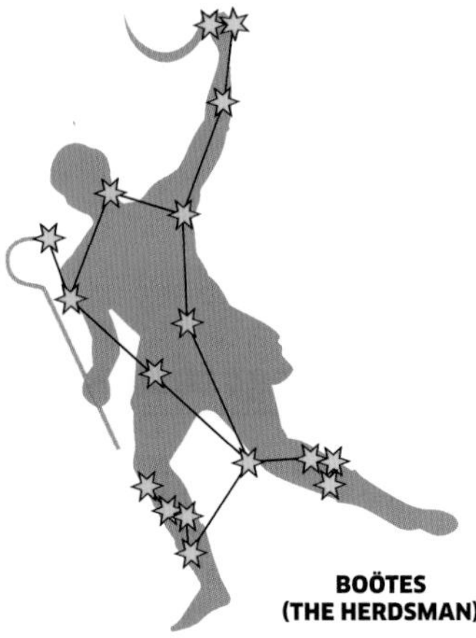
BOÖTES
(THE HERDSMAN)

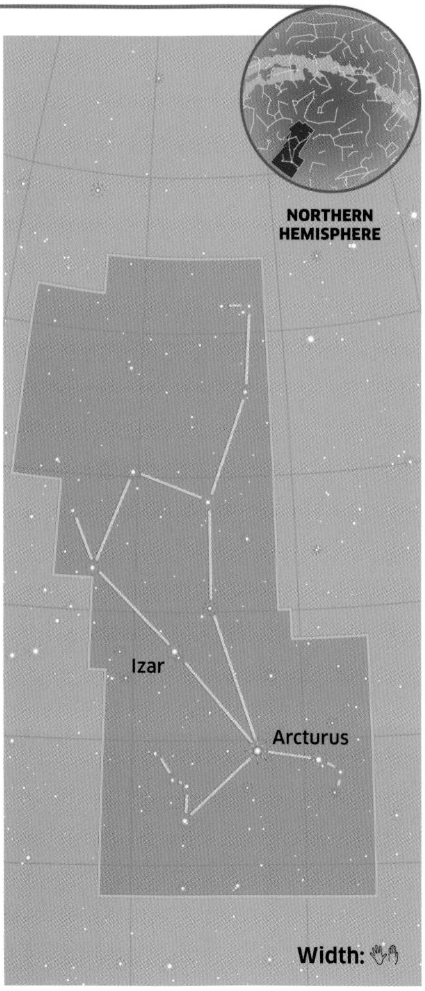
NORTHERN
HEMISPHERE
Izar
Arcturus
Width:

HERCULES

This constellation is named after Hercules, the strong man of Greek mythology. In star charts he is often depicted brandishing a club and with one foot on the head of Draco, the dragon, which he killed in a fight. The stars of Hercules are not particularly bright, so the constellation can be difficult to find. Its most noticeable feature is a squashed square of four stars known as the Keystone, which marks the body of Hercules. On one side of the Keystone lies the globular cluster M13.

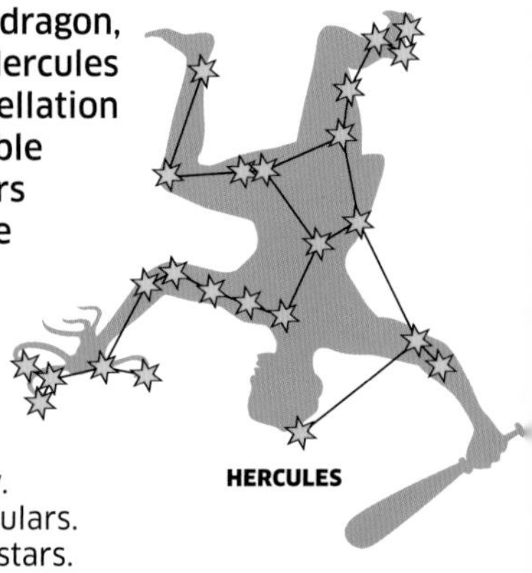
HERCULES

Star cluster M13
The globular cluster M13 is a ball of about 300,000 stars some 25,000 light years away. It can be seen as a hazy patch through binoculars. Telescopes are needed to see the individual stars.

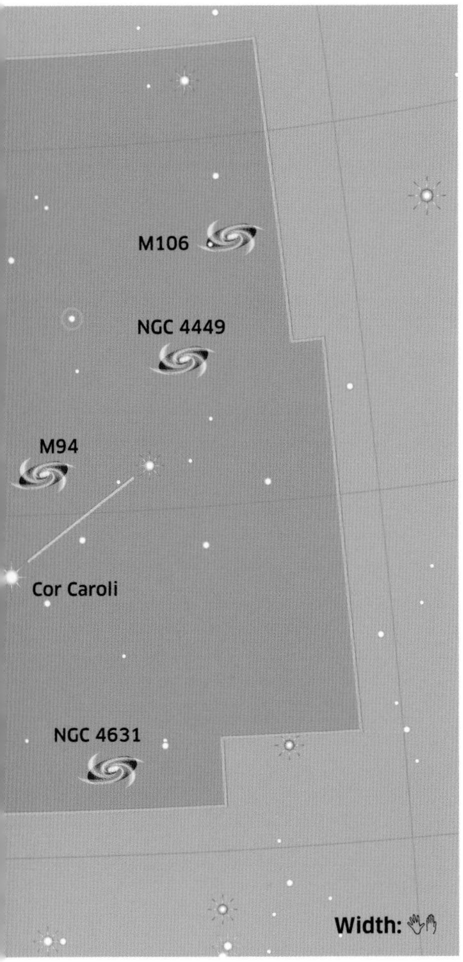
M106
NGC 4449
M94
Cor Caroli
NGC 4631
Width:

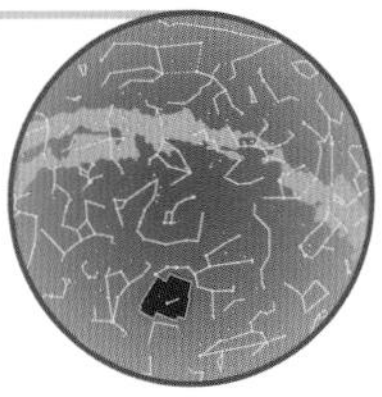

NORTHERN HEMISPHERE

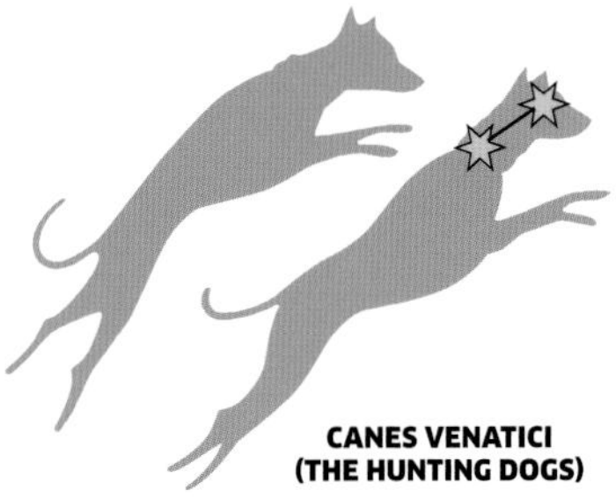

CANES VENATICI (THE HUNTING DOGS)

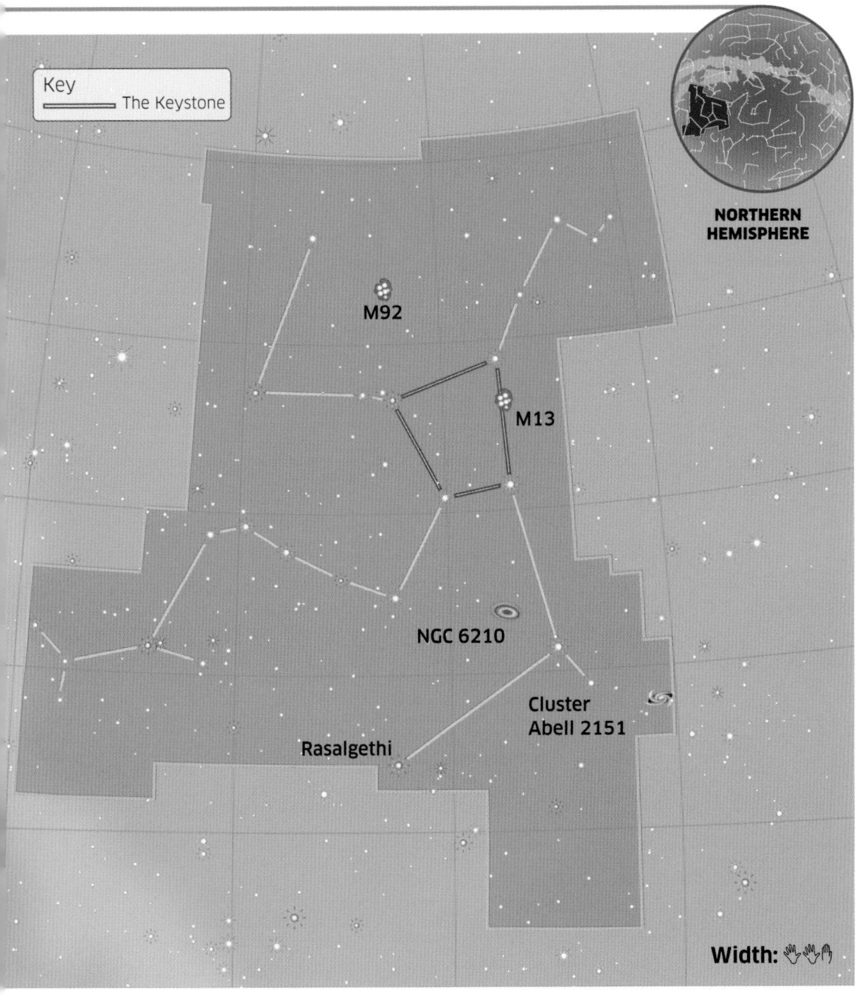
Key
The Keystone
M92
M13
NGC 6210
Cluster Abell 2151
Rasalgethi
Width:

NORTHERN HEMISPHERE

LYRA

The constellation Lyra represents a small harp, known to the Greeks as a lyre. In mythology, it was the instrument played by the musician Orpheus. Lyra is easy to spot because it contains Vega, the fifth-brightest star in the entire sky, 25 light years away. Vega forms one corner of the Summer Triangle – a triangle formed by bright stars in three different constellations.

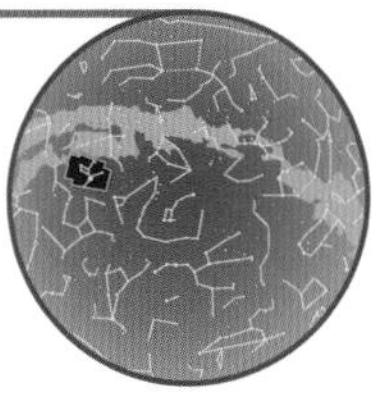

NORTHERN HEMISPHERE

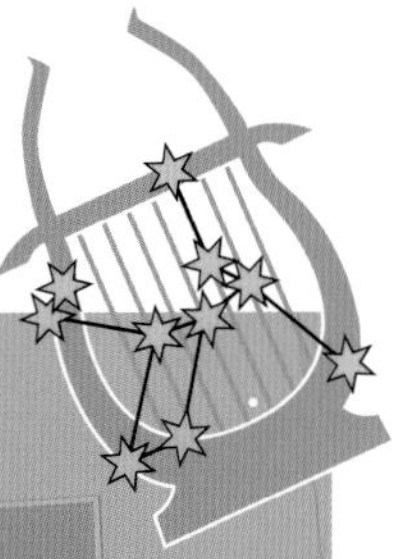

LYRA (THE LYRE)

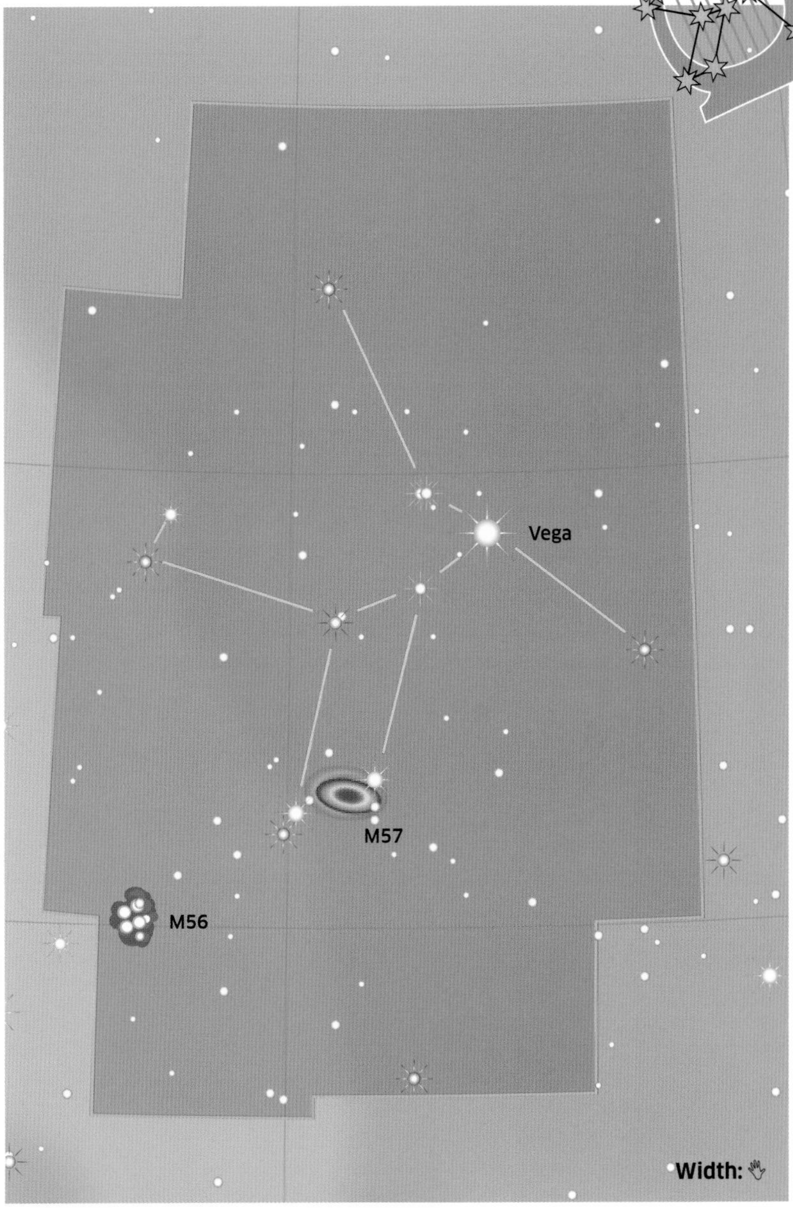
Vega
M57
M56
Width:

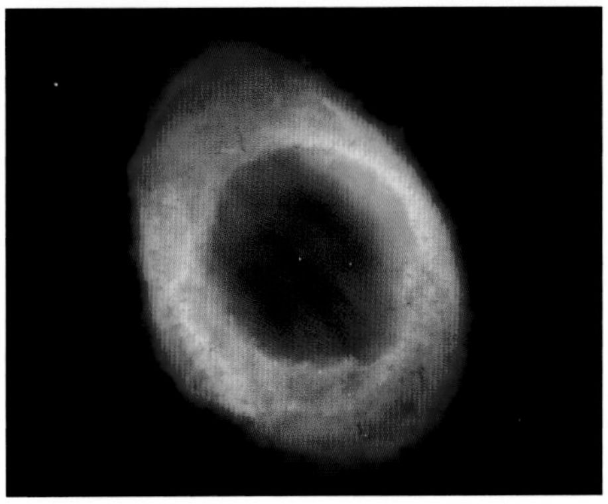

Ring Nebula
The Ring Nebula (M57), seen here through the Hubble Space Telescope, is a shell of glowing gas. At its centre is a white dwarf, the remains of the star that lost its outer layers to form the nebula.

CYGNUS

The ancient Greeks visualized Cygnus as a swan flying along the Milky Way. Its brightest star, Deneb, marks its tail, while the star Albireo is its beak. In mythology, the swan was the disguise used by the god Zeus when he visited Queen Leda of Sparta. The overall shape of the constellation resembles a large cross, so it is sometimes known as the Northern Cross. One of the most exciting objects in Cygnus lies in the swan's neck – a black hole called Cygnus X-1. The black hole itself cannot be seen from Earth, but satellites in space have detected X-rays from hot gas falling into it from a nearby star.

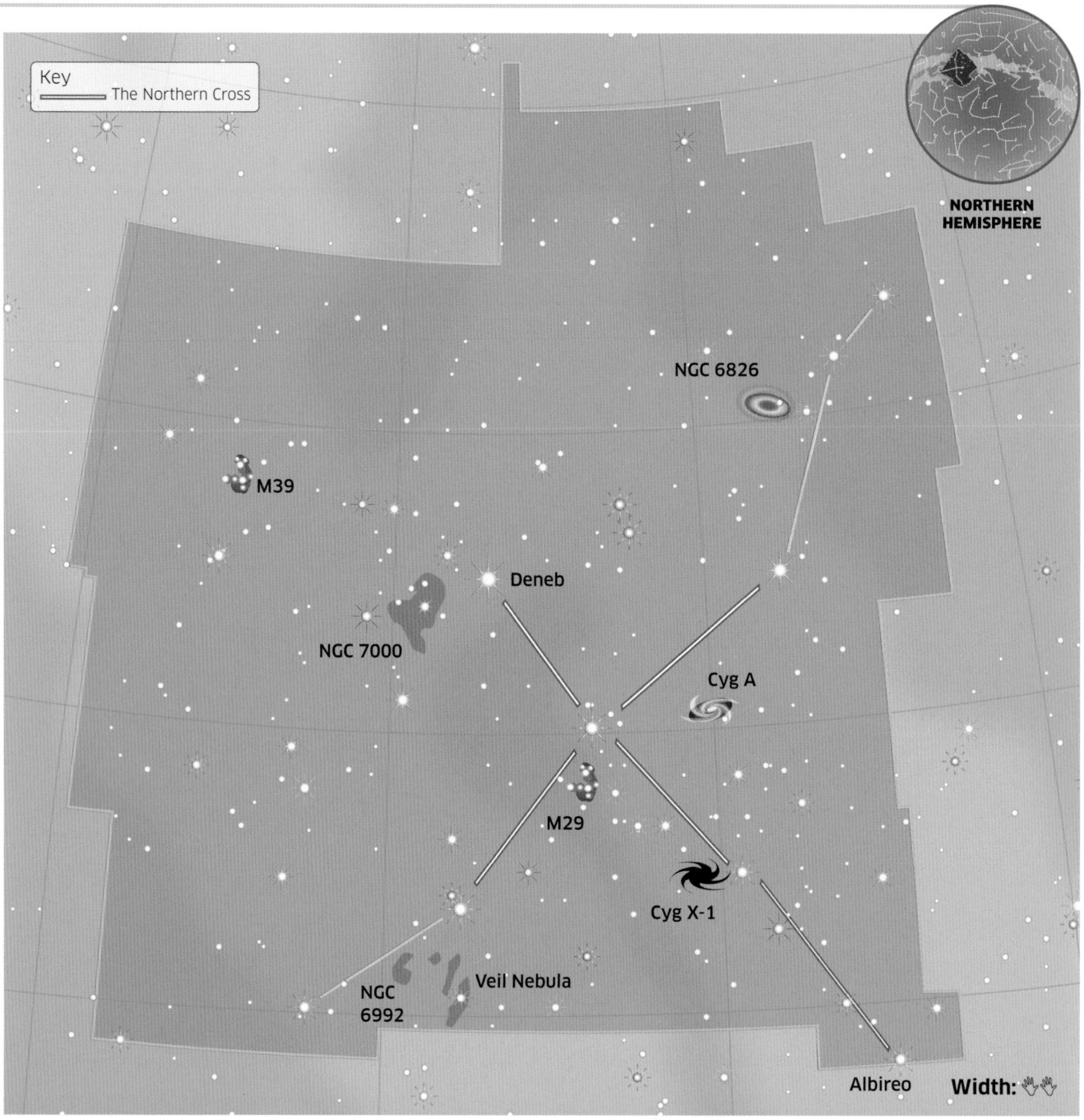
Key
The Northern Cross
NORTHERN HEMISPHERE
NGC 6826
M39
Deneb
NGC 7000
Cyg A
M29
Cyg X-1
NGC 6992
Veil Nebula
Albireo
Width:

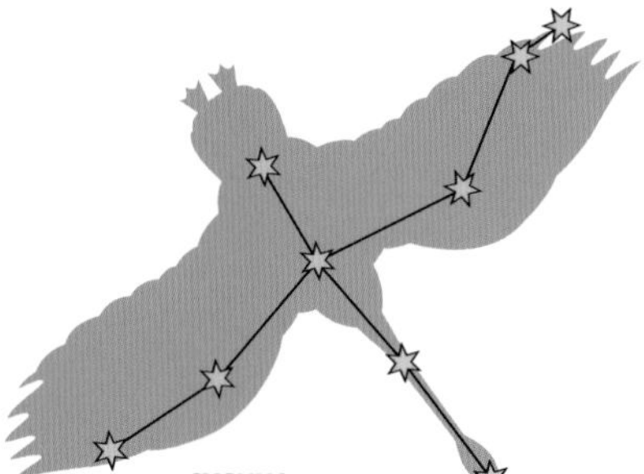

CYGNUS (THE SWAN)

Things to look for

Albireo In the head of the swan lies a beautiful coloured double star known as Albireo. To the naked eye it appears as a single star, but small telescopes show it as a pair. The brighter star is orange, and the fainter one is blue-green.

North America Nebula
Near Deneb lies a cloud of gas popularly known as the North America Nebula (NGC 7000) because of its shape, which resembles the continent of North America. The nebula cannot be seen without a telescope and shows up best on colour photographs like the one here.

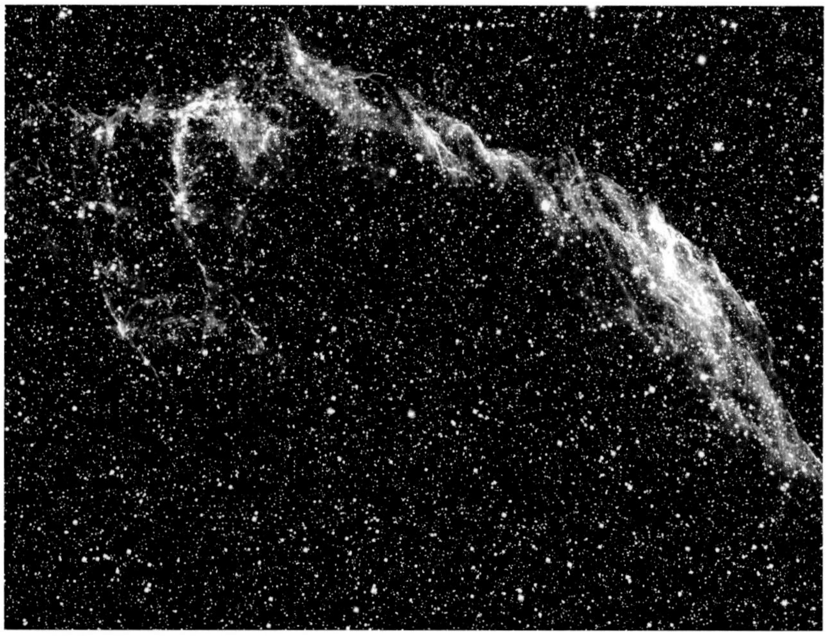

Veil Nebula
In one wing of the swan lie streamers of gas from a star that exploded as a supernova thousands of years ago. The shattered remains of that star are splashed across an area wider than six full moons, forming the Veil Nebula.

ANDROMEDA

This constellation is named after a princess of Greek mythology who was chained to a rock by her parents, King Cepheus and Queen Cassiopeia, as a sacrifice to a sea monster. Fortunately, she was rescued in the nick of time by the hero Perseus, who lies next to her in the sky. Andromeda's head is marked by the star known as Alpheratz. In ancient times, this star was shared with the constellation Pegasus.

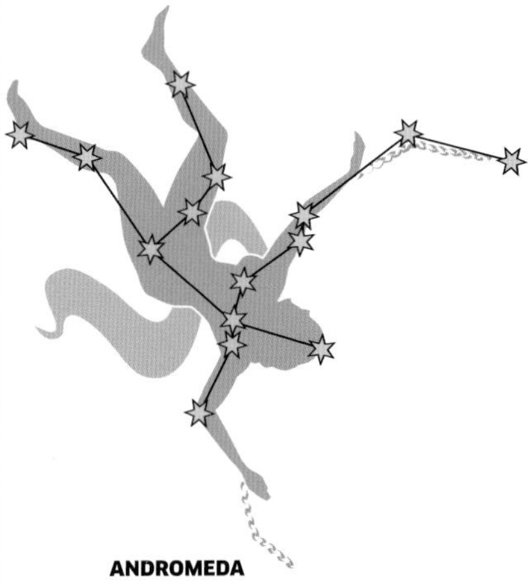

ANDROMEDA

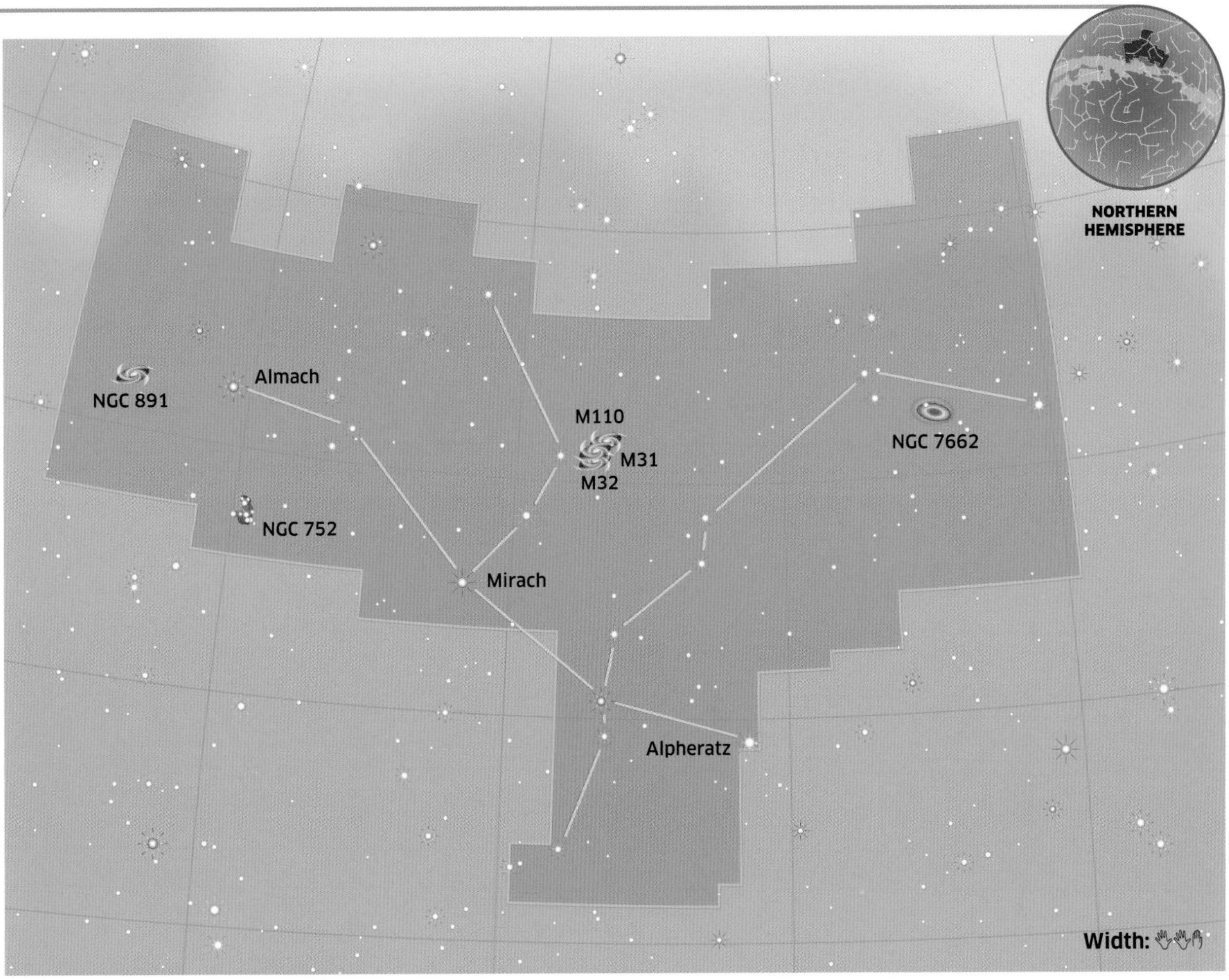
NORTHERN HEMISPHERE
Almach
NGC 891
M110
M31
M32
NGC 7662
NGC 752
Mirach
Alpheratz
Width:

LACERTA

This small figure represents a lizard scuttling between Andromeda and Cygnus. It was devised in 1687 by the Polish astronomer Johannes Hevelius from some faint stars that had not previously been part of any constellation. Of particular note is an object called BL Lacertae. Once thought to be an unusual variable star, it is now known to be the core of an active galaxy.

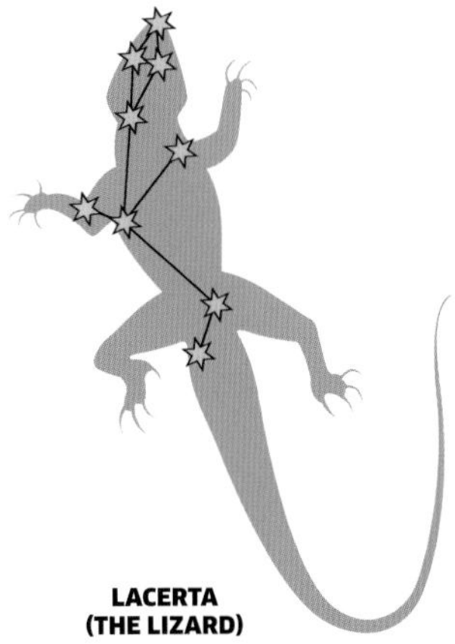

LACERTA (THE LIZARD)

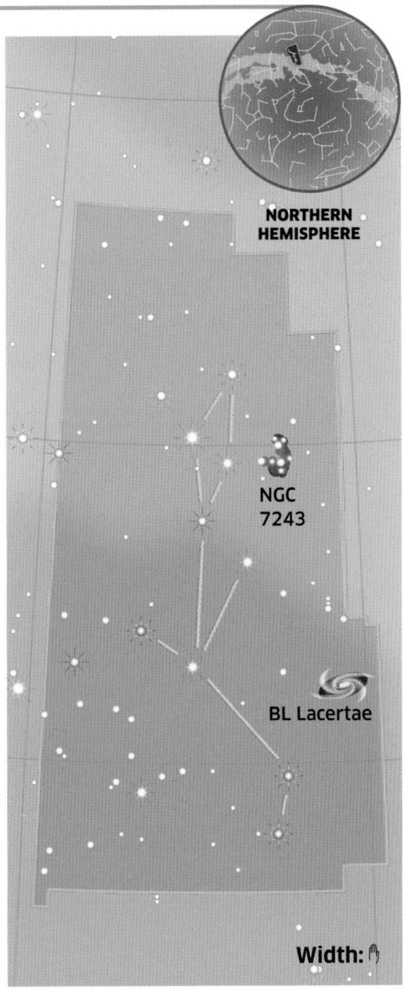
NORTHERN HEMISPHERE
NGC 7243
BL Lacertae
Width:

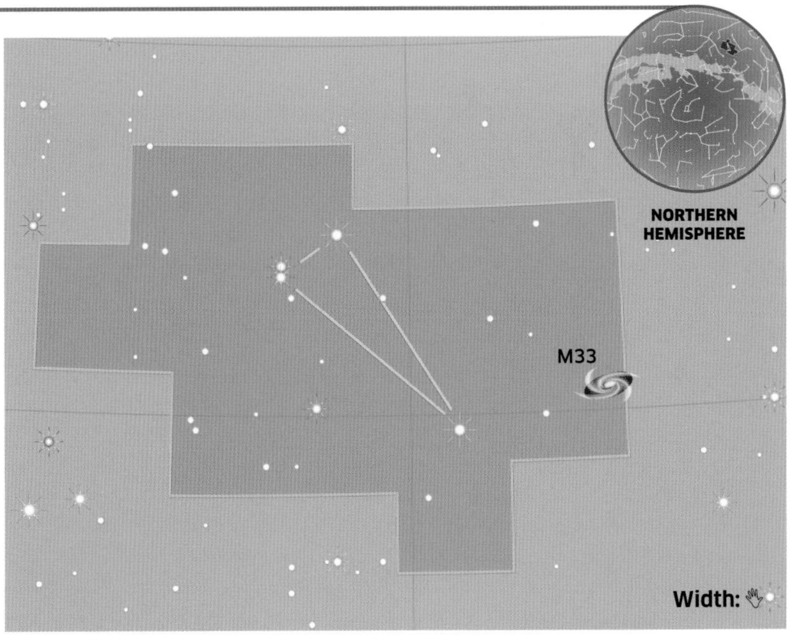
NORTHERN HEMISPHERE
M33
Width:

TRIANGULUM

To the ancient Greeks, this small, triangular-shaped constellation just south of Andromeda represented either the delta of the river Nile or the island of Sicily. Its main feature is M33, a spiral galaxy faintly visible through binoculars. M33 lies nearly 3 million light years away and is the third-largest member of our Local Group of galaxies.

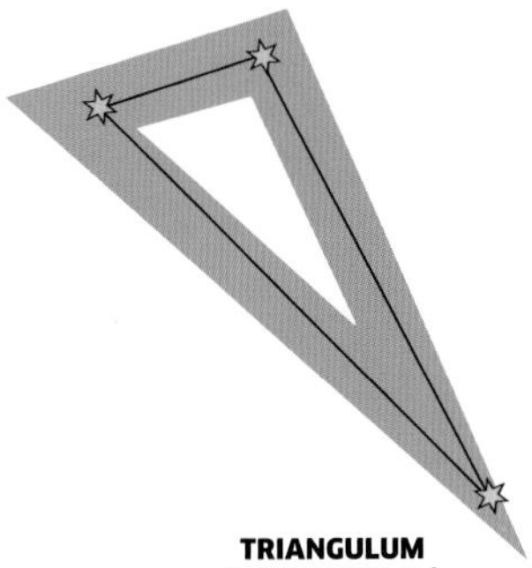

TRIANGULUM (THE TRIANGLE)

PERSEUS

The constellation Perseus is named after a hero of Greek mythology who was sent to cut off the head of Medusa, an evil character known as a Gorgon. In the sky Perseus is seen holding his sword aloft in his right hand, with the head of Medusa in his left. The head is marked by the variable star Algol.

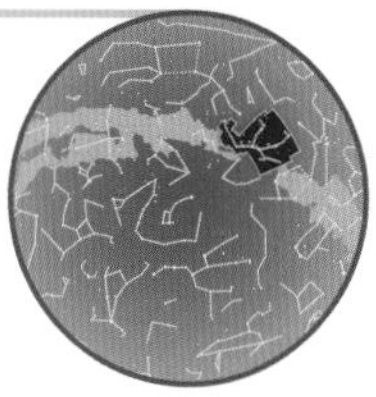

NORTHERN HEMISPHERE

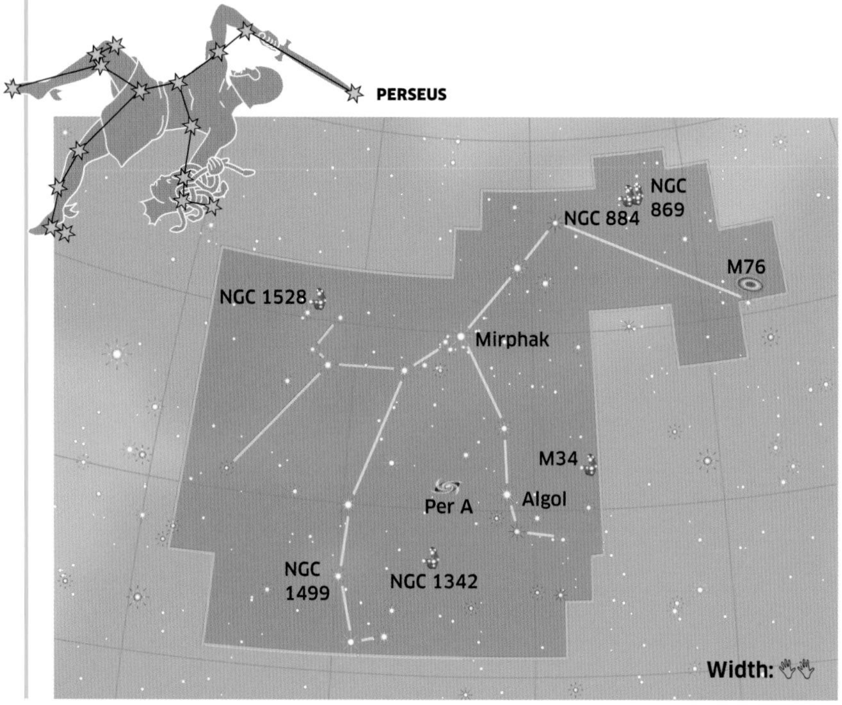
PERSEUS
NGC 869
NGC 884
M76
NGC 1528
Mirphak
M34
Per A
Algol
NGC 1499
NGC 1342
Width:

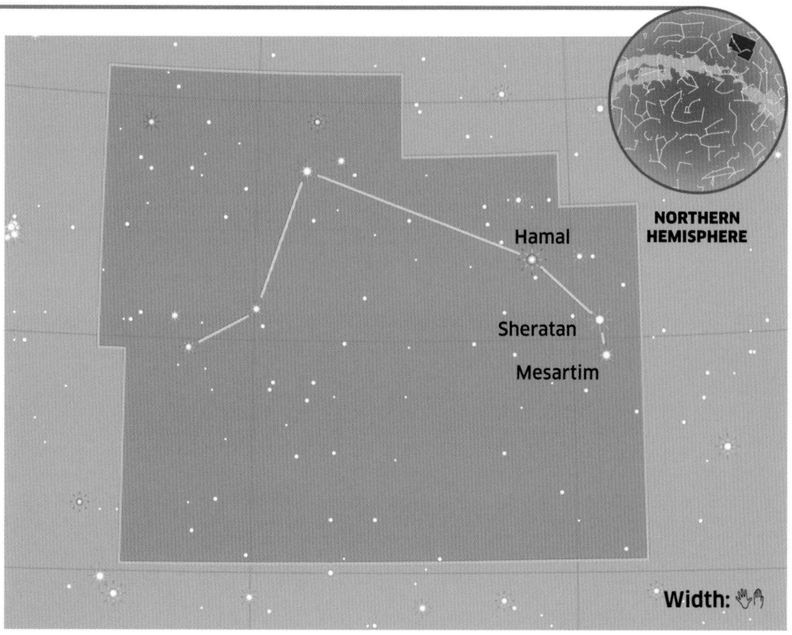
Hamal
Sheratan
Mesartim
Width:

NORTHERN HEMISPHERE

ARIES

Aries represents a ram with a golden fleece in Greek mythology. According to legend, Jason and the Argonauts made an epic voyage from Greece to the Black Sea to collect and bring back the fleece. The constellation's most obvious feature is a crooked line of three stars south of Triangulum. The most southerly (and faintest) of these stars, Mesartim, is a double star that is easily divided by small telescopes.

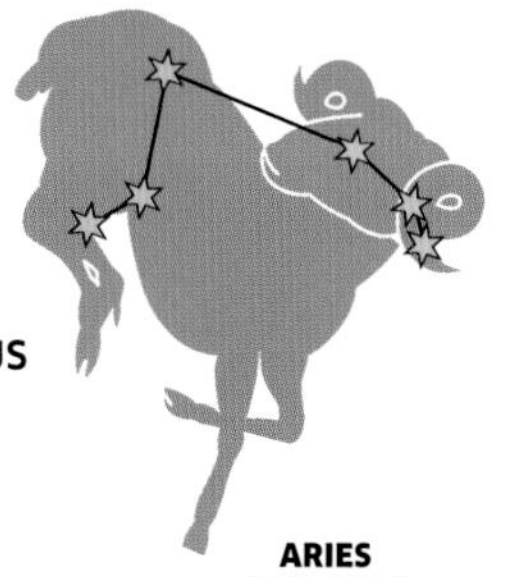

ARIES (THE RAM)

CANCER

This constellation represents a crab that had a minor role in Greek mythology. According to the story, when Hercules was fighting the multi-headed Hydra, the crab bit him but was then crushed underfoot. Cancer is the faintest of the 12 constellations of the zodiac. Near its centre is a large, hazy star cluster with several alternative names: the Beehive, Praesepe, the Manger, or simply M44.

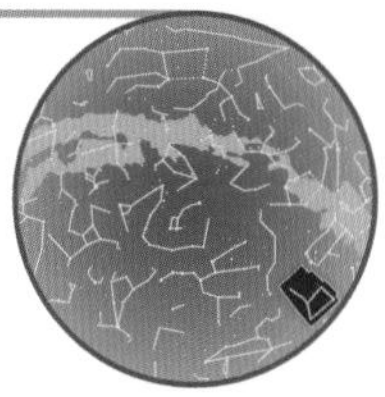

NORTHERN HEMISPHERE

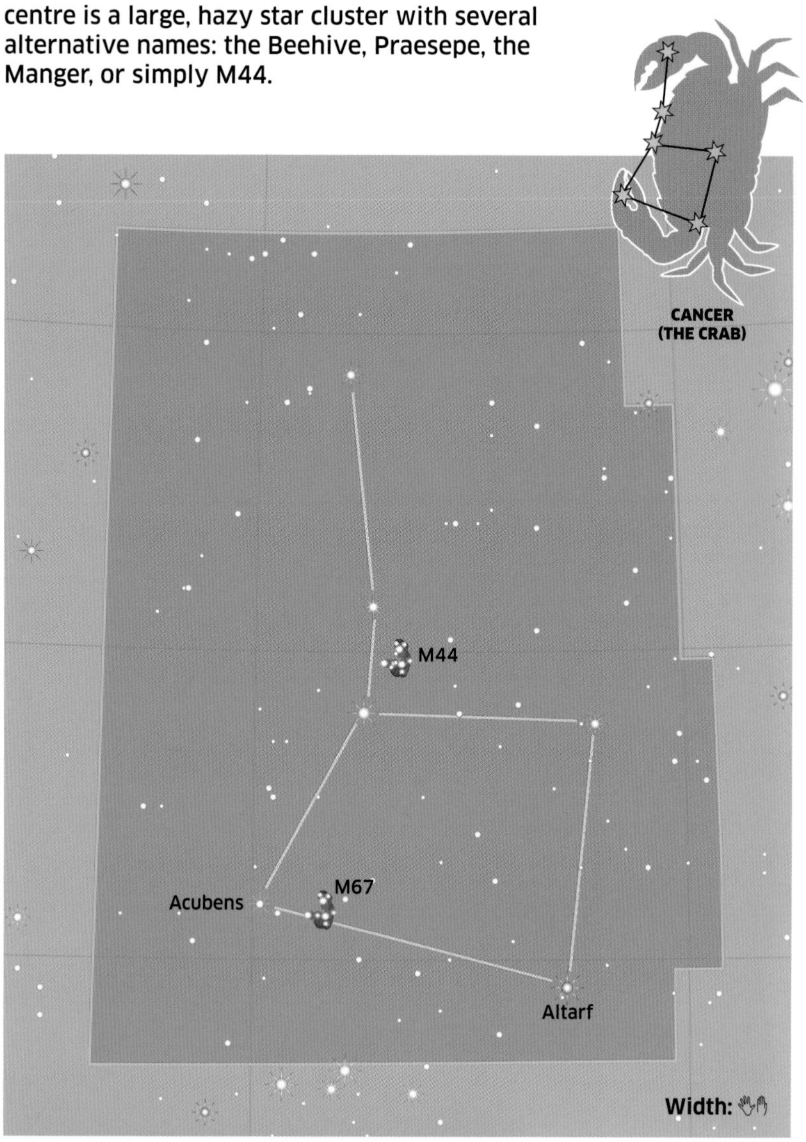
CANCER (THE CRAB)
M44
Acubens
M67
Altarf
Width:

Beehive Cluster
M44 is an open cluster made of stars that lie about 577 light years from Earth. While the cluster can be seen by the naked eye, most of its stars are visible only with binoculars or a telescope.

TAURUS

Taurus the bull is one of the most magnificent and interesting constellations in the sky. In Greek mythology, the god Zeus turned himself into a bull to carry off Princess Europa to the island of Crete. The brightest star in the constellation is Aldebaran, a red giant that marks the glinting eye of the bull. The star at the tip of the bull's right horn, Alnath (or El Nath), was once shared with Auriga to the north.

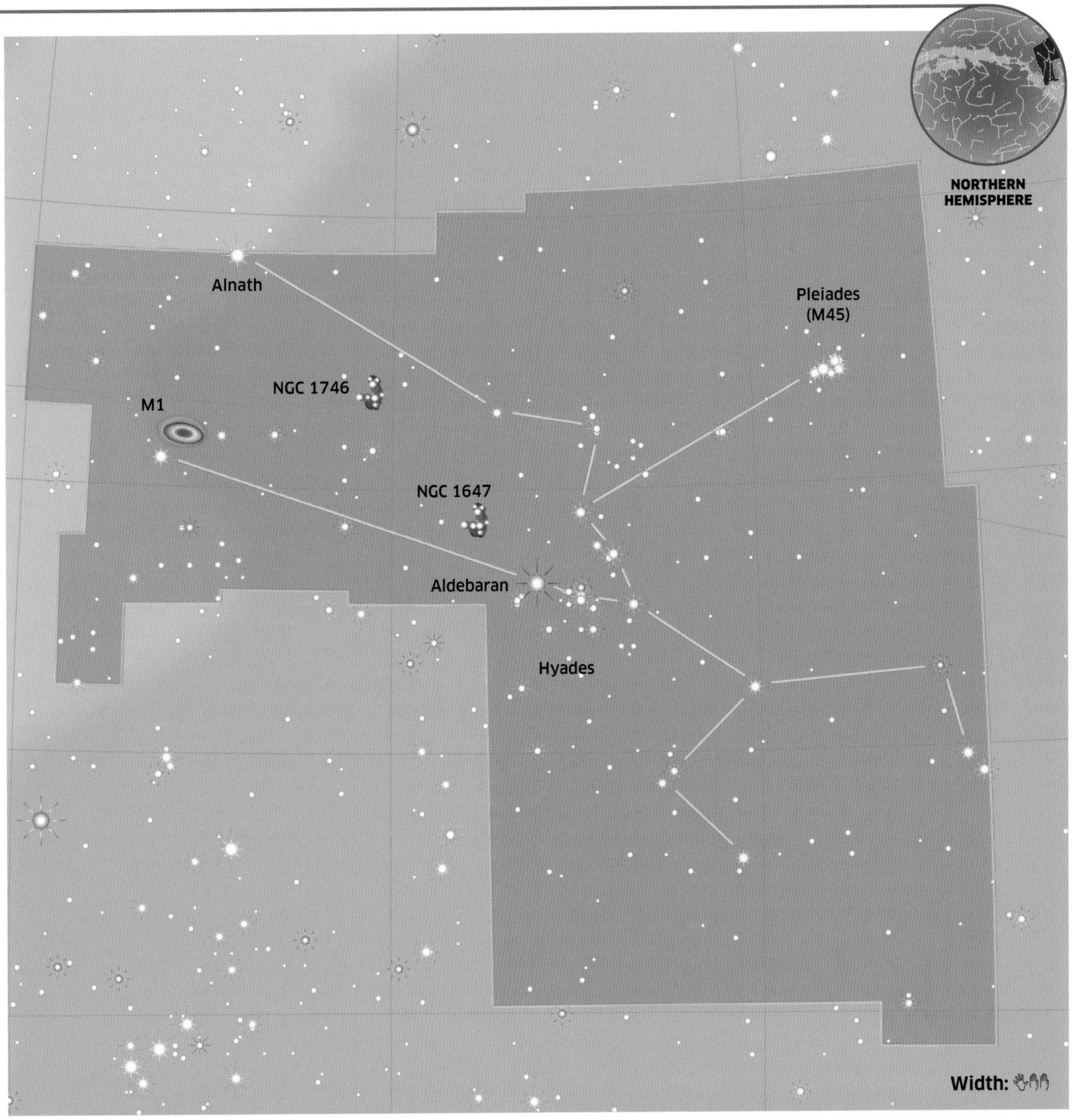
NORTHERN
HEMISPHERE
Alnath
Pleiades
(M45)
NGC 1746
M1
NGC 1647
Aldebaran
Hyades
Width:

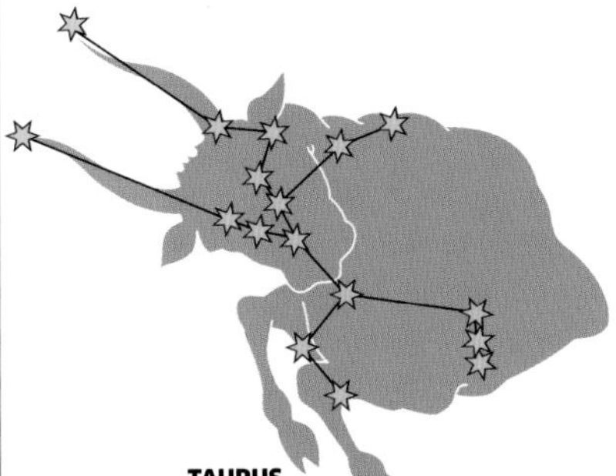
TAURUS
(THE BULL)

Pleiades
The Pleiades Cluster, popularly known as the Seven Sisters, is a beautiful star group. Six or more stars can be seen with the naked eye, and binoculars show dozens. Photographs reveal even more, along with a haze of dust that surrounds them.

Crab Nebula
In the year 1054, a new star appeared temporarily in Taurus. This was a supernova, the most violent form of stellar explosion. Now only visible through telescopes, the star's shattered remains can be seen as the Crab Nebula (M1). This image was taken with the Hubble Space Telescope.

Hyades
The face of the bull is marked by a V-shaped group of stars called the Hyades, easily visible to the naked eye. The bright star Aldebaran appears to be one of the Hyades but is, in fact, closer to us, and lies in front of the cluster by chance.

GEMINI

Gemini represents the mythical twins Castor and Pollux. The two brightest stars in the constellation are named after the twins and mark their heads. A small telescope shows that Castor is a double star. These two stars orbit each other every 500 years or so. Larger telescopes show a fainter red dwarf near them. Special instruments have revealed that each of these three stars is itself a close double, making Castor a family of six stars, all linked by gravity.

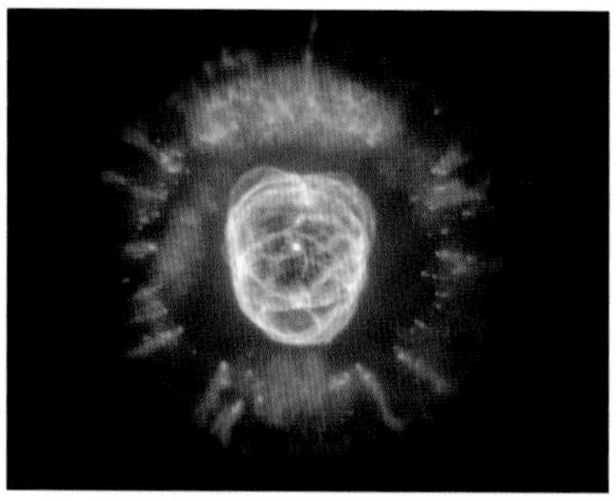

Eskimo Nebula
The Eskimo Nebula (NGC 2392) is a remarkable planetary nebula. It gets its popular name from its resemblance to a face surrounded by a fur-lined hood. Another name for it is the Clown-faced Nebula.

GEMINI (THE TWINS)

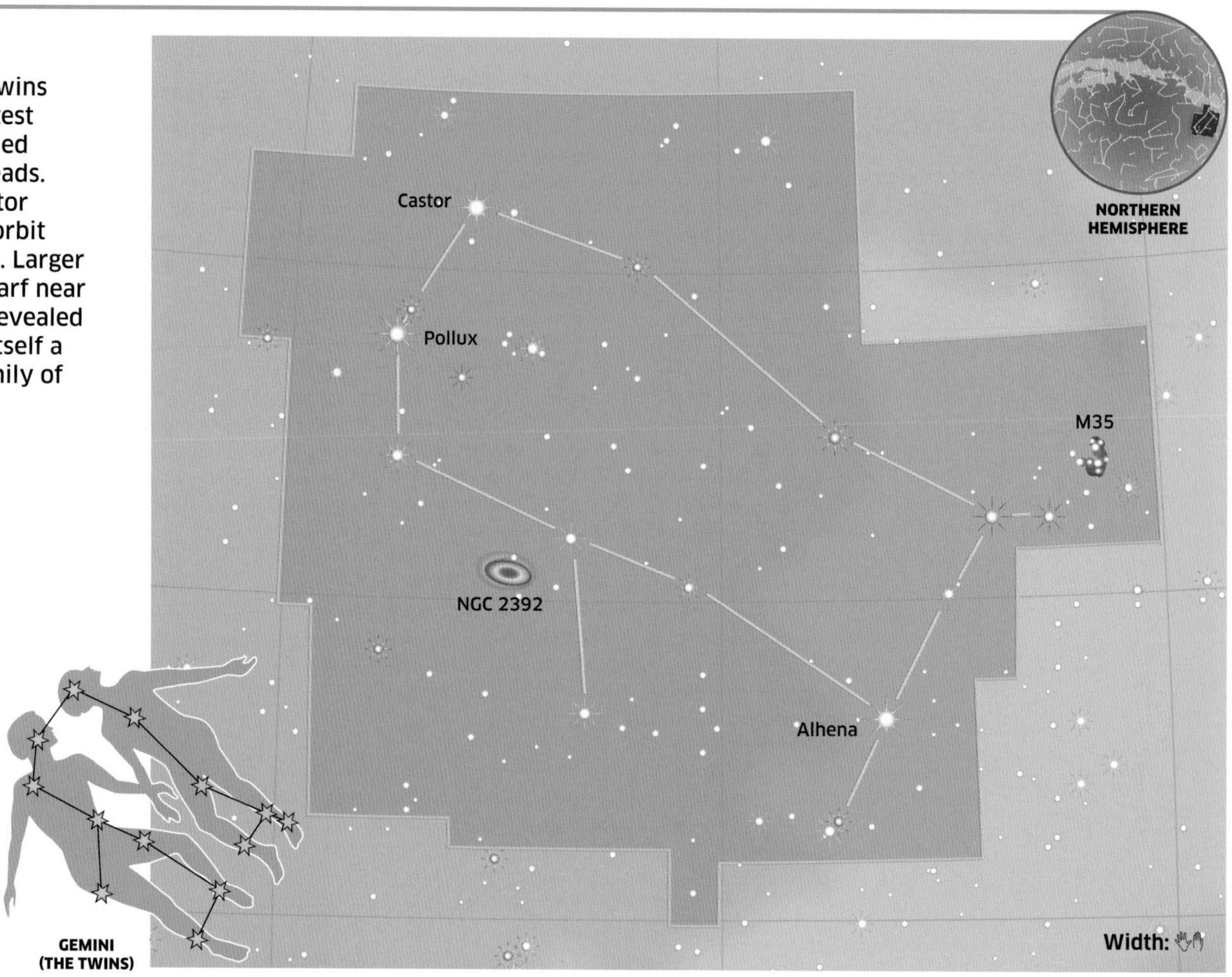
Castor
Pollux
M35
NGC 2392
Alhena
Width:
NORTHERN HEMISPHERE

LEO MINOR

This small constellation represents a lion cub. Polish astronomer Johannes Hevelius introduced it in 1687. Leo Minor contains very few objects of interest. The star R Leonis Minoris is a red giant. Its brightness varies at regular intervals – it can be seen with binoculars at its brightest but is not visible even through small telescopes at its dimmest.

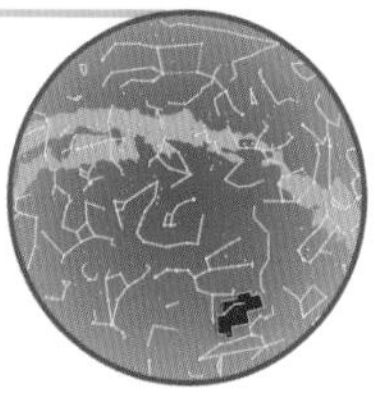
NORTHERN HEMISPHERE

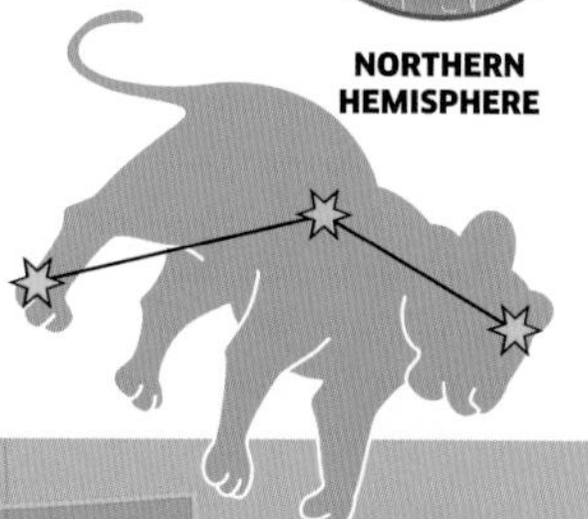

LEO MINOR (THE LITTLE LION)

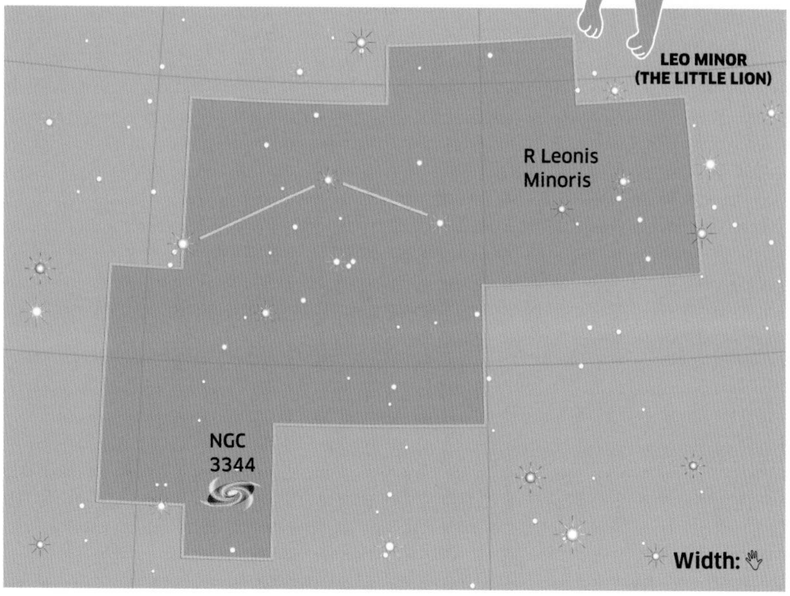
R Leonis Minoris
NGC 3344
Width:

COMA BERENICES

This is a faint but interesting constellation near the tail of Leo, the lion. The ancient Greeks imagined it as the hair of Queen Berenice of Egypt. She cut off her hair to thank the gods after her husband returned safely from fighting a war in Asia. Dozens of faint stars form a wedge-shaped group called the Coma Star Cluster, easily seen in binoculars.

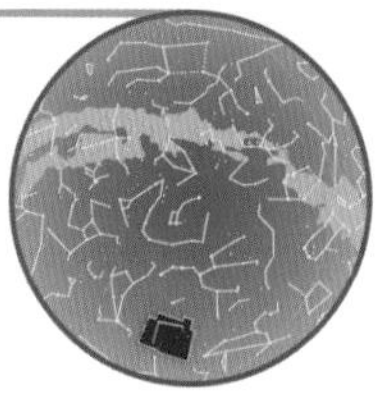
NORTHERN HEMISPHERE

COMA BERENICES (BERENICES' HAIR)

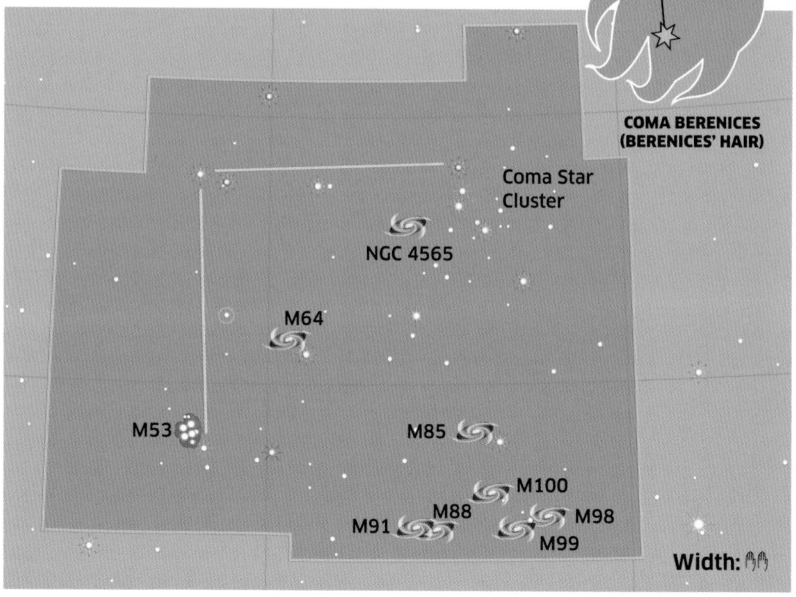
Coma Star Cluster
NGC 4565
M64
M53
M85
M100
M88
M91
M98
M99
Width:

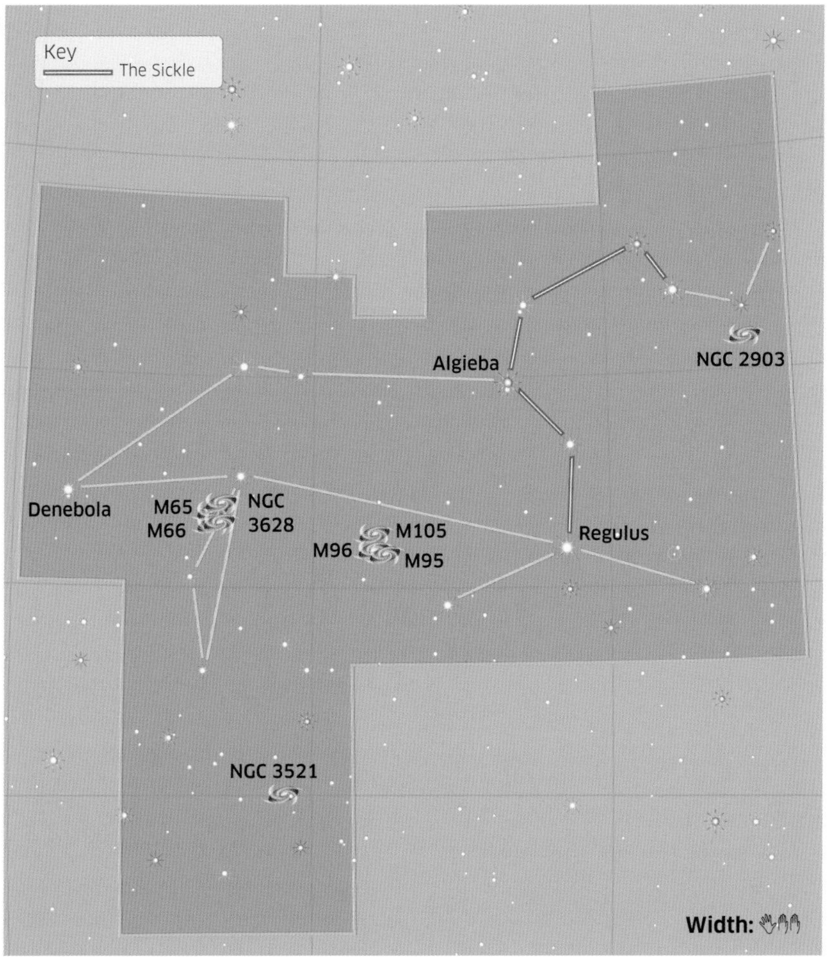
Key
The Sickle
Algieba
NGC 2903
Denebola
M65
M66
NGC 3628
M105
M96
M95
Regulus
NGC 3521
Width:

LEO

This is one of the few constellations that really looks like what it is supposed to represent – in this case, a crouching lion. In Greek mythology, it was said to be the lion slain by the warrior Hercules as one of his 12 labours. An arc of stars called the Sickle (marked here in purple) forms the lion's head and chest. Leo's brightest star, Regulus, lies at the base of the Sickle. One of the stars in the Sickle, Algieba, can be seen as a double star through small telescopes.

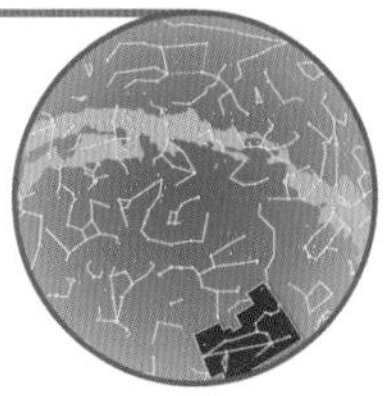

NORTHERN HEMISPHERE

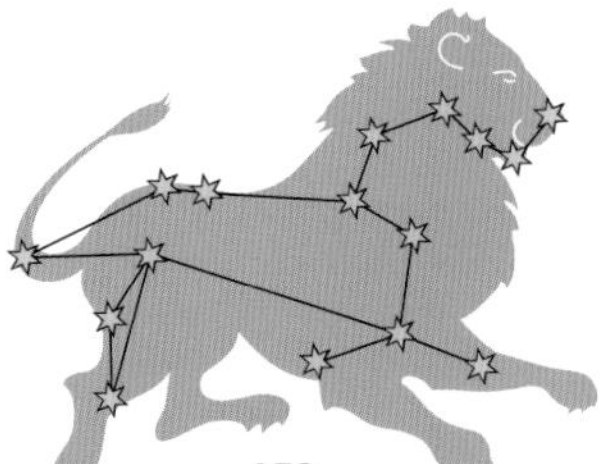

LEO (THE LION)

Spiral galaxy M66
M66 is a beautiful spiral galaxy that lies underneath the hind quarters of Leo, the lion. It forms a pair with another galaxy, M65. They can be glimpsed with small telescopes under good conditions, but large instruments help to see them clearly.

VIRGO

Virgo is the second-largest constellation. In Greek mythology, it represented both the goddess of justice and the goddess of agriculture. The main stars of Virgo form a lazy "Y" shape. The constellation's brightest star, Spica, is at the base of the Y. The star Porrima, in the middle of the Y, is a double star divisible with a small telescope. In the bowl of the Y is the Virgo Cluster – a cluster of more than 1,000 galaxies about 55 million light years away.

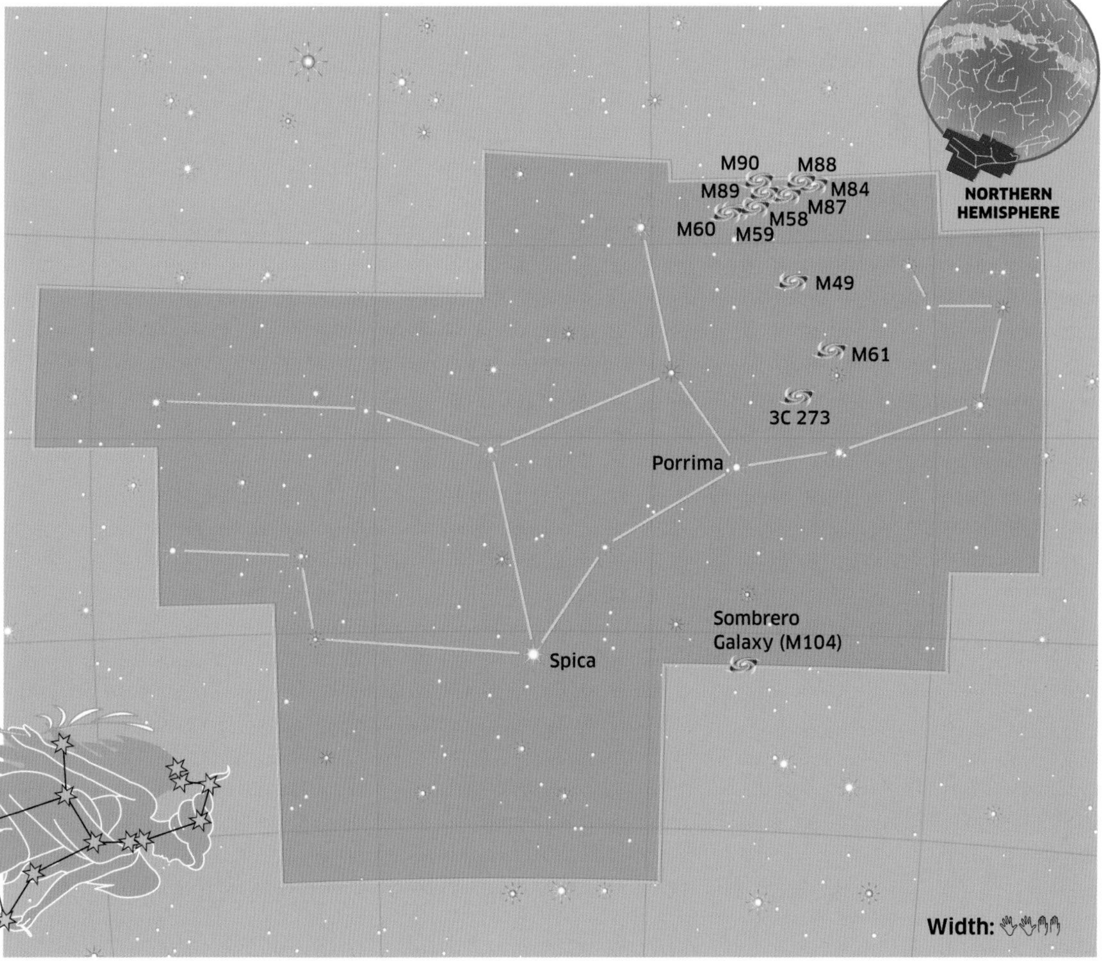
M90
M88
M89
M84
M87
M58
M60
M59
M49
M61
3C 273
Porrima
Sombrero Galaxy (M104)
Spica
Width:

NORTHERN HEMISPHERE

Sombrero Galaxy
The Sombrero Galaxy (M104) is a spiral galaxy seen edge-on that resembles a Mexican sombrero hat. This view of it was taken by the Hubble Space Telescope. The Sombrero is 30 million light years away, closer to us than the Virgo Cluster of galaxies.

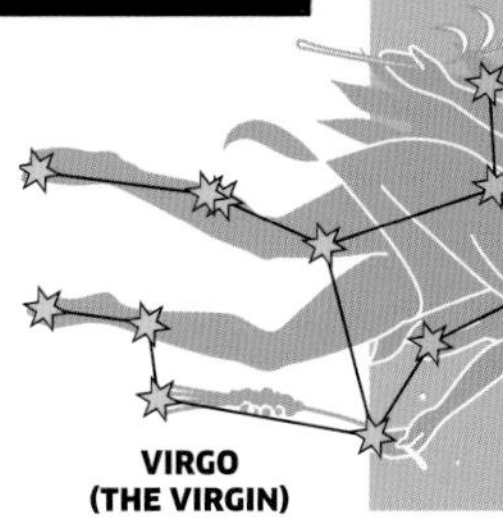

VIRGO (THE VIRGIN)

LIBRA

The scales of justice are represented by Libra and are held by the goddess of justice, Virgo, who lies next to Libra in the sky. Libra's stars represented the claws of the scorpion, Scorpius, until Roman times.

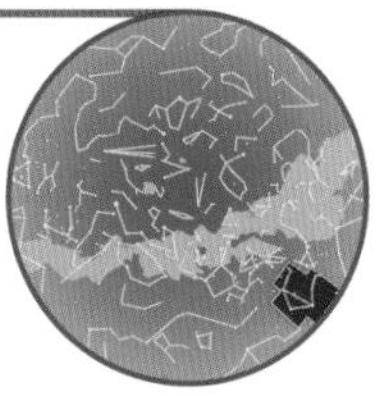

SOUTHERN HEMISPHERE

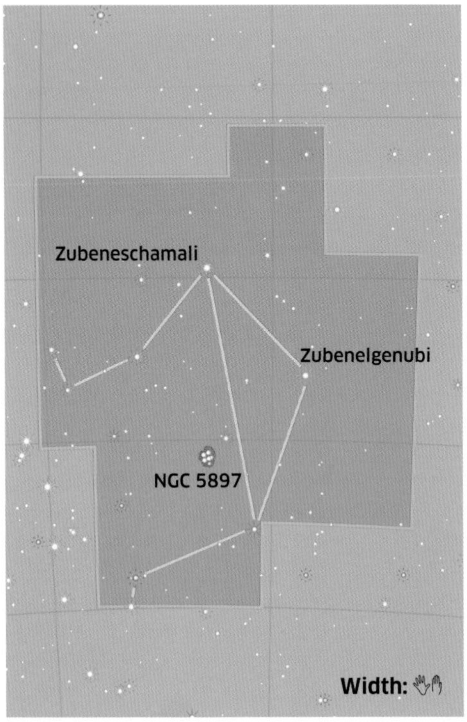
Zubeneschamali
Zubenelgenubi
NGC 5897
Width:

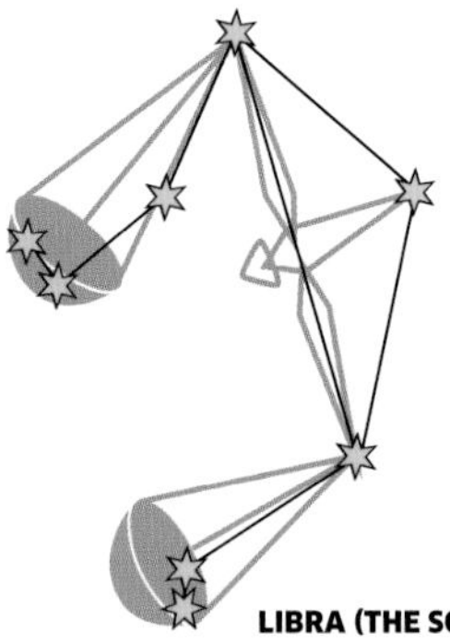

LIBRA (THE SCALES)

Things to look for

Zubenelgenubi This is a wide double star easily spotted with binoculars or even sharp eyesight. Its strange name comes from the Arabic for "the southern claw".

SERPENS

The constellation Serpens represents a large snake being held by the man in the constellation Ophiuchus. The head of the snake lies on one side of Ophiuchus, the tail on the other. This is the only example of a constellation being split into two. However, the two halves count as only one constellation. Near the neck of the snake lies M5, one of the best globular clusters in the northern skies, just visible through binoculars. Binoculars will also show an open cluster called IC 4756 near the snake's tail.

SERPENS (THE SERPENT)

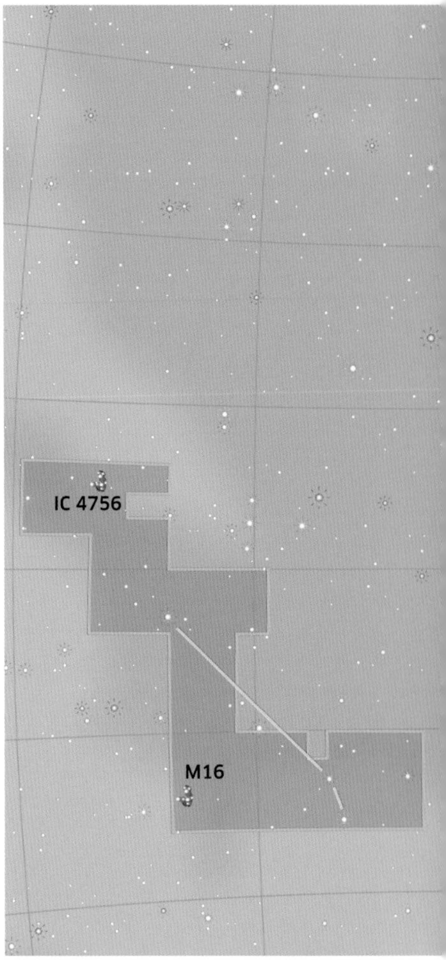
IC 4756
M16

CORONA BOREALIS

Shaped like a horseshoe, this constellation represents the jewelled crown worn by Princess Ariadne of Crete when she married the god Dionysus. Within the arc of the crown lies a most unusual variable star, R Coronae Borealis. This is a yellow supergiant that suddenly drops in brightness every few years.

CORONA BOREALIS (THE NORTHERN CROWN)

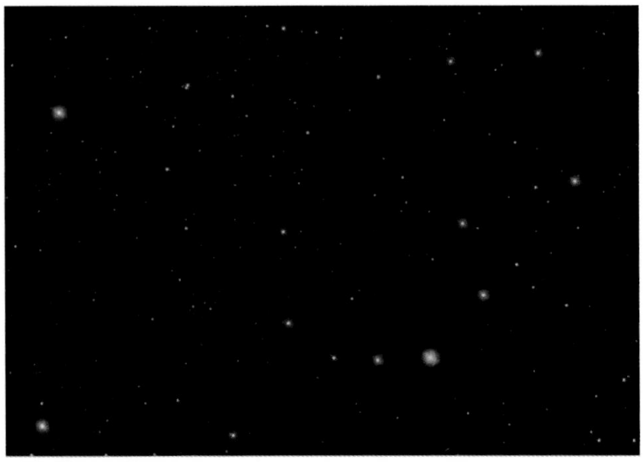

Jewel in the crown
Alphekka is the brightest member of the arc of seven stars that makes up the northern crown, Corona Borealis. The star is also known as Gemma.

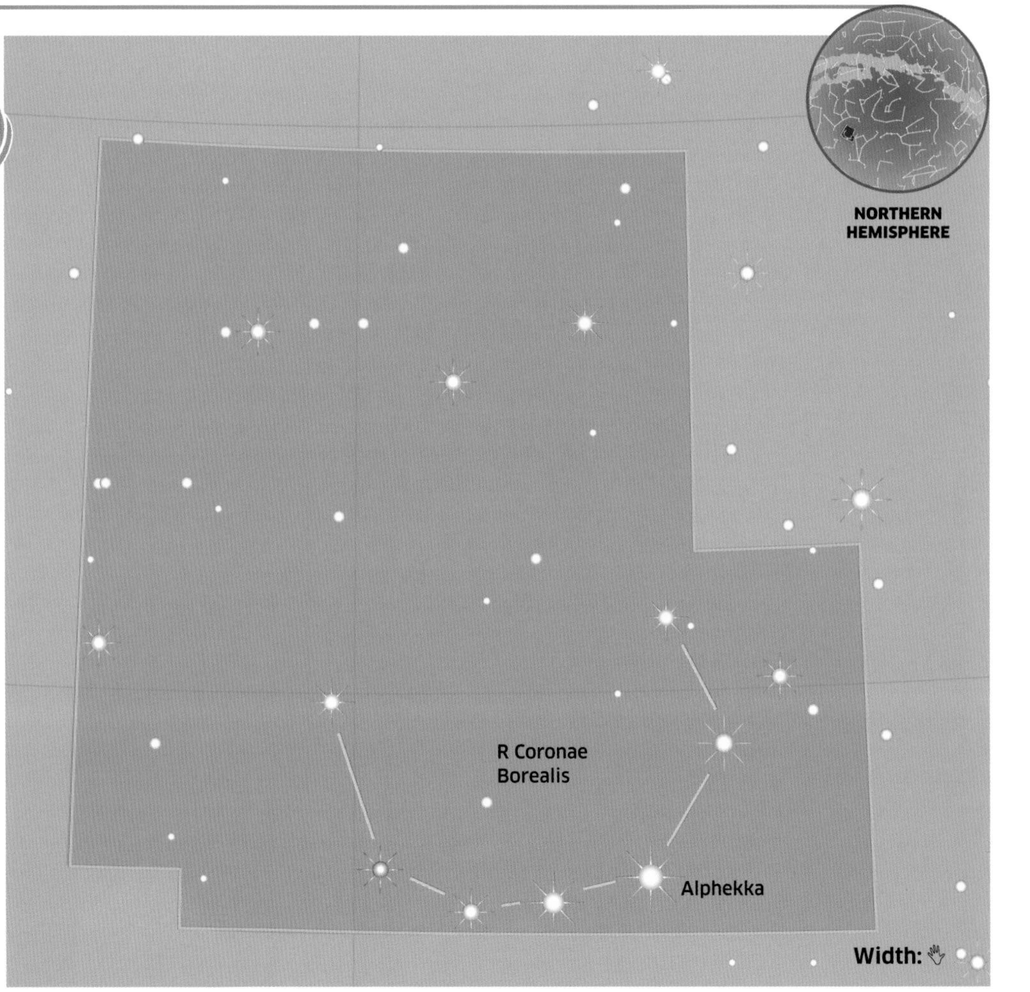
NORTHERN HEMISPHERE
R Coronae Borealis
Alphekka
Width:

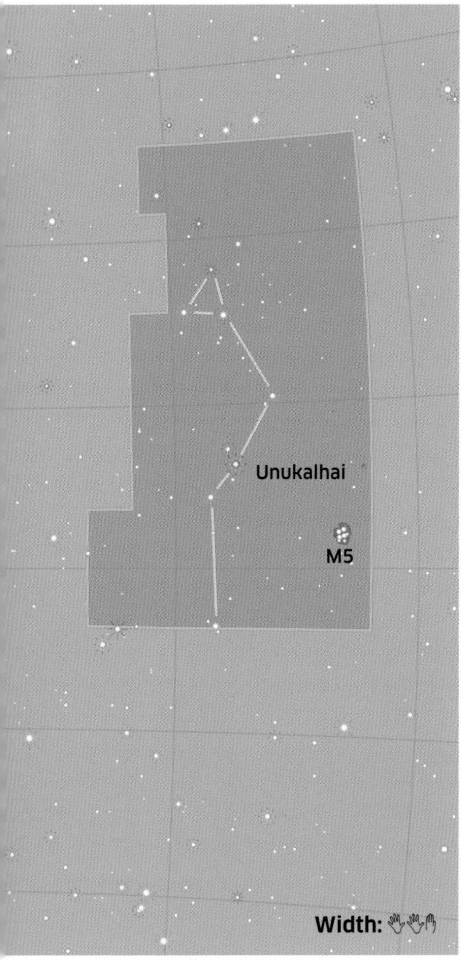
Unukalhai
M5
Width:

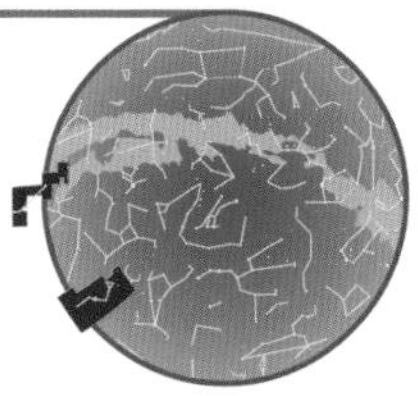

NORTHERN HEMISPHERE

Eagle Nebula
In the tail section of Serpens lies a star cluster called M16, visible through binoculars. Surrounding it is a glowing cloud of gas called the Eagle Nebula, seen here through the Hubble telescope.

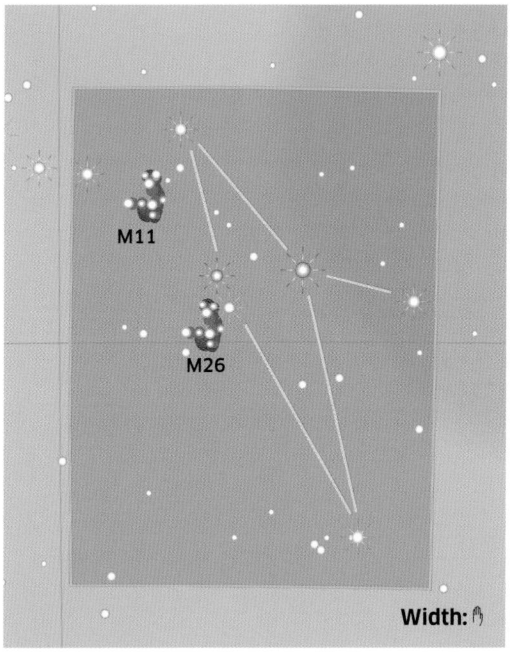
M11
M26
Width:

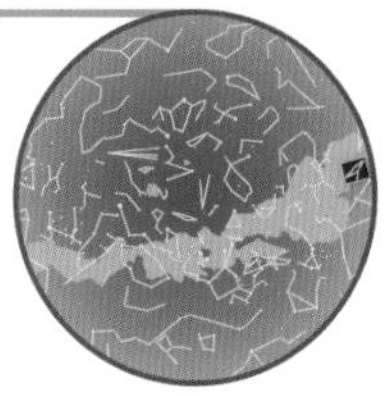

SOUTHERN HEMISPHERE

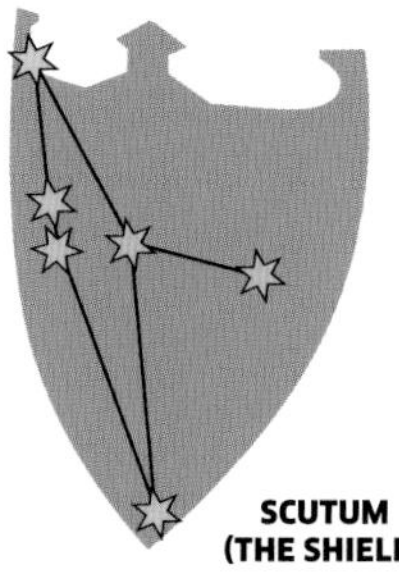

SCUTUM (THE SHIELD)

SCUTUM

This small constellation represents a shield. It was created in the late 17th century by the Polish astronomer Johannes Hevelius. One of the brightest parts of the Milky Way lies in the northern half of this constellation and is known as the Scutum Star Cloud. Near the border with the constellation Aquila is M11, a star cluster often called the Wild Duck Cluster because its shape resembles a flock of birds in flight.

OPHIUCHUS

This constellation represents the god of medicine. In the sky he is depicted holding a large snake: the constellation Serpens. Ophiuchus contains several globular clusters that can be seen with binoculars and small telescopes. The brightest of them are M10 and M12.

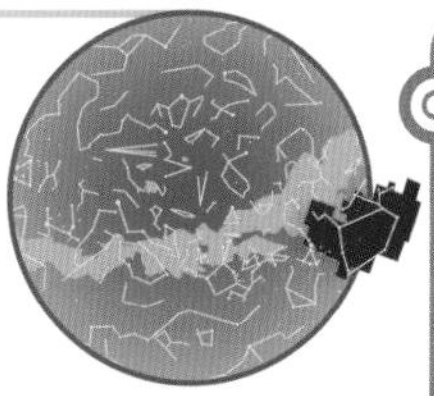

SOUTHERN HEMISPHERE

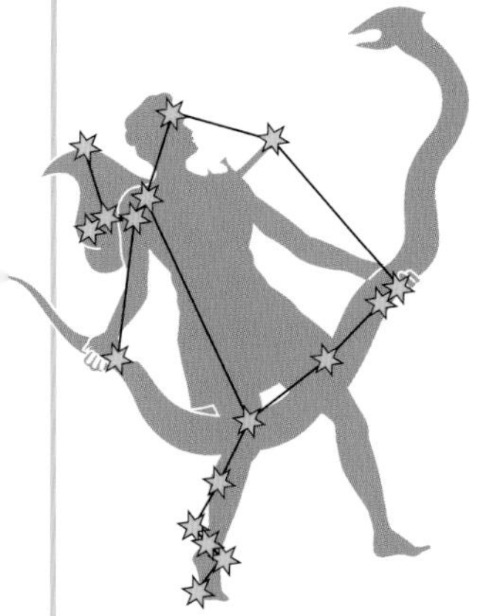

OPHIUCHUS (THE SERPENT HOLDER)

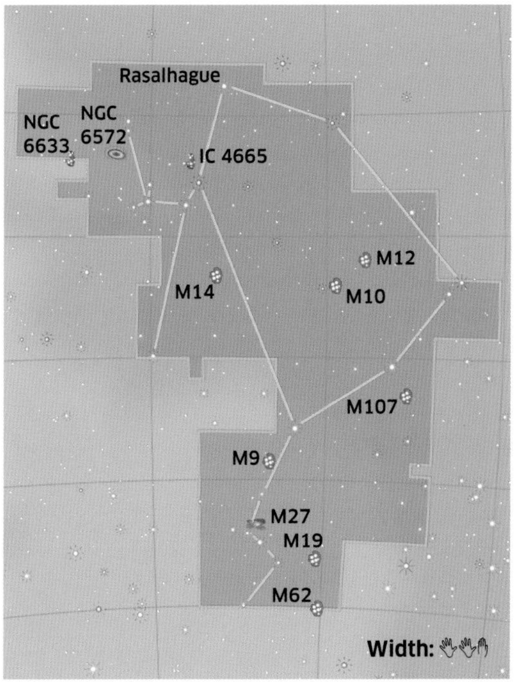
Rasalhague
NGC 6633
NGC 6572
IC 4665
M12
M14
M10
M107
M9
M27
M19
M62
Width:

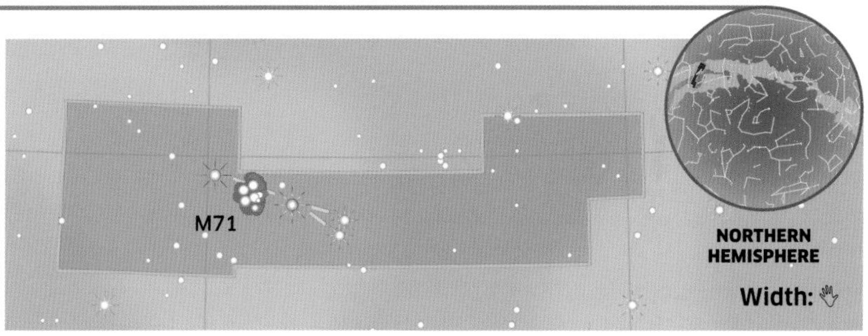
M71
Width:

NORTHERN HEMISPHERE

SAGITTA

The third-smallest constellation in the sky, Sagitta represents an arrow. It was one of the original constellations known to the ancient Greeks, who said that the arrow was shot either by Hercules, which lies next to it, or by one of the gods. Although its stars are faint, it is quite easy to recognize.

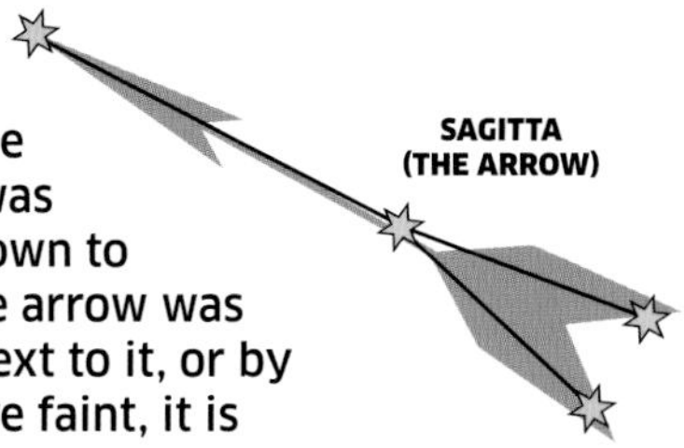

SAGITTA (THE ARROW)

Globular cluster M71
Sagitta contains a faint globular cluster, M71, visible through small telescopes. It measures about 27 light years wide and is thought to be about 10 billion years old.

AQUILA

Aquila represents a flying eagle, one of the disguises that was said in mythology to have been adopted by the Greek god Zeus. Its main star is Altair, which marks one corner of the Summer Triangle – a famous triangle made of bright stars from different constellations. The other two stars of the triangle are Vega in Lyra and Deneb in Cygnus. The most interesting feature in Aquila is Eta Aquilae, one of the brightest examples of the type of variable star known as a Cepheid.

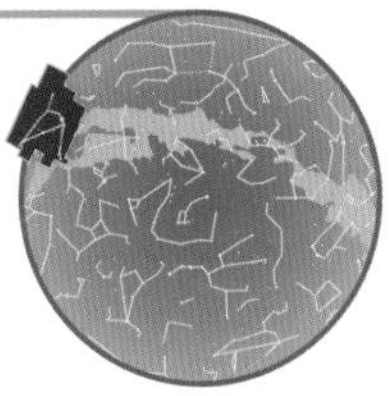
NORTHERN HEMISPHERE

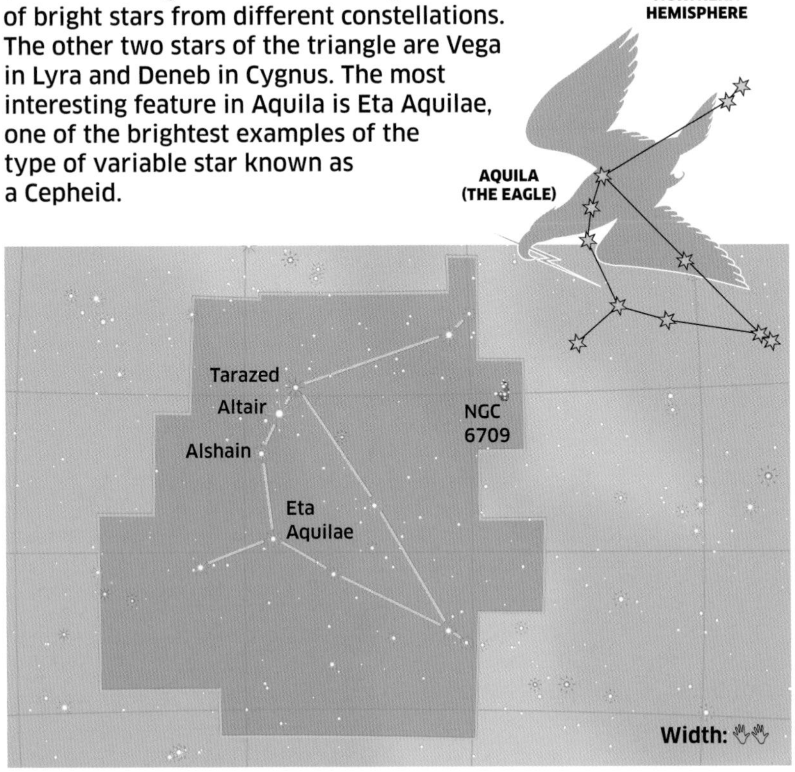
AQUILA (THE EAGLE)
Tarazed
Altair
Alshain
NGC 6709
Eta Aquilae
Width:

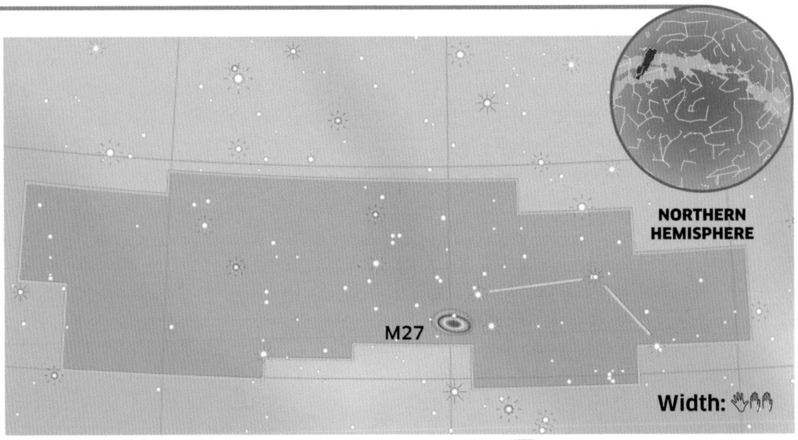
NORTHERN HEMISPHERE
M27
Width:

VULPECULA

Polish astronomer Johannes Hevelius named this faint constellation in the late 17th century. It represents a fox. An attractive object for binoculars is a group of stars called the Coathanger, shaped like a bar with a hook on top.

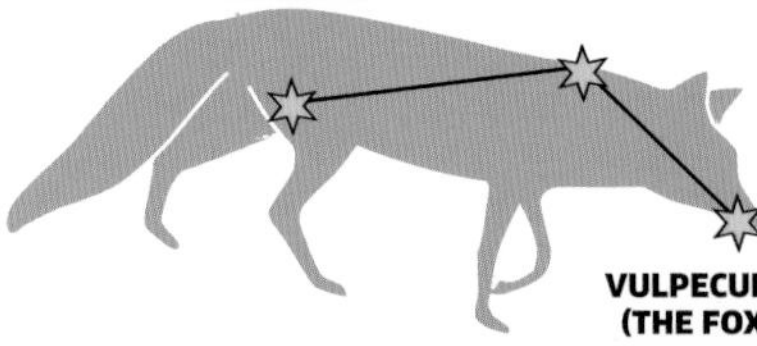
VULPECULA (THE FOX)

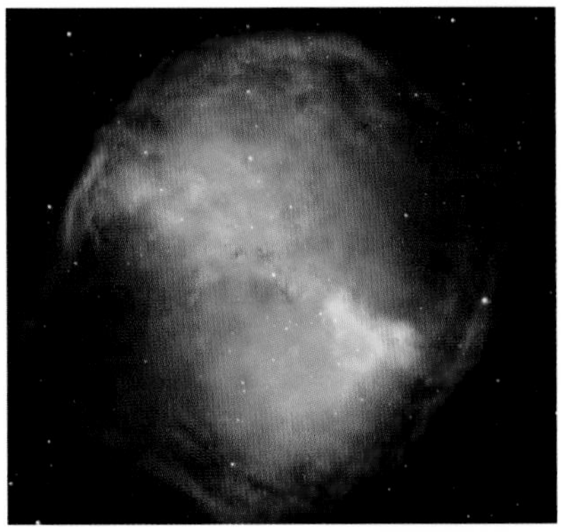

Dumbbell Nebula
A famous object in the constellation Vulpecula is the Dumbbell Nebula (M27). This planetary nebula (a shell of gas thrown off from a dying star) can be seen with binoculars on clear nights.

DELPHINUS

This attractive constellation represents a dolphin. In mythology, this was the dolphin that rescued the Greek musician Arion when he jumped overboard from a ship to escape a band of robbers. The constellation's two brightest stars bear the odd names Sualocin and Rotanev. Read backwards they spell Nicolaus Venator, the name of an Italian astronomer who is thought to have cunningly named them after himself.

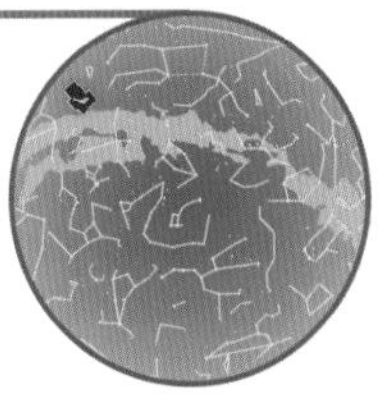
NORTHERN HEMISPHERE

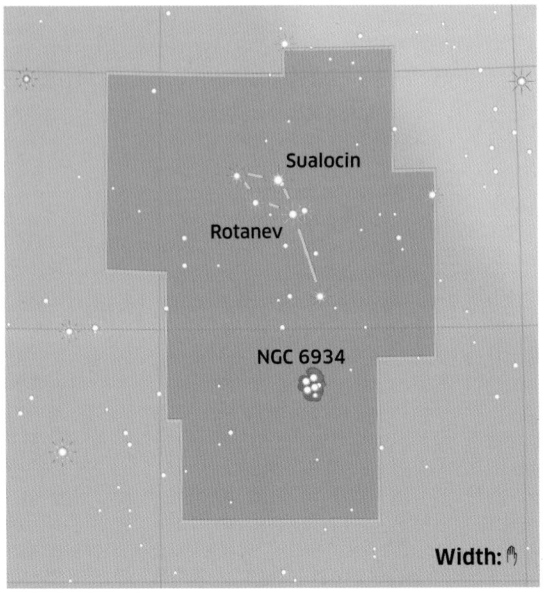
Sualocin
Rotanev
NGC 6934
Width:

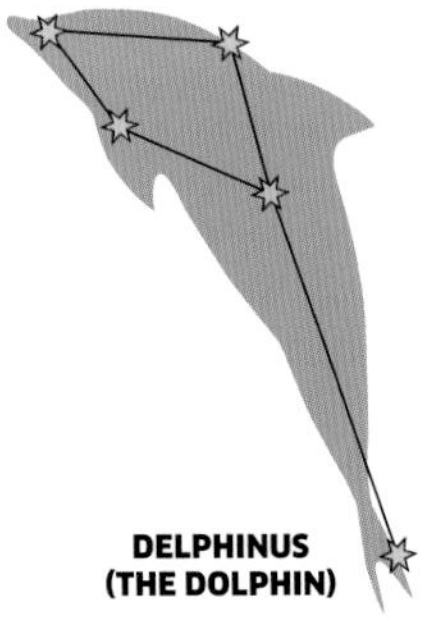
DELPHINUS (THE DOLPHIN)

EQUULEUS

Equuleus is the second-smallest constellation in the sky, representing the head of a foal. It lies next to the large flying horse Pegasus and was one of the constellations known to the ancient Greeks. There is little of interest in it apart from a double star, Kitalpha, that can easily be divided with binoculars.

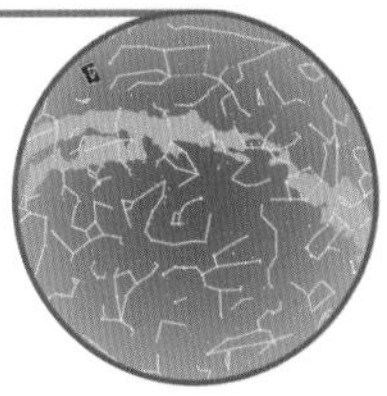
NORTHERN HEMISPHERE

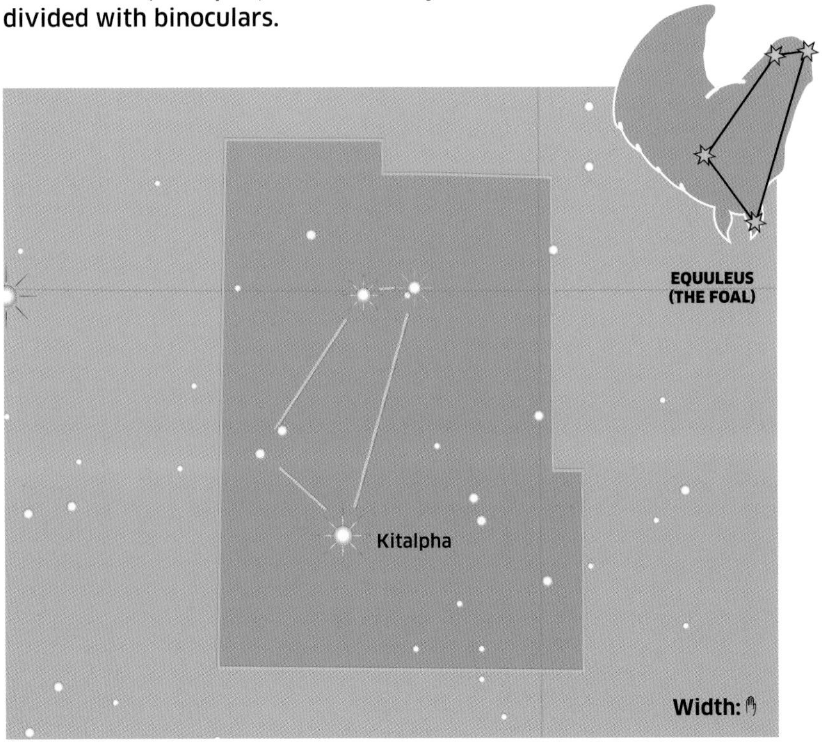
EQUULEUS (THE FOAL)
Kitalpha
Width:

PEGASUS

This large constellation of the northern sky represents a flying horse in Greek mythology. Its most noticeable feature is a pattern called the Great Square, formed by four stars that outline the horse's body. However, only three stars of the Square actually belong to Pegasus as the fourth is over the border in Andromeda (although in the past it was shared by the two constellations). The Square is so large that 30 full moons placed side by side could fit inside it. The horse's nose is marked by the star Enif.

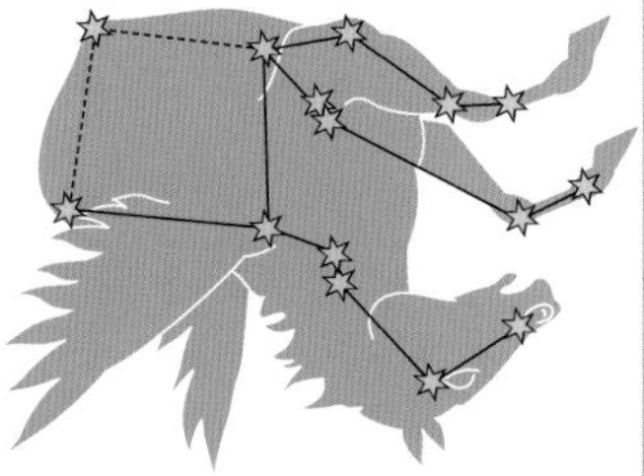

PEGASUS (THE WINGED HORSE)

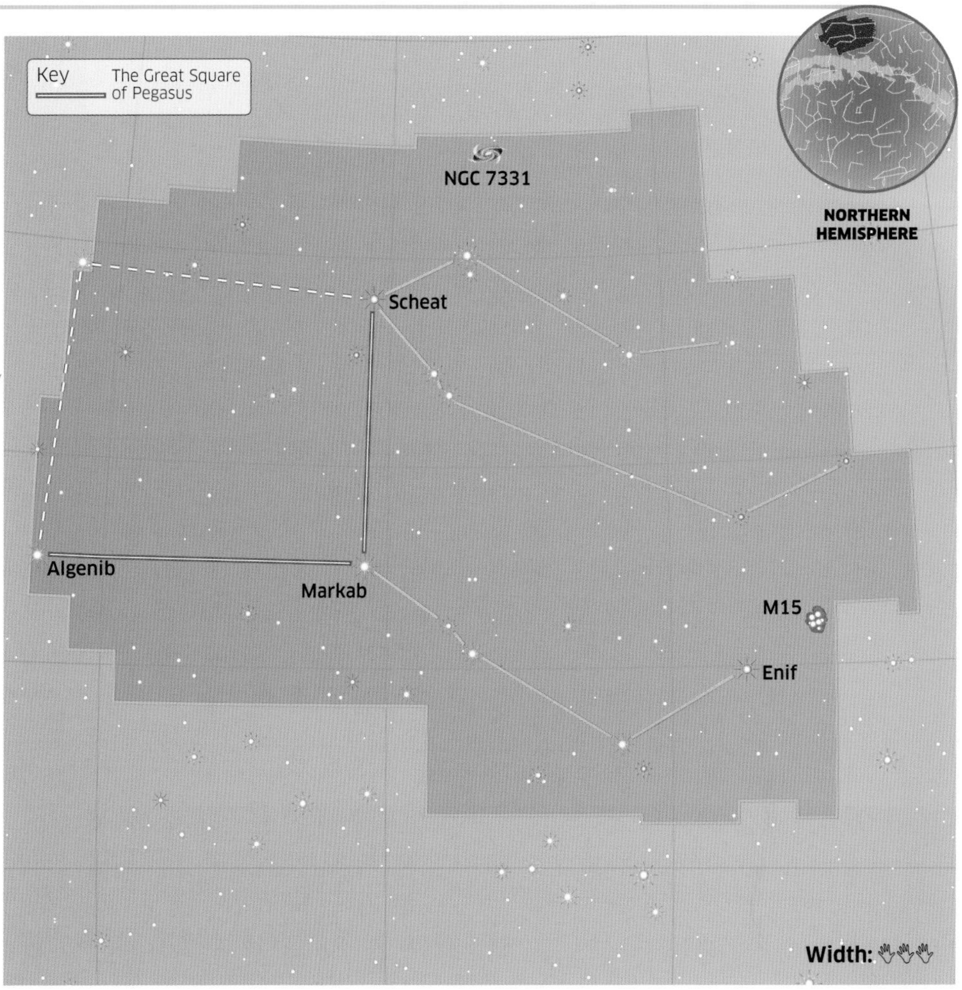
Key
The Great Square of Pegasus
NGC 7331
NORTHERN HEMISPHERE
Scheat
Algenib
Markab
M15
Enif
Width:

Globular cluster M15
Near the star Enif lies M15, one of the finest globular clusters in northern skies. This is easily visible through binoculars as a fuzzy patch. Telescopes reveal it as a vast ball of stars.

AQUARIUS

The constellation Aquarius represents a young man pouring water from a jar. The jar is represented by a little group of stars around Zeta Aquarii. A string of fainter stars cascading southwards represents the flow of water. In the north of the constellation lies the globular cluster M2, visible as a faint patch through binoculars. Two famous planetary nebulas (remains of dying stars) can be found in Aquarius with telescopes.

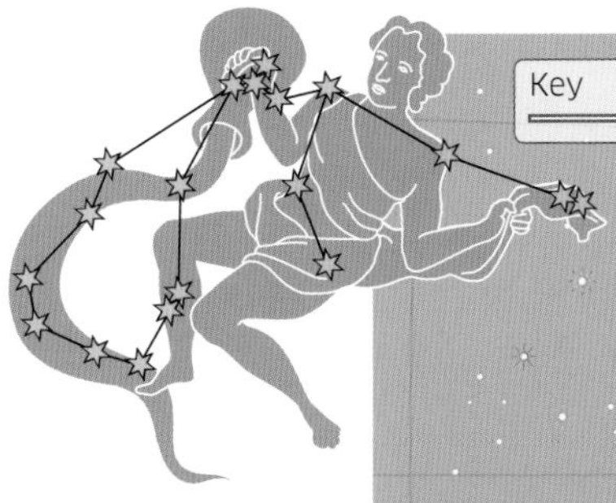

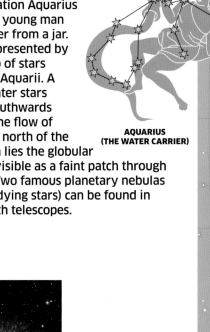

AQUARIUS (THE WATER CARRIER)

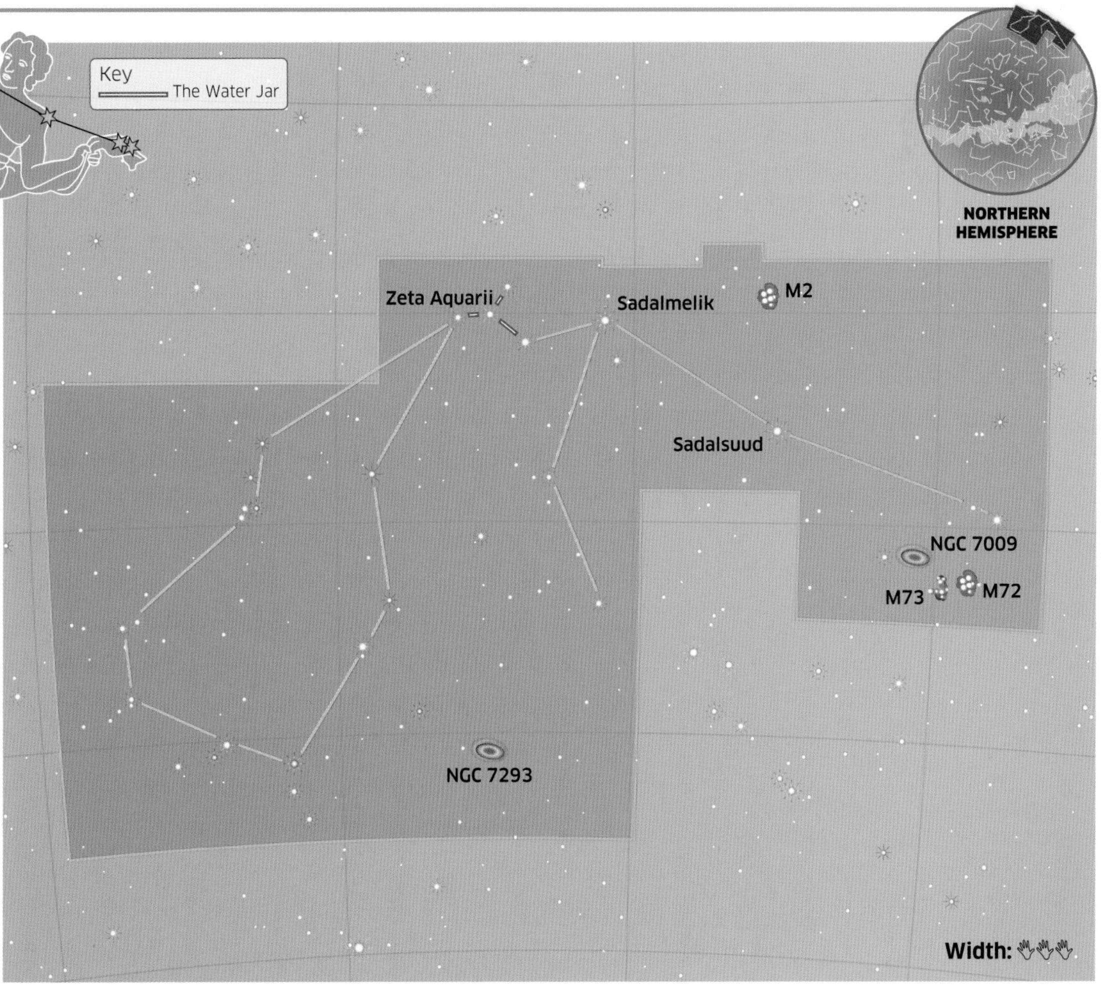
Key
The Water Jar
NORTHERN HEMISPHERE
Zeta Aquarii
Sadalmelik
M2
Sadalsuud
NGC 7009
M73
M72
NGC 7293
Width:

Helix Nebula
This looks like a beautiful flower. It is actually a shell of gas thrown off from the star at the centre of the nebula.

PISCES

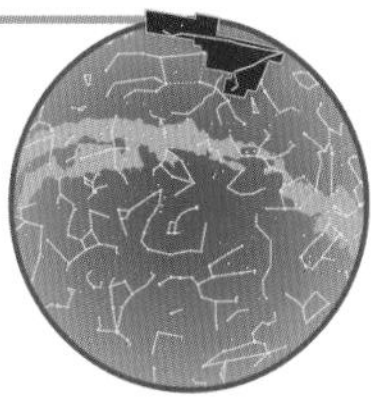
NORTHERN
HEMISPHERE

Pisces represents two fish with their tails tied together by ribbons. The star Alrescha marks the knot joining the two ribbons. The constellation depicts the Greek myth in which Aphrodite and her son Eros turned themselves into fish to escape from a monster, Typhon. A loop of seven stars called the Circlet marks the body of one of the fish. Pisces includes M74, a beautiful face-on spiral galaxy just visible through small telescopes.

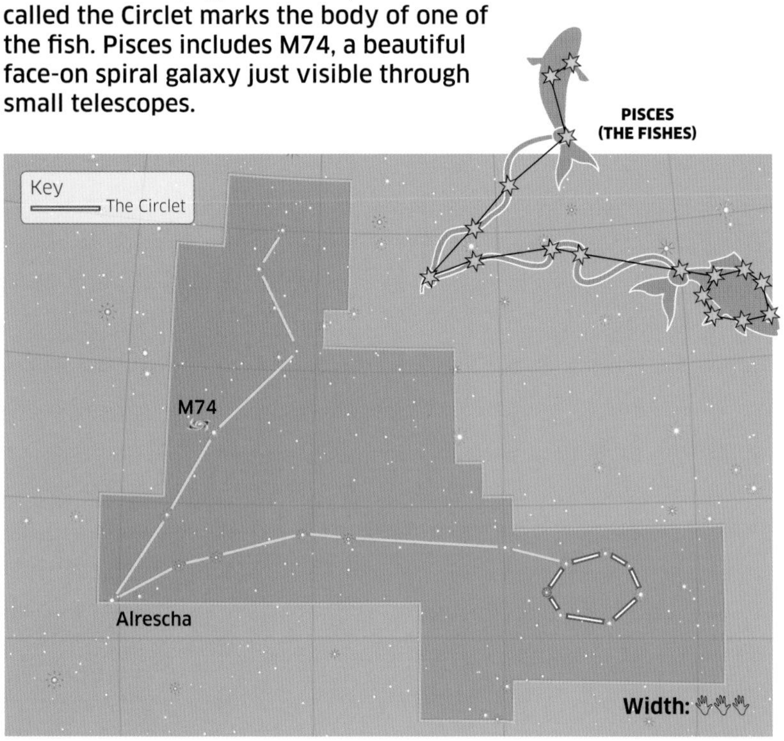
PISCES
(THE FISHES)
Key
The Circlet
M74
Alrescha
Width:

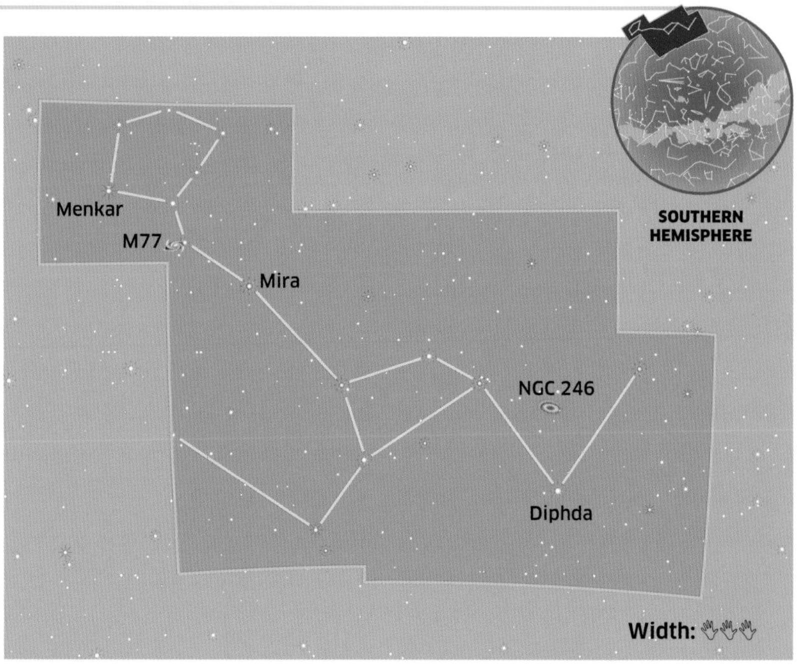
Menkar
M77
Mira
NGC 246
Diphda
SOUTHERN
HEMISPHERE
Width:

CETUS

Cetus, the sea monster, is the fourth-largest constellation. In Greek mythology, Andromeda was chained to a rock as a sacrifice to the monster, but Perseus saved her. In the neck of Cetus lies Mira, a famous variable star. When at its brightest, Mira is easily visible to the naked eye, but it fades from view for months at a time.

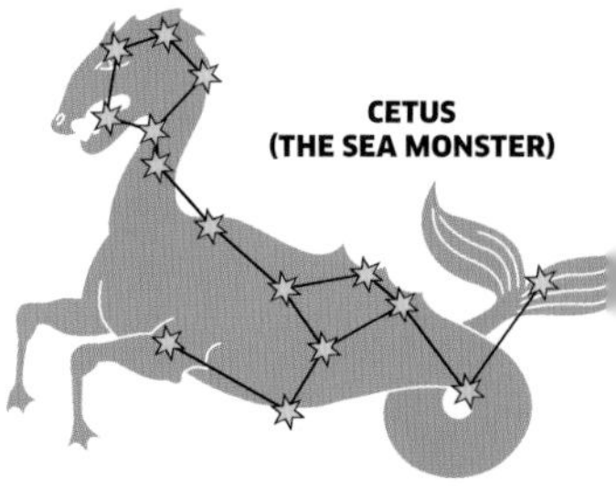
CETUS
(THE SEA MONSTER)

CANIS MAJOR

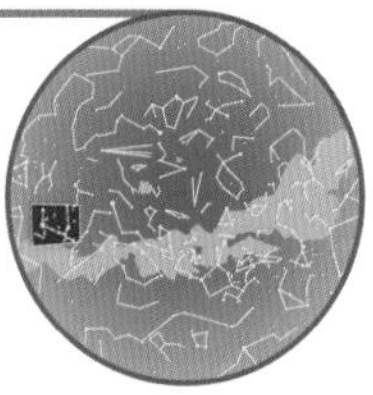
SOUTHERN
HEMISPHERE

The constellation Canis Major and nearby Canis Minor represent the dogs of Orion. Canis Major contains the brightest star in the night sky, Sirius, which lies 8.6 light years away. South of Sirius is the star cluster M41, which is just visible to the naked eye under clear dark skies and is a beautiful sight through binoculars.

CANIS MAJOR
(THE LARGE
DOG)

Sirius
NGC
2360
Mirzam
M41
NGC
2362
Adhara
Width:

CANIS MINOR

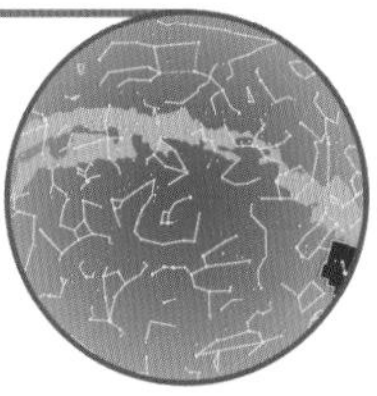
SOUTHERN
HEMISPHERE

Canis Minor is the smaller of the two dogs of Orion. Its main star, Procyon, is the eighth brightest in the sky. Procyon forms a large triangle with the other Dog Star (Sirius in Canis Major) and Betelgeuse in Orion. Both Procyon and Sirius are orbited by white dwarf stars, but these companions can be seen only with large telescopes. There is little else of interest in this constellation.

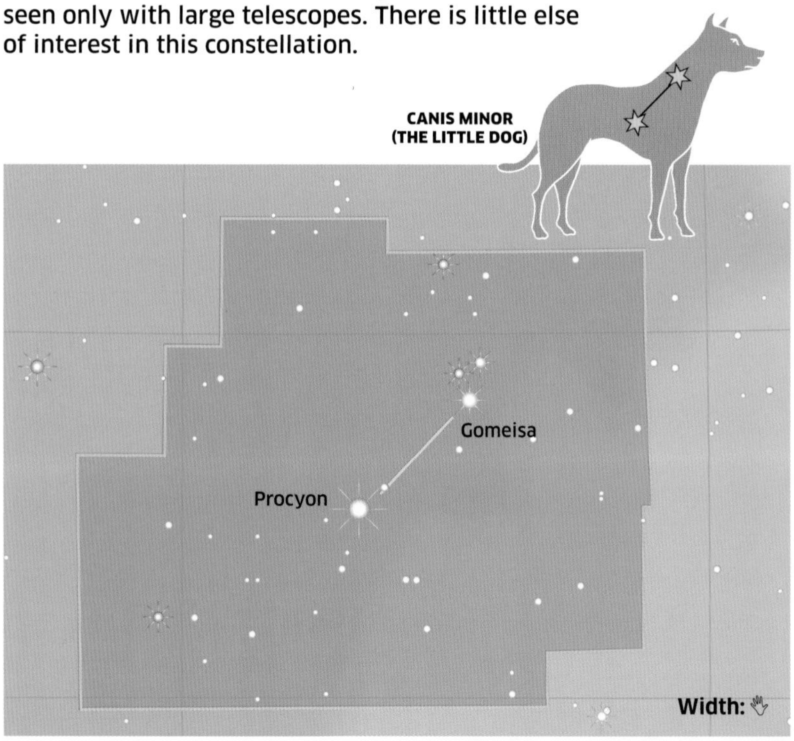
CANIS MINOR
(THE LITTLE DOG)
Gomeisa
Procyon
Width:

ORION

This constellation represents a giant hunter of Greek mythology. In the sky he is depicted raising his club and shield against Taurus the bull, the constellation next to him. The bright star Betelgeuse marks Orion's right shoulder and Rigel is his left foot. Betelgeuse is a red supergiant, which varies slightly in brightness, while Rigel, another supergiant star, is hotter and bluer. One feature that makes Orion easy to identify is the line of three stars that mark his belt. From the belt hangs his sword, which contains one of the treasures of the sky, the Orion Nebula.

ORION
(THE HUNTER)

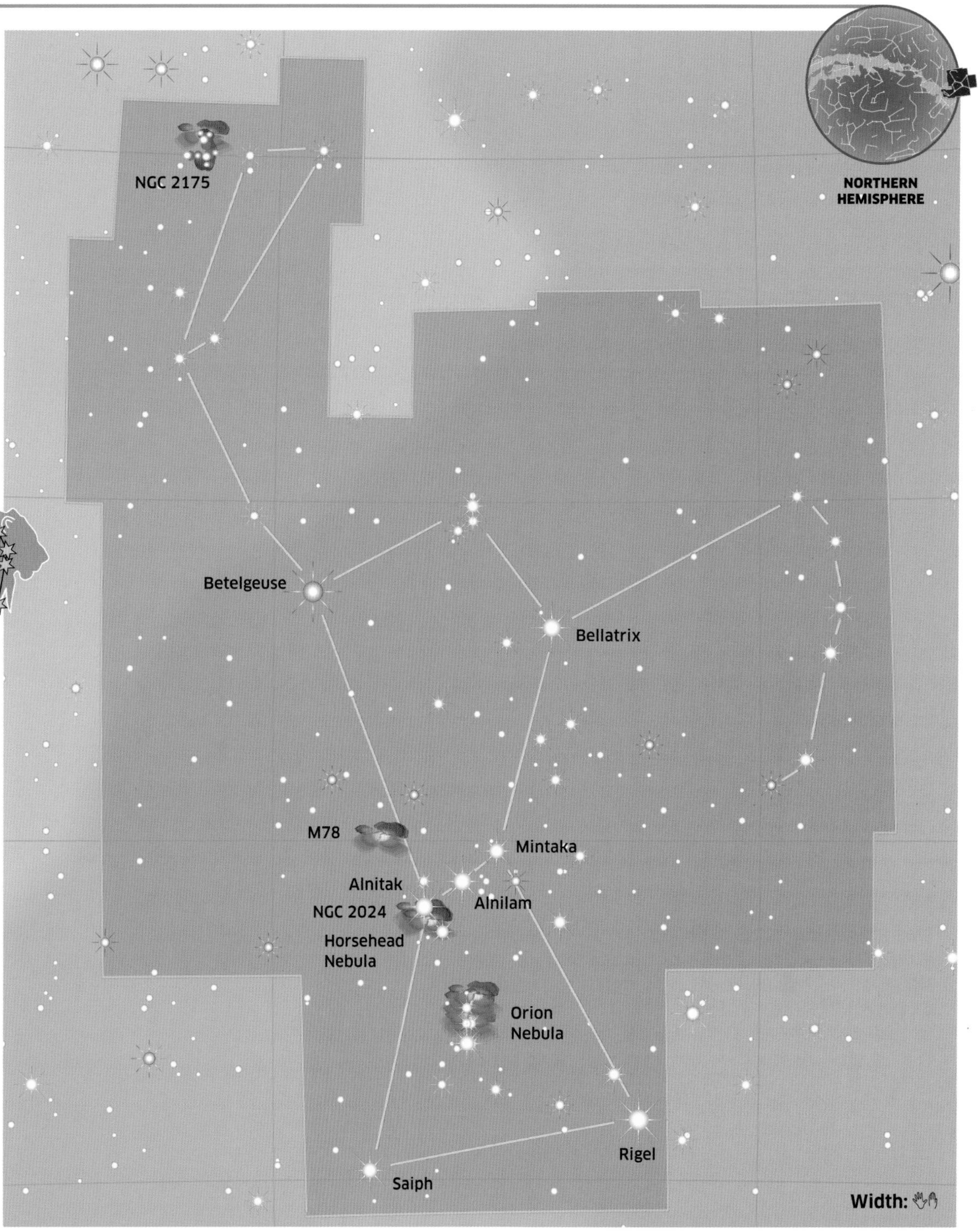
NORTHERN
HEMISPHERE
NGC 2175
Betelgeuse
Bellatrix
M78
Mintaka
Alnitak
Alnilam
NGC 2024
Horsehead
Nebula
Orion
Nebula
Rigel
Saiph
Width:

Trapezium
At the centre of the Orion Nebula lies a group of four stars called the Trapezium, which can be seen through small telescopes. Light from these new-born stars helps make the surrounding gas glow.

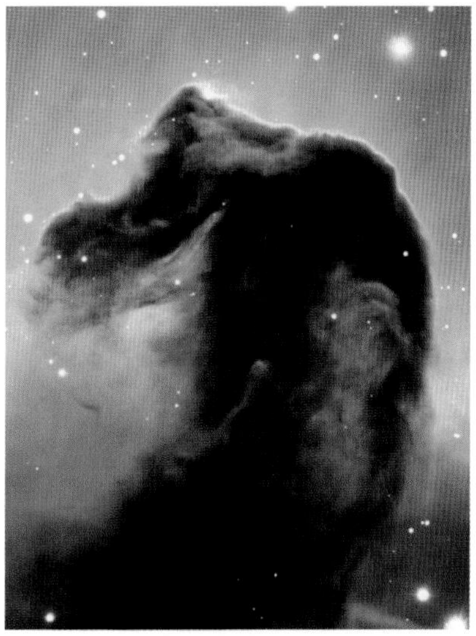

Horsehead Nebula
Looking like a knight in a celestial chess game, the Horsehead Nebula is a dark cloud of dust, seen here through the Hubble Telescope. The nebula is located just below the star Alnitak in Orion's belt. The background nebula is faint and the Horsehead shows up well only on photographs.

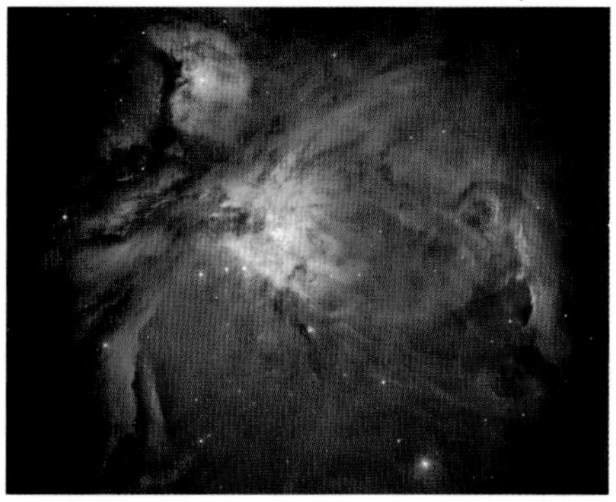

Orion Nebula
The Orion Nebula, a large star-forming cloud of gas, looks like a patch of mist in binoculars and small telescopes, but when pictured by the Hubble Space Telescope, its full complexity and colour can be seen.

MONOCEROS

This constellation represents a unicorn, the mythical beast with a single horn. Dutch astronomer and map-maker Petrus Plancius introduced it in the early 17th century in a gap between Greek constellations. One feature of interest is Beta Monocerotis, which is an excellent triple star for small telescopes. Three attractive star clusters for binoculars or small telescopes are M50, NGC 2244, and NGC 2264.

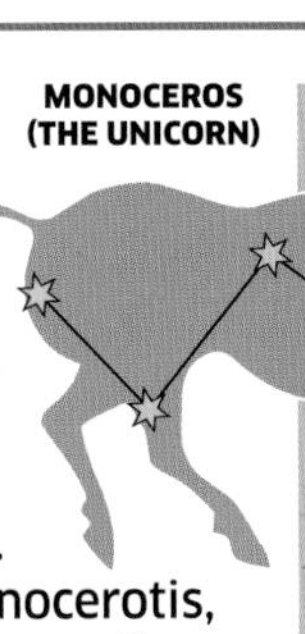
MONOCEROS
(THE UNICORN)

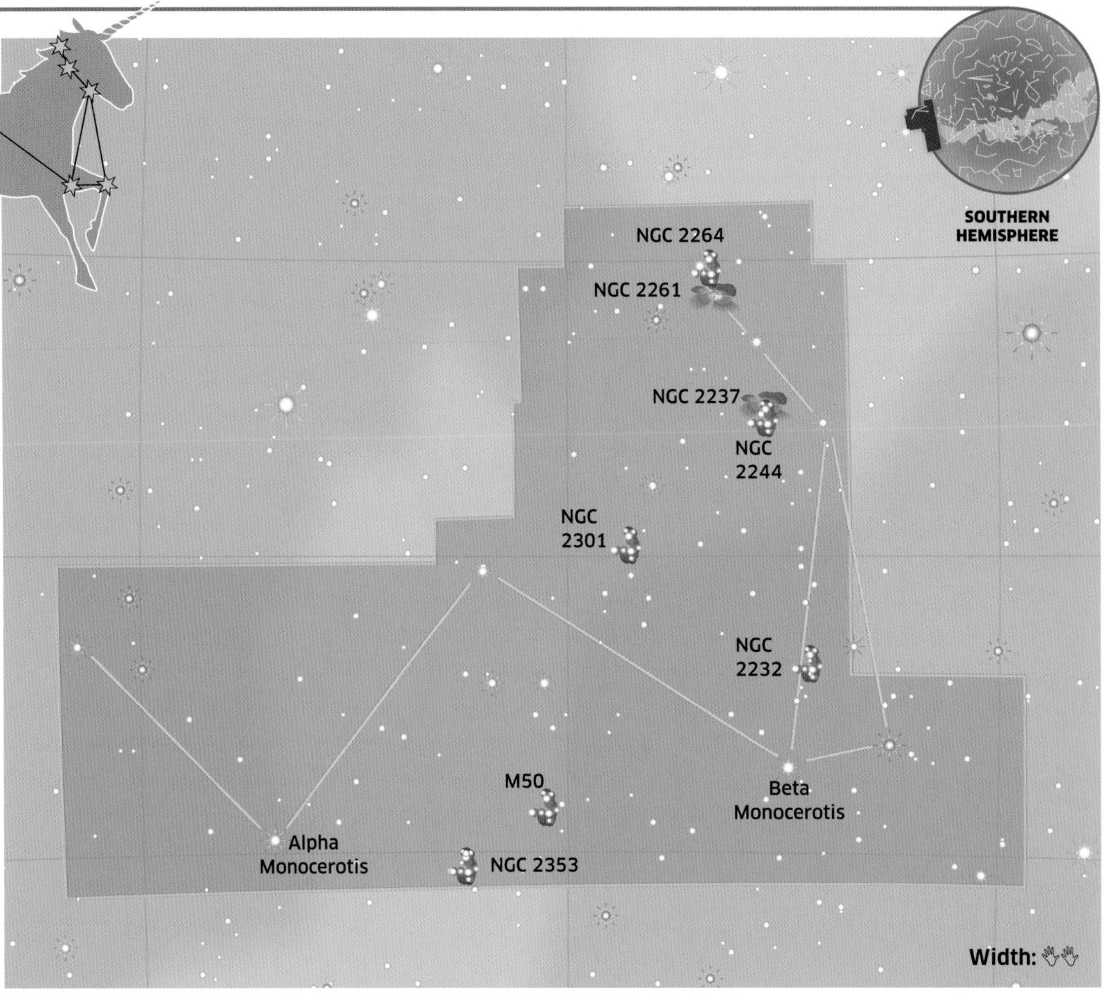
SOUTHERN
HEMISPHERE
NGC 2264
NGC 2261
NGC 2237
NGC
2244
NGC
2301
NGC
2232
M50
Beta
Monocerotis
Alpha
Monocerotis
NGC 2353
Width:

Rosette Nebula
The star cluster NGC 2244 lies within a flower-like cloud of gas known as the Rosette Nebula. The star cluster can easily be seen with binoculars, but the nebula, glowing like a pink carnation, shows up only on photographs.

HYDRA

This is the largest constellation of all, stretching more than a quarter of the way around the sky. In Greek mythology, Hydra was a monster with many heads, although in the sky it has only one head, represented by a loop of five stars. Its brightest star is called Alphard, meaning "the solitary one", since it lies in a fairly blank area of sky. M48, near the border with Monoceros, is a star cluster visible through binoculars and small telescopes.

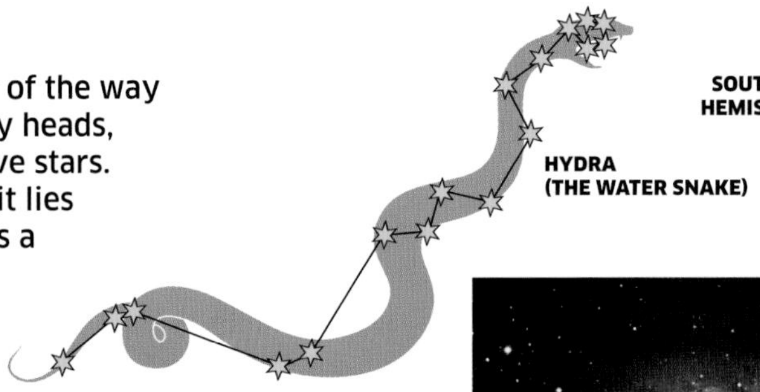
HYDRA
(THE WATER SNAKE)

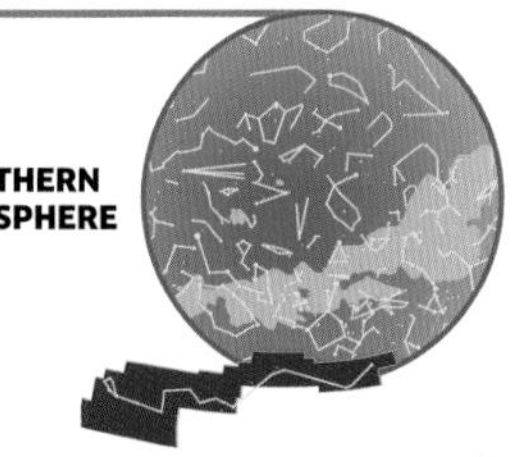
SOUTHERN
HEMISPHERE

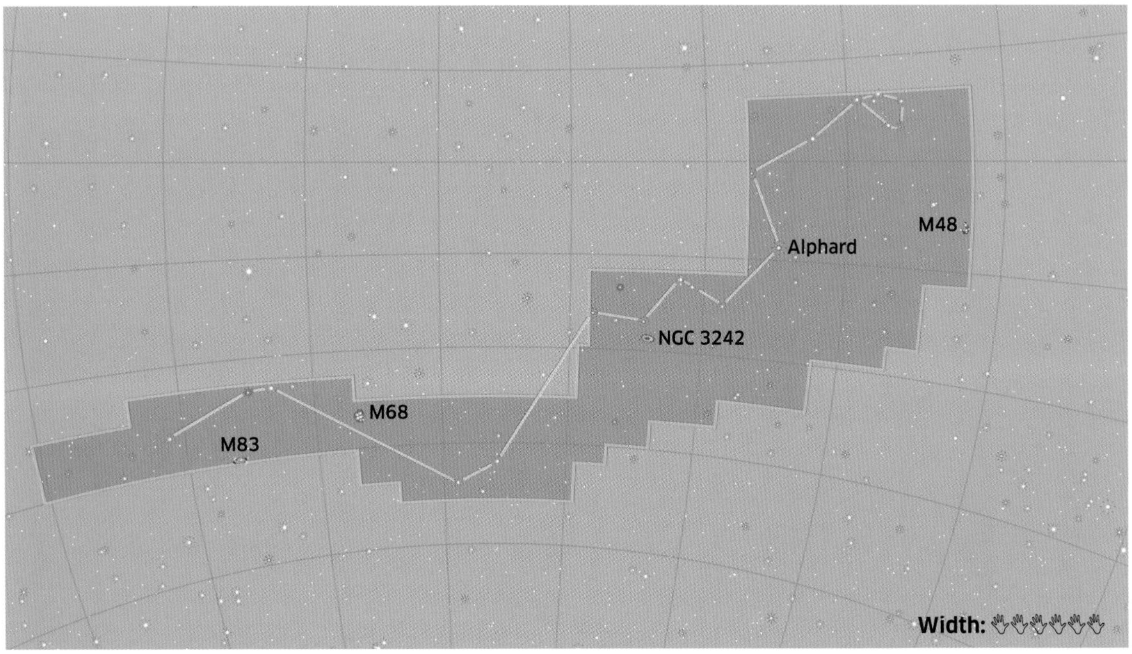
M48
Alphard
NGC 3242
M68
M83
Width:

Spiral galaxy M83
Sometimes known as the Southern Pinwheel, M83 is a beautiful spiral galaxy 15 million light years away. It can be seen as a faint patch through small telescopes, but larger instruments are needed to bring out the beauty of its spiral arms.

ANTLIA

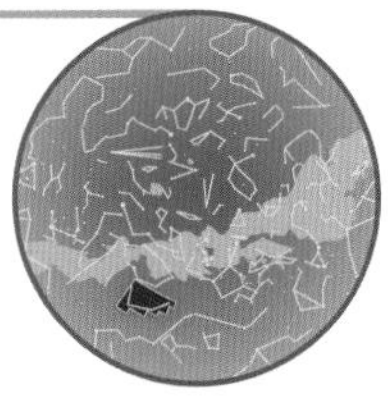

SOUTHERN HEMISPHERE

This is a small, faint southern constellation invented in the 1750s by the French astronomer Nicolas Louis de Lacaille. Its name, which means "pump", commemorates the invention of a kind of air pump. The constellation's most impressive feature is a spiral galaxy called NGC 2997. This is too faint to see with small telescopes but shows up beautifully on photographs, which reveal clouds of pink gas dotted along its arms.

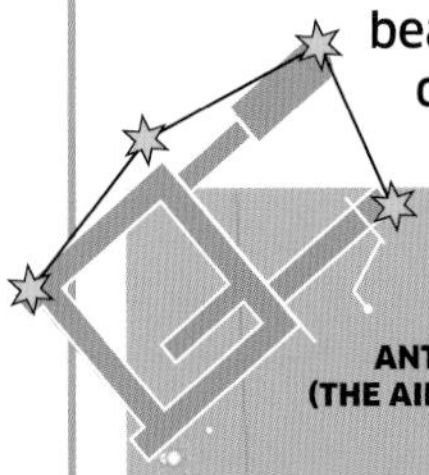
ANTLIA
(THE AIR PUMP)

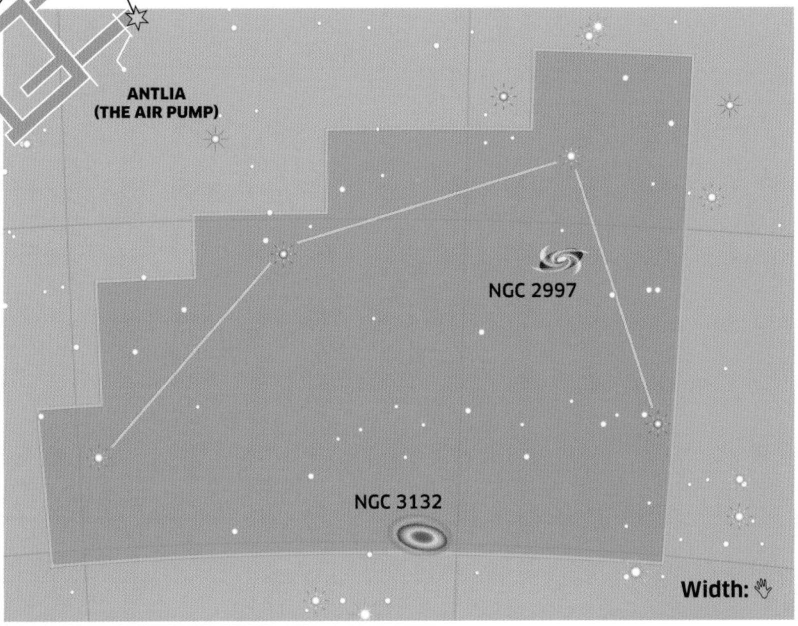
NGC 2997
NGC 3132
Width:

SEXTANS

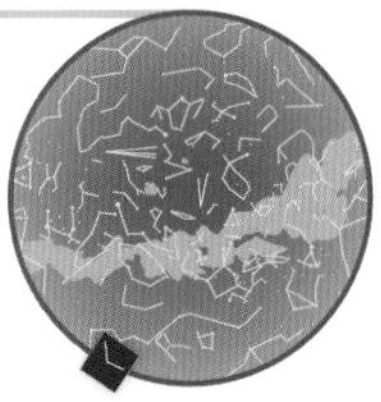

SOUTHERN HEMISPHERE

A faint constellation that was invented in the late 17th century by the Polish astronomer Johannes Hevelius, Sextans represents an instrument called a sextant, which was used for measuring star positions. Sextans contains the Spindle Galaxy (NGC 3115), a galaxy several times larger than our Milky Way.

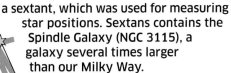

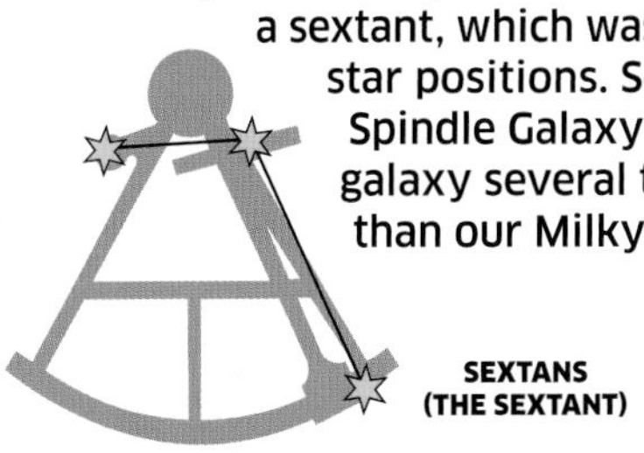
SEXTANS
(THE SEXTANT)

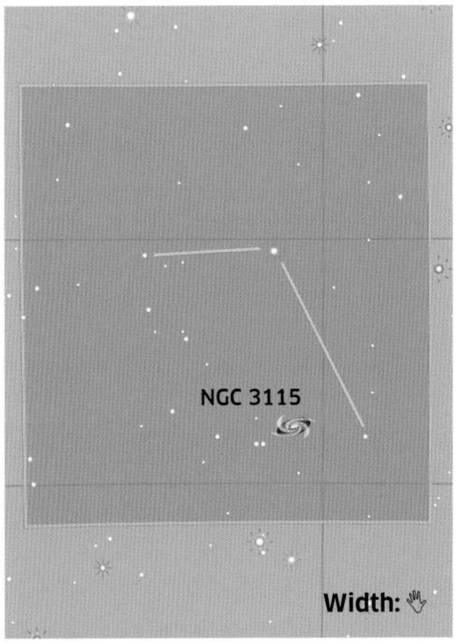
NGC 3115
Width:

Spindle Galaxy
This galaxy appears rod-shaped because we see it edge-on. It is also known by its catalogue number NGC 3115.

CRATER

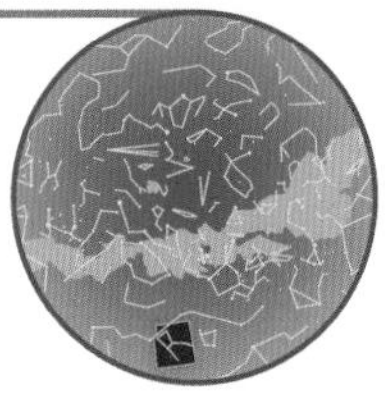

SOUTHERN HEMISPHERE

The word "crater" is Latin for cup, and this constellation represents the cup of the Greek god Apollo. In Greek mythology, Apollo sent a crow to fetch water in the cup. The greedy bird was late because it stopped to eat figs. It blamed the delay on a snake, but Apollo realized what had happened and punished the crow for lying by placing it in the sky, along with the cup and the snake. Crater contains no major objects of interest for users of small telescopes.

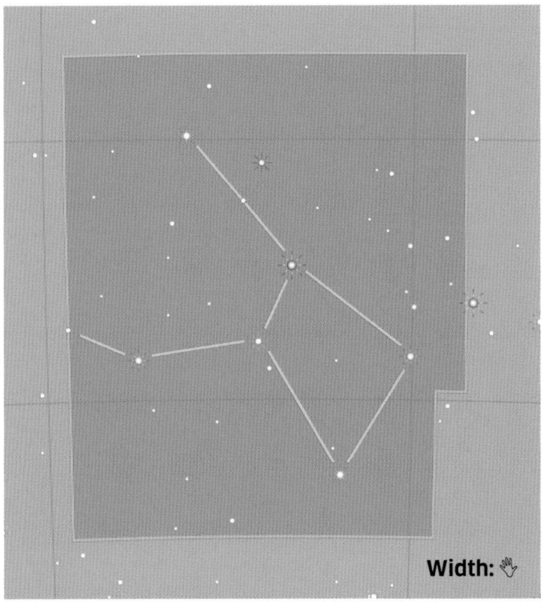
Width:

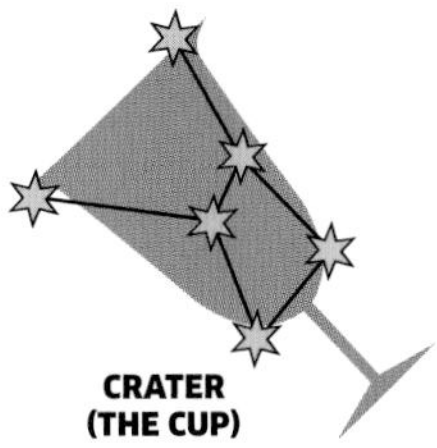
CRATER
(THE CUP)

CORVUS

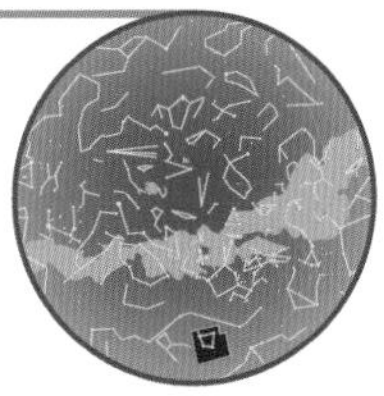

SOUTHERN HEMISPHERE

Corvus represents a crow that was sent to fetch water in a cup by the god Apollo. It lies next to Crater, which represents the cup. Both lie on the back of Hydra, the water snake. The constellation's most amazing feature is a pair of colliding galaxies called the Antennae – NGC 4038 and 4039. Large telescopes reveal long streamers of gas and stars stretching away from the galaxies like the antennae (feelers) of an insect.

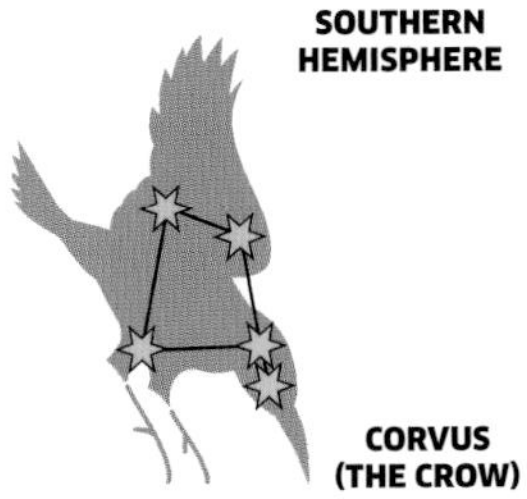
CORVUS
(THE CROW)

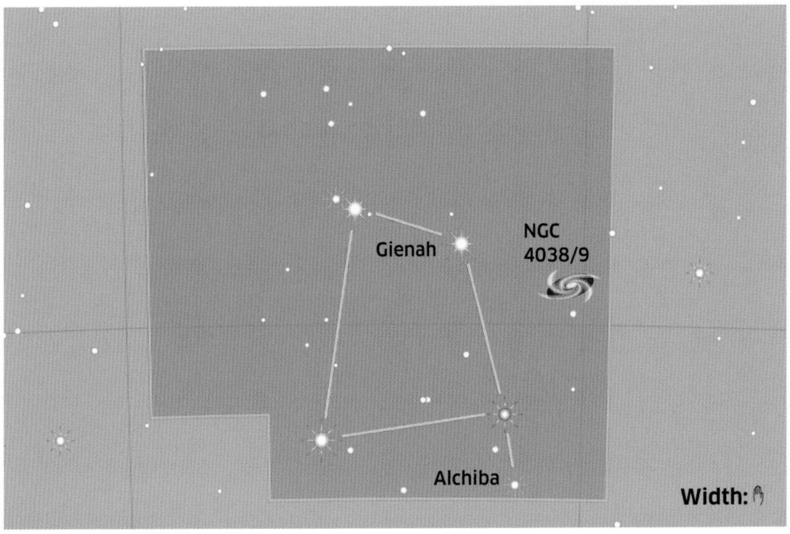
Gienah
NGC
4038/9
Alchiba
Width:

CENTAURUS

Centaurs were mythical creatures of ancient Greece, half-man, half-horse. This constellation represents a centaur called Chiron, who taught the children of the Greek gods. Small telescopes show that its brightest star, Alpha Centauri, is a double star. There is also a third star: a red dwarf called Proxima Centauri, which is the closest star to the Sun at 4.2 light years away.

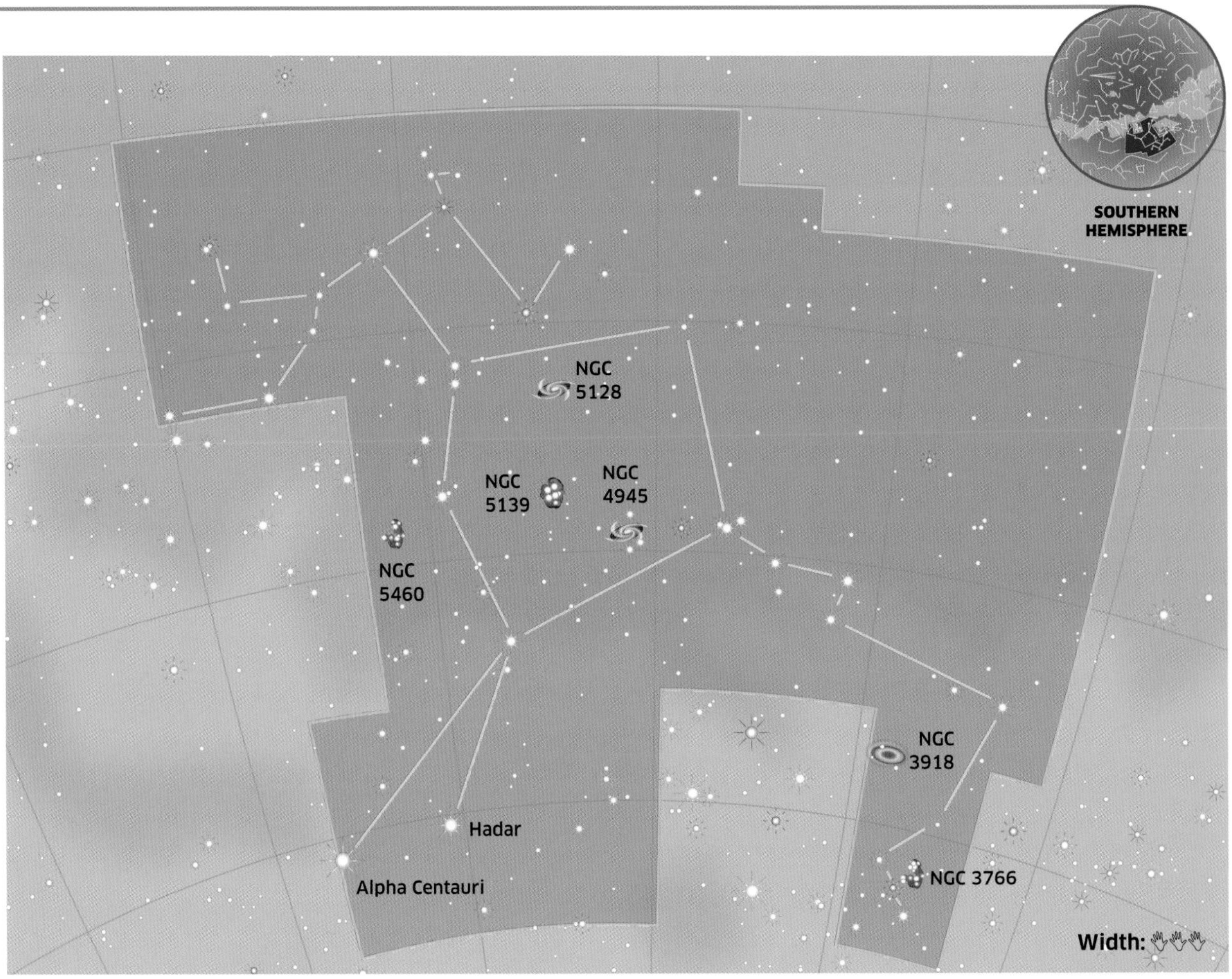
SOUTHERN HEMISPHERE

NGC 5128
NGC 5139
NGC 4945
NGC 5460
NGC 3918
Hadar
NGC 3766
Alpha Centauri
Width:

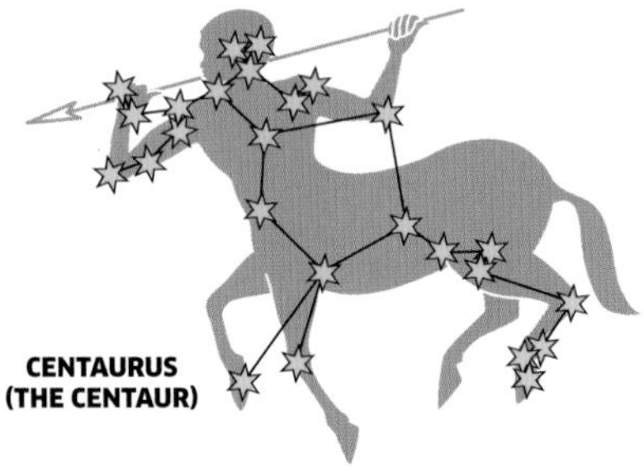
CENTAURUS (THE CENTAUR)

CRUX

Popularly known as the Southern Cross, this is the smallest of all the 88 constellations. Its brightest star, Acrux, is a double star that is easily separated by small telescopes. Near Becrux lies NGC 4755, popularly known as the Jewel Box, a beautiful cluster of stars easily visible through binoculars and small telescopes. A dark cloud of dust called the Coalsack Nebula can be seen against the bright Milky Way background.

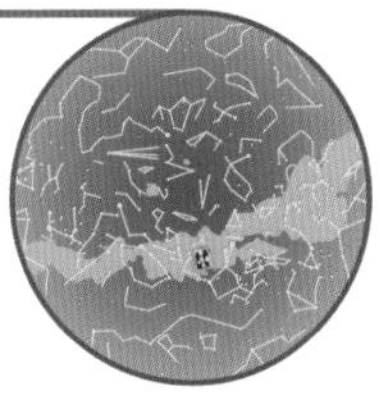
SOUTHERN HEMISPHERE

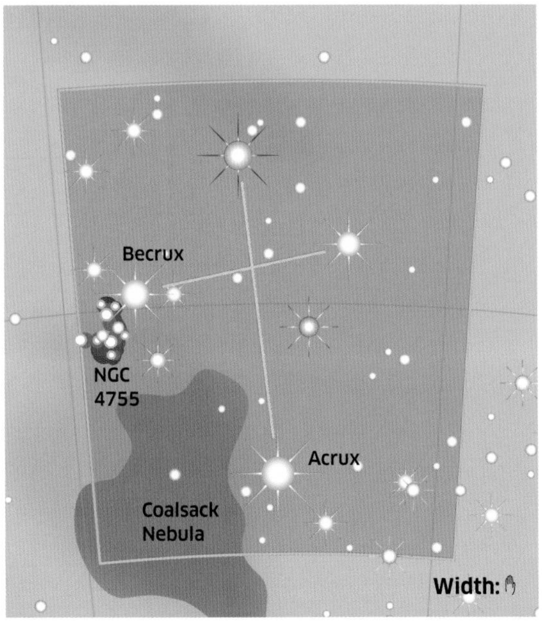
Becrux
NGC 4755
Acrux
Coalsack Nebula
Width:

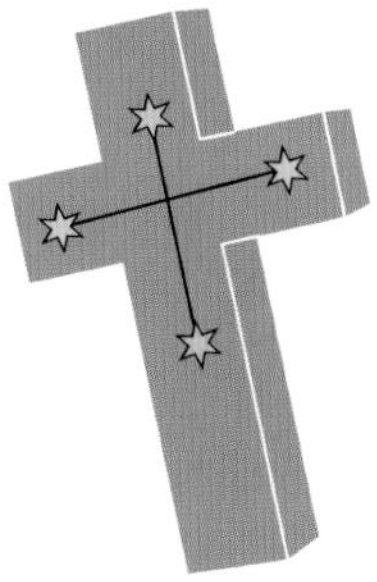
CRUX (THE SOUTHERN CROSS)

LUPUS

This constellation represents a wolf. Ancient Greek astronomers imagined it as being held on a spear by Centaurus, the centaur. Lupus contains several interesting double stars. In the southern part of the constellation lies a star cluster with the catalogue number NGC 5822.

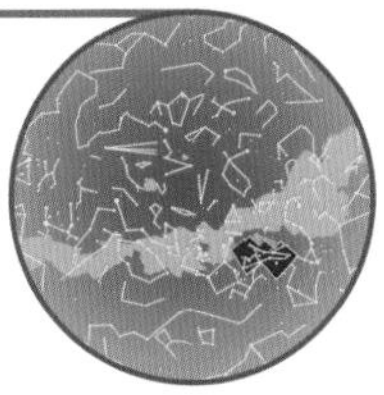
SOUTHERN HEMISPHERE

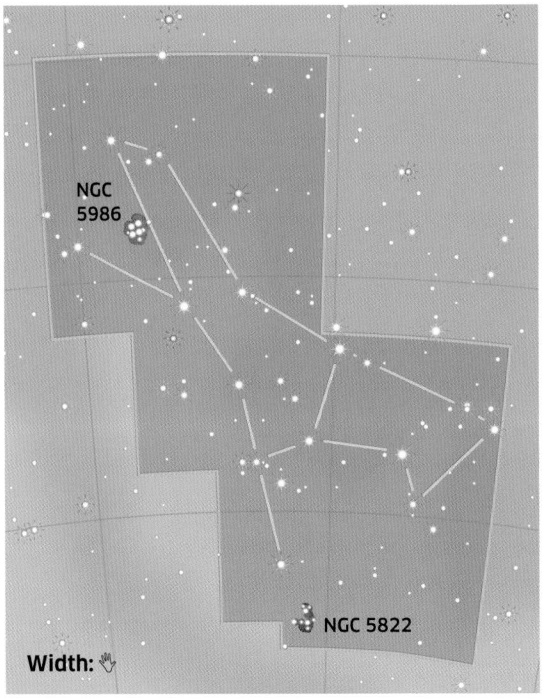
NGC 5986
NGC 5822
Width:

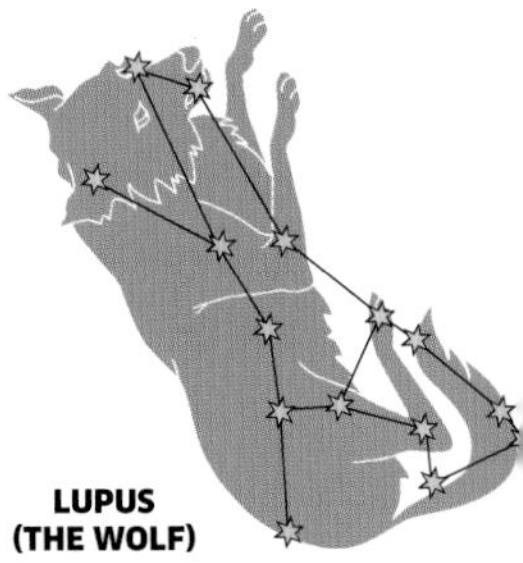
LUPUS (THE WOLF)

SAGITTARIUS

This constellation represents an archer drawing his bow and is depicted as a centaur. The eight main stars of Sagittarius form a shape known as the Teapot. Near the lid of the Teapot lies M22, a large globular cluster easily visible through binoculars. There are several fine nebulas in Sagittarius, including the Trifid Nebula (M20).

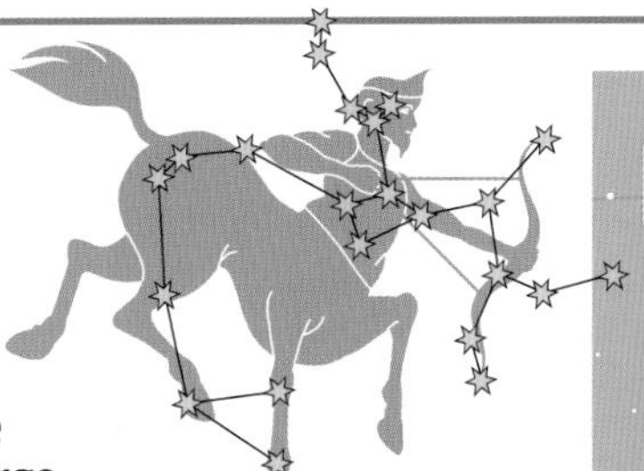

SAGITTARIUS (THE ARCHER)

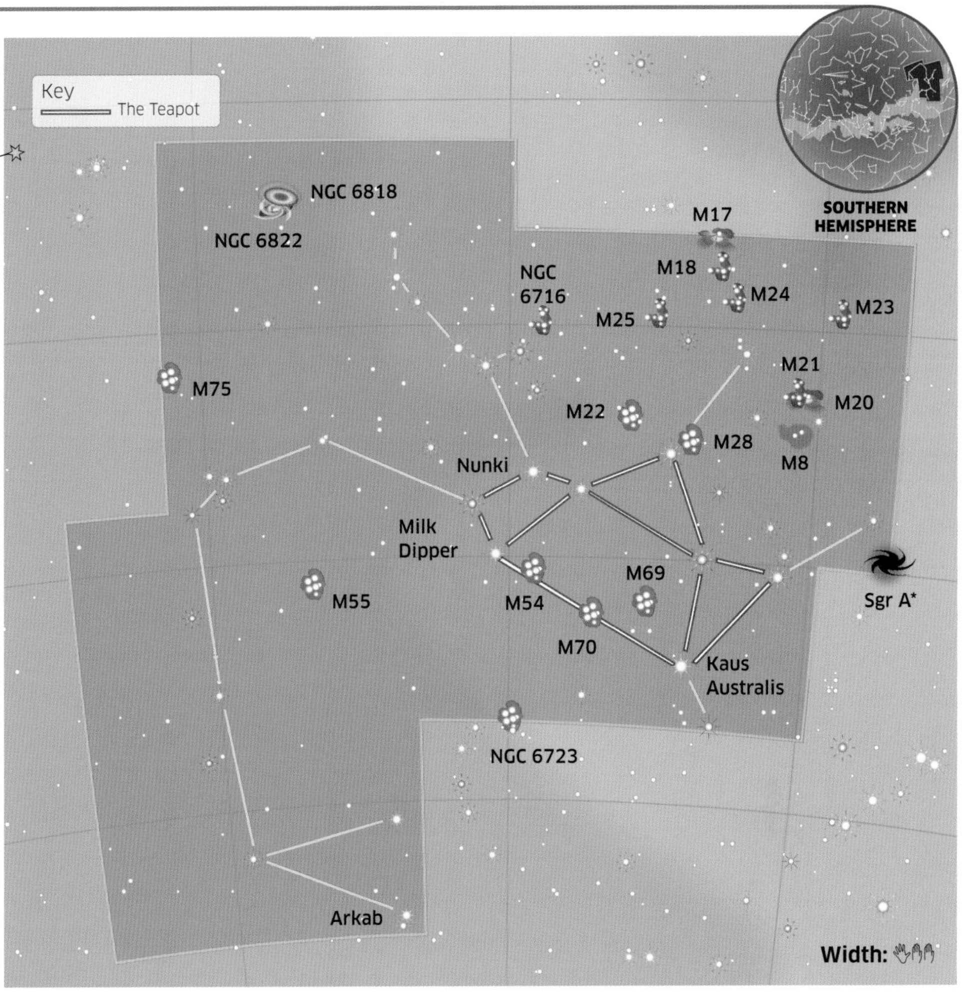
Key
The Teapot
SOUTHERN HEMISPHERE
NGC 6818
NGC 6822
M17
M18
M24
M23
NGC 6716
M25
M21
M20
M75
M22
M28
M8
Nunki
Milk Dipper
M55
M54
M69
M70
Sgr A*
Kaus Australis
NGC 6723
Arkab
Width:

Trifid Nebula
The Trifid Nebula (M20) is a colourful combination of pink gas and blue dust. Its full beauty is revealed on photographs taken with large telescopes, as seen here.

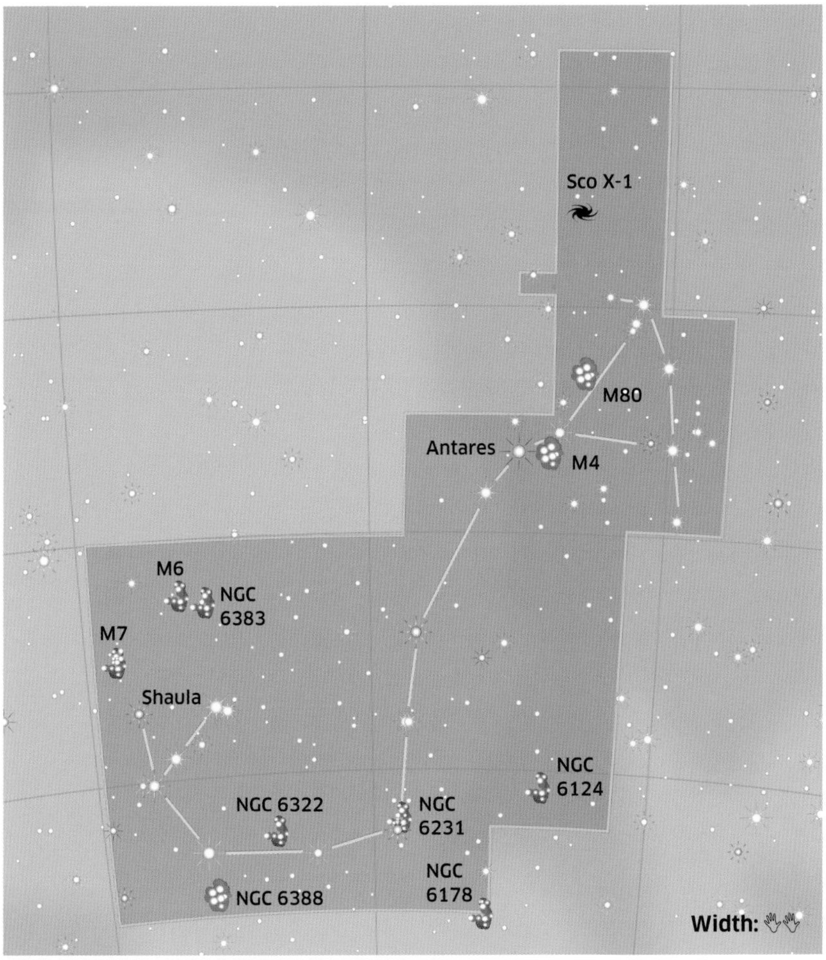
Sco X-1
M80
Antares
M4
M6
NGC 6383
M7
Shaula
NGC 6124
NGC 6322
NGC 6231
NGC 6388
NGC 6178
Width:

SCORPIUS

This constellation represents the scorpion that stung Orion to death in a story from Greek mythology. At the scorpion's heart lies Antares, a red supergiant hundreds of times larger than the Sun. Next to Antares is M4, a large globular cluster visible through binoculars. At the end of the scorpion's curling tail is a large star cluster, M7, just visible to the naked eye as a brighter spot in the Milky Way. Near to it is M6, smaller and best seen through small telescopes. Another beautiful star cluster for binoculars is NGC 6231.

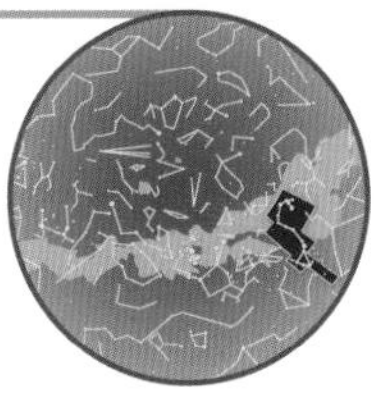

SOUTHERN HEMISPHERE

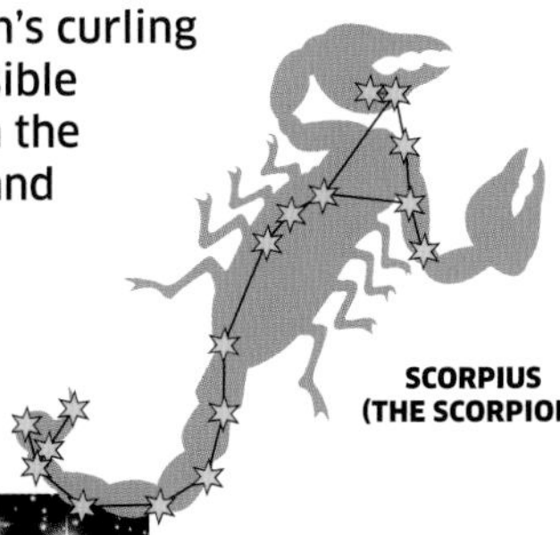

SCORPIUS (THE SCORPION)

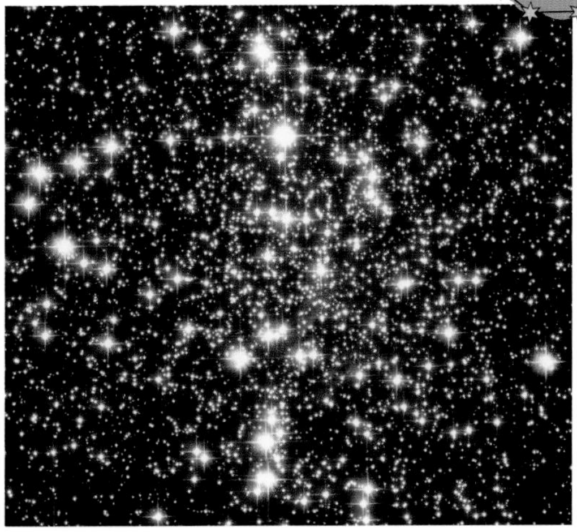

Star cluster M4
This sparkling photo from the Hubble Space Telescope shows the heart of the M4 globular cluster, 7,200 light years from Earth.

CAPRICORNUS

This constellation is shown as a goat with the tail of a fish. It is said to represent the Greek god Pan, who had the horns and legs of a goat. He grew the fish tail when he jumped into a river to escape from a monster called Typhon. A feature of interest is Algedi, a wide double star, which is easily divided with binoculars or even good eyesight. Dabih is another double, but needs binoculars or a small telescope to divide.

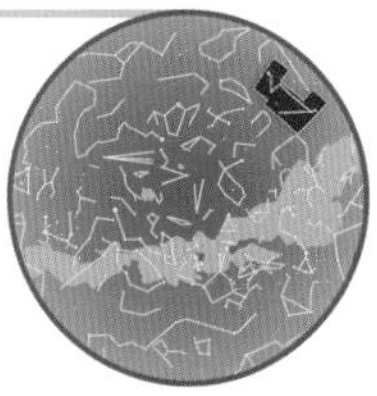

SOUTHERN HEMISPHERE

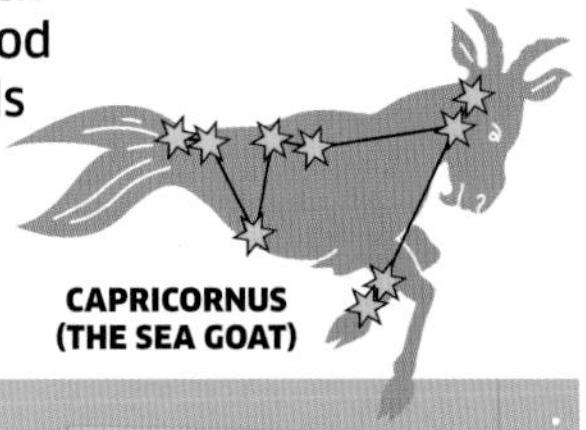

CAPRICORNUS (THE SEA GOAT)

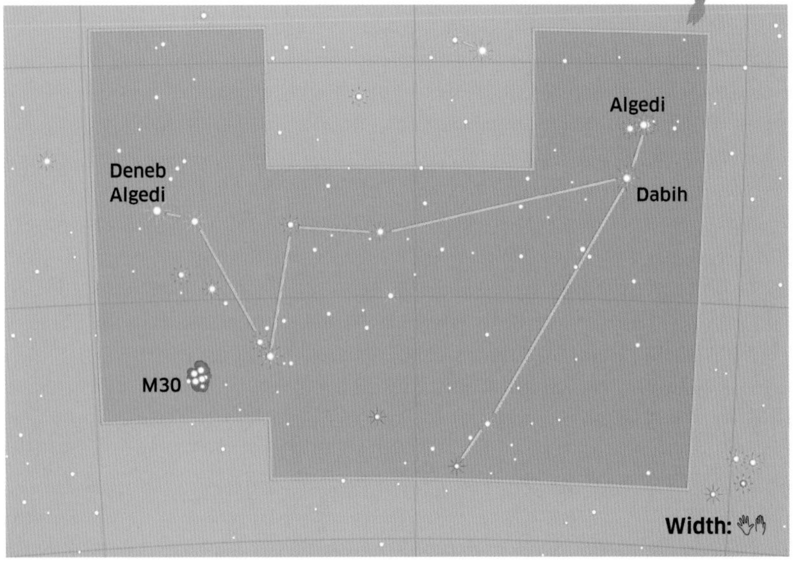
Algedi
Deneb Algedi
Dabih
M30
Width:

MICROSCOPIUM

This faint constellation of the southern sky was invented in the 1750s by the French astronomer Nicolas Louis de Lacaille, who studied the southern stars from the Cape of Good Hope in southern Africa. Lacaille invented many new constellations representing scientific instruments; in this case, a microscope.

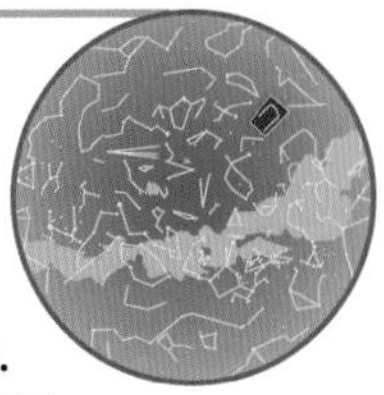

SOUTHERN HEMISPHERE

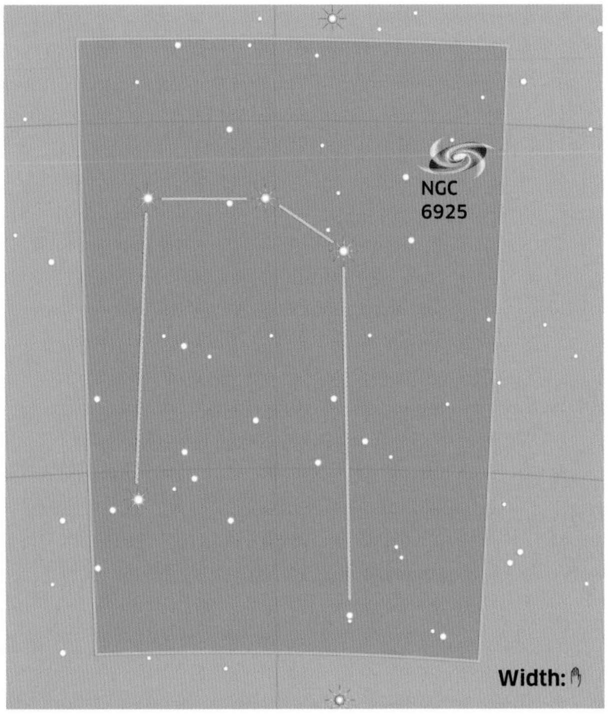
NGC 6925
Width:

MICROSCOPIUM (THE MICROSCOPE)

PISCIS AUSTRINUS

To the ancient Greeks, this constellation represented a large fish drinking water flowing from a jar held by Aquarius to its north. Its brightest star is Fomalhaut, which lies 25 light years away. The name Fomalhaut comes from Arabic and means "fish's mouth".

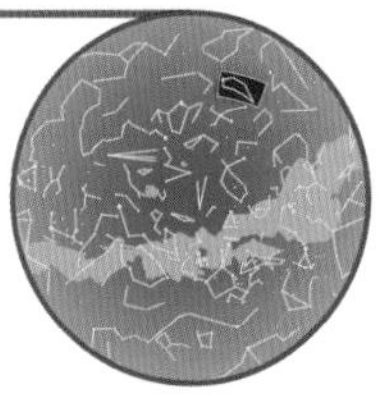

SOUTHERN HEMISPHERE

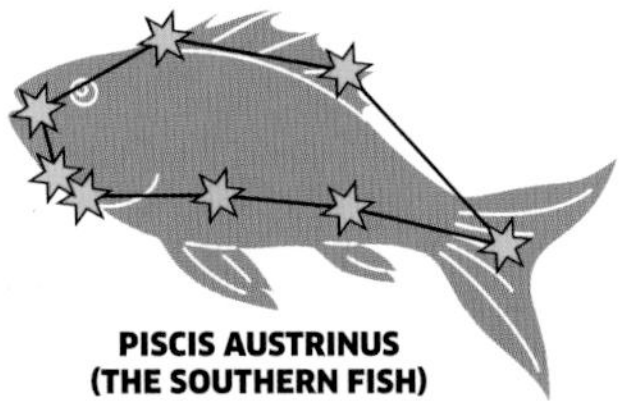

PISCIS AUSTRINUS (THE SOUTHERN FISH)

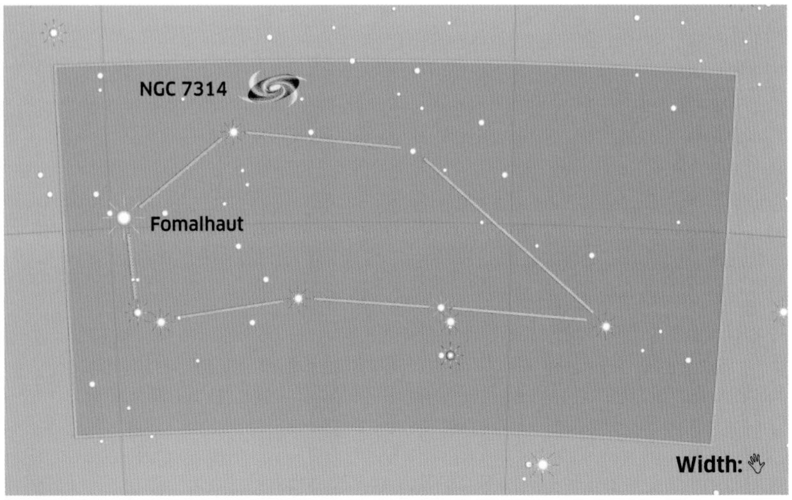
NGC 7314
Fomalhaut
Width:

SCULPTOR

Invented in the 1750s by the French astronomer Nicolas Louis de Lacaille, this constellation represents a sculptor's studio. Its stars are faint, but it contains a number of interesting galaxies. Most impressive of these is NGC 253, a spiral galaxy 13 million light years away, seen nearly edge-on and just visible in small telescopes. NGC 55 is another edge-on spiral. Dust clouds and areas of star formation make it look patchy, and it can be seen clearly only with larger telescopes.

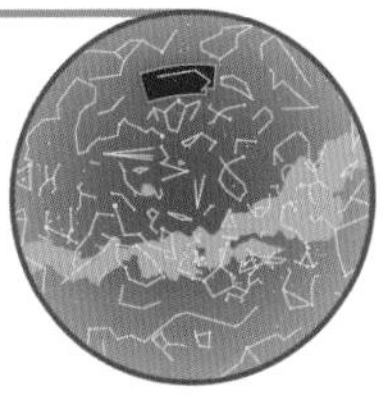

SOUTHERN HEMISPHERE

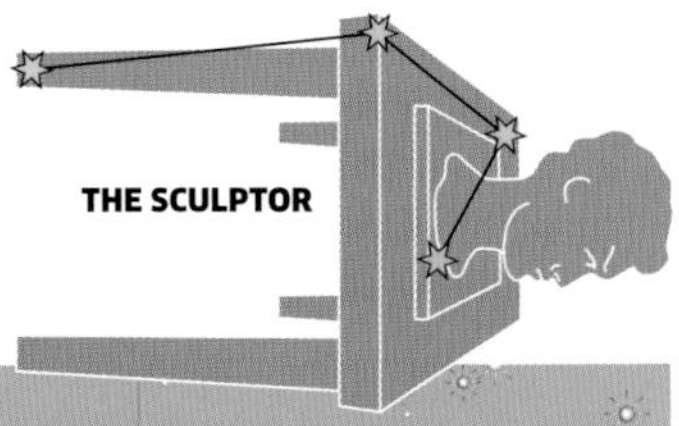

THE SCULPTOR

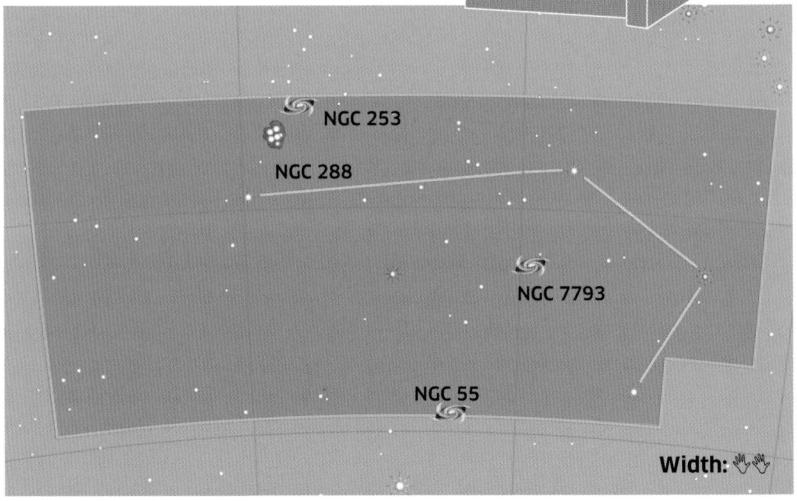
NGC 253
NGC 288
NGC 7793
NGC 55
Width:

FORNAX

French astronomer Nicolas Louis de Lacaille came up with this constellation in the 1750s. It represents a furnace used for chemical experiments. On its border lies the Fornax Cluster of galaxies, which is located about 65 million light years away.

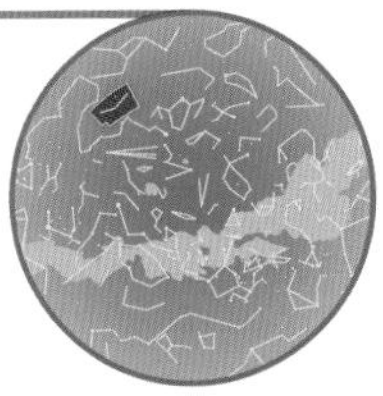

SOUTHERN HEMISPHERE

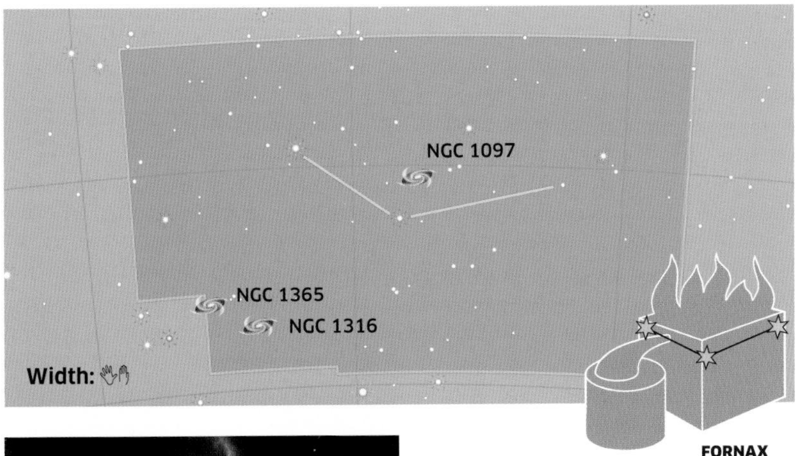
NGC 1097
NGC 1365
NGC 1316
Width:

FORNAX (THE FURNACE)

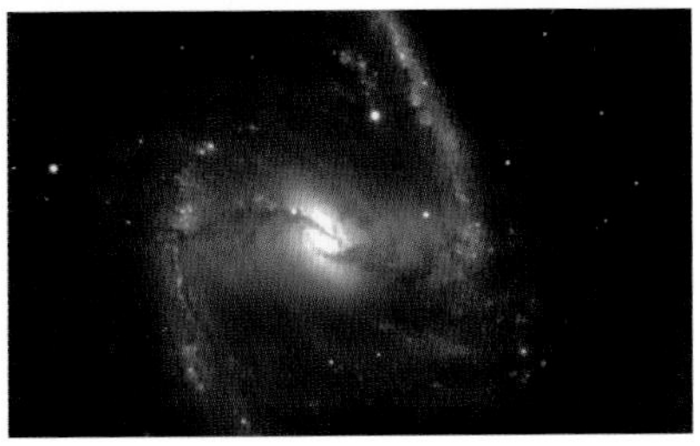

Barred spiral galaxy NGC 1365
A prominent member of the Fornax cluster, NGC 1365 is a barred spiral galaxy. Large telescopes are needed to see its full size and shape.

CAELUM

Caelum is another of the small, faint constellations of the southern sky that were invented in the 1750s by the French astronomer Nicolas Louis de Lacaille. It represents a chisel used by engravers. Caelum is squeezed into the gap between Eridanus and Columba. There is little in the constellation of interest to users of binoculars and small telescopes.

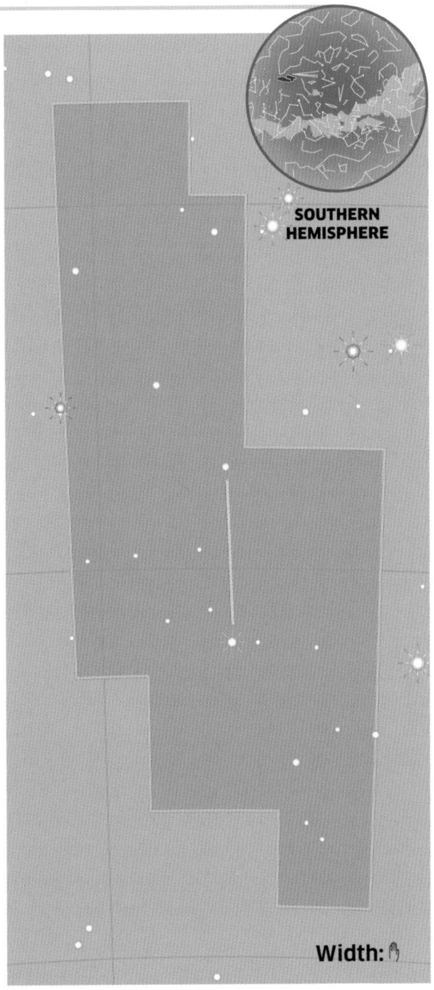

SOUTHERN HEMISPHERE
Width:

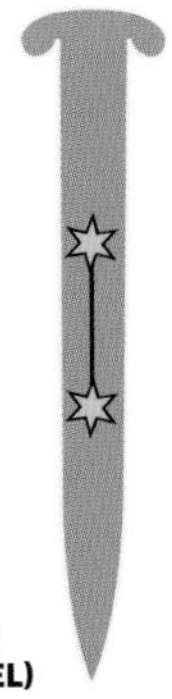

CAELUM (THE CHISEL)

ERIDANUS

To the ancient Greeks, this large constellation represented a river, either the Nile in Egypt or the Po in Italy. In the sky it meanders from the left foot of Orion deep into the southern sky. Its brightest star is Achernar, at the southern end of the river.

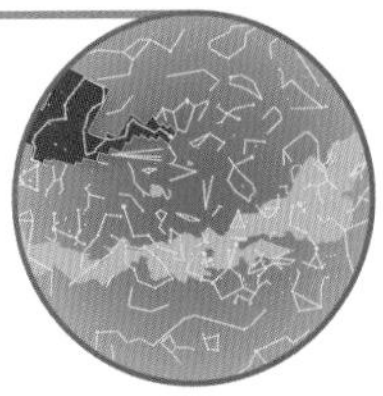

SOUTHERN HEMISPHERE

Barred spiral galaxy NGC 1300
Seen here in a Hubble view is a classic example of a barred spiral galaxy. NGC 1300 lies about 70 million light years from us. Large telescopes are needed to see it.

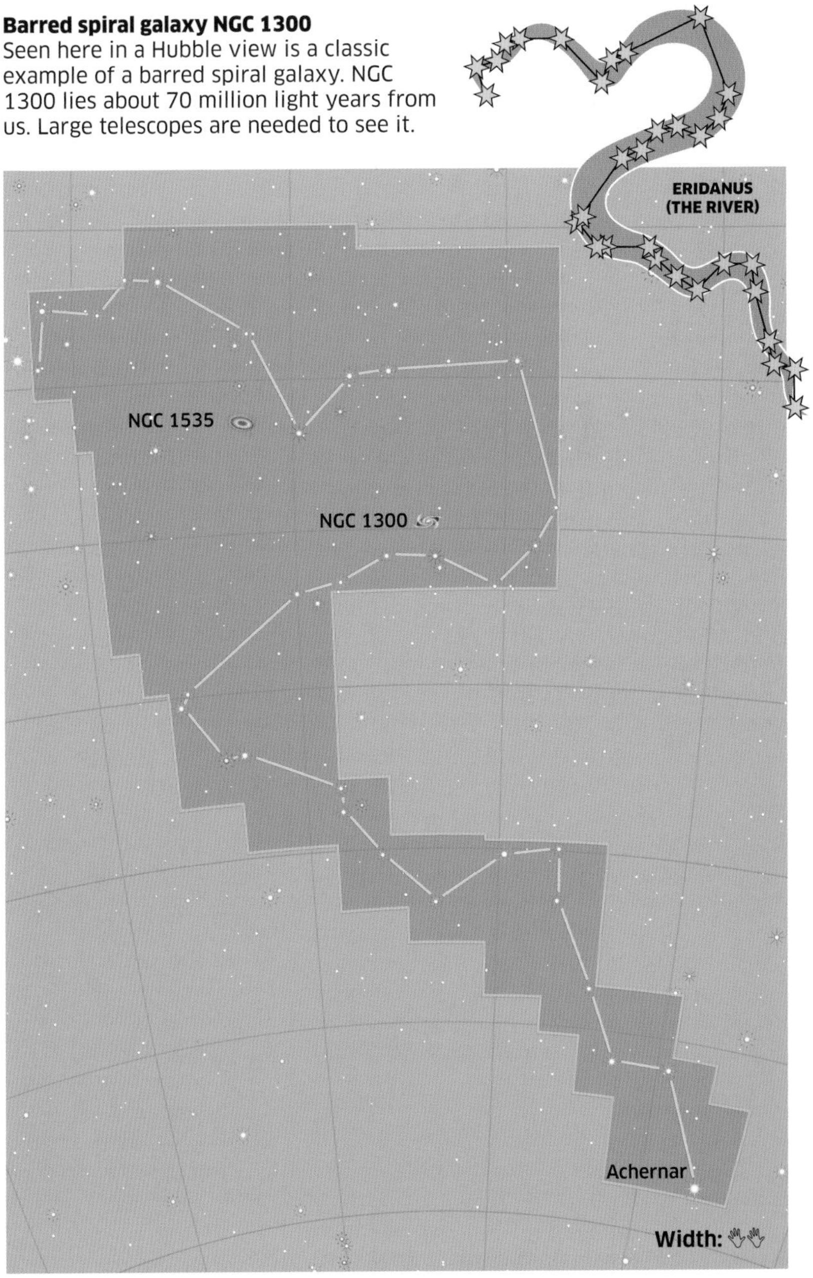

ERIDANUS (THE RIVER)
NGC 1535
NGC 1300
Achernar
Width:

LEPUS

Lepus represents a hare scampering under the feet of the hunter Orion. It was one of the constellations known to the ancient Greeks. The name of its brightest star, Arneb, means "hare" in Arabic. An interesting feature in this constellation is Gamma Leporis, an attractive double star that can be divided with binoculars. Another object of interest is NGC 2017, a small group of stars, the brightest of which can be seen through small telescopes.

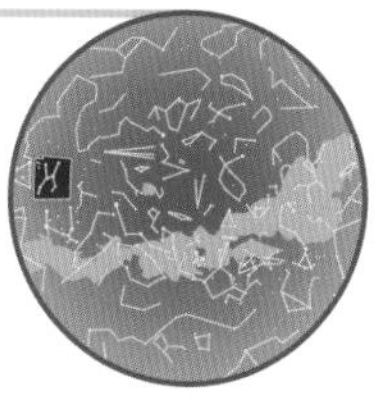

SOUTHERN HEMISPHERE

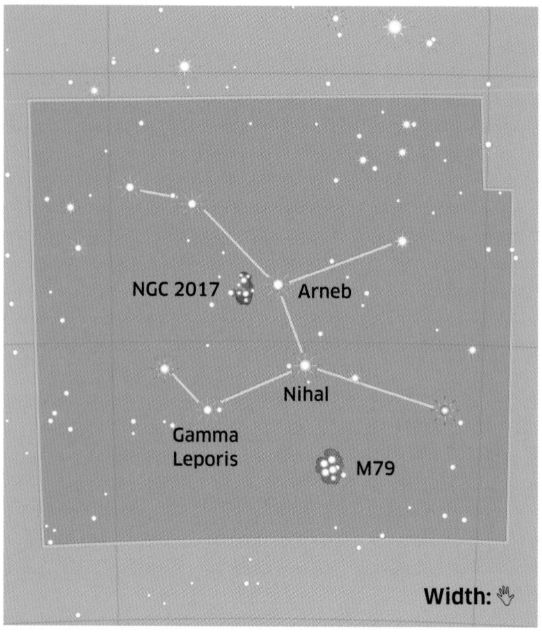
NGC 2017
Arneb
Nihal
Gamma Leporis
M79
Width:

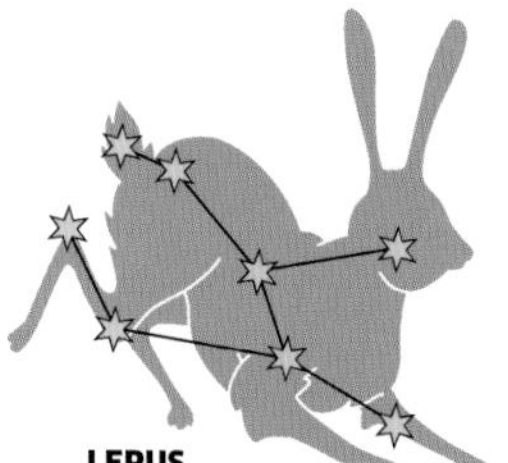

LEPUS (THE HARE)

COLUMBA

This constellation was devised in 1592 by the Dutch astronomer Petrus Plancius, using stars between Lepus and Canis Major that were not part of any Greek constellation. It is said to represent the dove that Noah sent from the biblical Ark to find dry land. Columba's brightest star is called Phact, from the Arabic meaning "ring dove".

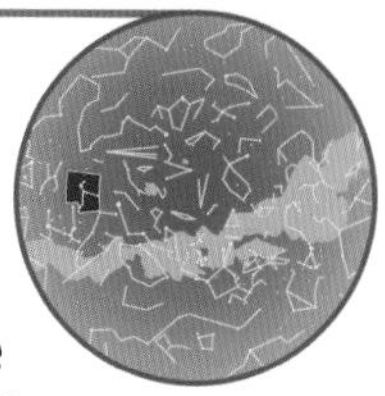

SOUTHERN HEMISPHERE

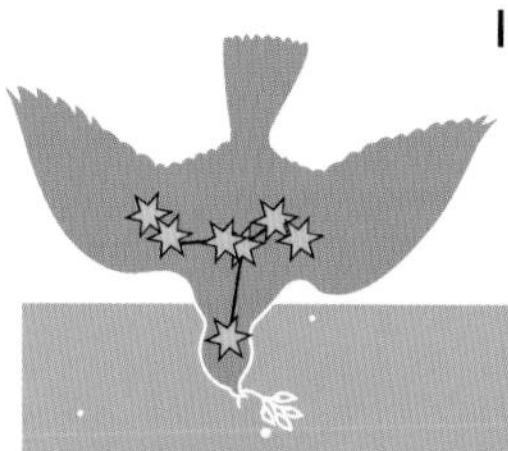

COLUMBA (THE DOVE)

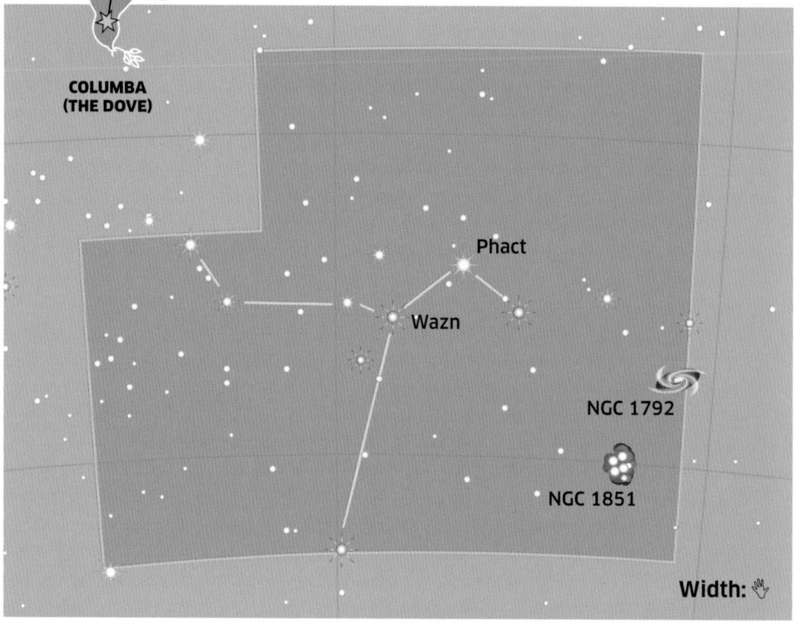
Phact
Wazn
NGC 1792
NGC 1851
Width:

PYXIS

French astronomer Nicolas Louis de Lacaille devised this faint southern constellation in the 1750s during his survey of the southern sky. Pyxis depicts a magnetic compass as used on ships. The constellation's most remarkable star is T Pyxidis, a recurrent nova – a kind of star that brightens from time to time. It has been seen to flare up six times since 1890. Further outbursts could occur at any time.

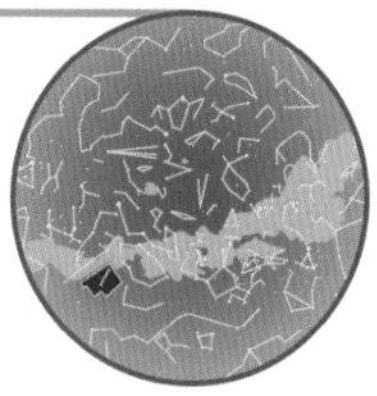

SOUTHERN HEMISPHERE

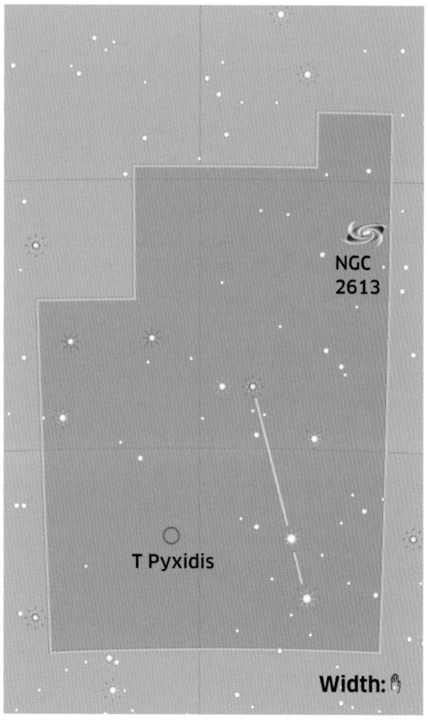
NGC 2613
T Pyxidis
Width:

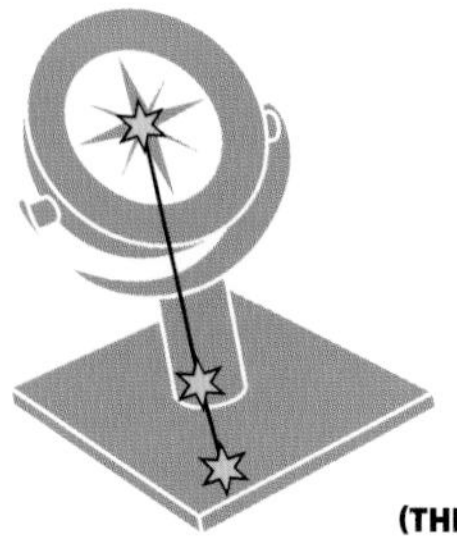

PYXIS (THE COMPASS)

PUPPIS

Puppis was once part of a much larger Greek constellation called Argo Navis, the ship of Jason and the Argonauts. It depicted the ship's stern. Puppis lies in a rich part of the Milky Way and contains many bright star clusters. M46 and M47 lie side by side and create a brighter patch in the Milky Way. NGC 2451 and NGC 2477 are two more clusters that lie close together. Binoculars give a good view of them both.

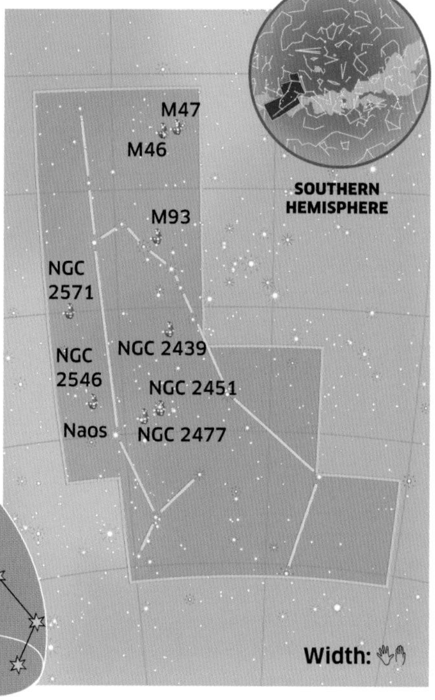
M47
M46
M93
NGC 2571
NGC 2439
NGC 2546
NGC 2451
Naos
NGC 2477
Width:

SOUTHERN HEMISPHERE

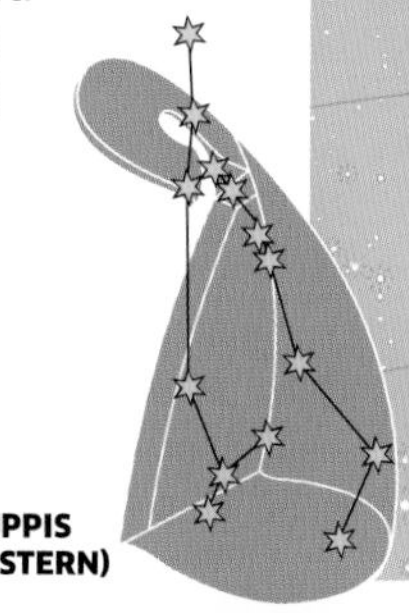

PUPPIS (THE STERN)

Star cluster M47
M47 is a large and scattered cluster of a few dozen stars in the north of Puppis, visible with binoculars. The rich view in this image was captured through a large professional telescope.

VELA

Vela represents the sails of Argo Navis, the ship of Jason and the Argonauts. Argo Navis was a large Greek constellation that was split into three smaller parts. The other two parts are Puppis and Carina. Two stars in Vela combine with a pair of stars in Carina to form the False Cross, sometimes mistaken for the real Southern Cross. Around another star is a large cluster called IC 2391, bright enough to be visible to the naked eye.

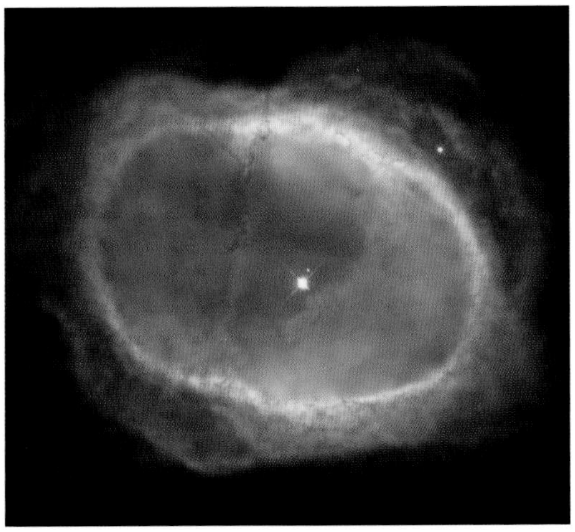

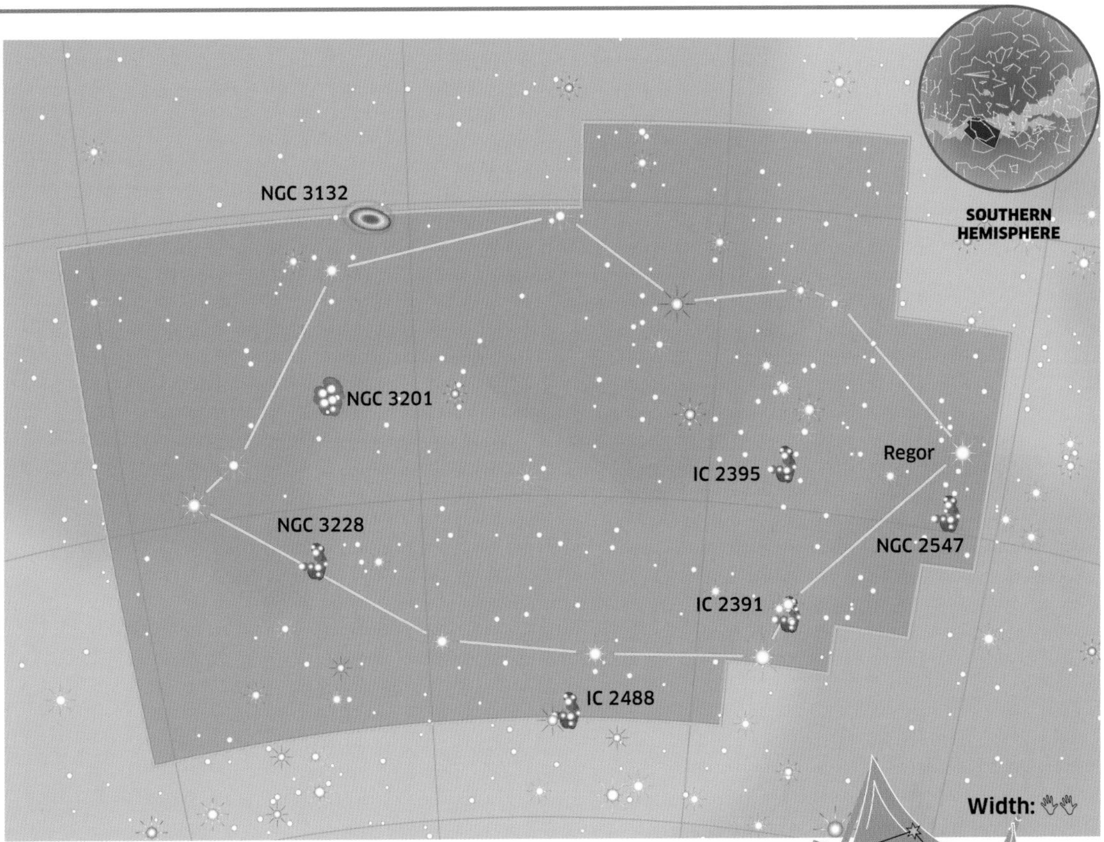
NGC 3132
NGC 3201
IC 2395
Regor
NGC 3228
NGC 2547
IC 2391
IC 2488
Width:
SOUTHERN HEMISPHERE

Eight-burst Nebula
This glowing cloud of wreckage from a dead star is called the Eight-burst Nebula (NGC 3132) because its loops of gas look like a figure of eight through telescopes. It is seen here as pictured by the Hubble Space Telescope.

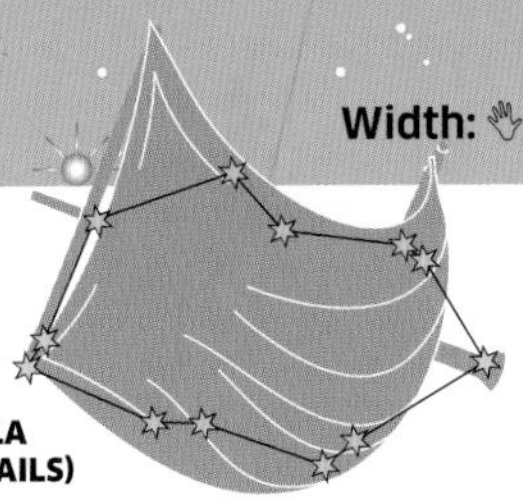
VELA
(THE SAILS)

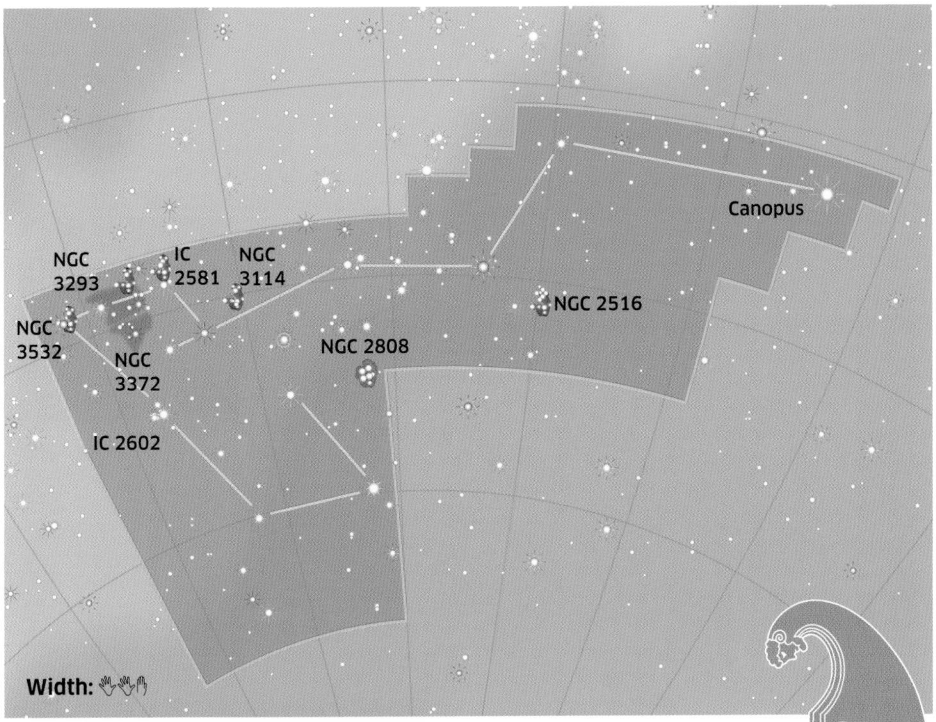
NGC 3293
IC 2581
NGC 3114
NGC 3532
NGC 3372
NGC 2808
NGC 2516
Canopus
IC 2602
Width:

CARINA

Carina is one of the three parts into which the large Greek constellation of Argo Navis, the ship of Jason and the Argonauts, was split. It depicts the ship's keel, or hull. This constellation contains the second-brightest star in the night sky, Canopus. A pair of stars in Carina form half of the False Cross, completed by two stars in Vela.

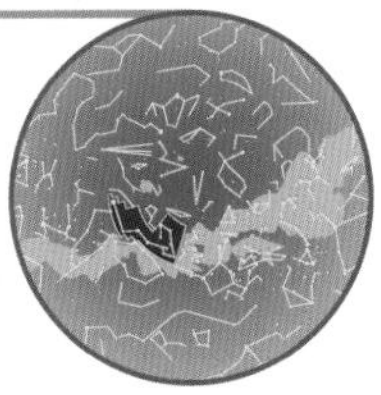
SOUTHERN HEMISPHERE

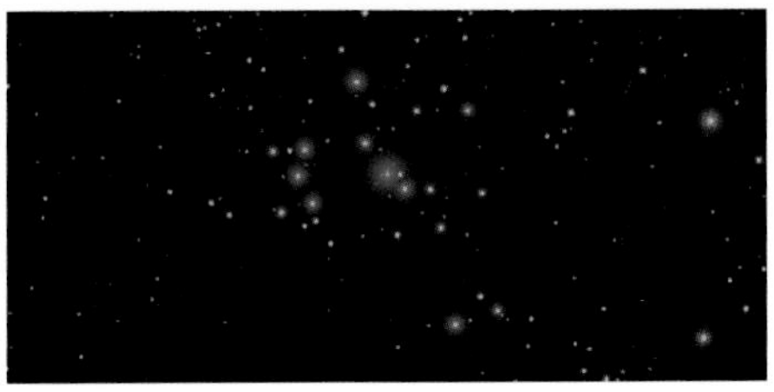

Southern Pleiades
The large star cluster IC 2602, called the Southern Pleiades, is a glorious sight through binoculars.

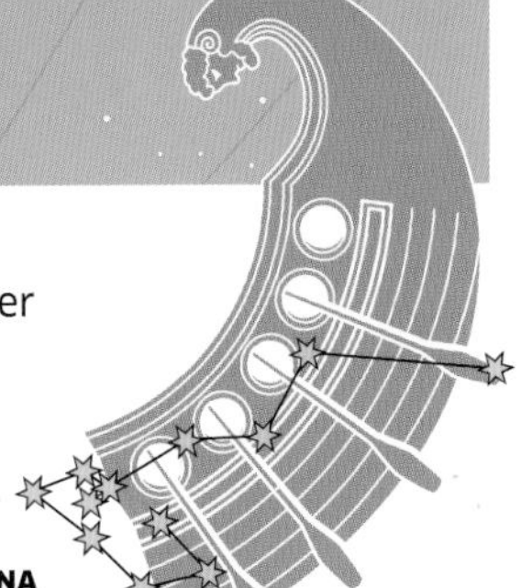
CARINA
(THE KEEL)

Carina Nebula
The Carina Nebula (NGC 3372) is a large, V-shaped cloud of gas visible to the naked eye. Its brightest part surrounds the star Eta Carina, a peculiar variable star that has thrown off shells of gas in the past.

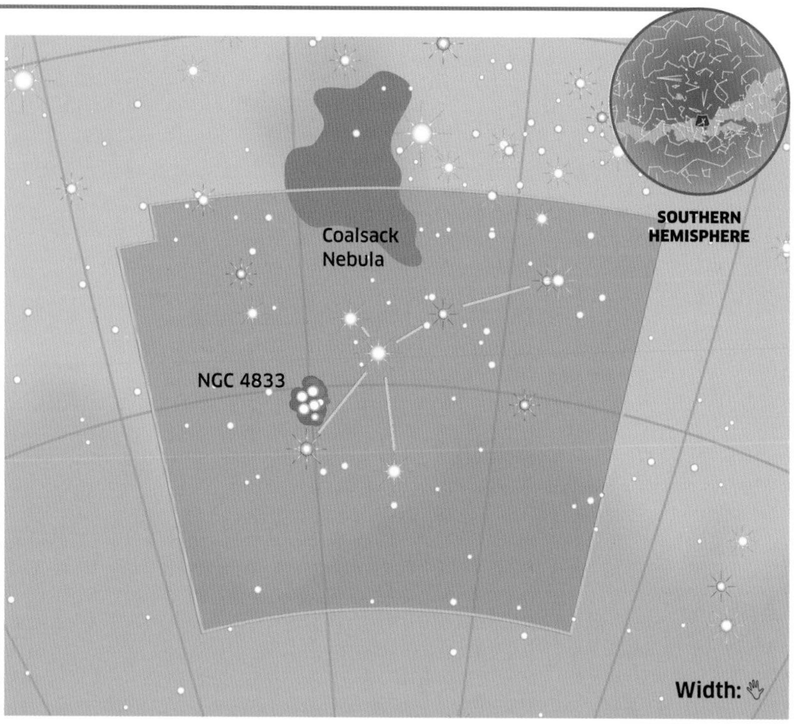
SOUTHERN HEMISPHERE
Coalsack Nebula
NGC 4833
Width:

MUSCA

This constellation of the southern sky was invented at the end of the 16th century by Dutch seafarers. It represents a fly. Part of the dark Coalsack Nebula spills into Musca from Crux, which lies to the north. Of note is NGC 4833, a globular cluster that can be seen through binoculars and small telescopes.

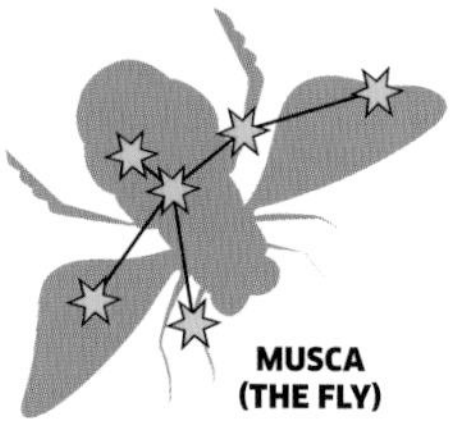
MUSCA (THE FLY)

CIRCINUS

This small southern constellation was created in the 1750s by the French astronomer Nicolas Louis de Lacaille. Most of his constellations represented instruments from science and the arts. He visualized Circinus as a pair of dividing compasses used by surveyors and navigators. Its brightest star is a double.

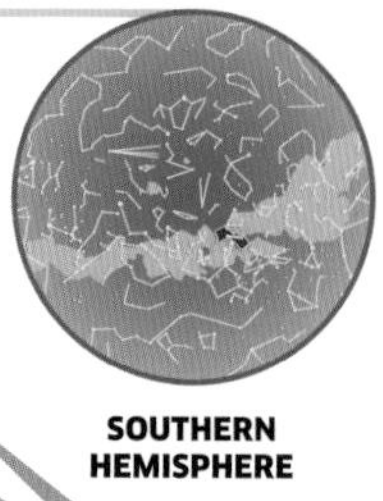
SOUTHERN HEMISPHERE

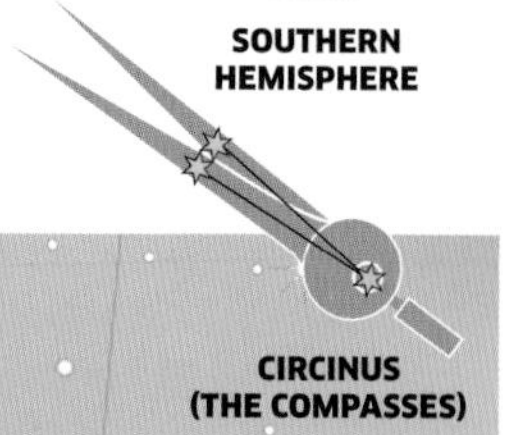
CIRCINUS (THE COMPASSES)

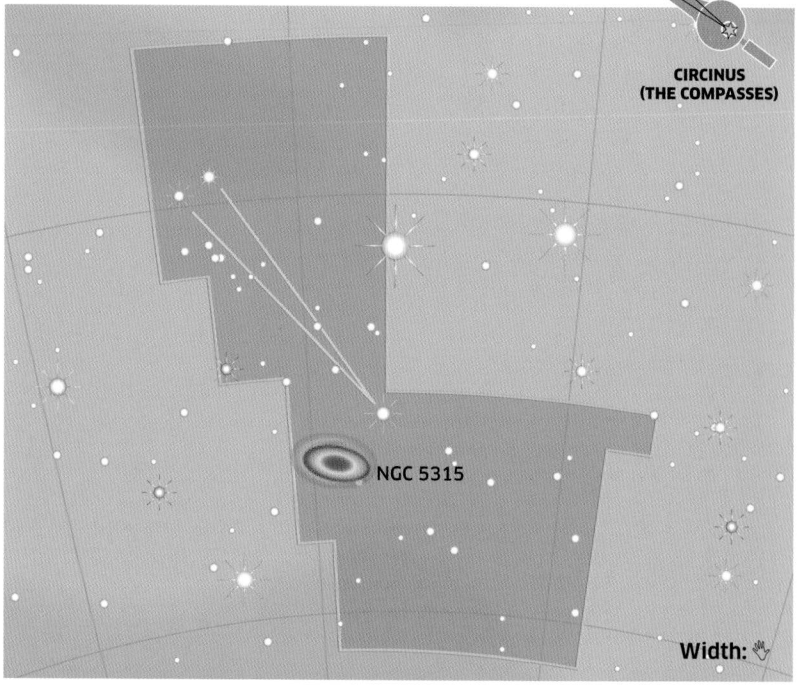
NGC 5315
Width:

NORMA

Norma was introduced in the 1750s by the French astronomer Nicolas Louis de Lacaille. It represents a set square as used by draughtsmen and builders. Objects of note include the star Gamma Normae, which consists of a wide pair of unrelated stars, both separately visible to the naked eye, and NGC 6087, a large, rich star cluster visible through binoculars.

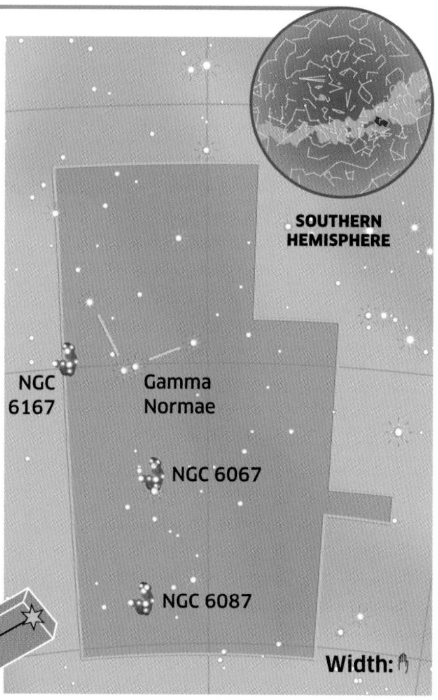
SOUTHERN HEMISPHERE
NGC 6167
Gamma Normae
NGC 6067
NGC 6087
Width:

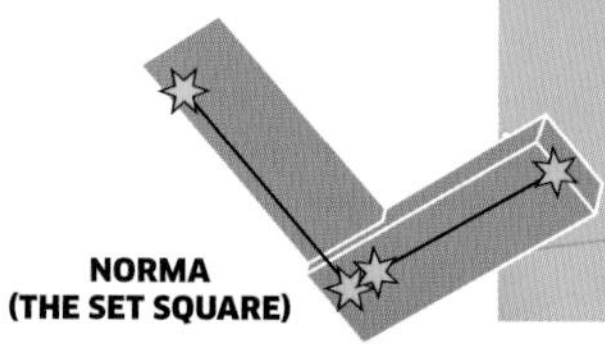
NORMA (THE SET SQUARE)

Star cluster NGC 6067
NGC 6067 is a rich cluster of stars in central Norma, visible through binoculars and small telescopes. It covers an area of sky about half the apparent diameter of the full moon.

TRIANGULUM AUSTRALE

At the end of the 16th century, Dutch explorers who sailed to the East Indies created a dozen new constellations among the southern stars. The smallest of them was Triangulum Australe, the southern triangle. It is smaller than the northern triangle, Triangulum, but its stars are brighter. The main object of interest in Triangulum Australe is the star cluster NGC 6025 on its northern border, visible through binoculars.

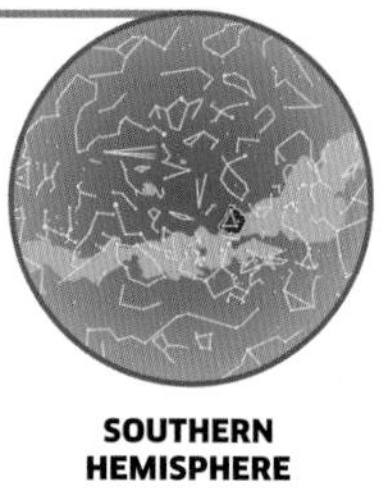
SOUTHERN HEMISPHERE

TRIANGULUM AUSTRALE (THE SOUTHERN TRIANGLE)

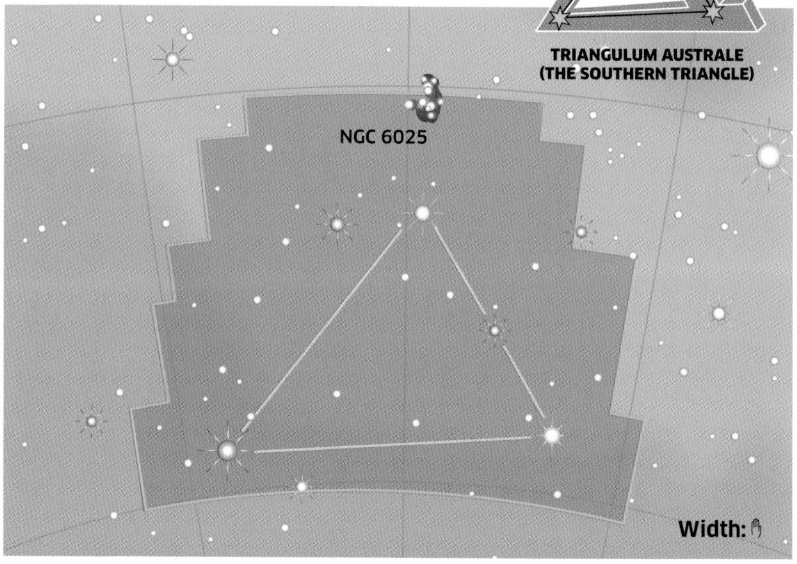
NGC 6025
Width:

ARA

The constellation Ara was known to the ancient Greeks. To them it depicted the altar on which the gods of Mount Olympus swore an oath of loyalty before fighting the Titans, their sworn enemies. An attractive star cluster in Ara is NGC 6193. None of the stars of Ara is of particular interest.

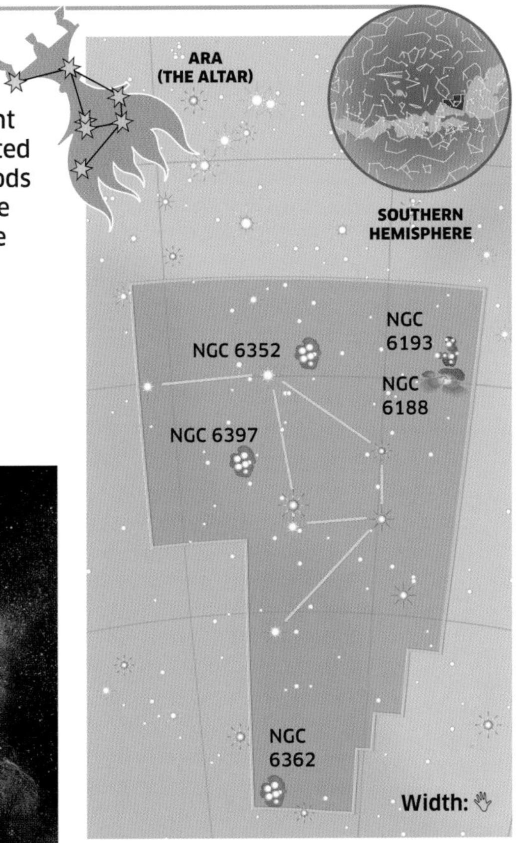
ARA
(THE ALTAR)
SOUTHERN
HEMISPHERE
NGC 6352
NGC
6193
NGC
6188
NGC 6397
NGC
6362
Width:

Starbirth nebula NGC 6188
Ultraviolet radiation from the stars in NGC 6193 lights up the sulphur, hydrogen, and oxygen atoms in the starbirth nebula NGC 6188, as seen in this Hubble photo.

CORONA AUSTRALIS

This small constellation lies under the feet of Sagittarius. It represents a crown or wreath, and was one of the constellations known to the ancient Greeks. Although faint, Corona Australis is fairly easy to spot as its main stars form a noticeable arc. An interesting object for small telescopes is the globular cluster NGC 6541.

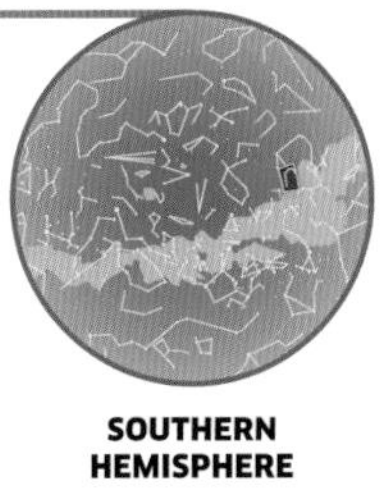
SOUTHERN
HEMISPHERE

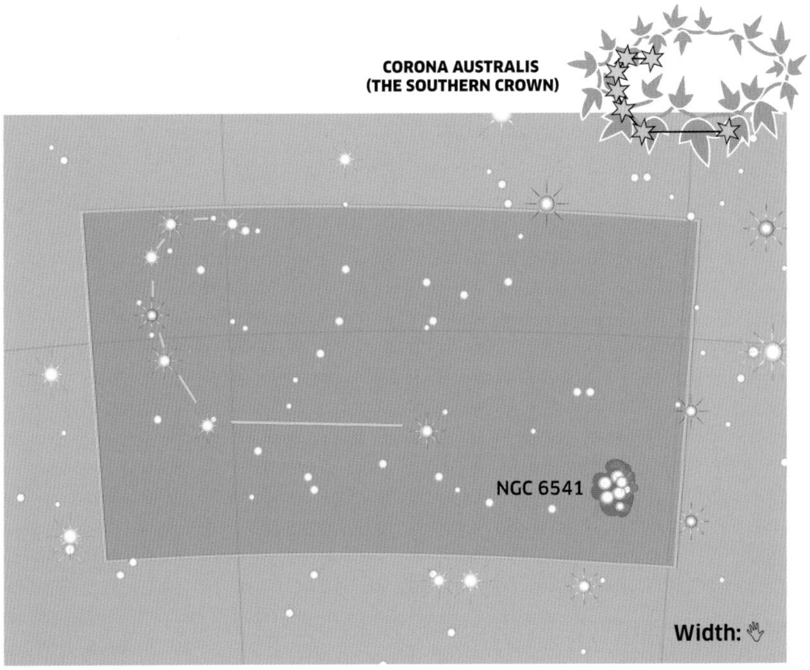
CORONA AUSTRALIS
(THE SOUTHERN CROWN)
NGC 6541
Width:

TELESCOPIUM

French astronomer Nicolas Louis de Lacaille came up with this faint constellation in the 1750s to commemorate the telescope, the astronomer's basic tool. The constellation has since been reduced in size. Besides a globular cluster and a wide pair of unrelated stars, which can be seen separately with binoculars or even good eyesight, there is little of note.

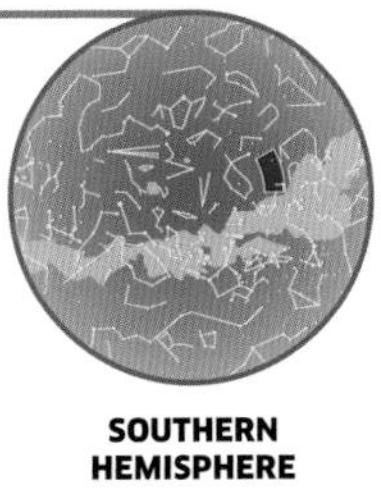
SOUTHERN
HEMISPHERE

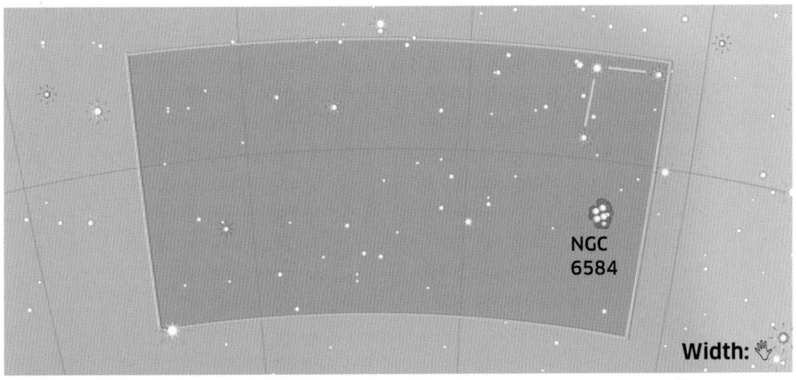
NGC
6584
Width:

Globular cluster NGC 6584
NGC 6584 is a faint and distant globular cluster and can be seen well through a large telescope. It is seen here as photographed by the Hubble Space Telescope.

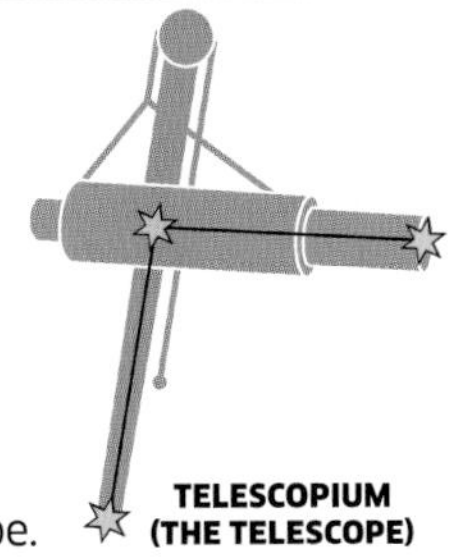
TELESCOPIUM
(THE TELESCOPE)

INDUS

Indus is one of the 12 southern constellations introduced at the end of the 16th century by Dutch seafarers. This constellation was visualized as a native hunter brandishing a spear. Indus has an interesting double star that can be divided by a small telescope.

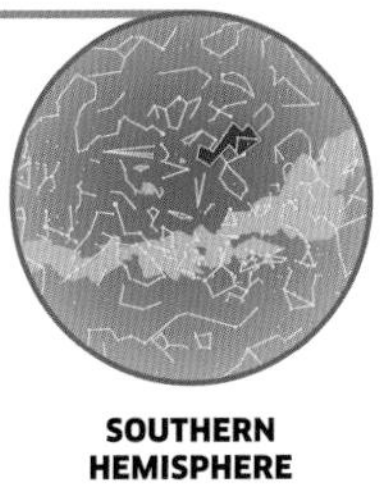
SOUTHERN
HEMISPHERE

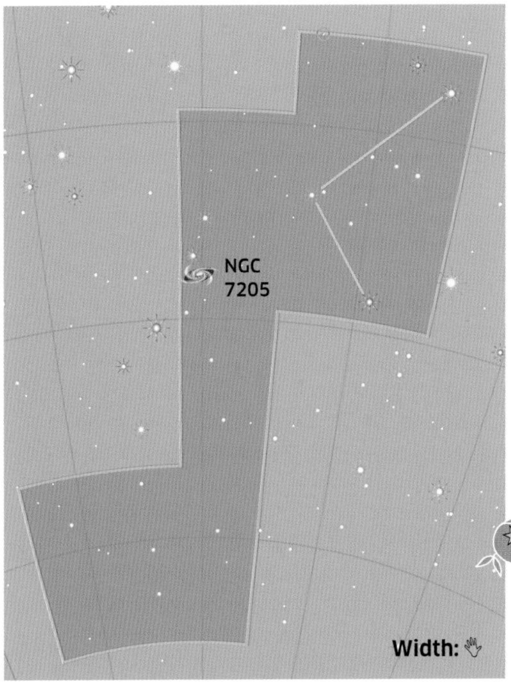
NGC
7205
Width:

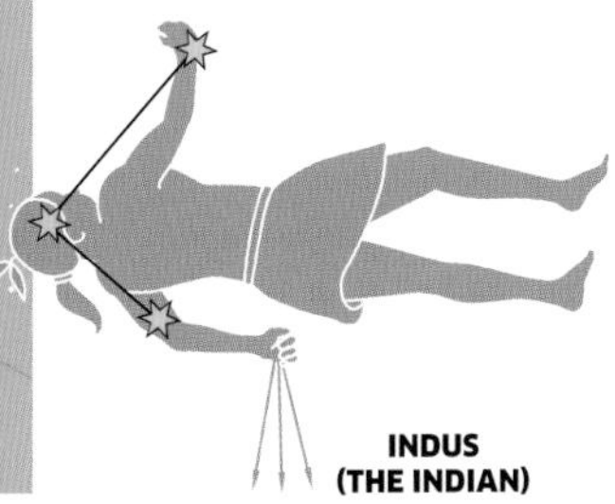
INDUS
(THE INDIAN)

GRUS

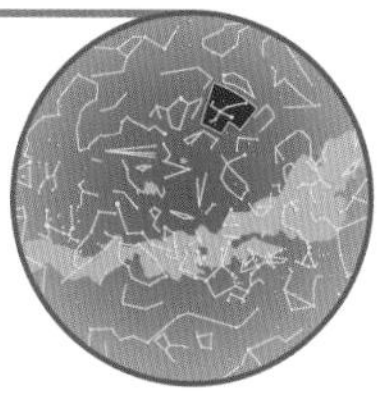
SOUTHERN
HEMISPHERE

Grus represents a crane, a long-necked wading bird. It is one of the constellations invented in the late 16th century by Dutch seafarers. In the bird's neck lie two wide double stars. Both pairs can be divided with the naked eye. The stars in each pair are actually at different distances from us and so not related – they are just optical doubles and not true binaries.

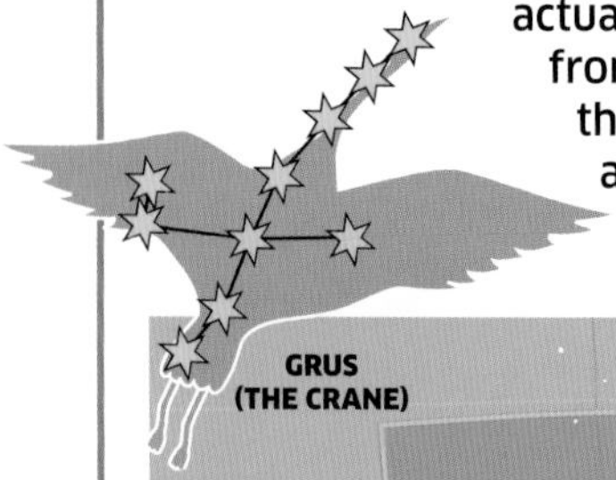
GRUS
(THE CRANE)

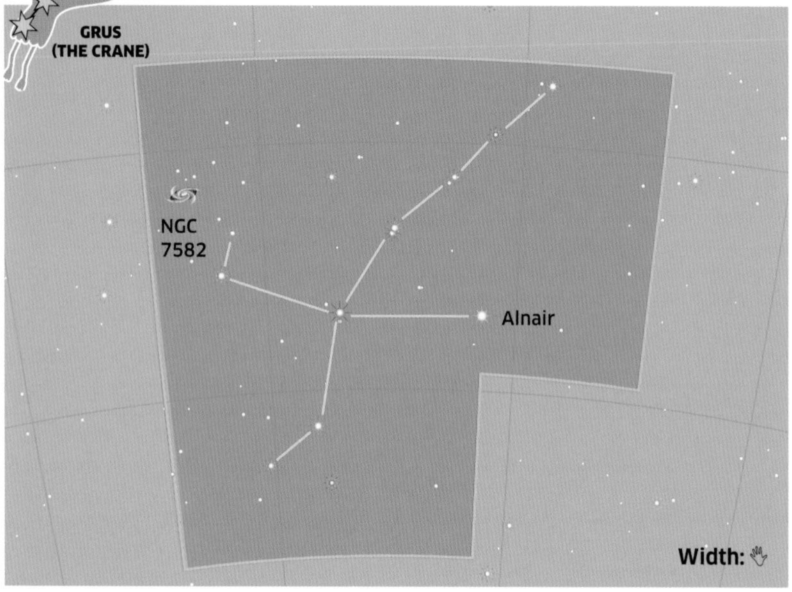
NGC
7582
Alnair
Width:

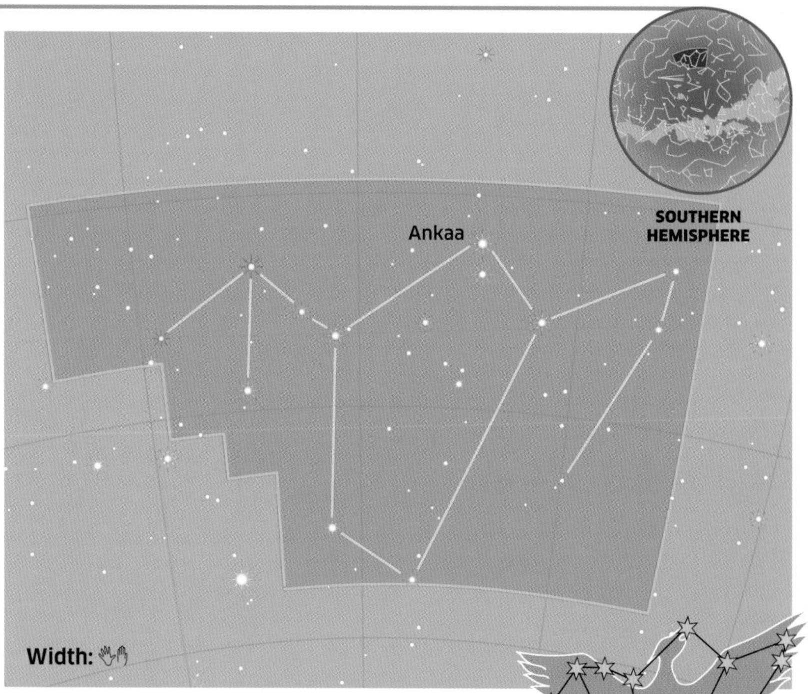
SOUTHERN
HEMISPHERE
Ankaa
Width:

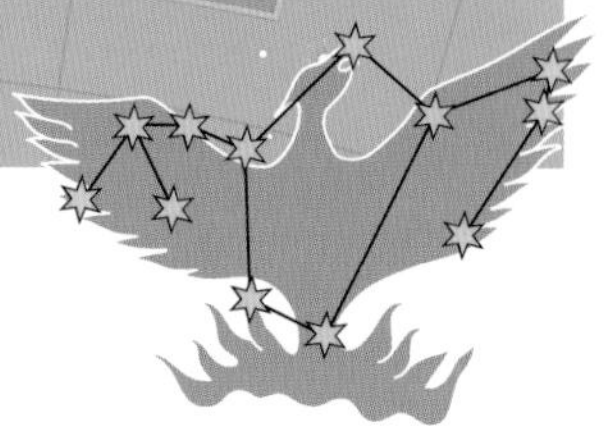
THE PHOENIX

PHOENIX

This constellation lies near the southern end of the river Eridanus. Phoenix is the largest of the 12 new constellations that were created at the end of the 16th century by Dutch explorers sailing to the East Indies. It represents the mythical bird that was said to be reborn from its own ashes every 500 years.

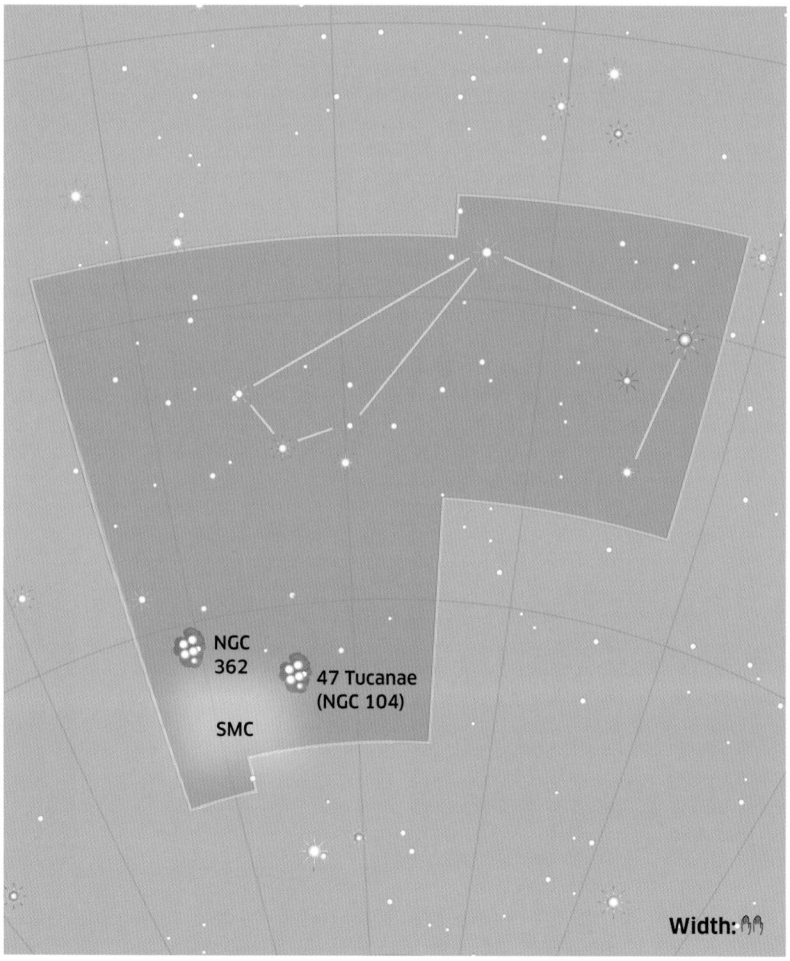
NGC
362
47 Tucanae
(NGC 104)
SMC
Width:

TUCANA

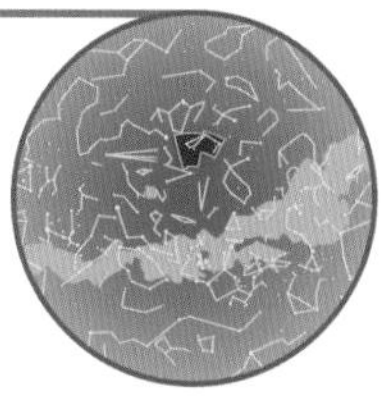
SOUTHERN
HEMISPHERE

Dutch navigators came up with this southern constellation in the late 16th century. It represents a toucan, a tropical bird with a large beak. Tucana contains the Small Magellanic Cloud (SMC), a mini-galaxy about 200,000 light years away from us. To the naked eye, the SMC looks like a separate part of the Milky Way. The globular clusters 47 Tucanae and NGC 362 lie on either side of the SMC but are actually much closer to us.

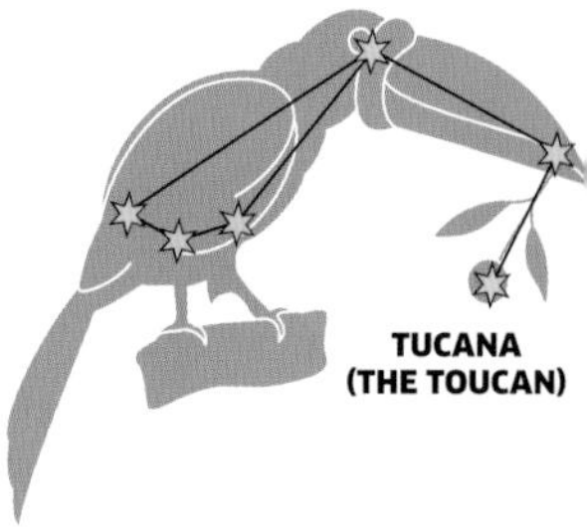
TUCANA
(THE TOUCAN)

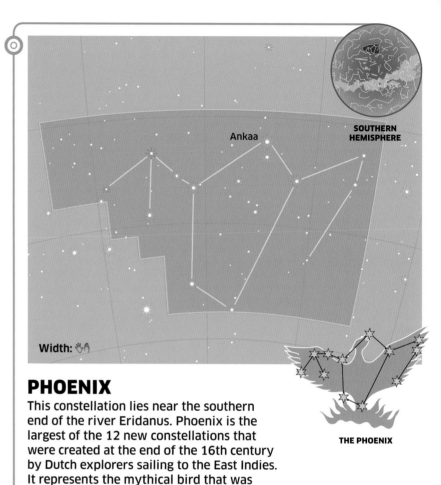

Globular cluster 47 Tucanae
To the naked eye, the globular cluster 47 Tucanae (NGC 104) looks like a single fuzzy star, but through large telescopes it breaks up into a swarm of individual points of light, as seen here. It lies about 16,000 light years away from us.

HYDRUS

Representing a sea snake, this constellation slithers between the Large and Small Magellanic Clouds (LMC and SMC). Hydrus was created by Dutch explorers in the 16th century. It should not be confused with Hydra, the large water snake, which has been known since ancient Greek times. Hydrus has a pair of red giants, Pi Hydri, that look like a double star but are unrelated and lie at different distances from us. Pi Hydri can be seen separately through binoculars.

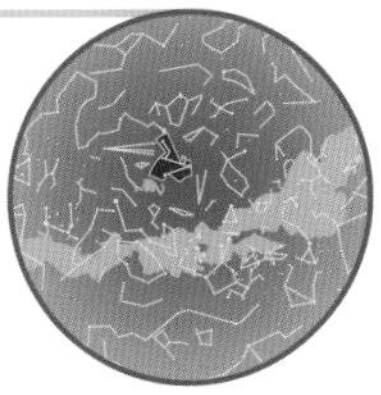

SOUTHERN HEMISPHERE

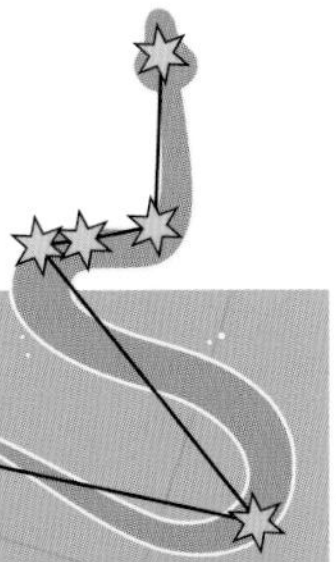

HYDRUS (THE LITTLE WATER SNAKE)

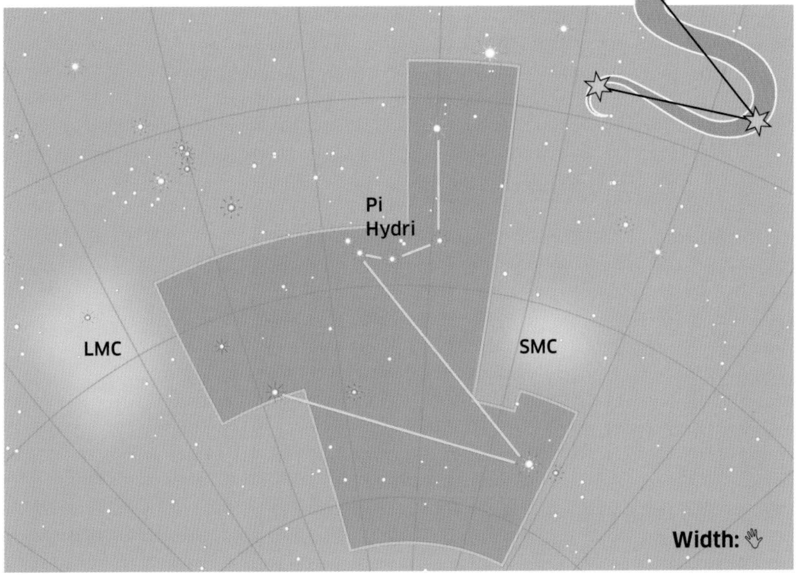
Pi Hydri
LMC
SMC
Width:

HOROLOGIUM

Horologium represents a clock with a long pendulum, as used in observatories for accurate timekeeping in the days before electronic clocks. It is one of the southern constellations honouring scientific and technical instruments that were introduced by the French astronomer Nicolas Louis de Lacaille in the 1750s. Horologium is faint and contains few objects of interest for small telescopes.

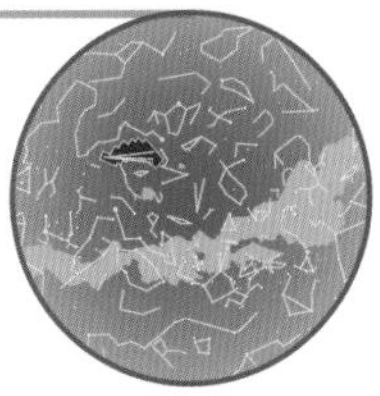

SOUTHERN HEMISPHERE

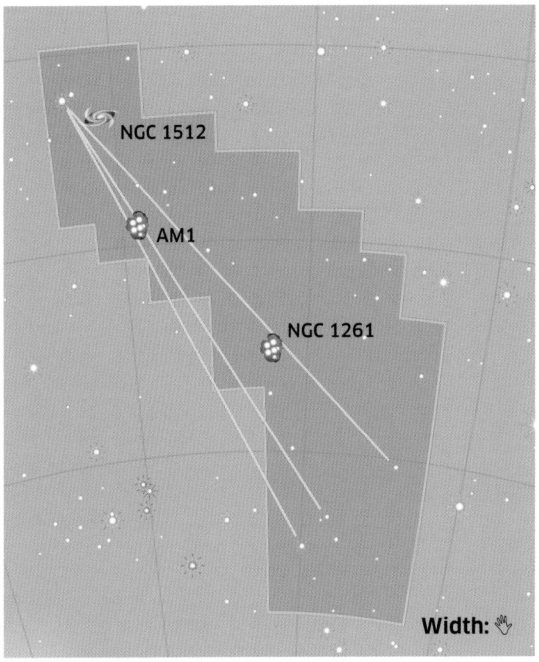
NGC 1512
AM1
NGC 1261
Width:

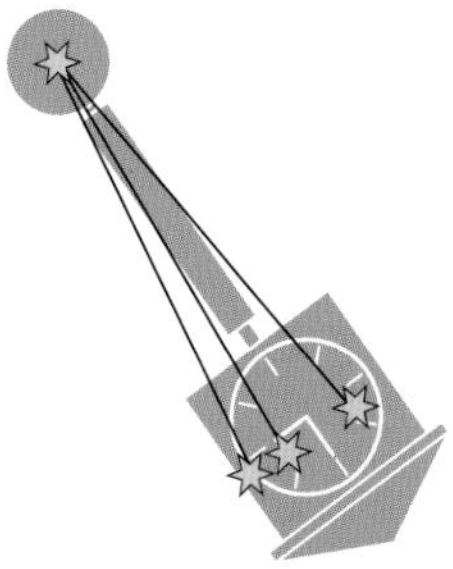

HOROLOGIUM (THE PENDULUM CLOCK)

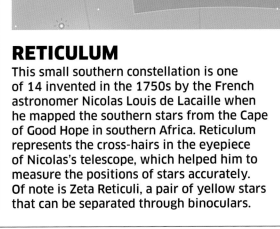

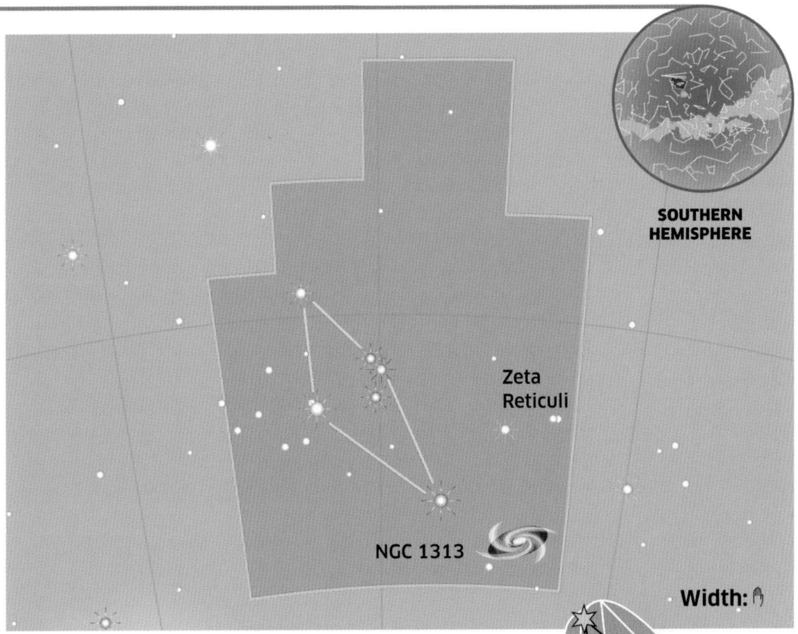
Zeta Reticuli
NGC 1313
Width:

SOUTHERN HEMISPHERE

RETICULUM

This small southern constellation is one of 14 invented in the 1750s by the French astronomer Nicolas Louis de Lacaille when he mapped the southern stars from the Cape of Good Hope in southern Africa. Reticulum represents the cross-hairs in the eyepiece of Nicolas's telescope, which helped him to measure the positions of stars accurately. Of note is Zeta Reticuli, a pair of yellow stars that can be separated through binoculars.

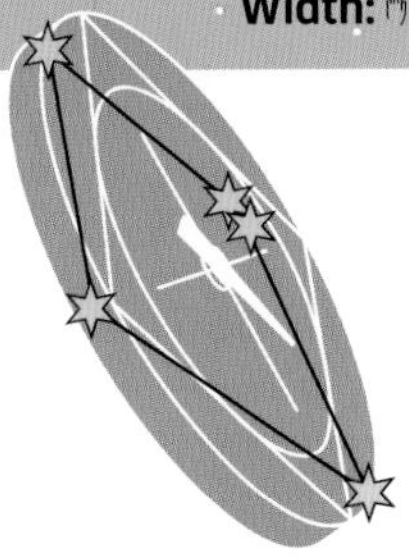

RETICULUM (THE NET)

PICTOR

This is yet another constellation invented in the 1750s by the French astronomer Nicolas Louis de Lacaille. It represents an artist's easel. Pictor contains an interesting double star, Iota Pictoris, which can be easily separated through small telescopes.

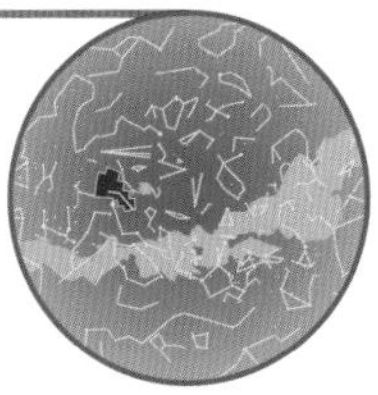

SOUTHERN HEMISPHERE

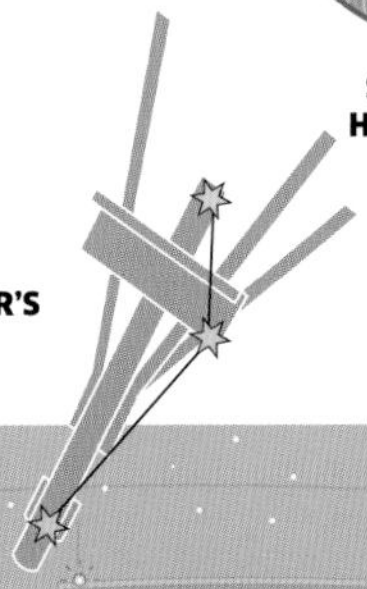

PICTOR (THE PAINTER'S EASEL)

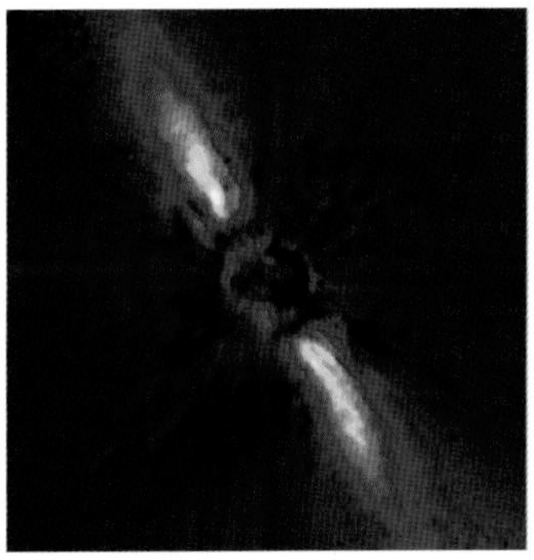

Beta Pictoris
The second brightest star in Pictor, Beta Pictoris is surrounded by a disc of dust and gas. Planets are thought to be forming from the disc. This disc can be seen only through large telescopes with special equipment.

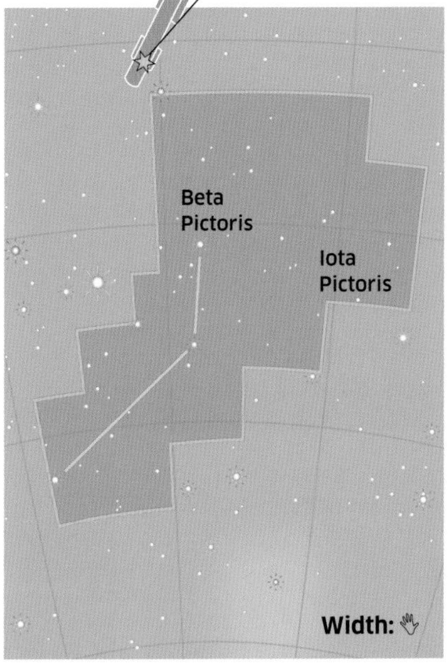
Beta Pictoris
Iota Pictoris
Width:

DORADO

Dutch seafarers created this southern constellation in the late 16th century. It represents a type of tropical fish called a dorado but is also known as the Goldfish. The main feature of Dorado is the Large Magellanic Cloud (LMC), the bigger of the two companion galaxies of the Milky Way. Another point of interest is the Tarantula Nebula (NGC 2070), which appears as a hazy star.

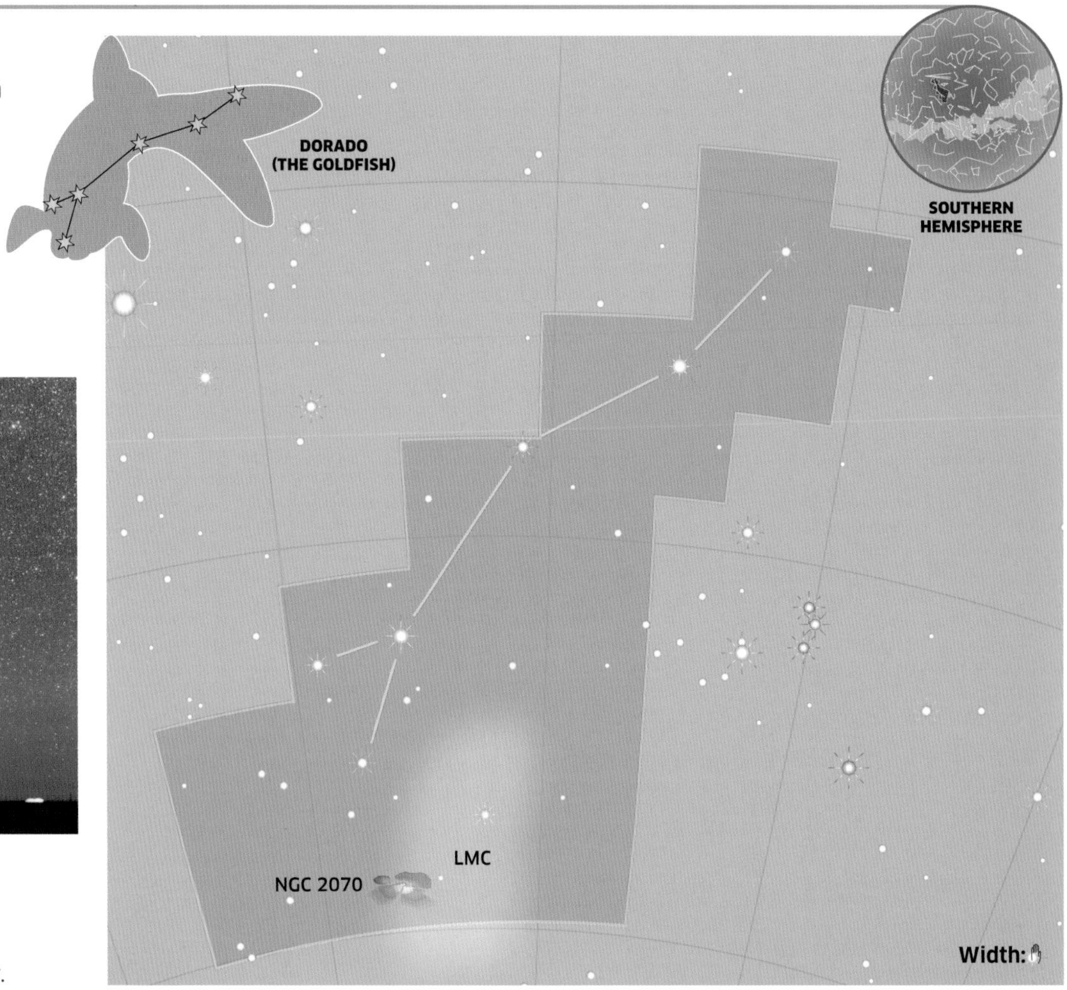
DORADO
(THE GOLDFISH)
SOUTHERN
HEMISPHERE
LMC
NGC 2070
Width:

Large Magellanic Cloud
The Large Magellanic Cloud (LMC) can be easily seen with the naked eye, and looks like a detached part of our galaxy. Binoculars reveal many star clusters and nebulas within it. It lies about 170,000 light years away.

VOLANS

This constellation was invented in the late 16th century by Dutch explorers who sailed to the East Indies, surveying the stars of the southern sky on the way. It represents a flying fish – one of the exotic creatures they saw on their voyages. Gamma and Epsilon Volantis are double stars that can easily be told apart by small telescopes.

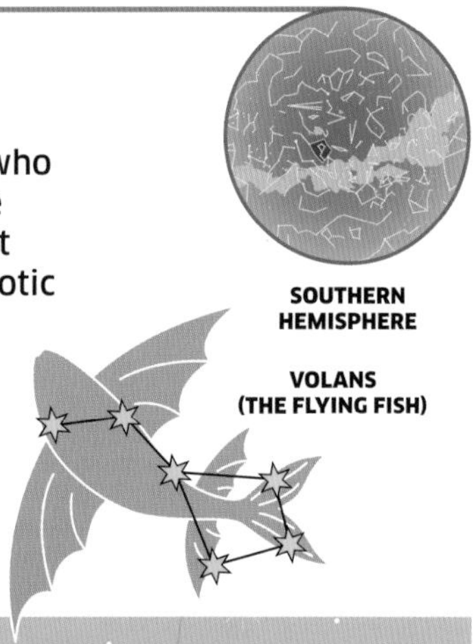
SOUTHERN
HEMISPHERE
VOLANS
(THE FLYING FISH)

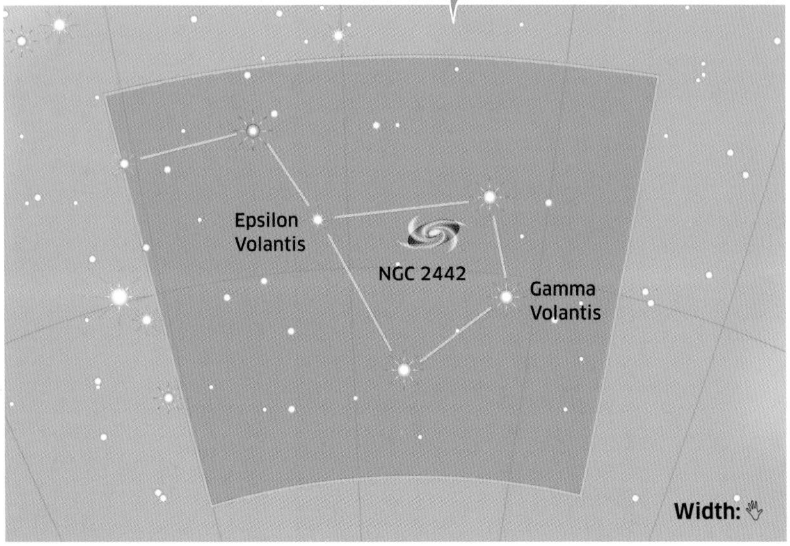
Epsilon
Volantis
NGC 2442
Gamma
Volantis
Width:

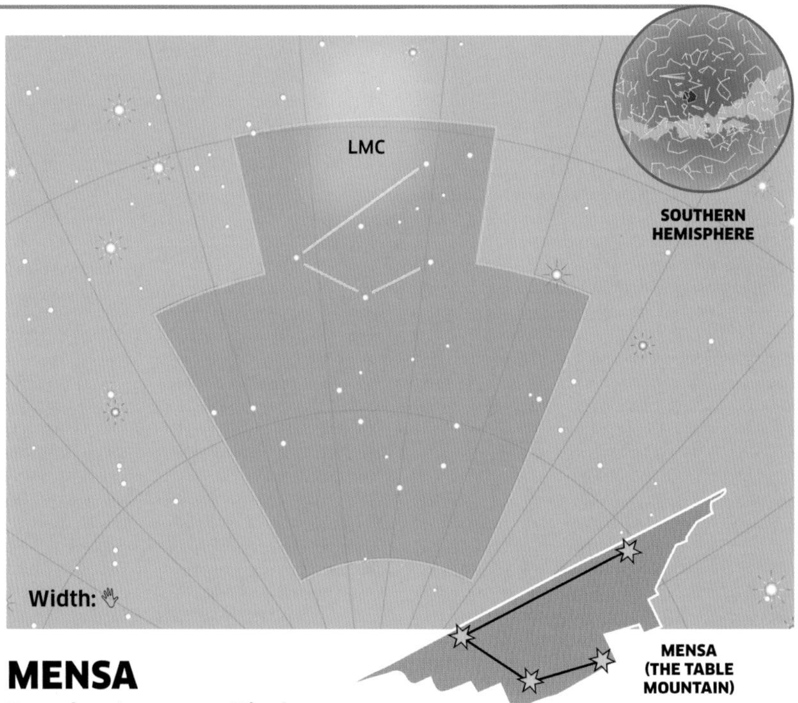
LMC
SOUTHERN
HEMISPHERE
Width:
MENSA
(THE TABLE
MOUNTAIN)

MENSA

French astronomer Nicolas Louis de Lacaille devised this constellation in the 1750s. He measured the positions of thousands of southern stars from an observatory near the foot of Table Mountain at the Cape of Good Hope, South Africa. This constellation was named Mensa – which means "table" in Latin – to celebrate the mountain. Mensa contains part of the Large Magellanic Cloud (LMC). All of Mensa's stars are faint, and none of them is of interest for users of small telescopes.

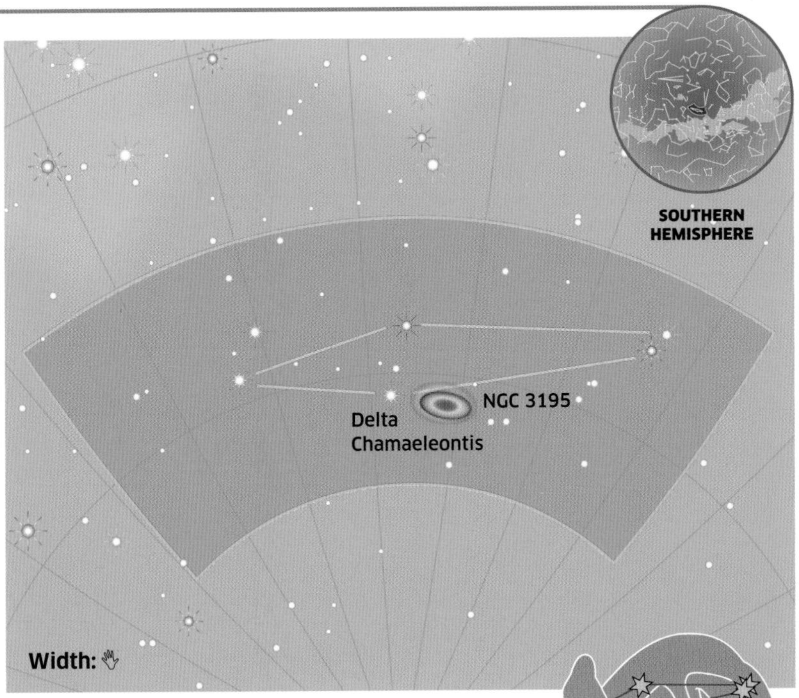
SOUTHERN
HEMISPHERE
NGC 3195
Delta
Chamaeleontis
Width:

THE
CHAMAELEON

CHAMAELEON

Chamaeleon is a small southern constellation invented in the late 16th century. It is named after the lizard that can change its skin colour to match its surroundings. Next to it lies Musca, the fly, which is appropriate because chameleons eat flies. Of interest is Delta Chamaeleontis, a wide double star that is easily seen with binoculars.

APUS

Dutch explorers sailing to the East Indies in the late 16th century devised Apus. This constellation represents a bird of paradise, a kind of bird known for its beautiful plumage, which in the past was used to decorate hats and other items of clothing. Delta Apodis is a wide pair of unrelated red giant stars, which can be seen separately with the naked eye or in binoculars.

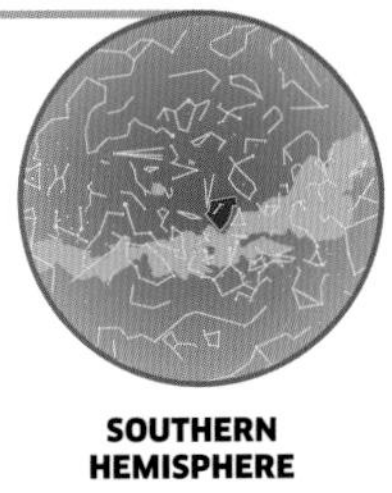
SOUTHERN
HEMISPHERE

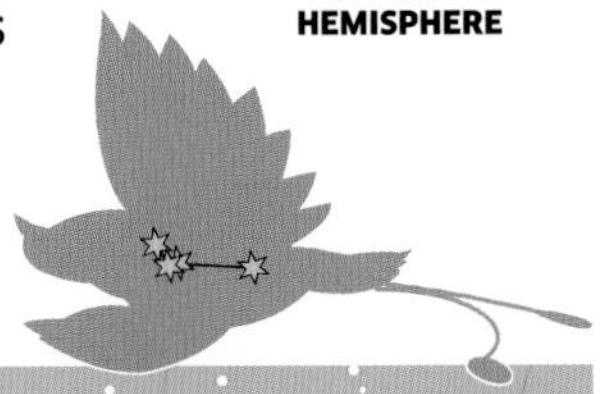
APUS
(THE BIRD OF PARADISE)

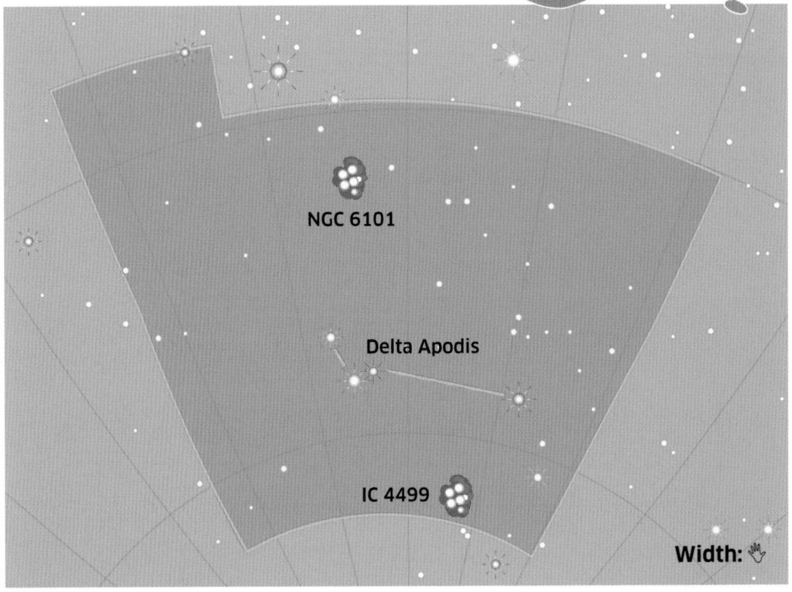
NGC 6101
Delta Apodis
IC 4499
Width:

PAVO

Pavo represents a peacock, a bird with a glorious, fan-like tail. It is one of the 12 southern constellations introduced by Dutch seafarers at the end of the 16th century. Items of note include NGC 6752, a large and bright globular cluster, easily visible in binoculars; and NGC 6744, a beautiful spiral galaxy with a short central bar, best seen on photographs.

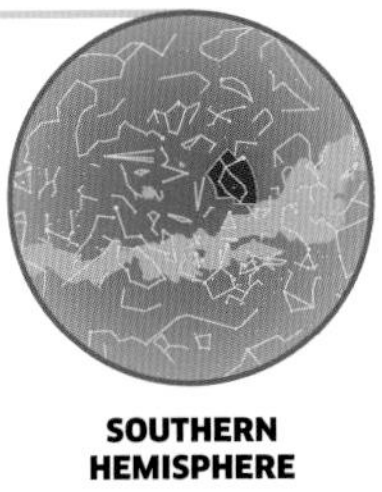
SOUTHERN
HEMISPHERE

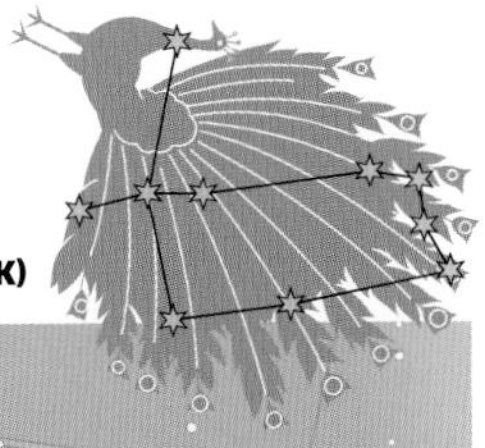
PAVO
(THE PEACOCK)

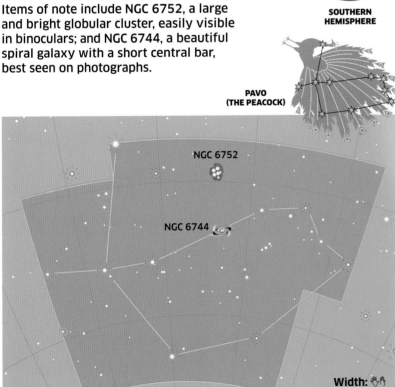

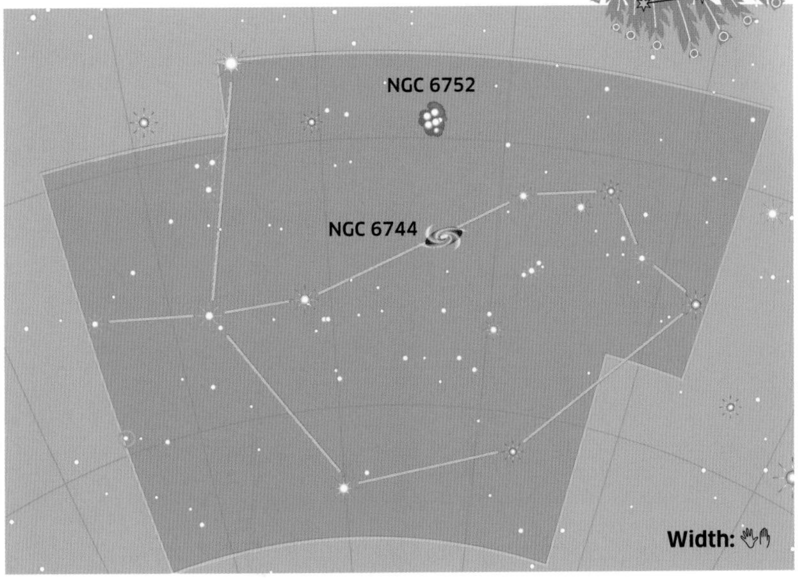
NGC 6752
NGC 6744
Width:

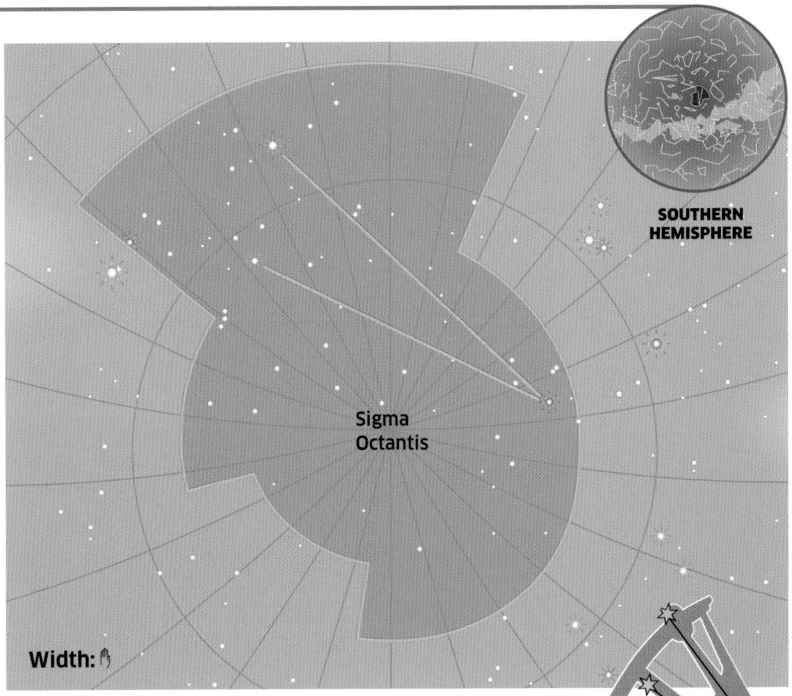
SOUTHERN
HEMISPHERE
Sigma
Octantis
Width:

OCTANS

Octans contains the south pole of the sky. Unlike the northern hemisphere, there is no bright pole star in the southern sky. The closest visible star to the south celestial pole is Sigma Octantis, but it is very faint. Octans was introduced in the 1750s by the French astronomer Nicolas Louis de Lacaille. It represents a navigation instrument known as an octant, the forerunner of the sextant.

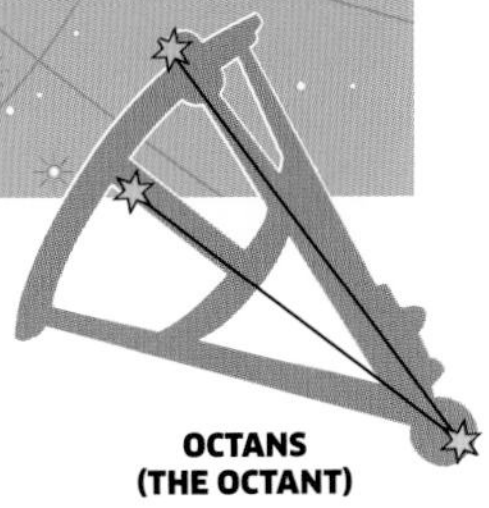
OCTANS
(THE OCTANT)

REFERENCE

The reference section is packed with facts and figures about planets, spacecraft missions, stars, and galaxies, and tells you the best time to see shooting stars, comets, and eclipses. A glossary explains many of the terms used in this book.

Solar System data

Our Solar System consists of the Sun and all the objects under its gravitational influence, including the eight planets and their moons, and an unknown number of dwarf planets, asteroids, comets, and smaller objects. The most distant objects – comets orbiting in the Oort Cloud – can be as far as a light year from the Sun.

The Sun weighs about 670 times as much as all the planets and other objects in the Solar System combined.

THE PLANETS

A planet is officially defined as an object in direct orbit around the Sun, with enough mass to pull itself into a ball, and strong enough gravity to force other objects out of broadly similar orbits. Today, astronomers recognize eight planets – four relatively small, rocky (or "terrestrial") worlds close to the Sun, and four much larger giant planets farther out.

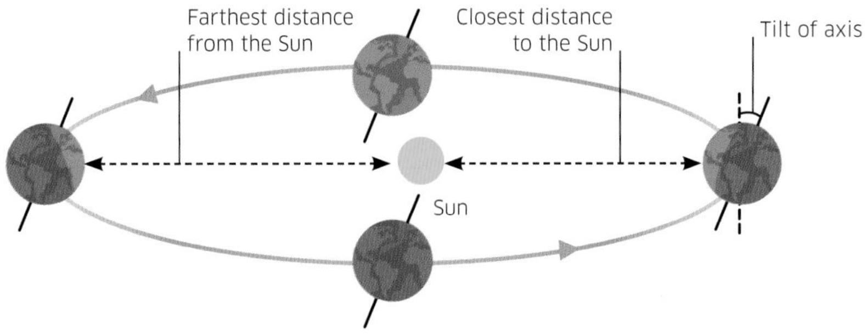
Farthest distance from the Sun
Closest distance to the Sun
Tilt of axis
Sun

A PLANET'S ORBIT AROUND THE SUN

PLANET DATA

	Mercury	Venus	Earth	Mars	Jupiter	Saturn	Uranus	Neptune
Diameter	4,880 km (3,032 miles)	12,104 km (7,522 miles)	12,756 km (7,926 miles)	6,792 km (4,220 miles)	142,984 km (88,846 miles)	120,536 km (74,896 miles)	51,118 km (31,762 miles)	49,528 km (30,774 miles)
Mass (Earth = 1)	0.06	0.82	1	0.11	318	95	14	17
Time of one rotation	1,408 hours	5,833 hours	23.9 hours	24.6 hours	9.9 hours	10.7 hours	17.2 hours	16.1 hours
Surface gravity (Earth = 1)	0.38	0.91	1	0.38	2.36	1.02	0.89	1.12
Tilt of axis	0.01°	2.6°	23.4°	25.2°	3.1°	26.7°	82.2°	28.3°
Number of moons	0	0	1	2	67+	62+	27+	14+
Closest distance to the Sun	46 million km (29 million miles)	107 million km (67 million miles)	147 million km (91 million miles)	207 million km (128 million miles)	741 million km (460 million miles)	1,353 million km (841 million miles)	2,741 million km (1,703 million miles)	4,445 million km (2,761 million miles)
Farthest distance from the Sun	70 million km (43 million miles)	109 million km (68 million miles)	152 million km (95 million miles)	249 million km (157 million miles)	817 million km (507 million miles)	1,515 million km (940 million miles)	3,004 million km (1,866 million miles)	4,546 million km (2,825 million miles)
Time to orbit the Sun	88 Earth days	225 Earth days	365.26 days	687 Earth days	12 Earth years	29 Earth years	84 Earth years	165 Earth years
Average orbital speed	48 km (30 miles) per second	35 km (22 miles) per second	30 km (19 miles) per second	24 km (15 miles) per second	13 km (8 miles) per second	10 km (6 miles) per second	7 km (4 miles) per second	5 km (3 miles) per second

METEOR SHOWERS

After being ejected from a comet or asteroid, many grains of rock get concentrated into narrow streams. When Earth's orbit crosses these streams, the grains burn up in our atmosphere as meteors (shooting stars), causing predictable meteor showers.

MAJOR METEOR SHOWERS

Name	Peak date	Most meteors	Parent comet/asteroid
Quadrantids	4 January	120 per hour	2003 EH1
Lyrids	22 April	10 per hour	C/1861 G1 (Thatcher)
Eta Aquarids	5 May	30 per hour	1P/Halley
Perseids	12 August	100 per hour	109P/Swift-Tuttle
Geminids	14 December	120 per hour	3200 Phaethon

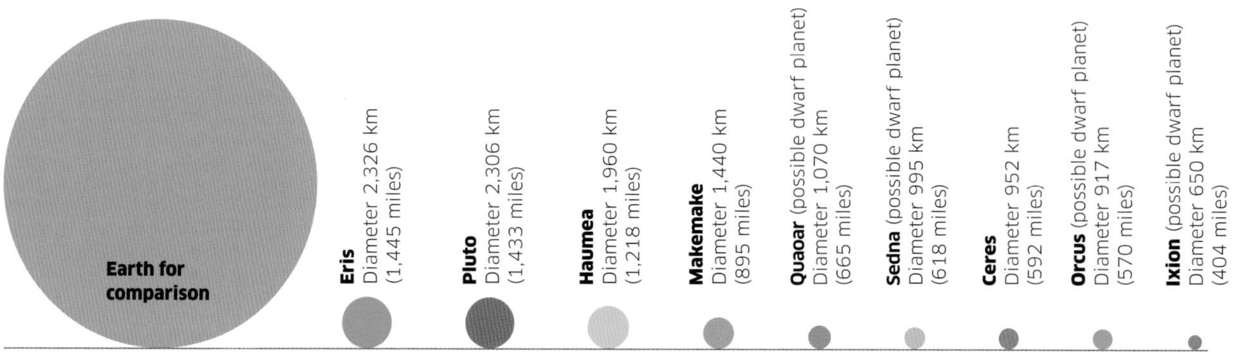
Earth for comparison
Eris Diameter 2,326 km (1,445 miles)
Pluto Diameter 2,306 km (1,433 miles)
Haumea Diameter 1,960 km (1,218 miles)
Makemake Diameter 1,440 km (895 miles)
Quaoar (possible dwarf planet) Diameter 1,070 km (665 miles)
Sedna (possible dwarf planet) Diameter 995 km (618 miles)
Ceres Diameter 952 km (592 miles)
Orcus (possible dwarf planet) Diameter 917 km (570 miles)
Ixion (possible dwarf planet) Diameter 650 km (404 miles)

DWARF PLANETS

A dwarf planet is a spherical object in an independent orbit around the Sun that lacks the strong gravity required to clear its orbit of other objects. Dwarf planets are mostly found in the Kuiper Belt and scattered disc zones beyond the orbit of Neptune, but they include the largest asteroid in the Main Asteroid Belt, Ceres.

COMETS

Most comets are deep-frozen, icy objects lurking at the outer edges of the Solar System, but a small number have fallen into orbits that periodically bring them closer to the Sun and cause them to burst into life.

COMET HALE-BOPP

SOME PERIODIC COMETS

Name	Orbital period	Sightings	Next due
1P/Halley	75 years	30	July 2061
2P/Encke	3 years, 3 months	62	March 2017
6P/d'Arrest	6 years, 5 months	20	September 2021
9P/Tempel	5 years, 5 months	12	August 2016
17P/Holmes	6 years, 8 months	10	February 2021
21P/Giacobini-Zinner	6 years, 6 months	15	September 2018
29P/Schwassmann-Wachmann	15 years	7	March 2019
39P/Oterma	19 years	4	July 2023
46P/Wirtanen	5 years, 4 months	10	December 2018
50P/Arend	8 years, 2 months	8	February 2016
55P/Tempel-Tuttle	33 years	5	May 2031
67P/Churyumov Gerasimenko	6 years, 4 months	7	December 2021
81P/Wild	6 years, 4 months	6	July 2016
109P/Swift-Tuttle	133 years	5	July 2126

ECLIPSES

By sheer coincidence, the Sun and Moon appear almost exactly the same size in Earth's skies. As a result, the Moon can sometimes pass in front of the Sun, blocking out its disc to create a solar eclipse. Total solar eclipses, which block the disc completely to reveal the tenuous outer solar atmosphere, are rare and very localized, but partial eclipses are more frequently seen.

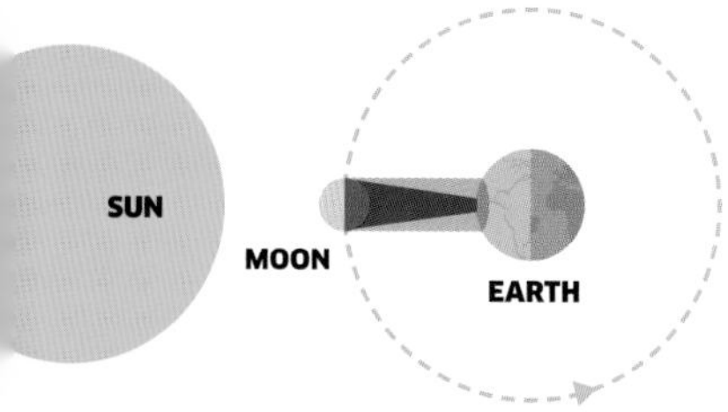
SUN
MOON
EARTH

SOLAR ECLIPSE

TOTAL SOLAR ECLIPSES

Date	Location
9 March 2016	Sumatra, Borneo, Sulawesi, Pacific
21 August 2017	North Pacific, USA, South Atlantic
2 July 2019	South Pacific, Chile, Argentina
14 December 2020	South Pacific, Chile, Argentina, South Atlantic
4 December 2021	Antarctica
8 April 2024	Mexico, central USA, east Canada
12 August 2026	Arctic, Greenland, Iceland, Spain
2 August 2027	Morocco, Spain, Algeria, Libya, Egypt, Saudi Arabia, Yemen, Somalia
22 July 2028	Australia, New Zealand
25 November 2030	Botswana, South Africa, Australia
30 March 2033	East Russia, Alaska
20 March 2034	Nigeria, Cameroon, Chad, Sudan, Egypt, Saudi Arabia, Iran, Afghanistan, Pakistan, India, China
2 September 2035	China, Korea, Japan, Pacific
13 July 2037	Australia, New Zealand
26 December 2038	Australia, New Zealand, South Pacific
15 December 2039	Antarctica

Exploring the planets

Since the late 1950s, we have sent dozens of robotic spacecraft beyond Earth's orbit, mostly aimed at other planets. Some perform brief flyby missions en route to another destination, but others stay longer. Orbiters become long-term satellites of planets, while landers and rovers touch down to examine or even explore the surface.

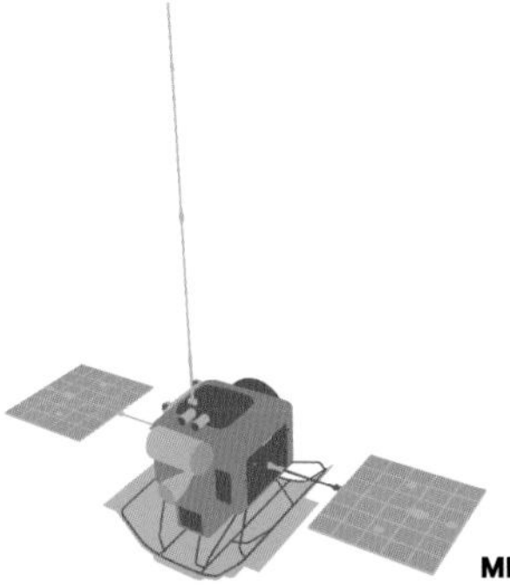
MESSENGER

Rocky worlds

Earth's immediate neighbours, Venus and Mars, have been subject to intense study by a variety of spacecraft, not all of which can be listed here – those mentioned below include all major successes as well as notable firsts and some interesting failures. The innermost planet, Mercury, moves so quickly in its orbit that it is hard to reach and rarely visited.

Mercury

Mission	Country of origin	Arrival date	Type	Status
Mariner 10	USA	1974	Multiple flybys	Success
MESSENGER	USA	2011	Orbiter	Success

Venera

Magellan

Venus

Mission	Country of origin	Arrival date	Type	Status
Mariner 2	USA	1962	Flyby	Success
Venera 4	USSR/Russia	1967	Flyby	Success
Mariner 5	USA	1967	Flyby	Success
Venera 7	USSR/Russia	1970	Lander	Success
Venera 9	USSR/Russia	1975	Orbiter/lander	Success
Pioneer Venus Orbiter	USA	1978	Orbiter	Success
Pioneer Venus Multiprobe	USA	1978	Atmospheric probe	Success
Venera 11	USSR/Russia	1978	Flyby/lander	Success
Venera 15	USSR/Russia	1983	Orbiter	Success
Vega 1	USSR/Russia	1985	Flyby/lander/balloon	Partial success (lander failure)
Vega 2	USSR/Russia	1985	Flyby/lander/balloon	Success
Magellan	USA	1990	Orbiter	Success
Venus Express	Europe	2006	Orbiter	Success

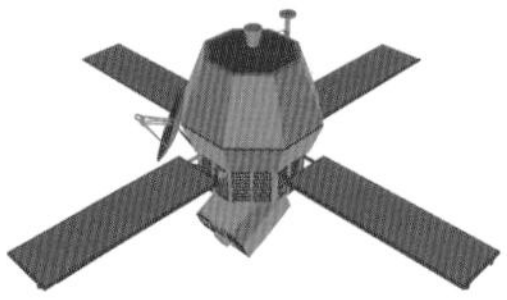
Mariner

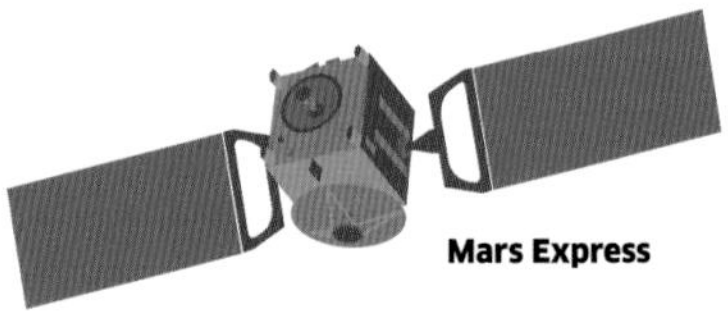
Mars Express

Mars

Mission	Country of origin	Arrival date	Type	Status
Mariner 4	USA	1965	Flyby	Success
Mariner 6	USA	1969	Flyby	Success
Mariner 7	USA	1969	Flyby	Success
Mariner 9	USA	1971	Orbiter	Success
Mars 2	USSR/Russia	1971	Orbiter/lander	Partial success (lander failure)

Viking 1	USA	1976	Orbiter/lander	Success
Viking 2	USA	1976	Orbiter/lander	Success
Phobos 2	USSR/Russia	1989	Phobos orbiter/lander	Partial success (lander failure)
Mars Pathfinder	USA	1997	Lander/rover	Success
Mars Global Surveyor	USA	1997	Orbiter	Success
Mars Odyssey	USA	2001	Orbiter	Success
Mars Express/Beagle 2	Europe	2003	Orbiter/lander	Partial success (lander failure)
MER-A Spirit	USA	2004	Rover	Success
MER-B Opportunity	USA	2004	Rover	Success
Mars Reconnaissance Orbiter	USA	2006	Orbiter	Success
Phoenix	USA	2008	Lander	Success
Curiosity	USA	2012	Rover	Success
Mars Orbiter Mission (Mangalyaan)	India	2014	Orbiter	Success
MAVEN	USA	2014	Orbiter	Success

Gas giants

The giant planets have no surfaces to investigate, but their atmospheres, rings, and moons are all intriguing. After an initial wave of flyby missions that surveyed the giants in the 1970s and 80s, Jupiter and Saturn have both been surveyed by long-term orbiters. A probe has entered Jupiter's atmosphere, and a lander has touched down on Saturn's largest moon, Titan.

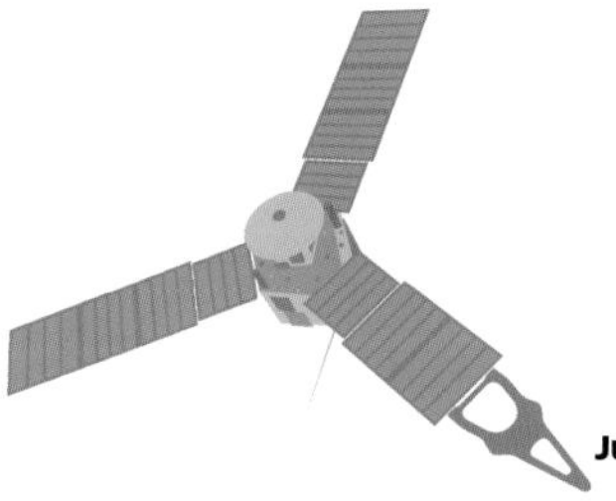

Juno

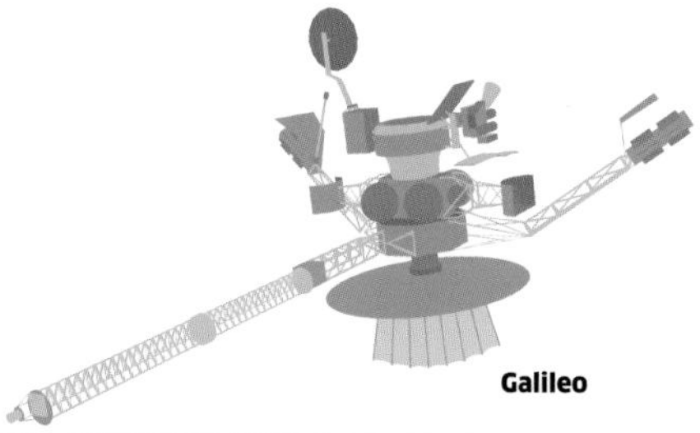

Galileo

Jupiter

Mission	Country of origin	Arrival date	Type	Status
Pioneer 10	USA	1973	Flyby	Success
Pioneer 11	USA	1974	Flyby	Success
Voyager 1	USA	1979	Flyby	Success
Voyager 2	USA	1979	Flyby	Success
Galileo	USA	1995	Orbiter/atmospheric probe	Success
Cassini	USA and Europe	2000	Flyby	Success
New Horizons	USA	2007	Flyby	Success
Juno	USA	2016 (planned)	Orbiter	En route

Saturn

Mission	Country of origin	Arrival date	Type	Status
Pioneer 11	USA	1979	Flyby	Success
Voyager 1	USA	1980	Flyby	Success
Voyager 2	USA	1981	Flyby	Success
Cassini/Huygens	USA and Europe	2004	Orbiter/Titan lander	Success

Uranus and Neptune

Mission	Country of origin	Arrival date	Type	Status
Voyager 2	USA	Uranus 1986, Neptune 1989	Flyby	Success

Stars and galaxies

The vast majority of objects in the night sky lie far beyond our Solar System. All the individual stars we can see are members of our own Milky Way galaxy, as are most of the star clusters and nebulas visible through amateur instruments. There are also countless other galaxies far beyond our own, most of them too distant to see.

There are about 200 billion galaxies in the observable Universe and about as many stars in the Milky Way.

Nearest stars

Many of the closest stars to Earth are red dwarfs, often in binary or multiple systems and so faint that they are hard to see despite their proximity. There are also a few Sun-like stars, and a couple of brilliant white stars, each paired with a burnt-out white-dwarf companion. Also close to Earth are many star-like objects called brown dwarfs – failed stars that are not massive enough to trigger nuclear fusion in their core.

KEY

- Red dwarf
- White main-sequence star
- Yellow main-sequence star
- White dwarf
- Orange main-sequence star
- Brown dwarf

Star type	Designation	Distance	Constellation	Apparent magnitude	Visibility
	Sun	8 light minutes	–	–26.7	Naked eye
	Proxima Centauri	4.2 light years	Centaurus	11.1	Telescope
	Alpha Centauri A/B	4.4 light years	Centaurus	0.01/1.34	Naked eye
	Barnard's Star	6.0 light years	Ophiuchus	9.5	Telescope
	Luhman 16 A/B	6.6 light years	Vela	10.7	Telescope
	WISE 0655-0714	7.2 light years	Hydra	13.9	Telescope
	Wolf 359	7.8 light years	Leo	13.4	Telescope
	Lalande 21185	8.3 light years	Ursa Major	7.5	Binoculars
	Sirius A/B	8.6 light years	Canis Major	–1.46/8.44	Naked eye/telescope
	Luyten 726-8	8.7 light years	Cetus	12.5/13.0	Telescope
	Ross 154	9.7 light years	Sagittarius	10.4	Telescope
	Ross 248	10.3 light years	Andromeda	12.3	Telescope
	Epsilon Eridani	10.5 light years	Eridanus	3.73	Naked eye
	Lacaille 9352	10.7 light years	Piscis Austrinus	7.3	Binoculars
	Ross 128	10.9 light years	Virgo	11.1	Telescope
	WISE 1506+7027	11.1 light years	Ursa Minor	14.3	Telescope
	EZ Aquarii A/B/C	11.3 light years	Aquarius	13.3/13.3/14.0	Telescope
	Procyon A/B	11.4 light years	Canis Minor	0.4/10.7	Naked eye/telescope
	61 Cygni A/B	11.4 light years	Cygnus	5.2/6.0	Naked eye/binoculars
	Struve 2398 A/B	11.5 light years	Draco	8.9/9.7	Telescope
	Groombridge 34 A/B	11.6 light years	Andromeda	8.1/11.1	Telescope

Brightest star

Star brightness is measured by apparent magnitude. The brightest stars have the lowest number; 6 is roughly the limit of naked-eye visibility in a clear, dark sky. The Sun, with a magnitude of –26.7, is the brightest object in our skies, but at night thousands of stars are visible to the naked eye, and millions more can be seen through binoculars or a telescope.

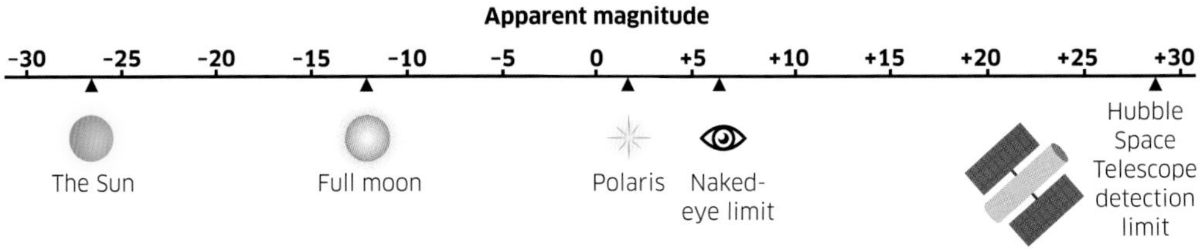
Apparent magnitude
–30
–25
–20
–15
–10
–5
0
+5
+10
+15
+20
+25
+30
The Sun
Full moon
Polaris
Naked-eye limit
Hubble Space Telescope detection limit

Nebulas

Nebulas are clouds of interstellar gas and dust of various shapes and sizes, ranging from huge star-forming complexes to the smoke rings puffed out by dying stars. Below are a few of the brightest nebulas.

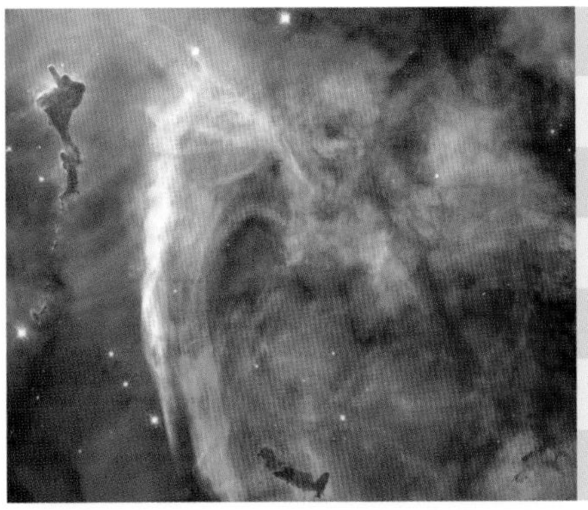

Name: Carina Nebula
Designation: NGC 3372
Constellation: Carina
Magnitude: 1
Distance: 6,500 light years
Type: Emission nebula
Visibility: Naked eye

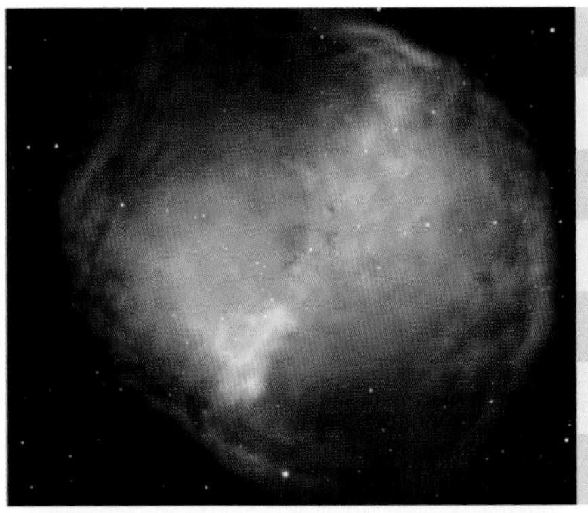

Name: Dumbbell Nebula
Designation: M27
Constellation: Vulpecula
Magnitude: 7.5
Distance: 1,360 light years
Type: Planetary nebula
Visibility: Binoculars

Name: Orion Nebula
Designation: M42
Constellation: Orion
Magnitude: 4
Distance: 1,340 light years
Type: Emission nebula
Visibility: Naked eye

Name: Helix Nebula
Designation: NGC 7293
Constellation: Aquarius
Magnitude: 7.6
Distance: 700 light years
Type: Planetary nebula
Visibility: Binoculars

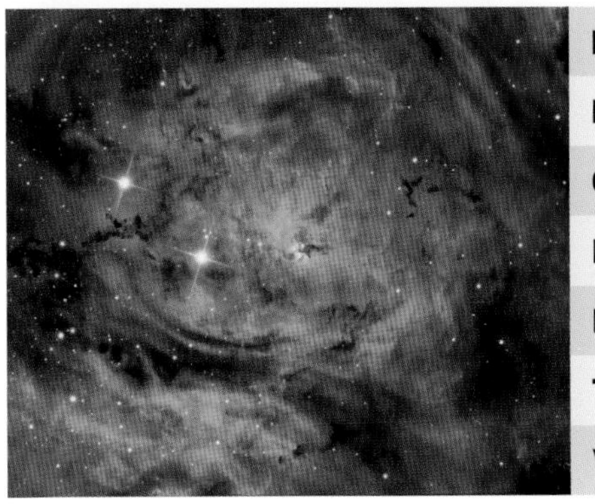

Name: Lagoon Nebula
Designation: M8
Constellation: Sagittarius
Magnitude: 6
Distance: 4,100 light years
Type: Emission nebula
Visibility: Naked eye

Name: Rosette Nebula
Designation: NGC 2237
Constellation: Monoceros
Magnitude: 9
Distance: 5,200 light years
Type: Emission nebula
Visibility: Binoculars

Galaxies

The brightest galaxies in the sky tend to be those closest to the Milky Way. This table lists some of the most interesting galaxies that can be observed with binoculars or the naked eye.

KEY
Irregular
Spiral
Barred spiral
Elliptical

Type	Name	Designation	Constellation	Apparent magnitude	Distance	Visibility
Barred spiral	Large Magellanic Cloud	LMC	Dorado/Mensa	0.9	160,000 light years	Naked eye
Irregular	Small Magellanic Cloud	SMC	Tucana	2.7	200,000 light years	Naked eye
Spiral	Andromeda Galaxy	M32	Andromeda	3.4	2.5 million light years	Naked eye
Spiral	Triangulum Galaxy	M33	Triangulum	5.7	2.9 million light years	Binoculars
Elliptical	Centaurus A	NGC 5128	Centaurus	6.8	13.7 million light years	Binoculars
Spiral	Bode's Galaxy	M81	Ursa Major	6.9	11.8 million light years	Binoculars
Spiral	Southern Pinwheel	M83	Hydra	7.5	15.2 million light years	Binoculars
Barred spiral	Sculptor Galaxy	NGC 253	Sculptor	8.0	11.4 million light years	Binoculars

Glossary

ANTENNA
A rod- or dish-like structure on spacecraft and telescopes used to transmit and receive radio signals.

APHELION
The point in the orbit of a planet, comet, or asteroid at which it is farthest from the Sun.

ASTEROID
A small, irregular Solar System object, made of rock and/or metal, that orbits the Sun.

ASTEROID BELT
A doughnut-shaped region of the Solar System, between the orbits of Mars and Jupiter, that contains a large number of orbiting asteroids.

ASTRONAUT
A person trained to travel and live in space.

ATMOSPHERE
The layer of gas that surrounds a planet. Also the outermost layer of gas around the Sun or a star.

ATOM
The smallest particle of a chemical element that can exist on its own.

AURORA
Patterns of light that appear near the poles of some planets. Solar wind particles are trapped by a planet's magnetic field and drawn into its atmosphere, where they collide with atoms and cause them to give off light.

AXIS
The imaginary line that passes through the centre of a planet or star and around which the planet or star rotates.

BIG BANG
The explosion that created the Universe billions of years ago. According to the big bang theory, the Universe began in an extremely dense and hot state and has been expanding ever since. The big bang was the origin of space, time, and matter.

BLACK HOLE
An object in space with such a strong gravitational pull that nothing, not even light, can escape from it.

BLAZAR
An active galaxy with a supermassive black hole at its centre.

CHARGED PARTICLE
A particle that has a positive or negative electrical charge.

CHROMOSPHERE
A gaseous layer above the surface of a star, such as the Sun. Along with the corona, it forms the star's outer atmosphere.

COMET
An object made of dust and ice that travels around the Sun in an elliptical orbit. As it gets near the Sun, the ice starts to vaporize, creating a tail of dust and gas.

CONSTELLATION
A named area of the sky (defined by the International Astronomical Union). The whole sky is divided into 88 constellations. Many are based around distinctive patterns of stars.

CORONA
The outermost part of the Sun or a star's atmosphere, seen as a white halo during a solar eclipse.

COSMONAUT
A Russian astronaut.

CRATER
A bowl-shaped depression on the surface of a planet, moon, asteroid, or other body.

CRUST
The thin, solid outer layer of a planet or moon.

DARK ENERGY
The energy that scientists believe is responsible for the acceleration in the expansion of the Universe.

DARK MATTER
Invisible matter that can be detected only by the effect of its gravity.

DENSITY
The amount of matter that occupies a certain volume.

DWARF PLANET
A planet that is big enough to have become spherical but hasn't managed to clear all the debris from its orbital path.

ECLIPSE
An astronomical event in which an object either passes into the shadow of another object or temporarily blocks an observer's view. During a solar eclipse, the shadow of the Moon falls on Earth. In a lunar eclipse, the shadow of Earth falls on the Moon.

ELECTROMAGNETIC RADIATION
Energy waves that can travel through space and matter. Visible light, X-rays, and microwaves are all forms of electromagnetic radiation.

EQUATOR
The imaginary line around the centre of a planet, halfway between its north and south poles.

ESCAPE VELOCITY
The minimum speed at which an object has to travel to escape the gravity of a planet or moon. Earth's escape velocity is 11.2 km (7 miles) per second.

EXOPLANET
A planet that orbits a star other than the Sun.

GALAXY
A collection of millions or trillions of stars, gas, and dust held together by gravity.

GAMMA RAY
An electromagnetic energy wave that has a very short wavelength.

GLOBULAR CLUSTER
A ball-shaped cluster of stars that orbit a large galaxy.

GRANULATION
Mottling on the surface of the Sun or another star.

GRAVITY
The force that pulls all objects that have mass and energy towards one another. It is the force that keeps moons in orbit around planets, and planets in orbit around the Sun.

HABITABLE
Suitable for living in or on.

HEMISPHERE
One half of a sphere. Earth is divided into northern and southern hemispheres by the equator.

HERTZSPRUNG-RUSSELL DIAGRAM
A diagram showing a star's temperature and brightness in relation to other stars.

INFRARED
Electromagnetic radiation with wavelengths shorter than radio waves but longer than visible light. It is the primary form of radiation emitted by many objects in space.

LAUNCH VEHICLE
A rocket-powered vehicle that is used to send spacecraft or satellites into space.

LIGHT YEAR
The distance travelled by light in a vacuum in one year.

LITHOSPHERE
The solid, hard outer layer of a planet or moon.

MAGNETIC FIELD
A field of force created by a planet, star, or galaxy, that surrounds it and extends into space.

MAGNITUDE
The brightness of an object in space given as a number. Bright objects have low or negative numbers and dim objects have high numbers.

MAIN-SEQUENCE STAR
An ordinary star, such as our Sun, that shines by converting hydrogen to helium. Main-sequence stars lie on the main band of the Hertzsprung-Russell diagram.

MANTLE
A thick layer of hot rock between the core and the crust of a planet or moon.

MARE
A large, flat area on the Moon's surface that looks dark when viewed from Earth. These areas were originally thought to be lakes or seas but are now known to be floods of solidified lava.

MATTER
Something that exists as a solid, liquid, or gas.

MESOSPHERE
The layer of atmosphere 50–80 km (30–50 miles) above Earth.

METEOR
A streak of light, also called a shooting star, seen when a meteoroid burns up due to friction on entering Earth's atmosphere.

METEORITE
A meteoroid that reaches the ground and survives impact. Meteorites are usually classified according to their composition as stony, iron, or stony-iron.

METEOROID
A particle of rock, metal, or ice travelling through space.

MICROWAVE
Electromagnetic radiation with wavelengths longer than infrared and visible light but shorter than radio waves.

MILKY WAY
The barred spiral galaxy that contains the Solar System and is visible to the naked eye as a band of faint light across the night sky.

MODULE
A portion of a spacecraft.

NEBULA
A cloud of gas and/or dust in space.

NEUTRINO
A subatomic particle produced by nuclear fusion in stars as well as in the big bang.

NEUTRON
A subatomic particle that does not have an electrical charge. It is found in all atomic nuclei except those of hydrogen.

NEUTRON STAR
A dense collapsed star that is mainly made of neutrons.

NUCLEAR FUSION
A process in which two atomic nuclei join to form a heavier nucleus and release large amounts of energy.

NUCLEUS
The compact central core of an atom. Also the solid, icy body of a comet.

ORBIT
The path taken by an object around another when affected by its gravity. The orbits of planets are mostly elliptical in shape.

ORBITER
A spacecraft that is designed to orbit an object but not land on it.

PARTICLE
An extremely small part of a solid, liquid, or gas.

PAYLOAD
Cargo or equipment carried into space by a rocket or a spacecraft.

PENUMBRA
The lighter outer shadow cast by an object. A person inside this region can see part of the source of light causing the shadow. Also the lighter, less cool region of a sunspot.

PERIHELION
The point in the orbit of a planet, comet, or asteroid at which it is closest to the Sun.

PHASE
The portion of a moon or planet that is seen to be lit by the Sun. The Moon passes through a cycle of different phases every 30 days.

PHOTOSPHERE
The thin gaseous layer at the base of the Sun's atmosphere from which visible light is emitted.

PLANET
A spherical object that orbits a star and is sufficiently massive to have cleared its orbital path of debris.

PLANETARY NEBULA
A glowing cloud of gas around a star at the end of its life.

PLANETESIMALS
Small rocky or icy objects formed in the early Solar System that were pulled together by gravity to form planets.

PLANISPHERE
A disc-shaped star map with an overlay that shows which part of the sky is visible at particular times and dates.

PLASMA
A highly energized form of gas. The Sun is made of plasma.

PROBE
An unmanned spacecraft that is designed to explore objects in space and transmit information back to Earth (especially one that explores the atmosphere or surface of an object).

PROMINENCE
A large, flame-like plume of plasma emerging from the Sun's photosphere.

PULSAR
A neutron star that sends out beams of radiation as it spins.

QUASAR
Short for "quasi-stellar radio source", a quasar is the immensely luminous nucleus of a distant active galaxy with a supermassive black hole at its centre.

RED GIANT
A large, luminous star with a low surface temperature and a reddish colour. It "burns" helium in its core rather than hydrogen and is nearing the final stages of its life.

ROVER
A vehicle that is driven remotely on the surface of a planet and moon.

SATELLITE
An object that orbits another object larger than itself.

SEYFERT GALAXY
An active galaxy, often spiral in shape, with a supermassive black hole at the centre.

SOLAR FLARE
The brightening of a part of the Sun's surface, accompanied by a release of huge amounts of electromagnetic energy.

SOLAR WIND
A continuous flow of fast-moving charged particles from the Sun.

SPACE-TIME
A combination of three dimensions of space – length, breadth, height – with the dimension of time.

SPACEWALK
Activity by an astronaut in space outside a spacecraft, usually to conduct repairs or test equipment.

STAR
A huge sphere of glowing plasma that generates energy by nuclear fusion in its core.

STRATOSPHERE
The layer of the atmosphere 8–50 km (5–30 miles) above Earth's surface.

SUBATOMIC PARTICLE
Any particle smaller than an atom.

SUNSPOT
A region of intense magnetic activity in the Sun's photosphere that appears darker than its surroundings.

THERMOSPHERE
The layer of the atmosphere 80–600 km (50–375 miles) above Earth's surface.

THRUST
The force from an engine that propels a rocket or spacecraft forwards.

TRANSIT
The passage of a planet or star in front of another, larger, object.

TROPOSPHERE
The layer of the atmosphere 6–20 km (4–12 miles) above Earth's surface.

ULTRAVIOLET RADIATION
Electromagnetic radiation with wavelengths shorter than visible light but longer than X-rays.

UMBRA
The darker central shadow cast by an object. A person inside this region cannot see the source of light causing the shadow. Also the darker, cooler region of a sunspot.

X-RAY
Electromagnetic radiation with wavelengths shorter than ultraviolet radiation but longer than gamma rays.

Index

E

F

G

H

I

J

K

L

M

Acknowledgments

The publisher would like to thank the following people for their assistance in the preparation of this book:
Ann Baggaley, Ashwin Khurana, Virien Chopra, and Rohini Deb for editorial assistance; Nick Sotiriadis, Bryan Versteeg, and the Maltings Partnership for additional illustrations; Steve Crozier for image retouching; Caroline Hunt for proofreading; Helen Peters for the index.

Smithsonian Enterprises:
Kealy Gordon, Product Development Manager
Ellen Nanney, Licensing Manager
Brigid Ferraro, Vice President, Consumer and Education Products
Carol LeBlanc, Senior Vice President, Consumer and Education Products
Chris Liedel, President

Curator for the Smithsonian:
Andrew Johnston, Geographer, Center for Earth and Planetary Studies, National Air and Space Museum, Smithsonian

The publisher would like to thank the following for their kind permission to reproduce their photographs:

(Key: a-above; b-below/bottom; c-centre; f-far; l-left; r-right; t-top)

2 NASA: Tony Gray and Tom Farrar (cl). **3 Dreamstime.com:** Peter Jurik (cb). **ESO:** The design for the E-ELT shown here is preliminary. http://creativecommons.org/licenses/by/3.0 (cr). **9 ESA:** OSIRIS Team MPS / UPD / LAM / IAA / RSSD / INTA / UPM / DASP / IDA (clb). **ESO:** E. Slawik http://creativecommons.org/licenses/by/3.0 (clb/Hale-bopp). **NASA:** (bl). **Science Photo Library:** Detlev Van Ravenswaay (clb/Pluto). **10 NASA:** JPL (tc). **12 Science Photo Library:** Jean-Claude Revy, A. Carion, ISM (br); Mark Garlick (clb). **13 NASA:** JPL-Caltech / T. Pyle (SSC) (bc). **14 BBSO / Big Bear Solar Observatory:** (clb). **15 Corbis:** Daniel J. Cox (crb). **16 NASA:** (clb). **17 NASA:** Johns Hopkins University Applied Physics Laboratory / Carnegie Institution of Washington (br). **18 NASA:** (tl); JPL (cra). **19 NASA:** JPL (tr). **20 FLPA:** Chris Newbert / Minden Pictures (cl). **21 Corbis:** Frans Lanting (cb, bc). **NASA:** Robert Simmon, using Suomi NPP VIIRS data provided courtesy of Chris Elvidge (NOAA National Geophysical Data Center). Suomi NPP is the result of a partnership between NASA, NOAA, and the Department of Defense. (crb). **22 Corbis:** Stocktrek Images (cra). **NASA:** Hal Pierce , NASA / GSFC (cl). **24 Getty Images:** Dana Berry (cla). **NASA:** (br). **25 NASA:** (tr). **29 Corbis:** Jim Wark / Visuals Unlimited (tc). **30 Science Photo Library:** Dr. Fred Espenak (tl). **31 Alamy Images:** Alexey Stiop (bc). **Corbis:** Brian Cassey / epa (tl). **32 Corbis:** Walter Myers / Stocktrek Images (bl). **NASA:** JPL / MSSS / Ed Truthan (tc). **33 NASA:** JPL-Caltech / University of Arizona (crb, fcrb). **34 ESA:** DLR / FU Berlin (cra). **NASA:** JPL / University of Arizona (ca). **34-35 NASA:** (tl). **Kees Veenenbos:** (b). **36 NASA:** (bc); Edward A. Guinness (bl). **37 ESA:** All Rights Reserved Beagle 2 (bl). **NASA:** JPL-Caltech (br). **38-39 NASA:** JPL-Caltech / MSSS. **41 Science Photo Library:** Joe Tucciarone (tr). **42 Corbis:** Bettmann (br). **44 NASA:** (bl). **45 NASA:** Hubble Heritage Team (STScI / AURA) Acknowledgment: NASA / ESA, John Clarke (University of Michigan) (tc); JPL, Galileo Project, (NOAO), J. Burns (Cornell) et al. (crb). **47 NASA:** JPL (c). **48 NASA:** JPL / University of Arizona (tr). **49 NASA:** JPL / University of Arizona (br). **51 NASA:** (br); JPL-Caltech / SSI (tl, tc, cr). **52 NASA:** JPL-Caltech / SSI (tr, clb). **54-55 NASA:** JPL-Caltech / SSI. **58 NASA:** ESA / NASA / JPL / University of Arizona (c); JPL-Caltech / ASI / JHUAPL / Cornell / Weizman (cl); JPL-Caltech / ASI / USGS (bl). **61 W.M. Keck Observatory:** Lawrence Sromovsky, University of Wisconsin-Madison (br). **62 Corbis:** NASA / Roger Ressmeyer (clb). **63 NASA:** JPL (cb). **Dr Dominic Fortes, UCL:** (tc). **64 NASA:** (tr). **65 ESO:** L. Calçada (tl) http://creativecommons.org/licenses/by/3.0. **NASA:** (tr); JPL-Caltech / UCLA / MPS / DLR / IDA (ca). **66 Corbis:** Andrew Bertuleit Photography (clb). **ESA:** Rosetta / MPS for OSIRIS Team MPS / UPD / LAM / IAA / SSO / INTA / UPM / DASP / IDA (clb/comet). **ESO:** E. Slawik (bc) http://creativecommons.org/licenses/by/3.0. **74 NASA:** ESA and L. Ricci (ESO) (cb); K.L. Luhman (Harvard-Smithsonian Center for Astrophysics, Cambridge, Mass.); and G. Schneider, E. Young, G. Rieke, A. Cotera, H. Chen, M. Rieke, R. Thompson (Steward Observatory, University of Arizona, Tucson, Ariz.) http://creativecommons.org/licenses/by/3.0 (cl). **75 NASA:** ESA, and the Hubble Heritage Team (AURA / STScI) (crb); ESA, M. Livio and the Hubble 20th Anniversary Team (STScI) (br). **77 ESO:** http://creativecommons.org/licenses/by/3.0 (tr). **Danielle Futselaar / SETI Institute (Collaborative work):** (cra). **79 NASA:** ESA / G. Bacon (cra); ESA, Alfred Vidal-Madjar (Institut d'Astrophysique de Paris, CNRS) (fcra). **82-83 NASA:** ESA and the Hubble SM4 ERO Team. **84 Science Photo Library:** Royal Observatory, Edinburgh (bl). **87 Corbis:** Chris Cheadle / All Canada Photos (crb). **88 NASA:** JPL-Caltech (bl). **89 A. Riazuelo, IAP/UPMC/CNRS:** (cr). **90 Adam Block/Mount Lemmon SkyCenter/University of Arizona (Board of Regents):** T. Bash, J. Fox (clb). **Sergio Eguivar:** (cla). **92-93 Two Micron All Sky Survey, which is a joint project of the University of Massachusetts and the Infrared Processing and Analysis Center/California Institute of Technology, funded by the National Aeronautics and Space Administration and the National Science Foundation**. **94 NASA:** ESA, S. Beckwith (STScI), and The Hubble Heritage Team (STScI / AURA) (cl). **96-97 Science Photo Library:** Take 27 Ltd. (bc). **97 Alamy Images:** Paul Fleet (br). **Chandra X-Ray Observatory:** X-ray: NASA / CXC / CfA / M.Markevitch et al.; Optical: NASA / STScI; Magellan / U.Arizona / D.Clowe et al.; Lensing Map: NASA / STScI; ESO WFI; Magellan / U.Arizona / D.Clowe et al. http://creativecommons.org/licenses/by/3.0 (tr). **Dorling Kindersley:** The Natural History Museum, London / National Maritime Museum, London (crb). **NASA:** R. Williams (STScI), the Hubble Deep Field Team (tl). **98-99 Mark Gee**. **100 CFHT/Coelum:** J.-C. Cuillandre & G. Anselmi (clb/M16). **NASA:** ESA, SSC, CXC, and STScI (clb). **101 NASA:** CXC / SAO, JPL-Caltech, Detlef Hartmann (cra); CXC / MSU / J. Strader et al, Optical: NASA / STScI (crb); ESA / Hubble (br). **SSRO:** R.Gilbert,D.Goldman,J. Harvey,D.Verschatse, D.Reichart (cr). **103 NASA:** DOE / Fermi LAT Collaboration (br); ESA, S. Baum and C. O'Dea (RIT), R. Perley and W. Cotton (NRAO / AUI / NSF), and the Hubble Heritage Team (STScI / AURA) (cra); ESA / Hubble & Flickr user Det58 (cr); John Bahcall (Institute for Advanced Study, Princeton) Mike Disney (University of Wales) and NASA / ESA (crb). **105 NASA:** ESA, Curt Struck and Philip Appleton (Iowa State University), Kirk Borne (Hughes STX Corporation), and Ray Lucas (STSI) (cra); ESA and the Hubble Heritage Team (STScI / AURA) (cr); ESA, and the Hubble Heritage Team (STScI / AURA)-ESA / Hubble Collaboration (crb); ESA; Z. Levay and R. van der Marel, STScI; T. Hallas; and A. Mellinger (br). **106 Adam Block/Mount Lemmon SkyCenter/University of Arizona (Board of Regents):** (cl). **CFHT/Coelum:** J.-C. Cuillandre & G. Anselmi (c). **ESO:** Digitized Sky Survey 2 http://creativecommons.org/licenses/by/3.0 (ca). **NASA:** ESA, the Hubble Heritage Team (STScI / AURA), J. Blakeslee (NRC Herzberg Astrophysics Program, Dominion Astrophysical Observatory), and H. Ford (JHU) (cla); ESA, Andrew Fruchter (STScI), and the ERO team (STScI + ST-ECF) (bl). **107 NASA:** ESA / Hubble & Digitized Sky Survey 2. Acknowledgment: Davide De Martin (ESA / Hubble) (crb); Swift Science Team / Stefan Immler (br). **110 NASA:** WMAP Science Team (tc). **114 Boeing:** (bc). **NASA:** (clb, bl); Tony Gray and Tom Farrar (ca); JPL-Caltech (cb). **116-117 Dreamstime.com:** Justin Black (tc). **116 Dreamstime.com:** Jahoo (cr). **NASA:** (ca, bl, crb); JPL (cb); Ames / JPL-Caltech (br); ESA and M. Livio and the Hubble 20th Anniversary Team (STScI) (bc). **117 Alamy Images:** DBI Studio (c); Danil Roudenko (br). **Dorling Kindersley:** The Science Museum, London (tr). **ESA:** Rosetta / MPS for OSIRIS Team MPS / UPD / LAM / IAA / SSO / INTA / UPM / DASP / IDA (bl). **Getty Images:** Universal History Archive (ca). **NASA:** (tc, cb); Hubble Heritage Team, D. Gouliermis (MPI Heidelberg) et al., (STScI / AURA), ESA (bc). **118-119 European Southern Observatory:** The design for the E-ELT shown here is preliminary http://creativecommons.org/licenses/by/3.0. **119 ESA:** Herschel / PACS / SPIRE / J. Fritz, U. Gent (br). **ESO:** L. Calçada http://creativecommons.org/licenses/by/3.0 (tc). **Adam Evans:** (crb/Visible). **NASA:** GALEX, JPL-Caltech (fcrb); ROSAT, MPE (crb); JPL-Caltech / Univ. of Ariz. (fcrb/mid-infrared). **Science Photo Library:** Dr. Eli Brinks (fbr). **121 NASA:** (tl); Hubble Heritage team, JPL-Caltech / R. Kennicutt (Univ. of Arizona), and the SINGS Team (cr); ESA, HEIC, and The Hubble Heritage Team (STScI / AURA), R. Corradi (Isaac Newton Group of Telescopes, Spain) and Z. Tsvetanov (NASA) (crb); ESA, and the Hubble Heritage Team (STScI / AURA) (br). **122 NASA:** (br, br/Earth); Artist concept (tl). **123 NASA:** (cra). **124 NASA:** F. Espenak , GSFC (bl). **125 Rex Features:** Sovfoto / Universal Images Group (c). **128 NASA:** JPL-Caltech / Cornell (bl). **129 NASA:** JPL-Caltech / Cornell University (ca). **130 ESA:** T. Peake (br). **NASA:** Bill Ingalls (cla). **132-133 NASA**. **134 NASA:** (cl). **135 Corbis:** Bettmann (cra). **NASA:** (tc). **137 NASA:** (crb, br). **139 NASA:** J.L. Pickering (cr). **141 NASA:** (br, cra, tr); JSC (crb). **142-143 NASA**. **144 NASA:** (crb). **145 NASA:** ESA (ca). **146-147 Bryan Versteeg:** (Mars Habitat artworks). **147 courtesy Virgin Galactic:** (crb). **World View:** (clb). **148 Ohio State University Radio Observatory:** North American Astrophysical Observatory (cr). **Science Photo Library:** David Parker. **149 ESA:** DLR / FU Berlin (G. Neukum) (c). **NASA:** (crb); Galileo Project, JPL, Ted Stryk (bc). **NRAO :** SETi (bl). **150 Corbis:** Rick Fischer / Masterfile (cl). **NASA:** NASA, ESA, K. Kuntz (JHU), F. Bresolin (University of Hawaii), J. Trauger (Jet Propulsion Lab), J. Mould (NOAO), Y.-H. Chu (University of Illinois, Urbana), and STScI, Canada-France-Hawaii Telescope / J.-C. Cuillandre / Coelum, G. Jacoby, B. Bohannan, M. Hanna / NOAO / AURA / NSF (c). **Peter Michaud (Gemini Observatory):** AURA, NSF (cr). **153 Corbis:** (cra). **154 Dreamstime.com:** Andrew Buckin (tr). **154-155 Corbis:** Bryan Allen (bc). **156 Corbis:** Rick Fischer / Masterfile (cra). **157 Corbis:** Alan Dyer, Inc / Visuals Unlimited (br). **Peter Michaud (Gemini Observatory):** AURA, NSF (cr). **Science Photo Library:** Eckhard Slawik (crb). **159 Corbis:** Alan Dyer, Inc / Visuals Unlimited (tr, br, cra). **Chris Picking:** (cr). **Science Photo Library:** Celestial Image co. (crb). **163 NASA:** J. P. Harrington (U. Maryland) and K. J. Borkowski (NCSU) (cr). **NOAO / AURA / NSF:** Hillary Mathis, N.A.Sharp (bl). **164 NOAO / AURA / NSF:** Adam Block (bl). **165 NASA:** NASA, ESA and the Hubble Heritage Team STScI / AURA). Acknowledgment: A. Zezas and J. Huchra (Harvard-Smithsonian Center for Astrophysics) (cl); NASA, ESA, K. Kuntz (JHU), F. Bresolin (University of Hawaii), J. Trauger (Jet Propulsion Lab), J. Mould (NOAO), Y.-H. Chu (University of Illinois, Urbana), and STScI, Canada-France-Hawaii Telescope / J.-C. Cuillandre / Coelum, G. Jacoby, B. Bohannan, M. Hanna / NOAO / AURA / NSF (bc). **NOAO / AURA / NSF:** (bl). **166 Adam Block/Mount Lemmon SkyCenter/University of Arizona (Board of Regents):** (c, br). **NASA:** ESA, S. Beckwith (STScI), and The Hubble Heritage Team (STScI / AURA) (tc). **167 NASA:** The Hubble Heritage Team (AURA / STScI / NASA) (br). **168 Adam Block/Mount Lemmon SkyCenter/University of Arizona (Board of Regents):** (bl). **NOAO / AURA / NSF:** N.A.Sharp, REU program (br). **170 NASA:** Stuart Heggie (br). **171 Corbis:** Rogelio Bernal Andreo / Stocktrek Images (br); Tony Hallas / Science Faction (bl). **NASA:** ESA / ASU / J. Hester (bc). **172 NASA:** Andrew Fruchter (STScI) (cla). **173 NASA:** The Hubble Heritage Team (STScI / AURA) (clb). **Science Photo Library:** NASA / JPL-CALTECH / CXC / Ohio State University / C. Grier et al. / STSCI / ESO / WFI (cr). **174 Corbis:** Roger Ressmeyer (bl). **175 ESO:** http://creativecommons.org/licenses/by/3.0 (ca). **NASA:** ESA / Hubble (br). **176 ESO:** http://creativecommons.org/licenses/by/3.0 (cr). **177 ESO:** VISTA / J. Emerson. Acknowledgment: Cambridge Astronomical Survey Unit http://creativecommons.org/licenses/by/3.0 (bl). **NOAO / AURA / NSF:** (cl). **179 ESO:** http://creativecommons.org/licenses/by/3.0 (bc). **NASA:** ESA, K.L. Luhman (Harvard-Smithsonian Center for Astrophysics, Cambridge, Mass.); and G. Schneider, E. Young, G. Rieke, A. Cotera, H. Chen, M. Rieke, R. Thompson (Steward Observatory, University of Arizona, Tucson, Ariz.) (bl); ESA, M. Robberto (Space Telescope Science Institute / ESA) and the Hubble Space Telescope Orion Treasury Project Team (br). **180 Corbis:** Visuals Unlimited (cla). **ESO:** http://creativecommons.org/licenses/by/3.0 (br). **181 Chandra X-Ray Observatory:** ESO / VLT (cra). **183 ESO:** http://creativecommons.org/licenses/by/3.0 (cla). **NASA:** STScI, Wikisky (br). **185 ESO:** http://creativecommons.org/licenses/by/3.0 (cl). **NASA:** ESA, and The Hubble Heritage Team (STScI / AURA). Acknowledgment: P. Knezek (WIYN) (cra). **186 ESO:** http://creativecommons.org/licenses/by/3.0 (bc). **187 Roberto Mura:** (bl). **NASA:** ESA, N. Smith (University of California, Berkeley), and The Hubble Heritage Team (STScI / AURA) (br); The Hubble Heritage Team (STScI / AURA / NASA) (cl). **188 Meire Ruiz:** (bl). **189 John Ebersole:** (cl). **Science Photo Library:** NASA / ESA / STScI (bl). **190 ESO:** M.-R. Cioni / VISTA Magellanic Cloud survey. Acknowledgment: Cambridge Astronomical Survey Unit http://creativecommons.org/licenses/by/3.0 (br). **191 ESO:** (crb). **192 ESO:** Y. Beletsky (LCO) http://creativecommons.org/licenses/by/3.0 (cla). **194 Corbis:** Dennis di Cicco (cr). **NASA:** JPL-Caltech (cl). **NOAO / AURA / NSF:** SSRO / PROMPT / CTIO (c). **197 Corbis:** Dennis di Cicco (cl). **201 Brian Davis:** (crb). **ESO:** (cra). **NASA:** ESA, The Hubble Heritage Team (AURA / STScI) (cla); ESA, M. Robberto (Space Telescope Science Institute / ESA) and the Hubble Space Telescope Orion Treasury Project Team (cl); JPL-Caltech (cr). **NOAO / AURA / NSF:** SSRO / PROMPT / CTIO (clb)

For further information see: www.dkimages.com